**MANFRED
DURNIOK
PRODUKTION
FÜR FILM UND
FERNSEHEN**
International Motion Picture
and Television Productions,
Co-Productions and Film Distribution.
Hausotterstraße 36, D-13409 Berlin,
Germany, Phone (030) 491 80 45
E-Mail 100722.2445@compuserve.com
Fax (030) 491 40 66

EDITED BY PETER COWIE

faber and faber
LONDON

Silman-James Press
LOS ANGELES

CONTENTS

Editor: Peter Cowie

Managing Editor: Daniel Rosenthal

Consulting Editor: Derek Elley

Editorial Assistants: Katrina Dodson, Meredith Luck, Nancy Tsuei

Advertising Co-ordination: Sandrine Bentata

Cover Design: Stefan Dreja

Book Design: John Harmer

Photo Consultants: The Kobal Collection

Editorial and Business Offices:
Variety
6 Bell Yard
London WC2A 2JR
Tel: (0171) 520 5222
Fax: (0171) 520 5219

*Published in the US by
Silman-James Press
Tel: (323) 661 9922
Fax: (323) 661 9933*

ISBN 0-571-19411-7 (United Kingdom)
ISBN 1-879505-47-9 (United States)
British Library Cataloging in Publication
Data
Variety International Film Guide 1999
1. Cowie, Peter
011.37

*Copyright © 1998 by
Variety Media Publications Ltd.*

*Photoset/Origination by Columns
Design Limited, Reading
Printed and bound in Great Britain by
Cromwell Press Ltd.*

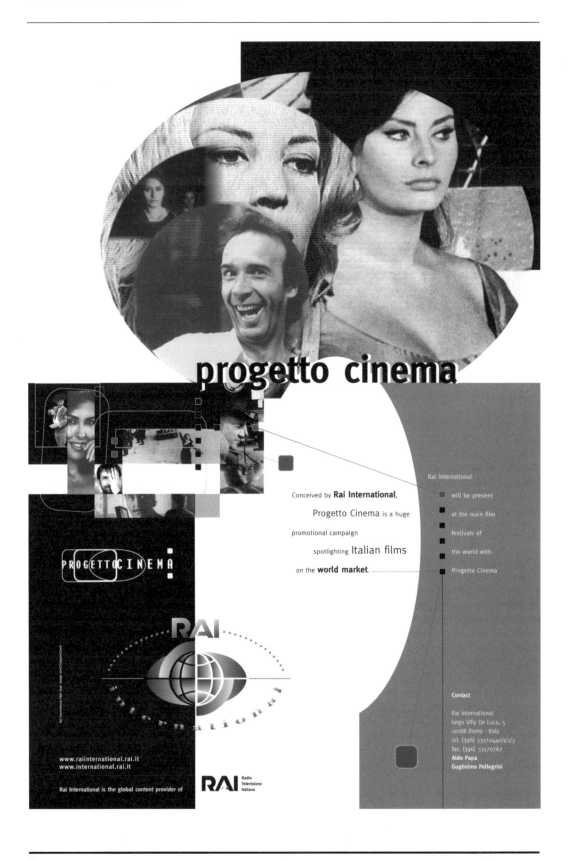

progetto cinema

PROGETTO CINEMA

Conceived by **Rai International**,

Progetto Cinema is a huge

promotional campaign

spotlighting Italian films

on the **world market**.

Rai International

will be present

at the main film

festivals of

the world with

Progetto Cinema

Contact

Rai International
largo Villy De Luca, 5
00188 Roma - Italy
tel. (396) 33172440/1/2/3
fax. (396) 33170767
Aldo Papa
Guglielmo Pellegrini

www.raiinternational.rai.it
www.international.rai.it

Rai International is the global content provider of

RAI Radio Televisione Italiana

CONTENTS

INTERNATIONAL LIAISON

Africa: Roy Armes (Algeria, Morocco, Tunisia); Judy Kendall (Burkina Faso, Senegal, Zimbabwe)
Australia: David Stratton, Peter Thompson
Austria: Beat Glur
Belgium: Patrick Duynslaegher
Bosnia & Hezegovina: Rada Šesić
Brazil: Nelson Hoineff
Bulgaria: Ivan Stoyanovich
Canada: Gerald Pratley
Chile: Hans Ehrmann
Croatia: Tomislav Kurelec
Czech Republic: Eva Zaoralová
Denmark: Ebbe Iversen
Egypt: Fawzi Soliman
Estonia: Jaan Ruus
Far East: Derek Elley (China, Hong Kong, Taiwan)
Finland: Antti Selkokari
France: Michel Ciment
Germany: Jack Kindred
Greece: Yannis Bacoyannopoulos
Hungary: Derek Elley
Iceland: Ásgrímur Sverrisson
India: Uma da Cunha
Indonesia: Marselli Sumarno
Iran: Jamal Omid
Ireland: Michael Dwyer
Israel: Dan Fainaru
Italy: Lorenzo Codelli
Japan: Frank Segers
Kazakhstan: Eugene Zykov
Latvia: Andris Rozenbergs
Lithuania: Gražina Arlickaite
Luxembourg: Jean-Pierre Thilges
Malaysia: Baharudin A. Latif
Mexico: Tomás Pérez Turrent
Netherlands: Pieter van Lierop
New Zealand: Peter Calder
Norway: Trond Olav Svendsen
Pakistan: Aijaz Gul
Peru: Isaac León Frías
Philippines: Agustin Sotto
Poland: Wanda Wertenstein
Portugal: Martin Dale
Puerto Rico: José Artemio Torres
Romania: Cristina Corciovescu
Russia: Michael Brashinsky
Serbia & Montenegro: Goran Gocić
Singapore: Yvonne Ng
Slovakia: Hana Cielová
South Africa: Martin Botha
South Korea: Frank Segers
Spain: Peter Besas
Sri Lanka: Amarnath Jayatilaka
Sweden: Bengt Forslund
Switzerland: Pierre Lachat
Syria: Rafik Atassi
Thailand: Anchalee Chaiworaporn
Turkey: Atilla Dorsay
Ukraine: Konrad Will
United Kingdom: Philip Kemp
United States: Harlan Jacobson
Venezuela: Irene Herrera

At the top of Scandinavia

From now on you can reach the entire Scandinavian market, with more than 20 million people, through one new powerful film company.

In key cities of Denmark, Finland, Norway and Sweden 140 screens are waiting for you. And more well-equipped multi-movie theatres are under way.

So, whenever you are ready to launch a new film, welcome to the number one film company of Scandinavia.

HEAD OFFICE P.O. BOX 5612, S-114 86 STOCKHOLM PHONE: +46 8 762 17 00, FAX: +46 8 10 38 50, http://www.sandrews.se

US Academy Awards: 1998

Best Film: *Titanic.*
Best Direction: James Cameron for *Titanic.*
Best Actor: Jack Nicholson for *As Good As It Gets.*
Best Actress: Helen Hunt for *As Good As It Gets.*
Best Supporting Actor: Robin Williams for *Good Will Hunting.*
Best Supporting Actress: Kim Basinger for *L.A. Confidential.*
Best Original Screenplay: Ben Affleck, Matt Damon for *Good Will Hunting.*
Best Adapted Screenplay: Brian Helgeland, Curtis Hanson for *L.A. Confidential.*
Best Cinematography: Russell Carpenter for *Titanic.*
Best Costume Design: Deborah L. Scott for *Titanic.*
Best Art Direction: Michael Ford, Peter Lamont for *Titanic.*
Best Editing: Conrad Buff, James Cameron, Richard A. Harris for *Titanic.*
Best Original Musical or Comedy Score: Anne Dudley for *The Full Monty.*
Best Dramatic Score: James Horner for *Titanic.*
Best Original Song: "My Heart Will Go On" from *Titanic.* Music by James Horner, lyrics by Will Jennings.

Jack Nicholson and Helen Hunt, Academy Award winners for AS GOOD AS IT GETS   photo: Columbia TriStar

Best Sound: Gary Rydstrom, Tom Johnson, Gary Summers, Mark Ulano for *Titanic.*
Best Make-up: Rick Baker, David LeRoy Anderson for *Men in Black.*
Best Visual Effects: Robert Legato, Mark Lasoff, Thomas L. Fisher, Michael Kanfer for *Titanic.*
Best Sound-Effects Editing: Tom Bellfort, Christopher Boyes for *Titanic.*
Best Foreign-Language Film: *Character* (The Netherlands).
Best Documentary Feature: *The Long Way Home.*
Best Documentary Short: *A Story of Healing.*
Best Animated Short: *Geri's Game.*
Best Live-Action Short: *Visas and Virtue.*
Career Achievement Award: Stanley Donen.

British Academy of Film and Television Awards: 1998

Best Film: *The Full Monty*.
Best British Film: *Nil By Mouth*.
Best Direction: Baz Luhrmann for *William Shakespeare's Romeo + Juliet*.
Best Actor: Robert Carlyle for *The Full Monty*.
Best Actress: Judi Dench for *Mrs. Brown*.
Best Supporting Actor: Tom Wilkinson for *The Full Monty*.
Best Supporting Actress: Sigourney Weaver for *The Ice Storm*.
Best Original Screenplay: Gary Oldman for *Nil By Mouth*.
Best Adapted Screenplay: Baz Luhrmann, Craig Pearce for *William Shakespeare's Romeo + Juliet*.
Best Foreign-Language Film: *L'Appartement* (France).
Audience Award: *The Full Monty*.
Fellowship Award: Sean Connery.

Judi Dench, BAFTA winner for MRS. BROWN
Photo: Mark Tillie/Miramax

European Film Awards: 1997

Best Film: *The Full Monty* (UK).
Best Actor: Bob Hoskins for *Twenty Four Seven* (UK).
Best Actress: Juliette Binoche for *The English Patient* (UK).
Best Screenwriter: Chris Vander Stappen, Alain Berliner for *Ma vie en rose* (Belgium/France)
FIPRESCI Award: *Viagem ao Principio do Mundo* (Portugal).
Documentary Award: Benoit Dervaux, Jean Pierre, Luc Dardenne for *Gigi, Monica...et Bianca* (Belgium).
Lifetime Achievement Award: Jeanne Moreau (France).

Australian Film Awards: 1998

Best Film: *Kiss or Kill*.
Best Direction: Bill Bennett for *Kiss or Kill*.
Best Original Screenplay: Santo Cilauro, Tom Gleisner, Jane Kennedy, Rob Sitch for *The Castle*.
Best Adapted Screenplay: Laura Jones for *The Well*.
Best Actress: Pamela Rabe for *The Well*.

Best Actor: Richard Roxburgh for *Doing Time for Patsy Kline*.
Best Supporting Actress: Cate Blanchett for *Thank God He Met Lizzie*.
Best Supporting Actor: Andrew Gilbert for *Kiss or Kill*.
Best Cinematography: Andrew Lesnie for *Kiss or Kill*.
Best Editing: Henry Dangar for *Kiss or Kill*.
Best Music Score: Peter Best for *Doing Time for Patsy Kline*.
Best Production Design: Michael Philips for *The Well*.
Best Costume Design: Louise Wakefield for *Doing Time for Patsy Kline*.
Best Foreign Film: *Secrets and Lies* (UK).
Byron Kennedy Award for Excellence: John Polson.
Best Documentary: *Mabo (Life of an Island Man)*.

Italian Donatello Awards: 1998

Best Film: *Life is Beautiful*.
Best Director: Roberto Benigni for *Life is Beautiful*.

Best Producer: Elda Ferri, Gianluigi Braschi for *Life is Beautiful.*
Best Debuting Director: Roberta Torre for *Tano da morire.*
Best Actor: Roberto Benigni for *Life is Beautiful.*
Best Actress: Valeria Bruni Tedeschi for *The Word Love Exists.*
Best Supporting Actor: Silvio Orlando for *Aprile.*
Best Supporting Actress: Nicoletta Braschi for *Ovosodo.*
Best Screenplay: Vincenzo Cerami, Roberto Benigni for *Life is Beautiful.*
Best Cinematography: Tonino Delli Colli for *Life is Beautiful.*
Best Music: Nino d'Angelo for *Tano da morire.*
Best Art Direction: Danilo Donati for *Life is Beautiful.*
Best Costumes: Danilo Donati for *Life is Beautiful.*
Best Editing: Jacopo Quadri for *Rehearsal for War.*
Best Sound: Tullio Morganti for *Ovosodo.*
Best Foreign Film: *The Full Monty* (UK).

French César Academy Awards: 1997

Best Director: Luc Besson for *The Fifth Element.*
Best Film: *On connait la chanson.*
Best Actor: Andre Dussollier for *On connait la chanson.*
Best Actress: Ariane Ascaride for *Marius et Jeannette.*
Best Supporting Actor: Jean-Pierre Bacri for *On connait la chanson.*
Best Supporting Actress: Agnès Jaoui for *On connait la chanson.*
Best Young Actor: Stanislas Merhar for *Nettoyage à sec.*
Best Young Actress: Emma de Caunes for *Un Frère.*
Best First Film: *Didier.*

Best Foreign Film: *Brassed Off* (UK).
Best Original or Adapted Screenplay: Agnès Jaoui, Jean-Pierre Bacri for *On connait la chanson.*
Best Music: Bernardo Sandoval for *Western.*
Best Photography: Thierry Arbogast for *The Fifth Element.*
Best Editing: Hervé de Luze for *On connait la chanson.*
Best Sets: Dan Weil for *The Fifth Element.*
Best Costumes: Christian Gasc for *On Guard.*
Best Short Film: David Fourier for *Des Majorêtes dans l'Espace.*

German Film Awards: 1998

Best Film: *Comedian Harmonists.*
Silver Filmband: (shared) *Wintersleeper; Train Birds.*
Best Director: Wim Wenders for *The End of Violence.*
Best Actor: Ulrich Noethen for *Comedian Harmonists.*
Best Actress: Katja Riemann for *Bandits, Die Apothekerin.*
Best Supporting Actor: Peter Lohmeyer for *Train Birds.*
Best Supporting Actress: Meret Becker for *Comedian Harmonists.*
Best Cinematography: Frank Griebe for *Wintersleeper* and *Train Birds.*
Best Editing: Peter R. Adam for *Comedian Harmonists.*
Best Foreign Film (shared): *Brassed Off* (UK); *The Full Monty* (UK).
Best Production Design: Rolf Zehetbauer for *Comedian Harmonists.*
Lifetime Achievement Awards: Heinz Badewitz, Gregory Peck.

Kevin Spacey in L.A. CONFIDENTIAL, winner of the Best Adapted Screenplay Oscar
photo: Merrick Morton/Regency

Peter Cattaneo directing Robert Carlyle in BAFTA winner, THE FULL MONTY

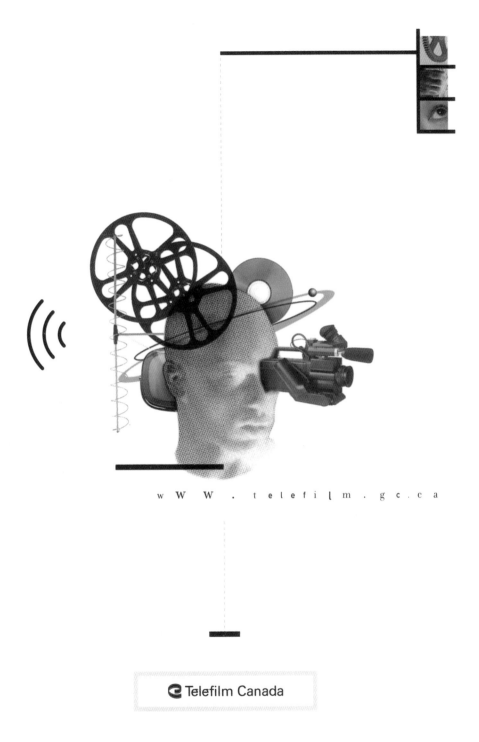

w W W . t e l e f i l m . g c . c a

Telefilm Canada

Canada

DIRECTORS
of the year

Pedro Almodóvar

by John Hopewell

In the late 1980s, a balmy breeze ruffled the cheerless climate of European cinema: the first mature films of Pedro Almodóvar. *The Law of Desire* (1987) and *Women on the Verge of a Nervous Breakdown* (1988) had foreign critics packing that old stand-by, alliteration, as they marched onto foreign territory. Here was a film-maker of "sensuous style", of, at first sight, "pure passion". At first sight. The problem when watching Almodóvar's films is that they are so 'sightly'. Plumb their more obscure shafts of significance, as his best critics (Paul Julian Smith, Peter Evans and Marsha Kinder, amongst others) have done, and you soon bump your head on some bedrock contradictions.

More than any other living artist, Almodóvar has changed the cultured cultural world's view of Spain. Yet he is something of an outsider in the Spanish film industry. His pictures have won a Best

Foreign Language César in France (*High Heels*) and a Donatella in Italy (*Live Flesh*), but only one Best Picture Goya in Spain (*Women On The Verge...*). Almodóvar's films subvert mainstream cinema; yet four of them figure among Spain's ten highest-grossing domestic features. Almodóvar has worked, he claims, "as if Franco never existed"; yet his characters' sexual suffering often seems best attributed to mental hostages left by the society Franco perpetuated. Religious icons abound in his films.

When he approaches gender and sexuality, Almodóvar seems to champion not so much a freedom of speech as a freedom of desire. Yet, with almost perverse timing, his follow-up to the feminist *Women On The Verge...*, was *Tie Me Up! Tie Me Down!* (1990), with a former psychiatric ward inmate kidnapping and binding an actress; and the final consequence is that they fall in love. Almodóvar is more than just passion and palette.

PEDRO ALMODÓVAR was born in 1949, a full decade before Spain's industrial revolution, in the dozing hamlet of Calzada de la Calatrava in La Mancha, south of Madrid. His father was a humble carter; his mother, a housewife and unpublished poet, wore traditional black. He studied with Salesian monks, sang solos in their choir and felt, he later recalled, like an astronaut at the Court of King Arthur. After seeing Richard Brooks' *Cat on a Hot Tin Roof* he marked himself

The outrageous nuns in DARK HABITS
photo: Ana Muller

Carmen Maura wonders WHAT HAVE I DONE TO
DESERVE THIS?!   *photo: Antonio de Benito*

down, at 12, for "a life of sin and degeneracy".

Almodóvar's childhood left some fairly obvious marks: notably deafness in one ear from a botched medical operation, and a hatred of hypocrisy, whose flipside is an adoration of deep feeling plainly expressed, as in the boleros which preface many of his films. His key film influences came from directors whose work he caught as a teenager: the comedies of Frank Tashlin, Blake Edwards and Billy Wilder; Buñuel, Hitchcock and the melodramas of Douglas Sirk; the Spanish neo-realism of Marco Ferreri or Fernando Fernán-Gómez. Almodóvar's career describes a curve on which, having established his independence, he has been able in full maturity – from *The Flower of My Secret* (1995) onwards – to reacknowledge his origins.

On the verge of a breakthrough

First, however, Almodóvar had to get the hell out of La Mancha. He moved to the nearest big city – Madrid – in 1969, worked in administration at the Telefónica telephone company, at night wrote short stories, invented mock newsreels, spoof commercials for products such as fart-recycling panties (which appear in *Pepi, Luci, Bom...*), made 11 Super-8 shorts and, in 1978 a Super-8 feature: *Fuck, Fuck, Fuck Me...Tim* which he later called "the typical *feuilleton* about a poor girl who works in a department store. Her blind boyfriend plays the guitar. He becomes famous, she goes blind as well."

Commissioned in 1978 to pen a "really dirty" photo-novel for a fanzine, Almodóvar turned the project into his first 35mm feature, the summery, joyous pop farce *Pepi, Luci, Bom...* (1980). It forms a diptych with the more tempered screwball comedy *Labyrinth of Passions* (1982), which tracks the surprisingly chaste romance between Sexilia, the nymphomaniac daughter of a 'biogynaecologist', and Riza Niro, the (seemingly) homosexual son of the Emperor of Tiran. Contemporary period pieces exposing the thoroughly modern milieu of Madrid, the two pictures mark high points of the early 1980s *movida*, Spain's riposte to punk, in which social jaundice was replaced by camp pop art and a hedonistic relish for affairs of the groin.

These films were perilously budgeted (*Pepi...* came in at some $40,000), disjointed, louche, almost impossibly kitsch and doggedly vulgar (*Pepi...* features a 'How long is your penis?' contest), but they still possess magnificent scenes of camp hokum: Bom's nonchalant golden shower, for example, or Almodóvar singing "Gran Ganga" ("Great Bargain") in *Labyrinth...*, tarted up in fish-net tights and a plastic raincoat which would embarrass a Siberian housewife. Their point, at the time at least, seemed to be that they had no serious point. They cocked a snook at Spain's earnest "quality" film establishment, which still portrayed a country living in the long psychological shadow of Francoism. This left-wing, right-minded and wrong-headed establishment never quite forgave Almodóvar for signalling its sell-by date.

Critics had by now clamped two albatrosses around Almodóvar's neck: he was superficial and too modern by half. Almodóvar fought back with *Dark Habits* (1983) and *What Have I Done To Deserve This?!* (1984). Both represented departures. The first, not necessarily for the better. A mock melodrama following a cabaret chanteuse who evades the police by shacking up in a convent for fallen woman, *Dark Habits* discovers its emotional centre – the Mother Superior's unrequited love for the singer – far too late in the day.

Gloria in extremis

In contrast, *What Have I Done...?!* is a desperately funny comic melodrama in which the accent is very much on desperation. It chronicles the travails of Gloria, a lumpen drudge of a housewife who lives with her family in a God-awful high-rise block with a wonderful view of the Madrid ring-road. Next door is a prostitute (allowing Almodóvar to debunk porn flicks); above a girl with supernatural powers (Almodóvar parodies the terror genre). Cluttered and claustrophobic, the camera's medium-shots recall the superbly poky, Spanish neo-realism of the late 1950s.

What Have I Done ...?! is also the first film consistently to demonstrate Almodóvar's magnificent ability to melt and modulate tones, creating, as he puts it, "screwball drama". One example: after a hard day's work, Gloria finally has time to put her feet up. Will she watch telly? Gawp at *Hola* magazine? No, slumped on the sofa, she takes a surreptitious sniff at a tube of glue. This is at once funny and sad. But pathos wins out, as Bernardo Bonezzi's score returns, and Gloria, once more a mother, goes next door to tuck up the children. Swamped by her work, Gloria shows the resourcefulness of a heroine of Hollywood melodrama, but her sufferings are not driven by overwhelming passion, just an overwhelming struggle to get by: she knows little human warmth.

What Have I Done...?! set Almodóvar up as a semi-fledged auteur, establishing his distinctive traits: forefronting female desire and women's independence and solidarity, alongside a post-modernist stress on film style and performance. Most significantly, despite his professed lack of interest in politics or social issues, Almodóvar was developing what could be called a social and sexual democracy. Characters of radically different origins or sexuality can inhabit the same house (*What Have I Done...?!*) and cinematic frame – and avoid social pigeonholing (the nuns in *Dark Habits* take heroin, write best-sellers and keep a pet tiger).

Three steps to cult status

Having begun to develop an international cachet (the *New York Times* called *What Have I Done...?!* "a small masterpiece"), Almodóvar was to deepen his politics of desire in three films which, along with his two most recent pictures, some critics still see as his finest work: *Matador* (1986), *The Law of Desire* (1987) and *Women on the Verge of a Nervous Breakdown* (1988).

Matador charts the fatal attraction between two natural born killers: Diego, a bullfighter ("matador" in Spanish also means "killer") and Maria, a feisty lawyer turned serial murderer. Having taunted each other like a *torero* passes a bull, they consummate their passion in simultaneous orgasm and suicide – which coincides with an eclipse. *Matador* presents a typical Almodóvar challenge for the viewer by keying into the sexual attraction of death. The bizarre plot is especially hard to take for those who think of death more in terms of hospital wards than as a kind of mental Viagra. But through droll irony, including a sharply-drawn mother-son relationship played by Julieta Serrano and Antonio Banderas, the funny ha-ha humanises what could remain just funny peculiar.

Above all, *Matador* offers the spectator an extensive menu of sexual choice: female and male fetishism; heterosexual and (closet) gay voyeurism; sadism, necrophilia; (frustrated) male rape, and even female penetration (Maria reaches orgasm

Nacho Martínez and Assumpta Serna in MATADOR
photo: Jorge Aparilio

as she plunges a hair-pin into her murder victims' napes).

The voluptuously-shot and gloriously physical *The Law of Desire* offers even more of the same, opening with a three-quarters rear shot of an actor, Juan, jerking off for a scene in a movie. When Antonio (Banderas, in his first major lead role) falls for the film's director, Pablo, he asks explicitly if Pablo wants anal sex; charmingly affectionate bedroom-scenes follow.

Almodóvar's grand theme – desire, its ineluctability and pain – received a further gloss in *Women On The Verge...*, which established him as a women's director par excellence. His attraction to women was almost inevitable. In 1987 there were three types of Spanish women who had been in short supply just two decades earlier: the educated, the employed and the divorced. Their standards of living had improved dramatically, not so their standards of love. *Women On The Verge...*'s protagonist, Pepa (a marvellously plucky Carmen Maura), is a case in point. Modelled on the penthouse from Jean Negulesco's *How to Marry a Millionaire*, Pepa's flat has all the mod-cons, including a boyfriend, Ivan. Or it did have. At the beginning of the film, Ivan dumps Pepa, who has just discovered she is pregnant. She finally tracks him down, saves him from being shot by another ex, and decides to have their child on her own.

The women in the movie still need male affection, still don their sexual battle-kit of make-up et al. But their men? Mere saps.

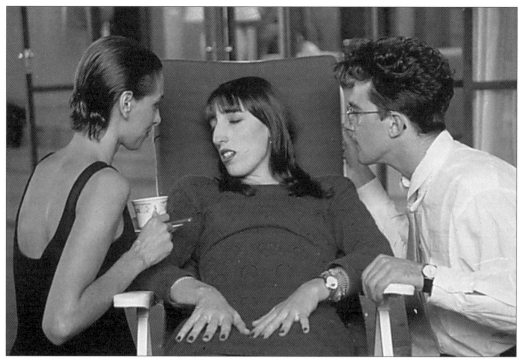

Rossy de Palma (centre) and Antonio Banderas in WOMEN ON THE VERGE OF A NERVOUS BREAKDOWN

Victoria Abril (centre) in HIGH HEELS

The cops who come by Pepa's flat are numbskulls; Ivan, a heel, slips into chat-up auto-drive whenever sees a girl, seeming to lack authentic sentiments. Women made $7.8m in Spain, remained the highest-grossing domestic film in Spanish history for a decade, and clinched Almodóvar's cult status world-wide.

Brotherly love, family values

Yet Almodóvar's next three films – the bonding drama *Tie Me Up! Tie Me Down!* (1989), the mother and daughter reunion melodrama *High Heels* (1991) and a radical portrait of urban dystopia, *Kika* (1993) – confused his fans and delighted his nay-saying Spanish critics, who claimed that he had lost not just Carmen Maura (publicly disgusted at not having a good enough seat at the 1989 Oscar ceremony when *Tie Me Up...* was nominated for Best Foreign Language Film), but also his sense of direction.

The films can also be viewed, however,

as a period of research and development from a director who had by now evolved a degree of artistic and financial autonomy. From *The Law of Desire* onwards, he had found his perfect producer, his brother Agustín Almodóvar. They founded El Deseo SA in 1986. *High Heels* kicked off a co-production pact with the Paris-based auteur powerhouse CiBy 2000, a deal which ensured that, as long as Almodóvar films came in on (their not very high) budget, its sales arm, CiBy Sales, could reasonably write off most of their production costs against foreign sales.

Although differing widely in texture, from the lushness of *High Heels* to the Euro-trash tones of *Kika*, two motifs mull through all three films. One is the increasing importance of the family. The Banderas character in *Tie Me Up!...* only charms Abril's actress when he acquires a domestic "femininity", running around collecting her black-market painkillers, worrying if she is getting enough to eat. The daughter's murder in *High Heels* is a desperate cry for attention from a mother who has put her performing career before maternal affection. *Kika* marks a pæan to Spain's bastion of social cohesion: a spit-and-grin housewife who somehow muddles through her husband's infidelity, her lover's serial murders and her rape, which becomes a star item on a TV reality show.

A second theme is Almodóvar's palpably growing discomfort with his unofficial status as the voice, and assumed advocate, of a new Spain, which by the 1990s seemed to offer a dire future to the dispossessed and the young, and had sunk into a mire of cultural commercialism, most evident in its TV programming (a point forced home in *Kika*).

He returns to this theme in *The Flower of My Secret* (1995). Leo, a romantic pulp novelist, pines for a visit from her husband Paco, a member of NATO's peace-mission force based out of Brussels. He finally floats in to tell her that their marriage is over. An emotional El Niño now seems to have swept over Spain. The film is shot in

Almodóvar with Veronica Forqué filming KIKA
photo: Jean Marie Leroy

Arctic blue, steel red, drab green. Paco, one of Spain's new European powerbrokers, is emotionally straight, stresses control, ironises about late Madrid nights. *The Flower of My Secret* marks the first appearance of Almodóvar's more positively-viewed "New Man", here a pillow-bellied, sentimental editor of Spanish broadsheet *El País*.

Another "New Man" is the long-suffering but caring Victor in *Live Flesh*, Almodóvar's most recent film and one which seems to mark a third creative period, after his early comedies and mature mock melodramas. A superb, if loose, adaptation of Ruth Rendell's novel of the same name, it charts with mellow humanism the moral flux of right and wrong, and the final, inescapable passion between Victor, disenfranchised son of a prostitute, a cop paralysed from the waist downwards, and his ex-junkie wife. In its single narrative, stylised realism and strong male characters, *Live Flesh* is perhaps the closest Almodóvar has come to mainstream film-making.

A talent to surprise

Beyond the superb marketing and appeal to camp sensibilities, Almodóvar's huge popularity at home and abroad may stem from his tapping with good humour into the central modern search of where to go next; how, especially to refashion relationships between the sexes. Yet Almodóvar still remains hard to pin-down. His desire to capture the full expressive potential of each scene means that the true trunk of his films is often obscured by a rich foliage of ideas and sensations.

Perhaps at the heart of his work there lies a deep distrust of the uniformity of mankind, whether their uniforms are grey suits or psychological -isms. He will approach themes, scenes and shots from a different angle, metaphorically and literally. He still surprises, as in the sex sequence of *Live Flesh*, in which he manages to convey democratically the sensuality of both male and female lover.

It seems very likely that his next film but one, following 1998's *All About My Mother*, will be an English-language co-production with the US, possibly an adaptation of Pete Dexter's *The Paperboy*. That would offer an exciting opportunity for Almodóvar to enhance still further the options by which a disorientated modern world can live.

JOHN HOPEWELL has written two books on Spanish film-making: *Out of the Past: Spanish Cinema After Franco* (London, British Film Institute, 1985) and *El cine español despues de Franco* (Madrid, Ediciones el Arquero, 1989). He heads *Variety*'s bureau in Spain and is European Editor of *Moving Pictures International*.

Almodóvar at work on LIVE FLESH
photo: Daniel Martinez

Almodóvar Filmography

Shorts

From 1974 onwards, Almodóvar made a series of mainly silent Super-8 shorts, mostly between five and 12 minutes in length. He would screen them and then present mock newscasts and commercials in the 'intervals' between shorts, as a parody of the interval entertainment offered during old-style Spanish double-bills. He also provided an off-screen live soundtrack, with the aid of a tape recorder, dubbed the actors' voices and offered a running commentary on their performances.

The Super-8s comprise: *Dos Putas, o Historia de amor que termina en boda* (Two Whores, or Love Story Ending in a Wedding), 1974; *Film político* (Political Film),1974; *La caída de Sodoma* (The Fall of Sodom), 1975: *Homenaje* (Hommage), 1975); *El sueño o La estrella* (The Dream or The Star), 1975; *Blancor* (Whiteness), 1975; *Trailer de Who's Afraid of Virginia Woolf?* (Trailer For Who's Afraid of Virginia Woolf?), 1976; *Sea caritativo* (Be Charitable), 1976; *Las tres ventajas de Ponte* (Ponte's Three Advantages), 1977; *Sexo va, sexo viene* (Sex Comes, Sex Goes), 1977, and the feature-length *Folle... Folle... Fólleme... Tim* (Fuck... Fuck... Fuck Me... Tim), 1978. He shot the 16mm *Salomé* in 1978 and a made-for-TV medium-feature *Trailer para amantes de lo prohibido* (Trailer For Love Things Which are Prohibited) in 1985.

1980 PEPI, LUCI, BOM Y OTRAS CHICAS DEL MONTON (Pepi, Luci, Bom...)

Script and Direction: PA. Photography: Paco Femenia. Editing: José Salcedo. Music: Little Nell, The Pegamoides, "My Mad Youth". Players: Carmen Maura (*Pepi*), Félix Rotaeta (*Policeman*), Olvido Gara "Alaska" (*Bom*), Eva Silva (*Luci*). Produced by Pepón Corominas for Figaro Films. 80 mins.

1982 LABERINTO DE PASIONES (Labyrinth of Passion)

Script and Direction: PA. Photography: Angel Luis Fernández. Editing: José Salcedo. Music: "Suck It To Me", Bernardo Bonezzi Fanny McNamara and PA; "Great Bargain", Bonezzi and PA. Players: Cecilia Roth (*Sexilia*), Imanol Arias (*Riza Niro*), Helga Line (*Toraya*), Marta Fernández Muro (*Queti*), Fernando Vivanco (*Doctor*), Ofelia Angelica (*Susana*), Angel Alcázar (*Eusebio*), Concha Grégori (*Angustias*), Cristina S. Pascual (*Eusebio's girlfriend*), Fanny McNamara (*Fabio*), Antonio Banderas (*Sadec*), Luis Ciges (*Tintorero*), Agustín Almodóvar (*Hassan*). Produced by Javier Garcillán and Mariel Guiot for Alphaville. 100 mins.

1983 ENTRE TINIEBLAS (Dark Habits)

Script and Direction: PA. Photography: Angel Luis Fernández. Editing: José Salcedo. Music: "I Left Because I Left", Curel Alonso; "Tell Me", Morris Abert; "Chained", Carlos Arturo Briz and Lucho Gatica. Art Direction: Pin Morales, Román Arango. Players: Cristina Sánchez Pascual (*Yolanda*), Julieta Serrano (*Mother Superior*), Marisa Paredes (*Sister Manure*), Mary Carrillo (*Marquesa*), Lina Canalejas (*Sister Víbora*), Manuel Zarzo (*Chaplain*), Carmen Maura (*Sister Perdida*), Chus Lampreave (*Sister Rata de Callejón*). Produced by Luis Clavo for Tesauro S.A. 115 mins.

1984 ?QUE HE HECHO YO PARA MERECER ESTO! (What Have I Done To Deserve This?!)

Script and Direction: PA. Photography: Angel Luis Fernández. Editing: José Salcedo. Music: Bernardo Bonezzi. Art Direction: Pin Morales, Román Arango. Players: Carmen Maura (*Gloria*), Angel de Andrés Lopez (*Antonio*), Chus Lampreave (*Grandmother*), Veronica Forque (*Cristal*), Kiti Manver (*Juani*), Juan Martínez (*Toni*), Gonzalo Suarez (*Lucas*), Amparo Soler Leal (*Patricia*), Emilio Gutierrez Caba (*Pedro*). Produced by Hervé Hachuel for Tesauro. 102 mins.

1986 MATADOR

Script: PA and Jesus Ferrero. Direction: PA. Photography: Angel Luis Fernández. Editing: José Salcedo. Music: Bernardo Bonezzi. Art Direction: Roman Arango, José Morales, Josép Rosell. Players: Assumpta Serna (*María Cardenal*), Antonio Banderas (*Angel*), Nacho Martinez (*Diego*), Eva Cobo (*Eva*), Julieta Serrano (*Berta*), Chus Lampreave (*Pilar*), Carmen Maura (*Julia*), Eusebio Poncela (*Comisario*), Bibi Andersen (*Flower seller*). Produced by Andrés Vicente Gómez for Iberoamericana de TV. 96 mins.

1987 LA LEY DEL DESEO (The Law of Desire)

Script and Direction: PA. Photography: Angel Luis Fernández. Editing: José Salcedo. Music: Tango (Stravinsky), Symphony No. 10 (Shostakovich), Bernardo Bonezzi. Set Design: Javier Fernández. Players: Eusebio Poncela (*Pablo Quintero*), Carmen Maura (*Tina Quintero*),

Antonio Banderas (*Antonio*), Miguel Molina (*Juan*), Manuela Velasco (*Ada*), Bibi Andersen (*Ada's mother*), Fernando Guillen (*Police inspector*), Nacho Martinez (*Doctor*), Helga Liné (*Antonio's mother*). Produced by Miguel Angel Pérez Campos for El Deseo in co-production with Lauren Films. 100 mins.

1987
MUJERES AL BORDE DE UN ATAQUE DE NERVIOS (Women on the Verge of a Nervous Breakdown)

Script and Direction: PA. Photography: José Luis Alcaine. Editing: José Salcedo. Music: Bernardo Bonezzi. Set Design: Félix Murcia. Players: Carmen Maura (*Pepa*), Fernando Guillen (*Iván*), Julieta Serrano (*Lucía*), Antonio Banderas (*Carlos*), Maria Barranco (*Candela*), Rossi de Palma (*Marisa*), Kiti Manver (*Paulina*). Produced by Agustín Almodóvar for El Deseo. 95 mins.

1989
¡ATAME! (Tie Me Up! Tie Me Down!)

Script and Direction: PA. Photography: José Luis Alcaine. Editing: José Salcedo. Music: Ennio Morricone. Set Design: Ferrán Sánchez. Players: Victoria Abril (*Marina*), Antonio Banderas (*Ricki*), Francisco Rabal (*Máximo Espejo*), Loles Leon (*Lola*), Julieta Serrano (*Alma*), Maria Barranco (*Berta*), Rossy de Palma (*Girl on moped*), Lola Cardona (*Director of psychiatric hospital*). Produced by Agustín Almodóvar for El Deseo.101 mins.

1991
TACONES LEJANOS (High Heels)

Script and Direction: PA. Photography: Alfredo Mayo. Editing: José Salcedo. Music: Ryuichi Sakamoto. Set Design: Pierre-Louis Thevenet. Players: Victoria Abril (*Rebeca*), Marisa Paredes (*Becky del Páramo*), Miguel Bosé (*The Judge/*

Marisa Paredes in HIGH HEELS

Hugo/Femme Letal), Pedro Diez del Corral (*Alberto*), Feodor Atkine (*Manuel*), Bibi Andersen (*Chon*), Miriam Diaz Aroca (*Isabel*), Nacho Martinez (*Juan*), Mairata O'Wisiedo (*Judge's mother*). Produced by Agustín Almodóvar for El Deseo and CiBy 2000. 113 mins.

1993
KIKA

Script and Direction: PA. Photography: Alfredo Mayo. Editing: José Salcedo. Music: "Love's Broken For Us", Fernanda and Bernarda, "Moonlight", Chavela Vargas. Players: Verónica Forqué (*Kika*), Victoria Abril (*Andrea*), Peter Coyote (*Nicholas*), Alex Casanovas (*Ramon*), Rossy de Palma (*Juana*), Santiago Lajusticia (*Paul Bazzo*), Anabel Alonso (*Amparo*), Bibi Andersen (*Beautiful stranger*), Charo Lopez (*Ramon's mother*). Produced by Agustín Almodóvar for El Deseo and CiBy 2000. 112 mins.

1996
LA FLOR DE MI SECRETO (The Flower of My Secret)

Script and Direction: PA. Photography: Affonso Beato.

Editing: José Salcedo. Music: "Full Moon Tune", Caetano Velasco, "The Last Drop", Chavela Vargas, "Oh, Love", Bola de Nieve. "Soleá", Miles Davis. Set Design: Wolfgang Burmann. Players: Marisa Paredes (*Leo*), Juan Echanove (*Angel*), Imanol Arias (*Paco*), Rossy de Palma (*Rosa*), Chus Lampreave (*Jacinta*), Carmen Elias (*Betty*), Joaquín Cortés (*Antonio*), Manuela Vargas (*Blanca*). Produced by Agustín Almodóvar for El Deseo and CiBy 2000. 90 mins.

1997
CARNE TREMULA (Live Flesh)

Script: PA, Ray Loriga, Jorge Guerricaechevarria, based on the novel *Live Flesh*, by Ruth Rendell. Direction: PA. Photography: Affonso Beato. Editing: José Salcedo. Music: Alberto Iglesias. Art Direction: Antxon Gómez. Players: Javier Bardem (*David*), Francesca Neri (*Elena*), Liberto Rabal (*Victor*), Angela Molina (*Clara*), José Sancho (*Sancho*), Penélope Cruz (*Isabelle*), Pilar Bardem (*Dona Centro*), Alex Angulo (*Bus driver*). Produced by Agustín Almodóvar for El Deseo, CiBy 2000 and France 3 Cinema. 100 mins.

Patrice Leconte

by Philippe Rouyer

Patrice Leconte is not an easily defined film-maker, as the release of *Half a Chance* earlier this year proved. After the sophisticated and much-honoured *Ridicule*, Leconte chose to deliver an action comedy with no ambitions other than to entertain, while playing with the image of its cast (superstars Jean-Paul Belmondo and Alain Delon, acting together more than 25 years after *Borsalino*, and the young Vanessa Paradis). *Half A Chance* has confused those who still viewed Leconte as the prototype of the director who renounces the "commercial" successes of his early years (*French Fried Vacation* and other café-theatre hits) in favour of the rewarding virtues of *cinéma d'auteurs*. The timeless wonderings of *Tandem* certainly marked a turning point in his career, but anyone wishing to understand Leconte's universe should not neglect his early films.

With the exception of *Ridicule*, Leconte has co-written all his films. However, *The Scent of Yvonne* is the only scenario he directed and produced. Unlike many French auteurs since the Nouvelle Vague, he understood straightaway that "one can never work too much on a script", and that at this stage of creation, it is often in a director's interest to work with a professional writer: scriptwriter Patrick Dewolf, author Claude Klotz and even writer-actor Michel Blanc.

Convinced that he should explore different styles in order to avoid boring himself or his audience, Leconte therefore alternates between box-office hits and pet productions, screen adaptations of literary material (novels, plays or comic strips), and original scenarios. It would be a mistake to label the dozens of commercials he has shot between each full-length feature since 1983 as merely a good source of income. These rather off-beat shorts have enabled him to adapt himself to stylistic constraints and to refine the image of his films. Long before he decided to launch into the advertising business, his career in the comic strip industry had helped him acquire his sense of ellipsis and economy (until *Ridicule*, none of his features was longer than 90 minutes).

PATRICE LECONTE was born in Paris on November 12, 1947. He decided at a very early age to become a moviemaker. To realise his ambition, he attended the renowned IDHEC (France's most prestigious film school), graduating in 1969. Regular visits to the Paris Cinémathèque helped him develop a strong cinematography culture. At the end of his studies, he veered away from tradition and decided not to start out as an on-set assistant. Instead, he worked as a cartoonist for the French magazine *Pilote*.

Until 1975, he spent as much time as possible shooting shorts such as *The Laboratory of Anxiety* , combining gags and fantasy, but made his living from the cartoon strips whose rectangular format hinted at his future predilection for cinemascope. The amount of effort needed for each new story line obliged him to concentrate on the essential. His work developed a cool and sophisticated humour, which would later be the trademark of his most personal comedies, and which would bring him closer to the universe of Marcel Gotlib, a friend and colleague at *Pilote*.

Cops flop, Splendid succeeds

When Leconte launched into feature films, one of his first productions was a screen adaptation of the investigations of Inspector Bougret, a character amalgamated from Inspector Bourel (hero of the famous French TV series *Les Cinq Dernières Minutes*) and Inspector Maigret. Gotlib had featured Bougret in his *Rubriques à Brac*, strip in *Pilote*, and the two men co-wrote the script of *The Toilets Were Locked from the Inside*, a pastiche of both *The Mystery of the Yellow Room* and the French whodunits of the 1950s.

In spite of photography by Bruno Nuytten – future director of *Camille Claudel* and Leconte's classmate at IDHEC – and the presence of two French stars, Jean Rochefort and stand-up comedian Coluche, this first attempt at comedy had a very poor reception. Its sense of humour, by turns surreal (a naked woman in a train) and alienating (running commentary by the characters in the midst of the action), did not go down well with a French public used to more conventional entertainment. Moreover, the film suffers from mediocre acting and the repetitive nature of certain incidents, which seem like running gags from a comic-book serial. The director later admitted that his lack of understanding of human relationships and of life on set had led to mistake after mistake. He would learn his lesson.

This failure led to a break in Leconte's career, but he bounced right back. An amateur of the Café theatre scene, Leconte wrote a script for the famous theatre company, Le Splendid, whose members included Gérard Jugnot, Michel Blanc, Thierry Lhermitte and Josiane Balasko. This new form of comedy (which had already launched Coluche) was at that time all the rage in France. In spite of the actors' enthusiasm, the project never got off the ground. However, when Yves Rousset-Rouard, the wealthy producer of *Emmanuelle*, now keen to change his image, decided to finance the screen adaptation of their play, *Amours, coquillages et crustacés*, the actors insisted on Leconte as director.

This satire, based on a holiday in an African Club Med resort, was filmed as *French Fried Vacation* (*Les Bronzés*). It was a much bigger success on screen than it had ever been on stage. It reveals its true colours right from the start, with Serge Gainsbourg's singing "Sea, Sex and Sun", and the French found its humour an agreeable change from the eternal tomfoolery of Louis de Funès and Pierre Richard. The entire film is a good-natured comedy but, with hindsight, one gag (the accidental death of one of the reps) is the first appearance of the black comedy of *Tango*.

The rapport between the director and the Splendid actors was such that they decided to shoot a sequel right away – a unique event in the filmography of an artist haunted by the fear of repeating himself. The sequel, *Les Bronzés Go Skiing*, was not as original, but still filled cinemas, before enjoying a second life on video. Today, its dinner scene, featuring outrageous mountain hillbillies, has cult status.

Free at last

Now associated with a certain kind of comedy, Leconte was asked by producer Christian Fechner to adapt the play *Come to My Place, I'm Staying at a Girlfriend's*, by Didier Kaminka and Luis Rego (one of the actors in *French Fried Vacation*). This marked the start of a very profitable collaboration with Michel Blanc, one of the pillars of the Splendid company. He wrote the script and played the main character, Guy, a sour, unemployed parasite, whose dubious shenanigans threaten to disrupt the harmonious relationship of the couple

Michel Blanc and Jane Birkin in CIRCULEZ, Y A RIEN A VOIR

at whose house he is crashing. *Come to My Place...* was a huge hit. Leconte's next two comedies, *I Want My Wife Back*, and *Move Along, There's Nothing to See*, also starring Blanc, were not as successful, but still sold over one million tickets. By this stage, in 1983, Leconte felt that he ought to change register, and accepted without hesitation Christian Fechner's offer to shoot an action comedy, *The Specialists*.

The story of two escaped convicts who hold up a Mafia-owned casino in the South of France, it resembles a draft version of *Half a Chance*, and brings to mind the light-hearted detective novels of Henri Vernueil and Georges Lautner. The style is the same (witty remarks and spectacular stunts) but Bernard Giraudeau and Gérard Lanvin, in the leading roles, add a breath of fresh air to parts previously played by Delon and Belmondo. Far from being Leconte's best film, *The Specialists* remains his biggest box-office hit to date, drawing in more than four million cinemagoers. Now the director at last felt free to produce the kind of feature he had always wanted, and unearthed *Tandem*, an old personal project from 1981 that had languished since being rejected by all prospective financial backers.

This road movie, accompanied by a haunting Richard Cocciante score, concerns the ongoing battle between an ageing, pretentious and disconsolate radio presenter and his loyal assistant, who desperately tries to conceal from him the management's decision to axe their programme. Comedy of manners in the

Michel Blanc and Sandrine Bonnaire in MONSIEUR HIRE
photo: Kobal Collection

style of the Splendid is never far from the surface throughout (notably in the dinner scene with small-town dignitaries), but the story of the pair's gruelling flight along the roads of France, punctuated by stays in seedy hotels, gradually takes on a more nightmarish quality, as the protagonist infects his companion with his madness. The motif of male friendship, which, from *The Toilets...* to *The Specialists*, had always fascinated Leconte, is enriched in *Tandem* by the spectre of death, symbolised by a mysterious red dog.

Reality is delicately observed and a subtle analysis of human relationships throws into relief the brief descents into the irrational – classic moments where the film, like the characters, slips towards a frightening void. Rochefort is sensational in the role of radio presenter. As his associate, Jugnot's performance mirrored Leconte's direction: offering proof that he could do better than the light, entertaining work for which he had been too quickly typecast.

The bald and the beautiful

The same can be said of Michel Blanc, whose bald head in *Monsieur Hire* is more evocative of Murnau's *Nosferatu* than the luckless philanderer he played in *French Fried Vacation*. The script is an adaptation of a Simenon novel first filmed by Julien Duvivier in the 1946 classic *Panique*. It describes the perverse relationship between Hire, a lonely man in his forties, and his young neighbour, whom he observes from his window every night.

By not revealing until the film's half-way point the secret which binds the pair together (Hire saw his neighbour's lover hiding the proof of a vicious crime), Leconte backgrounds the thriller plot in order to concentrate on the story of an impossible love. The greenish and expressionist visuals (in contrast to the grainy look of *Tandem*, which was shot in exteriors with no artificial light) adds to the claustrophobic and oppressive atmosphere. Leconte's incongruous close-ups of inanimate objects (a boiled egg, tomatoes rolling down stairs) and his insistence on Hire's odd habits (he listens to the same record night after night) suggest a deviant sexuality which adds soul to this brilliant exercise in style.

Sexuality and mental illness are again closely linked In Leconte's next film, *The Hairdresser's Husband*. This is again a kind of *huis-clos*, as most of the action takes place in the hairdressing salon, but this time the tone is light and poetic. Antoine, played by an enigmatic and inspired Jean Rochefort, fulfils his childhood dream when he marries Matilde and becomes a hairdresser's husband. From then on, life with his beloved is peaceful and quiet. His days are spent complacently watching her at work, and in the salon after hours he ardently embraces her.

Whether fantasy or reality, this happiness is too strong to endure. Matilde commits suicide in order to keep their love alive. Antoine is now alone in the salon with his memories and his Arab tunes, which no longer inspire in him the trances of old. Using insignificant details – a wool swimming costume decorated with cherry pompoms, a dance in amongst the hair products – the director invents a fantastical universe which, without ever crossing over into pure fantasy, keeps its distance from reality .

On the road again – twice

After a short break from cinema, during which he directed *Ornifle*, a play by Jean Anouilh, at the Bouffes-Parisiens theatre, Leconte made *Tango*, which cynically picks up the theme of the impossibility of a happy relationship. Incapable of living with or without his wife, a pilot (crazed Thierry Lhermitte) decides to murder her. The result is a rather bizarre road movie teaming the pilot, who goes off his head after killing his wife, with a misogynist judge bent on freeing criminal husbands (Philippe Noiret in an unlikely role) .

The plot and dialogue make one think of Bertrand Blier's cinema. Vertiginous scope set-ups (aerial shots at the beginning),

Richard Bohringer in TANGO

delicious portraits of the women encountered on the road, and the weird nature of the situations (a killer armed with blanks, a fisherman without his rod) link this entertaining musical comedy (tango music played at full blast in the car) to Leconte's last three previous success.

It was not for lack of talent that Leconte's next two films did not conjure up much enthusiasm. Due to a certain superficiality, created more on the part of the characters than the mise en scène, *The Scent of Yvonne* was disappointing. Leconte illuminates the beauty of Dutch model Sandra Majani by casting her with Jean-Pierre Marielle as an ageing queen past his sell by date, and a romantic, dreamy Hippolyte Girardot. More than ever, Leconte refuses to reveal the true nature of his characters, in order to revive, alongside solid intrigue, the nostalgic charm of a bygone era and languid scenery – the shores of Lake Geneva at the end of the 1950s.

Quite different from the sensuous nature of *The Scent of Yvonne*, *The Grand Dukes* is about the unlikely escapades of three failing actors while on tour. Quite frankly it is a farce. Rochefort, Noiret and Marielle clearly enjoyed playing fuddy-duddies who find renewed success by sabotaging an already disastrous play: lampshades falling on to the stage, actresses disappearing through trap doors, and a producer who tries to decimate his own troupe during every performance. Behind this burlesque madness, however, Leconte gives us a glimpse of broken destinies.

The wittiest Western

This despair shows in *Ridicule*, shot while *The Grand Dukes* was being edited (the two titles could be interchangeable). This subtle comedy, focusing on the dynamics of power and social appearances, owes its success to liberties taken in its historical reconstruction. Concentrating more on the flavour than the exact circumstances of life in the late eighteenth century, the director allows himself full poetic licence in order to expose the superficiality of court life.

Chosen as the opening film at Cannes in 1996, this period piece about the obstacle-strewn journey of an idealistic provincial nobleman who comes up to Versailles seeking finance for his humanitarian project (the draining of the swamps back home), is, at first glance, funny and witty. However, behind the smiles and powdered faces lies a bitter social game in which each player risks his or her life. Jean Rochefort, who plays the good-natured scientist, summed it up perfectly: *Ridicule* is "a Western where witticisms have replaced

Anna Galiena and Jean Rochefort in LE MARI DE LA COIFFEUSE   *photo: Kobal Collection*

six-shooters". It won four Césars, including Best Film and Best Director.

Firearms and wisecracks are the flavour of the day in *Half a Chance*, but the stakes are not the same. In this cocktail made up of equal parts action, humour and emotion, the question of who will win the war between the three heroes and the Russian Mafia generates no suspense. The heart of the film lies elsewhere, in the way that Leconte plays with the image of Delon and Belmondo, who, now much older, find themselves obliged to repeat the stunts of

Leconte with Fanny Ardant and Jean Rochefort shooting RIDICULE

photo: Catherine Cabrol

their old movies. The theme of ageing and male friendship does not quite reach the same heights as in *Tandem*. But what does it matter? Leconte has the luxury of changing the period, register and even the style of each film.

PHILIPPE ROUYER teaches cinema at the Sorbonne. He is a critic for *Positif* and contributes to numerous publications, including *Canal + Magazine*. He is the author of two books: *Initiation au cinéma* (1990) and *Le Cinéma gore: une esthétique du sang* (1997).

Leconte Filmography

SHORT FILMS

1968: *Autoportrait*; 1969: *L'Espace vital*; 1970: *Tout à la plume ou au pinceau*; 1971: *Le Laboratoire de l'angoisse*; 1972: *La Famille heureuse*; 1993: *Le Batteur de boléro*.

Contributions (one segment) to portmanteau films:

1991: *Contre l'oubli*; 1995: *Lumière et Compagnie*.

Leconte has made dozens of commercials for Guerlain, Chanel, Caprice des Dieux, Humex de Fournier, plats cuisinés Marie, Club Méditerranée, Volkswagen, Lotus, anti-drugs campaign.

1975
LES VÉCÉS ÉTAIENT FERMÉS DE L'INTÉRIEUR
(The Toilets Were Locked from the Inside)

Script: PL, Marcel Gotlib. Direction: PL. Photography: Bruno Nuytten. Editing: Catherine Michel. Production Design: Jacques d'Ovidio. Music: Paul Misraki. Players: Jean Rochefort (*Pichard*), Coluche (*Charbonnier*), Roland Dubillard (*Gazul*), Billy Bourbon (*Joseph Ordure*), Jean-Pierre Sentier (*Doctor Buffard*), Olga Valéry (*Mrs Buffard*), Patrick Guillemain (*Angelo*), Robert Dalban (*Trainer*), Danièle Évenou (*Kermadet Gwendoline*), Virginie Vignon (*Odette Jeandrin*), Jean-Louis Castelli (*Piazzorossicelli*), Darling Légitimus (*Rose*). Produced by Alain Poiré for Gaumont/Production 2000. 79 mins.

1978
LES BRONZÉS
(French Fried Vacation)

Script: PL and the Splendid (based on the play by the Splendid *Amours, coquillages et crustacés*). Direction: PL. Photography: Jean-François Robin. Editing: Noëlle Boisson. Production Design: Jacques d'Ovidio. Music: Alain Bernholc. Song: Serge Gainsbourg. Players: Michel Blanc (*Jean-Claude*), Gérard Jugnot (*Bernard*), Josiane Balasko (*Nathalie*), Christian Clavier (*Jérôme*), Thierry Lhermitte (*Popeye*), Michel Creton (*Bourseault*), Martin Lamotte (*Miguel*), Dominique Lavanant (*Christiane*), Marie-Anne Chazel (*Gigi*), Luis Rego (*Bobo*), Bruno Moynot (*Man with black briefs*), Guy Laporte (*Headman*). Produced by Yves Rousset-Rouard for Trinacra Films. 90 mins.

1979
LES BRONZÉS FONT DU SKI

Script: PL and the Splendid. Direction: PL. Photography: Jean-François Robin. Editing: Noëlle Boisson. Production Design: Jacques d'Ovidio. Music: Pierre Bachelet. Players: Michel Blanc (*Jean-Claude*), Gérard Jugnot (*Bernard*), Josiane Balasko (*Nathalie*), Christian Clavier (*Jérôme*), Thierry Lhermitte (*Popeye*), Dominique Lavanant (*Christiane*), Bruno Moynot (*Météo*), Maurice Chevit (*Marius*). Produced by Yves Rousset-Rouard for Trinacra Productions. 90 mins.

1980
VIENS CHEZ MOI, J'HABITE CHEZ UNE COPINE (Come To my Place, I'm Staying at a Girlfriend's)

Script: PL, Michel Blanc, Jean-

Delon, Vanessa Paradis and Belmondo filming UNE CHANCE SUR DEUX
photo: Patrick Camboulive

Luc Voulfow, Jean-Paul Sèvres, based on the play by Luis Rego and Didier Kaminka. Dialogues: Michel Blanc. Direction: PL. Photography: Bernard Zitzerman. Editing: Jacqueline Thiédot. Production Design: Ivan Maussion. Music: Renaud, Ramon Pipin, Jean-Philippe Goude. Players: Michel Blanc (*Guy*), Bernard Giraudeau (*Daniel*), Thérèse Liotard (*Françoise*), Anémone (*Adrienne*), Christine Dejoux (*Cécile*), Gaëlle Legrand (*Daphné*), Sylvie Granotier (*Girl in the car*), Marie-Anne Chazel (*Catherine*), Jean Champion (*Manager*), Isabelle Duthil-Lafrance (*Annie*), Marie-Pierre Casey (*Concierge*). Produced by Films Christian Fechner/Antenne 2. 90 mins.

1981
MA FEMME S'APPELLE REVIENS
(I Want My Wife Back)

Script: PL, Michel Blanc, Joseph Morhaim. Dialogues: Michel Blanc. Direction: PL. Photography: Robert Fraisse. Editing: Jacqueline Thiédot. Production Design: Ivan Maussion. Music: William Sheller. Players: Michel Blanc (*Bernard*), Anémone (*Nadine*), Xavier Saint-Macary (*Philippe*), Catherine Gandois (*Mireille*), Pascale Rocard (*Anne*), Christophe Malavoy (*Terry*), Michel Rivard (*Alexandre*), Sylvia Zerbib (*Girl in estate agent's office*), Charlotte de Turckheim (*Unwell woman*), Patrick Bruel (*François*), Jean-Michel Ribes (*Superintendent*), Ellen von Unwerth (*Kerstin*). Produced by Fildebroc/Films Christian Fechner. 85 mins.

1982
CIRCULEZ, Y'A RIEN À VOIR
(Move Along, There's Nothing To See)

Script: PL, Martin Veyron. Direction: PL. Photograph: Robert Fraisse. Editing: Joëlle Hache. Production Design: Éric Moulard. Music: Ramon Pipin, Jean-Philippe Goude. Players: Michel

Blanc (*Leroux*), Jane Birkin (*Hélène Duvernet*), Jacques Villeret (*Pélissier*), Michel Robbe (*Marc*), Gaëlle Legrand (*Martine*), Luis Rego (*Reska*), Martin Lamotte (*Cook*), Dominique Faysse (*Maid*), Jean-Michel Ribes (*Café owner*), Alan Adair (*Mr Muller*). Produced by Films Christian Fechner/Films A2. 90 mins.

1984
LES SPÉCIALISTES

Script: Bruno Tardon. Adaptation and dialogues: PL, Patrick Dewolf, Michel Blanc. Direction: PL. Photography: Eduardo Serra. Editing: Joelle Hache. Production Design: Ivan Maussion, Jacques Bufnoir. Music: Éric Demarsan. Players: Bernard Giraudeau (*Paul Brandon*), Gérard Lanvin (*Stéphane*), Christiane Jean (*Laura*), Bertie Cortez (*Gaetan Mazetti*), Maurice Barrier (*Kovacs*), Daniel Jegou (*Casino manager*), Jacques Nolot (*Gendarme*). Produced by Gaumont/Films Christian Fechner. 90 mins.

1986
TANDEM

Script: PL, Patrick Dewolf. Direction: PL. Photography: Denis Lenoir. Editing: Joëlle Hache. Production Design: Ivan Maussion. Music: François Bernheim. Players: Jean Rochefort (*Michel Mortez*), Gérard Jugnot (*Rivetot*), Sylvie Granotier (*Bookseller*), Julie Jézéquel (*Waiter*), Jean-Claude Dreyfuss (*Adviser*), Pierre-François Dumeniaud, Marie Pillet (*Hotel managers*), Albert Delpy (*Motorist*), Gabriel Gobin (*Barman*), Jacques Rousselot (*Mr. Vaillant*), Ged Marlon (*Picnicker*). Produced by Cinéa/Hachette Première et Cie/Films A2. 91 mins.

1988
MONSIEUR HIRE

Script: PL, Patrick Dewolf, from

the novel by Georges Simenon *Les Fiançailles de Monsieur Hire*. Direction: PL. Photography: Denis Lenoir. Editing: Joëlle Hache. Production Design: Ivan Maussion. Music: Michael Nyman, Brahms. Players: Michel Blanc (*M. Hire*), Sandrine Bonnaire (*Alice*), André Wilms (*Police Inspector*), Luc Thuillier (*Émile*), Philippe Dormoy (*François*), Marie Gaydu (*Masseuse*), Éric Béranger (*Bowling manager*). Produced by Cinéa/Hachette Première et Cie/FR3 Films Production in association with Sofinergie, Sofimage Créations, CNC. 80 mins.

1990
LE MARI DE LA COIFFEUSE
(The Hairdresser's Husband)

Script: PL, Claude Klotz. Direction: PL. Photography: Eduardo Serra. Editing: Joëlle Hache. Production Design: Ivan Maussion. Music: Michael Nyman. Players: Jean Rochefort (*Antoine*), Anna Galiena (*Mathilde*), Roland Bertin (*Antoine's father*), Maurice Chevit (*Agopian*), Philippe Clévenot (*Morvoisieux*), Jacques Mathou (*Mr. Chardon*), Claude Aufaure (*Gay customer*), Albert Delpy (*Donecker*), Henri Hocking (*Antoine, aged 12*), Ticky Holgado (*Morvoisieux's son-in-law*), Michèle Laroque (*Adoptive mother*), Anne-Marie Pisani (*Mrs Shaeffer*) Yvelyne Ailhaud (*Antoine's mother*). Produced by Lambart Productions/TF1 Films Production in association with Investimage 2 and 3, CNC. 80 mins.

1992
TANGO

Script: PL, Patrick Dewolf. Direction: PL. Photography: Eduardo Serra. Editing: Geneviève Winding. Production Design: Ivan Maussion. Music: Angélique and Jean-Claude Nachon. Players: Philippe Noiret (*François de Nemours, l'Élégant*),

Thierry Lhermitte (*Paul*), Richard Bohringer (*Vincent Baraduc*), Miou-Miou (*Marie*), Judith Godrèche (*Madeleine*), Carole Bouquet (*Lady in hotel*), Jean Rochefort (*Boots*), Michèle Laroque (*Hélène Baraduc*), Maxime Leroux (*Mariano Escobar*), Jean Benguigui (*Lefort*), Ticky Holgado (*Waiter*), Jacques Mathou (*Truck driver*). Produced by Cinéa/Hachette Première et Cie/TF1 Films Production/Zoulou Films, in association with Sofinergie, Canal+, Région Languedoc-Roussillon. 88 mins.

1993
LE PARFUM D'YVONNE
(The Scent of Yvonne)

Script: PL, from the novel by Patrick Modiano, *Villa Triste*. Direction: PL. Photography: Eduardo Serra. Editing: Joëlle Hache. Production Design: Ivan Maussion. Music: Pascal Estève. Players: Hippolyte Girardot (*Victor*), Sandra Majani (*Yvonne*), Jean-Pierre Marielle (*René Meinthe*), Richard Bohringer (*Yvonne's uncle*), Paul Guers (*Daniel Hendrickx*), Corinne Marchand (*Les Tilleuls manager*), Philppe Magnan (*Pulli*), Claude Dereppe (*Roger Fossorié*). Produced by Lambart Films/Zoulou Films in association with Le Centre Européen Cinématographique Rhöne-Alpes, M6 Films, Canal+. 89 mins.

1995
LES GRANDS DUCS

Script: PL, Serge Frydman. Dialogues: Serge Frydman. Direction: PL. Photography: Eduardo Serra. Editing: Joëlle Hache. Production Design: Ivan Maussion. Music: Angélique and Jean-Claude Nachon. Players: Jean-Pierre Marielle (*Georges Cox*), Philippe Noiret (*Victor Vialat*), Jean Rochefort (*Eddie Carpentier*), Catherine Jacob (*Carla Milo*), Michel Blanc (*Shapiron*), Clotilde Courau (*Juliette*), Pierre-Arnaud Juin

Gérard Jugnot and Christian Clavier in LES BRONZÉS

(*Pat*), Jacques Mathou (*Janvier*), Marie Pillet (*Clémence*), Jacques Nolot (*Marceau*), Jean-Marie Galey (*Markus*), Olivier Pajot (*Brami*). Produced by Lambart Films/M6 Films/Zoulou Films in association with le Centre Européen cinématographique Rhöne-Alpes, Cofimage 7. 85 mins.

1996
RIDICULE

Script: Rémi Waterhouse. Direction: PL. Photography: Thierry Arbogast. Editing: Joëlle Hache. Production Design: Ivan Maussion. Music: Antoine Duhamel. Players: Charles Berling (*Ponceludon de Malavoy*), Fanny Ardant (*Comtesse de Blayac*), Bernard Giraudeau (*Abbé Vilecourt*), Judith Godrèche (*Mathilde de Bellegarde*), Jean Rochefort (*Marquis de Bellegarde*), Bernard Dhéran (*de Montalieri*), Carlo Brandt (*Chevalier de Milletail*), Jacques Mathou (*Abbé de l'Épée*), Urbain Cancelier (*Louis XVI*), Albert Delpy (*Baron de Guéret*), Bruno Zanardi (*Paul*), Marie Pillet (*Charlotte*), Maurice Chevit (*Lawyer*). Produced by Épithète/Cinéa/France 3 Cinéma, in association with Canal+, CNC. 100 mins.

1998
UNE CHANCE SUR DEUX
(Half a Chance)

Script: PL, Patrick Dewolf. Dialogues: Serge Frydman. Photography: Steven Poster. Editing: Joëlle Hache. Production Design: Ivan Maussion. Music: Alexandre Desplat. Players: Jean-Paul Belmondo (*Léo Brassac*), Alain Delon (*Julien Vignal*), Vanessa Paradis (*Alice Tomaso*), Eric Defosse (*Carella*), Michel Aumont (*Ledoyen*), Alexandre Iakovlev (*"The Raincoat"*), Valery Gataev (*Anatoli Sharkov*), Jacques Roman (*Varinot*), Philippe Magnan (*Judge*), Olivier Parenty (*Carella's assistant*), Mbembo (*Maryline*), Guillaume Rannou (*Yob*). Produced by Films Christian Fechner/UGCF/TF1 Films Production, in association with Cofimage 8, Sofinergie 3 and 4, Canal+. 109 mins.

LA FILLE SUR LE PONT (The Girl on the Bridge)
[*shooting from August 1998*]

Players: Vanessa Paradis, Daniel Auteuil.

LA VEUVE DE SAINT-PIERRE
(The Widow of Saint-Pierre)
[*shooting from March 1999*]

Players: Daniel Auteuil, Juliette Binoche.

Gus van Sant

by Sheila Johnston

The peer group recognition conferred on *Good Will Hunting* proved a mixed blessing for Gus van Sant. In critical and commercial terms, the film was indisputably a triumph. It drew raves for its two young writer-stars, Ben Affleck and Matt Damon, the latter also playing the plum lead role, a gifted working-class youngster frittering away his mathematical genius in a dead-end job. The pair won an Oscar for their screenplay, and Robin Williams was similarly rewarded for his supporting turn as the psychiatrist who draws Damon out of his shell by acknowledging his own weaknesses and troubles. Van Sant himself received a nomination – his first – for Best Director.

The film boasted palpable strengths. The dialogue was finely textured, the performances captivating, the Boston blue-collar setting captured with insight and sympathy. But the basic storyline was very much in the traditional Hollywood mould, with a healthy dose of moral uplift, clearly signposted psychological revelations and a neat resolution. Many viewed it as a surprisingly old-fashioned movie to have come from such a resolutely off-Hollywood director.

Van Sant had shot to prominence in 1985 with *Mala Noche*, a gay love story which marked him out as a strikingly original talent with a penchant for unconventional subjects, a unique, hip but poetic sensibility and a highly idiosyncratic story-telling style. His emergence coincided with the revival of American independent cinema in the mid-1980s, sparked by directors like Spike Lee, Jim Jarmusch and, subsequently, Hal Hartley, Steven Soderbergh, Richard Linklater and Quentin Tarantino. But with *Good Will*, like so many before him, he appeared to be surrendering his maverick status.

GUS VAN SANT was born in Louisville, Kentucky, in 1952. His father, Gus Snr, was a travelling salesman working his way up the corporate ladder (he eventually became President of McGregor Doniger sportswear before branching out into women's fashion), so the family moved continually: about five or six times while Gus Jr was a child. While still at school he became interested in painting, producing what he later described as semi-figurative, Dali-esque landscapes, and in Super-8 film-making, and began making semi-autobiographical shorts for between $30 and $50. In 1970, he went to the Rhode Island School of Design, where he was a contemporary of David Byrne and other members of the Talking Heads pop group. Here he was introduced to avant-garde American directors like Stan Brakhage, Jonas Mekas and Andy Warhol, and swiftly changed his major from painting to cinema.

Turned away by Tinseltown

In 1976, after spending some time in Europe, he went to Los Angeles, where he secured a job at Paramount as production assistant to the writer-director Ken Shapiro. Shapiro had a measure of clout, having recently scored a hit with *The Groove Tube*, a film based on a cult television comedy show. But the climate was changing in Hollywood, and this kind of anarchic countercultural satire was being displaced by the new breed of *Jaws*-style event movies. Though van Sant and Shapiro developed several ideas together, none came to fruition.

In 1981, he vented some of this frustration in *Alice in Hollywood*, a film about a naive young actress who goes to Tinseltown and rapidly abandons her ideals. This project, which started life as a full-length feature but was later cut down by van Sant to 45 minutes, was never released. While living in LA, he spent some time in the insalubrious district around Hollywood Boulevard, observing the teenage hustlers and runaways who hung out there, and became fascinated by this parallel universe co-existing in close proximity to, but completely isolated from the ordinary "straight" world. Despite his own privileged, middle-class background, his work would return repeatedly to these beautiful losers on the margins of society.

In 1983, van Sant went to New York to work in an advertising agency as an assistant producer. Within two years he had saved $25,000, which enabled him finally to make his first feature, *Mala Noche*. This tale of the homosexual love of a liquor store clerk for a young Mexican immigrant, in Portland, Oregon, was based on a semi-autobiographical novella by Walt Curtis, a street writer whom van Sant had met in the 1970s while working in Portland as a sound recordist on a friend's film, and to whom he paid $500 for the rights.

Mala Noche bore several of what were to become its director's hallmarks. The central relationship was portrayed with a yearning romanticism, mingled with deadpan absurdity, while his non-judgmental manner declined to present homosexuality as a "problem" or, indeed, a special case in any way. Van Sant was openly gay, at the height of the Aids epidemic when homosexuality was regarded with enormous suspicion. Many homosexual film-makers reacted to this prejudice with fiercely radical and partisan movies, but, while van Sant would touch frequently on same-sex love in his work, he declined to adopt an overtly political agenda.

Shot in black-and-white, with looming close-ups and expressionistic camera angles, *Mala Noche* looked exceedingly handsome for its $25,000 budget, and it earned him instant acclaim on the festival circuit. It also attracted interest in Hollywood and, invited by Universal to pitch projects, he came up with three stories: one about drug-addicted pharmacy thieves; a tale about teenage male prostitutes; and a prison drama featuring a transvestite, a psychotic killer and a victim of a gang rape. None of them was taken up.

And so the director returned to Portland, which became his home and the backdrop for his next few movies. He found the city congenial: modern, but contained and near open country. The Pacific Northwest was also becoming a creative centre for independent musicians and film-makers – David Lynch would later set his influential TV series *Twin Peaks* in neighbouring Washington State. Above all, Portland was the perfect base for anyone wishing to maintain a reasonable proximity to, but healthy distance from Hollywood.

Sex 'n' drugs and surprising roles

In Portland, with the aid of independent production company Avenue, the first

Left to right: Heather Graham, Matt Dillon, James Le Gros and Kelly Lynch in DRUGSTORE COWBOY
photo: Kobal Collection

*River Phoenix and Keanu Reeves in MY OWN PRIVATE
IDAHO*   *photo: New Line/Kobal Collection*

script idea van Sant had pitched to
Universal became *Drugstore Cowboy*, a
picaresque road movie about a quartet of
junkies who feed their habit by raiding
pharmacies: the story was based on
another real-life case, that of James Vogle, a
convicted felon serving time for a series of
robberies in the 1970s, the period in which
the movie was also set. Matt Dillon played
the charming, feckless leader of the band,
who loves the chemical highs and the
outlaw lifestyle (van Sant's energetic,
mobile camerawork and surreal hal-
lucination scenes conveyed something of
its seductiveness), but who eventually sees
the need to cut free.

The film's release in 1989 coincided with
Nancy Reagan's "Just Say No" anti-drugs
campaign, but, unlike other movies at that
time, such as the John Belushi biopic,
Wired, it declined to occupy the high moral
ground. The playful tone was established
from the outset, in Dillon's laconic, ironic
voice-over: "I was once a shameless, full-
time dope fiend," he confides
unrepentantly. The director insisted that
Drugstore Cowboy did not endorse its
characters' behaviour, and the ending –
Dillon speeding to hospital in an
ambulance after being shot by a couple of
low-lifes – could scarcely be regarded as
glamorising narcotics abuse. This did not
prevent Avenue from asking for reshoots to
make the message less ambiguous. But
Drugstore Cowboy was released in the form
that van Sant intended.

Drugstore Cowboy gave Dillon his best

role in years and rejuvenated his ailing
career, confirming van Sant's gift for
bringing out the best in his actors and
allowing them to reveal facets they had not
been allowed to display before. And his
next film – based on the second rejected
script idea – did this again to brilliant
effect. *My Own Private Idaho* took two hot
teen idols, River Phoenix and Keanu
Reeves, and enabled each spectacularly to
reinvent his image.

Phoenix played a young gay prostitute
afflicted by narcolepsy, while Reeves was a
rich kid slumming it on the streets. The
story traced their relationships with their
parents (Phoenix was obsessed with his
lost mother; Reeves was rebelling against
his politician father); with each other
(Phoenix's character was unrequitedly in
love with Reeves); and with the
community of rent boys – social outcasts
who, as so often in van Sant's films, sought
solace and security in their alternative
"family".

Told from Phoenix's spaced-out
perspective, the narration was dreamlike
and fractured: it was, van Sant admitted,
spliced together from three entirely
separate screenplays. The action was
punctured by bizarre images dredged up
from somewhere deep in the subconscious,
such as a house suddenly crashing down
out of the sky (presumably a nod to *The
Wizard of Oz*), or a shoal of salmon leaping
upstream. In one sequence, the cover boys
from the porn magazines on a newsagents'
rack come to life and muse on their
profession. Midway through, the story
digressed into a long romp based on a
scene from *Henry IV*, via Orson Welles'
Chimes at Midnight, complete with cod-
Shakespearean dialogue.

Reeves, whose main claim to fame had
hitherto been as Ted in the dopey teen
comedy *Bill and Ted's Excellent Adventure*,
could at last hope to be taken seriously,
while Phoenix was named Best Actor at the
Venice Film Festival for his performance.
And for van Sant himself, *My Own Private
Idaho* was his greatest success yet, both
critically and commercially.

Thumbs down for the hitch-hiker

Van Sant's next film, however, was a severe disappointment. Based on Tom Robbins' 1970s novel, *Even Cowgirls Get The Blues* marked a new departure for its director. He would have, for the first time, a female protagonist, a hitch-hiker with giant thumbs whose adventures on the road include a spell in New York with decadent Warholian trendies, an affair with an oriental mystic and an interlude at a ranch run by a posse of militant lesbian cowgirls.

Van Sant had a relatively opulent budget to play with – $8.5m – and was able to attract an interesting, eclectic cast: Uma Thurman in the lead role, supported by John Hurt, Angie Dickinson, Lorraine Bracco, Buck Henry, Keanu Reeves and Rain Phoenix (River's sister). The project had all the makings of a cult movie. But, like many a self-conscious cult before it, it flopped dismally when it was premiered at the 1993 Venice Film Festival, which had received Idaho so enthusiastically only two years before.

The hippy early 1970s setting seemed dated and irrelevant, and van Sant had probably been unwise to import so many of the novel's long declamatory speeches wholesale into his script. Abruptly pulled from US release – although a full-scale marketing campaign was already in place – the film was thrown back to van Sant for re-editing. But when the reworked version finally appeared, it fared no better, although the director would continue to defend it loyally, insisting it was the movie he wanted to make.

Van Sant appeared to be suffering a reversal of fortune. Phoenix, who, according to rumour, had become seriously involved with heroin while immersing himself in his *My Own Private Idaho* role, had been unable to shake off his addiction and died of a lethal cocktail of drugs outside a West Hollywood club in 1993. The director subsequently explored his grief, in thinly fictionalised form, in his first novel, *Pink* (1997) whose narrator, a director of "independent infomercials", mourns the

Uma Thurman in EVEN COWGIRLS GET THE BLUES
photo: Kobal Collection

young star of his ads when the latter dies in similar circumstances to Phoenix.

Another of his own projects, *The Mayor of Castro Street*, based on a biography of Harvey Milk, the openly homosexual San Francisco politician who was assassinated in 1978, had run into difficulties. Robin Williams had been lined up to star, but the project collapsed when van Sant fell out with his producer, Oliver Stone, over a script which van Sant, as determined as ever not to pander to the gay lobby, felt depicted Milk as too much of a one-dimensional hero.

A murderous forecast

He struck back with *To Die For*, a comedy about an airheaded but ruthlessly ambitious television weather girl who murders her husband (Dillon again, sweetly slobbish) in her pursuit of a career. This film was intricately and cleverly constructed as a mock-documentary, with flashbacks, home video sequences and characters addressing the camera. In many ways it looked like a curiously impersonal piece: it was van Sant's first for a major

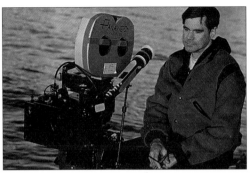

Van Sant shooting TO DIE FOR
photo: Kerry Hayes/Columbia TriStar

studio, Columbia, and he forewent the right to final cut. And the script, by Buck Henry from a book by Joyce Maynard, was a mordant but very broad attack on an easy target: the superficiality of American television and celebrity culture.

Still, *To Die For* relaunched yet another career, that of Nicole Kidman (previously known chiefly as Mrs Tom Cruise) whose wickedly accurate and funny performance won her a Golden Globe. And the

Matt Dillon and Nicole Kidman in TO DIE FOR
photo: Rank-Castle Rock/Turner

director's affinity for society's underdogs emerged in the touching and farcical sub-plot, in which her character befriends a trio of no-hope high-school kids (including another Phoenix sibling, Joaquin) and seduces them into her schemes.

After the success of *To Die For* and *Good Will Hunting* (world-wide takings of more than $220m in addition to the Oscar recognition), one might have thought van Sant in a sufficiently strong position to return to a small-scale, defiantly eccentric project. Instead, he announced his intention to remake Alfred Hitchcock's *Psycho* for Universal, with Vince Vaughn as Norman Bates and Anne Heche in the Janet Leigh role. It was his most astonishing choice yet. *Psycho* belongs to a genre, the thriller, entirely at odds with his freewheeling, laid-back approach. It represents the kind of classical Hollywood storytelling from which, he had claimed, he wanted to distance himself. And the original comes from a director whose sexual politics would seem diametrically opposed to van Sant's.

Moreover, the self-declared discipline of following someone else's storyboards virtually shot-for-shot – while filming in colour and speeding up the editing for the 'needs' of a modern audience – was a curious move for a director who had declared his preference for creating an atmosphere of controlled chaos and encouraging his actors to improvise on set.

In between his feature projects, he had taken an executive producer's credit on *Kids*, a nihilistic story of New York teenagers mired in a quagmire of sex, drugs and Aids. It might once have been a quintessential van Sant movie. Instead, *Kids* was directed in 1995 by the photographer Larry Clark, whose portraits of junkies had served as a visual point of reference for *Drugstore Cowboy*. Van Sant seemed to be turning his keenest attention to other artforms, with the publication in 1997 of *Pink*, and the pursuit of his long-standing interest in music: he has directed music videos for David Bowie, Elton John, The Red Hot Chili Peppers and Tracy

Chapman, and plays guitar and writes songs; in the winter of 1997-98 he released two albums, *18 Songs About Golf* and *Gus van Sant*.

Withdrawn and enigmatic in person, he has always kept his cards close to his chest and his next move is anyone's guess. Meanwhile, to those who reproach him for moving perhaps irretrievably into the mainstream – or, depending on how one looks at it, selling out to Hollywood – the director's riposte is that the most unadventurous thing he could do would be to go on making the same kind of films with which he made his name.

Van Sant with Matt Damon, shooting GOOD WILL HUNTING   *photo: George Kraychyk*

SHEILA JOHNSTON is a critic and writer on film who contributes regularly to *The Times*, *Evening Standard* and *Daily Telegraph*, London, as well as *Variety* and other publications. She is the author of a PhD thesis (University College London) on Rainer Werner Fassbinder and the New German Cinema, and of *Keanu*, a biography of Keanu Reeves.

Van Sant Filmography

1985
MALA NOCHE

Script: GvS, based on the novella by Walt Curtis. Direction: GvS. Photography: John Campbell, with Eric Alan Edwards. Editing: GvS. Music: Creighton Lindsay. Players: Tim Streeter (*Walt*), Doug Cooeyate (*Johnny*), Ray Monge (*Roberto Pepper*), Nyla McCarthy (*Betty*), Sam Downey (*Hotel clerk*), Bob Pitchlynn (*Drunk man*), Eric Pedersen (*Policeman*), Marty Christiansen (*Bar friend*), Bad George Connor (*Wino*), Don Chambers (*Himself*), Walt Curtis (*George*). Produced by GvS for the Northern Film Company. 78 mins.

1989
DRUGSTORE COWBOY

Script: GvS, Daniel Yost, based

on the novel by James Fogle. Direction: GvS. Photography: Robert Yeoman, with Eric Alan Edwards. Editing: Curtiss Clayton, Mary Bauer. Production Design: David Brisbin. Music: Elliot Goldenthal. Players: Matt Dillon (*Bob Hughes*), Kelly Lynch (*Dianne Hughes*), James Le Gros (*Rick*), Heather Graham (*Nadine*), Beah Richards (*Drug counsellor*), Grace Zabriskie (*Bob's mother*), Max Perlich (*David*), William S Burroughs (*Tom the Priest*), Eric Hull (*Druggist*), James Remar (*Gentry*), John Kelly (*Cop*). Produced by Nick Wechsler, Karen Murphy for Avenue Entertainment. 101 mins.

1991
MY OWN PRIVATE IDAHO

Script: GvS, with additional

dialogue by William Shakespeare. Direction: GvS. Photography: Eric Alan Edwards, John Campbell. Editing: Curtiss Clayton. Production Design: David Brisbin. Music: Bill Stafford. Players: River Phoenix (*Mike Waters*), Keanu Reeves (*Scott Favor*), James Russo (*Richard Waters*), William Reichert (*Bob Pigeon*), Rodney Harvey (*Gary*), Chiara Caselli (*Carmella*), Michael Parker (*Digger*), Jessie Thomas (*Denise*), Flea (*Budd*), Grace Zabriskie (*Alena*), Tom Troupe (*Jack Favor*), Udo Kier (*Hans*), Sally Curtice (*Jane Lightwork*), Robert Lee Pitchlynn (*Walt*), Mickey Cottrell (*Daddy Carroll*), Wade Evans (*Wade*). Produced by Laurie Parker for New Line Cinema. 104 mins.

1993
EVEN COWGIRLS GET THE BLUES
Script: GvS, based on the novel by Tom Robbins. Direction: GvS. Photography: John Campbell, Eric Alan Edwards. Editing: Curtiss Clayton. Production Design: Missy Stewart. Music: k.d. lang, Ben Mink. Players: Uma Thurman (*Sissy Hankshaw*), Rain Phoenix (*Bonanza Jellybean*), Lorraine Bracco (*Delores del Ruby*), John Hurt (*The Countess*), Angie Dickinson (*Miss Adrian*), Noriyuki 'Pat' Morita (*The Chink*), Keanu Reeves (*Julian*), Sean Young (*Marie Barth*), Crispin Glover (*Howard Barth*), Ed Begley Jnr (*Rupert*), Carol Kane (*Carla*), Roseanne Arnold (*Madame Zoe*), Buck Henry (*Dr Dreyfus*), Ken Kesey (*Sissy's daddy*), Grace Zabriskie (*Mrs Hankshaw*), Udo Kier (*Film director*). Produced by Laurie Parker for New Line Cinema. 108 mins.

1995
TO DIE FOR

Script: Buck Henry, based on the novel by Joyce Maynard. Direction: GvS. Photography: Eric Alan Edwards. Editing: Curtiss Clayton. Production Design: Missy Stewart. Music: Danny Elfman. Players: Nicole Kidman (*Suzanne Stone*), Matt Dillon (*Larry Maretto*), Joaquin Phoenix (*Jimmy Emmett*), Casey Affleck (*Russell Hines*), Illeana Douglas (*Janice Maretto*), Alison Folland (*Lydia Mertz*), Dan Hedaya (*Joe Maretto*), Wayne Knight (*Ed Grant*), Kurtwood Smith (*Earl Stone*), Buck Henry (*Mr Finlaysson*), Joyce Maynard (*Lawyer*). Produced by Laura Ziskin for Columbia Pictures. 107 mins.

1997
GOOD WILL HUNTING
Script: Matt Damon, Ben Affleck. Direction: GvS. Photography: Jean Yves Escoffier. Editing: Pietro Scalia. Production Design: Melissa Stewart. Music: Danny Elfman. Players: Robin Williams (*Sean McGuire*), Matt Damon (*Will Hunting*), Ben Affleck (*Chuckie*), Stellan Skarsgård (*Professor Gerald Lambeau*), Minnie Driver (*Skylar*), Casey Affleck (*Morgan*), Cole Hauser (*Billy*), John Mighton (*Tom*), Rachel Majorowski (*Krystyn*), Colleen McCauley (*Cathy*). Produced by Lawrence Bender for Miramax Films. 126 mins.

Michael Winterbottom

by Geoff Brown

L isten to Derek Jarman fulminating in 1987, in his book *Kicking the Pricks*: "I watch the new crop of British films and smile at their authors' claims. What have these sitcom writers (who can barely grope their way past the TV) got to do with cinema? And those responsible for visualising them, where ever did they learn their language? In some blind institute."

The intervening decade has brought no overwhelming changes to the visual landscape of British films. True, the *Trainspotting* team, led by director Danny Boyle, have set out to jolt us from complacency. Just consider the opening line of the published *Trainspotting* script: "INTERIOR. HORRIBLE TOILET. DAY." But the British movies that reach the screen remain largely in the hands of new film-makers with little cinema experience, too tethered to their past lives as television directors, music video merchants, actors or scriptwriters to employ the medium's own special language with ease.

Then there is Michael Winterbottom. He caused a stir at home in 1994 with his gritty direction of the television series *Family*. Eyebrows were raised internationally the following year when his first cinema feature, *Butterfly Kiss*, was presented in competition at Berlin. Images, emotions, situations: all were pushed to unfamiliar extremes in a grotesque tale of murder and devotion. Then came a television film, *Go Now*, which broke the boundaries of disease-of-the-week movies with its urgent, unorthodox account of a man battling multiple sclerosis.

Literary adaptation, mainstay of the posh end of British cinema, was the next genre to receive a kick in the pants. Hardy's *Jude the Obscure* was the source, *Jude* the result: lean and mean, with no rolling hills or picturesque interiors. The ambitious and prickly war drama *Welcome to Sarajevo*, in 1997, further consolidated Winterbottom's position as British cinema's hottest property, maker of films uneven at times in achievement, but unparalleled for passion and visual flair.

Not to mention exciting casts. From his earliest work in television, Winterbottom has shown an empathy with youth, and – by luck or judgement – has worked with several of British cinema's rising stars, securing some of their best performances. Kate Winslet's suffering in *Titanic* was nothing compared to the tragic reversals experienced as Sue Bridehead in *Jude*. Robert Carlyle shone equally brightly as the defiant MS sufferer in *Go Now*; while in Winterbottom's latest, the seaside mood piece *I Want You*, Rachel Weisz is potent enough to obliterate memories of her vacuous outcast heroine in *Amy Foster* (aka *Swept from the Sea*).

MICHAEL WINTERBOTTOM was born in Blackburn, Lancashire, on March 29, 1961. His film education began in his teens: the local film society introduced him to Werner Herzog and the other gods of the New German cinema, to Ingmar Bergman, and the French New Wave, Godard and Truffaut especially. This was a crucial experience. You can tell from Winterbottom's work how much he gained from European art films of the late 1950s and 1960s.

He learned the delights of narrative fragmentation and jump-cut editing; he absorbed the film-makers' sympathy for characters, often young, living beyond the fringe of conventional society; he saw the creative benefits of freewheeling shooting on location, and maintaining a family of technicians from project to project.

Conventional British film-making practice could never have taught him these skills and sympathies; nor could mainstream Hollywood.

From documentary to drama

Winterbottom read English at Oxford University. Then the film and television courses offered by Bristol University beckoned, followed by the Polytechnic of Central London, from where he graduated in 1984 with an MA in film and television. He entered the industry via the cutting rooms of Thames Television, in London, where he worked initially as an assistant editor. Within two years he was assisting the veteran British iconoclast Lindsay Anderson on the director's tetchy and schoolmasterly contribution to a three-part series, *British Cinema: Personal View*, produced by Kevin Brownlow and David Gill to mark the end of British Film Year in 1986.

Two years later, Winterbottom demonstrated greater warmth and love of his subject when he made his directing debut with two television documentaries about Ingmar Bergman, *The Magic Lantern* (for Channel 4) and *The Director* (for Thames). By 1989, Winterbottom was beginning to direct dramatic television, mostly series episodes. He made *Rosie the Great* for the children's series *Dramarama*, and collaborated with Frank Cottrell Boyce, who would later write *Butterfly Kiss*, on an hour-long drama, *The Strangers*. There was work for Central TV's popular hero-for-hire series,

Saskia Reeves (left) and Amanda Plummer in BUTTERFLY KISS

Boon, and one episode for *Shrinks*, a 1991 series about a psychiatric institute.

Some of this work allowed little scope for personal expression: it is hard to imagine Winterbottom deriving much satisfaction from directing "Death at the Bar" for the BBC, one of five cosy *Inspector Alleyn Mysteries*, based on Ngaio Marsh's detective stories. An eminent barrister had died in a village pub, apparently from a lethal dart. But how was the dart prepared – and by whom? One trusts the audience wanted to know. But all the time, Winterbottom was gaining experience, and forging creative partnerhips with writers, producers and technicians like Trevor Waite, now his regular editor, then a supervising editor at Thames. In some cases we can see future themes and sensibilities emerging.

Hitting the road

Forget About Me, his first feature-length film, began as a Thames Television commission for two half-hour programmes for teenagers; what emerged in 1990, however, was a 72-minute film on 16mm, made in collaboration with Hungarian television, fit to be shown at the London, Cologne and Lisbon film festivals. Footloose youth was the topic: Frank Cottrell Boyce's script followed the fortunes of two Scots youths stationed at an army base in West Germany, who pick up an exuberant Hungarian girl while travelling to Hungary to drink in the New Year. It was fresh; it was energetic; it cared for its characters.

Winterbottom's next film, *Under the Sun*, made for Thames in 1991, enlarged on the road movie feeling. Susan Campbell's script underwent regular changes to reflect new thoughts and events as they emerged during shooting in Spain. Kate Hardie was the heroine, a reclusive 19-year-old on a world trip, left high and dry in Malaga when her companion takes off with a local Romeo. Working with cameraman Dafydd Hobson, another key member of his film family, Winterbottom described the

heroine's plight in a nuanced European style, and showed once again his intuitive grasp of the confusions and pressures felt by young people. The film was shown at the 1992 London, Montreal and Turin festivals.

By shooting these one-off TV ventures on location, outside England, Winterbottom found a new freedom of expression, closer in style to the European film-makers he loved: Bergman, Truffaut, these were his models. The press book for *Butterfly Kiss* humorously informed journalists that "in an ideal world, [Winterbottom] would gather round him a Bergman-like entourage of actors and production crew to work on a series of low-budget, personal films for which the finance would always be available".

While waiting for this ideal world to materialise, Winterbottom kept busy on other TV ventures. *Love Lies Bleeding*, made for BBC2's ScreenPlay series, earned a silver medal at the New York Television Festival in 1993. Mark Rylance gave a subtle performance as a Republican inmate of the Maze Prison, Belfast, given a day release to help track the killers of his former girlfriend. However, novelist Ronan Bennett's script, though knowledgeably couched in prison slang and street talk, shed no new light on the Irish troubles. Winterbottom found wider success with his direction of "The Mad Woman in the Attic", the opening two-hour episode of the popular Granada series *Cracker*, written by another strong regional voice, Liverpool's Jimmy McGovern.

Fear and loathing in Dublin

But the work that secured Winterbottom's future was *Family*, in 1994, a four-part TV series written by the hugely successful Irish author Roddy Doyle. Readers and viewers weaned on the rollicking humour of *The Commitments*, *The Snapper* and *The Van* – Doyle's Barrytown trilogy – were taken aback by the harshness of these slices of life from the Dublin suburbs. Each episode observed the chaos from the viewpoint of one member in the family of

Charlo Spencer, played by Sean McGinley, who ruled his wife and two teenage children with a cocktail of fear and violence.

Winterbottom chose a deliberately raw and rough-edged style to match the fiery dialogue. Artful compositions were outlawed; the camera almost lunged at the characters as they fought, drowned sorrows in drink, ran away or were thrown out of the house.

Doyle remained the dominant creative personality; but you can see the director of *Butterfly Kiss* and *Welcome to Sarajevo* in Winterbottom's knack for bringing us close to dangerous situations. "You like these characters much more," he said, "when you know you can safely return them to a box in the corner once the programme is finished." Among other awards, *Family* won the Prix Europa for the year's best European television programme. A two-hour feature version made an impact at festivals in Toronto, Galway, Telluride, London and Chicago.

During post-production on *Family*, Winterbottom took a decisive step, away from television, into films made directly for cinema. His power base was Revolution Films, a company he formed with *Family* producer Andrew Eaton, who announced their intention to make movies "that will cause a stir". Films, in fact, like *Butterfly Kiss*, Winterbottom's cinema debut, made for his producer on *Time Riders*, Julie Baines, through her own fledgling company, Dan Films. Shooting started in June 1994, one month after the television transmission of *Family*.

Once again, Winterbottom showed his flair for location shooting: no other British film has captured so well the country's desolate motorway landscape of tarmac, service stations and motels. Into this bleak setting, Winterbottom and his writer, Cottrell Boyce, placed two extraordinary characters. Eunice, played by Amanda Plummer, wears chains and bruises round her chest, and thinks nothing of murdering passers-by. Miriam (Saskia Reeves), a

Kate Winslet in JUDE   *photo: Kobal Collection*

mousy shop assistant, becomes her devoted friend, and the two embark on a corpse-laden spree along the motorways of northern England. Besides this pair, so powerfully portrayed, Thelma and Louise seem like a couple of Shirley Temples.

Winterbottom drives the bizarre story along with real cinematic flair: audiences are given a hell of a ride. But to what purpose? Cottrell Boyce's script raises matters of punishment and hell, and gives scattered biblical references, though the

Winterbottom on location for WELCOME TO SARAJEVO
photo: Laurie Sparham/Miramax

film ends up as more of an exercise in grotesquerie than a rewarding exploration of human nature's darker corners.

No sentiment allowed

Butterfly Kiss certainly set people talking, and ensured immediate interest in the first product of Revolution Films, *Go Now*, financed and transmitted in Britain by the BBC, but given some theatrical exposure abroad. Freed from Cottrell Boyce's fondness for pretentious fantasy, Winterbottom buckled down with energy and compassion to the simple human predicament of a man fighting MS. Daf Hobson's camera leaped about Bristol; jokes peppered the script, written by Jimmy McGovern and MS sufferer Paul Powell. In these speedy 80 minutes there was no time, and no room, for maudlin sentiment, the usual tone of films about diseases. Robert Carlyle was immensely appealing as the ordinary Joe hero, a plasterer and amateur soccer player, put to the test when MS strikes.

Winterbottom then moved into a crowded British field with a classic literary adaptation, *Jude*, mostly shot in the summer of 1995, far from Hardy's Dorset (too twee, said the director) in harsher locations, like Yorkshire and Edinburgh. The opening scene banished all prospect of the usual prettified celluloid. Rooks circled above a ploughed field, starkly shot in widescreen black-and-white by Eduardo Serra. Instead of scaring the birds, young Jude feeds them, and gets whipped for his pains.

Subsequent scenes moved into colour. The sun sometimes shone, but the mood remained bleak. Winterbottom encouraged his scriptwriter, Hossein Amini, to scratch period words from the script: all talk had to be forceful, modern-sounding. His direction caught the fierceness and grit of Hardy's novel so effectively that he risked emotional monotony. But Kate Winslet set the film ablaze as Sue, cousin of the doomed stonecutter Jude (Christopher Ecclestone), life drained out of her by fate's hard knocks and society's demands.

Stephen Dillane (right) and Emirea Nusević in
WELCOME TO SARAJEVO

Casualties of war and love

Winterbottom always wants an immediacy in his films, and he achieved it in spades in his most ambitious project to date, *Welcome to Sarajevo*, which began shooting in the summer of 1996, four years after the events it describes. Shooting on location caused practical problems, but Winterbottom still created a vivid picture of the civil war in Bosnia, and the surrounding media circus, and made cutting use of archive footage of various visitations by politicians and the UN.

The film drew on the experiences of Michael Nicholson, the British television reporter moved to smuggle out and adopt an orphaned child. Stephen Dillane, Nicholson's fictional representative, was quietly persuasive; Woody Harrelson and Marisa Tomei were less helpful presences in a film otherwise eager to do without Hollywood gloss.

Winterbottom's most recent film, *I Want You*, shown in competition at Berlin in 1998, sees him returning, in part, to the intimate and bizarre mood of *Butterfly Kiss*. This is his most European film to date. In a depressed seaside town (Hastings supplied locations), a hairdresser (Rachel Weisz), suffers the loving gazes of a silent 14 year-old refugee and the unwanted attentions of her former boyfriend, convicted of murder but now on parole.

Eoin McNamee's script craves an audience's indulgence with its sketchy characterisations and poetic posturings (lovingly rendered by Slawomir Idziak, cameraman on Kieślowski's *A Short Film about Killing*). But Winterbottom keeps us glued to the screen with the unbuttoned sex scenes (there is something definitely un-English about him here) and a visual flair that puts him head and shoulders above other new British directors.

In June, Winterbottom started shooting the romantic comedy *Old New Borrowed Blue*, set in Northern Ireland and starring *Jude*'s Christopher Eccleston. We know we can expect something exciting.

Rachel Weisz plays a hairdresser in I WANT YOU
photo: Marcus Robinson/PolyGram

GEOFF BROWN has been film critic of *The Times* in London since 1990. He has written extensively on British film-makers like Launder and Gilliat, John Baxter and Michael Balcon, and is currently preparing a book on the English character as depicted in films.

Winterbottom Filmography

TELEVISION

1988: *Ingmar Bergman: The Magic Lantern*; *Ingmar Bergman: The Director*. 1989: *Rosie the Great*; *The Strangers*. 1990: *Forget About Me*. 1992: *Under the Sun*. 1993: *Love Lies Bleeding*; *Cracker: The Mad Woman in the Attic*; *Cinema Europe – The Other Hollywood: Art's Promised Land* (Co-Dir: Dan Carter); *The Inspector Alleyn Mysteries: Death at the Bar*. 1994: *Family* [four-part series].

1994
FAMILY

Script: Roddy Doyle. Direction: MW. Photography: Daf Hobson. Editing: Trevor Waite. Art Direction: Mark Geraghty. Music: Elvis Costello, John Harle. Players: Sean McGinley (*Charlo*), Ger Ryan (*Paula*), Neili Conroy (*Nicola*), Barry Ward (*John Paul*), Des McAleer. Produced by Andrew Eaton, for the BBC. 118 minutes. [Feature-length version of the television series].

BUTTERFLY KISS

Script: Frank Cottrell Boyce. Direction: MW. Photography: Seamus McGarvey. Editing: Trevor Waite. Art Direction: Rupert Miles. Music: John Harle. Players: Amanda Plummer (*Eunice*), Saskia Reeves (*Miriam*), Paul Bown (*Gary*), Freda Dowie (*Elsie*), Fine Time Fontayne (*Tony*), Des McAleer (*Eric*), Ricky Tomlinson (*Robert*), Emily Aston (*Katie*). Produced by Julie Baines, for Dan Films. 85 mins.

1995
GO NOW

Script: Paul Powell, Jimmy McGovern. Direction: MW. Photography: Daf Hobson. Editing: Trevor Waite. Production Design: Hayden Pearce. Music: Alastair Gavin. Players: Robert Carlyle (*Mick Cameron*), Juliet Aubrey (*Karen Walker*), James Nesbitt (*Tony*), Sophie Okonedo (*Paula*), John Brobbey (*Geoff*),

Darren Tighe (*Dell*), Berwick Kaler (*Sammy*), Sean McKenzie (*George*), Sara Stockbridge (*Bridget*), Sean Rocks (*Charlie*). Produced by Andrew Eaton, for Revolution Films and the BBC. 81 mins.

1996
JUDE

Script: Hossein Amini, from the novel *Jude the Obscure* by Thomas Hardy. Direction: MW. Photography: Edouard Serra. Editing: Trevor Waite. Production Design: Joseph Bennett. Music: Adrian Johnston. Players: Christopher Eccleston (*Jude Fawley*), Kate Winslet (*Sue Bridehead*), Liam Cunningham (*Phillotson*), Rachel Griffiths (*Arabella*), June Whitfield (*Aunt Drusilla*), Ross Colvin Turnbull (*Little Jude*), James Daley (*Jude as a Boy*). Produced by Andrew Eaton, for Revolution Films. 123 mins.

1997
WELCOME TO SARAJEVO

Script: Frank Cottrell Boyce, based on the book *Natasha's Story* by Michael Nicholson. Direction: MW. Photography: Daf Hobson. Editor: Trevor Waite. Production Design: Mark Geraghty. Music: Adrian Johnston. Players: Stephen Dillane (*Henderson*), Woody Harrelson (*Flynn*), Marisa Tomei (*Nina*), Emirea Nusević (*Emira*), Kerry Fox (*Jane Carson*), Goran Visnjic (*Risto*), James Nesbitt (*Gregg*), Emily Lloyd (*Annie McGee*), Igor Dzambazov (*Jacket*), Gordana Gadzic (*Mrs Savic*), Juliet Aubrey (*Helen Henderson*), Drazen Sivak (*Zeljko*).

1998
I WANT YOU

Script: Eoin McNamee. Direction: MW. Photography: Slawomir Idziak. Editing: Trevor Waite/ White. Production Design: Mark Tildesley. Music: Adrian Johnston. Players: Rachel Weisz (*Helen*), Alessandro Nivola (*Martin*), Luka Petrusic (*Honda*), Labina Mitevska (*Smokey*), Carmen Ejogo (*Amber*), Ben Daniels (*Bob*), Graham Crowden (*Old Man*), Geraldine O'Rawe (*Sonja*), Steve J. Shepherd (*Sam*), Phyllida Law, Mary MacLeod (*Women at Hair Salon*), Kenny Doughty (*Smokey's Friend*). Produced by Andrew Eaton for Revolution Films. 87 mins.

John Woo

by Derek Elley

Neither film school graduate nor professional journeyman, John Woo is a member of that sizeable but often disregarded middle category among Hong Kong-raised directors: the movie buff who has worked his way up through the industry and is content to work within commercial genres.

Though rightly lauded (and almost exclusively known in the West) for a swathe of heroic, in-your-face action dramas exploring modern codes of chivalry and friendship, Woo is a far more versatile film-maker than his output of the past decade suggests. Of the 25 features he has directed to date – averaging one per year throughout his directing career – only 11 have been in the genre that made his name internationally and propelled him from Hong Kong to Hollywood in the early 1990s.

Woo's career has in fact been marked by several false starts, sudden setbacks and a variety of non-directing jobs. Now in his early fifties, and with an unassailable reputation as the man who led the "exodus" of Hong Kong directors to Hollywood, he still has far more to offer than the narrow genre into which he has been placed in the past decade or so. Some of his best, and most human work resides in the 14 pictures he made prior to his breakthrough in 1986 with *A Better Tomorrow*: the nine comedies, four martial arts movies and even one Cantonese Opera film on which he honed his skills in the take-no-prisoners industries of Hong Kong and Taiwan.

JOHN WOO was born on October 22, 1946, in Guangzhou (Canton), China, to parents from Pingnan, in neighbouring Guangxi province. Soon after the Communist take-over, his family moved to Hong Kong, where he later studied at Matteo Ricci College. A devout film fan during his teens, he acted in student plays and, in the late 1960s, made several 8mm and 16mm semi-experimental films, one, *Fast Knot*, with the future well-known film critic Sek Kei. Another that survives, the 8mm silent black and white short *Ngauyin* (known in English as *Chance* or *Accidentally*), is a kind of amateur version of *The Collector*, with Woo himself playing a dreamer who ties up a beautiful young woman. Shot on a veranda overlooking

Hong Kong, it is a typically fanciful and roughly made student work.

The master's apprentice

In 1969, Woo entered the industry at the bottom, getting a job as a script boy at Cathay Film, where he graduated to working as an assistant director to Chang Sen. In 1971, he switched to the mighty Shaw Bros., then at the height of its domination, and for 18 months was an assistant director to Chang Cheh, the then undisputed master of heroic martial arts pictures. It was, Woo admits, the defining experience of his career.

In 1973, Woo left Shaws and, with some money invested by a friend, Ronald Lui, made the costume martial arts movie *Farewell Buddy* with another friend, Wang Kai-yi. Too violent for the local censor, it was initially released in Taiwan; however, the heads of Golden Harvest, a talent-hungry new studio that had struck gold with the films of Bruce Lee, saw it and were sufficiently impressed to offer Woo a job as a contract director. They also bought *Farewell Buddy*, recut and rescored it, and finally released it in autumn 1975 as *The Young Dragons*.

Woo's first film to make it to Hong Kong cinemas was *The Dragon Tamers*, a typically cheap and cheerful Golden Harvest movie, shot, like many at the time, in South Korea, starring contract players James Tien and Carter Wong, and centred on rival martial arts schools (here, Japanese karate and Chinese taekwondo girl students). Spiced up with lots of cuties in tracksuits (and sometimes less), it is an uneasy mix of titillation and kung-fu, its one really memorable moment being the sudden appearance at the end of the Japanese villainess in a black belt and pink costume to take on Tien.

Here, and in the subsequent *Countdown in Kung Fu* – a cheapie also shot in Korea and most notable now for an early supporting role by Jackie Chan, then a struggling actor-cum-fight arranger – one searches in vain for any later Woo

"trademarks". These are typical production line efforts, learning experiences, making heavy use of the zoom lens (then very popular) and clearly influenced by his spell under Chang Cheh.

Broader horizons

Woo, however, was being heavily promoted by Golden Harvest as a new young talent and, in between helping the studio's new discovery, TV comedian Michael Hui, to find his directing legs on a series of massively popular comedies, Woo himself started to branch out. First, he made the Cantonese opera film *Princess Chang Ping* (a gorgeously shot movie that failed, however, to revive this once-popular genre) and then the first of many knockabout comedies, *The Pilferers' Progress*, starring Richard Ng and Ricky Hui (Michael's gormless-looking younger brother) as two get-rich-quick hustlers.

Full of clever visual gags, verbal jokes, likeable characters and energetic stunts, the six comedies that Woo made for Golden Harvest between 1977 and 1982 show a real flair and inventiveness that mirror Hong Kong's frenetic lifestyle, the resurgence of its Cantonese-language industry and its celebration of the ordinary guy, the underdog, rather than the heroic characters that had dominated Mandarin-language film-making of the past decade or more.

Almost all are based around the themes of money and success: *Follow the Star* is

Rowena Cortes and Roy Chiao (centre, by altar) in Woo's FOLLOW THE STAR

basically one long chase, and *From Riches to Rags* a series of close shaves, as lottery winner Ricky Hui fends off an assassin he has hired to kill himself in the mistaken belief that he has a fatal disease. In their simple humanity, these movies could not be farther from those for which Woo is currently famous, and their existence raises hopes that some time in the future he will again demonstrate his talent for comedy. Woo himself has recently said he is keen to move into other genres.

By late 1983, however, Woo was ready for a move from Golden Harvest's production line, especially after his Golden Triangle mercenaries movie, *The Sunset Warrior*, shot in Thailand, was shelved (it was finally released three years later, as *Heroes Shed No Tears*, and did poorly). Joining the rapidly expanding Cinema City Co. – for which he had pseudonymously made *Laughing Times*, an uncredited remake of Chaplin's *The Orphan*, a couple of years earlier – he left Hong Kong to work in its new affiliate in Taiwan, where a New Wave of directors was energising the local industry.

The two years he spent there were the lowest point in his career, resulting in directing credits on two largely forgettable comedies and associate producer credits on two dramas by young Taiwanese directors. However, his return to Hong Kong in 1986 was one of the most spectacular in the history of the territory's film industry. Largely thanks to Tsui Hark, a Hong Kong New Wave director whose company Film Workshop was in the same group as Cinema City, Woo was given the job of directing the crime picture *A Better Tomorrow*.

Crime makes a comeback

Following the success of the realistic gangland movie *Long Arm of the Law* (1984), the genre was coming back into fashion, and *Tomorrow* was partly designed by Cinema City to relaunch the stalled career of Ti Lung, a 1970s Shaw Bros. star of Chang Cheh martial arts movies. Against opposition, however, Woo pressed for Chow Yun-fat, a former TV actor still struggling to make a major mark in films, to play the lead, as Ti's counterfeiting partner; in the third main role, as Ti's cop brother, who is ignorant of his elder's occupation, he had young babyfaced pop star Leslie Cheung.

The strange chemistry, united by Woo's all-stops-out approach to the story as a kind of martial arts picture with guns and designer sunglasses, worked magically. Released in August 1986, *Tomorrow* ran for an unprallelled two months and became the highest-grossing film in Hong Kong's history. A new genre – slick, bloody gunplay movies, celebrating the same brotherly codes and heroic virtues as Chang Cheh's historical epics of the 1960s and 1970s – was definitively born.

Woo largely disowns the hastily-made sequel, *A Better Tomorrow II*, on which he and Tsui failed to agree on the focus. The film's first half shows signs of heavy cutting, as too much plot is squeezed in, but the final hour, climaxing in a 10-minute guns-and-grenades assault on the bad guy's villa by Chow, Ti and Dean Shek, has an elemental, Sergio Leone-ish power that beats anything in the more tightly-wound original.

Woo found his feet again with *The Killer*, a very slick pairing of Chow and Danny Lee as, respectively, a professional assassin and a policeman who form an uneasy partnership to dispose of a psycho gunman. The two equally crazed characters end up fighting side by side, the moral dividing line between their occupations totally erased, and the Doppelganger theme – explored literally in the later *Face/Off* – attains the quality of a heroic ballad. Helped by a well-received festival screening, *The Killer* was the first of Woo's films to catch the attention of American critics and audiences – thereby launching him on the international stage. It is a fluid piece of work, heavy on style and symbols (religion, doves, candles), and very Leone-ish in its mixture of hommages and near self-parody, but it is not Woo at his best, and lacks a genuinely human core.

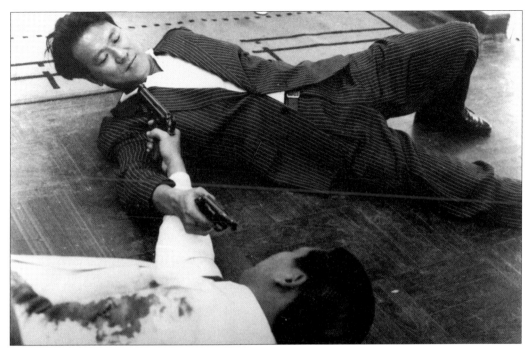

Chow Yun-fat (foreground) and Danny Lee in THE KILLER

After co-directing the star-laden triad movie *Just Heroes* – an uneven but unjustly neglected project made by Chang Cheh's industry pals to provide him with a retirement fund – Woo went independent, setting up his own production company for his next picture, the epic two-and-a-half hour saga *Bullet in the Head*. It is his finest and most heartfelt film to date, tracing the friendship among three young men (sensible Tony Leung Chiu-wai, reckless Jacky Cheung, ruthless Waise Lee) as they are caught up in the horrors of the Vietnam War and finally settle scores back in Hong Kong.

Here, the gunplay and action are at the service of the characters rather than being simply bolted on as stylistic showpieces; this obviously very personal film, which seems like an elegy for a lost age of youthful commitment, is about real friendship rather than fictional heroic codes, and as a result the violence is among the most shocking in Woo's oeuvre.

Hong Kong farewell, Hollywood debut

The financial failure of the film was a huge blow to Woo, who cranked out a glossy caper movie, *Once a Thief* (a romantic *Jules et Jim*-like comedy set in Nice and Hong Kong), to restore his box-office credibility before returning to gangland pastures. If *Bullet in the Head* is his most emotionally wrenching movie, *Hard-Boiled* is the best of his Hong Kong gunplay films, a totally gripping tale of a renegade cop (Chow) teamed with an undercover agent (Leung) against arms smugglers whose cache is hidden beneath a hospital. Climaxing in a final hour set entirely within the hospital, this is the Woo film that comes closest to those of fellow Hong Kong action dramatist Ringo Lam in its natural melding of action, character, gradually mounting suspense and exaggerated realism.

In retrospect, it was the perfect farewell to Hong Kong, a mature, totally assured movie that seemed to close a chapter in Woo's career. However, as his compatriots have since discovered, going Hollywood involves more than just a trip across the Pacific: for Woo, faced with incessant studio politics and ingrained rules and tastes, it was almost like starting over again. The Jean-Claude Van Damme extravaganza *Hard Target* emerged as watered-down Woo, neither fish nor fowl, and it was three years (and several on-off

Chow Yun-fat in HARD-BOILED

Nicolas Cage starts a riot in FACE/OFF
photo: Stephen Vaughn/Paramount

projects) before his next US picture, *Broken Arrow*, hit screens.

By this time, Woo and Hollywood had learned to co-exist: the studios accepted the leaps of imagination that make Hong Kong directors so special, and in *Broken Arrow* the director cleverly used American actors' personae to his own ends, continuing the post-*Pulp Fiction* revival in John Travolta's career with a role (psychotic bomber pilot) for which Hollywood would never have selected him.

Woo has never stopped working since, tossing off the relaxed and highly enjoyable TV movie *Once a Thief* (unrelated to his earlier film) before embarking on *Face/Off*, an extremely elaborate revenge-cum-personality transference saga that shows him comfortably settling into the Hollywood mainstream. If *Broken Arrow* was six parts Hong Kong to four parts America in flavour, *Face/Off* is at least seven parts America to three parts Hong

Kong, especially in its cosy, family reunion ending. Not for the first time in his career, it looks like Woo is getting ready to reinvent himself yet again.

DEREK ELLEY has been associated with *IFG* for more than 25 years, during which time he has written extensively on East Asian cinema. Currently Senior Film Critic of *Variety*, he is also editor of the annual *Variety Movie Guide*, a distillation of the paper's reviews of the past 90 years.

Still from BULLET IN THE HEAD
photo: Kobal Collection

Woo on location for BROKEN ARROW
photo: Richard Foreman/Fox

Woo Filmography

During his career, JW has also been known under the names Wu Yu-sheng, John Ng and John Y.S. Woo (Wu, Woo and Ng being alternate versions of the same Chinese surname). In addition to his directing credits below, he also worked as assistant director on Chang Cheh's *The Boxer from Shantung*, *The Water Margin*, *Four Riders* (all 1972) and *The Blood Brothers* (1973); as production consultant on Michael Hui's *Games Gamblers Play* (1974), *The Private Eyes* (1976) and *The Contract* (1978); as associate producer on the Taiwanese productions *Super Citizen* (Dir. Wan Jen, 1985) and *Love, Lone Flower* (Dir. Lin Ching-chieh, 1985).

He was one of the leading actors in Raymond Lee's *Rebel from China* (1990). He also appears in *Love, Lone Flower*, Patrick Leung's *Task Force* (1997), and in his own films *The Hand of Death*, *A Better Tomorrow*, *Bullet in the Head* and *Hard-Boiled*.

1975
NUZI TAIQUAN QUNYING HUI
(The Dragon Tamers)

Script and Direction: JW. Photography (scope): Li Cheng-chun. Editing: Peter Cheung. Music: Joseph Koo. Martial Arts Direction: Chen Chuan. Players: James Tien (*Nan-kung*), Carter Wong (*Fang*), Chin Chang-shu, Yang Wei, Ryoko Ina, Keiko Hara, J. Han Jae. For Golden Harvest. 107 mins. Mandarin. Known as *Belles of Tae Kwon Do* in its English-dubbed version.

TIE HAN ROU QING
(The Young Dragons)

Script: I Kuang, JW. Direction: JW. In scope. Players: Hu Chin (*Hung*), Tien Ni (*Yeh Feng*), Yu Yang (*Chien*), Liu Chiang (*Fan Ming*), Cheng Lei, Chiang Nan, Feng Ko-an, Dean Shek, Li Feng, Wu Ming-tsai, Ho Kuang-ming.

Executive produced by Wang Kai-yi for Lui Bros. Mandarin. Shot in 1973. First released in Taiwan in April 1974, as *Guoke yu shuang yan* (*Farewell Buddy*), with a co-direction credit to producer Wang Kai-yi. 98 mins.

1976
DAI NUI FA
(Princess Chang Ping)

Script: Tang Ti-chiang. Direction: JW. Photography (scope): Cheung Yiu-cho. Editing: Peter Cheung. Music Direction: Joseph Koo. Players: Long Kim-sung (*Chou Shih-hsien*), Mui Shuet-sih (Princess Chang Ping), Lang Chih-pai (*Emperor Chung*), Yen Suet-fun (Queen), and The Young Phoenix Opera group. For Golden Phoenix, for Golden Harvest. 98 mins. Cantonese. Reissued in 1977 with its official English title "Canton-ised" to *Princess Cheung Ping*.

SHAOLIN MEN
(Countdown in Kung Fu)

Script and Direction: JW. Photography (scope): Liang Yung-chi. Editing: Peter Cheung. Music: Joseph Koo. Martial Arts Direction: Sammo Hung. Players: Dorian Tan (*Yun-fei*), James Tien (*Shih Shao-feng*), Jackie Chan (*Tan Feng, the woodcutter*), Chu Ching (*Chiu-yeh*), Sammo Hung (*Tu Ching, Shih's deputy*), Yang Wei (*"Zorro," the swordsman*), Kao Chiang (*Tan Hsiung*), Chin Chi-chu (*Ma Lieh*), John Woo (*Chang Yi, the scholar*), Chen Feng-chen. For Golden Harvest. 96 mins. Mandarin. Known as *The Hand of Death* in its English-dubbed version and on posters (but not prints) of the original version at the time.

1977
FATCHIN HON
(The Pilferers' Progress)

Script and Direction: JW. In scope. Players: Richard Ng,

Ricky Hui, Agee Chiu. For Golden Harvest. Cantonese. Also known under the English titles *Money Crazy* and *Money Chasers*. 98 mins.

1978
DAI SATSING YU SIU MUITAU
(Follow the Star)

Script: Lau Tin-chi, JW. Direction: JW. Photography (scope): Cheung Yiu-cho. Editing: Peter Cheung. Music: Chan Sin-kei. Players: Roy Chiao (*Sing*), Rowena Cortes (*Ka*), Fung Hak-on, Chin Yut-sang, Wong Ching, Lee Hoi-sang, Chung Chai-sam, David Wu, Chan Pak-san, Cheng Siu-ping, Tsui Kwai-heong. For Golden Harvest. Cantonese. 98 mins.

HALO! YE GWAI YAN
(Hello, Late Homecomers)

Script and Direction: JW, Louis Sit, Lau Tin-chi. In scope. Players: Louis Lo, Angel Chan, Lam Hau-yi, Yick Kar, Karl Maka. For Golden Harvest. Cantonese. Three-story portmanteau film. JW directed the first episode. 102 mins.

1979
HO HAP
(Last Hurrah for Chivalry)

Script and Direction: JW. Photography (scope): Cheung Yiu-cho. Martial Arts Direction: Fung Hak-on. Players: Ngai Chau-wah (*Sau-sau*), Wai Pak (*Cheung Sam*), Damian Lau (*Ching-yi*), Chan Yiu-lam (*Ko-pang*), Lee Hoi-sang (*Pak Chung-tong*), Cheung Hung-cheung (*Mang Ping*), Wong Kwong-yu (*Lok-san*), Yick Kar (*Cheung's sister*). For Golden Harvest. Cantonese. 100 mins.

1980
CHIN CHOK GWAI
(From Riches to Rags)

Script and Direction: JW. Photography (scope): Bill Wong.

Editing: Peter Cheung. Action Direction: Lam Ching-ying, Billy Chan. Players: Ricky Hui, Johnny Koo, Jo Jo Chan, Yick Kar, Tong Ching. For Golden Harvest. Cantonese. 98 mins.

GWATKAI SIDOI
(Laughing Times)

Script and Direction: JW (under pseudonym Wu Shang-fei). Photography (scope): Ho Ming. Editing: Tony Chow. Art Direction: Yuen Tai-yung. Music: Frankie Chan. Players: Dean Shek (*Tramp*), Wong Wai (*Orphan*), Wong Sau-man (Singer), Karl Maka, Wu Ma, Lau Nga-lai, Lee Chung-keung. Executive produced by Raymond Wong for Cinema City Co. Cantonese. 100 mins.

1982
MODANG TINSI
(To Hell with the Devil)

Script: Sze-to Cheuk-hon, Shu Kei, JW. Direction: JW. Photography (scope): Bill Wong. Editing: Peter Cheung. Art Direction: Alex Ma. Music: Tang Siu-lam. Players: Ricky Hui (*Lee Kit*), Jade Hsu (*Pui-chi*), Fung Shui-fan (*Piu*), Paul Chun (*Marco*), Chan Pak-cheung (*Rocky*), Paul Chung (*The Devil*), John Sham (*Manager*). For Golden Harvest. Cantonese. 96 mins.

BATCHOI LAM A-CHAN
(Plain Jane to the Rescue)

Script: JW, Lam Chun-fat. Direction: JW. In scope. Players: Josephine Siao (*Lam*), Ricky Hui (*Her suitor*), Wu Fung, Maggie Li, Chan Sing, Lau Hak-sun, David Wu. For Golden Harvest/High Pitch Co. Cantonese. 100 mins.

1984
XIAO JIANG
(The Time You Need a Friend)

Script: Raymond Wong, JW, Lin Neng-kuan. Direction: JW. Players: Sun Yueh (*Ku Jen*), Tao

Ta-wei (*Shen Pin*), Liu Jui-chi (*Liu Ya-nan*), Wu Shao-kang (*Peter*), Liu Meng-yen (*Nancy Huang*), Hsiao Yu-chi (*Hsiao-lan*), Chiang Hsia (*Manager Liang*). Produced by Karl Maka, Dean Shek and Wang Ying-hsiang for Cinema City Co. (H.K.)/Long Shong (Taiwan). Mandarin. 98 mins. Also known under the English title *A Friend In Need*.

1985
LEUNGCHEK LOFU
(Run Tiger Run)

Script: Raymond Wong. Direction: JW. Players: Teddy Robin, Tsui Hark, Bin Bin. Produced by Karl Maka, Wang Lung-hsiang, Dean Shek and Raymond Wong for Cinema City (H.K.)/Long Shong (Taiwan). Cantonese. 97 mins.

1986
YINGHUNG BUNSIK
(A Better Tomorrow)

Script: JW, Chan Hing-kar, Leung Suk-wah. Direction: JW. Photography: Wong Wing-hang. Editing: Kam Ma. Art Direction: Bennie Lui. Music: David Wu (theme by Joseph Koo). Action Direction: Blackie Ko, Tung Wai. Players: Chow Yun-fat (*Mark*), Leslie Cheung (*Sung Chi-kit*), Ti Lung (*Sung Chi-ho*), Waise Lee (*Tam Sing*), Emily Chu (*Jackie*), Kent Tseng (*Kin*), Shek Yin-chi, Tien Feng, Kam Hing-yin, Wang Hsia, JW, Sing Fui-on, Leung Ming, Tsui Hark. Executive produced by Tsui Hark for Film Workshop, for Cinema City Co. Cantonese. 95 mins.

YINGHUNG MO LUI
(Heroes Shed No Tears)

Script and Direction: JW. Photography: Kenichi Naragawa. Editing: Peter Cheung. Production Design: Fung Yuen-chi. Music: Chung Siu-fung. Action Direction: Chin Yut-sang. Players: Eddy Ko (*Chan Chung – "Kirk"*), Lam Ching-ying (*Vietnamese colonel*), Chin Yut-

sang, Lau Chau-sang, Lee Hoi-suk, Jang Doo-hee, Kum Ho-kon, Phillip Loffredo, Cecile Le Bailly, Ma Ying-chun. Executive produced by Leonard Ho for Golden Harvest. Cantonese. 84 mins. Shot in 1983 as *Wongfan chinsi* (*The Sunset Warrior*).

1987
YINGHUNG BUNSIK II
(A Better Tomorrow II)

Script: JW, from a story by Tsui Hark. Direction: JW. Photography: Wong Wing-hang. Editing: Cinema City Editing Unit. Art Direction: Andy Lee. Music: Joseph Koo. Action Direction: Ching Siu-tung. Players: Dean Shek (*Lung*), Ti Lung (*Sung Chi-ho*), Leslie Cheung (*Sung Chi-kit*), Chow Yun-fat (*Ken*), Kwan San (*Ko*), Emily Chu (*Jackie*), Kent Tseng (*Kin*), Regina Kent (*Peggy*), Lung Ming-yan, Chindy Lau, Paul Francis, Ken Boyle, Marco Wo, Wai Sing-chow, Sammy Lee, Sing Fui-on, Lau Siu-ming, Ng Mang-tat, Peter Wang. Executive produced by Tsui Hark for Film Workshop, for Cinema City Co. Cantonese. 103 mins.

1989
DIP HUT SEUNG HUNG
(The Killer)

Script and Direction: JW. Photography: Wong Wing-hang, Peter Pao. Editing: Fan Kung-ming. Art Direction: Ben Luk. Music: Lowell Lo. Action Direction: Ching Siu-tung, Lau Chi-ho. Players: Chow Yun-fat (*Jeff/John*), Danny Lee (*Insp. Li Ying*), Sally Yeh (*Jennie*), Chu Kong (*Sidney Fung*), Kent Tseng (*Tseng*), Sing Fui-on (*Johnny Wong Hoi*), Ricky Wong (*Frank*), Tommy Wong (*Wong Hung*), Yip Wing-cho (*Wong Tung-yun*), Barry Wong (*To*), Parkman Wong (*Chan Pak-man*), Alan Ng (*Killer*), Yeung Sing, Ngan Chiu-hung (*Bodyguards*). Executive produced by Tsui Hark for Film Workshop/Magnum Films, for Golden Princess. Cantonese. 110 mins.

YIDAM KWANYING
(Just Heroes)

Script: I Kuang, Tommy Hau. Direction: JW, Wu Ma. Photography: Cho Wai-ki, Yee Tung-lung. Editing: Choi Hung. Art Direction: Ringo Cheung, Andy Lee. Music: Romeo Diaz, James Wong. Players: John Chiang (*Wai*), Danny Lee (*Sau*), Chen Kuan-tai (*Tai*), Kelly Chu (*Annie*), Cally Kwong (*Shum Sing-fai*), Wu Ma (*Ma*), James Wong, Stephen Chiau (*Jacky*), Sing Fui-on, Joe Nieh, Ti Lung (*Lung*), Chao Lei, Yueh Hua (*Opera manager*), Ku Feng, Paul Chun (*Tai*), Lo Lieh, Tang Chia, Yuen Woo-ping, Lau Kar-yung, Philip Ko, Bill Tung (*Kwai*), Fung Hak-on, James Ha. Executive produced by Tsui Hark for Magnum Films. Cantonese. 96 mins. By his own reckoning, JW directed about 60 per cent of the movie.

1990
DIP HUT GAITAU
(Bullet in the Head)

Script: JW, Patrick Leung, Janet Chun. Direction: JW. Photography: Ardy Lam, Chan Pui-kai, Somchai Kittikun, Wong Wing-hang. Editing: JW. Production Design: James Leung. Music: James Wong, Romeo Diaz. Action direction: Lau Chi-ho. Players: Tony Leung Chiu-wai (*Ben*), Jacky Cheung (*Frank*), Waise Lee (*Paul*), Simon Yam (*Luke*), Fennie Yuen (*Jane*), Yolinda Yam (*Sally*). Produced by JW for John Woo Film Production. Cantonese. 146 mins.

1991
CHUNGWANG SEIHOI
(Once a Thief)

Script: JW, Clifton Ko, Janet Chun, from a story by JW. Direction: JW. Photography: Poon Hang-seng. Editing: David Wu. Art Direction: James Leung. Music: Violet Lam. Action Direction: Philip Kwok.

Players: Chow Yun-fat (*Joe*), Leslie Cheung (*Jim*), Cherie Chung (*Cherie*), Chu Kong (*Chu*), Kent Tseng, Wu Fung. Produced by JW for Milestone Pictures, for Golden Princess. Cantonese. 107 mins.

1992
LAT SAU SAN TAM
(Hard-Boiled)

Script: Barry Wong, from a story by JW. Direction: JW. Photography: Wong Wing-hang. Editing: JW, David Wu, Kai Kit-wai, Jack. Production Design: James Leung. Music: Michael Gibbs, James Wong. Action Direction: Philip Kwok. Players: Chow Yun-fat (*Insp. Yuen – "Tequila"*), Tony Leung Chiu-wai (*Tony*), Teresa Mo (*Teresa*), Philip Chan (*Pang*), Anthony Wong (*Johnny*), Kwan Hoi-shan (*Hoi*), JW (*Barman*), Philip Kwok, Bowie Lam, Bobby Ah Yuen, Ng Shui-ting, Tung Wai, Y. Yonemu. Produced by JW for Milestone Pictures, for Golden Harvest. Cantonese. 125 mins.

1993
HARD TARGET

Script: Chuck Pfarrer. Direction: JW. Photography (scope): Russell Carpenter. Editing: Bob Murawski. Production Design: Phil Dagort. Music: Graeme Revell. Stunt Co-ordination: Billy Burton. Players: Jean-Claude Van Damme (*Chance Boudreaux*), Lance Henriksen (*Fouchon*), Arnold Vosloo (*Van Cleaf*), Yancy Butler (Natasha Binder), Carmine (*Kasi Lemmons*), Wilford Brimley (*Douvee*), Bob Apisa (*Mr. Lopaki*), Chuck Pfarrer (*Binder*), Douglas Forsythe Rye (*Frick*), Michael D. Leinert (*Frack*), Willie Carpenter (*Elijah Roper*). Produced by James Jacks and Sean Daniel for Alphaville/ Renaissance, for Universal. 94 mins. (UK: 95 mins.)

1996
BROKEN ARROW

Script: Graham Yost. Direction: JW. Photography (scope): Peter Levy. Editing: John Wright, Steve Mirkovich, Joe Hutshing. Production design: Holger Gross. Music: Hans Zimmer. Stunt Co-ordination: Alan Graf. Players: John Travolta (*Vic Deakins*), Christian Slater (*Riley Hale*), Samantha Mathis (*Terry Carmichael*), Delroy Lindo (*Col. Max Wilkins*), Bob Gunton (*Pritchett*), Frank Whaley (*Giles Prentice*), Howie Long (*Kelly*), Vondie Curtis-Hall (*Lt.-Col. Sam Rhodes*), Jack Thompson (*Joint Chiefs of Staff Chairman*). Produced by Mark Gordon and Bill Badalato, in association with WCG Entertainment, for Twentieth Century Fox. 108 mins.

1997
FACE/OFF

Script: Mike Werb, Michael Colleary. Direction: JW. Photography (scope): Oliver Wood. Editing: Christian Wagner, Steven Kemper. Production Design: Neil Spisak. Music: John Powell. Stunt Co-ordination: Brian Smrz. Players: John Travolta (*Sean Archer*), Nicolas Cage (*Castor Troy*), Joan Allen (*Eve Archer*), Alessandro Nivola (*Pollux Troy*), Gina Gershon (*Sasha Hassler*), Dominique Swain (*Jamie Archer*), Nick Cassavetes (*Dietrich Hassler*), Harve Presnell (*Lazzaro*), Colm Feore (*Dr. Malcolm Walsh*), John Carroll Lynch (*Walton*), CCH Pounder (*Hollis Miller*), Robert Wisdom (*Tito*), Margaret Cho (*Wanda*), Jamie Denton (*Buzz*), Matt Ross (*Loomis*). Produced by David Permut, Barrie M. Osborne, Terence Chang and Christopher Godsick for Douglas-Reuther/WCG Entertainment/ David Permut, for Paramount/ Touchstone. 139 mins.

By Peter Cowie

The past few months have made it plain that laser discs are being eliminated from their future strategy by the major studios, in favour of DVD. Stores in the US like Barnes and Noble are no longer stocking LDs, and the respected trade weekly, *Video Business*, has banished all mention of the format since the spring of 1998 – save reporting Image Entertainment's decline in sales of the product.

This is harsh news indeed for the millions of LD enthusiasts in the US, Europe and the Far East. Are they all expected to throw in the towel, purchase a DVD player (with the many glitches that entails), and replace their software library with new DVDs at $25 a film? When the CD revolution occurred in the early to mid-1980s, the music companies wisely continued to produce vinyl ('black') records, to cater for the masses who still used turntables. That overlap of technologies continued until at least the early 1990s.

The problem for LD buffs is that they are not the masses. Hollywood will continue to churn out cassettes because the hundreds of millions of VCR owners around the world need a medium that allows them to record sports, sitcoms and movies off air. Until DVD offers recording abilities, it will simply be a refined version of laser disc.

Add to this situation a handicap of the studios' own making. DVD discs cannot be played outside their specific region. So an Australian cannot purchase DVDs in London, and a Japanese cannot purchase

them in New York. Of course the machines can be doctored to cheat the system, but the net effect will be to inhibit production of software outside the US and Japan. The sales potential will not be sufficiently attractive for any but the most mainstream of Hollywood movies to be released in the format.

Looking on the bright side

DVD does, however, hold several advantages for the prosperous collector only now coming into the marketplace. A DVD can hold most movies on one disc, making the 'turning over' of the LD format redundant. A DVD can include subtitles in several languages, as well as a menu of options and interactivity. Most important of all, it is both less cumbersome and less expensive than LD.

In short, if the industry handles the situation intelligently, then DVD will become the format of choice in every respect. Until that day arrives, however, we will continue to champion the cause of those companies that continue to put out sophisticated LDs, with commentaries in the US, and who publish rare foreign classics as well as the latest exercises in slam-bang surround sound. Next year will see reviews of DVDs alongside the last of the LDs. Meanwhile, here is a round-up of highlights for the 1997-1998 season.

Restorations

Coppola's masterpiece, **The Godfather**, has been re-released in a widescreen version (Pioneer PLFED 37031 in PAL, and Paramount Home Video in NTSC) that both looks and sounds infinitely better than earlier versions on LD. The colours are rich, almost refulgent in their evocation of 1940s Kodachrome, and Walter Murch has enhanced the soundtrack with some subtlety. For example, you can now hear the cat purring on Brando's lap in the first sequence, and the gunshots that destroy Sonny at the tollbooths have a dry, rasping intensity in the Dolby Surround mode.

More of an unexpected revelation is Scorsese's **The Last Temptation of Christ** (Criterion CC 1503L/NTSC). Transferred with absolute brilliance by Maria Palazzola under the watchful eye of cinematographer Michael Ballhaus, the disc features commentary by Scorsese, Dafoe, Schrader and Jay Cocks, as well as an interview with composer Peter Gabriel. Add a cornucopia of location footage, production stills, costume designs, and an enlightening liner note by David Ehrenstein, and this film acquires a fresh dimension.

The same company has issued a pristine transfer of Woody Allen's **Crimes and Misdemeanors** (Criterion CC1475L). Sven Nykvists, predominantly sombre lighting (at Allen's request) looks excellent in this new digital version, although the plot appears more schematic than it did when the film came out in 1989.

Two black-and-white treasures resurrected from the vaults. **Advise and Consent**, hailed by Peter Bogdanovich as "by far the best political movie ever made [in the US]", is available on NTSC from Warner Home Video (catalogue 35691) in full 'scope format. The monochrome is crisp on side one, but goes a little hazy on sides 2 and 3. The new transfer demonstrates how a savvy Preminger used every inch of the 'scope screen and how well he could direct actors like Franchot Tone, Don Murray, Lew Ayres and even Peter Lawford. Pioneer have published an admirable PAL transfer of the 1950s semi-camp classic **Creature from the Black Lagoon** (PLFEB 350801). The film was at first released in 3-D, but even so the image looks sharp and the allusive nature of the plot prevents Jack Arnold's masterpiece from being absurd or even incredible. Pioneer have added the

Willem Dafoe in THE LAST TEMPTATION OF CHRIST, in a magnificent transfer to LD by Criterion

original trailer, and also a trailer for *Dragonheart*.

Special Editions

Those stalwart defenders of the LD format, The Criterion Collection, continue to release around 40 new titles a year. Each is presented with the same care and devotion as *King Kong* was some 15 years ago – the first of the modern LD classics as we know

Juliette Binoche and Lena Olin in Criterion's superb restoration transfer of Kaufman's masterpiece, THE UNBEARABLE LIGHTNESS OF BEING

them. Criterion's most ambitious special edition in the past season has been **Evita** (CC1488L, 4 discs). Director Alan Parker provides a lucid and trenchant commentary on the analogue track, there is a 42-minute documentary featuring Madonna, Antonio Banderas, Jonathan Pryce and of course Parker, while Criterion's Nancy Bauer has corralled a host of trailers, TV spots, stills and articles on the Peróns and Argentina. Also included in the set are the music video for "You Must Love Me", and Parker's full shooting script. Altogether an album that sets a benchmark in its category, with terrific packaging and a transfer that does full justice to the soundtrack and to Darius Khondji's autumnal lighting.

Only slightly less essential is the widescreen version of David Cronenberg's **Crash** (Criterion CC1500L). Savaged by the right-wing press on its arrival at Cannes in 1996, this faithful adaptation of the J.G. Ballard novel is brought into accurate perspective by one of the best director commentaries in recent years. Indeed, it is probably better to see *Crash* on this LD, listening to Cronenberg's explanation of each scene, than it is to watch it in a theatre.

Saul Zaentz has been collecting any number of awards this past year, as if the film world had only just awoken to his indomitable spirit as a maverick producer. Now Criterion has paid tribute to two of his most successful works. **The English Patient** (CC1487L, 2 discs) is presented in a director-approved widescreen transfer supervised by Walter Murch, with audio commentary by Anthony Minghella, Michael Ondaatje and Zaentz himself. This sumptuous release also contains a 24-minute documentary, trailers and TV spots, and readings from the novel.

An even richer, and more authentically European masterpiece is **The Unbearable Lightness of Being**. Hitherto available only in a washed-out full-screen version, Phil Kaufman's inspiring adaptation of Milan Kundera's novel about the Czech experience in the late 1960s receives such sensitive treatment at the hands of the Criterion team that it recovers all the wit

and emotional force it delivered on first release in 1988. On the commentary track, Kaufman, editor Walter Murch and star Lena Olin all talk well, while screenwriter Jean-Claude Carrière's remarks sound especially wise and illuminating.

Foreign-language

The Criterion Collection does not permit a dubbed version to darken its towels, but every so often it pays homage to a film that uses English almost by default (or for reasons of a distribution deal). Liliana Cavani's notorious **The Night Porter** (CC1511L) uses English because both its stars, Dirk Bogarde and Charlotte Rampling, hail from the sceptred isle. But the new transfer, in widescreen, recaptures the authentic bleakness and Manichaean outlook of this study of decadence in the wake of the Nazi camps. Annette Insdorf contributes a thoughtful liner note.

Death in Venice, however, poses another problem altogether. In this Warner Home

Dirk Bogarde in DEATH IN VENICE, finally released on disc by Warners   photo: Kobal Collection

Video re-release (catalogue 11060, 2 discs), care is paid to the accurate 2.35:1 ratio, and to finessing the soundtrack with its recurrent use of Mahler's Fifth Symphony. But many of the minor characters are woefully dubbed from Italian into English, and only Bogarde looks authentic (despite his heavy make-up). Still, who would cavil when this engrossing example of the art of Luchino Visconti has been unavailable on LD for so long?

Another courageous revival is Criterion's double-disc version of the complete **Olympia** (CC1489L), which showcases the undeniable art of Leni Riefenstahl for some 200 minutes as it records the entire spectrum of the 1936 Berlin Olympic Games – with a commentary in the most "BBC-type" English of the time. The most engaging part of the film may well be its 20-minute prologue, showing the flame being lit in Greece, despite the repellent implication that the Aryan body is sublime. The nonagenarian director even helped with the transfer from original 35mm elements.

Three Japanese classics have also been issued in recent months. **Good Morning** (Criterion CC1523L) is better known as *Ohayo*. Directed in 1959 by Yasujiro Ozu, it is less poignant than much of this director's work and offers an amusing look at suburban Japan in the heyday of American influence. The colour remains a little hazy, but the subtitles have been updated, and the film is a gorgeous example of Ozu's discreet talent. So too is **Early Summer** (Criterion CC1483L, 2 discs), made eight years earlier in black-and-white. The film describes, as do many Ozu pictures, the erosion of family life and values in the chaos of a post-war world.

The most vivid of all Criterion's recent Japanese LDs is **Double Suicide** (CC1522L). Masahiro Shinoda never became an art-house staple in the West, but this single masterpiece demonstrates the abiding relevance of the *bunraku* puppet play tradition. One can only extol the rigorous compositions, the extraordinary use of blacks and whites (in an even more

extraordinary transfer), and the flitting back and forth between contemporary backstage reality and the aching drama of the Chikamatsu source.

Finally, a word for the luscious pastel colours of Pedro Almodóvar's **Women on the Verge of a Nervous Breakdown** (Criterion CC1499L). Made ten years ago, Spain's finest screwball comedy established Almodóvar on the international festival circuit, and introduced several of his favourite actors. The excellent subtitles, and the accurate transfer, make this disc worth grabbing while stocks last.

Mainstream

Among the numerous standard issues of new Hollywood product, five titles stand out through a combination of excellent technical achievement and visual imagination. Oliver Stone's **U Turn** (Columbia TriStar Home Video 32526) provides persuasive evidence that this maverick director's mind is as fertile and fiery as it was in the 1980s. Part film noir, part Western, *U Turn* owes something to Sergio Leone and a lot more to David Lynch. The images are rendered with tactile appeal, the sweat drips off the screen, and Morricone's antic score ricochets around the home cinema.

Louder still and louder, Paul Verhoeven's **Starship Troopers** (Columbia TriStar Home Video 71716) benefits on LD from an audio commentary by the director and his screenwriter, Ed Neumeier. Palpably misunderstood in the States, this witty and subversive sci-fi spectacular debunks the American dream of idealistic youth, perfect of complexion and gleaming of teeth, as it joins up to ward off the enemy in true 1950s Cold War style. The transfer sets altogether new standards for laser.

In the same idiom, but refracted through the gloating eyes of French director Jean-Pierre Jeunet (*Delicatessen*), the latest episode in the *Alien* saga was shot on Super 35 with a 2.35: 1 aspect ratio. **Alien Resurrection** (Fox Home Video 0032585)

WHO FRAMED ROGER RABBIT?
photo: Touchstone/Amblin Entertainment

offers a gallery of bizarre and repugnant characters, while the action is restricted to a decrepit spaceship, captured in Darius Khondji's queasy, bilious-looking cinematography.

On a lighter note, there is a PAL version of **Who Framed Roger Rabbit?** (Encore/Laser UK, EE 1168, 2 discs), with the laser format a perfect vehicle for Richard Williams' brightly-spangled animation. Encore throw in a bonus CAV

disc with three short cartoons featuring Roger Rabbit and produced by Steven Spielberg's stable.

Finally, in a splendid display of all that is good about PAL compared to NTSC, Pioneer's **Mission: Impossible** (PLFEB 35741) deserves a place on every LD collector's shelf. The surround sound, the meticulous direction by Brian De Palma, and set-pieces like the raid on the computer-room, recreate as near as dammit the "big screen experience".

PETER COWIE is founding Editor of the *IFG*, and has written some 20 books on the cinema. He is International Publishing Director of Variety Inc.

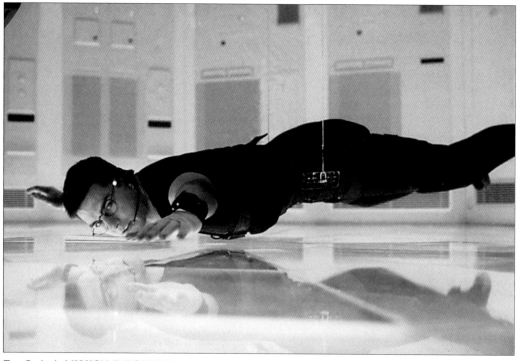

Tom Cruise in MISSION: IMPOSSIBLE

photo: Murray Close/Paramount

Jerry Goldsmith – Boldly scoring for 40 years

by Jon Burlingame

Who is the most respected composer in Hollywood? Ask practically any working film musician this question and the answer, likely as not, will be Jerry Goldsmith. At 69, Goldsmith, has been writing original music for films for more than 40 years, and remains as strongly in demand as ever. His music has accompanied some of the most important, and memorable, films of our time: *Planet of the Apes*, *Patton*, *Chinatown*, *Star Trek: The Motion Picture*, *Rambo*, *Basic Instinct* – and about 170 more.

The past year has been one of Goldsmith's most successful. He scored a huge commercial hit in *Air Force One*, received his seventeenth Oscar nomination for *L.A. Confidential*, and wrote the music for this summer's Disney animated hit, *Mulan*. In addition, he composed the new Oscars ceremony fanfare, and became one of only a handful of Hollywood composers to have a major concert work performed by the Los Angeles Philharmonic (*Music for Orchestra*, conducted by Esa-Pekka Salonen last March). Goldsmith's own take on this hot streak: "I'm 69-years-old and suddenly everything starts to happen!"

Charles Bernstein, an Emmy-nominated composer and governor of the Academy of Motion Picture Arts and Sciences music branch, explains Goldsmith's standing within the music community: "Jerry has been consistently creative, original, and on-target, year after year, picture after picture.

Jerry's a musician's musician. He does things beyond what is necessary simply to serve the dramatic function. There is a level of musicality that musicians recognise and appreciate with Jerry that sets him apart." That is probably because – unlike many of today's hot film scorers, who come from a pop-music background – Goldsmith is not only classically trained, he also paid his dues in radio, episodic television and low-budget movies throughout the 1950s and early 1960s.

Goldsmith likes to tell the story of how he got hooked on movies, and movie music: "I remember when I was around 14 or 15, I saw *Spellbound*. I came out of the theatre in love with Ingrid Bergman and in

Goldsmith's score for PATTON is now regarded as a classic
photo: CBS Fox/Kobal Collection

Jerry Goldsmith at work circa 1980

love with the score that Miklós Rózsa had written. At that point I made up my mind to do two things: marry Ingrid Bergman and write music for motion pictures." Well, one out of two ain't bad.

Television trains a cinema star

Born in Los Angeles on February 10, 1929, Goldsmith majored in music at LA City College and studied with pianist Jakob Gimpel and composer Mario Castelnuovo-Tedesco; he later studied film composition with Rózsa at the University of Southern California. His showbiz break occurred in 1950, when he took a job typing radio scripts at CBS. By 1953 he was composing for radio, and by 1955 he was composing original music for CBS's *Climax*, the first live weekly anthology series to emanate from the West Coast.

Climax was a baptism of fire for the young composer. Each week he wrote a full score for a chamber-sized ensemble (often just three musicians plus himself playing piano, organ and the now-extinct Novachord) and conducted it during the show's live, coast-to-coast one-hour

broadcast, improvising changes on the spot as necessitated by shifts in pacing or alternate line readings from earlier rehearsals. "From a technical point of view, you never knew what was going to happen. It was a wonderful training ground," Goldsmith recalls. With the death of live TV, the excitement and adrenaline rush disappeared. "There was something about counting off and going on the air live to a zillion people. I never experienced that energy again."

Although Goldsmith scored his first feature in 1957 (the forgotten George Montgomery western *Black Patch*), he continued to work mainly in TV through the early 1960s. As live broadcasts were gradually replaced by recorded programmes, he scored such classic series as *The Twilight Zone* and *Thriller*, and penned the themes for such fondly remembered shows as *Dr Kildare* and *The Man from U.N.C.L.E.*

In 1961, he scored his first major studio film, the contemporary Western *Lonely Are the Brave*, starring Kirk Douglas. He received his first Oscar nomination for the cerebral score for John Huston's *Freud*, in 1962. An all-percussion score for *Seven Days in May* (1964) won him a Golden Globe nomination; his gentle music for *A Patch of Blue* (1965) and the Oriental touches and large-scale orchestral sounds for Robert Wise's epic *The Sand Pebbles* (1966) earned him additional Oscar nominations.

Oscar duet for ape and General

His groundbreaking, avant-garde score for *Planet of the Apes* (1968) – an impressionistic, otherworldly soundscape created entirely without trendy electronic instruments – solidified his reputation as a master of his profession. This was the first of many Goldsmith-scored films where unusual instruments were used to create strange sounds. Whenever Goldsmith's long-time orchestrator Arthur Morton heard a weird noise coming from outside the recording stage, he would say: "Find

Goldsmith's score for PAPILLON was nominated for an Academy Award

out who that guy is and bring him in here. We can use that in Jerry's next picture."

Planet of the Apes was the second of his seven films with director Franklin J. Schaffner. It was nominated for a Best Original Score Oscar, as were *Patton* (1970), *Papillon* (1973) and *The Boys from Brazil* (1978). *Patton* is now used in many film-scoring classes as a textbook case of using music to define character: Goldsmith used echoing trumpets for the controversial general's belief in reincarnation, martial music for Patton the military man, and organ to suggest his religious beliefs.

"Frank and I had a very special relationship," says Goldsmith of Schaffner. "It was so succinct, it was almost laconic. We would discuss not very much of anything. We'd have lunch and talk about anything except the movie, and then finally it would be like one sentence, what he wanted me to do or what he expected in the music. And that would be it until [we saw each other on] the scoring stages."

Since that time, Goldsmith has forged strong relationships with other directors, including Paul Verhoeven (*Total Recall*, *Basic Instinct*), Fred Schepisi (*The Russia House*) and Joe Dante (*Gremlins*, *The 'Burbs*). Dante, whose summer hit *Small Soldiers* is his eighth film with the composer, points out: "When we're on the set and things aren't working out, we just say, 'Oh, it's okay, Jerry will save it.' All of the drama of

Lee Remick in THE OMEN, which earned Goldsmith his only Oscar for Best Original Score

a movie comes up eight notches once Jerry's music is in it."

Producer Robert Evans recently said that Goldsmith's music – written in nine days as a replacement for another score that was not working – saved *Chinatown* (1974) from disaster. Written for an unusual ensemble of four pianos, four harps, strings, two percussionists and trumpet, it is now a classic of the private eye genre.

Frights, sci-fi, action!

The winner of five television Emmys (for such landmark mini-series as *QB VII* and *Masada* and, most recently, the theme for *Star Trek: Voyager*), Goldsmith has won the Best Original Score Oscar just once, for his unsettling and powerful choral and orchestral work on *The Omen* in 1976. He went on to write the music for both sequels (which, although disappointing as movies, contain equally impressive scores, with Latin texts).

The frightening dissonance of *Alien* (1979), the heroics of *Star Trek* (1979), plus sequels *Star Trek V* and *Star Trek: First Contact*, the ferocious action music of all three *Rambo* movies (1982, 1985, 1988) and the surprising ethnic sounds of such exotic-locale movies as *Under Fire* (1983, Latin America), *Congo* and *The Ghost and the Darkness* (1995 and 1996, African rhythms) and *Mulan* (1998, ancient China), are the product of one musical imagination.

Exactly how Goldsmith conjures up the music remains a mystery – even to the man himself. "It just happens. To describe how one writes music is impossible. I can't intellectually tell you how it gets from the head and the heart, through my arm, down to my hand and onto the paper. But being an artist means being self-critical. You can put anything down on paper, but you have to be the judge of how good it is. If you have the talent, the ability, it's going to happen."

Goldsmith scores an average of four or five films a year and turns down at least as

BASIC INSTINCT, the second Paul Verhoeven film to boast a score by Jerry Goldsmith

many. With *Small Soldiers* approaching its summer 1998 premiere, he was writing the music for the medieval Viking picture *The 13th Warrior* for writer-producer Michael Crichton (with whom he previously teamed on *Coma* and *The Great Train Robbery*) and preparing to write the music for the ninth in the hugely successful *Star Trek* series.

The circumstances under which Goldsmith works have changed radically over his 40-plus years in the business. In the 1960s, he says, he often had 10 weeks to write 30 or 40 minutes of music for a movie; now, due to the truncated post-production schedules on many films, he is lucky to have four or five weeks in which to churn out 60 to 70 minutes of music.

Despite those pressures, Goldsmith still enjoys his work. "Some mornings I wake up and the thought of going to work is appalling. But then I sit down at the piano and all of a sudden I get an idea. I'm off and running and it's great." For that reason, Goldsmith says, he will never retire. "Why should I? I'm still having fun." He would like to write more concert music, but will continue to write film scores "as long as somebody wants me.

Hey, I like doing it. There are very few composers who can sit down and write an hour of music and hear it played and recorded the next day, under the best technical conditions, with some of the greatest musicians in the world. A composer would kill for that."

New lives for classic themes

by Philip Kemp

Over the past few years, film music – for so long a despised and disparaged genre – has come in from the cold. The film scores of 'proper' composers like Copland, Vaughan Williams or Shostakovich, once dismissed as mere hack work, an embarrassment to be tactfully disregarded, have been readmitted to full membership of their oeuvres. At the same time, the concert-hall works of composers who largely concentrated on cinema – Bernard Herrmann, Miklós Rósza, Nino Rota – are being

Wolfgang Erich Korngold, who wrote the memorable score for THE ADVENTURES OF ROBIN HOOD, is among the composers enjoying reissue success

photo: Kobal Collection

rediscovered. The lush Hollywood scores of Erich Wolfgang Korngold are no longer seen as proof that this wunderkind of the Austro-German tradition sold out to Mammon, but as evidence of his soaring romantic talent in whatever musical field. It is at last being accepted that composers can write for the movies without debasing themselves – and more, that movie scores can be great music.

A few film scores, suitably reworked for the concert hall, have always achieved respectability: Walton's music for *Henry V*, for example, or Prokofiev's *Lieutenant Kijé*. But the net is now being cast far wider, opening up the whole territory of film music for exploration. The scores of Franz Waxman or Max Steiner are recorded and rerecorded, just like Mahler symphonies, and played by the BBC on Radio 3 alongside Bartok and Stravinsky. Classical record companies not only include movie scores in their catalogues, but, where necessary, painstakingly recreate them, lavishing on them the kind of close musicological research that used to be reserved for lost fragments by Mozart or Schubert.

A pioneer in this kind of rescue work is the Hong Kong based record company Marco Polo, also behind the enterprising budget label Naxos. As the name suggests, Marco Polo is essentially an explorer label, unearthing neglected composers (or lesser-known works by more famous figures), and their ever-widening range of film music fits this strategy. Alongside the great names of the Hollywood golden age, like Waxman, Steiner and Korngold, the label features such European film composers as Bliss, Ibert (whose score for Welles's *Macbeth* is a revelation), Auric, Honegger and Khachaturian. Each score is given the full studio treatment, restoring lost cues and revealing orchestral detail obscured by congested early soundtracks.

Where do discs like these find their market: among classical music lovers exploring a new field of composition, or movie buffs venturing into the fringes of classical? Some of both, but predominantly the latter, believes Matthew Freeman, A&R manager of Marco Polo. "The sales reflect that. In general, a film disc will sell twice or even three times as many as a non-mainstream classical recording. It's not that the general public's heard of Steiner any more than of [Russian symphonist] Arensky – but they immediately relate to *King Kong*." Film music discs, it seems, are expanding the classical market sideways and pulling more customers into its ambit. Marco Polo's disc of Steiner's ground-breaking score for *King Kong*, played by the Moscow Symphony Orchestra under William Stromberg, has become one of the company's all-time best-sellers.

Painstaking reconstruction

A co-begetter of the Steiner recording is John Morgan, an LA-based composer and arranger. Working with Stromberg, he has reconstructed some 14 classic Hollywood scores. Since written scores and original tapes were junked once a film was finished, Morgan has had to work from a viewing copy of the movie – and often, in the case of early sound movies, make an educated guess at the exact orchestration. "Sometimes you have the composer's later work to use as a guide," says Morgan, "or even, when it comes to the 1950s, a full score. Though you often have to restore those if they're badly damaged. It can take months. But every score is like a college education for me. Korngold studied with Mahler, so did Steiner. It's a privilege to get inside the heads of composers like these."

Another classical company extending its reach into screen composers is the leading

British independent Chandos. The company has always specialised in British music, and its catalogue features film scores by Walton, William Alwyn and Malcolm Arnold. "We get more calls asking for more film music than for almost anything else," says Chandos' press officer Paul Westcott. "Film buffs will hunt out the available recordings, almost regardless of label, but there's bound to be a lot of crossover from our traditional customers. The Alwyn film music disc has sold amazingly well, so has Malcolm Arnold." Chandos is actively expanding into this field: a new series of contemporary Film & TV music has just been launched with a disc of work by David Ferguson (featuring his music for British TV dramas *Cracker* and *The Woman in White*), and a series of classic movie scores is planned.

The market is growing so rapidly, that it can support dedicated labels. One such is the London-based Silva Screen, whose catalogue covers almost the whole screen music spectrum from Korngold to Jerry Goldsmith, from *The World of Gerry Anderson* to the best-selling Lesley Garrett disc *Diva! A Soprano at the Movies*. "I think

Max Steiner at work   photo: Kobal Collection

it's because of the lack of popular music coming from the concert hall," says Silva Screen's director James Fitzpatrick. "You now have to find it in the cinema. The big symphonic splendoured stuff that John Williams writes, like *Star Wars* – it's the equivalent of what Beethoven would have been asked to write. Being commissioned to write an oratorio or a set of dances – it's no different from having Paramount commission a film score." Jerry Goldsmith as the new Wagner? That's a less outrageous thought than it might have seemed a few years ago.

Steiner scored Huston's classic THE TREASURE OF THE SIERRA MADRE *photo: Kobal Collection*

Cover of Marco Polo's reissue of the KING KONG score by Max Steiner *photo: HNH International*

World Box-Office Survey

ARGENTINA

	Admissions
1. Wild Cards (Argentina)	1,385,125
2. Dibu – The Movie (Argentina)	1,162,905
3. The Fury (Argentina)	1,046,000
4. The Lost World	1,030,000
5. Hercules	927,044
6. Men in Black	744,681
7. Ashes From Paradise (Argentina)	721,305
8. Batman & Robin	679,000
9. The English Patient	628,871
10. Ransom	618,251

AUSTRALIA

	$
1. Men in Black	15,434,640
2. Liar Liar	14,360,240
3. The Lost World	13,648,280
4. Bean (UK)	13,059,400
5. The Full Monty (UK)	12,992,760
6. My Best Friend's Wedding	11,696,680
7. Jerry Maguire	9,538,360
8. Batman & Robin	9,162,320
9. Romeo + Juliet	8,763,160
10. Star Wars: Special Edition	7,707,800

$1 = AUS$1.60

AUSTRIA

	Admissions
1. Men in Black	575,500
2. Bean (UK)	542,000
3. The Lost World	460,000
4. The First Wives Club	404,500
5. 101 Dalmatians	397,500
6. Ransom	342,000
7. The Fifth Element (France)	340,000
8. Con Air	276,000
9. Evita	275,000
10. Seven Years in Tibet	264,000

BELGIUM

	$
1. The Hunchback of Notre Dame	4,556,145
2. The Lost World	4,437,812
3. Men in Black	3,689,657
4. Bean (UK)	3,454,731
5. 101 Dalmatians	3,429,395
6. Oesje! (Belgium)	3,092,105
7. The Fifth Element (France)	3,076,960
8. My Best Friend's Wedding	2,999,591
9. Ransom	2,972,947
10. The English Patient	2,858,680

$1 = 38 Belgian francs

BRAZIL

	Admissions
1. The Lost World	2,613,545
2. Batman & Robin	1,918,283
3. Men in Black	1,757,473
4. English Patient	1,486,925
5. Space Jam	1,295,564*
6. Ransom	1,266,131
7. Hercules	1,259,037
8. My Best Friend's Wedding	1,257,269
9. Evita	1,043,021
10. The Fifth Element (France)	981,979

* Excl. 341,146 in 1996

BULGARIA

	Admissions
1. Star Wars: Special Edition	117,046
2. Anaconda	98,521
3. Men in Black	93,176
4. The Empire Strikes Back	72,934
5. Double Team	70,399
6. Batman & Robin	64,674
7. Romeo + Juliet	64,121
8. Return of the Jedi	61,935
9. The Lost World	60,415
10. Face/Off	56,286

All films are US productions unless otherwise indicated.
All figures are for January to December 1997 unless otherwise indicated.

CHILE

		Admissions
1.	The Lost World	282,655
2.	Hercules	230,845
3.	Star Wars	204,437
4.	Space Jam	189,348
5.	The English Patient	167,347
6.	Men in Black	161,757
7.	101 Dalmatians	149,745
8.	The Fifth Element (France)	133,598
9.	Batman & Robin	111,567
10.	My Best Friend's Wedding	107,719

Figures are for Santiago only

CROATIA

		Admissions
1.	Bean (UK)	238,485
2.	The Strange Adventures of Apprentice Hlapic (Croatia)	208,901
3.	The Fifth Element (France)	200,221
4.	Men in Black	161,777
5.	The English Patient	71,824

CZECH REPUBLIC

		Admissions
1.	Kolya (Czech)	449,877
2.	Men in Black	437,427
3.	Bean (UK)	408,071
4.	101 Dalmatians	382,925
5.	The Lost World	364,865
6.	The Wonderful Years that Sucked (Czech)	328,733
7.	The People Versus Larry Flynt	312,485
8.	Cop Story II (Czech)	255,864
9.	Evita	238,031
10.	Lotrando and Zubejda (Czech)	219,349

DENMARK

		$
1.	Smilla's Sense of Snow	2,808,178
2.	The Lost World	2,760,930
3.	Barbara (Denmark)	2,622,811
4.	Men in Black	2,437,137
5.	The English Patient	2,432,112
6.	Bean (UK)	2,333,464
7.	Ransom	2,056,220
8.	The Fifth Element (France)	1,800,908
9.	Wild Flowers (Denmark)	1,744,559
10	My Best Friend's Wedding	1,658,504

$1 = 6.5DKK

KOLYA, hugely successful in the Czech Republic

Niels Olsen and Ditte Gråbøl in WILD FLOWERS, popular in Denmark

ESTONIA

	Admissions
1. Bean (UK)	66,638
2. 101 Dalmatians	40,937
3. Men in Black	40,571
4. Con Air	30,915
5. Face/Off	25,674
6. Evita	25,035
7. The Lost World	24,448
8. The Nutty Professor	22,933
9. Liar Liar	20,455
10. Romeo + Juliet	18,891

BEAN, mugging his way to No. 1 in Finland
photo: Susan Hanover/PolyGram

FINLAND

	Admissions
1. Bean (UK)	386,976
2. Men in Black	288,902
3. The Lost World	258,983
4. 101 Dalmatians	211,304
5. Liar Liar	206,181
6. The English Patient	197,997
7. Tomorrow Never Dies	182,285
8. Romeo + Juliet	157,746
9. The First Wives Club	150,461
10. The Fifth Element (France)	135,839

FRANCE

	Admissions
1. The Fifth Element (France)	7,514,000
2. Men in Black	5,608,000
3. Le Vérité si je mens (France)	4,769,000
4. The Lost World	4,742,000
5. 101 Dalmatians	3,996.000
6. Hercules	3,627,000
7. Le Pari (France)	3,614,000
8. Bean (UK)	2,992,000
9. Didier (France)	2,845,000
10. Alien Resurrection	2,489,000

GERMANY

	Admissions (millions)
1. Men in Black	7.30
2. Bean (UK)	5.80
3. The Lost World	5.52
4. Knockin' on Heaven's Door (Germany)	3.54
5. Rossini (Germany)	3.25
6. The Fifth Element (France)	3.22
7. The English Patient	3.07
8. The Little Arsehole (Germany)	3.06
9. Ransom	2.63
10. Con Air	2.62

GREECE

	Admissions
1. Titanic	850,000
2. As Good As It Gets	240,000
3. The Full Monty (UK)	200,000
4. My Best Friend's Wedding	190,000
5. Bean (UK)	185,000
6. The Devil's Advocate	170,000
7. Tomorrow Never Dies	170,000
8. Great Expectations	145,000
9. Men in Black	145,000
10. Balkanisator (Greece)	140,000

Figures are for Greater Athens area only, September 1997 to May 1998; unconfirmed officially and based on information from distribution offices.

HONG KONG

$ (millions)

1. The Lost World	7.5
2. Mr Nice Guy (Hong Kong)	5.85
3. All's Well Ends Well 97 (Hong Kong)	5.2
4. Once Upon a Time in China & America (HK)	3.9
5. Face/Off	3.9
6. Men in Black	3.8
7. Lawyer Lawyer (Hong Kong)	3.5
8. Titanic	3.45*
9. Armageddon (Hong Kong)	3.05
10. Lifeline (Hong Kong)	2.7

* After two weeks in release. Gross was $15.3m by mid-June 1998. $1 = HK$7.75

CON AIR, a soaring hit in Hungary and Iceland
photo: Frank Masi/Touchstone Pictures

HUNGARY

1. The Lost World	739,941
2. 101 Dalmatians	574,935
3. Dollybirds (Hungary)	501,519
4. Men in Black	473,289
5. Liar Liar	466,525
6. Bean (UK)	414,773
7. Star Wars: Special Edition	370,913
8. The Fifth Element (France)	363,167
9. Con Air	354,415
10. Out of Order (Hungary)	351,100

ICELAND

Admissions

1. Bean (UK)	60,100
2. Liar Liar	51,025
3. Men in Black	43,300
4. Tomorrow Never Dies	37,996
5. The Full Monty (UK)	34,300
6. Face/Off	30,625
7. The Lost World	29,300
8. Con Air	27,817
9. My Best Friend's Wedding	27,300
10. Space Jam	26,820

INDIA

Second half of 1997
1. Border
2. Pardes
3. Dil To Pagal Hain
4. Ishq
5. Chachi 420
First half of 1998
1. Pyaar Kiya To Darna Kya
2. Chota Chetan
3. Kamasutra (Hindi version)
All titles are Indian.

INDONESIA

1. The Lost World
2. Air Force One
3. Con Air
4. Romeo + Juliet
5. Liar Liar
6. Men in Black
7. The English Patient
8. Evita
9. Face/Off
10. Bean (UK)

IRAN $

1. The Snowman	434,000
2. Leila	307,000
3. Soltan	238,000
4. The Unforgiven	150,000
5. Cardboard Hotel	146,000
6. The Sportsman	140,000
7. Speed	139,000
8. The Scorpion	133,000
9. The Wedding Key	127,000
10. The Miracle of Laughter	109,000

All titles are Iranian.

IRELAND

1. The Full Monty (UK)
2. Men in Black
3. The Lost World
4. Bean (UK)
5. Ransom
6. Sleepers
7. 101 Dalmatians
8. Liar Liar
9. Jerry Maguire
10. My Best Friend's Wedding

Compiled from a survey of Irish film distributors and exhibitors.

Rupert Everett in MY BEST FRIEND'S WEDDING, wooing audiences in Ireland and Italy
photo: Kobal Collection

ITALY $

1. Titanic	45,699,725
2. Fireworks (Italy)	29,424,985
3. Life is Beautiful (Italy)	25,694,939
4. Three Men and a Leg (Italy)	17,948,617
5. Bean (UK)	13,657,600
6. My Best Friend's Wedding	13,461,044
7. Hercules	10,965,925
8. Seven Years in Tibet	10,919,082
9. The Fifth Element (France)	9,991,875
10. The Devil's Advocate	9,942,577

Source: *Giornale dello spettacolo*. $1 = 1,700 Lire .
Figures to end of May 1998.

JAPAN $ (millions)

1. Princess Mononoke (Japan)	75.9
2. Independence Day	61.4
3. The Lost World	41.1
4. Lost Paradise (Japan)	16.3
5. Doraemon (Japan)	14.2
6. Speed 2	14.2
7. Star Wars Trilogy	13.5
8. The Fifth Element (France)	12.1
9. Sleepers	10.6
10. The End of Evangelion (Japan)	10.3
11. Ransom	9.9

$1 = 141 yen

LATVIA   Admissions

1. 101 Dalmatians	88,000
2. Bean (UK)	55,000
3. Romeo + Juliet	44,900
4. Mill of Fate (Latvia)	37,900
5. Space Jam	29,800
6. Con Air	28,400
7. Men in Black	25,600
8. Liar Liar	25,300
9. Sleepers	24,200
10. Face/Off	22,000

LUXEMBOURG 1997

	Admissions
1. Men in Black	44,000
2. Bean (UK)	43,000
3. The Fifth Element (France)	30,000
4. Space Jam	29,000
5. Knockin' on Heaven's Door (Germany)	26,000
6. Tomorrow Never Dies*	25,500
7. The English Patient	25,000
8. Hercules	24,500
9. My Best Friend's Wedding	24,000
10. The Hunchback of Notre Dame	23,500

* Still in release in 1998, for final total of 44,000.

MEXICO

	Admissions
1. The Lost World	1,906,959
2. Men in Black	1,452,058
3. Hercules	1,301,053
4. Batman & Robin	1,203,385
5. Volcano	1,202,559
6. Dante's Peak	1,174,408
7. Anaconda	924,142
8. Anastasia	840,123
9. My Best Friend's Wedding	907,030
10. Scream	739,551

NETHERLANDS

	Admissions
1. Bean (UK)	1,009,981
2. 101 Dalmatians	812,969
3. The Lost World	796,728
4. Men in Black	730,361
5. The English Patient	693,977
6. Liar Liar	683,808
7. Ransom	591,446
8. Space Jam	569,858
9. Face/ Off	516,920
10. Tomorrow Never Dies	468,859

Gary Sinise in RANSOM, a favourite in the Netherlands and New Zealand   photo: Lorey Sebastian/Touchstone

NEW ZEALAND

	$ (millions)
1. Men in Black	2,220,000
2. The Lost World	1,700,000
3. The Full Monty (UK)	1,600,000
4. The English Patient	1,550,000
5. Bean (UK)	1,450,000
6. Star Wars: Special Edition	1,300,000
7. Romeo + Juliet	1,250,000
8. Ransom	1,170,000
9. Shine (Australia)	1,160,000
10. Liar Liar	1,100,000

$1= NZ$2

NORWAY

	Admissions
1. Men in Black	304,345
2. Bean (UK)	289,376
3. 101 Dalmatians	277,974
4. The English Patient	259,666
5. Liar Liar	238,755
6. The Full Monty (UK)	184,873
7. The Lost World	173,413
8. The First Wives Club	169,917
9. Tomorrow Never Dies	163,864
10. My Best Friend's Wedding	153,941

Jim Carrey's LIAR LIAR convinced the crowds in Puerto Rico and Romania
photo: Melinda Gordon/Universal

The Bard scored well in Poland and Romania with ROMEO + JULIET
photo: Merrick Morton/Fox

PAKISTAN

1. Love Crazy
2. Lost and Found
3. Reunion
4. Pious
5. Mafia
6. Heartless
7. Miracle
8. From the Heart
9. Bastard
10. Promise

All films are Pakistani.

POLAND   Admissions

1. Killer (Poland)	1,627,524
2. Space Jam	1,431,911
3. The Lost World	949,456
4. Bean (UK)	859,824
5. 101 Dalmatians	851,972
6. Men in Black	830,913
7. Sara (Poland)	703,866
8. Night Graffiti (Poland)	604,861
9. Star Wars Trilogy	576,680
10. Romeo + Juliet	562,761

PUERTO RICO $

1. The Lost World	2,030,908
2. Men in Black	2,016,000
3. Liar Liar	1,000,000
4. Face/Off	995,000
5. Daylight	900,000

ROMANIA   Admissions

1. 101 Dalmatians	594,280
2. Double Team	337,137
3. Maximum Risk	311,029
4. Liar Liar	284,111
5. Men in Black	241,564
6. Con Air	240,396
7. The Lost World	.210,732
8. Anaconda	203,138
9. Romeo + Juliet	192,001
10. Star Wars: Special Edition	184,676

THE DEVIL'S ADVOCATE, scaring up big numbers in Spain   photo: Brian Hamill/Warner Bros.

THE HUNCHBACK OF NOTRE DAME set tills ringing in Slovakia   photo: Disney

SERBIA & MONTENEGRO   Admissions

1. Bean (UK)	387,003
2. The Fifth Element (France)	228,236
3. Space Jam	208,858
4. To The Bone (Serbia)	171,117
5. Balkan Rules (Serbia)	170,477
6. The English Patient	111,588
7. The Lost World	142,299
8. Men in Black	135,397
9. My Best Friend's Wedding	109,188
10. Microcosmos (France)	108,023

SLOVAKIA   Admissions

1. 101 Dalmatians	220,171
2. Men in Black	169,450
3. Bean (UK)	161,977
4. The Lost World	145,040
5. Space Jam	133,588
6. Evita	107,431
7. The Hunchback of Notre Dame	95,122
8. The Fifth Element (France)	86,573
9. Kolya (Czech)	82,050
10. The Glimmer Man	75,915

SOUTH AFRICA

1. Men in Black
2. The Lost World
3. Liar Liar
4. Ransom
5. Con Air
6. Bean (UK)
7. Speed 2
8. 101 Dalmatians
9. The Saint
10. Face/Off

SPAIN $

1. The Lost World	12,314,000
2. The Full Monty (UK)	9,717,000
3. Men in Black	9,271,000
4. The English Patient	9,157,000
5. My Best Friend's Wedding	8,098,000
6. Airbag (Spain)	7,589,000
7. Space Jam	7,234,000
8. Ransom	7,162,000
9. Bean (UK)	6,992,000
10. The Devil's Advocate	6,269,000

SWEDEN

	Admissions
1. Tomorrow Never Dies	790,000
2. Adam & Eva (Sweden)	650,000
3. 101 Dalmatians	595,000
4. Men in Black	585,000
5. Bean (UK)	525,000
6. Svensson, Svensson (Sweden)	510,000
7. Hercules	500,000
8. The Lost World	480,000
9. The Full Monty (UK)	475,000
10. The English Patient	370,000

Includes admissions up to March 1998, but excludes all-time record of Titanic: 1,400,000 admissions in first 11 weeks.

SWITZERLAND

	Admissions
1. Men in Black	475,284
2. Bean (UK)	472,443
3. The English Patient	450,458
4. Tomorrow Never Dies	416,302
5. The Fifth Element (France)	380,802
6. Seven Years in Tibet	373,095
7. The Lost World	355,450
8. Evita	328,275
9. The Full Monty (UK)	322,511
10. 101 Dalmatians	321,585

THAILAND

	$
1. Titanic*	5,300,000
2. The Lost World	3,750,000
3. Anaconda	2,250,000
4. Daeng Bailey & Young Gangsters (Thai)	1,875,000
5. Con Air	1,825,000
6. Men in Black	1,725,000
7. Batman & Robin	1,475,000
8. Face/Off	1,375,000
9. Air Force One	1,325,000
10. The Red Bike Story (Thailand)	1,200,000

$1 = 40 baht   Figures are kept until April 1998 and in Bangkok only. Figures are unconfirmed officially, based on information from distribution offices. *Still in release.

THE RED BIKE STORY – a big local hit in Thailand

TURKEY

	Admissions
1. The Bandit (Turkey)	2,750,000
2. Titanic	1,900,000
3. The Jackal	940,000
4. The Devil's Advocate	870,000
5. Cholera Street (Turkey)	850,000
6. My Best Friend's Wedding	780,000
7. As Good As It Gets	510,000
8. Face/Off	438,000
9. The English Patient	402,000
10. The Fifth Element (France)	390,000

UK

	$ (millions)
1. The Full Monty (UK)	65.3
2. Men in Black	57.3
3. The Lost World: Jurassic Park	41.3
4. 101 Dalmatians	32.6
5. Bean (UK)	28.1
6. Star Wars: Special Edition	21.8
7. Batman & Robin	23.5
8. Evita	22.7
9. Ransom	20.5
10. The English Patient	20.2

MEN IN BLACK: Will Smith and Tommy Lee Jones captured the biggest audiences of the year in the US and Canada
photo: Melinda Gordon/Columbia TriStar

US & CANADA $ (millions)

1.	Men in Black	250.0
2.	The Lost World	229.1
3.	Liar Liar	181.4
4.	Air Force One	171.9
5.	Star Wars: Special Edition	138.3
6.	My Best Friend's Wedding	126.7
7.	Titanic	112.6
8.	Face/Off	112.3
9.	Batman & Robin	107.3
10.	George of the Jungle	105.2

VENEZUELA $

1.	The Lost World	642,229
2.	Independence Day	551,737
3.	Hercules	542,126
4.	Men in Black	458,921
5.	The Hunchback of Notre Dame	398,483
6.	Twister	390,668
7.	Batman & Robin	344,925
8.	Space Jam	323,127
9.	101 Dalmatians	307,570
10.	My Best Friend's Wedding	296,907

WORLD SURVEY

ALGERIA

Roy Armes

The handful of film-makers who have managed to continue working in Algeria amid the terror and chaos of the 1990s have followed the path mapped by Belkacem Hadjadj in his first feature *Once Upon A Time* (*Machaho*; described in *IFG* 1997): a retreat from the city into the mountains and deserts to tell simple, allegorical tales. Like **Hadjadj,** two members of this group, Abderrahmane Bouguermouh and Azzedine Meddour, also use the Berber language, which was banned from the mid-1960s until the mid-1990s, when Algeria had its flourishing but tightly-controlled state cinema.

Bouguermouh, who trained at IDHEC in Paris, and began his career with several feature-length works for Radio-Télévision Algérienne, made his first cinema release, *Cry of Stone*, in 1986. His new work, **The Forgotten Hillside** (*La Colline Oubliée*), was shot in 1992, but technical problems delayed its release for five years. Adapted from a well-known novel by Mouloud Mammeri (who died in 1989), the film is set on the eve of the Second World War, but its tale of young people's loves and friendships in a time of change has a very contemporary feel.

Life in the warren-like Berber mountain village is ruled by tradition, with elders setting the rules according to age-old custom. Whatever path the young people choose – study or emigration, settling down or trying to make money – they all share a real sense of malaise, of inescapable suffering. Spread over two-and-a-quarter hours, *The Forgotten Hillside* is a slow-moving, sincere slice of life which treats its subject with respect and avoids most of the traps of folklore.

Mountain language, desert love

Meddour's **Baya's Mountain** (*La montagne de Baya*) is another Berber-language film set at high altitude. Meddour, who studied for seven years at VGIK (the Moscow film school), has hitherto been known for feature-length documentaries made for Algerian television, in particular his six-part series, *Colonialism Without Empire*, which dealt with the struggle against neo-imperialism in Vietnam, Cuba, Egypt and numerous other countries. *Baya's Mountain* is set at the beginning of the century and tells the story of a woman, Baya, torn between love and the resistance struggle, who personifies the spirit of the Berber villagers' opposition to the French occupying forces who have driven them up into the mountains.

The move away from the present is perhaps most striking in the case of the former actor Mohamed Chouikh, whose previous feature, *Youssef: The Legend of the Seventh Sleeper* (1993), was a savage denunciation of contemporary political corruption, written shortly before the army take-over in 1992. But with **The Desert Ark** (*L'arche du désert*), Chouikh has created what he himself calls "an allegory on violence and its origins".

In a Saharan oasis, the love of two young people from different ethnic groups, Myriam and Amin, causes conflict. After much suffering the lovers are reunited, but as crisis follows crisis the once united village is destroyed by long submerged hatreds and rivalries. As if in mockery of the inhabitants' dreams, the only 'escape route' is the version of Noah's ark, built in the middle of the desert by the village madman.

The events are observed through the eyes of a child who finally walks off into the desert, denouncing his elders: "I'm going to another country where they don't kill children and don't burn down houses. May God forgive you. I don't ever want to see you again. You adults have become mad." *The Desert Ark* is a passionately committed work, shaped as a fable rather than as a systematic demonstration of the escalation of violence, and marred only by the inclusion of documentary-style footage of the dances and music performed by the inhabitants of the community where the film was shot.

Home thoughts from abroad

Many Algerian film-makers now live in virtual permanent exile in Europe. In Italy, Rachid Benhadj, best known for his sensitive debut feature *Desert Rose*, has completed **The Tree Hung With Destinies** (*L'albero dei destini sospesi*). Samir, a Moroccan youth, and Maria, a young Italian woman, meet up and travel south on what becomes a voyage of initiation.

Along the way they encounter the eponymous tree, which is hung with ribbons and other tokens marking the hopes and dreams of the people who pass by. The couple's love is genuine but does not last.

In France, Mahmoud Zemmouri's career has come full circle with **100% Arabica**. The director's first feature, *Take a Thousand Quid and Get Lost* (1991), traced the adventures in Algeria of two second-generation immigrants who choose to 'return home' via a French government repatriation scheme, even though they have always lived in France and speak no Arabic. In *100% Arabica*, the Parisian exploits of two young Algerians give Zemmouri an excuse to paint a satiric portrayal of a poor Paris neighbourhood and, above all, to enjoy the *raï* music of Algerian stars Cheb Khaled and Cheb Mami.

Another recent release is **The Night of Destiny** (*La nuit du destin*), made by Abdelkrim Bahloul who came to Paris aged 20 to study at IDHEC and has made all his films in France. The new work, like *The Hamlet Sisters* (mentioned in *IFG 1997*), is a low-budget independent feature, this time dealing with a criminal investigation which brings together a police officer and the daughter of a Muslim witness.

ROY ARMES is the author of several books on film history and specialises in African cinema. He teaches film in London.

Recent Films

LA COLLINE OUBLIÉE
(The Forgotten Hillside)

Script and Dir: Abderrahmane Bouguermouh, from the novel by Mouloud Mammeri. Phot: Rachid Merabtine. Players: Mohamed Chabane, Samira Abtout, Saïd Hilmi, Djamila, Rachid Ould Mohand, Djamila Amzal, Saïd Amrane. Prod: CAAIC – ENPA – Wilaya de Tizi-Ouzou – Wilaya de Béjaïa.

L'ARCHE DU DÉSERT
(The Desert Ark)

Script and Dir: Mohamed Chouikh. Phot: Mustapha Belmihoud. Players: Myriam Mouffen, Messaouda Adami, Shyraz Aliane, Amin Chouikh, Abdelkader Belmokadem, Fatyha Nesserine, Lynda. Prod: Atlas Films (Algeria), K Films (France), ENPA (Algeria), Vulkan Kultur GmbH (Germany).

LA MONTAGNE DE BAYA
(Baya's Mountain)

Script and Dir: Azzedine Meddour. Dial: Boualem Rabia. Phot: Bachir Sellami. Players: Djamila Amzal, Ali Ighil Ali, Ouardia Kessi, Abderrahmane Debiane, Dahmane Aidrous. Prod: Imago – Caro-Line – ENTV – ENPA.

L'ALBERO DEI DESTINI SPOSITI

Script and Dir: Rachid Benhadj. Phot: Gianni Mammolotti. Players: Giusi Cataldo, Said Taghmaoui. Prod: Albatros – RAI (Marco Bellocchio) (Italy).

100% ARABICA

Script: Mahmoud Zemmouri and A-Lawrence Attias. Dir: Zemmouri. Players: Cheb Khaled, Cheb Mami, Mouss, Najim Laouriga. Prod: Fennec Productions (France) – Les Films de la Toison d'Or (Belgium) – Incoprom S A (Switzerland).

LA NUIT DU DESTIN (The Night of Destiny)

Script and Dir: Abdelkrim Bahloul. Players: Philippe Volter, Gamil Ratib, Sonia Mankai, Marie-Jose Nat. Prod: Les Films sur la Plage (France).

Useful Addresses

Entreprise Nationale de Production Audiovisuelle (ENPA)
3 avenue de l'Indépendence
BP 76
Didouche Mourad
Algiers
Tel: (213 2) 665 140
Fax: (213 2) 662 520

Agence Nationale des Actualitées Filmées (ANAF)
12 rue Ali Bedjaoui
El Biar
Algiers
Tel: (213 2) 791 029
Fax: (213 2) 788 349

Cinémathèque Algérienne
rue Larbi-Ben-M'Hidi
Algiers
Tel: (213 2) 638 301

Centre Algérien pour l'Art et l'Industrie Cinématographique (CAAIC)
Immeuble les Asphodèles
16030 Ben Aknoun
Algiers
Tel: (213 2) 781 657
Fax: (213 2) 784 104

ARGENTINA
Alfredo Friedlander

While none of the ten top-grossing films in Argentina in 1996 were local productions, in 1997 local features accounted for the top three positions. **Wild Cards** (*Comodines*), which was the biggest hit of the year, was shot by newcomers Jorge Nisco and Daniel Barone. The script followed a pattern very familiar from American movies: a team of mismatched cops go from strong distrust to true friendship. Their main duty: to foil a drug-dealing organisation whose members include high-ranking police officers. The film's use of special effects – such as a spectacular helicopter explosion – is unusual in Argentine cinema, but is overshadowed by excessive product placement of well-known international brands.

Released just two weeks before

Comodines, **The Fury** (*La Furia*) shared a drug-related theme. Set on the border between Argentina and Paraguay, it dealt with the misfortunes of a judge's son, who is unfairly arrested for drug trafficking. The judge's stern and stubborn position, convinced at first that his son is guilty, contrasts with the devoted attitude of his girlfriend, who finally convinces the judge of his son's innocence.

Sons of the judiciary who fall foul of the law featured in another big hit, **Ashes from Paradise** (*Cenizas del Paraíso*), Marcelo Piñeyro's third movie after *Tango Feroz* and *Wild Horses*. This crime story starts with two suspicious deaths, including that of a judge (played by Héctor Alterio, star of Piñeyro's two earlier films). The second victim is a 22-year-old girl and each of the judge's three sons accuses himself of being

Still from THE LIGHTHOUSE

responsible for her death. Like all Piñeyro's movies, it played very successfully with critics and public alike.

Back for good

In November 1997, the 13th International Film Festival of Mar del Plata took place. This was the second consecutive festival after the 20-year hiatus which ended in 1996. Among the celebrities in attendance were Peter Fonda and Victor Nunez, promoting *Ulee's Gold*, Catherine Deneuve, Jacqueline Bisset, Alain Delon, Sofia Loren and Kathleen Turner. First prize went to **The Tango Lesson**, Sally Potter's UK/Argentina co-production.

Other Argentine movies in competition in Mar del Plata were: **Pizza, Beer, Smoke** (*Pizza, Birra, Faso*), the tale of five young

kidnappers, and **Soul's Square** (*Plaza de Almas*). The former was the first local movie released in 1998. It opened in January, in the middle of the summer season, which is highly unusual for an Argentine movie, and was acclaimed by the critics and successful with the public. Another successful movie released in the first half of 1998 was Eduardo Mignogna's **The Lighthouse** (*El Faro*), which portrays two very different sisters in a story which reaches a dramatic conclusion.

It looks as though the number of Argentine releases in 1998 will outnumber the 28 from last year. But with perhaps more than 100 features completed and awaiting release, finding screens is very difficult. The decision of the Argentine Film Institute to open a new cinema, increasing the number of theatres solely devoted to Argentine films to four, gave several of the new local films a much-needed alternative route to their audience.

Alejandro Agresti, whose ninth movie, *Buenos Aires Viceversa*, was the first Argentine hit of 1997, has already finished his twelfth film, **The Wind Gone With** (*El viento se llevó lo que*), which features a Patagonian cinema projectionist whose habit of mixing up reels explains the film's jumbled-up title.

ALFREDO FRIEDLANDER is a freelance film critic who writes regularly for the monthly *Cinetop* magazine. He also broadcasts on movie history and, above all, is a film buff.

Recent and Forthcoming Films

COMODINES (Wild Cards)

Script: Gustavo Bellati, Mario Segade. Dir: Jorge Nisco & Daniel Barone. Phot: Ricardo De Angelis. Music: Ivan Wyszogrod. Players: Carlos Andrés Calvo, Adrián Suar, Rodolfo Ranni, Víctor Laplace, Nancy Dupláa, Patricia Viggiano, Nelly Prono. Prod: Artear, Pol-ka, Flehner Films.

The first special effects-heavy Argentinian film teams two very different cops against

drug dealers who are in league with senior figures in the Police Department. Top grossing film in 1997's box-office chart.

LA FURIA (The Fury)

Script: Juan Bautista Stagnaro, Matías Stagnaro. Dir: Stagnaro. Phot: Carlos Torlaschi. Music: Leo Sujatovich. Players: Luis Brandoni, Diego Torres, Laura Novoa, Rubén Stella, Ingrid Pellicori, Rodolfo Ranni, Pepe Novoa, Horacio

Novoa. Prod: Argentina Sono Film.

A judge presiding over a drugs investigation lets his innocent son go to jail. The young man's girlfriend fights to clear his name.

CENIZAS DEL PARAISO (Ashes From Paradise)

Script: Aída Bortnik, Marcelo Piñeyro. Dir: Piñeyro. Phot: Alfredo Mayo. Music: Osvaldo Montes. Players: Héctor Alterio, Cecilia

Roth, Leonardo Sbaraglia, Daniel Kuznieka, Leticia Bredice, Nicolás Abeles, Chela Ruiz, Jorge Marrale. Prod: Patagonik Films, Artear, Buena Vista Corporation.

A woman investigates a murder and the suspicious death of a judge who falls from the roof of the Federal Courthouse.

PIZZA, BIRRA, FASO
(Pizza, Beer, Smoke)

Script: Bruno Stagnaro, Adrián Caetano. Dir: Bruno Stagnaro, Adrián Stagnaro. Phot: Marcelo Lavintman. Music: Leo Sujatovich. Players: Héctor Anglada, Jorge Sesán, Pamela Jordán, Alejandro Pous, Walter Díaz, Tony Lestingi, Martín Adjemián. Prod: INCAA, Hubert Bals Fund (Netherlands).

Outstanding debut feature from two young directors, which focuses on five jobless youths, played by amateur actors, who make their living through kidnapping.

PLAZA DE ALMAS
(Soul's Square)

Script and Dir: Fernando Díaz. Phot: Abel Peñalba. Music: Luis Robinson. Players: Olga Zubarry, Norman Briski, Alejandro Gancé, Vera Fogwill, Villanueva Cosse, Roberto Carnaghi, Prod: Díaz.

SUS OJOS SE CERRARON
(His Eyes Closed)

Script: Oscar Plasencia, Raœl Brambilla with the participation of Jaime Chávarri and José María Paolantonio. Dir: Chávarri. Phot: Carlos Gusi. Music: Luis María Serra, Daniel Berardi, Rodolfo Mederos. Players: Darío Grandinetti, Aitana Sánchez-Gijón, Juan Echanove, Ulises Dumont, Pepe Soriano, Carlos Carella, Raœl Brambilla. Prod: Buena Vista International, Patagonik Films.

FUGA DE CEREBROS
(Brain Drain)

Script: Fernando Musa, Branko Andjic. Dir: Musa. Phot: Carlos Torlaschi. Music: Luis María Serra. Players: Nicolás Cabré,

Victor Laplace in SHARED SECRETS

Luis Quiroz, Roberto Carnaghi, Enrique Liporace, Federico D'Elía, Alberto Busaid, Nicolás Pauls, Ana María Picchio, Jimena Anganuzzi, Manuel Callau, Brian Forcinitti. Prod: Fernando Musa Producciones.

ASESINATO A DISTANCIA
(Murder At Distance)

Script and Dir: Santiago Carlos Oves. Phot: Jorge Ruíz. Music: Emilio Kauderer. Players: Héctor Alterio, Patricio Contreras, Laura Novoa, Fabián Vena, Carlos Weber, Martín Adjemián . Prod: Proafilme S.R.L, Negocios Cinematográficos S.A.

Agatha Christie-like murder mystery set in 1950s Uruguay. A lawyer investigates the apparent suicide of an industrialist's son.

TINTA ROJA (Blood Ink)

Script: Carmen Guarini, Jorge Goldenberg, Marcelo Céspedes. Dir: Guarini, Céspedes. Phot: Libio Pensavalle. Music: Olivier Manoury. Prod: Cine-Ojo, ISKRA

Experienced documentary-makers Guarini and Céspedes turn their attention to press exploitation of pain, death and fear.

EL FARO (The Lighthouse)

Script and Dir: Eduardo Mignogna.

Phot: Marcelo Camorino. Sound: Goldstein & Steinberg. Players: Ingrid Rubio, Ricardo Darín, Jimena Barón, Florencia Bertoti, Norma Aleandro, Norberto Díaz, Boy Olmi, Mariano Martínez, Jorge Marrale, Paola Krum. Prod :Artear Argentina, Raœl J. Naya Producciones, Alfredo Odorisio, Promofilm SA, Film Suez SA, Prime Films (Spain).

Ten years in the lives of two sisters who are the sole survivors of a family car crash.

SECRETOS COMPARTIDOS
(Shared Secrets)

Script: Alberto Lecchi, Daniel Romañach, Leandro Siciliano. Dir: Lecchi. Phot: Hugo Colace. Music: Iván Wyszogrod. Players: Victor Laplace, Leonor Benedetto, Gabriel Goity, Antonio Grimau, Alicia Zanca, Enrique Pinti. Prod: Zarlek producciones S.A., America Show Business.

A surprising plot and an outstanding performance from Laplace as a serial killer who befriends a shy clown.

UN CRISANTEMO ESTALLA EN CINCOESQUINAS
(A Chrysanthemum Blows in Cincoesquinas)

Script and Dir: Daniel Burman. Phot: Esteban Sapir.

Music: Antonio Tarragó Ros. Players: José Luis Alfonso, Pastora Vega, Martín Kalwill, Valentina Bassi, Millie Stegman, Walter Reyno. Prod: Burman, Diego Dubcovsky.

Erasmo sets out to avenge the rape and murder of the nanny who raised him after he was abandoned by his parents.

LA SONAMBULA
(The Sleepwalker)

Script: Ricardo Piglia, Fernando Spiner. Dir: Spiner. Phot: José Luis García. Music: Leo Sujatovich. Players: Sofía Viruboff, Lorenzo Quinteros, Patricio Contreras, Gastón Pauls, Norman Briski, Alejandro Urdapilleta, Noemí Frenkel, Pastora Vega, Martín Adjemián. Prod: Spiner, Rolo Azpeitía, Jorge Poleri.

Extremely original sci-fi vision of Buenos Aires in 2010. An explosion releases a huge amount of "psychic gas" which wipes the memories of the entire population and forces the authorities into drastic action.

BUENOS AIRES ME MATA
(Buenos Aires Kills Me)

Script: Beda Docampo Feijoó, Laura Ramos. Dir: Docampo Feijoó. Phot: Ricardo Rodriguez. Music: Iván Wyszogrod. Players: Imanol Arias, Fernán Mirás, Eleonora Wexler, Nancy Dupláa, Claudio Tolcachir, Leonardo Saggese, Nicolás Pauls, Osvaldo Santoro, Pastora Vega. Prod: Kompel Producciones, Jorge Estrada Mora S.A.

One night in a disco transforms the lives of a group of young people.

DOÑA BARBARA

Script and Dir: Betty Kaplan. Phot: Carlos González. Music: Bigen Mendizabel. Players: Esther Goris, Jorge Perugorría, Ruth Gabriel, Víctor Laplace, Ulises Dumont, Juan Fernández, Guillermo Angelelli, Víctor Cárdenas, Horacio Rocca, Sandra Ballesteros. Prod: Austral Films, U.I.P. (Spain).

A young lawyer is caught up in a story of violence, lust and black magic, set in the fascinating and savage landscape of an unidentified Latin American country.

LA NUBE (The Cloud)

Script and Dir: Fernando Pino Solanas. Phot: Juan Diego Solanas. Music: Gerardo Gandini. Players: Tato Pavlovsky, Laura Novoa, Angela Correa, Leonor Manso, Franklin Caicedo, Cristina Banegas, Bernard LeCoq, Christophe Malavoy, Jorge Petraglia, Carlos Paez, Horacio Peña. Prod: Cinesur SA, Les Films du Sud (France), Film Welt (Germany), Bim (Italy).

TANGO

Script and Dir: Carlos Saura. Phot: Vittorio Storaro. Music: Lalo Schifrin. Players: Miguel Angel Solá, Cecilia Narova, Mía Maestro, Juan Carlos Copes, Carlos Rivarola, Julio Bocca, Juan Luis Galiardo, Enrique Pinti. Prod: Argentina Sono Film, Terraplén Prod., Alma Ata Intl., Astrolabio, Adela Pictures, Beco Films, Saura Films and Pandora Cinema (international distribution).

Budget of $6m makes this the most expensive Argentinian movie ever made. A story of love and death, beautifully shot by Storaro.

UN ARGENTINO EN NUEVA YORK (An Argentinian in New York)

Script: G. Maglie, C.Civale. Dir: Juan José Jusid. Phot: Juan Carlos Lenardi. Music: Federico Jusid. Players: Guillermo Francella, Natalia Oreiro, Diana Lamas, Jessica Schultz, Cristina Albero, Boris Rubaya, Frenando Siro, Gabriel Goity, María Valenzuela. Prod: Argentina Sono Film, in association with TELEFE.

Comedy about a father who travels to New York to bring home his errant daughter.

EL VIENTO SE LLEVO LO QUE (The Wind Gone With)

Script and Dir: Alejandro Agresti.

Players: Angela Molina, Jean Rochefort, Vera Fogwill, Fabián Vena, Ulises Dumont, Carlos Roffé, Sergio Povés Campos, Mario Paolucci, Sebastián Polonsky. Prod: Agresti Films S.R.L., Orler Films S.A., DMVB Films and Canal Plus (France), Nieuwe Gronden (Netherlands), Maestranza Films (Spain).

Soledad (Fogwill), one of only three women taxi drivers in Buenos Aires in the early 1970s, travels to a small village in Patagonia, where the only contact with the outside world is through a cinema whose projectionist mixes up the reels (hence the film's title).

CORAZON ILUMINADO
(Foolish Heart)

Script: Héctor Babenco, Ricardo Piglia. Dir: Babenco. Phot: Lauro Escorel. Music: Zbigniew Preisner. Players: Walter Quiroz, Miguel Angel Solá, María Luisa Mendonca, Xuxa Lopes, Oscar Ferrigno, Villanueva Cosse, Alejandra Awada, Arturo Maly, Norma Aleandro, Daniel Fanego. Prod: Oscar Kramer S.A., HBFilmes Ltda. (Brasil), Flach Film and Canal Plus (France).

Juan, a young Jewish student, faces hostility in the early 1970s. He returns to Argentina 20 years later after making his name as a film director in Los Angeles and discovers that the great love of his youth is still alive.

Producers

Aleph Producciones S.A.
Maipú 853 – 3° Piso
1006 Buenos Aires
Fax: (54 1) 312 6876

Arena Films
Callao 1057 – 4° Piso
1023 Buenos Aires
Fax: (54 1) 811 1181/2

Argentina Sono Film
Lavalle 1860
1051 Buenos Aires
Fax: (54 1) 374 9250

Artear Group S.A.
Lima 1261
1138 Buenos Aires
Fax: (54 1) 370 1309

Cine-Ojo
Lavalle 1619 – 3° Piso
1048 Buenos Aires
Fax: (54 1) 373 8208
e-mail: cineojo@interlink.com.ar

Imágen Satelital S.A.
Avenida Melián 2752
1430 Buenos Aires
Fax: (54 1) 546 8001

**Jorge Estrada Mora
Producciones**
Esmeralda 570 – Piso 13° Of.48
1007 Buenos Aires
Fax: (54 1) 393 9814

Negocios Cinematográficos
Lavalle 1943
1051 Buenos Aires
Fax: (54 1) 372 2807

Oscar Kramer Producciones
Figueroa Alcorta 3351 –
Piso 1° Of.104
1425 Buenos Aires
Fax: (54 1) 807 3254
e-mail: okafilms@overnet.com.ar

Patagonik Film Group S.A.
Godoy Cruz 1540
1414 Buenos Aires
Fax: (54 1) 778 0046

Telefe S.A.
Pavón 2444
1248 Buenos Aires
Fax: (54 1) 308 0054

Distributors

Artistas Argentinos Asociados
Lavalle 1977/79
1051 Buenos Aires
Fax: (54 1) 811 5016

**Buena Vista Columbia Tristar
Films of Argentina S.A.**
Ayacucho 533
1026 Buenos Aires
Fax: (54 1) 954 3819/952 9168

Cinemania Films Group S.A.
Riobamba 477
1025 Buenos Aires
Fax: (54 1) 374 0648/374 8435
e-mail: orlersa@comnet.com.ar

Distribution Company S.A.
Ayacucho 595
1026 Buenos Aires
Fax: (54 1) 372 9945/371 3662

Eurocine S.A.
Tucumán 1980 – P.B-
1050 Buenos Aires
Fax: (54 1) 373 0547

IFA Argentina
Riobamba 339 2° Piso A
1025 Buenos Aires
Fax: (54 1) 373 7967

Líder Films S.A.
Lavalle 2086
1051 Buenos Aires
Fax: (54 1) 953 7355

**UIP (United International
Pictures) S.R.I.**
Ayacucho 520
1026 Buenos Aires
Fax: (54 1) 373 5098

Warner Bros. – Fox
Tucumán 1938
1050 Buenos Aires
Fax: (54 1) 372 6094/97

Useful Address

**INCAA (Instituto Nacional de
Cine y Artes Audiovisuales)**
Lima 319
1073 Buenos Aires
Fax: (54 1) 383 0029

ARMENIA
Sousanna Haroutiunian

Only three films at last year's Gothenburg International Film Festival attracted the attention of Elisabeth Sorenson, critic of the *Svensk Tagbladet* newspaper, and one was the Armenian feature **Outflow** (*Hosk*). Sorensen was particularly struck by the innovative and luminous dramaturgy directed by Edgar Baghdassarian. How ironic, then, that this fine film, shot in black-and-white on a tiny budget, has never and probably will never be seen by Armenian audiences in a cinema.

This situation arises partly from the financial crisis suffered by Armenia and partly because of the ridiculous and unwise privatisation of its cinemas. The state film distribution agencies have collapsed and have not been replaced by private enterprise because the people who bought the cinemas have turned their properties into car showrooms or supermarkets. Those few cinemas still in operation are in a dreadful condition, their high electricity costs cannot even be covered by the prices of tickets sold and in any case most of the population have hardly any disposable income. Only video saloons make money.

The only Armenian distribution agency that keeps providing films for the only state-run cinema still in operation, The Moscow, is Paradise. But the firm does this mainly out of charity, as its main source of income is film distribution abroad, as well as video rentals and TV advertisements. Only with the help of enormous investment will it be possible to renovate and technically equip the cinemas and develop an internal market. Tax breaks are needed to encourage exhibitors and to stimulate the flow of private capital into Armenian film production.

Armenian cinema somehow survives on the small subsidy allocated to production by the government. That sum, which has hardly changed since 1995, is only about $250,000 per year and, according to old-style Soviet thinking, is allocated to just two state studios: Haifilm and Haik. The clamour for a new system of subsidy grows by the month. Some favour the awarding of grants to individual films on a competitive basis, with producers guaranteeing that additional private funding will be available to cover the remainder of each budget. The state studios could then become a production base.

From Holland with love

This method worked successfully in 1998 with **Her Name, His Name**, directed by David Safarian. Having first gained financial support from Holland's Hubert Bals Foundation and then acquired a Dutch producer, Jan Heijs of Jura Filmproducties, the Armenian Ministry of Culture and Haifilm Studio, where the film is being shot, came on board. The plot focuses on a married couple of average years in the early 1990s, while the Soviet Union was collapsing and Armenia was suffering a severe energetic and economic blockade.

Haroutiune Khachatrian is widely respected within the Armenian industry, and has been awarded a number of prizes at international festivals. For the last 10 years, Khachatrian has worked masterfully on the border between documentary and fiction – and he occupies the same territory in his latest film, **Documentalist**, released late in 1997. Its main character is an imaginary hero – a film director, whom Khachatrian installs in a documentary environment to create a very interesting picture of city life.

Armen Dovlatian's **Dreams** (Haifilm Studio) is a mystically-flavoured criminal drama, exploring the complex relationship between a man and his ex-wife in the wake of the illness and death of their daughter. Another film in production is **Crazy Angel** (working title), directed by Souren Babayan. The script is based on Swedish writer Pier Lagerquist's novel, *Barraba*, and its prevailing biblical motives are supposed to be dedicated to the forthcoming tercentenary of the adoption of Christianity as a state religion in Armenia in 1700.

Another Haifilm project worth mentioning is **An Armenian World**, the new feature by internationally-known director Arthur Peleshian. Now 60, Peleshian has not shot an astonishing number of films in a 30-year career, but each piece of work, including *The Beginning, Seasons of The Year* and *Our Century*, was born out of opposition to the Soviet system and was amazingly innovative. Peleshian's new project is being partially financed by the Armenian Ministry of Culture, and France's Centre National du Cinéma.

SOUSANNA HAROUTIUNIAN graduated from Moscow's State Cinematographic Institute in 1987. She has contributed to numerous Armenian and Russian publications, such as *Film*, *Kino* and *Sovetskaya Kultura*, and has been film expert of the daily *Respublica Armenia* since 1991. She is president of Armenia's Association of Film Critics and Cinema Journalists.

Recent and Forthcoming Films

CRAZY ANGEL (working title)

Script: S. Babayan, A. Hovsepian. Dir: Babayan. Phot. A. Mirakian. Players: M. Poghossian, K. Djanibekian. Prod: Haifilm Studio.

HER NAME, HIS NAME

Script and Dir: David Safarian. Phot: A. Mkrtchian. Players: A. Safarian, Y. Drouz. Prod: Haifilm Studio, Armenia & Jura Filmproducties (Holland).

AN ARMENIAN WORLD

Script and Dir: Arthur Peleshian. Phot: V. Ter-Hakopian.

DREAMS

Script and Dir: Armen Dovlatian. Phot: A. Yavourian. Players: A. Shougarov, N. Gevorkian, A. Elbakian. Prod: Haifilm.

Producers

Haifilm Studio
50 Gevork Chaush
375088 Yerevan
Tel: (374 2) 343 000

Haik Documentary Studio
50 Gevork Chaush
375088 Yerevan
Tel: (374 2) 354 590
Fax: (374 2) 357 032

Paradise
18 Abovian
375001 Yerevan
Tel: (374 2) 521 271
Fax: (374 2) 521 302

Useful Addresses

Armenian Union of Cinematographers
18 Vardanats
Yerevan
Tel: (374 2) 570 528
Fax: (374 2) 571 136

Armenian National Cinematheque
25A Tbilisskoye shosse
Yerevan
Tel: (374 2) 285 406

Association of Film-Critics and Cinema-Journalists of Armenia
5 Toumanian St.
375001 Yerevan
Tel: (374 2) 521 517
Fax: (374 2) 523 922

Association of Film Producers of Armenia
15 Armiryan St., Apt. 85
375010 Yerevan
Tel/Fax: (374 2) 535 322
Fax: (374 2) 907 141

Film Department Ministry of Culture
5 Toumanian St.
375001 Yerevan
Armenia
Tel: (374 2) 529 319)

AUSTRALIA — David Stratton

Writing in *IFG* a year ago, I referred to the enormous difficulties faced by Australian film-makers in finding a cinema audience. Despite the mushrooming of shiny new suburban multiplexes all over the country (which naturally boost overall cinema attendance considerably), Australian films hardly ever get space outside the city centres. With occasional exceptions (*Shine, Babe, Muriel's Wedding*), local producers find themselves swamped by big-budget, extensively-publicised Hollywood films – and, like foreign language films, are also directly competing for screen space with the so-called Sundance productions, the small-scale independent American films which have become so ubiquitous in the last couple of years.

When Australian films perform poorly, in some cases catastrophically, at the local box-office, potential overseas distribution deals suffer accordingly: if a film does not work at home, why would it work abroad? Part of the problem seems to be that Australian films with minority appeal are opened too wide. It used to be that an Australian film would open in one cinema in each city and be given time to find its audience. Twenty years ago, films which have now become classics, like *Picnic at*

Heather Rose as Julia in DANCE ME TO MY SONG

Hanging Rock, Sunday Too Far Away, Breaker Morant and *Newsfront*, ran for months in this way. No longer.

Now, many Australian films open in several cinemas, including big city multiplexes, and so audience attendance is scattered over a much wider area. Unless a film clicks immediately (as only *The Castle* did last year) it tends to disappear. Peter Duncan's engaging, low-budget comedy **A Little Bit Of Soul**, despite a cast that included Oscar-winner Geoffrey Rush, barely scraped through one week's release, though it was handled by Columbia Pictures and given a major launch.

Spokesmen for the outsiders

Despite these difficulties, production in the last year remained buoyant. Twenty features were completed and screened during the year (five more than in 1996), and they were a pretty diverse and, for the most part, worthwhile bunch. Confrontational, too. Rolf De Heer's Cannes competition entry **Dance Me To My Song** is, like most of this maverick director's work, about outsiders: in *Bad Boy Bubby*, his protagonist emerges into the real world after spending his entire life in a locked room; *Epsilon* features a female extra-terrestrial, *The Quiet Room* a child whose parents are separating. In the new film, Julia (Heather Rose) suffers from severe cerebral palsy. Rose, who wrote the screenplay (with Frederick Stahl) is similarly afflicted in real life, but this is not a documentary – it is a fictional drama

about an intelligent woman yearning for love but trapped in a stunted and twisted body.

With tenderness and understanding, De Heer uncompromisingly depicts the painfully restricted world of his protagonist, who is appallingly treated by her carer (Joey Kennedy) and who finds herself falling in love with a 'normal' man (John Brumpton) who befriends her. A remarkable, challenging film with a deliciously upbeat conclusion.

The Boys, one of the year's (modest) commercial successes, also challenges the viewer. Inspired by a singularly brutal rape-murder case which shocked Australia a few years ago, the film – based on a play – unfolds during a 24-hour period, the day Brett (David Wenham) comes out of prison after serving a term for grievous bodily harm. Filled with anger at the world, this walking time-bomb gets drunk with his brothers and terrorises his mother and girlfriend (Toni Collette) before setting out into the night looking for trouble. The film ends before the 'boys' commit the savage killing for which (in brief flash-forwards which punctuate the action) they are eventually captured and punished. This corrosive exploration of the seeds of violence is directed with menacing skill by first-timer Rowan Woods, and is a considerable achievement.

Night and day

Ana Kokkinos' **Head On**, another abrasive first feature which unfolds in a 24-hour time-frame, also deals with a young man's frustrations, but in a very different context. Ari (Alex Dimitriades) is a gay Greek-Australian who has grown up in a traditional family. The film follows him through a long night of confrontations and sexual entanglements. Kokkinos does a remarkable job in keeping up the momentum of Ari's night-time activities, and Dimitriades gives a remarkably brave performance, taking part in some fairly full-on sexual encounters.

A restricted time-frame also distinguishes another accomplished feature

Alex Dimitriades as Ari in HEAD ON

debut, Craig Monahan's **The Interview**, which has some similarities to the Claude Miller classic *Garde à Vue*. Early one morning, police violently break into the lodgings of a man (Hugo Weaving), who is taken to the station and interrogated by cops Tony Martin and Aaron Jeffrey. At first, the police seem to be uncommonly brutal; in true Kafka style they refuse to tell the bemused victim what he is supposed to have done; but gradually it emerges that he is a suspected serial killer. Monahan skilfully switches sympathy back and forth between the police and the suspect, and the claustrophobic atmosphere of the police station is beautifully controlled. A small film, but a serious and intriguing one.

James Bogle's third feature, **In The Winter Dark**, was chosen to open the 45th Sydney Film Festival; not the happiest of choices, because this eerie mood-piece, based on a Tim Winton novel, was not seen at its best in a cavernous 2,000-seat picture palace. The film, which in theme and mood has similarities to last year's *The Well*, but which also evokes William Wellman's *Track of the Cat*, is set in a chilly, remote farming area where an elderly couple (Brenda Blethyn, Ray Barrett), a pregnant woman (Miranda Otto) abandoned by her lover, and a loner (Richard Roxburgh), find themselves threatened by something out there in the dark. Bogle, assisted by four flawless performances, beautifully creates a quietly chilling atmosphere of mystery and dread.

Novelist Richard Flanagan used a similarly dank, bleak setting – wintry Tasmania – for his first feature, **The Sound of One Hand Clapping**, which he wrote and directed with Rolf De Heer producing. Kerry Fox plays the daughter of a Slovenian migrant (Kristof Kaczmarek) and the film delves into the problems of assimilating (and of overcoming bitter memories of war-torn Europe) in a strange new land. Another novelist-turned-film-maker, Robert Carter, made **The Sugar Factory**, in which Matt Day plays a disturbed young man traumatised when a child he is baby-sitting is accidentally killed.

Betting on co-production

On a vastly bigger scale, two ambitious co-productions with the US produced decidedly mixed results. Gillian Armstrong's bold attempt to adapt Peter Carey's novel **Oscar and Lucinda** for the screen was generally received better in America than it was at home. The quixotic story of a pair of gamblers (Ralph Fiennes, Cate Blanchett) who become (non-

Cate Blanchett as Lucinda in OSCAR AND LUCINDA
photo: Fox Searchlight

romantically) connected, this ambitious film, with its very handsome photography and production design, is flawed by the overly mannered performance of Fiennes (whose Oscar is more irritating than eccentric) and by the story's arc, which just fails to deliver on expectations.

More successful is Alex Proyas' visually exciting **Dark City**, an often dazzling mixture of science-fiction and film noir, with a classic story (amnesiac suspected of murder) attached to a space invaders theme. The mixture does not entirely work, but Proyas' feature, like his two earlier efforts, is filled with amazing images. Sad to report that a third ambitious co-production, this time with France, turned out a complete disaster. **Love In Ambush**, directed by the usually excellent Carl Schultz, is a soggy romantic mish-mash set in Cambodia, and unconvincing on every level.

In the wake of *Babe*, animal films have been coming thick and fast, including **Joey** (baby kangaroo) and **The Real Macaw** (talking parrot). The best of them is **Paws**, Karl Zwicky's amusing tale of a computer-literate dog; the others are best forgotten. A handful of good comedies brightened the year. **Road To Nhill** is an unexpected delight from first-time director Sue Brooks, in which the inhabitants of a small town are thrown into disarray by a car accident involving four women members of the bowling club. With its roll-call of well-observed eccentrics, and a magnificent ensemble cast, this is a joy from start to finish.

Peter Duncan's follow-up to his clever *Children of the Revolution*, **A Little Bit Of Soul**, is another small film, privately financed on a minuscule budget. David Wenham, in complete contrast to his role in *The Boys*, portrays a Cary Grant-like absent-minded scientist on the verge of a major discovery for which he needs funds; Geoffrey Rush, in his first post-*Shine* role, is Australia's befuddled Treasurer. A dialogue-led comedy of considerable charm, it completely failed to find an audience.

Like *Road To Nhill*, **Crackers**, directed by David Swann, is an ensemble piece, this time about members of a family who gather for a "typical" Aussie Christmas. There are plenty of laughs here, more so than in David Parker's rather sad **Diana & Me**, in which Toni Collette plays Diana Spencer's namesake who, while in London hoping to meet the Princess of Wales, falls in love with a member of the paparazzi. Talk about bad timing; the film was released not long after Princess Diana's tragic death, and was a box-office disaster, but the concept would not have been very funny under any circumstances.

Broken silence, sad censorship

Parker scripted the altogether more interesting **Amy**, which was directed by his wife, Nadia Tass. This takes the familiar story of a child traumatised into silence when she witnesses the death of her father (a rock singer electrocuted on stage), but gives it a fresh twist by enabling the youngster to communicate through song. Winning performances from Rachel Griffiths, as Amy's mum, Ben Mendelssohn and the talented Alana de Roma, as Amy, lift this amiable but uneven film out of the rut.

Similarly, John Ruane invests potentially unpromising material with intelligence and charm in **Dead Letter Office**, in which Miranda Otto plays a young woman forlornly searching for her long-lost father and getting a job in the dead letter section of the city post office, where she falls for her boss, a refugee from Chile. Thanks to Otto's delicious performance, the film is both amusing and emotionally satisfying.

On the other hand, the much-praised **Radiance**, based on a play by Louis Nowra, proved to be derivative (the plot, about three sisters who are reunited for the funeral of their mother, is almost identical to that of *Hotel Sorrento*, filmed by Richard Franklin a few years back) and overly theatrical. It is hard to escape the suspicion that those who profess to admire the film do so because it is a rare example of an all-aboriginal production (director Rachel

Rachel Griffiths (left) and Alana de Roma in AMY

Perkins) rather than because of its achievements as a piece of cinema.

Censorship is, sad to report, on the rise, with the government overseeing the banning of Pier Paolo Pasolini's *Salo*, which had been circulating for a few years with an R classification. More insidiously, mainstream films (*Men In Black* is a good example) have been modified to achieve the PG rating initially denied their distributors by increasingly hard-line bureaucrats, spurred on by crusading right-wing politicians. Unfortunately, this situation will probably get worse.

Still from DEAD LETTER OFFICE photo: PolyGram

DAVID STRATTON was Director of the Sydney Film Festival (1966–1983) and is co-host of *The Movie Show*, a weekly programme on the SBS TV network. He also contributes reviews to *Variety* and *The Australian*, and lectures on film history at the University of Sydney.

Still from RADIANCE photo: Beyond Films

Industry Survey

by Peter Thompson

'TROPFEST' is a good place to start. As mentioned in last year's *IFG*, this amazing festival brings thousands onto Sydney's streets on a summer evening to watch a new crop of short films on giant video screens. Various intoxicants are consumed and substantial financial rewards go to the winning films. To nurture the seeds planted by Tropfest, its instigator, actor-director John Polsen, has expanded his dream into Tropnest, a workshop for screenwriters. Occupying (rent free) a restored bungalow within the precinct of the new Fox studio complex, Tropnest will supply facilities and guidance, via mentors drawn from the industry, to a hand-picked group of budding scribes.

This is a significant development for two reasons: it reflects continuing concern that Australian scripts lack substance; and it also bodes well for the film production facility which has sprouted in the former Royal Agricultural Society grounds in Moore Park, where Sydney's Easter Show was held for generations before moving to the site of the 2000 Olympic Games.

Fox Studios Australia (FSA), a joint venture between Rupert Murdoch's News Corporation and Lend Lease Development, is the biggest thing to happen to Australia's film industry in recent times. Opened in May 1998, amid protests from residents in neighbouring suburbs, who feared a raucous movie theme park, and grumblings from many in the film community resentful of another corporate conquest, it is an impressive facility, quickly dubbed the most advanced in the world (!). Boasting six large stages, and comprehensive support services, FSA has fibre-optic cable links which instantly bridge the distance between Sydney and international production centres – i.e. Hollywood.

Therein lies the main fear of many local film-makers. While FSA means substantial employment opportunities for a potentially stable workforce – and we could use more stability – it also means a major shift in existing power relationships. Ever-fearful of the Hollywood cultural juggernaut, many see the new player as a black hole which will suck up indigenous creative energy and convert it into homogenised American product. This is a complex debate which will never end. But many people are simply ignoring it. On the one hand, there are those busting to produce scripts which will suit the tastes of the new monster. On the other, there are those within a diverse local industry who will go their merry ways, regardless of Murdoch and his lieutenants.

Missing the mainstream

This diversity is reflected at the Australian box-office. Gross receipts continued to climb, and, based on previous year-on-year increases, 1999 should bring another boom period, with a projected total of around $435m (AUS$700m), up from $365m in 1997. But Australian movies only enjoy a dismal five to ten per cent of the total. There is still resistance to local product amongst audiences who associate the word 'movie' with Hollywood, in spite of a thin but steady stream of popular successes such as Working Dog's *The Castle* and Arenafilm's *The Boys*.

The fact is that very few Australian film-makers are aiming at the mainstream audience. Although *Titanic* has only recently overtaken *Crocodile Dundee* as the all-time Australian box-office champ, the success of the latter remains the exception rather than the rule. Australians are so used to a diet of movies filtered through the commercial networks of other countries that the raw and inevitably variable quality of new local work often sticks in their throats.

Of just as much potential danger as the spectre of foreign domination are the ills of the sheltered workshop. And yet you would have to say that the strategy adopted three decades ago to grow a local industry from the colonial ashes has worked. Generous injections of public money have led to astonishing levels of activity and an industry showing increasing signs of being able to stand on its own feet. While taxpayers' money continues to flow at stable levels into a substantial arts bureaucracy, and into the pockets of local producers, more and more private money is being invested.

Several local distributors, such as Village Roadshow, Southern Star and Beyond, are continuing their expansion into film production. Other investment is coming from newer players, such as the cable channel Showtime, which is legally obliged to increase the proportion of local content in its schedule.

Who needs big budgets?

With around 40 feature films completed, 1997-98 has been a significant year in terms of sheer quantity – and diversity. George Miller has completed the *Babe* sequel, *Babe: Pig in the City*, and there were new films from other established directors such as Bill Bennett (*In a Savage Land*), Jane Campion (*Holy Smoke*), Rolf de Heer (*Dance Me to My Song* and *Dead Dolphins*), Peter Duncan (*Passion*) and Emma-Kate Croghan (*Strange Planet*). But there was also a posse of newcomers, including Rachel Perkins (*Radiance*), Rowan Woods (*The Boys*), Ana Kokkinos (*Head On*), James Bogle (*In the Winter Dark*), Gregor Jordan (*Two Hands*), Kate Woods (*Looking for Alibrandi*), Craig Monaghan (*The Interview*) and Chris Cudlipp (*Dear Claudia*).

Defying any swing towards big studios, higher costs and global homogenisation, there has also been increasing activity in the 'no-budget' sector. As predicted here last year, many have taken inspiration from the success of Emma-Kate Croghan's *Love*

and Other Catastrophes and Mike Cordell's *The Year of the Dogs* (a documentary shot on DVC video format and blown up to 35mm for theatrical distribution). Watch out for Maurice Murphy's *Fifteen Amore*, Marque Owen's *All the Way*, Alan White's *Erskineville Kings*, Iren Koster's *Dead End*, Vicki Fisher's *The Beggar's Opera Café* and Michelle Warner's *The Pumpkin's Big Night Out*.

If you go to the movies in the UK, Germany, Holland, the US, Mexico, Chile, the Middle East or even Argentina, there is an increasingly good chance that you will be watching an Australian-owned screen. Major exhibitors such as Hoyts, Greater Union and Village Roadshow are reaching out aggressively, building multiplexes all over the globe. This international thrust is matched by many production companies in film and television, with a growing realisation that borders no longer offer protection from or barriers to growth. Meanwhile, the opportunities for film-makers eager to fill this expanding demand show no sign of diminishing.

PETER THOMPSON is a writer, film-maker and critic who appears regularly on Australian national television.

Sinister cops at work in THE INTERVIEW
photo: The Globe Film Co.

Producers

Arenafilm Pty Ltd
(Robert Connolly,
John Maynard)
270 Devonshire Street
Surrey Hills NSW 2010
Tel: (61 2) 9317 7011
Fax: (61 2) 9319 6906

Artist Services Pty Ltd
(Andrew Knight,
Steve Vizard)
33 Nott Street
Port Melbourne VIC 3207
Tel: (61 3) 9646 3388
Fax: (61 3) 9646 7644

Bazmark Inq. Pty Ltd
(Baz Luhrmann)
PO Box 430
Kings Cross NSW 1340
Tel: (61 2) 9361 6668
Fax: (61 2) 9361 6667
Web: www.bazmark.com

Beyond Productions Ltd
(Mikael Borglund)
53-55 Brisbane Street
Surrey Hills NSW 2010
Tel: (61 2) 9281 1266
Fax: (61 2) 9281 1261
e-mail: beyond.com.au

Bill Bennett Productions Pty Ltd
(Bill Bennett)
PO Box 117
Castlecrag NSW 2068
Tel: (61 2) 9417 7744
Fax: (61 2) 9417 7601

Binnaburra Film Company Pty Ltd
(Glenys Rowe)
PO Box 2124
Clovelly NSW 2031
Tel: (61 2) 9665 6135
Fax: (61 2) 9665 4378

Cascade Films
(David Parker, Nadia Tass)
117 Rouse Street
Port Melbourne VIC 3207
Tel: (61 3) 9646 4022
Fax: (61 3) 9646 6336

David Hannay Productions
(David Hannay)
PO Box 175
Leura NSW 2780
Tel: (61 2) 4782 7111
Fax: (61 2) 4782 3711
e-mail: memdah@hermes.net.au

Filmside
(Richard Brennan, Al Clark, Andrena
Finlay, Ross Mathews)
33 Riley Street
Woolloomooloo NSW 2011
Tel: (61 2) 9361 4164
Fax: (61 2) 9332 3427

Fox Icon Productions Pty Ltd
(Tim White)
Fox Studios Australia FSA No 24
Driver Avenue
Moore Park NSW 1363
Tel: (61 2) 9383 4600
Fax: (61 2) 9383 4605

Fox Studios Australia
(Kim Williams)
Driver Avenue
Moore Park NSW 1363
Tel: (61 2) 9383 4000
Fax: (61 2) 9361 3106

Great Scott Productions
(Jane Scott)
27 Elizabeth Street
Paddington NSW 2021
Tel: (61 2) 9331 3535
Fax: (61 2) 9360 5875
e-mail: greats@netspace.net.au

House & Moorhouse Films
(Lynda House, Jocelyn Moorhouse)
117 Rouse Street
Port Melbourne VIC 3207
Tel: (61 3) 9646 4025
Fax: (61 3) 9646 6336

Jan Chapman Productions
(Jan Chapman)
PO Box 27
Potts Point NSW 1335
Tel: (61 2) 9331 2666
Fax: (61 2) 9331 2011

Kennedy Miller Pty Ltd
(George Miller)
The Metro Theatre
30 Orwell Street
Kings Cross NSW 2011
Tel: (61 2) 9357 2322
Fax: (61 2) 9356 3162

Matt Carroll Films Pty Ltd
(Matt Carroll)
12 Sloane Street
Newtown NSW 2042
Tel: (61 2) 9516 2400
Fax: (61 2) 9516 2099
e-mail: mcfilms@pop.real.com.au

Palm Beach Pictures Pty Ltd
(David Elfick)
33 Edward Street
Bondi NSW 2026
Tel: (61 2) 9365 1043
Fax: (61 2) 9365 1380
e-mail: palmbeach@infolearn.
com.au

RB Films
(Rosemary Blight)
9 Knox Street
Chippendale NSW 2008
Tel: (61 2) 9281 9550
Fax: (61 2) 9211 2281
e-mail: rbfilms@ozemail.com.au

Samson Productions Pty Ltd
(Sue Milliken)
119 Pyrmont Street
Pyrmont NSW 2009

Tel: (61 2) 9660 3244
Fax: (61 2) 9692 8926

Southern Star Group Limited
(Errol Sullivan)
Level 9/8 West Street
North Sydney NSW 2060
Tel: (61 2) 9202 8555
Fax: (61 2) 9925 0849
e-mail: general@sstar.com.au

Stamen Films Pty Ltd (Jonathan
Shteinman)
PO Box 3226
Tamarama NSW 2026
Tel: (61 2) 9365 2284
Fax: (61 2) 9300 0264
e-mail: stamen@ozemail.com.au

Tristram Miall Films Pty Ltd
(Tristram Miall)
270 Devonshire Street
Surrey Hills NSW 2010
Tel: (61 2) 9310 2422
Fax: (61 2) 9318 2542
e-mail: tmfilm@zeta.org.au

Vertigo Productions Pty Ltd (Rolf
de Heer)
3 Butler Drive
Hendon SA 5014
Tel: (61 8) 8348 9382
Fax: (61 8) 8348 9347
e-mail: vertigo@adelaide.on.net

Village Roadshow Pictures
(Michael Lake)
Warner Roadshow Movie World
Studios
Pacific Highway
Oxenford QLD 4210
Tel: (61 7) 5588 6666
Fax: (61 7) 5573 3698
Web: www.village.com.au

Wintertime Films Pty Ltd (John
Winter)
48 Lamb Street
Lilyfield NSW 2040
Tel: (61 2) 9810 5271
Fax: (61 2) 9818 3640
e-mail: nomad@s054.aone.net.au

Working Dog Pty Ltd (Santo
Cilauro, Tom Gleisner, Michael
Hirsh, Jane Kennedy, Rob Sitch)
PO Box 488
South Yarra VIC 3141
Tel: (61 3) 9826 4344
Fax: (61 3) 9826 4355
e-mail: dog@fox.net.au

Distributors

Note: The Beyond Group and Southern Star are important distributors (see producer list for contact details).

Columbia TriStar Films Pty Ltd
GPO Box 3342
Sydney NSW 2001
Tel: (61 2) 9272 2900
Fax: (61 2) 9272 2991

Footprint Films Pty Ltd
(same address as Arenafilm Pty Ltd)

The Globe Film Company
373 Liverpool Street
Darlinghurst NSW 2010
Tel: (61 2) 9332 2722
Fax: (61 2) 9332 2888
e-mail: info@globefilm.com.au

Newvision Film Distributors Pty Ltd
252 Bay Street
Port Melbourne VIC 3207
Tel: (61 3) 9646 5555
Fax: (61 3) 9646 2411

Palace Films
233 Whitehorse Road
Balwyn VIC 3103
Tel: (61 3) 9817 6421
Fax: (61 3) 9817 4921
e-mail: palace@netspace.net.au

PolyGram Filmed Entertainment
PO Box 17
Millers Point NSW 2000

Tel: (61 2) 9207 0500
Fax: (61 2) 9251 9654

REP Film Distribution
PO Box 130
St Leonards NSW 2065
Tel: (61 2) 9438 3377
Fax: (61 2) 9439 1827

Roadshow Film Distributors
GPO Box 1411M
Melbourne VIC 3000
Tel: (61 3) 9667 6666
Fax: (61 3) 9662 1449

Ronin Films
PO Box 1005
Civic Square ACT 2600
Tel: (61 6) 248 0851
Fax: (61 6) 249 1640
e-mail: roninfilms@netinfo.com.au

Sharmill Films
4/200 Toorak Road
South Yarra VIC 3141
Tel: (61 3) 9826 9077
Fax: (61 3) 9826 1935

20th Century Fox Film Distributors Pty Ltd
505 George Street
Sydney NSW 2000
Tel: (61 2) 9273 7300
Fax: (61 2) 9283 2191

United International Pictures
208 Clarence Street
Sydney NSW 2000
Tel: (61 2) 9264 7444
Fax: (61 2) 9264 2499

Useful addresses

Australian Film Finance Corporation
130 Elizabeth Street
Sydney NSW 2000
Postal address: GPO Box 3886
Sydney NSW 2001
Tel: (61 2) 9268 2555
Fax: (61 2) 9264 8551
Web: www.ffc.gov.au

Australian Film Commission
150 William Street
Wooloomooloo NSW 2011
GPO Box 3984
Sydney 2001
Tel: (61 2) 9321 6444
Fax: (61 2) 9357 3737
e-mail: info@afc.gov.au
Web: www.afc.gov.au

Australian Film, Television and Radio School
PO Box 126
North Ryde NSW 2113
Tel: (61 2) 9805 6611
Fax: (61 2) 9887 1030
e-mail: direct.sales@syd.aftrs.edu.au

Film Australia
101 Eton Road
Lindfield NSW 2070
Tel: (61 2) 9413 8777
Fax: (61 2) 9416 9401

Useful information can be found via the Web on www.nla.gov.au/oz/gov/

AUSTRIA — Beat Glur

Last year was one of the most important in Austrian cinema's recent history. The country's film-makers have rarely been so well represented at international festivals; rarely has their work been so widely discussed. The film that made it all happen was Michael Haneke's **Funny Games**, the first Austrian feature to be accepted for competition at Cannes since the early 1960s. That recognition gave

Austrian cinema a welcome boost which lasted well into 1998.

The disturbing story of a Viennese family – husband, wife and son – who are slaughtered by two bored youngsters while on a weekend break, *Funny Games* divided critics and audiences. It was sold to more than 30 countries – an unprecedented figure for an Austrian feature in recent times – and Haneke was invited to dozens of festivals all over the globe, many of which screened *Funny Games* alongside his other 1997 release, **The Castle**, based on the Kafka novel.

Martin Schweighofer, Managing Director of the Austrian Film Commission, called 1997 "the most successful year for Austrian cinema since the beginning of New Austrian Cinema", with a total of 180 Austrian placements at international festivals. These included Stefan Ruzowitzky's **Tempo**, about an adolescent Vienna bicycle courier; Robert Dornhelm's **The Unfish** (*Der Unfisch*), with German star Maria Schrader as a young woman who ends up sleeping inside the stomach of a huge, magic whale, with fantastical consequences; **Inheritance, or A Love Withheld** by Andreas Gruber, with French star Sandrine Bonnaire in search of her father; and Serb director Goran Rebic's **Jugofilm**, about a family in exile in Vienna after being torn apart by the war in the former Yugoslavia.

Truth and consequences

Austria's international profile was boosted further by documentaries like Nikolaus Geyrhalter's Venice and Berlin entry **The Year After Dayton**, a much acclaimed profile of post-war Bosnia, Ruth Beckermann's **East of War**, about "War of Extermination" (Vernichtungskrieg), the exhibition about the Wehrmacht which recently toured museums in Austria and Germany, and Robert-Adrian Pejo's **R.I.P. – Rest in Pieces**, a profile of New York artist Joe Coleman.

This year began with more high-profile festival exposure. Stefan Ruzowitzky's **The One-Seventh Farmers** (*Die Siebtelbauern*),

Still from Michael Haneke's FUNNY GAMES

about seven farm hands who inherit their dead master's land between the World Wars, was invited to Rotterdam, Florian Flicker's emigration drama, **Suzie Washington**, was shown in competition in Saarbrücken, and Edgar Honetschlger's first feature, **Milk**, shot in Tokyo and New York, premiered in the Forum section at Berlin.

However, the production roster for the year as a whole is not so promising. "In quantity, 1998 looks rather like a down year," said Schweighofer. Upcoming productions are Johannes Fabrick's first feature, **Beastie Girl**, Houchang Allahyari's **Black Flamingos**, Nikolaus Leytner's black comedy, **Three Gentlemen** (*Drei Herren*), Reinhard Schwabenitzky's **An Almost Perfect Divorce** (*Eine fast perfekte Scheidung*), the sequel to his 1995 comedy hit, *An Almost Perfect Affair*, Franz Novotny's eagerly awaited **Escort Service** and Niki List's new comedy, **Helden in Tyrol.**

Home, sweet home?

Austrian film's major problem remains its poor commercial performance on home turf. Although there was a general rise in admissions, up by more than ten per cent, from 12.3 million in 1996 to 13.7 million in 1997, Austrian films, despite frequently being acclaimed by the press, failed to meet the great hopes pinned on them and reach large audiences.

Since 1995, when no fewer than three Austrian films (historical drama *The Quality of Mercy* and comedies *Replay* and *An Almost*

Perfect Affair) were major box-office hits, with about 150,000 admissions each, almost no homegrown movie has reached more than a few thousand admissions, including *Funny Games*, which drew about 10,000. Even *The Unfish*, distributed by Buena Vista, was, with 20,000 admissions, somewhat disappointing. "The situation is pitifully bad," said Schweighofer. "We really have to work on this problem." The gap between the market shares of domestic and imported films again widened in 1997. Austria's top ten films were all US productions, or mass-market European films like *Bean* or *The Fifth Element*. No Austrian film came close to making the list.

Still, as in many European countries, a shortage of local hits did not prevent 1997 from being a very good year in Austria for distributors and exhibitors. The market was, as usual, dominated by the six majors, with Columbia TriStar, Buena Vista, UIP, Constantin Film, WarnerBros and Centfox accounting for more than 90 per cent of box-office takes (almost 30 per cent for Buena Vista alone). The remaining share goes to some ten independent distributors, with Filmladen, Polyfilm and Stadtkino standing out.

The major increase in admissions comes as Austria feels the effects of the global multiplex revolution. Since 1994, when UCI opened Austria's first multiplex, the nine-screen Kinowelt, in Vienna, there has been a boom in multiplexing. Last year, four more opened, in Linz, Graz, St Pölten and Innsbruck. Further projects in Salzburg, Linz and, especially, Vienna are set to change the Austrian cinema landscape dramatically, increasing the country's seating capacity by as much as 20 per cent.

BEAT GLUR is a Swiss film and music critic, editor of the cultural department of the Swiss News Agency. A member of the Swiss Federal Film Commission and of the Cultural Commission of Suissimage, he is adviser to the Locarno International Film Festival.

Still from Robert Dornhelm's THE UNFISH

Recent and Forthcoming Films

BLUTRAUSCH (Bloodlust)
Dir: Thomas Roth. Prod: DOR Film.

**DAS JAHR NACH DAYTON
(The Year after Dayton)**
Dir and Prod: Nikolaus Geyrhalter.

DER SEE (The Lake)
Dir: Thomas Roth. Prod: MR Film.

**ES WAR DOCH LIEBE
(Was it not Love?)**
Dir: Wolfgang Glück. Prod: Wega Film.

FUNNY GAMES
Dir: Michael Haneke. Prod: Wega Film.

**IN SCHWIMMEN-ZWEI-VÖGEL
(Two Birds Swimming)**
Dir: Kurt Palm. Prod: Fischer Film.

JUGOFILM
Dir: Goran Rebic. Prod: Lotus Film.

DAS SCHLOSS (The Castle)
Dir: Michael Haneke. Prod: Wega Film.

STILLE WASSER (Still Water)
Dir: Max Linder. Prod: Allegro Film.

**DIE TOTALE THERAPIE
(Total Therapy)**
Dir: Christian Frosch. Prod: Prisma Film.

DER UNFISCH (The Unfish)
Dir: Robert Dornhelm. Prod: Terra Film.

**ALLES BUNT UND WUNDERBAR
(Shrill, Bright World)**
Dir: Barbara Albert, Michael Grimm, Reinhard Jud. Prod: Novotny & Novotny/Epo Film.

BEASTIE GIRL
Dir: Johannes Fabrick. Prod: DOR Film.

BLACK FLAMINGOS
Dir: Houchang Allahyari. Prod: Terra Film.

DAS SIEGEL (The Seal)
Dir: Xaver Schwarzenberger. Prod: Fernsehfilmproduktion Dr. Heinz Scheiderbauer.

**DIE NEUE GENERATION
(The New Generation)**
Dir: Andreas Riedler.

**DREI HERREN
(Three Gentlemen)**
Dir: Nikolaus Leytner. Prod:

Allegro Film/Home Run Pictures (D).

EINE FAST PERFEKTE SCHEIDUNG (An Almost Perfect Divorce)

Dir: Reinhard Schwabenitzky. Prod: Star Film/Drefa (D).

ESCORT SERVICE

Dir: Franz Novotny. Prod: Novotny & Novotny/Epo Film.

HELDEN IN TIROL (Heroes in Tyrol)

Dir: Niki List. Prod: Cult Film/ Bernard Lang AG (CH)/Zeitsprung Film und TV Produktions GmbH (D).

HINTERHOLZ 8

Dir: Harald Sicheritz. Prod: DOR Film.

MILK

Dir: Edgar Honetschläger. Prod: Fischer Film/OSY Limited (J).

NORDRAND

Dir: Barbara Albert. Prod: Lotus – Film.

DIE SIEBTELBAUERN (The One-Seventh Farmers)

Dir: Stefan Ruzowitzky. Prod: DOR Film with ORF and Bayrischer Rundfunk (BR).

SUZIE WASHINGTON

Dir: Florian Flicker. Prod: Allegro Film.

WAR REQUIEM – EIN FILMEPOS

Dir: Theodor Eisner. Prod: Studio West/R Film Adrian Zschokke (CH).

WOLKEN ÜBER DEM PARADIES (Clouds Over Paradise)

Dir: Bernhard Semmelrock.

Producers

Allegro Film Produktionsges.m.b.H.
(Helmut Grasser)
Krummgasse 1a
A-1030 Vienna
Tel: (43 1) 712 5036
Fax: (43 1) 712 5036-20

Dor Film Produktionsges.m.b.H.
(Danny Krausz/Kurt Stocker)
Neulerchenfelderstrasse 12
A-1160 Vienna
Tel: (43 1) 402 2138
e-mail: dorfilm@magnet.at

Eclypse Filmpartner Gmbh
(Arno Ortmair)
Hietzinger Hauptstrasse 11
A-1130 Vienna
Tel: (43 1) 877 6393
Fax: (43 1) 877 3564
e-mail: 106037,2557@compuserve. com

Epo-Film Produktionsges.m.b.H.
(Dieter Pochlatko)
Edelsinnstrasse 58
A-1120 Vienna
Tel: (43 1) 812 3718
Fax: (43 1) 812 3718-9
e-mail: office@epo-film.co.at

Extrafilm
Arbeitsgemeinschaft Film & Video Ges.m.b.H.
(Bernd Neuburger/Lukas Stepanik)
Grosse Neugasse 44/24
A-1040 Vienna
Tel: (43 1) 581 7896
Fax: (43 1) 587 2743
e-mail: stepanik@aon.at

Neue Studio Film GmbH
(Peter Pochlatko)
Hietzinger Hauptstrasse 11
A-1130 Vienna
Tel: (43 1) 877 6253
Fax: (43 1) 877 3564
e-mail: 106037,2557@compuserve. com

Satel Fernseh- und Filmproduktionsges.m.b.H.
(Michael Wolkenstein)
Computerstrasse 6
A-1101 Vienna
Tel: (43 1) 661 090

Fax: (43 1) 667 5650
e-mail: 106114,2540@compuserve. com

Terra Film Produktionsges.m.b.H.
(Norbert Blecha)
Lienfeldergasse 39
A-1160 Vienna
Tel: (43 1) 484 1101-0
Fax: (43 1) 484 1101-27
e-mail: terrafilm@magnet.at

Wega-Filmproduktionsges.m.b.H.
(Veit Heiduschka)
Hägelingasse 13
A-1140 Vienna
Tel: (43 1) 982 5742
Fax: (43 1) 982 5833

Distributors

Buena Vista (Austria) Gmbh
(Ferdinand Morawetz)
Hermanngasse 18
A-1071 Vienna
Tel: (43 1) 526 9467
Fax: (43 1) 526 9468-5
e-mail: ferdinand_morawetz@ studio.disney.com

Centfox-Film Ges.m.b.H.
(Roman Hörmann)
Neubaugasse 35
A-1070 Vienna
Tel: (43 1) 523 2629
Fax: (43 1) 526 7297

Columbia TriStar Filmverleih Ges.m.b.H.
(Hermann Hobodides)
Wallgasse 21
A-1060 Vienna
Tel: (43 1) 597 1515
Fax: (43 1) 597 1516
e-mail: columbiatristaraustria@ compuserve.com

Concorde Media Beteiligungs GmbH
(Herbert Kloiber)
Seilergasse 15
A-1010 Vienna
Tel: (43 1) 513 2728

Constantin-Film Verleih-, Vertriebs- & Produktionsges.m.b.H.
(Ing.Christian Langhammer)
Siebensterngasse 37

A-1070 Vienna
Tel: (43 1) 521 28-150
Fax: (43 1) 521 28-160

Filmladen
(Michael Stejskal)
Mariahilferstrasse 58
A-1070 Vienna
Tel: (43 1) 523 4362
Fax: (43 1) 526 4749
e-mail: m.stejskal@vip.at

Polyfilm Verleih
(Hans König, Christa Auderlitzky)
Margaretenstrasse 78
A-1050 Vienna
Tel: (43 1) 581 3900-20
Fax: (43 1) 581 3900-39
e-mail: polyfilm@polyfilm.at

Stadtkino
(Franz Schwartz)
Spittelberggasse 3
A-1070 Vienna
Tel: (43 1) 522 4814
Fax: (43 1) 522 4815

U.I.P. Filmverleih GmbH.
(Steven O'Dell)
Neubaugasse 1, P.O.Box 280
A-1071 Vienna
Tel: (43 1) 523 4631
Fax: (43 1) 526 7548

Warner Bros Ges.m.b.H.
(Ingeborg König)
Zieglergasse 10
A-1070 Vienna
Tel: (43 1) 523 8626-0
Fax: (43 1) 523 8626-31

Useful Addresses

Austrian Audiovisual and Film Industry Association
(Prof. Dr. Elmar A. Peterlunger)
017 Wiedner Hauptstrasse 63
PO Box 327, A-1045 Vienna
Tel: (43 1) 501 05-3010
Fax: (43 1) 502 06-276
e-mail: faf@wk.or.at

Austrian Film Commission
(Martin Schweighofer)
Stiftgasse 6
A-1070 Vienna
Tel: (43 1) 526 3323-200
Fax: (43 1) 526 6801
e-mail: afilmco@magnet.at
www.afc.at

Austrian Film Institute
(Mag. Gerhard Schedl)
Spittelberggasse 3
A-1070 Vienna
Tel: (43 1) 526 9730-400
Fax: (43 1) 526 9730-440
e-mail: fi@filminstitut.or.at

Media Desk
MMag. Gerlinde Seitner
Österreichisches Filminstitut
Spittelberggasse 3
1070 A-1010 Vienna
Tel: (43 1) 526 9730-406
Fax: (43 1) 526 9730-440
e-mail: Media@filminstitut.or.at

Vienna Film Financing Fund
(Wiener Filmfinanzierungsfonds)
Wolfgang Ainberger
Stiftgasse 6/2/3
A-1070 Vienna
Tel: (43 1) 526 5088
Fax: (43 1) 526 5088-20
e-mail: wff@wff.at

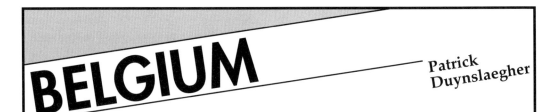

BELGIUM — Patrick Duynslaegher

The child sex scandal that rocked Belgium during 1996 raised so many fundamental questions about the country's police, judicial and political malfunction that local film-makers inevitably had to reflect on the malaise. The economical context of the crisis was somewhat prophetically evoked by the Dardenne brothers' *La Promesse*, made months before the case exploded, but the first feature directly to expose something rotten in the state of Belgium was **Out of Range** (*Le Bal Masqué*).

Though not dealing in any direct way with the case of Marc Dutroux, the man who allegedly abducted, raped and murdered at least four underage girls, this story about a police detective and a magistrate investigating a brutal double murder at a petrol station is very much in tune with the conspiracy climate and the sense of public outrage in a country dogged by government scandals, unsolved political murders, inter-police force rivalry, fraud, embezzlement and corruption on every level.

Still from OUT OF RANGE

The script is based on a still-unsolved killing spree from the 1980s that became the focus of renewed interest in the wake of the Dutroux-related investigations. At least 34 people were slaughtered during supermarket raids by an armed gang, the so-called "Nivelles gang" (named after the southern Belgian city where the enquiry into the murders began). Former television director Julien Vrebos adheres to a far-fetched conspiracy theory which suggests that the seemingly random killings were in fact a cover-up for the execution of key witnesses to videotaped sex parties with minors, where the participants included people from the highest, even royal ranks – a plot so outrageous it might even shock Oliver Stone.

Nobody can deny, however, the cinematic flair Vrebos demonstrates in his debut feature. The highly stylised proceedings are based on a simple concept: by eliminating most medium shots, scenes are made up either of confusing, rapid-fire montages of close-up details, or long establishing shots inviting the audience to pick up the meaningful elements and actions within the exquisite wide-screen compositions.

This formalist conceit, while irritating to some, proves in fact an apt visual metaphor for how the "Nivelles gang" case was perceived by the Belgian population. At the time, people were bombarded with fragmented, seemingly unconnected information, but when one took a step back to see the big picture, one was still left in the dark regarding the identity and motivation of the killers, and allegations of official interference in the investigation.

Polar opposites

Also based on a criminal true story is **Thief**, written (presumably in the space of a rainy afternoon) and directed by distributor and now also film-maker Marc Punt. This is the life story of local thief Frans Van Reeth, a master at his profession, so we are told – so why does he get caught all the time? This is far from the largest absurdity in a film aiming for the lowest common denominator by poorly imitating straight-to-video American action flicks – as vulgar as it is cliché-ridden.

Two more reliable Flemish film-makers offered disappointing new works. Stijn Coninx's eagerly-awaited **When the Light Comes** proved to be a total failure. It tells the tale of a wilful young girl in search of outdoor adventure, who decides to spend a year with a fur trapper at the North Pole. These two have absolutely nothing in common, and are obviously not made for each other, but, with nobody else around, as the isolation takes its toll their relationship develops into a love story of sorts. The motivation of the lead character is intermittently stupid and irritating and the drama is as frozen as the landscape. Although shot on location at Spitsbergen, close to the North Pole, Coninx makes little use of the icy environment, except to shoot pretty pictures.

After the failure of *Suite 16*, his ambitious erotic thriller, Dominique Deruddere comes back strongly with **Hombres Complicados**, a black comedy about the love-hate relationship between two brothers who hit the road together after the death of their mother. The duelling siblings' antics are mildly amusing, but the whole film verges toward cheap caricature of their conflicting personalities, with a lot of second-hand philosophy and scatological humour thrown in for good measure.

The whole truth?

Two films joined the world-wide trend for mixing documentary and fiction. In **State of Dogs**, co-directors Peter Brosens and Dorjkhandyn Turmunkh offer a pointedly poetic account of the life and death of a stray dog in Mongolia, but their tale gets paralysed by a redundant voice-over. Jan Bucquoy delivered the third instalment of his *Sexual Life of the Belgians* cycle, **The Closing Down of the Renault Factory at Vilvoorde**. What starts off as a subjective documentary about the loss of more than 3,000 jobs grows into a fictionalised narrative, involving the kidnapping and

Still from STATE OF DOGS   photo: *Progrès Films*

murder of Renault chief executive Louis Schweitzer.

As usual, the box-office in Flanders was dominated by a comedy of only local interest, **Oesje!** This first feature by TV comedian and impressionist Chris van den Durpel was an embarrassing, amateurish affair. Certainly not a very distinctive calling card for this first feature film from the Kinepolis Group, the largest exhibitor in Belgium. The biggest industry news of the year was Kinepolis' decision to float their company on the stock market, a move which gave it the capital necessary for international expansion and the export of the Kinepolis multiplex brand to France, Spain and the Netherlands.

Yvan Le Moine based **The Red Dwarf** (*Le Nain Rouge*), his first feature, on a short story by Michel Tournier about a dwarf who works for a law firm and uses his virility to rise through society. He becomes involved with a voluptuous diva, played by an overblown Anita Ekberg of *La Dolce Vita* fame. Other echoes of Fellini abound in a film that shifts from Kafkaesque bureaucracy to a travelling circus. Its dream-like black-and-white world was obviously a dream for the production designer, but what the film really needed was a script doctor.

To kill a priest

Among established film-makers, Marion Hänsel produced one of her best features. Shot in English on location in South-Africa, **The Quarry** tells the story of a man (played by Irish actor John Lynch) on the run after

John Lynch plays a murderer in THE QUARRY

killing a reverend. He takes on his victim's identity and presents himself as the new priest a township has been waiting for, and tries to carry out pastoral tasks. But others become entangled in the deception. When the priest's body is found, two young black brothers become murder suspects, while a white police captain searches desperately for the truth.

Hänsel gradually builds up the tension between the characters. Very much a mood piece, *The Quarry* offers less action and suspense than the material might suggest; the director is more interested in the often ambiguous relationships and the themes of identity, guilt and redemption. The scorching heat of the sun-dried South African landscape and the wide-screen images give the film a spaciousness and luminosity that clashes with the feeling of claustrophobia and entrapment.

Battle of Beasts (*Combat de Fauves*), Benoit Lamy's comeback film, deserved better than its lacklustre performance in cinemas. It is a dark thriller about a businessman who gets stuck in an elevator and the female neighbour who refuses to save him. A highly symbolic clash of the sexes ensues, a game of seduction and humiliation. Lamy cannot carry off his story's literary conceits, but he succeeds nevertheless in making the minimal action absorbing, thanks mainly to his elegant *mise en scène* and strong performances from French star Richard Bohringer and the hypnotic Ute Lemper, transformed by the camera into a Garbo-like sphinx.

Renowned animator Raoul Servais won the main prize at this year's Annecy festival for his short film *Nocturnal Butterflies*, inspired by the paintings and etchings of Paul Delvaux, the famous Belgian surrealist.

PATRICK DUYNSLAEGHER is film critic for *Knack*, the leading Belgian weekly. His articles have appeared in *Variety*, *Sight and Sound* and other periodicals. He has written a book on André Delvaux, a guide for films on television and video, and a history, through 2,000 reviews, of a hundred years of cinema.

Recent and Forthcoming Films

ROSIE

Script and Dir: Patrice Toye. Players: Aranka Coppens, Sara Deroo, Dirk Roofthooft, Frank Vercruysse. Prod: Antonino Lombardo (Prime Time).

MARIE ANTOINETTE ISN'T DEAD

Script and Dir: Irma Achten. Phot: Tinus Holthuis. Players: Antje De Boeck, Lucas Van den Eynde, Gilda De Bal, Chris Lomme. Prod: Kees Kasander (Kasander and Wigman Productions), Jan

Hintjens and Linda Van Tulden (Nieuwe Media Produkties).

PECCATO

Animation. Script and Dir: Manuel Gomez. Prod: Martine Lambrechts and Gomez.

THE YOUNG VAN GOGH AT THE BORINAGE

Dir: André Huyghe. Script: René De Bok. Phot: Eddy Van Der Enden. Prod: Huyghe (Media Projects).

BEHEMOTH

Script and Dir: Marian Handwerker. Phot: Pierre Gordower. Players: Michel Kartchevsky, Patrick Goossens. Prod: George Géron and Handwerker.

THE BALL

Script and Dir: Dany Deprez and Jean-Claude Van Rijckeghem. Phot: Pjotr Kukla. Players: Hilde Van Mieghem, Rijk De Gooijer, Julien Schoenaerts, Michael Pas, Luc Philips. Prod: Deprez and Van Rijckeghem (A Private View).

THE JUST JUDGES

Dir: Vincent Rouffaer. Script: Paul Pourveur and Dominique Mys. Phot: Jan Vancaillie. Prod: Eric Kint (Itinera Films).

SOEUR SOURIRE

Dir: Robbe De Hert. Script: Luc Maddelein and Leen Van Den Berg. Prod: Samuel Cerulus (Kladaradatsch ! Films).

THE ALZHEIMER FILES

Dir: Erik Van Looy. Script: Carl Joos and Van Looy. Prod: Erwin Provoost (Multimedia/VRT/AFI).

MAX ET BOBO

Dir: Frédéric Fonteyne. Script: Philippe Blasband. Phot: Virginie Saint-Martin. Players: Alfredo Pea, Jan Hammenecker. Prod: Artémis Productions/ Samsa Film/ Les Productions Lazennec.

LA PATINOIRE (The Skating Rink)

Script and Dir: Jean-Philippe Toussaint. Phot: Jean-François Robin. Players: Tom Novembre, Mireille Perrier, Marie-France Pisier, Jean-Pierre Cassel. Prod: Les Films de l'Etang/ les Films des Tournelles/ Studio Canal+/ Fandango.

Producers

Corsan Productions
J. De Hasquestraat 7
2000 Antwerp
Tel: (32 3) 234 2518
Fax: (32 3) 226 2158

D.D.D. 1867
Avenue de la Jonction
1190 Brussels
Tel: (32 2) 344 0201
Fax: (32 2) 344 0201

Emotion Pictures
Volaardestraat 250
5200 Dendermonde
Tel: (32 52) 413 783

Favorite Films
Vandenbusschestraat 3
1030 Brussels
Tel: (32 2) 242 4510
Fax: (32 2) 242 1408

Fugitive Cinema
Prinsesstraat 35
2000 Antwerp
Tel: (32 3) 234 3674
Fax: (32 3) 232 8684

Independent Productions
Sphere Business Park
Doornveld 1 Box 42
1731 Zellik
Tel: (32 2) 463 1130
Fax: (32 2) 466 9460

Kunst en Kino
Avenue Louise 32/4
1050 Brussels
Tel: (32 2) 511 6341
Fax: (32 2) 512 6874

La Nouvelle Imagerie
Avenue Jacques Pastur 90
1080 Brussels
Tel: (32 2) 646 3946
Fax: (32 2) 646 3946

Lamy Films
Moensberg 57,
1180 Brussels
Tel: (32 2) 375 3442
Fax: (32 2) 375 3271

Les Films de la Drève
Rue de la Victoire 175
1060 Brussels
Tel: (32 2) 537 8894

Man's Films
Avenue Mostinck 65
1150 Brussels
Tel: (32 2) 771 7137
Fax: (32 2) 771 9612

Multimedia
Nieuwstraat 99
1730 Asse
Tel: (32 2) 453 0304
Fax: (32 2) 453 0920

Useful Addresses

Communauté Française de Belgique
Boulevard Léopold II, 44
1080 Brussels
Tel: (32 2) 413 2221
Fax: (32 2) 413 2068

Decatron
(technological support and general contractor in multiplex theatres)
Kampioenschapslaan 1
1020 Brussels
Tel: (32 2) 478 3197
Fax: (32 2) 478 3385

Flanders Image
Handelskaai 18/2
1000 Brussels
Tel: (32 2) 219 3222
Fax: (32 2) 219 3402

Ministry of the Flemish Community
Koloniënstraat 29-31
1000 Brussels
Tel: (32 2) 510 3411
Fax: (32 2) 510 3651

Wallonie Bruxelles Image
Boulevard Adolphe Max 13
1000 Brussels
Tel: (32 2) 233 2304
Fax: (32 2) 218 3424

BOSNIA & HERZEGOVINA
Rada Šešić

Describing the present situation as "the worst in the last 50 years of our cinema history", Bosnian and Herzegovinan film-makers made a special appeal to the government early in 1998. "After living for three years in peace, and now faced with the prospect of Bosnian and Herzegovinan cinema production dying a slow death, film-makers have the right to ask all relevant government institutions to start reviving the cinema scene in this country."

When the split-up of the former Yugoslavia into five different states became a fact, Bosnian cinema, apart from being systematically destroyed by shelling and bombing, was completely cut off from all technical facilities. In the past, Bosnian feature films were always shot with high-quality 35mm equipment, hired either in Belgrade or Zagreb. Film negative developing took place in the big laboratories of these two cities. Film crews often included people hired from Croatia or Serbia.

Now, the wounds of the war are too fresh to continue old partnerships, and international co-production is rare. Film-makers are completely deprived of the means necessary to produce professional features on 35mm. "The State without film is not a state, no matter how democratic it is," emphasised the film-makers. Before the war, up to 75 per cent of film budgets were paid by the state, but it remains to be seen how the government will respond to the film-makers' demand for the creation of a new state fund for cinema.

Those in power are, however, realising that film is an important medium, and have recognised how powerful it was during the war. President Izetbegovic himself gave a special decoration to the French philosopher and film-maker Bernard Henry-Levi for his contribution during the war, especially for the films *One day in the death of Sarajevo* and *Bosnia*.

Shooting of a different kind

After the Dayton peace agreement, Bosnia's cinegenic locations (bombed and burned-out buildings etc.) made it a very busy shooting ground. Among numerous western projects shot in Bosnia, the most successful was Michael Winterbottom's *Welcome to Sarajevo*. Unlike many other films about the war in the former Yugoslavia, this one was well received in Sarajevo and closed the city's third Film Festival, in September 1997.

The festival is the biggest cinema event in the country, professionally organised and offering the people of Sarajevo new and interesting world movies, and sometimes famous guests. John Malkovich and Julia Ormond were some of the celebrities who attended last year's festival. The event is also an opportunity to connect the country with potential co-producers or distributors.

At the festival, Branko Lustig, the Croatian producer now based in the US (he co-produced *Schindler's List*), agreed to be chairman of a committee dedicated to raising international aid for Bosnian cinema. At the same time, a representative of Buena Vista made a deal for the distribution of their big hits in Bosnia and in the Republic of Srpska, the part of the Federation that is mainly covered by Serbian distributors.

While the money flowing into the Bosnian film industry is mainly the result of "renting" the post-war landscape and the local workforce, some directors do succeed in raising overseas finance for their projects. One of those is Haris Pasovic, whose long, well-received documentary **Greta** was a Dutch/Bosnian co-production. The film focuses on the academic architect Greta Luburic, a survivor of Auschwitz, and tells the story of her two horrible imprisonments: first in the death camp and then, 50 years later, in Sarajevo during the siege.

Veteran's controversial epic

The forthcoming project which will be made in Bosnia and which raised enormous discussion for months, is **Sarajevo**. It is going to be a spectacular epic about the war in the former Yugoslavia, with 12,000 extras and 250 real soldiers, members of special army units. The focus of the verbal battles has been the film's 70-year-old director, Veljko Bulajic. A Montenegrin living in Croatia, he became famous in the former Yugoslavia in the 1950s and 1960s for directing epics about the Second World War partisans.

His projects were always extremely expensive and glamorous. For *Sarajevo*, he was trying to cast Catherine Deneuve and Claudia Cardinale. Bosnians were angry that a non-Bosnian or Herzegovinan citizen was going to make such a costly film about their war (with co-production finance pledged by a Bosnian company, Bosnafilm), while domestic directors remain jobless.

Recently, books about cinema have once again been published in Bosnia. Vefik Hadzismajlovic, a retired documentary film-maker, produced a book of film essays, and *Recollection*, the memoirs of the recently deceased director, Mirza Idrizovic, were published. Film critic Rajko Radovanovic, from Banja Luka (the Serbian part of the Bosnian Federation), published a book called *American film and how to avoid it*, while film magazine *SINEAST*, which never ceased publication during the war, went back to colour printing and celebrated its hundredth issue.

Even the national festival for film

The cover of SINEAST magazine

amateurs has been organised in Sarajevo again. With state-regulated film production, Bosnian and Herzegovinan cinema might come up with its second post-war feature film in the next season. The first, Ademir Kenović's **Perfect Circle**, did excellent business at the domestic box-office (12,000 viewers in its first ten days on release) and was shown at dozens of festivals, including Cannes, Rotterdam and Tokyo, where it won a major award.

RADA ŠEŠIĆ was born in Croatia and lived in Sarajevo until the war broke out in Bosnia. She was a film critic for Yugoslavian newspapers and magazines for 15 years and is now a freelance film journalist in The Netherlands. She recently finished a 16mm documentary, *Room without a view*.

Useful Addresses

SAGA Production Company
71 000 Sarajevo
Tel: (387 71) 663 352
Fax: (387 71) 471 145

Ton & Light Production
R. Abazovica 2
71 000 Sarajevo
Tel/Fax: (387 71) 520 897

Igman Production
Paris 75 011
Tel: (33 1) 4700 0610
Fax: (33 1) 4700 0402

International Sarajevo Film Festival
Obala Kulina Bana 10
71 000 Sarajevo
Tel: (387 71) 668 186
Fax: (387 71) 664 547

Kino Savez B&H Film magazine SINEAST
Strosmajerova 1
71 000 Sarajevo
Tel/Fax: (387 71) 212 377

The National Film Archive of Bosnia & Herzegovina
Alipasina 19
71 000 Sarajevo
Tel/Fax: (387 71) 668 678

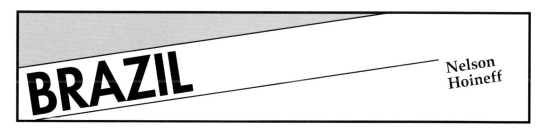

BRAZIL

Nelson Hoineff

Brazil's film activity in 1997-98 was characterised by three main events: the strengthening of local production in the wake of improved tax breaks, the domestic and international success of many home-grown features and, above all, the revolution in the exhibition sector.

By the end of this year, Spean Bridge should have opened Brazil's first megaplex, a 31-screen complex at Barra da Tijuca, in Rio de Janeiro. UCI is building an 18-screen multiplex nearby (in partnership with Luiz Severiano Ribeiro). In all, the Barra da Tijuca sector will soon have 79 screens - three years ago, there were fewer than 10. The picture is similar all over the country. Cinemark has opened nine multiplexes and, by 2000, is expected to be operating 220 screens in Brazil, with UCI another 169. Attendance in 1997 rose to 43.4 million, up from 41m the year before, and box-office revenue climbed to $190m (221m reais), against $165m in 1996.

Tax breaks remained the most important ally of local producers. Total investment via the two main laws governing film production went up from $60m in 1996 to $78m in 1997. This increase helped launch 27 Brazilian films in 1997 and, in May 1998, 54 new titles were in production, post-production or awaiting release.

These laws allow deductions up to three per cent of the income tax payable by companies investing in film production. Other sources of financing are directly linked to state or municipal governments, with states such as Rio de Janeiro, Sao Paulo and Cearo offering substantial aid to producers shooting in their areas. Private companies (Grupo Novo de Cinema e Video), foundations (Rio Cine) and government (the Secretary of Culture) are currently investing to help re-establish foreign distribution of Brazilian pics.

An award-winning search

Titanic became the first film since *Jaws* to break the 13-million ticket barrier and attendance was also great for local productions. *Sound of Music* parody **O Novico Rebelde**, the first film in more than three years to star celebrated Brazilian comedian Renato Aragao (he played the singing nun), drew 1.4 million cinema-goers. Walter Salles' **Central Station** (*Central do Brasil*) was expected to reach one million by the end of 1998. Focusing on a little boy's search for his father in the Brazilian interior, Salles' third feature won the Golden Bear at Berlin and Fernanda Montenegro won the festival's best actress award.

Central Station was sold for $1m to Sony Classics for distribution in the US and Canada, and for $1.3m to Miramax for parts of Europe. Other excellent local productions which enjoyed box-office success were **The War of Canudos** (*Guerra de Canudos*), directed by Sergio Rezende, in which nineteenth-century Brazilian Republicans are challenged by a religious

Location shooting for ORFEU

The success of *Central Station* followed on from the nomination in 1995 for the best foreign language film Oscar of *Four Days in September* (*O Que Isso, Companheiro?*), Bruno Barreto's film about the kidnapping of US Ambassador to Brazil, Charles Elbrick. Together with the continuing stabilisation of the Brazilian economy, recognition for these features provides welcome encouragement for the country's film-makers .

These developments also contributed to Globo's decision to open its own film production company, Globo Filmes, which is being directed by Daniel Filho and Marco Aurelio Marcondes. Globo, the biggest Brazilian media complex (and one of the biggest in the world), is already investing in several projects, including Cacá Diegues' *Orfeu* (inspired by the Camus film), *Senhorita Simpson*, by Bruno Barreto, and *A Partilha*, by Daniel Filho.

fanatic and his followers, and **The Killers** (*Os Matadores*), a low-budget feature from Beto Brant exploring the ethical codes of assassins on the Brazil/Paraguay border.

NELSON HOINEFF, chief film critic for the daily paper *O Dia*, is a regular contributor to weekly *Variety*. Founder and vice-president of the Association of Film Critics of Rio de Janeiro, he has written several books on electronic media.

Recent and Forthcoming Films

ORFEU

Dir: Caca Diegues. Players: Tony Garrido, Patricia Franca, Isabel Filiardis Prod: Rio Vermelho Filmes and Globo Filmes.

XANGO DE BAKER STREET

Dir: Miguel Faria. Players: Joaquim de Almeida, Jo Soares. Prod: Skylight and Sony.

ESTORVO

Dir: Ruy Guerra Players: Jorge Perrugoria, Leonor Arrocha. Prod: Skylight.

MAUA, O IMPERADOR E O REI (Maua, the Emperor and the King)

Dir: Sergio Rezende. Players: Malu Mader, Paulo Betty. Prod: Joaquim Vaz de Carvalho.

MISS SIMPSON

Dir: Bruno Barreto Players: Amy Irving. Prod: by L.C.Barreto.

Producers and distributors

Rio Vermelho Filmes

(Cacá Diegues)
Rua Ataulfo de Paiva 527 s.702
22420-030 Rio de Janeiro
Tel: (55 21) 259 2289

Cinédia

(Alice Conzaga)
Estrada do Soca, Jacarepagua
Rio de Janeiro
Tel: (55 21) 445 6868
Fax: (55 21) 445 8215

Comunicacao Alternativa

(Marcos Rezende)
Rua do Russel, 450
22210-010 Rio de Janeiro
Tel: (55 21) 558 2825
Fax: (55 21) 557 5848
e-mail:comalt@ibm.net

Filme B

(Paulo Sergio Almeida/Andrea Queiroga)
Rua Alcindo Guanabara 24 s.801
20038-900 Rio de Janeiro
Telefax: (55 21) 240 8439

Grupo Novo de Cinema e TV
(Antonio Urano/Tarcisio Vidigal)
Rua Marechal Neimeyer 24
22251-060 Rio de Janeiro
Tel: (55 21) 266 3637

L. C. Barreto
(Luiz Carlos Barreto)
Av. Franklin Roosevelt, 194

Rio de Janeiro
Tel: (55 21) 240 8161

Morena Filmes
(Marisa Leão)
Rua Visconde de Pirajá, 596/204
Rio de Janeiro
Telfax: (55 21) 511 0754

HB Filmes
(Hector Babenco)
Rua Emmanoel Kant, 39
Jardim Paulista – S. Paulo
Tel: (55 11) 883 7755

BULGARIA

Ivan Stoyanovich

Political and economic figures in the West have been pleasantly surprised at Bulgaria's speedy recovery from the catastrophic regression brought about by the short-lived communist comeback. The country has regained political and financial stability and intensified its partnership with NATO and the European Union. Moreover, its painful divorce from Russia – on which it is still dependant for fuels and some technology- has come a step closer .

But in a poverty-stricken nation, the needs of the stomach remain the top priority, and the arts are bound to be at the bottom of the list of problems posed by reform – especially the costly art of making films. Still, the state is trying to help in several ways. Although the government's long-term strategy envisages gradual privatisation of the entire film business, the National Television (including fiction and documentary film production) is still supported by the National Budget. The Ministry of Culture, through the National Film Centre, subsidises some feature films, with special committees ensuring that tax-payers' money goes to the highest-quality audio-visual projects.

New cinema and TV laws are being drafted to bring Bulgaria into harmony with the EU. The legislation is also designed to foster closer co-operation between the country's cinema and television industries with regard to repertory and finances, in a bid to compensate for the fall in cinema attendance. Filmgoers, discouraged by rising ticket prices, are increasingly relying on television for film entertainment. At the same time, local government, public organisations and private companies, some of them from abroad, are being encouraged to invest in film-making. Eurimages, France's Centre National du Cinéma and George Soros's Open Society are amongst the international investors to have come forward recently.

Fruits of a painful transition

Everybody in the film business tries to adapt to market conditions, and, to strengthen their collective power, dozens of individual producers have joined the Bulgarian Film Producers Association. The Bulgarian Private Film Distributors Association now includes leading companies such as Sunny Films, Alexandra Films, Duga Entertainment and Radivision. The fully equipped Cinema Centre in Boyana provides excellent services for an increasing number of co-productions. The likes of Richard Chamberlain, Ornela Muti and Jennifer Tilly have recently been filming at Bulgarian locations.

In a year of painful transition, Bulgarian

Still from Boris Livanov's DON QUIXOTE COMES BACK

film-makers completed some ten titles – an output which contained no masterpieces. The emphasis tended towards the lighter side, as in **Spanish Fly** (*Ispanska muha*), directed by Kiran Kolarov, and Marko Stoychev's crime comedy, **Murder Squad** (*Mordburo*). We also had **Sulami**, Hristo Hristov's twentieth-century retelling of an ancient saga, Marius Kurkinski's version of Gogol's **Diary of a Madman** (*Dnevnikat na edin lud*) and the award-winning Russian-Bulgarian co-production **Don Quixote Comes Back** (*Don Kihot se zavrashta*)

Features nearing completion when this article went to press included Petar Popzlatev's mock tragedy about the cult of personality, **Touched by Grace** (*Poseteni ot Gospod*), and **After the End of the World** (*Sled kraya na sveta*), directed by Ivan Nichev, which looks at the plight of ethnic minority children.

Bulgarian films were selected for festivals in 25 countries in 1997, including Germany, Italy, France, Russia, Canada, Argentina and Australia. Those winning awards included Lyudmil Todorov's **Emily's Friends** (*Priyatelite no Emilia* – FIPRESCI Award, Salonika, Greece); **The Black Swallow** (*Chernata lyastovitza* – Grand Prix at the Golden Eagle, Batumi, Georgia) and **Shock** (*Shok*), directed by Zlatin Radev, which took first prize at the International Anima Film Festival in the Ukraine, and second prize at Ankara. Such successes give cause for optimism, and demonstrate that the painful rebirth of Bulgarian Cinema is well underway. Democratic reforms will, in the long run, help it to emerge as a lovingly anticipated expression of the national spirit.

IVAN STOYANOVICH is the author of ten books, plays and film scripts and more than 1,000 articles. For 30 years he has been Editor-in-Chief of *Bulgarian Film Magazine* and has served as Executive Director of Bulgarian National Television and Animation Film Studio 'Sofia'. He is now consulting expert in the Ministry of Culture.

Recent and Forthcoming Films

WAGNER
Dir: Andrey Slabakov

An Orwell-style comedy.

VAGLISHTARYAT
(The Coal-Burner)
Dir: Ilian Simeonov

SANS CHANGEMENT
(Without Change)
Script: Milena Andonova, Vera Petrova. Dir: Andonova

The protagonist sets out on a journey to Europe that turns out to be a journey to his own inner self.

POSLEDNA LYUBOV (Last Love)
Script: Dunya Smirnova. Dir: Aleksey Outchitel.

The script, which won a Hartley-Merrill International Scriptwriter's Jury Award, deals with an episode from the life of exiled Russian author Ivan Bunin.

Producers

Boyana Film Company
Kinocentar Boyana
Sofia 1616
Tel: (359 2) 91917*/596 055/
597 159
Fax: (359 2) 593 115

Animation Film Studio
Kinocentar Boyana
Sofia 1616
Tel: (359 2) 91917*/595 061/
671 126
Fax: (359 2) 597 165

Documentary Film Studio
"Vreme"
67 Dondukov Blvd
Sofia 1504
Tel: (359 2) 442 823*/442 977
Fax: (359 2) 442 453

Army Audio-Visual Centre
23 Stoletov Blvd
Sofia
Tel: (359 2) 324 014/317 155/
323 037
Fax: (359 2) 320 018

Bulgarian Film Producers Association
67 Dondukov Street
Sofia 1504
Tel: (359 2) 447 326
Fax: (359 2) 463 676

Distributors

Sofia Film
Maria Luiza Blvd 26
Sofia 1000
Tel: (359 2) 835 584/835 759
Fax: (359 2) 833 707

Alexandra Film
Naycho Tzanov Street 17
Sofia 1000
Tel: (359 2) 980 6040
Fax: (359 2) 981 0715

Duga Entertainment
141 Knyaz Boris I Street
Sofia 1304
Tel: (359 2) 981 9584
Fax: (359 2) 980 8842 *

Sunny Films
17a Tzar Osvoboditel
Sofia 1000
Tel: (359 2) 943 4849
Fax: (359 2) 943 3703

Ady Films
3 Gerlovo Street
Sofia 1504
Tel/Fax: (359 2) 946 1212/468 048

Eurocom
30 Vasil Levski Blvd
Sofia 1000
Tel/Fax: (359 2) 981 2070/963 1529

Useful Addresses

Ministry of Culture
17 Stamboliski Blvd
Sofia 1000
Tel: (359 2) 86111*
Fax: (359 2) 877 339

National Film Centre
2a Dondukov Blvd
Sofia 1000
Tel: (359 2) 803 134/883 831
Fax: (359 2) 873 626

Bulgarian National Film Library
36 Gurko Street
Sofia 1000
Tel: (359 2) 802 749/870 296/
871 392
Tel/Fax: (359 2) 876 004

Union of Bulgarian Film-Makers
67 Dondukov Blvd
Sofia 1504
Tel/Fax: (359 2) 946 1068/946
1069/946 1062

Bulgarian National Television
29 San Stefano Street
Sofia 1000
Tel/Fax: (359 2) 43481*/871 871

*telephone exchange operator

BURKINA FASO
Judy Kendall

In September 1997, Burkina Faso held its first conference on the Burkinabe film industry. Spurred on by the imminent collapse of the national film distribution company, the conference was dominated by the question of the distribution of local and regional films. Would Burkina Faso be able to save its film heritage? The fear was that privatisation of the distribution and exhibition structures could only result in poorer exhibition of Burkinabe films.

The biannual Panafrican Film and TV Festival of Ouagadougou (FESPACO) is the largest of any African festival, reflecting the high regard in which Burkinabe film-makers are held. The next edition of FESPACO (in Ferbruary/March 1999) has as its proposed theme "Cinema and Distribution Channels in Africa", indicating a growing concern: major funding of Burkinabe film from traditional sources, such as the European Union, the Agence de la Francophonie and the French Ministry of Co-operation, shows signs of drying up.

One effect of cuts in funding could be an increase in the number of co-productions, such as **Kini and Adams** (1997), an obvious success story. Directed by Burkinabe Idrissa Ouedraogo, shot in Zimbabwe and starring South African actors, it won an award at the 1997 FESPACO and was in official competition at Cannes. However, even if Burkinabe films do reasonably well on the festival circuits, is such critical success sufficient? As Professor Samba Gadjigo said in a recent FESPACO newsletter: "Almost invisible in African countries themselves, African films are hibernating in European film libraries, when they are not simply adorning international film festivals."

Treacherous healer

In a bid to widen local audiences, and provide television with fresh material, the Burkinabe Ministry of Communication and Culture has launched a series of TV films co-produced by the National Film Board and National TV. The first of these ventures is **Le Secret**, directed by Raymond Tiendrebeogo and adapted from Ansonavin Ignace Hien's novel, *Au Gré du Destin*. *Le Secret*, set in west Burkina Faso, deals with the subjects of incest and traditional medicine and the treacherous power of the healer. Future projects include a film of Jacques Bazie's novel *La Dérive des Bozos*, to be directed by Abdoulaye Dao and Guy Desire, and Roger Nikiema's **Deux Adorables Rivales**, to be directed by Issouf Ouedraogo and Zacharia Hema.

Idrissa Ouedraogo has also been preparing a new feature. **Naba Wobgo**, due to start shooting in October 1998, is about the reign of an African emperor, Boukay Koutou (also known as Naba Wobgo). Generally perceived as a hero in Burkina Faso, he ruled for seven years at the end of the nineteenth century. He refused to co-operate with European colonial intentions and was eventually overcome by French military intervention.

A name to watch out for is Fanta Regina Nacro, an up-and-coming Burkinabe director, who won a laureate in the 17th Amiens Film Festival for her latest project, *La Nuit de la Verité*.

JUDY KENDALL lived in Africa for four years, and is a freelance journalist on African film and music.

Useful Addresses

Centre Nationale du Cinéma du Burkina Faso
Ministère de la Communication et de la Culture
Ouagadougou 01
Tel: (226) 302 551/57

FESPACO African Film Library
Ardionnia Soma
Ouagadougou 01
Tel: (226) 307 538
Fax: (226) 312 509
email: soma@fespaco.bf

Secretariat Permanente de FESPACO
01 BP 2505
Ouagadougou 01
Tel: (226) 307 538
Fax: (226) 312 509

CANADA — Gerald Pratley

The business, if not the art, of film production in Canada appears to be brisk, bountiful and booming. This country surely holds the record for the number of events of all kinds which proliferate annually under the guise of improving Canadian films and business in general. No one will be surprised to hear that yet another government enquiry is going on into the support of film-making, including television because of its importance as a means of exhibition for feature films, documentaries and television movies.

Talkative Sheila Copps, the Minister of Heritage, whose knowledge of the business of film is minimal, has been carrying on before trade delegates about the absence of Canadian films in cinemas – the majority get shown, most of them to empty houses, other than Quebec films in that province. Those elusive figures used to represent Hollywood's domination of our screens (do Canadian films account for three per cent of screen time, or is it five?) are being bounced around again. The fact that a great many other countries live with the same situation is seldom mentioned – but Ms Copps and her blinkered believers keep telling us that we should be like "the other European countries who have quotas", despite the fact that the only concrete European example they can find is France, lauded for "standing up to Hollywood" with a third of screen time

devoted to homegrown films. Ms Copps' ideas included the introduction of quotas for Canadian cinemas and a chain of government-supported speciality theatres showing only Canadian films.

These suggestions have all been put forward time and time again by these endless government commissions, only to fail for many good reasons, one being that setting up quota regulations comes under provincial and not federal jurisdiction – and to expect the provinces to agree on working together is wishful thinking. And should the taxpayers pay for a chain of cinemas? There are independently-owned specialist cinemas in most towns and cities showing Canadian films on a regular basis – and usually lose money doing so.

All Hollywood's fault?

The problems of our "cultural industries" are mostly laid at Hollywood's door. It is seldom anyone asks if it is the nature of the feature films we are making that is responsible for the lack of support? Many perceptive observers have written Letters to Editors saying that if we could make a *Full Monty*, or emulate the many other pictures from Britain and Australia that play successfully here, we would have no difficulty reclaiming more screen time.

The only film to make a dent in English

Alberta Watson and Bruce Greenwood in THE SWEET HEREAFTER

Canadian cinema this past year was Egoyan's minimalist *The Sweet Hereafter* – due entirely to the inordinate amount of media hype accompanying it. And so whenever the politicians get restless in Ottawa, MPAA chairman Jack Valenti trots up or telephones to deliver stern warnings, as he has done so often in the past, pointing out that our subsidised film production is contrary to the Free Trade Agreement and observing that the majority of Canadian films have little to do with art and culture.

Meanwhile, provincial premiers hurry to follow each other down to Los Angeles to be wined and dined as they promise various forms of tax concessions in return for increased location shooting in their provinces. And they all talk enthusiastically about the "Canadian production" resulting from their blandishments. Even the Yukon Territories have joined the throng, while the entire media went into mourning when the producers of *The X-Files* announced they were moving the show from Vancouver back to Los Angeles!

Talk of quotas has turned attention away from making Canadian films to the question of which cinemas do, or do not, show them, and who owns the screens? This came about with the news that the US Department of Justice and Investment Canada had approved the purchase by Sony's Loew's Theatres of New York, of Cineplex-Odeon – which began life in the mid-1940s as J. Arthur Rank's Canadian Odeon circuit. Rank sold to Canadian interests in the mid-1970s. Cineplex, after becoming Canadian, then became American with MCA, and then Canadian again two years ago when Seagram's Edgar Bronfman, the Canadian-US business tycoon, purchased Universal Studios. With Cineplex losing money he could hardly resist Sony's takeover bid. Top executives of Cineplex received golden handshakes and the head office moved to New York.

Ottawa would not allow Cineplex's distribution arm to be sold to a non-Canadian company however, and Alliance Releasing, knowing a good deal when it sees one, stepped in to purchase it. The worrying aspect is this: Cineplex showed all the films it invested in under the Cineplex name. It remains to be seen whether Loews'-Cineplex will show Alliance's Canadian films and the other, usually foreign, pictures it distributes in Canada; or whether Sony itself will invest in Canadian films.

Inconsistencies abound in the decision of Investment Canada; Spielberg's Dream-Works has been given a license to open an office to distribute its own productions, but Polygram, which has been trying for two years to get a licence as a distributor, can only distribute its own pictures and not those it has bought from other companies – even though it promised to invest in Canadian productions. But with Seagram (Universal) buying Polygram, the wheel has come full circle again.

A powerful Alliance

The most surprising development of the year came in July with the announcement that Atlantis Films (mainly a production house for American television) was 'merging' with its much larger rival, Alliance Communications. Following its purchase of Norstar Films and Cineplex-Odeon's distribution arm, Alliance had become Canada's largest producer and distributor of television programmes and theatrical features. Alliance founder and boss Robert Lantos has left to become an independent producer and the new man in charge is Michael MacMillan of Atlantis, whose declared goal – to create more American programming – could deal another blow to indigenous feature film-making. Before the merger, Atlantis had completed production of David Cronenberg's $30m *Existenz*, billed as "a futuristic thriller".

Telefilm cannot avoid controversy as it travels to far corners of the earth anxiously looking for more countries to sign its co-production deals. Its latest blow-up came when it announced there was no more money for French-language films. It resolved this difficulty by taking money from the English-language budget. Telefilm's movie budget: $21.1m for English-language films, and $11.83m for those in French.

At the box-office, **Les Boys**, a boisterous comedy about an incompetent hockey team, directed by Louis Saia, has made $5.8m in Quebec alone, an all-time record for a Canadian film. When the video was released it immediately sold 11,000 copies to video clubs for rental. This makes it the best-selling VCR in the history of Quebec French-language films.

Survivor's tales

The once vibrant National Film Board (NFB), still a public body within the Federal government, has survived some drastic cost-cutting measures and continues to make documentaries for television in partnership with independent film-makers. Some recent titles: *Under the Willow Tree* (Chinese-Canadian women), *One Man's Paradise* (netting swordfish and tuna), *McGill, Mahler and Montreal* (McGill University's Symphony Orchestra) and the animations *When the Dust Settles*, *Narco Blues*, *Duel*, *Locked* and *How Wings are Attached to the Backs of Angels*, all shown at the Annecy Film Festival.

The NFB's widest exhibition of its films today is on the speciality cable channels. The CBC, after years of saying 'no' will show the superb six-part documentary series on Canada in the Second World War

entitled *No Price Too High*, directed by Richard Neilson. It had already been shown in the UK, on the Bravo! cable channel, and PBS in the US. It is considered to right the wrongs of the atrocious CBC-NFB Second World War documentary *The Valour and the Horror*.

Features sent to Cannes in 1998 included **Babyface**, directed by Jack Blum, a psychological study of the relationship between a mother, her lover and her teenage daughter, and **Last Night**, directed by Don McKellar, in which various characters try to arrange the perfect way to spend December 31, 1999. Also at Cannes were Denis Villeneuve's **August 32nd on Earth** (*Un 32 Aout Terre*), about a young woman's attempt to come to terms with life after an horrific car accident, François Girard's **The Red Violin**, an epic journey across five cities and four centuries, the bicycle courier drama **Two Seconds**, directed by Manon Briand, and **No**, Robert Lepage's third film, this one about an actress appearing at the 1970 World's Fair in Osaka who finds her life turned upside down. Patricia Rozema will write and direct Jane Austen's *Mansfield Park* in the UK for Miramax.

Edgar Bronfman of Universal has suggested that moviegoers should pay admission prices according to the film's budget. Howard Lichtman, when still executive vice-president of Cineplex replied that the system would leave an averagely-budgeted movie such *As Good As It Gets* with a ticket price of the standard $8. But *Titanic* would cost $28 a ticket and *The Full Monty* about 40 cents. Latest figures as reported by Statistics Canada and the indispensable *Film Canada Year Book*: 667 theatres (77 drive-ins), 2,200 screens (Famous Players and Loews Cineplex), box-office receipts (excluding taxes) $418m; paid admissions 87.5 million.

GERALD PRATLEY has been reporting on the Canadian scene for *Variety* since 1956. He teaches film history at Ryerson Polytechnic University, Toronto.

Sandva Oh in Don McKellar's LAST NIGHT   *photo: Cylla von Tiedemann*

Funding Agencies

Telefilm Canada
Tour de la Banque Nationale
600 rue de la Gauchetière ouest
14 étage
Montréal, PQ H3B 4L8
Tel: (1 514) 283 6363
Fax: (1 514) 283 8212
Telex: 055 60998
Budget: $207.5m

**Ontario Film Development
Corporation**
175 Bloor St. E.
North Tower, Ste. 300
Toronto, ON M4W 3R8
Tel: (1 416) 314 6858
Fax: (1 416) 314 6876
Budget: $15m

**Société de développement des
enterprises culturelles (SODEC)**
1755 boul. René Levesque est,
bur. 200
Montréal, PQ H2K 4P6
Tel: (1 514) 873 7768
Fax: (1 514) 873 4388
Budget: $14.5m

British Columbia Film Fund
2225 W. Broadway
Vancouver, BC V6K 2E4
Tel: (1 604) 736 7997
Fax: (1 604) 736 7920
Budget: $5m

Producers and Distributors

**Alliance Communications
Corporation**
121 Bloor St. E., Ste. 1500
Toronto, ON M4W 3M5
Tel: (1 416) 967 1174
Fax: (1 416) 960 0971

Atlantis Releasing
65 Heward Ave.
Toronto, ON M4M 2T5
Tel: (1 416) 462 0246
Fax: (1 416) 462 0779

Cinar Films Inc.
1055, boul. René Levesque est
Montréal, PQ H2L 4S5
Tel: (1 514) 843 7070
Fax: (1 514) 843 7080

**Ellis Enterprises & Keg
Productions**
1300 Yonge St., Ste. 300
Toronto, ON M4T 1X3
Tel: (1 416) 924 2186
Fax: (1 416) 924 6115

Film line International Inc.
410 St. Nicolas St., Ste. 105
Montréal, PQ H2Y 2P5
Tel: (1 514) 288 5888
Fax: (1 514) 288 8083

Films Transit International Inc.
402 East Notre Dame St., Ste. 100
Montréal, PQ H2Y 1C8
Tel: (1 514) 844 3358
Fax: (1 514) 844 7298

Imax Corporation
38 Isabella St.
Toronto, ON M4Y 1N1
Tel: (1 416) 960 8509
Fax: (1 416) 960 8596

**Lions Gate Films Inc.
formerly Cinepix Film Properties**
2 Bloor St. W., Ste. 1901
Toronto ON M4W 3E2

Motion International Inc.
A coacient Group Company
465 McGill St.
Montréal, QC H2Y 4A6
(1 514) 844 3542
Fax: (1 514) 985 4461

National Film Board
3155 Côté de Liesse Rd.
Ville Saint Laurent
Montréal, PQ H3C 3H5
Tel: (1 514) 283 9246
Fax: (1 514) 283 8971

(London Office)
No. 1 Grosvenor Square
London, England
W1X 0AB
Tel: 011 44 171 258 6481

Nelvana Enterprises Inc.
32 Atlantic Ave.

Toronto, ON M6K 1X8
Tel: (1 416) 588 5571
Fax: (1 416) 588 5588

Productions La Fête
225 rue Roy est., bur. 203
Montréal, PQ H2W 1M5
Tel: (1 514) 848 0417
Fax: (1 514) 848 0064

Red Sky Entertainment
Ste. 635 The Landing
375 Water St.
Vancouver, BC V6B 5C6
Tel: (1 604) 899 0609
Fax: (1 604) 899 0819

Rhombus International
489 King St. W., Ste. 102
Toronto ON M4C 1L3
Tel: (1 416) 971 7856
Fax: (1 416) 971 9647

Salter Street Films International Limited
2507 Brunswick St.
Halifax, NS B3K 2Z5
Tel: (1 902) 420 1577
Fax: (1 904) 425 8260

Societe De Distribution
Cinema Libre Inc.
460 Ste. Catherine o, bur. 500
Montréal, QC H3B 1A7
(1 514) 861 9030
Fax: (1 514) 861 3634

Sullivan Entertainment International Inc.
110 Davenport Road
Toronto, ON M5R 3R3
Tel: (1 416) 921 7177
Fax: (1 416) 921 7538

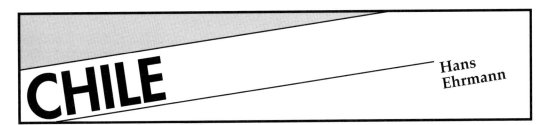

CHILE

Hans
Ehrmann

T he hopes of early 1997 have become solid facts and, after almost a decade of decreasing cinema audiences, there was a terrific 55 per cent rise during the first third of 1998. There was also a parallel increase in the consumption of popcorn and sodas, which had not previously been an integral part of Chilean cinema-going. Now refreshments are raising the cost of a night at the movies.

The facts of the multiplex revolution speak for themselves. At the start of 1997, there were 45 commercial screens in Santiago; by May 1998, there were 97 (excluding five art houses and half a dozen soft-core screens). Australia's Hoyts, America's National Amusement International and Cinemark (the latter associated with Chile's Conate) are by now well-established, constantly growing and spreading into the provinces.

The above is of course a world-wide

trend but, at this stage, it is by no means clear where it will lead. In Chile it has not yet led to an increase in the number or variety of films that are being screened – a situation not unrelated to the virtual extinction of independent distributors, and the market controls exerted by multi-national distribution and exhibition companies.

Bad guys and tall stories

Film production in Chile has, over the years, developed in stop-go cycles and is once again showing increased activity, although two of the four most recently completed films had not been seen when this article went to press. **Southern Cross**, produced by Chela Bon, a Chilean US resident, and directed by James Beckett, had a cast including Malcolm McDowell, Michael Ironside and Esai Morales; and several local actors. It deals with "bad guys

Still from Andres Wood's FOOTBALL STORIES

trying to take over a Chilean mine to store nuclear waste".

The second hybrid, also shot in English, was **Last Call**, produced by Juan Harting, owner of Chile's Roos Films. It combines Chilean actors with the likes of Peter Coyote and Elizabeth Berkley and has been described as an urban thriller which cuts back and forth between three stories unfolding on different floors of the same building. This is Chilean director Christine Lucas' second film. Producer Harting's as yet untested premise is that by shooting in English and including internationally recognisable actors, his global sales will prosper.

The two strictly local films were a different matter. **Football Stories** (*Historias de Futbol*), a promising debut from 31-year-old Andres Wood, consists of three episodes. In one, a factory worker who is the star of a neighbourhood soccer club is offered the bribe of a trial with a big-time team if he fails to score in a decisive match. In another, a group of little boys are having a kick-about outside a provincial stadium after failing to gain admittance to the match. Suddenly, due to a powerful kick, the match ball lands beside the kids and, for the first time in their lives, they have a real football to play with instead of a rag and paper bundle.

The last and best part takes place in the southern Chile archipelago, where a Santiago student is stranded on the eve of one of Chile's 1982 World Cup matches. With several fishermen he finds his way to the house of two middle-aged spinsters who own the district's only rickety TV set and, when the occasion arises, use it as a magnet for their private agenda. Close to neo-realism and working on a minimal budget, Wood keeps things simple and his characters true to life.

Scandal in the cemetery

Sergio Castilla's **Gringuito** became the most controversial film of the year. Exiled after the 1973 military coup, Castilla first lived in Sweden and then in the US, where his last film was *The Girl in a Watermelon* (1994). In *Gringuito*, he deals with the touchy subject of the thousands of exiles' children who grew up overseas and, on eventually returning to Chile, found themselves strangers in their native country. Castilla's hero, eight-year-old Ivan (Sebastián Pérez), is utterly unhappy at leaving New York and, on arriving home, even rebels by refusing to speak Spanish.

He runs away from home and his adventures all over Santiago, during which he pals up with a picturesque push-cart vegetable salesman (Mateo Iribarren), become a voyage of discovery. Although Castilla sometimes overplays the magic realism (particularly in a whorehouse scene) and the reconciliation between the exiled father and pro-Pinochet mother-in-law is simplistic, this is an impressive fable.

The director could not have predicted that a song-and-dance routine filmed in the Santiago General Cemetery would cause such scandal. The great grand-daughter of Claudio Vicunia Guerrero, a Chilean senator in the 1880s, saw the film and

Sébastian Pérez and Mateo Iribarren in the controversial GRINGUITO

realised that the sequence had been shot on the steps of her ancestor's mausoleum. She tried to have *Gringuito* banned for "desecrating the memory of those that repose" in the cemetery and "violating their psychic integrity". Happily, the court of appeal refused to have the film withdrawn from exhibition.

HANS EHRMANN is a columnist and the film critic for Santiago's daily *La Nación*.

Useful Addresses

Arauco Film
(production facility)
Silvina Hurtado 1789
Santiago
Tel: (56 2) 209 2091
Fax: (56 2) 204 5096

Conate and Chile Films
(studio, lab, distributor and exhibitor)
La Capitania 1200
Santiago
Tel: (56 2) 220 3086
Fax: (56 2) 211 9826

Filmocentro
(production facility)
Jorge Washington 302
Santiago
Tel: (56 2) 341 3100
Fax: (56 2) 209 1671

Hoyts Cinemas Chile S.A.
(exhibitors)
Roger de Flor 2736, Las Condes
Santiago
Tel/Fax: (56 2) 234 4456

Oficina de Difusión de la Cinematografia Chilena
Villavicencio 352
Santiago
Tel: (56 2) 632 6565 or 632 6607
Fax: (56 2) 632 6389

Roos Films
(production facility)
Ricardo Matte Pérez 0216
Santiago
Tel: (56 2) 341 1188
Fax: (56 2) 341 1199

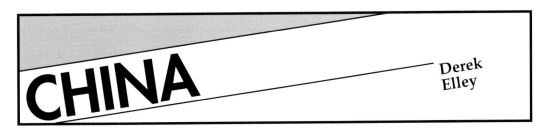

CHINA — Derek Elley

Though change in China's film industry is marked more by small increments than sudden upheavals, there have been encouraging signs in the past 12 months that things may be on the move again after the paralysis of the last couple of years. Several new films have shown a new way forward in production, and the dramatic events across the border in Hong Kong (see separate section) may even help to bind the two industries closer together.

As of summer 1998, there was definitely a sense of change afoot. Widely circulating rumours suggested that the Film Bureau (the industry's regulator and censor) might be closed down in its present form and its functions absorbed by the Culture Ministry, and that, even more dramatically, August First Film Studio (the country's richest entity, funded by the People's Liberation Army) might abandon pro-

duction and concentrate on services and facilities.

Even official sources now admit that feature film production is now around 100 titles a year, down from the 150 that was for years quoted as an immutable figure. In 1997, total investment in production was estimated at $16m (129m yuan). A hefty chunk of that amount came from private sources, channelled through the part-privatised studios in order to obtain the official production permits that ensure distribution. As of January 1, 1998, however, film companies can apply directly to the Ministry of Radio, Film & Television for production permits, rather than going through one of the 16 official studios.

Though the vast majority of the 100 films were purely of local interest – crime movies, action movies, ethnic stories, political makeweights etc. – there have been signs that the middle ground between these and the high-art "festival films" is being filled by quality, accessible items that could prove a fruitful way forward.

Generation next

One of the most notable in this category was **Spicy Love Soup** (*Aiqing mala tang*), by 30-year-old Zhang Yang. A smoothly shot and brightly played collection of vignettes about love and married life, it proved popular locally on release in late spring 1998 and could help to change the image of mainland Chinese movies if given half a chance by western festivals. The problem is that festival directors seem locked into outdated preconceptions of what Chinese cinema should be: either by a Fifth or Sixth Generation director, preferably set in the countryside or the past, and ideally mimicking western-style 'art cinema'.

In *Spicy Love Soup*, Zhang – who has made clear he does not want to wear any Generation tag, and is committed only to making good, accessible movies – has come up with an enjoyable look at a wide range of modern Pekingers' lives, well-acted by a large cast and directed with technical verve that never slips into MTV-like slickness. The $300,000 budget came from Taiwanese sources, marshalled by a Peking-based American, Peter Loehr, with ties in the music industry. The film was the first of its kind also to get a simultaneous soundtrack release.

A similar shift towards accessibility can be seen in Li Shaohong's **Happiness Street** (*Xingfu dajie*), an involving look at an average, blue-collar Peking family in which the husband (the excellent Wang Xueqi) suddenly loses his job and tries to hide the news from his wife (Song Dandan, equally fine). Realistic without being grungy, warm without becoming syrupy, and often very funny, the film is a far cry from Li's previous features, such as *Bloody Morning*, which was a more self-consciously arty movie, tailored for the festival circuit. *Happiness Street* is also known under the less suitable title *Red Suit* (*Hong xizhuang*), imposed by the Film Bureau.

Though not on quite the same level, but representing a quantum leap for journeyman director Hu Bingliu, is **Live in Peace** (*An ju*), a potentially melodramatic tale about a young Canton business couple (Sun Min, Wang Hong) and their problems with the husband's grouchy old mother-in-law (Pan Yu). Free of the usual official homilies about caring for old people, the film manages to tap into the pulse of modern-day China and draws fully-rounded performances from its entire cast.

After several re-edits, one film finally came off the shelf and was made available for foreign sales (but not, reportedly, festival screenings). **The Making of Steel** (*Zhangda chengren*; shot three years ago as *Gangtie shi zenyang lianchengde*) is the first film from Lu Xuechang, now 34, and was produced by Tian Zhuangzhuang at his unit attached to Bejing Film Studio. It is an ambitious portrait of changes in Chinese society during the past 20 years, through the story of a young man whose childhood idealism is slowly eroded as free-market reforms and western influences make their mark on the country. Despite gaps in the narrative, it is still a frank portrait of young people's modern rootlessness and loss of traditional values, finely observed and free of the pure nihilism that tainted Zhang Yuan's similarly-themed *Beijing Bastards* (1993).

Teacher, crook and killer

Xia Gang, a director who has done interesting work in the past (e.g. *Letting Go*), came up with **Concerto of Life** (*Shengming ru ge*), a beautifully shot and well acted story of a piano teacher's personal and professional travails over almost 40 years. However, like Xia's *Yesterday's Wine* (1996), it is a Janus movie, with an almost art-film approach lavished on an essentially melodramatic script (by Xia's wife, Meng Zhu) about a valid subject – a lament for a generation whose talents

Still from XIAO WU

were wasted by the upheavals of the Cultural Revolution.

As several of the above films demonstrated, use of direct sound is on the rise, adding immensely to the movies' realism and performances. *Live in Peace* also included some brief scenes in the Hakka dialect, rather than officially-sanctioned Mandarin. With no new films from established names like Chen Kaige, Zhang Yimou or Zhang Yuan in the past year, mainland Chinese representation at the major festivals has been sparse.

However, one independent production, **Xiao Wu**, made by first-timer Jia Zhangke, with financial help from Hong Kong, made a minor impact. It is a modest portrait of a petty crook-cum-hustler in a small town, shot on 16mm and with an almost documentary flavour. Acted by non-pros, and very loosely structured as a series of incidents, it is over-long and leisurely paced, but interesting nonetheless.

Also showcased at Berlin in 1998 was the first film of Mainland-born, San Francisco-

based actress Joan Chen. Though officially a US production (but in fact funded by Hong Kong, mainland Chinese and Taiwanese sources), **Xiu Xiu: The Sent-Down Girl** (*Tian yu*) is a highly impressive directorial debut, a chamber drama about a teenager's sexual and emotional loss of innocence in the wilds of Tibet, whither she is "sent down" during the Cultural Revolution. Secretly shot in a remote location on the border between Tibet and Sichuan province, without official

Lu Lu in Joan Chen's XIU XIU: THE SENT-DOWN GIRL

permission, the film (from the novella by Yan Geling) is beautifully observed and, finally, very moving, with a knockout performance from young actress Li Xiaolu in the lead role.

Curiously overlooked by festivals was **Dragon Town Story** (*Long cheng zhengyue*), a co-production with Hong Kong directed by Yang Fengliang, best known as the associate director on Zhang Yimou's *Code Name "Cougar"* (1989) and *Ju Dou* (1990). Credited as executive producer, Zhang had a considerable hand in shaping and casting the film, an artily shot revenge drama set in the early days of Republican China, with an impressive, stylised reality that' is perfectly mirrored by the leading performances of Wu Chien-lien (as the vengeful widow) and mainland actor You Yong (as the professional killer she meets along the way).

Hong Kong 'homecoming'

Most of the more interesting work the past year has come from Peking-based companies, rather than from those clustered around Shanghai Film Studios, whose output has been thoroughly local and commercial. More than ever, directors are hopping backwards and forwards between film and the booming TV drama sector (with commercials and music video work providing a lucrative sideline), and during the past year Hong Kong actors have been an increasing presence on the mainland as work has thinned out at home.

Despite Hong Kong's "return" to China in mid-1997, the territory is still not considered part of the motherland when it comes to film imports, which are officially still under quota. In practice, however, huge numbers of Hong Kong films are viewed in China, mostly on video compact disc (VCD), which has rapidly taken over from videocassettes as the preferred home viewing medium. In 1997, some 53 million VCDs were sold, compared with a mere four million cassettes.

Hong Kong's economic woes could well force it into closer co-operation with the mainland, as well as diminshing its perceived 'threat' in mainland eyes. For some years, the flow of money, talent and product between China and Hong Kong (and Taiwan) has been considerable, despite official regulations, and the signs of a Greater China market slowly evolving are already there. China needs Hong Kong's energy and experience to invigorate its own movie industry, and, following the collapse of many of its East Asian outlets, Hong Kong now needs China's cheap facilities and huge market to sell into.

The endless game of distribution ping-pong with the US majors continued as usual, with the Chinese authorities frowning on *Kundun*, *Red Corner* and *Seven Years in Tibet*, and rapping Disney, MGM and Columbia/TriStar over the knuckles. Twentieth Century Fox, however, managed to get *Titanic* onto mainland screens in April 1998, and around a dozen US movies continue to be imported every year. China's displeasure with Disney over *Kundun* only lasted so long: *Mulan* was allowed in, with the main character dubbed by local pop star Ai Jing.

The 17th Golden Rooster Awards

The awards were made in Foshan in December 1997, alongside those for the 20th Hundred Flowers Awards (voted by readers of the large-circulation monthly, *Popular Cinema*). Main prizes:

Best Film: *The Opium War.*
Best Director: Wei Lian (*The Turning Point*).
Best Script: Wang Xingdong (*The Days without a Hero*).
Best Actor: Liu Peiqi (*The Days without a Hero*).
Best Actress: Yu Hui (*Happy Lotus*).
Best Supporting Actor shared: Lin Liankun (*The Opium War*), Sun Chun (*Drug-Busting Heroes*).
Best Supporting Actress: Ma Xiaoqing (*My Daddy*).
Best Photography: Hou Yong (*The Opium War*).
Best Art Direction: Cui Denggao, Sun Yongyin, Zhang Biao (*The Turning Point*).
Best Editing: Feng Sihai (*Red River Valley*).

Best Music: Jin Fuzai (*Red River Valley*).
Best Sound: Lai Qizhen, Wang Xueyi (*The Opium War*).
Best First Work by a Director (shared prize): Lu Wei (*The Journey to the Western Xia Empire*), Zhou Bo (*A Life Catching Wolves*).
Best Documentary: *The Ridge.*
Best Musical: no award.
Best Children's Film: *My Daddy.*
Best Feature Film Co-production: *The Soong Sisters* (Dir: Mabel Cheung).
Special Jury Prize: *Surveillance* (Dir: Huang Jianxin and Yang Yazhou).

20th Hundred Flowers Awards

Best Films: *Red River Valley, The Turning Point, The Days without a Hero.*
Best Actor: Gao Ming (*Kong Fansen*).
Best Actress: Ning Jing (*Red River Valley*).
Best Supporting Actor: Niu Ben (*Husband Sings and Wife Too*).
Best Supporting Actress: Song Chunli (*The Days without a Hero*).
Special Prize: Kong Fansen.

Forthcoming Films

JING KE CI QIN WANG (Ch'in/The Assassin)

Players: Li Xuejian, Zhang Fengyi, Gong Li, Sun Zhou. Prod: NDF (Japan)/Foundry Communications (New York)/Beijing Film Studio.

YIGE BU NENG SHAO (Not One Less)

Players: Wei Minzhi, Tian Zhengda, Zhang Huike. Prod: Guangxi Film Studio.

FEICHANG AIQING (A Special Kind of Love)

Dir: Wu Tianming. Players: Yuan Li, Liu Yunlong, Zhu Daoxian. Prod: Beijing Film Studio.

HONGSE LIANREN (Red Lover)

Dir: Ye Daying. Players: Leslie Cheung, Mei Ting.

XIARI QING DONG (Summer Affaires)

Script and Dir: Jules Gilfillan. Players: Sarita Choudhury, Catherine Kellner, Josh Lucas, Matt Faber, David Wu, Chen Hsiang-chi, Geng Le, Hu Xin, Chen Daming.

CHONGMAN GANQINGDE CHENGSHI (A City Full of Emotion)

Dir: Mi Jiashan. Players: Pan Hong. Prod: Emei Film Studio.

WO AI BEIJING (I Love Beijing)

Dir: Ning Ying. Prod: Eurasia Communications.

STORY ABOUT LOVE

Dir: Zhou Xiaowen. Prod: Shanghai Film Studio.

APPEAL FOR LOVE

Dir: Wu Tianming. Players: Liu Yunlong, Yuan Li. Prod: Nande Group/Beijing Xinying Jia/Beijing Film Studio.

Useful Addresses

Film Bureau
(regulation, censorship)
129 Lishi Hutong
Dongcheng District
Beijing 100010
Tel: (86 10) 6512 1278
Fax: (86 10) 6512 6864

China Film Archive
3 Wenhuiyuan Rd.
Haidian District
Beijing 100088
Tel: (86 10) 6225 4422
Fax: (86 10) 6225 0362

China Film Corp.
(import, export)
25 Xinjiekouwai St
Beijing 100088
Tel: (86 10) 6225 4488
Fax: (86 10) 6225 0652

China Film Coproduction Corp.
5 Xinyuan South Rd
Chaoyang Distruct
Beijing 100027
Tel: (86 10) 6466 3330
Fax: (86 10) 6466 3983

August First Film Studio
A1, Beili
Liuliqiao
Guanganmenwai
Beijing 100073
Tel: (86 10) 6681 2329
Fax: (86 10) 6326 7324

Beijing Film Institute
4 Xitucheng Rd
Haidian District
Beijing 100088
Tel: (86 10) 6201 8899
Fax: (86 10) 6201 3895

Beijing Film Studio
77 Beisanhuan Central Rd
Haidian District
Beijing 100088
Tel: (86 10) 6201 2067
Fax: (86 10) 6201 2312

Shanghai Film Studio
595 Caoxi North Rd
Shanghai 200030
Tel: (86 21) 6438 7100
Fax: (86 21) 6439 1650

Xi'an Film Studio
70 Xiying Rd
Xi'an 710054
Tel: (86 29) 552 2526
Fax: (86 29) 552 2611

Pearl River Film Production Co.
352 Xingang Central Rd
Guangzhou 510311
Tel: (86 20) 8420 2238
Fax: (86 20) 8420 9584

Guangxi Film Studio
26 Youai North Rd
Nanning 530001
Tel: (86 771) 313 4261
Fax: (86 771) 313 3739

Changchun Film Studio
20 Hongqi St
Changchun 130021
Tel: (86 431) 595 3511
Fax: (86 431) 595 2747

CROATIA
— Tomislav Kurelec

In spite of considerable financial difficulties, which are usually solved through co-production with HRT (Hrvatska Televizija, the Croatian Television), Croatia has managed to produce six feature films in each of the last few years. These films are first presented at the national film festival in Pula, at the beginning of August, but none of the half-dozen or so entries for the 1998 event had been finished when this report went to press.

The 1997 festival was dominated by movies like Hrvoje Hribar's **Tranquilizer Gun** (*Puška za uspavljivanje*) and Lukas Nola's **Russian Meat** (*Rusko meso*), both mentioned in last year's *IFG* and both interestingly combining elements of *film d'auteur* and thriller. The first movie by young director Goran Rušinović, **Mondo Bobo**, fitted in neatly alongside this pair.

The very effective black-and-white photography by Ven Jemeršić was characterised by a roughness that went beyond naturalism and enabled Rušinović to place his vision of a thriller as a conflict between the individual and society within the frame of the alternative film tradition that stretches from Jean-Luc Godard to Jim Jarmusch. It was precisely this difference

from other Croatian films that enabled *Mondo Bobo*, the story of an outsider who stops fighting for justice and becomes a criminal, to gain more points from the festival jury, and from critics, than it really deserved.

A Welles-made return

Another film that aroused great interest in Pula was **The Third Woman** (*Treća žena*), the first picture, after a seven-year break, from the best Croatian director of the 1980s, Zoran Tadić. In it, he varies the themes and motifs of *The Third Man*, shifting the setting from post-war Vienna

Alma Prica in Zoran Tadić's THE THIRD WOMAN

to Zagreb in 1991-92, and transforming the heroes into heroines; but the main line of the plot remains the same. Scenes of alarms and blackouts contributed to an impressive presentation of the fight for independence, with superb work from cinematographer Goran Trbuljak.

The ominous atmosphere owed much to Tadić's decision to shoot the movie in black-and-white, and the imaginative use of light in dark scenes was reminiscent not only of *The Third Man*, but also of German expressionism and Tadić's first (and, according to many, best) film, *The Rhythm of Crime* (*Ritam zločina*, 1981).

Tadić has certainly not lost his masterful touch during his time away, and he conducts the action in a rapid rhythm. The decision to make the leading characters women did not completely prove Tadić's thesis that in the Croatian war for independence women were psychically stronger, but did produce excellent performances from Ena Begović and Alma Prica (maybe the best Croatian actress today) in, respectively, the Joseph Cotton and Orson Welles roles.

The remaining two films did not match the quality of these authorial thrillers, although **Christmas in Vienna** (*Božić u Beču*), a story of a musician who has a hard time deciding whether he should return to Croatia and the war after he has spent the Christmas holiday in the Austrian capital, is a well-made drama by Branko Schmidt, a director whose previous two movies disappointed those impressed by his 1980s work. Much less successful was **Pont Neuf**, directed by a very good scenographer, Željko Senečić, which pictures the suicide of the prominent Croatian painter Josip Račić during his stay in Paris in the years before the First World War.

The final verdict on the 1997 film season would still be a positive one, had not the audience for Croatian film again fallen.

Bojana Gregorić and Filip Šovagović in CHRISTMAS IN VIENNA

After Vinko Brešan's *How the War Started on my Island* (*Kako je počeo rat na mom otoku*) beat all the American blockbusters of 1996, with an audience of 300,000, the animated **The Strange Adventures of the Apprentice Hlapić** (*Čudnovate zgode šegrta Hlapića*) was the only Croatian feature to sell more than 200,000 tickets in 1997, while few feature films broke 10,000.

Those figures can be attributed to the superiority of the American commercial movie, and Hollywood's ability to offer people an escape from the everyday problems which feature, in some form, in all Croatian films. Another quite alarming problem is the fact that the distribution of subsidy to film production in Croatia by the Ministry of Culture is controlled by people who do not favour the young authors who have in the past few years been most successful (perhaps because they view the Croatian social situation quite critically). Yet the powers that be do not hesitate to give money to those directors who have been responsible for some of the greatest failures in the last few years. In such circumstances it is hard to talk about continuity and development in Croatian cinema.

TOMISLAV KURELEC has been a film critic since 1965, mostly on radio and television, and has directed five short films and many TV features.

Recent and Forthcoming Films

MONDO BOBO (Mondo Bobo)

Script and Dir: Gorn Rušinović. Phot: Ven Jemeršić. Players: Sven Medvešek, Nataša Dorčić, Lucija Šerbedžija, Svebor Kranjc, Nino Bantić. Prod: DSL Film

TREĆA ŽENA (The Third Woman)

Script: Pavao Pavličić, Zoran Tadić. Dir: Zoron Tadic. Phot: Goran Trbuljak. Players: Ena Begović, Vedran Mlikota, Alma Price, Filip Šovagović, Vlatko Dulić. Prod: G.D. Histrioni/HRT

BOŽIĆ U BEČU
(Christmas in Vienna)

Script and Dir: Branko Schmidt. Phot: Vjekoslav Vrdoljak. Players: Filip Šovagović, Bojana Gregorić, Ljubo Kapor, Vjera Zagar Nardelli. Prod: Inter-film/HRT.

PONT-NEUF

Script and Dir: Željko Senečić. Phot: Enes Midžić. Players: Ivan Marević, Senka Bulić, Glorija Šoletić, Dražen Kühn, Filip Šovagović, Ana Karić. Prod: HRT.

KAD MRTVI ZAPJEVAJU
(When the Dead Men Sing)

Script: Mate Matišić and Krsto Papić. Dir: Krsto Papić. Phot: Vjekoslav Vrdoljak. Players: Ivo Gregurević, Ivica Vidović, Mirjana Majurec, Ksenija Pajić, Boris Miholjević, Matija Prskalo. Prod: Jadran Film, Heiser Production – München, HRT.

TRANSATLANTIK (Transatlantic)

Script and Dir: Mladen Juran. Phot: Goran Trbuljak. Players: Filip Šovagović, Melita Jurišić, Alen Liverić, Boris Dvornik, Prod: Jadran Film/HRT.

U AGONIJI (In Agony)

Script: Jakov Sedlar, Georgij Paro. Dir: JAKOV Sedlar. Phot: Karmelo Kursar. Players: Božidar Alić, Ena Begovic, Sven Medvešek, Tarik Filipović, Nives Ivanković, Zoja Odak, Franjo Kuhr. Prod: Patria film/HRT.

DUBROVNIK '91

Script and Dir: Željko Senečić. Phot: Enes Midžić. Players: Filip Šovagović, Jasna Ančić, Milka Kokotović.

TRI MUŠKARCA MELITE ŽGANJER (Three males of Melita Žganjer)

Script and Dir: Snježana Tribuson. Players: Mirjana Rogina, Sanja Vejnović, Suzana Nikolić, Gorn Navojec. Phot: Goran Mećava. Prod: Kvadar/HRT.

GARCIA

Script and Dir: Dejan Šorak. Phot: Vjekoslav Vrdoljak. Prod: Studio K 36.

HRVATSKA BOGORODIC
(Croatian Mother of God)

Script: Hrvoje Hitrec. Dir: Neven Hitrec. Phot: Stanko Herceg. Players: Ljubomir Kerekeš, Ivo Gregurević, Vanja Drach. Prod: Maxima film/Jadran film/HRT.

CRVENA PRAŠINA
(Red Dust)

Script: Goren Tribuson, Zrinko Ogresta. Dir: Zrinko Ogresta. Phot: Davorin Gecl. Players: Josip Kučan, Ivo Gregurević, Slaven Knezović, Marko Matanopvić. Prod: Inter film/HRT.

CZECH REPUBLIC
Eva Zaoralová

While it was anticipated that almost two dozen features would be made during the latter half of 1997 and the first half of 1998, a shortage of funding obliged several film-makers to postpone their projects. Private producers are becoming less inclined to use the costly services offered by Prague's Barrandov Studios. The studios themselves are resorting to foreign commissions and are also undergoing complex procedures with regard to property rights.

Thus one of Europe's largest film studios – once also the largest producer of Czech films – is gradually deteriorating and faces an extremely uncertain future. This is prompting fears that, if Barrandov were sold, the copyright for Czech feature films made after 1965, which Barrandov owns, might be transferred into the wrong hands and become the subject of purely commercial interests. Furthermore, Krátký Film, the company which had governed the copyright for the majority of Czech animated films, has declared itself insolvent. Now, more than ever, it has become essential to revise the law on audio-visual production.

Six of the best

Kolya, the top box-office hit of the last two years, has found a dignified successor in **The Buttoners** (*Knoflíkáři*), the second film by Petr Zelenka, a recent scriptwriting graduate from FAMU (Prague's Academy of Arts), whose first film, *Happy End*, captured the attention of audiences and critics alike. Produced by Czech Television, *The Buttoners* addresses the young generation, in particular, with its intelligent humour, absurdist elements and tragic undercurrents. The film's six short stories are set both in the present day and within a strange time loop (one unfolds in

1945) which alters the relationship between cause and effect.

The common denominator of these tragicomic episodes, set in contemporary Prague, in a Japanese town and on board the bomber en route for Hiroshima, lies in the mysterious contexts which affect the course of events. Characters and motifs move freely between the episodes. *The Buttoners* enjoyed great success with the public and critics, winning four of the most important Czech Lion awards and being named as one of the three best films at the Rotterdam Film Festival.

Pavel Marek's feature debut, **Dead Beatle** (*Mrtvej Brouk*), also enjoyed considerable success at Rotterdam. This melancholy account of a love affair between two unstable young people in a mental asylum was admirably authentic, not least because many of the actors were themselves asylum patients.

After six troubled years in theatre and television, the young Czech director Tomáš

Still from THE BUTTONERS

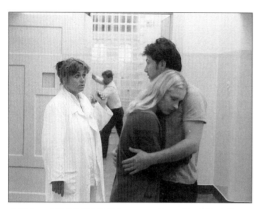

Still from DEAD BEATLE   *photo: David W. Černý*

Vorel finally completed his third feature film, **The Stone Bridge** (*Kamenny Most*). Its story – a director called Tomáš tries to break out of a personal rut – gave the film a certain autobiographical slant and reflected to a great extent Vorel's views on contemporary Czech life. Vorel's idea of torment is rooted in kitsch, amorality and self-betrayal, epitomised by the world of television advertising, which "steals" the two women in the hero's life, and his film was tendentious and stylistically un-balanced.

Bewildered in black-and-white

Lack of public interest and the bewilderment of the critics plagued the launch of the feature debut of successful director of photography and documentarist Ivan Vojnar, **The Way Through The Black Wood** (*Cesta Pustým Lesem*). Shot in black-and-white, this is an extremely melancholic portrait of a remote mountain settlement just before the start of the First World War. The leisurely camera tracking intensifies the almost dreamy ambience of a film whose characters are overwhelmed by in-significant and petty conflicts that will ultimately be swept away by the war.

While the new film by Věra Chytilová, **Traps, Traps, Little Traps** (*Pasti, Pasti, Pastičky*), attracted only marginal enthusiasm from the critics, it was nevertheless applauded by the public. One of the greatest names of the Czechoslovak New Wave, Chytilová had already succumbed to the temptation to make a film directed at the general public in *The Inheritance* (1993), thereby yielding to indelicacy and mass appeal. On this occasion, the style of this grotesque story is more restrained. A young veterinary surgeon punishes two men for raping her by using her medical skills to castrate them (reportedly a true story). During the second half of the film in particular, however, the director attempts a somewhat cumbersome criticism of "odious capitalist society" and her tone becomes almost hysterical.

Oskar Reif's debut, **The Bed** (*Postel*), divided its audience into two opposing camps; some viewers were even incensed by the film. Far removed from Chytilová's feminism, the work brings us a ruthless portrayal of women and their attitudes to men. Although Reif's film has yet to be fully appreciated on its home ground, the director was given the satisfaction of seeing it included in the International Critics' Week at Cannes 1998.

The oldest profession

Another feature to pick up mixed reviews at home was **The Mandrake Root**, although it attracted considerable interest in the US and also took away one of the awards at the Geneva festival. It was directed by Polish-born Wiktor Grodecki, who lives in Prague and the US, and made a name for himself in recent years with two controversial feature-length documentaries, *Angels Are No Angels* and *Body Without Soul*, which both explored adolescent male prostitution. This theme was incorporated into *The Mandrake Root*,

Still from TRAPS, TRAPS, LITTLE TRAPS

the story of Marc, a 15-year-old country boy who comes to Prague and, desperate for money, becomes a prostitute. Its striking authenticity owed much to former male prostitute David Švec, who served as co-scriptwriter, co-star (as one of Marc's hustler friends) and assistant editor.

Undeniably the most promising film project for the 1998 season is the third feature by the talented Vladimír Michálek, **Sekal Has To Die** (*Je Třeba Zabít Sekala*). The screenplay for this timeless parable about good and evil, human courage and cowardice, was written by the experienced Jiří Křižan, who viewed this ambitious rural story, set at the end of the war, as a classic western.

This and *The Way Through The Black Wood* were the only two films of the year to explore the past. Contemporary film production in the Czech Republic is clearly dominated by contemporary themes, reflecting the artists' attitude to certain modern phenomena. It seems that Czech film currently provides a platform chiefly for the generation which took shape at the end of the old regime and the beginning of the new era. It is young film-makers such as Zelenka who are able to perceive film expression without buckling under the burden of the past, who are not afraid to break up old aesthetic schemes and who discover new themes around them and within themselves.

EVA ZAORALOVÁ is a Czech film critic and editor of the magazine *Film a doba*. The author of many essays and books on Italian, French and Czech cinema, she taught film history for ten years at FAMU in Prague, and is artistic director of the Karlovy Vary International Film Festival.

Recent and Forthcoming Films

CESTA PUSTÝ LESEM (The Way Through the Black Woods)

Script: Ivan Arseniev. Dir: Ivan Vojnár. Phot: Jaromír Kačer. Players: Václav Koubek, Pavel Landovský, Jana Dolanská, Jiří Soukup. Prod: Gaga Productions

JE TŘEBA ZABÍT SEKALA (Sekal Has to Die)

Script: Jiří Křižan. Dir: Vladimír Michálek. Phot: Martin Štrba. Players: Oiaf Lubaszenko, Boguslaw Linda, Jiří Bartoška, Vlasta Chramostová. Agnieszka Sitek. Prod: Buc-Film

KAMENNY MOST (The Stone Bridge)

Script: Tomáš Vorel, Jaroslav Dušek. Dir: Vorel. Phot: Marke Jícha. Players: Tomáš Hanák, Romas Sittová, Milena Dvorská, Jan Slovák, Václav Strasser. Prod: Vorel Film/Czech Television/Barrandov Biografia/ Krátký film a.s.

KNOFKLÍKÁŘI (Buttoners)

Script and Dir: Petr Zelenka. Phot: Martin Gábor. Players: Rudolf Hriušínský, Eva Holubová, Jiří Kodet, Antonín Navrátil, Vladimír Dlouhý. Prod: Czech Television.

MRIVEJ BROUK (Dead Beatle)

Script and Dir: Pavel Marek. Phot: Diviš Marek. Players: Jan Zuska, Pavlína Jirásková, Ondřej Malý, Vladimír Drha, Radim Špaček. Prod: Whisconti, Telexport Praha.

PASTI, PASTI, PASTIČKY (Traps, Traps, Little Traps)

Story: Eva Kačírková. Script: Věra Chytilová, Michal Lázňovská, David Vávra, Tomáš Hanák. Dir: Chytilová. Phot: Štěpán Kučera. Players: Mirsolav Donutil, Tomáš Hanák, Zuzana Stivínová, Dagmar Bláhová, Eva Holubová, Luboš Svoboda, Milan Lasica. Prod: Cineart, TV NOVA.

POSTEL (The Bed)

Script and Dir: Oskar Reif. Phot: Igor Luther. Players; Michal Przebinda, Stanislava Jachnická, Jana Hrušková, Sylva Langová-Williams, Prod: Silver Screen.

Producers

Barrandov Biografia
(also distributor)
Kříženeckého nám. 322
151 00 Praha 5
Tel: (420 2) 6707 1111
Fax: (420 2) 6707 2273

Bonton Films Production
Severozápadní IV 39
140 00 Praha 4
Tel: (420 2) 746 529
Fax: (420 2) 745 750

CINEART Productions
Vzdušná 817
140 00 Praha 4
Tel: (420 2) 6171 1108/6171 1044
Fax: (420 2) 6171 1048

ETAMP Film
U továren 261
102 00 Praha 10
Tel: (420 2) 705 257
Fax: (420 2) 706 077

Febio, Ltd
Růžová ul. 13
110 00 Praha 1
Tel: (420 2) 2421 3933
Fax: (420 2) 2421 4254

KF a.s. (also distributor)
Jindřišská 34
112 07 Praha 1
Tel: (420 2) 2421 2410
Fax: (420 2) 644 5111

Space Films s.r.o.
(also distributor)
Karlovo nám. 19
120 00 Praha 2
Tel: (420 2) 2491 3043
Fax: (420 2) 2491 3045

VaC – Vachler Art Company
Na Žertvách 40
180 00 Praha 8
Tel: (420 2) 683 2600

Distributors

Bonton Films
Národní tř. 28
1120 00 Praha 1
Tel: (420 2) 2110 5248
Fax: (420 2) 2422 5263

CINEMART a.s.
Národní 28
110 00 Praha 1
Tel: (420 2) 2110 5235
Fax: (420 2) 2110 5220

FALCON
Stroupežnického 6
150 00 Praha 5
Tel: (420 2) 538 085
Fax: (420 2) 533 194

Filmexport Prague
Na Moráni 5
128 00 Praha 2
Tel: (420 2) 2491 5239
Fax: (420 2) 293 312

Gemini Film
V jámě 1
110 00 Praha 1
Tel: (420 2) 2416 2471
Fax: (420 2) 2422 6562

Intersonic Taunus Prod. Ltd
Palackého 15
110 00 Praha 1
Tel/Fax: (420 2) 2422 9007

Useful Addresses

Ministry of Culture
Milady Horákové 139
160 00 Praha 6
Tel: (420 2) 5708 5111
Fax: (420 2) 2431 8155

**FITES (Association of Czech
Film Artists)**
Pod Nuselskými schody 3
120 00 Praha 2
Tel: (420 2) 691 0310
Fax: (420 2) 691 1375

Union of Czech Distributors
U Rajské zahrady 14
130 00 Praha 3
Tel: (420 2) 9000 2651

**Association of Producers in the
Audiovisual Industry c/o SPACE
Film**
Karlovo nám. 19
120 00 Praha 2
Tel: (420 2) 2491 3043

DENMARK — Ebbe Iversen

The inclusion of two Danish features in competition for the Palme d'Or at Cannes was the most notable event in the Danish film world in 1998. *The Celebration*, by Thomas Vinterberg (who turned 29 during the festival), and Lars von Trier's *Idiots* were both based on the so-called Dogma 95 (also known as The Vow of Chastity) which was devised by the two directors in 1995. The ten commandments of Dogma 95 state that, among others things, films must be shot on location, sound must never be produced separately from images (or vice versa), the camera must be hand-held, there must be no superficial action and genre movies are unacceptable.

DANISH FILM INSTITUTE

Presenting DANISH FILMS worldwide

Bogota
Paris
Riga
Medellin
Brussels
Tromsø
Rotterdam
Belgrade
Göteborg
Tel Aviv
Oporto
Berlin
Portland
Lillehammer
Málaga
Lübeck
Bonn
Rio de Janeiro
Zürich
Dublin
London
Munich
Santa Barbara
Tokyo
Malmö
Cleveland
Rouen

Toronto	Sitges			Salzburg
Augsburg	São Paulo			Jerusalem
Laon	Poznan			Durban
New York	Vilnius	Bangkok		Giffoni
Montevideo	Tammerfors	Zlin		Haugesund
Montreal	San Francisco	Varna		Mexico City
Istanbul	Philadelphia	Troia	Pesaro	Burgsvik
Madrid	Greifswald	Freiburg	Valencia	Strasbourg
Prague	Cannes	Helsinki	St. Petersburg	San Sebastian
Singapore	Ljubljana	Potsdam	La Rochelle	Rimouski
Frankfurt am Main	Seattle	Hannover	Hong Kong	Hamburg
				Vancouver
				Kuala Lumpur
				Chicago

DANISH FILM INSTITUTE

VOGNMAGERGADE 10 · DK-1120 COPENHAGEN K

TEL +45 3374 3430 · FAX +45 3374 3435

The Celebration shared the Jury Prize in Cannes with Claude Miller's *La Classe de Neige*. Vinterberg's dark and disturbing comedy is the story of a family reunion on the occasion of the father's sixtieth birthday, disrupted by the subsequent revelation that he had sexually abused a son and a daughter when they were kids. As most members of the family desperately try to preserve a sense of normality, events spin further and further out of control.

Von Trier's follow-up to the internationally successful *Breaking the Waves*, **Idiots** (*Idioter*), is even more disturbing than Vinterberg's film. The idiots of the title are a group of young people living in a large house north of Copenhagen. They spend their time pretending they are mentally retarded – perhaps to liberate themselves psychologically, perhaps as a protest against bourgeois society. Gradually their feigned madness becomes real, reality and fiction become blurred, and von Trier shifts from grotesque comedy to serious drama.

Idiots contains an extremely bold sex scene which will probably get it into trouble with censors in several countries, but even before Cannes it had been sold to more territories than *Breaking the Waves*. The buyers may find the film – which, technically, is deliberately amateurish – more controversial than they expect.

New team at the top

The most important event for the Danish film industry over the last 12 months was the introduction by the Danish Film Institute (DFI) in April of an ambitious four-year plan calling for a dramatic increase in government financial support for production and distribution of Danish feature films, as well as shorts and documentaries.

According to the plan, which was still being considered by the politicians when this article went to press, production funding should be raised from $15m to $42m (from DKK100m to 278m) per year; annual funding for distribution and promotion from $3.8m to $10m, and

annual funding for the Film Museum (including the national film archives) from $2.5m to $4.3m. The plan also calls for an appropriation of $12m to make the nondescript, gloomy-looking Film House (home to the DFI and Film Museum) in the centre of Copenhagen more attractive to the public.

During the year, the DFI took on a new management structure. Its chief executive is Henning Camre, former head of the Danish Film School, and, more recently, controversial renovator of England's National Film and Television School. Thomas Stenderup heads production and development, Peter Wolsgaard is chief of distribution and marketing, Dan Nissen is the principal of the Film Museum, and Christian Kofoed-Enevoldsen is head of administration.

Optimism reigns in the Danish film world, as 1997 was a good year for the domestic cinemas, partly due to the success of homegrown films. Overall admission increased to 10.8 million, the highest figure for ten years, and Danish films drew 35 per cent more cinemagoers than in 1996, securing an overall market share of 21 per cent. That figure does not include the year's most successful film, Bille August's German-Danish co-production, *Smilla's Sense of Snow*.

Slackers triumphant

Of the new Danish films, Nils Malmros' **Barbara** was in competition at the Berlin International Film Festival. Based on a classic novel by Jørgen Frantz Jacobsen, it is a love story unravelling in the remote Faroe Islands in the eighteenth century, but its rather old-fashioned style is, unfortunately, pretty to look but short of real passion. The film critics' Bodil Award for best Danish film of the year went to young director Jonas Elmer's first feature **Let's Get Lost**, a charming black-and-white account of the lives of a bunch of likeable Copenhagen slackers.

Susanne Bier's **Credo** (*Sekten*) is a mildly exciting feminist thriller about a young

Sidse Babett Knudsen and Nicolaj Kopernikus in LET'S GET LOST

woman (played by the admirable Sofie Gråbøl) attempting to help a friend who has been drawn into a dangerous sect. Lone Scherfig's **On Our Own** (*Når mor kommer hjem*) is a very likeable story of three children managing on their own while their single mother is in jail for shoplifting.

Jannik Hastrup's **Hans Christian Andersen and the Long Shadow** (*H. C. Andersen og den lange skygge*) is an ambitious and very well crafted feature-length cartoon about the great Danish writer. First-time director Jakob Grønlykke's **Heart of Light** (*Lysets hjerte*), shot in Greenland, is the first feature ever made in the indigenous Inuit language. Its well-meaning, but rather feeble story, centres on an alcoholic trying to come to terms with life after his son has committed a double murder and then suicide.

Amongst recent comedies, Mette Louise Knudsen's **Honey, It's Your Turn!** (*Skat, det er din tur!*) is a completely out-dated take on the reversal of the sexes' traditional roles, and Hans Kristensen's **Sune's**

Family (*Sunes familie*) is a harmless movie for children.

Shakespearean comedy cocktail

Michael Wikke and Steen Rasmussen mixed elements from Shakespeare's *Hamlet*, *Othello* and *Macbeth* in their contemporary comedy **Motello**, which is not nearly as funny as intended, but also not nearly as bad as Kasper Wedendahl's embarrassing **Stars Without Brains**

Still from Lone Scherfig's ON OUR OWN

Still from BABY DOOM

(*Stjerner uden hjerner*), about a couple of ridiculous stand-up comedians. Prior to *Idiots*, von Trier shot the highly original, funny and scary TV series **The Kingdom 2** (*Riget 2*), and Peter Gren Larsen revealed promising talent in the satirical **Baby Doom**, whose computer programmer hero struggles to combine work with life as the father of a new-born baby.

Another debutant director, Simon Staho, tells in **Wildside** (*Vildspor*) – shot in Iceland – the dramatic story of the confrontation between two former friends and drug smugglers, and a third first-time director, Anders Dalgaard, made **Nether World** (original title) in America with his own money. Unfortunately, the story of two professional killers waiting to carry out a hit goes nowhere.

Amongst the numerous films currently in production or post-production, veteran director Henning Carlsen's **I Wonder Who's Kissing You Now** (original title) depicts with humour the effects of a husband's raging jealousy, and Trine Piil Christensen's

Max is a thriller about a young female criminal. Thomas Borch Nielsen's **The Shadow** (*Skyggen*) is a futuristic techno-thriller, Morten Lorentzen's **Diving** (*Rungsted*) is a contemporary love story, and Christian Braad Thomsen's **The Blue Monk** (*Den blå munk*) describes the lives and dreams of the regular customers in a Copenhagen bar.

Linda Wendel's **Mimi & The Movers** (*Mimi & Madammerne*) is a tale of five women who gather in a countryside cottage to celebrate the tenth anniversary of their friendship; Torben Skjødt Jensen's **Ved jorden at blive** (no English title yet) is the weird story of a man who, after losing his wife and child in a fire, spends the next 20 years in a box in his basement, and Ole Christian Madsen's **Pizza King** deals with a group of young immigrant hustlers in Copenhagen.

Two more films based on Dogma 95 principles are on the way, directed by Søren Kragh-Jacobsen and Kristian Levring. Last, but not least, the beloved Olsen Gang, who delighted Danes in 13 films between 1968 and 1981, are to make one final appearance. **Olsen Bandens sidste stik** (no English title yet) has the same main cast as the previous films, but the veteran Erik Balling has handed directorial duties to his younger colleague, Tom Hedegaard. A huge success in Denmark seems assured.

EBBE IVERSEN has been a professional journalist since 1966. He has been film critic of *Berlingske Tidende* since 1973, and is a former co-editor of the magazine *Kosmorama*.

Producers

ASA Film Production ApS
Mosedalvej
DK-2500 Valby
Tel: (45) 3618 8200
Fax: (45) 3116 8502

Crone Film Produktion A/S
Blomstervænget 52
DK-2800 Lyngby
Tel: (45) 4587 2700
Fax: (45) 4587 2705

Danish Film Studio
Blomstervænget 52
DK-2800 Lyngby
Tel: (45) 4587 2700
Fax: (45) 4587 2705
Telex: 37798 (studio dk)

Domino Film & TV Production
Langebrogade 6 A
København N
DK-1411

Tel: (45) 3296 6644
Fax: (45) 3296 0644

Film & Lyd Produktion A/S
Bredgade 63A
DK-1260 København K
Tel: (45) 3312 1050
Fax: (45) 3312 1093

Grasten Film, Regner
Lykkevej 6

DK-2920 Charlottenlund
Tel: (45) 3163 4424
Fax: (45) 3163 4823

Holst Film A/S, Per
Klampenborg 50
DK-2930 Klampenborg
Tel: (45) 3963 8866
Fax: (45) 3963 5575

Lense-Møller Film ApS, Lise
Fortunvej 56
DK-2920 Charlottenhund
Tel: (45) 3164 2284
Fax: (45) 3164 2269

Locomotion Kofod Schiller Film
Nannasgade 28
DK-2200 København N
Tel: (45) 3183 8900
Fax: (45) 3582 1737

**Madsen, Kenneth
Filmproduktion A/S**
Guldbergsgade 29 F
DK-2200 København N
Tel: (45) 3536 0036
Fax: (45) 3536 0011

Mandart Production
H. P. Ørumsgade 47
DK-2100 København

Metronome Productions A/S
Søndermarksvej 16
DK-2500 Valby

Nordisk Film Production A/S
Mosedalvej
DK-2500 Valby
Tel: (45) 3630 1033
Fax: (45) 3116 8502

Obel Film, ApS
A.N. Hansens Allé 23
DK-2900 Hellerup
Tel: (45) 3161 0666
Fax: (45) 3161 0667

**Panorama Film International
Ltd.**
The Old Mill, London Road, Hook,
Hants AG27 9EH, England
Tel: (44) 256 766868
Fax: (44) 256 768747

Penta Film
Strandgade 4 B

DK-1401 København K
Tel: (45) 3296 6230
Fax: (45) 3296 0014

Ravn Film og Media Aps
Mosedalvej 11 B
DK-2500 Valby
Tel: (45) 3645 5800
Fax: (45) 3645 0808

Such Much Movies ApS
Blomstervænget 52
DK-2800 Lyngby
Tel: (45) 4587 2700
Fax: (45) 4587 2705

Superfilm Productions
Forbindelssvej 5
DK-2100 København Ø
Tel: (45) 3142 4611
Fax: (45) 3142 4611

Vestergaard Film, Jørgen
Gadekøret 24, Sennels
DK-7700 Thisted
Tel: (45) 9798 50020
Fax: (45) 9798 5020

Victoria Film
Frederiksberggade 16
DK-1459 København K
Tel: (45) 6260 1595
Fax: (45) 6260 1534

Zentropa Entertainments ApS
Ryesgade 106, st.
DK-2100 København Ø
Tel: (45) 3142 4233
Fax: (45) 3142 429

Distributors

AB Collection
Hirsemarken 3
DK-3520 Farum
Tel: (45) 4499 6200
Fax: (45) 4295 1786

Camera Film
Mikkel Bryggers Gade 8
DK-1460 København K
Tel: (45) 3313 6112
Fax: (45) 3315 0882

Constantin Film ApS
Skelbækgade 1
DK-1717 København V
Tel: (45) 3325 2424
Fax: (45) 3325 0707

Egmont Audio Visual A/S
Skelbækgade 1
DK-1717 København V
Tel: (45) 3325 4000
Fax: (45) 3325 4002

Holland House
Vesterbrogade 26, 2
DK-1620 København V

Gloria Film
Vesterbrogade 149
DK-1620 København V
Tel: (45) 3327 0022
Fax: (45) 3327 0099

Nordisk Film Distribution A/S
Skelbøkgade 1
DK-1717 København V
Tel: (45) 3123 2488
Fax: (45) 3123 0488

Scala Film
Centrumpladsen
DK-5700 Svendborg
Tel: (45) 6221 8866
Fax: (45) 6221 0821

20th Century Fox
Skelbækgade 1, 3
DK-1717 København V
Tel: (45) 3325 4000
Fax: (45) 3325 4002

**United International Pictures
(UIP)**
Hauchsvej 13
DK-1825 Frederiksberg C
Tel: (45) 3131 2330
Fax: (45) 3123 3420

Warner & Metronome ApS
Søndermarksvej 16
DK-2500 Valby
Tel: (45) 3146 8822
Fax: (45) 3644 0604

Useful Addresses

Danish Film Institute
Vognmagergade 10
DK-1120 København K
Tel: (45) 3374 3430
Fax: (45) 3374 3435
Tlx: 31465 dfilm dk

The Danish Film Studio
Blomstervænget 52
DK-2800 Lyngby
Tel: (45) 4587 2700
Fax: (45) 4587 2705

Risby Studios
Ledøjevej 1
DK-2620 Albertslund
Tel: (45) 4262 9646

Danish Film Institute Workshop
Vognmagergade 10
DK-1120 København V
Tel: (45) 3374 3480
Fax: (45) 3374 3490

National Film Board of Denmark
Statens Filmcentral
Film House Denmark
Vognmagergade 10
DK-1120 København K
Tel: (45) 3374 3500
Fax: (45) 3374 3565

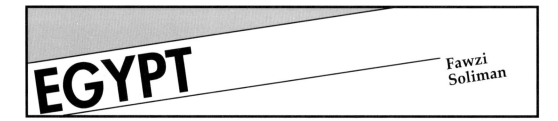

EGYPT

Fawzi Soliman

Just 16 Egyptian films were released in 1997 – the smallest number for 50 years – and, inevitably, the debate over the impasse in which Egyptian cinema finds itself continued. The advent of 1998, however, gave rise to hopes that this would be the year of revival, with new life breathed into Egyptian film by new directors and companies.

Last year did provide one highlight, however, when Egyptian director Youssef Chahine was awarded the Anniversary Prize at the 50th Cannes Film Festival for his life-time achievements, and his most recent film, **The Destiny**, was screened in the official competition. Egyptian cinema achieved further recognition when **The Captain**, the first film by the director and critic Sayed Saeed, won the golden award at the Damascus Film Festival.

The efforts exerted by the prime minister and the investment authority to boost film production are starting to pay off. Two new companies with sizeable capitals have finally been set up, with contributions from businessmen and cinema people. Some new, high-tech cinemas have opened, including a drive-in, and there have been proposals to build 100 new cinemas in the next 10 years.

There is cause for optimism in the emergence of new directors like Fakhr El-din Negeida, whose **Harmonica** was chosen to represent Egypt at the Cairo International Film Festival in December 1997, winning the award for best Arab picture, and young Atet Hatata, whose debut film **(90–91)**, about the impact of the Gulf War, was eagerly awaited. Another young film-maker, Adel Adeeb, showed great talent with his first feature, **Hysteria**. He was greatly helped by scriptwriter Mohamed Helmy Helal, whose focus on the minute details in the lives of the under-privileged captured the innate tragedy of simple people in a mixed-up society. All in all this was a funny and sincere movie.

In his second movie, **The Champ**, Magdy Ahmad Ali took us to 1920s

Still from Adel Adeeb's HYSTERIA

Still from Magdy Ahmad Ali's THE CHAMP

Alexandria, during the national struggle against British occupation. The film was costly, with art director Salah Marei's lavish production design beautifully capturing the period atmosphere. The film offered some good opportunities to promising actresses, as well as a popular singer who proved successful in his first role in the cinema.

Sex, women and song

Enas El-Degheidi is Egypt's only persistent female director, with 10 films to her credit in 13 years. She dedicated her new feature, **Lace** (*Dantella*), "to every woman who thought she might lose her friend because of a man". It deals with a conflict between two women friends from different social strata over the same man, and ends with them rejecting him and dedicating themselves instead to raising the little girl who is the fruit of their love triangle. The numerous sex scenes caused some controversy, but the director evidently did not care – her next film is entitled **Nudism**!

Ismailia Back and Forth (*Ismailia Rayeh Gaey*) was the surprise hit of 1997–98.

Without the benefit of stars, a large budget or a distinguished director, it still became the biggest box-office success in Egyptian history, thanks to a winning blend of humour, songs, romance, chivalry and warmly characterised relationships. Two traditional star vehicles directed by 58-year-old Nader Galal offered plenty of action and suspense. **48 Hours in Israel** saw star and producer Nadia El Guindy's character transformed from spy to reborn nationalist, while **Message to the Ruler**, the second film starring comedian Adel Imam, jumped forward suddenly from the backward nineteenth century to 1990s Cairo.

By the end of the year we should have seen the second film from Radwan El Kashef, **Dates Wine** (an Egypt/France co-production), a new film by Daud Abdel Sayed, **Land of Fear**, and a film by Khairy Beshara about Princess Diana and her tragic death. Anwar Kawadri, Syrian-born but resident in Britain, has completed **Nasser**, which deals with the life of the leader of the 1952 revolution. Egyptian Television produced Mohamed Kamel El Kaliouby's third film, **Stolen Dreams**, a terrorist drama. A new monthly film magazine, *The Seventh Art*, has been launched, staffed by young critics and published by a famous actor, Mahmoud Hemeda.

FAWZI SOLIMAN is Vice-President of the Egyptian Film Critics Association. He has contributed to magazines and newspapers in Egypt and the Arab world.

Recent and Forthcoming Films

ISMAILIA RAYEH GAEY
(Ismailia Back and Forth)

Script: Ahmad El-Bey. Dir: Karim Dia' Eddin. Phot: Kamal Abdel Aziz. Players: Mohamed Fouad, Mohamed Heneidy, Khaled El Nabawy. Prod: H. Ibrahim.

RESALA ILA EL WALI
(Message to the Ruler)

Script: Bassam Ismail, Bassiony Othman. Dir: Nader Galal. Phot: Samir Farag. Players: Adel Imam, Yusra, Mustapha Metwalli. Prod: Misr Al-Arabiya Film.

DANTELLA (Lace)

Script: Mustapha Moharram and Rafik Sabban. Dir: Inas El-Degheidi. Phot: Samir Bahzan. Players: Yusra, Elham Shahin, Mahmoud Hemeda. Prod: Five Stars (Inas Film).

HYSTERIA

Script: Mohamed Helmi Hilan. Dir: Adel Adeeb. Phot: Ayman Abul Makarem. Players: Ahmad Zaki, Abla Kamel, Sherif Mounir. Prod: Nahid Farid Shawqi.

EL BATAL (The Champ)

Script: Medhat El Adl. Dir: Magdi Ahmad Ali. Phot: Tarek El Telmissany. Players: Ahmad Zaki, Mustapha Kamar, Mohamed Heneidy, Abir Sabry. Prod: El Adl Film.

AFRIT AL NAHAR
(Daylight Devil)

Script: Bassyouny Othman. Dir:

Adel El Aassar. Phot: Samir Farag. Players: Nour El Sherif, Elham Shahin, Hassan Hosny. Prod: Oyun Cine.

AHLAM MASROUKA
(Stolen Dreams)

Script: Mohamed El Refae. Dir: Mohamed Kamel El Kaliouby. Phot: Ramses Marzouk. Players: Farouk El Feshawi, Salway Khattab, Ahlam El Greitly. Prod: Egyptian TV.

Producers and Distributors

Al-Ahram for Cinema & Video
1 Au El Karamat Square
Mohandessin
Cairo
Tel: (20 2) 346 5396
Fax: (20 2) 347 0286

Al-Alamia for TV & Cinema
10 Naguib El-Rehani St.
Cairo
Tel: (20 2) 770 359/770 259
Fax: (20 2) 770 029

Danna Prod. & Dist.
20 Mussadeq St.
Giza
Tel: (20 2) 349 0057
Fax: (20 2) 376 6797

Egyptian Radio & TV Union
Kornish El-Nil, Maspero,
Cairo
Tel: (20 2) 769 584, 575 9313
Fax: (20 2) 574 6989

El-Sultan Film
102 Al Aharam Av.
Giza
Tel: (20 2) 385 5561
Fax: (20 2) 386 000

Hani Fawzi Film
40 Talaat Har St.

Cairo
Tel: (20 2) 767 430
Fax: (20 2) 575 6840

Misr Al Arabiya Films
12 Soliman El-Halaby St.
Cairo
Tel: (20 2) 574 8879
Fax: (20 2) 574 8878

Misr International
35 Champollion St.
Cairo
Tel: (20 2) 578 8034/578 8124
Fax: (20 2) 578 8033

El Adl Film
4 Oraby Sq.
Cairo
Tel: (20 2) 579 0290
Fax: (20 2) 579 5295

Sphinx Film
2 Behlar St. (Kasr El-Nil St.)
Cairo
Tel: (20 2) 392 0709
Fax: (20 2) 392 0710

Studio 13
Soliman El-Halaby St.
Cairo
Tel: (20 2) 574 8807
Fax: (20 2) 578 1406

Tamido
55 Mohamed Farid St.
Nozha, Heliopolis
Cairo
Tel: (20 2) 247 0461
Fax: (20 2) 247 1203

Useful Addresses

Academy of Arts
City of Arts
Gamal El-Din El-Afghany St.
Giza
Tel: (20 2) 561 3995
Fax: (20 2) 561 1034

Chamber of Film Industry
33 Oraby St.
Cairo
Tel: (20 2) 574 1677
Fax: (20 2) 575 1583

Cultural Development Fund
Opera Area, Gezira
Cairo
Tel: (20 2) 340 4234/340 7001
Fax: (20 2) 340 6759

National Film Centre
City of Arts
Al Ahram Avenue
Giza
Tel: (20 2) 585 4801
Fax: (20 2) 585 4701

Still from MESSAGE TO THE RULER

ESTONIA

Jaan Ruus

Following long debates in oversized commissions, the Estonian Minister of Culture finally signed the edict establishing the Estonian Film Foundation in May 1997. The goal of this Scandinavian-type institution is to develop and support national film culture, including film development, production and distribution. Its first annual budget was $1.2m (17.8m crowns). Its first major task was to take over the buildings and properties of Tallinnfilm, the former state monopoly corporation, sell them and use the revenue to build a new cinema centre (screening halls, editing rooms, laboratory etc), which should be completed in 2000.

Sixty-five small production companies are active in Estonia, mostly producing video documentaries and commercials. After last year's silence, however, a feature has been produced: Hardi Volmer's **All My Lenins** (*Minu Leninid*). It takes real-life Estonian secret agent Aleksander Keskküla, and involves him in a fantasy in which, in pre-First World War Europe, the German government helps him establish a school for Lenin clones in Switzerland. Volmer delivers a fascinating and darkly comic tale of the illegal machinations of Bolsheviks. The temperamental and amusing Lenin, played by Viktor Sukhorukov, from St Petersburg, is the sixteenth performance of the role in a film from the former Soviet Union. Sukhorukov was awarded the year's Best Film Actor award.

Scriptwriters and directors have prepared various features, but the chronic shortage of finance has prevented them from proceeding beyond the development stage. Only a few producers have succeeded in breaking out of the isolation of the domestic market. The minimum budget of a feature is approximately $350,000, but the state – the principal and,

Viktor Sukhorukov with his Best Estonian Film Actor award *photo: Sven Tupits*

practically non-existent, while promotion and distribution outside Estonia are totally chaotic. In 1997, total cinema attendance was 973,844 – falling below a million for the first time in Estonian history. The number of cinemagoers falls as ticket prices rise. The average in 1997 was $2.40, up 25 per cent on 1996.

The number of cinemas decreases as well: in 1995, there were 134, but in 1997 just 110, and only 34 of these show films at least three days a week. Only one cinema has two screens. Approximately one in five Estonian households has a video recorder and video piracy has become a serious problem, attracting much media coverage. In 1997 there were 83 new films screened (68 from the US). Approximate calculations suggest a total box office take of $2.35m, but the statistical base is inadequate, and some distribution companies keep their revenue secret.

often, the only financier – has fixed the maximum subsidy at $175,000 per project. Total state support for film production in 1997 was $1.2m, plus $106,000 for distribution. In addition, Cultural Endowment, which receives its income from taxes on alcohol, tobacco and gambling, provided the film industry with $525,000.

Rise and fall

Most films' only route to audiences is via the country's four TV channels (one public and three commercial). Marketing is

Estonian FIPRESCI named Mark Soosaar's **Father, Son and Holy Torum** as Film of the Year. It contrasted the ways of life of an Ostyak shaman living in western Siberia and his son, who does business with Russian dealers. The film drew a striking parallel with the American Indians' fight against oil companies, and proved that, in this crisis situation when producers yearn for an increase in state subsidy, documentaries are perhaps the only solution.

JAAN RUUS is film critic for the biggest Estonian weekly, the Tallinn-based *Eesti Ekspress*. He is a member of the board of the Estonian Film Foundation and is Chairman of its Commission of Experts.

Recent and Forthcoming Films

KOLM KIUSATUST (Me, Myself and I)

Script: Jaak Kilmi, Peter Herzog, Rainer Sarnet, Taavi Eelma. Dir: Kilmi, Herzog, Sarnet. Prod: Exitfilm (Estonia)/Zentropa (Denmark).

Three picaresque short stories following the exploits of Jan the adventurer, Florian the playboy and Paul the singer.

LURJUS (An Affair of Honour)

Script and Dir: Valentin Kuik. Players: Taavi Eelma. Prod: OnFilm F-Film

What would happen in today's world if men solved questions of honour by duelling? Based on the story by Vladimir Nabokov.

VEE JOON (Waterline)

Script: Toomas Raudam. Dir: Peeter Simm. Prod: Lege Artis.

A tragi-comic story of a curious little town.

SOO (Swamp)

Script: Arvo Valton. Dir: Renita and Hannes Lintrop. Prod: SEE.

A French artist travels to Estonia and meets a mysterious girl and a group of smugglers on a swampland farm.

K'IK MOONID ON PIKAD (All Poppies Are Tall)

Script and Dir: Aare Tilk. Prod: Aristo.

Tragi-comic tale of a rock band in an Estonian market town in the late 1960s.

LEND (MEES VINCIST)

Script: Indrek Ude, Toomas Sula, Toomas Muru. Prod: Nikodemus Film.

Romantic comedy about Lobatchevsky's images of a man and a woman.

Producers

A Film
Kaare 15
EE 0016 Tallinn
Tel: (372) 670 6485
Fax: (372) 670 6433
e-mail: afilm@online.ee

Allfilm
Saue 11
EE 0006 Tallinn
Tel: (372) 502 1989
Fax: (372) 642 7115
e-mail: allfilm@datanet.ee

Cumulus Project
Köleri 32-2
EE 0010 Tallinn
Tel: (372 2) 426 645
Fax: (372) 640 9118
e-mail: iho@dpu.ee

Eesti Joonisfilm
Laulupeo 2
EE 0001 Tallinn
Tel: (372) 641 9047
Fax: (372) 641 9047
e-mail: joonis@online.ee

Eesti Telefilm
Faehlmanni 12
EE 0100 Tallinn
Tel: (372 2) 434 540
Fax: (372) 631 2089

Taavi Eelmaa in AN AFFAIR OF HONOUR

EXITfilm
Kaupmehe 10-11
EE 0001 Tallinn
Tel: (372) 631 7995
Fax: (372 2) 448 416

Faama Film
Pärnu mnt 67 A
EE 0001 Tallinn
Tel: (372) 646 2027
Fax: (372) 646 2028
e-mail: faama@saturn.zzz.ee

FilmiMAX
Uus 3
EE 0001 Tallinn
Tel: (372) 244 3436
Fax: (372) 646 4164

Freyja Film
Regati 8
EE 0019 Tallinn
Tel/Fax: (372 2) 238 682

F-Seitse
Narva mnt 63
EE 0001 Tallinn
Tel: (372 2) 421 808
Fax: (372 2) 421 803
e-mail: fseitse@online.ee

Gaviafilm
Kivila 42-61
EE 0038 Tallinn
Tel: (372) 523 2554

Kairiin
Säpruse pst 175-53
EE 0034 Tallinn
Tel/Fax: (372 2) 520 182
e-mail: jyri@datanet.ee

Lege Artis Film
Narva mnt 5
EE 0001 Tallinn
Tel: (372) 437 733
Fax: (372) 648 8014

Myth Film
Söstra 3-11
EE 0006 Tallinn
Tel/Fax: (372) 656 6117

Nikodemus Film
Kaupmehe 6
EE 0001 Tallinn
Tel/Fax: (372) 642 6682
e-mail: niko@online.ee

Nukufilm
Kaupmehe 6
EE 0001 Tallinn
Tel/Fax: (372 2) 442 770

OMAfilm
Tatari 21B-12
EE 0001 Tallinn
Tel/Fax: (372) 646 6249
e-mail: omafilm@online.ee

ONfilm
Lasnamäe 24-12
EE 0014 Tallinn
Tel: (372 2) 215 296

Polarfilm
Gonsiori 29
EE 0001 Tallinn
Tel: (372 2) 421 880
Fax: (372) 626 9973

Raamat-film
Tähe 5-3
EE 0016 Tallinn
Tel/Fax: (372) 670 0778

Rao Heidmets Filmstudio
Tartu mnt 47-48
EE 0001 Tallinn
Tel: (372) 502 4906
e-mail: eva@er.ee

SEE
Uus 3
EE 0001 Tallinn
Tel/Fax: (372 2) 446 644

Weiko Saawa Film
Nikolai 15-4
EE 3600 Pärnu
Tel: (372) 444 3869
Fax: (372) 443 0774
e-mail: doctest@Chaplin.ee

Distributors

BDG
Vana-Posti 8
EE 0001 Tallinn
Tel: (372) 631 4394
Fax: (372) 631 3023
e-mail: bdg@bdg.ee

FilmiMAX
Uus 3
EE 0001 Tallinn
Tel: (372 2) 443 436
Fax: (372) 646 4164

MPDE
Pärnu mnt 45
EE 0001 Tallinn
Tel: (372) 631 4546
Fax: (372) 631 3671
e-mail: info@mpde.ee

Useful Address

Estonian Film Foundation
Harju 9
EE 0001 Tallinn
Tel: (372) 641 1120
Fax: (372) 644 2356
e-mail: estfilm@estpak.ee

FINLAND

Antti Selkokari

After a decade of depressingly low attendance figures between 1987 and 1996, cinema admissions in Finland in 1997 rose to 5.9 million, up more than eight per cent on the previous year. With Finns flocking to see *Titanic* in the same huge numbers as every other nationality, audience figures for the first half of 1998 had increased by an astonishing 37 per cent compared to 1997.

One of the domestic films contributing to this leap was **A Summer By The River**, written and directed by Markku Pölönen. His film about father and son lumberjacks in the 1950s was a big hit by Finnish standards, with 265,000 admissions by August. With its vulgar humour and nostalgic touch, it hit all the right buttons in the Finnish psyche.

Some domestic films also did fairly well in 1997. The best was Jarmo Lampela's **Freakin Beautiful World** (*Sairaan kaunis maailma*), with 67,815 admissions. Lampela's debut feature, with its music

video-style editing and youth-oriented marketing, attracted more people than popular comedies, which used to rule the domestic box-office in the 1970s and 1980s. **Kummeli Gold Fever** (*Kummeli kultakuume*), a spin-off from a popular TV series, was the most successful domestic film (fourteenth in the annual chart), with 100,051 admissions.

In February 1998 the Finnish Film Foundation and the four national television channels agreed to commit about $5.5m (30 million marks) to support the making of ten feature films a year over the next three years. Many of the films financed this way will be shown on the small screen as mini-series after their theatrical release. Television remains the most important arena for films, with the TV companies using movies as a key weapon in the battle for a larger audience share.

Now that the former distribution and exhibition monopoly of Finnkino has been

Still from the hugely popular A SUMMER BY THE RIVER

broken down, the American majors, which previously worked with Finnkino, have branch offices in Helsinki. Distributors are convinced that business will boom from November 1998, when two new multiplexes open their doors in Helsinki, with ten and 14 screens, respectively, and state-of-the-art technology. Finnkino and Sandrew-Metronome are eagerly awaiting opportunities to build multiplexes in all of Finland's key cities.

Cutting crew under scrutiny

Finnish film censors have become notorious for their intolerance, especially of gory horror movies. But the rating system hitherto controlled by the state-run Finnish Board of Film Classification seems certain to change. Since the ban on *The Texas Chainsaw Massacre* was lifted in November 1996, there has been much wider discussion about the relevance of film censorship and when Antti Alanen, former programming director of the Finnish Film Archive, was appointed as director of the classification board he declared he wished to make himself unemployed.

The film classification law was reviewed by a committee appointed by the Ministry of Culture in April 1998. The committee's report proposes a standardisation of classification for all audio-visual products, with the same rules applying to cinema, video, DVD (scheduled for launch in Finland in autumn 1998) and television. At press time the government had yet to decide between continuing with state-run

censorship or setting up a self-regulatory system, modelled on the American MPAA ratings, with the film business itself determining the borders of taste and decency.

Looking down the list of forthcoming films, it is clear that Finnish directors are relying heavily on literary sources. How successfully films inspired by Finnish literature will travel remains to be seen. One of the most interesting features in production is **Rolling Stone** (*Rolling Stone - Aleksis Kiven elämä*), directed by Jari Halonen, the former *enfant terrible* of Finnish theatre and the director of films such as *Back to the USSR* and *Christmas Part*.

Literary horizons

Halonen is sure to make a provocative film out of the life of the hugely respected Finnish writer, Aleksis Kivi, who died in poverty and has acquired the status of a national treasure. It will also be interesting to see what will become of Kaisa Rastimos' **A Respectable Tragedy** (*Säädyllinen murhenäytelmä*), based on a novel depicting the life of the Finnish upper middle class just before the Second World War.

The brothers Kaurismäki are back at work. Mika Kaurismäki's **Los Angeles Without A Map** is based on British writer Richard Reyner's novel about a young Brit bound for Hollywood. An international cast star alongside the Leningrad Cowboys. While Mika is working hard to achieve the international acclaim he so badly wants, Aki Kaurismäki chooses his own individual path with **Juha**, based on a classic nineteenth-century Finnish novel. The black-and-white film will be silent, with captioned dialogue (a familiar device in Aki's earlier films) and a score by Anssi Tikanmäki.

Finally, Finnish cinema lost one of its most distinguished figures when Jaakko Talaskivi died at home in March 1998. The son of Paula Talaskivi, for decades the chief film critic for *Helsingin Sanomat*, he dedicated his life to film. He began his

career as a child actor in 1955 and worked his way up through Finnish film studios in a variety of jobs. In the 1970s he directed and produced two children's musicals, and in the 1980s worked as a production director on several Kaurismäki films, including *Worthless*. Talaskivi was highly respected by his industry colleagues and film critics.

ANTTI SELKOKARI is a film critic for Tampere-based morning newspaper *Aamulehti*, and president of the film section of the Finnish Critics' Association.

Still from Pirjo Honkasalo's FIRE-EATER
photo: Marja-Leena Hukkanen

Recent and Forthcoming Films

KESKIYÜN AURINKO (Midnight Sun)

Script: Patrick Amos. Dir: Ilkka Järvi-Laturi. Players: Bill Pullman, Irène Jacob.

Post-Cold War romantic espionage comedy set in Helsinki, with Jacob as a KGB agent and Pullman a seasoned CIA man.

PITKÄ KUUMA KESÄ (A Long Hot Summer)

Script and Dir: Perttu Leppä. Prod: Johannes Lassila, Talent House/MRP Oy.

Story of an aspiring rock star who moves from Helsinki to a small town and ends up managing an eccentric band.

HÄJYT (The Tough Ones)

Script: Aleksi Bardy. Dir: Aleksi Mäkelä. Players: Samuli Edelman, Teemu Lehtillä, Julia Veijonen. Prod: Solar Films Inc. Oy.

A young law student gets a summer job as district police superintendent in his hometown and helps two ex-con friends build a new life.

RIKOS JA RAKKAUS (Love and Crime)

Script: Pekka Milonoff, based on a novel by Jari Tervo. Dir: Milonoff. Prod: Claes Olsson and Petteri Pasanen.

The mysterious murder of a charismatic

small-time criminal sets off a series of absurd events.

VIENA 1941 (Ambush)

Script: Antti Tuuri and Olli Saarela, based on Tuuri's novel. Dir: Saarela. Prod: Marko Röhr and Ilkka Matila.

Drama based on the experiences of a Finnish army major during the first days of the Continuation War between Finland and the Soviet Union.

ROLLING STONE – ALEKSIS KIVEN ELÄMÄ (Rolling Stone)

Script: Jari Halonen and Jorm Tommila. Dir and Prod: Halonen.

A poor young man falls in love with the daughter of a rich master tailor and determines to become a writer to overcome the class barrier obstructing his romantic chances.

MARKET (Kiss Me in the Rain) [working titles]

Script: Antii Karumo. Dir:Veikko Aaltonen. Prod: Lasse Saarinen.

Drama about the relationship between a policeman's widow and a compassionate housewife who becomes obsessed with the widow's tragedy.

KULKURI JA JOUTSEN (The Swan and the Wanderer)

Script: Timo Koivusalo and Juha

Numminen. Dir and Prod: Koivusalo.

Story of a hugely popular musical trio.

LOS ANGELES WITHOUT A MAP

Script: Mika Kaurismäki and Richard Reyner, from the novel by Reyner. Dir: Kaurismäki. Phot: Michel Amathieu. Players: David Tennant, Vanessa Shaw, Vincent Gallo, Julie Delpy. Prod: Marianna Films.

JUHA

Script and Dir: Aki Kaurismäki. Phot: Timo Salminen. Players: Sakari Kuosmanen, Kati Outinen, Andre Wilms, Kati Outinen, Esko Nikkari. Prod: Sputnik Films.

POIKA JA ILVES (The Boy And The Lynx)

Script and Dir: Raimo O. Niemi and Ville Suhonen. Phot: Kari Sohlberg. Players: Konsta Hietanen, AnttiVirmavirta, Kristiina Halttu, Jarmo Mäkinen and Väiski (the lynx). Prod: Wildcat Production.

HIEKKAMORSIAN(Sand Bride)

Script: Eeva Tikka and Pia Tikka. Dir: Pia Tikka. Phot: Olli Varja. Players: Liisi Tandefelt, Rui Polanah, Maria Järvenhelmi,

Juha Mäkelä, Kristo Salminen.
Prod: Oblomovies and Marianna
FilmsProd: MRP Matila & Röhr
Productions.

KULTALA (Goldfish)
Script: Heikki Vuento. Dir: Åke
Lindman. Prod: Åke Lindman
Film-Productions.

**MUSTA KISSA LUMIHANGELLA
(Black Cat On The Snow)**
Dir: Anu Kuivalainen. Phot:
Marita Hällfors. Prod: Lasse
Saarinen/Kinotar.

Producers

Dada-Filmi Oy/Fennada-Filmi Oy
Kolmas linja 5
FIN-00530 Helsinki
Tel: (358 9) 737 788
Fax: (358 9) 730 734

GNU-films Oy
Aleksis Kiven katu 26 C
FIN-00500 Helsinki
Tel: (358 9) 726 1525
Fax: (358 9) 726 1536
e-mail: tero@gnn.pp.fi

Jörn Donner Productions Oy
Pohjoisranta 12
FIN-17000 Helsinki
Tel: (358 9) 135 6060
Fax: (358 9) 135 7568

Kinofinlandia Oy
Maurinkatu 2
FIN-00170 Helsinki
Tel: (358 9) 278 1783
Fax: (358 9) 278 1763

**Kinotar Oy/
For Real Productions Oy**
Meritullinkatu 33
FIN-00170 Helsinki
Tel: (358 9) 135 1864
Fax: (358 9) 135 7864
e-mail: kinotar@co.inet.fi

**Kinotuotanto Oy/
Kinoproduction Ltd**
Katajanokankatu 6
FIN-00160 Helsinki
Tel: (358 9) 663 217
Fax: (358 9) 662 048

Marko Röhr Productions Oy
Tallberginkatu 1A/141
FIN-00180 Helsinki
Tel: (358 9) 685 2227
Fax: (358 9) 685 2229
e-mail mrp@surfnet.fi

Reppufilmi Oy
Pohjoinen Rautatienkatu 17 A 16
FIN-00100 Helsinki
Tel: (358 9) 498 284/498 378
Fax: (358 9) 441 843

**Villealfa Filmproductions
Oy/Sputnik Films/Marianna
Films/Oblomovies Oy**
Pursimiehenkatu 25
FIN-00150 Helsinki
Tel: (358 9) 622 1811
Fax: (358 9) 622 3855

Solar Films Oy
Kiviaidankatu 1, 4 krs
FIN-00210 Helsinki
Tel: (358 9) 682 3622
Fax: (358 9) 682 3410
e-mail: markus.selin@solarfilms.com

Åke Lindman Film-Productions
Elimäenkatu 14-16C
FIN-00150 Helsinki
Tel: (358 9) 736 300
Fax: (358 9) 737 700

Distributors

Buena Vista Int. Finland Oy
Kaisaniemenkatu 1 C 110
FIN-00100 Helsinki
Tel: (358 9) 2530 3200, 2530 3224
Fax: (358 9) 2530 3220

Cinema Mondo Oy
Unioninkatu 10
FIN-00130 Helsinki
Tel: (358 9) 629 528/177 501
Fax: (358 9) 631 450

**Columbia TriStar Egmont Film
Filmdistributors**
Runeberginkatu 60 B
FIN-00260 Helsinki
Tel: (358 9) 4764 460
Fax: (358 9) 4764 4660

Finnkino Oy
Koivuvaaranjuja 2

FIN-01640 Vantaa
Tel: (358 9) 131 191, 1311 9323
Fax: (358 9) 852 7206

Kamras Film Group Oy
Mikonkatu 19
FIN-00100 Helsinki
Tel: (358 9) 6220 0260
Fax: (358 9) 6220 0261

Kinoscreen Oy
Katajanokankatu 6
FIN-00160 Helsinki
Tel: (358 9) 663 717
Fax: (358 9) 622 048

Scanbox Finland Oy
Vapaalantie 2 B 26
FIN-01650 Vantaa
Tel: (358 9) 854 5560
Fax: (358 9) 8545 5611

United International Pictures Oy
Kaisaniemenkatu I C 98
FIN-00100 Helsinki
Tel: (358 9) 684 1007
Fax: (358 9) 6841 0010

Warner Bros Finland Oy
Kaisaniemenkatu 1 b
FIN-00100 Helsinki
Tel: (358 9) 8624 5806, 8624 5808
Fax: (358 9) 8624 5810

Useful Addresses

**Central Organisation of Finnish
Film Producers**
Kaisaniemenkatu 3 B 29
FIN-00160 Helsinki
Tel: (358 9) 636 305
Fax: (358 9) 176 689

Finnish Film Foundation
Kanavakatu 12
FIN-00160 Helsinki
Tel: (358 9) 622 0300
Fax: (358 9) 6220 3060, 6220 3050
Internet: lumo@kaapeli.fi

Finnish Cinema Association
Finnish Film Chamber
Kaisaniemenkatu 3 B
FIN-00100 Helsinki
Tel: (358 9) 636 305
Fax: (358 9) 176 689

FRANCE — Michel Ciment

In the 1980s, the fashion among a number of French intellectuals was to announce the death of cinema. Disillusioned ex-Maoists, such as the well-known critic Serge Daney, were proclaiming the disappearance of their once beloved art. A hundred years ago, Louis Lumière himself saw no future for his invention. Strangely for the end of a millennium – historically a time to expect disasters – the tendency today is to celebrate the good health of the medium.

Attendance is rising, and in many countries production levels are soaring. France is no exception. The 1998 Cannes Film Festival witnessed no backlash after the celebration of its fiftieth anniversary last year: there had never been larger crowds, nor so many journalists. The event itself embodies some of the contradictions inherent in this industrial art, or artistic industry. The phenomenal success of the festival, the importance of its market and all the media coverage all go hand in hand with highly sophisticated choices for its main awards in recent years: Theo Angelopoulos, Shohei Imamura, Abbas Kiarostami, Atom Egoyan, Mike Leigh and Chen Kaige are hardly huge crowd-pleasers.

This was also the year when the Minister of Culture, Catherine Trautmann, finally announced the opening, in 2000, of the House of Cinema (formerly less modestly labelled the Palace of Cinema), which will be located in the now disused American Centre built by Frank Gehry in 1993. The building will contain three screening rooms, a library, the Langlois Museum, a restaurant and a bookstore. The Cinémathèque Française and the BiFi will thus be united in one space, at long last offering French filmgoers a place to study cinema's past (as well as its present, one hopes) in the best possible surroundings.

Soaring to new heights

Cinema attendance in 1997 rose to 148.1 million, 12 million more than the previous year, and total box-office receipts were $873m (5.15 billion francs). This was a spectacular rise, following year-on-year increases of six million in 1995 and 1996. American films took 53.8 per cent of the market (the lowest share in Europe), French films 34.5 per cent. British films *Bean* and *The Full Monty* did very well, but the total attendance for non-French, non-English-speaking pictures was less than four per cent of the total. There is obviously less and less curiosity for outlandish films, while just 30 titles accounted for half the total box-office take.

While an average viewer watches 85 hours' worth of cinema films a year on television, the high levels of small-screen consumption through TV or video rentals do not slacken the public's appetite for movies in theatres. Almost 40 per cent of the audience go to the movies at least once a month (as against 33.6 per cent in 1990). The slight decrease in ticket prices (the average is now $5.50), combined with the rapid development of multiplexes, and a dissatisfaction with poor-quality television programmes explain cinema's growing popularity.

In 1997, 185 new screens in 57 new theatres opened, 80 per cent of them in multiplexes. Multiplexes claimed 17.3 per cent of the box-office total (up from 10.8 per cent in 1996). This explains the increase in attendance on the outskirts of Paris (up 17.3 per cent) and in towns of more than 100,000 inhabitants (up 12.5 per cent), the areas where most multiplexes are sited, whereas in Paris itself there was a meagre one per cent rise. The few remaining independent theatre owners continue to fear the defection of their audiences to these huge screen complexes.

In the best of health

But it is the vitality and the variety, both economic and artistic, of production which is a flourishing industry's strongest asset. In 1997, 163 films were produced in France, as against 134 the year before. Of these, 125 had wholly or predominantly French financial backing (as against 104 in 1996). These figures make France the most prolific producer in Europe, with the largest number of screens to project the films (4,519). Production investment also rose sharply: $780m, compared to $560m in 1996. The average budget was $4.7m ($4.1m in 1996) – not taking into account the cost of *The Fifth Element*, defined as a French film because it was produced by Gaumont, but made in English and marketed like a Hollywood movie.

As usual, the industry benefited from strong external support, with almost 40 per cent of finance coming from television channels; half the films produced were international co-productions. Film-making trends followed twin paths: more films with big budgets and, conversely, more with small budgets. Among the latter group were many first films. There were 46 debuts this season (the most for ten years) and 13 film-makers directed their second feature.

In all, 394 films were distributed (an average of eight per week!): 151 French, 145 American and 98 for the rest of the world, including 25 British. There was an increase in the number of films opening in more than 100 theatres; 52 opened in more than 300 theatres, as against 39 in 1996. The danger, of course, is that wide releases become huge flops while simultaneously stifling smaller films. French films exported well, to bring in international income of $68.5m (an increase of 12 per cent).

A unique combination

The best French films are by no means the most popular, and even Hollywood, which was able in its heyday to combine quality and large box-office grosses, has lost the secret. So the huge commercial and critical success of Alain Resnais' marvellous **On Connait la chanson** was a formidable and unexpected event: it sold 2.6 million tickets to rank fifteenth in the year's box-office

Still from Alain Resnais' ON CONNAIT LA CHANSON

chart and won Césars for best film, best screenplay, best actress and best supporting actor and actress. Resnais' triumph, and that of Eric Rohmer with his latest, *Conte d'Automne*, show that directors in their seventies, still at the top of their creative powers, continue to co-exist on the French scene with daring newcomers: a situation seemingly unparalleled in any other country.

The most disturbing and audacious first film of the year was probably Gaspar Noé's **Seul contre tous** (winner of the Critics' Week award in Cannes), an interior monologue by a former butcher who hates the world, his wife, unemployment, the state of the country and anything that confronts his eye. This was a hurricane of despair and nihilism, shot in splendid cinemascope with a rare sense of composition.

Its dark humour can be contrasted with another first feature, Bruno Podalydes' **Dieu seul me voit**, in which the director's brother, Denis, plays a protagonist always hesitating between two paths, two women, two ideas. One thinks of Tati in front of this intelligent, graphic portrayal, rich in slow-burning gags, of a fumbling hero. Already responsible for a brilliant short, *Versailles, Rive Gauche*, the Podalydes brothers may become the most inventive comedy authors of their generation.

Olivier Ducastel and screenwriter Jacques Martineau have trodden fearlessly on Jacques Demy's territory in **Jeanne et le garçon formidable**, a musical comedy with some inventive lyrics that concentrates on a love story between a free-spirited woman (splendid Virginie Ledoyen) who falls in love with a young man (Mathieu Demy, son of Jacques) stricken by Aids. One forgets the pastiche to enjoy a sad story transformed into a hymn to life.

Reality bites

Another debut, **La Vie rêvée des anges**, by Erick Zonca, caused a sensation in Cannes, its two leads, Elodie Bouchez and Natacha Régnier, jointly winning Best Actress. In

Elodie Bouchez and Natacha Régnier in LA VIE REVEE DES ANGES

Still from JEANNE ET LE GARÇON FORMIDABLE

the realistic manner so heavily favoured by young French film-makers, *La Vie...* depicts the complex relationship between a heroine who stays for a while with another girl, a stranger whose mystery she will slowly learn to approach. The quality of the writing and the exceptionally natural acting lift this far above an ordinary slice of life.

Jacques Nolot's **L'Arrière pays** chooses a minimalist style to follow the return of its hero (played by the director), a homosexual, to his home village to attend his mother's funeral. Christophe Ruggia warmly depicts a more traditional realism in **Le Gone de Chaaba**, following a bunch of kids of Algerian origin in the Lyons suburbs.

The diversity of talent amongst France's novice film-makers is also well illustrated by four more features: Manual Pradal's **Marie Baie des Anges**, with flamboyant, virtuoso camerawork evoking a story of tragic young love; Olivier Peray's

Sandrine Kiberlain in Laetitia Masson's A VENDRE

hommage to Rohmer in **Petits désordres amoureux** (named Best First European Film in Berlin) is a witty portrait of a Don Juan who finds himself impotent in front of a dominant woman. **Mange ta soupe**, by Mathieu Amalric (who also plays the lead), explores the comic, strained relationship between a young man and his domineering, book-worm mother, while talented François Ozon, with **Sitcom**, fails in his would-be sexually scandalous comedy about a family's incestuous relationships.

Women on top form

Six female cinéastes confirmed their vigour and audacity with second or third features, especially in confronting their heroines' sex lives. Frankest of all was Laetitia Masson's **A Vendre**, with Sandrine Kiberlain in the lead – as in Masson's first feature, *En Avoir (Ou Pas)* – as a woman who sells herself and is pursued by an emotionally troubled private eye. Masson avoids all the trappings of her theme by refusing a naturalistic approach in favour of an intense, Romanesque style. The same qualities surface in Nicole Garcia's third feature, **Place Vendome**, where she cracks the veneer of fellow actress Catherine Deneuve, who is particularly effective as a jeweller's widow dealing with her equally complex past and present.

In **Si je t'aime, prends garde à toi**, Jeanne LaBrune plunges us headlong into a physical passion between a sexually overwhelmed Nathalie Baye and Daniel Duval as her bullying lover. The spiral of self-destruction is described with relentless energy. As for Sandrine Veysset, after *Y Aura-t-il de la Neige a Noël?* she retained the same mix of realism and fantasy in **Victor ... pendant qu'il est trop tard** to describe the relationship between a prostitute and a drifting kid who has killed his father.

Anne Fontaine, in **Nettoyage à sec**, describes with meticulous realism the disorder created in a couple of provincial dyers (Miou-Miou, Charles Berling) by the arrival of a beautiful stranger who – *Teorema*-like – seduces both husband and wife. Noémie Lvovsky's second feature, **Petites** (made for television), demonstrates incredible energy in painting the maverick, reckless behaviour of a group of teenage schoolgirls.

Some of these women's male counterparts are on a par when it comes to hard-hitting approaches, sexual or otherwise, whether it be Cedric Kahn in **L'Ennui**, his adaptation of Alberto Moravia's novel, *La Noia*, in which a square young man (Charles Berling) is sexually intoxicated by a dumb, plump and uncouth girl, or Claude Mouriéras, whose **Dis moi que je rêve** mixes humour and harsh realism à la Pialat in his portrayal of a peasant family in which a retarded son finally discovers that he has a brother even less intellectually capable than himself.

This new generation of talented directors also includes Pierre Salvadori, whose off-beat humour is particularly evident in **Comme elle respire**, where Marie

Still from Claude Mouriéras' DIS-MOI QUE JE REVE
photo: Frédéric Goujon

Trintignant plays a compulsive liar whose crazy fantasies lead her to impossible ordeals, and Tony Gatliff's **Gadjo Dilo** where he continues his portrayal of the gypsy world, this time with the journey of a Frenchman in search of a lost song in Eastern Europe.

Favourite themes

More established directors also delivered accomplished works. After several forays into new thematic territories (such as *Tous les matins du monde*), Alain Corneau comes back to his favourite genre, crime, with **Le Cousin**, a realistic, morally complex portrait of a police inspector and his drug dealer informant (Patrick Timsit). Jacques Doillon, in **Trop (Peu) d'amour**, resumes his psychodrama of seduction and sexual strategies: a married film director welcomes into his country house a teenager who offers to help him write a screenplay, while playing – half innocently, half mischievously – with him, his wife and his daughter's boyfriend.

In **Une Chance sur deux**, Patrice Leconte reunited Alain Delon and Jean-Paul Belmondo for the first time in decades, in an adventure film where the two ageing stars make fun of themselves as tired heroes, an ironical treatment that did not seem to please their fans. Patrice Chéreau, in **Ceux qui m'aiment prendront le train**, wants to escape from his theatrical training by using dazzling camera work à la Lars von Trier in telling the story of a group of people going by train to a funeral and the complex relationships which ensue.

Benoît Jacquot scored twice (at the Venice and Cannes competitions, though without winning any prizes), with **Le Septième Ciel**, a comedy-drama (starring real-life couple Sandrine Kiberlain and Vincent Lindon) about a frigid woman who consults a hypnotist and, once cured, sees her husband become impotent, and **L'Ecole de la chair**, adapted from a Mishima novel about a middle-aged woman (Isabelle Huppert) who falls in love with a young man.

Claude Miller's forte has always been to create a feeling of unease within a rigorous narration, a talent in evidence in his adaptation of Emmanuel Carrère's best-seller **La Classe de neige**, winner of the Jury Prize in Cannes and the first film produced by Warner Brothers-France. The story of a child sent to a winter sports camp who starts to develop feelings of anxiety proves a powerful exercise in the uncanny. Unease is also the subject of Christian Vincent's **Je ne vois pas ce qu'on me trouve**, but in a lighter mood, as melancholy mixes with deadpan humour. A stand-up comic (Jacky Beroyer) goes back to his native town as guest of honour for an evening at a film club, tries in vain to seduce the club's PR woman and eventually decides not to show up at the event.

Most of French cinema's elder statesmen were active this season. Philippe de Broca's talent for swashbucklers was conspicuous in his new version of **Le Bossu**, with Daniel Auteuil in the lead, a costume film with gusto and a sense of action. Claude Lelouch, forgetting his sometimes dubious tendency to philosophise, was at his best in **Hasards ou coincidences**, in which, as is his wont, he playfully jumps from place to place: Venice, Canada, Mexico, New York, Istanbul serve as locations in a story of love and loss which has the charm and grief of a light romance.

Claude Chabrol celebrated his fiftieth film with **Rien ne va plus**, a minor but pleasant comedy of two civilised crooks (Michel Serrault and Isabelle Huppert)

Michel Serrault and Isabelle Huppert in RIEN NE VA PLUS

who face unexpected entanglements in the West Indies. With the help of a splendid Sandrine Bonnaire, Jacques Rivette tried his hand at criminal melodrama and produced the overlong **Secret Defense**.

Still masters of their art

But probably the two greatest achievements came from Resnais, 75, and Rohmer, 78. Resnais' *On connait la chanson*, weaves a tale of chance meetings and family relationships in contemporary Paris, using old and new popular songs to express the inner feelings of the protagonists. The dialogue switches seamlessly to singing thanks to technically perfect post-synchronisation, where an actress surprisingly may be dubbed by a male singer and vice versa. But this brilliant and funny comedy hides beneath its surface a melancholy commentary about death, illness, ageing couples, selfishness and unemployment.

Rohmer's *Tales of Four Seasons* ended with **Conte d'automne**. Set in the south of France, it has a mellower mood than the other three tales, probably due to the age of protagonists enjoying their Indian summer. The director views with tenderness two of his former actresses (Beatrice Romand and Marie Rivière), now in their forties, as the latter tries to find a husband for the former. Rohmer's delicious strategies again work beautifully; the autumn of the tale is also the triumphant season of its patriarch director.

Often accused, somewhat unfairly, of not being sufficiently in tune with contemporary social and political issues in its features (as opposed to the topical trend in British movies), French cinema nevertheless offers a nice spectrum of documentaries. With many specialised festivals in this field (including Marseilles, Brest and Lussas), a cable station, Planète, devoted to the genre, and substantial production support from ARTE and Canal+, this is a very active field.

For example, Yamina Benguigui's **Mémoires d'immigrées** is a complex and brilliant three-hour panorama on the lives and dreams of Algerian women in France. Raymond Depardon, in **Paris**, interviews various young women (including some professional actresses) picked up at the Gare Saint Lazare for a possible role in a forthcoming film, and delivers a kaleidoscopic portrait of today's youth. Dominique Cabrera, in **Demain et Encore Demain**, offers a home video about her private life, while Alain Ferrari's **Milice Film Noir** investigates an obscure and particularly shameful part of France's past: the over-zealous extreme-right militia that killed people during the occupation with a brutality comparable to that of the SS.

MICHEL CIMENT is one of France's most eminent critics and commentators on the cinema. An editor of *Positif*, and a lecturer on film at universities in France and abroad, he has also made documentaries on various directors.

The copious archives of the late François Truffaut have been entrusted to BiFi, the excellent new repository for books, magazines, posters, and documents in Paris. They will be available to students and professionals for consultation from late 1998 onwards.

photo: Kobal Collection

Producers

Alexandre Films
14 rue de Marignan
75008 Paris
Tel: (33 1) 4495 8989
Fax: (33 1) 4289 2689

Alter Films
4 Rue Treilhard
75008 Paris
Tel: (33 1) 4256 1297
Fax: (33 1) 4256 4574

Caméra One
38 rue du Bac
75007 Paris
Tel: (33 1) 4549 0979
Fax: (33 1) 4549 9 69

Cinéa
87 rue Taitbout
75009 Paris
Tel: (33 1) 4491 9414
Fax: (33 1) 4016 1911

Film Par Film
10 avenue George V
75008 Paris
Tel: (33 1) 4073 8420
Fax: (33 1) 4723 9568

Films Alain Sarde
17 rue Dumont d'Urville
75116 Paris
Tel: (33 1) 4443 4370
Fax: (33 1) 4720 6150

Films Christian Fechner
39 Rue des Tilleuls
92100 Boulogne
Tel: (33 1) 4699 0202
Fax: (33 1) 4699 0343

Flach Films
47 rue de la Colonie
75013 Paris
Tel: (33 1) 4416 4000
Fax: (33 1) 4580 4001

Gaumont
30 avenue Charles de Gaulle
92200 Neuilly
Tel: (33 1) 4643 2000
Fax: (33 1) 4643 2168

Hachette Première
10 rue de Marignan
75008 Paris
Tel: (33 1) 4225 1970
Fax: (33 1) 4256 0081

IMA Productions
3 rue de Liège
75009 Paris
Tel: (33 1) 4023 4810
Fax: (33 1) 4082 9701

MACT Productions
27 Rue de Fleurus
75006 Paris
Tel: (33 1) 4549 1010
Fax: (33 1) 4559 3060

MK2 Productions
55 rue Traversière
75012 Paris
Tel: (33 1) 4467 3000
Fax: (33 1) 4341 3230

Les Productions Lazennec
5 rue Darcet
75017 Paris
Tel: (33 1) 4387 7171
Fax: (33 1) 4387 1774

Renn Productions
10 rue Lincoln
75008 Paris
Tel: (33 1) 4076 9 00
Fax: (33 1) 4225 1289

Le Studio Canal+
17 rue Dumont d'Urville
75116 Paris
Tel: (33 1) 4443 9800
Fax: (33 1) 4720 1358

Téléma
26 rue Danton
92300 Levallois Perret
Tel: (33 1) 4758 6730
Fax: (33 1) 4758 8116

UGC Images
(also UGC distributors)
24 avenue Charles de Gaulle
92200 Neuilly
Tel: (33 1) 4640 4400
Fax: (33 1) 4624 3728

Distributors

AFMD
18 rue Troyon
75017 Paris
Tel: (33 1) 4409 0808
Fax: (33 1) 4764 1427

A.M.L.F.
10 rue Lincoln
75008 Paris
Tel: (33 1) 4076 9100
Fax: (33 1) 4225 1289

Bac Films
10 Avenue de Messine
75008 Paris
Tel: (33 1) 5353 5252
Fax: (33 1) 5353 5253

Diaphana Distribution
50 rue de Paradis
75010 Paris
Tel: (33 1) 4479 9292
Fax: (33 1) 4246 5448

Gaumont/BVI
5 rue du Colisée
75008 Paris
Tel: (33 1) 4643 2453
Fax: (33 1) 4643 2047

Mars Films
95 Bd Haussmann
75008 Paris
Tel: (33 1) 4494 9500
Tel: (33 1) 4494 9501

Metropolitan Filmexport
116 bis avenue des Champs Elysées
75008 Paris
Tel: (33 1) 4563 4560
Fax: (33 1) 4563 7731

MKL
55 rue Traversière
75012 Paris
Tel: (33 1) 4307 1510
Fax: (33 1) 4344 2018

PolyGram Distribution (ex Pan Européenne)
107 Boulevard Péreire
75017 Paris
Tel: (33 1) 4415 6666
Fax: (33 1) 4764 3638

Pyramide Film
5 rue Richepanse,
75008 Paris
Tel: (33 1) 4296 0101
Fax: (33 1) 4020 0221

UFD
2 avenue Montaigne
75008 Paris
Tel: (33 1) 5367 1717
Fax: (33 1) 5367 1700

GERMANY
Jack
Kindred

It was the best of times for German film. In a boom year for the cinema industry, home-grown productions captured 17.3 per cent of the market in 1997, continuing a five-year upward trend. After years in the celluloid doldrums, audiences for German movies started growing in 1993 with 8.4 million patrons, 11 million in 1995, 20.8 million in 1996 and 23.9 million last year. Overall attendance amounted to 143.1 million paying patrons in 1997, the highest figure in the 1990s.

Contributing to the euphoria among the nation's producers, distributors and exhibitors were such hit comedies as Helmut Dietl's **Rossini**, with a stellar cast featuring Götz George, Mario Adorf, Heiner Lauterback and Gudrun Landgrebe, and Thomas Jahn's road movie **Knockin' on Heaven's Door**, toplining "buddies" Til Schweiger and Jan Josef Liefers. Even the small, low-budget **Life Is All You Get** (*Das Leben Ist Eine Baustelle*) scored with the public.

Another far-out comedy, Tom Gerhard's slapstick **Ballermann 6,** a lampoon of German tourists' outlandish behaviour on the Spanish resort island of Majorca, drew two million cinemagoers. In a more serious vein, Caroline Link's surprising and moving story of a musically gifted girl born to deaf parents, **Beyond Silence** (*Jenseits der Stille*), capped a banner year by receiving an Academy Award nomination for best foreign language film.

However, with no potential blockbusters in sight in the 1998 line-up, the widely acclaimed renaissance of German film has taken on sober overtones. During the first quarter of 1998, the market share of German films slumped to 7.9 per cent, evoking memories of the dismal years when domestic productions consistently failed to account for even a tenth of the market.

Hopes, talent and yearning

Increased support from the Federal Film Board in Berlin, and subsidies from Hamburg, North Rhine Westphalia and Bavaria, as well as from public and private television broadcasters, has brought total funds available to upwards of $110m (DM 200m) annually. Compare that with Hollywood, where production and marketing costs for a single project frequently top $100m.

Since the German language territory is too small to sustain high-budget films, domestic producers have to make do with modest budgets, pinning their hopes on talent, promising scripts and the public's yearning for German stories and characters with whom they can identify. German film's bid to grab a fair share of the market in view of the perennially popular American movies appeared to falter during the first quarter of 1998, as a number of promising releases failed to meet box-office expectations.

Tom Gerhardt, Diana Frank and Hilmi Sözer in BALLERMANN 6

Heiner Lauterbach and Sandra Speichert in THE CAMPUS

1920s musical stars in COMEDIAN HARMONISTS

One of these was **The Campus** (*Der Campus*), produced by Bernd Eichinger. Following his success with Eichinger's smash hit *Der bewegte Mann* (6.5 million admissions) a couple of years ago, Sönke Wortmann turned his directing skills to Dietrich Schwanitz's best-selling ironic comedy of university society, lining up versatile actor Heiner Lauterbach for the lead opposite Barbara Rudnik and Axel Milberg.

Lauterbach plays Professor Hackmann, whose reckless affair with a student causes his downfall at a time when he is in line to become the university's president. Hackmann becomes a victim of intrigues from envious rival professors, capped when Babsy, his student, says he has sexually molested her. The scandal ends his teaching career. Released at a time when Germany's students were out in force protesting against university conditions and budget cuts, the movie only pulled a disappointing 675,000 visitors after a seven-week run, falling well short of the one million benchmark for a successful movie in Germany.

Perfect harmony

Josef Vilsmaier's **Comedian Harmonists** was completed too early to be selected for Berlin's International Film Festival, since the director wanted to release the movie when the cinema season was at its height. His historically accurate film recalled the rise and fall of a legendary vocal group, whose global success in the roaring Twenties was abruptly terminated during the Nazi era. Attendance soared to 2.5 million during a 13-week run early in 1998, reflecting young Germans' interest in the history of the Third Reich, and evoking nostalgic memories in the older generations.

Many still remember the Harmonists, a pianist and five singers, whose 1920s popularity can be compared to the hysteria surrounding some of today's pop stars. In line with Nazi persecution of Jews, propaganda minister Joseph Goebels banned the sextet, forcing its three Jewish members to go into exile. Vilsmaier's $10m feature is an opulent, entertaining costume film whose anecdotal plot revolves around the love affairs and rivalries of six diverse characters. Katja Riemann, one of Germany's foremost actresses, took the female lead as the wife who converts to Judaism out of love for her husband. Vilsmaier had his actors lip-synch to some of the original Comedian Harmonists' recordings.

The current dearth of attractive German films was highlighted at the 1998 Berlinale, when festival director Moritz de Hadeln could only fill the gap in the competition with director-actor Michael Gwisdek's debut, **The Mambo Game** (*Das Mambospiel*). An unbalanced mixture of urban drama and relationship comedy laced with gags, it failed to obtain a favourable response. The only other quasi-German entry in the competition was a German-financed film, *The Commissioner*, shot with an English-language soundtrack.

A series of comedy flops early in 1998, including Vivian Naefe's **Two Men, Two Women, Four Problems** (*Zwei Manner, Zwei Frauen, Vier Probleme*), Sherry Hormann's **Widows** and Hermine Huntgeburth's **Das Trio**, saw the reputation of Germany's top female directors take a dive. *Widows* failed to amuse despite a top cast featuring Katja Flint, Eva Mattes, Ornella Muti and Uwe Ochsenknecht; nor could Götz George and Christian Redl rescue *Das Trio* .

Spanish odysseys

Nevertheless, hopes are high for the long-delayed fall release of Doris Dörrie's **Am I Beautiful?** (*Bin ich schön?*), whose filming in Spain was cut short by the untimely death of her cameraman husband, Helge Weindler. The movie charts the quest for happiness of a group of discontented Germans who wander through Spain seeking love. The lovers find each other at last in Seville, against the colourful background of a religious procession during the Semana Santa.

Also in a Spanish setting, the comedy **Rettich, Czerni and Me** (*Frau Rettich, die Czerni und ich*) has a plot revolving around three ladies on the loose in Spain: Frau Rettich hopes to marry her Barcelona lover, Czerni seeks free-loading amusement and Sophie wants to forget a hapless Frankfurt romance. But despite the efforts of Iris Berben, Martina Gedeck and Jeanette Hain, limp dialogue, slapstick comedy and a thin plot made for another flop.

Director Michael Juncker chose a familiar theme – the search for a perfect partner – in yet another comedy with a foreign setting (Italy this time), **Good Girls Don't Lie** (*Frauen lügen nicht*). The cast included Jennifer Nitsch and Martina Gedeck, both well known to German film fans.

Wim Wenders' **The End of Violence**, with Bill Pullman, Andie MacDowell and Gabriel Byrne, found such little favour at the 1997 Cannes festival that the director re-edited it, re-arranging some scenes and

Mario Adorf provided one of the animal voices for THE FEARLESS FOUR

cutting about 25 minutes. But Wenders, an icon of auteur film-making, especially in Cannes, still failed to save the film, not least because a story concerned with the subject of violence itself in a Los Angeles atmosphere was hardly an enticing prospect for an entertainment-hungry public.

Worth mentioning is the full-length, colour animation musical **The Fearless 4**, produced by Eberhard Junkesdorf with a $15m budget. Four singing animals (a cat, a dog, a donkey and a rooster) are in the leading roles in an adaptation of a Bremen fairytale. Their adventures, including confrontations with villainous robbers, drew a creditable 792,000 admissions.

Homage to noir

Volker Schlöndorff followers were on the watch for the director's latest project, **Palmetto**, a homage to film noir which starred Woody Harrelson, Elisabeth Shue and Gina Gershon. Based on English pulp novelist James Hadley Chase's *Just Another Sucker*, this was the tale of a hard-boiled court reporter who winds up in jail after attempting to expose a corruption scandal. After two years in the slammer, Harry Barber (Harrelson) returns to his home town bitter and disillusioned, and becomes involved in a blackmailing scheme. Harrelson's fans must have been disillusioned, too, since the thriller drew fewer than 30,000 patrons in its first fortnight. The movie hardly did any better in America, taking just $5.8m.

Hollywood films again dominated the

German market in 1997, with the top ten headed by *Men in Black*, followed by *Bean* and *The Lost World*, although it was good to see three German films (*Knockin' on Heaven's Door*, *Rossini* and *The Little Arsehole*) making the list. German productions early in 1998 found the going rough, with *Titanic* dominating all other releases.

The boom in exhibition saw the number of screens in Germany rise to 4,284 in 1997, compared with 4,070 the previous year, partly attributed to over 900 new or renovated theatres and the 52 multiplexes in operation at year's end. Despite the fall-off of domestic productions, Johannes Klingsporn, head of the Association of German distributors, is still optimistic for the future of the industry, predicting that by the end of 1998, attendance will rise to at least 160 million.

JACK KINDRED, non-practising musicologist and classical pianist, turf specialist and former *Variety* bureau chief, covers Germany's film, TV and video scene from Munich.

Recent and Forthcoming Films

ASTERIX & OBELIX

Script and Dir: Claude Zidi. Phot: Tony Pierce-Roberts. Players: Christian Clavier, Gérard Depardieu, Roberto Benigni, Gottfried John Laetitia Casta, Marianne Sägebrecht. Prod: Renn Productions, Paris/Bavaria Film, Munich/Melampo Cinematografica, Rome.

BALLERMANN 6

Script and Dir: Tom Gerhardt. Phot: Germot Roll. Players: Gerhardt. Prod: Constantin Film.

DER CAMPUS

Script: Dieter Schwanitz, Jürgen Egger. Dir: Söhnke Wortmann. Phot: Tom Fährmann. Players: Heiner Lauterbach, Axel Milberg, Barbara Rudnik, S. Canonica. Prod: Constantin.

COMEDIAN HARMONISTS

Script: Klaus Richter. Dir: Joseph Vilsmaier. Phot: Vilsmaier. Players: Ulrich Noethen, Ben Becker, Heino Ferch, Kai Wiesinger, Max Tidof, Heinrich Schafmeister. Prod: Senator/Bavaria/Iduna.

DIAMANTENTANZ (Diamond Dance)

Script, Dir, Phot: Ulrike Ottinger.

Players: Dianne Wiest, F. Murray Abraham, Carol Kane, Joe Mantello. Prod: Ulrike Ottinger Filmproduktion.

THE END OF VIOLENCE

Script and Dir: Wim Wenders. Phot: Pascal Rabaud. Players: Bill Pullman, Andie MacDowell, Gabriel Byrne, Loran Dean, Traci Lind. Prod: Road Movies Film Production.

FETTE WELT (Fat World)

Script: Klaus Richter, Jan Schütte. Dir: Schütte. Phot: Thomas Plenert. Players: Jürgen Vogel, Julia Filimonow, Stefan Dietrich, Sibylle Canonica. Prod: MTM Cineteve/Senator Filmproduktion/Novoskop Film.

FRAU RETTICH, DIE CZERNI UND ICH (Rettich, Czerni and Me)

Script: Sinone Borowiak, Hans Kantereit. Dir: Markus Imboden. Phot: Benedict Neuenfels. Players: Iris Berben, Martina Gedeck, Jeanette Hain, Olli Dittrich, Thomas Heinze. Prod: Bavaria Film/Lunaris Film.

GEORGIA O'KEEFFE "TILL THE END OF TIME"

Script: Hans-Jörg Weyhmüller.

Dir: Jeremy Kagan. Phot: Igor Luther. Players: Sean Young, Christopher Walken, Jan Niklas, Barbara Auer. Prod: ArtOko.

HÄRTETEST (Hard Test)

Script and Dir: Janek Rieke. Phot: Florian Ballhaus. Players: Janek Rieke, Lisa Martinek, Gerhard Garbers, Katrin Sass. Prod: Lichtblick.

JIMMY THE KID

Script: Martin Rauhaus, Peter Wohlgemuth. Dir: Wolfgang Dickmann. Phot: Dickmann. Players: Rufus Beck, Herbert Knaup, Christiane Hörbiger, Sophie Moser. Prod: Wohlgemuth Filmproduktion.

LONG HELLO AND THE SHORT GOODBYE

Script and Dir: Rainer Kaufmann. Players: Til Schweiger, Nicolette Krebitz, Katja Riemann. Prod: Studio Hamburg Filmproduktion.

LIEBE DEINEN NÄCHSTEN (Love Your Neighbour)

Script and Dir: Detlev Buck. Phot: Joachim Berc. Players: Lea Mornar, Heike Makatsch, Moritz Bleibtreu, Heribert Sasse. Prod: Boje Buck Produktion.

DAS MAMBOSPIEL
(The Mambo Game)

Script and Dir: Michael Gwisdek. Phot: Roland Dressel. Players: Corinna Harfouch, Michael Gwisdek, Jürgen Vogel, Franziska Petri. Prod: Neue Deutsche Filmgesellschaft.

DAS MERKWÜRDIGE VERHALTEN (The Remarkable Behaviour of Sexually Mature City Dwellers in the Mating Season).

Script: Peter Gersina. Dir: Marc Rothemund. Phot: Hans-Günther Bücking. Players: Christoph Waltz, Gudrun Landgrebe, Michaela May, Anica Dobra, Dieter Landuris. Prod: SamFilm, Munich.

DIE MUSTERKANABEN
(Role Models)

Script: Dominic Raacke, Ralf Huettner. Dir: Huettner. Phot: Hannes Hubach. Players: Oliver Korritke, Jürgen Tarrach, Ellen Ten Damme, Herbert Knaup. Prod. ndF.

NEUE FREIHEIT - KEINE JOBS
(New Freedom - No Jobs)

Script and Dir: Herbert Achternbusch. Phot: Michael Wagner. Players: Achternbusch, Dieter Dorn, Georg Ringsgwandl, Jörg Hube. Prod: Achternbusch Film Productions.

PALMETTO - DUMMEN STERBEN NICHT AUS (Palmetto)

Script: E. Max Frye. Dir: Volker Schlöndorff. Phot: Thomas Kloss. Players: Woody Harrelson, Elisabeth Shue, Gina Gershon, Chloe Sevigny, Michael Rapaport, Tom Wright, Rolf Hoppe. Prod: Rialto.

REQUIEM FÜR EINE ROMANTISCHE FRAU (Requiem for a Romantic Woman)

Script and Dir: Dagmar Knöpfel. Phot: Igor Luther. Players: Sylvester Groth, Janina Sachau,

Felix von Manteuffel, Anne Bennert. Prod: Dagmar Knöpfel Filmproduktion.

ST. PAULI NACHT
(St. Paul's Night)

Script: Frank Göhre. Dir: Sönke Wortmann. Players: Detlev Buck, Katja Flint, Benno Fürmann. Herbert Knaup. Prod: Hager Moss Film.

SIEBEN MONDE
(Seven Moons)

Script: Nils-Morten Osburg. Dir: Peter Fratzscher. Phot: Thomas Merker. Players: Jan Josef Liefers, Ulrich Mühe, Marie Bäumer, Christoph Walz, Peter Lohmeyer, Burkhard Driest. Prod: Avista/Roxy.

SILVESTER COUNTDOWN

Script and Dir: Oskar Roehler. Phot: Lorenz Haarmann. Players: Rolf Peter Kahl, Marie Zielcke, Robert Victor Minich, Juliane Werner, Harry Hass, Wolfgang Wimmer. Prod: Erdbeermund Filmproduktion/FGV Schmidel.

SOLO FÜR KLARINETTE (Solo for Clarinet)

Script: Susanne Schneider. Dir: Nico Hofmann. Phot: Hans-Günther Bücking. Players: Götz George, Corinna Harfouch, Tim Bergmann, Barbara Auer. Prod: Regina Ziegler Filmproduktion.

DER TAG DES CLOWNS (Day of the Clowns)

Script: Paul Döblin. Dir: Roger Christian. Phot: Mike Southon. Players: Klaus Maria Brandauer. Prod: Ecco Film/Screen Parnters.

EIN TÖDLICHES VERHÄLTNIS
(A Fatal Affair)

Script and Dir: Michael Bartlett. Phot: Ekkehart Pollach. Players: Dominique Horwitz, Floriane Daniel, Julia Jäger, Dorothea Moritz. Prod: Rialto.

DAS TRIO

Script: Horst Scerba. Dir: Hermine Hundgeburth. Phot. Martin Kukula. Players: Götz George, Jeanette Hain, Felix Eitner, Christian Redl. Prod: Next Film Produktion.

ZWEI MÄNNER - ZWEI FRAUEN – VIER PROBLEME (Two Men – Two Women - Four Problems)

Script and Dir: Vivian Naefe. Phot: Peter Dötting. Players: Heino Ferch, Aglaia Szyszkowitz, Gedeon Burkhard, Hilde van Mieghem, Clemens Jakubetz, Pamela Marquardt. Prod: Olga Film.

WIDOWS

Scrpt: Kit Hopkins. Dir: Sherry Hormann. Phot: Hans-Günther Bücking. Players: Katja Flint, Eva Mattes, Ornella Muti, Uwe Ochsenknecht. Prod: Hager Moss.

Producers

Allianz Filmproduktion GmbH
Leibnitzstr. 60
10625 Berlin
Tel: (49 30) 323 9011
Fax: (49 30) 323 1693

Anthea Film GmbH
Widenmayerstr. 4
80538 Munich
Tel: (49 89) 226 194
Fax: (49 89) 221 251

Bavaria Film GmbH
Bavariafilmplatz 7
80336 Geiselgasteig/Munich
Tel: (49 89) 6499 2389
Fax: (49 89) 649 2507

BioSkop-Film GmbH
Türkenstr. 91/111
80799 Munich
Tel: (49 89) 394 987
Fax: (49 89) 396 820

Capitol Film + TV International GmbH & Co. Vertriebs KG
Harvestehuder Weg 43
20149 Hamburg 13

Tel: (49 40) 411 79-0
Fax: (49 40) 411 70-199

Connexion-Film Vertriebs & Produktions GmbH & Co.
Harvestehuder Weg 45
20149 Hamburg
Tel: (49 40) 411 79 300
Fax: (49 40) 411 79 399

Constantin Film GmbH
Kaiserstr. 39
47441 Munich
Tel: (49 89) 3860 9221/2
Fax: (49 89) 3860 9242

Franz Seitz Produktions GmbH
Beichstr. 8
80802 Munich
Tel: (49 89) 391 1123
Fax: (49 89) 340 1291

Willy Bogner Film GmbH
Sankt Veitstr. 4
81673 Munich
Tel: (49 89) 436 06-0
Fax: (49 89) 436 06 429

CCC Filmkunst GmbH
Verlangerie Daumstr. 16
13599 Berlin
Tel: (49 30) 334 200-1
Fax: (49 30) 334 0418

CineVox Film GmbH
Bavaria Filmplatz 7
80336 Geiselgasteig
Tel: (49 89) 641 80-0
Fax: (49 89) 649 3288

Manfred Durniok Produktion
Hausotterstr. 36
13409 Berlin
Tel: (49 30) 491 8045
Fax: (49 30) 491 4065

Hermes Film GmbH
Kaiserplatz 7
47441 Munich
Tel: (49 89) 394 368
Fax: (49 89) 344 363

Oko-Film GmbH
Mauerkircherstr. 3
81679 Munich
Tel: (49 89) 987 666
Fax: (49 89) 987 602

Olga Film GmbH
Tengstr. 16
80798 Munich
Tel: (49 89) 271 2635
Fax: (49 89) 272 5768

PolyGram Filmed Entertainment GmbH
Glockengiesserwall 2
20035 Hamburg
Tel: (49 40) 308 706
Fax: (49 40) 308 7944

Regina Ziegler Filmproduktion
Budapesterstr. 35
10789 Berlin
Tel: (49 30) 261 8071
Fax: (49 30) 262 8213

Rialto Film GmbH
Bismarckstr. 108
13469 Berlin
Tel: (49 30) 310 0000
Fax: (49 30) 3100 0559

Roxy-Film GmbH
Schützenstr. 1
80335 Munich 2
Tel: (49 89) 555 341
Fax: (49 89) 594 510

Studio Hamburg
Tonndorfer Hauptstr. 90
22045 Hamburg
Tel: (49 40) 66 880
Fax: (49 40) 665 601
(49 40) 6688 4370

Tele-München GmbH
Kaufingerstr. 25
80331 Munich
Tel: (49 89) 290 930
Fax: (49 89) 290 93129

Vision Film GmbH
Kurfürstenplatz 4
80796 Munich
Tel: (49 89) 390 025
Fax: (49 89) 395 569

Von Vietinghoff Filmproduktion
Potsdamerstr. 199
10783 Berlin
Tel: (49 30) 216 8931
Fax: (49 30) 215 8219

Distributors

Ascot Filmverleih GmbH
St. Annastr. 16
80538 Munich
Tel: (49 89) 296 995
Fax: (49 89) 331 839

Columbia TriStar Filmgesellschaft GmbH
Ickstattstr. 1
80469 Munich
Tel: (49 89) 236 90
Fax: (49 89) 264 380

Concorde Filmverleih GmbH
Rosenheimerstr. 143 B
81671 Munich
Tel: (49 89) 4506 100
Fax: (49 89) 4506 1014

Futura/Filmverlag GmbH
Rambergstr. 5
80799 Munich
Tel: (49 89) 381 701
Fax: (49 89) 3817 0020

Helkon Media Filmvertrieb GmbH
Widenmayerstr. 36
80538 Munich
Tel: (49 89) 2916 0490
Fax: (49 89) 291 3720

Jugend Film Verleih GmbH
Reichsstrasse 15
14052 Berlin
Tel: (49 30) 300 6970
Fax: (49 30) 3006 9711

Kinowelt Filmverleih GmbH
Schwere-Reiterstrasse 35
Building 14
80797 Munich
Tel: (49 89) 307 960
Fax: (49 89) 3079 6701

Nil Film GmbH
Bnd Brunnthal 3
81657 Munich
Tel: (49 89) 9980 5800
Fax: (49 89) 9980 5810

Pandora Film
Egenolffstrasse 13
60316 Frankfurt
Tel: (49 69) 9434 280
Fax: (49 69) 9434 2899

ScotiaFilm GmbH
Possartstr. 14
81679 Munich
Tel: (49 89) 413 0900
Fax: (49 89) 470 6320

SenatorFilm GmbH
Kurfürstendamm 65
10707 Berlin
Tel: (49 30) 8809 1700
Fax: (49 30) 8809 1790

20th Century Fox of Germany GmbH
Postfach 70 11 22
60561 Frankfurt am Main
Tel: (49 69) 609 020
Fax: (49 69) 627 716

TiMe Filmverleih GmbH
Brüsselerstr. 89–93
50672 Cologne

Tel: (49 221) 952 9680
Fax: (49 221) 19529 6866

Transit Film GmbH
Dachauerstrasse 35
80335 Munich
Tel: (49 89) 555 261
Fax: (49 89) 596 122

United International Pictures GmbH
Hahnstr. 31-35
60528 Frankfurt am Main
Tel: (49 69) 669 8190
Fax: (49 69) 666 6509

Warner Bros Film GmbH
Hans-Henny-Jahn-Weg 35
22085 Hamburg
Tel: (49 40) 226 500
Fax: (49 40) 2265 0259

Useful Addresses

Verband der Filmverleiher e.V (49 VDI)
(49 Assn. of Distributors)
Kreuzberger Ring 56
65205 Wiesbaden
Tel: (49 611) 778 920
Fax: (49 611) 778 9212

Export Union
Türkenstr. 93
80799 Munich
Tel: (49 89) 390 095
Fax: (49 89) 395 223

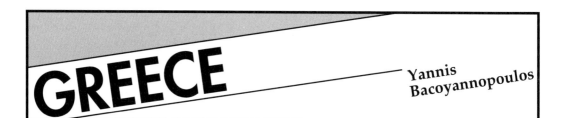

GREECE

Yannis Bacoyannopoulos

This year witnessed the greatest distinction ever won by a Greek film, when Theo Angelopoulos' **Eternity and a Day** was honoured with the Palme D'Or at Cannes. Angelopoulos has, of course, garnered countless awards all over the world, including Cannes, where three years ago he won the Grand Jury Prize for *Ulysses' Gaze*. Yet, as *Le Figaro* wrote, Angelopoulos, despite forming "part of the constellation of Antonioni and Tarkovsky, was, at the same time, a film-maker who was... forgotten as far as the Palme D'Or was concerned. At last he has been rewarded."

As noted, Angelopoulos belongs to the modernist movement that began with Antonioni and included Rocha, Jancso, Oshima, Bertolucci, the Taviani brothers and Wenders. Most of them have gone, fallen silent or chosen to follow lesser routes. But Angelopoulos is always present on the bulwarks, with a film every two or three years, films that are landmarks in an unwavering and renewable course. Why? Because he addresses the great crises of our time: man's confrontation with ideologies, his defeats and his persistent and painful comebacks. Angelopoulos finds ways of giving this progression creative and ultimately poetic form.

Greek cinema also scored another hit, a commercial one, on the home front. For the first time in many years a Greek film was ranked among the year's top ten grossers, successfully competing against the American giants. Sotiris Goritsas' **Balkanisator** racked up 140,000 admissions in the statistically controlled Greater Athens area, and around 220,000 in the whole country. Satisfactory box-office figures were obtained for Nikos Perakis's **Paterfamilias** (almost 100,000 admissions), Antonis Kokkinos' **My Brother and I** (50,000) and

Bruno Ganz in ETERNITY AND A DAY, a worthy Palme d'Or winner at the 1998 Cannes Festival

Pericles Hoursoglou's **The Man in Grey** (40,000) while Vangelis Serdaris' **Vassili** and Pantelis Voulgaris **It's a Long Road** also did well.

Between October 1997 and May 1998, 13 new Greek films were released, attracting almost 500,000 admissions, compared to 300,000 in 1997. Yet about half of them failed to find any kind of audience. The problem facing Greek cinema remains acute despite extensive state aid, chiefly through the Greek Film Centre. A new law drawn up by the Minister of Culture, Evangelos Venizelos, provides for greater scriptwriting and production development support. It also encourages the participation of independent producers and more systematic promotion and marketing for films, as well as greater creative collaboration with other European and Balkan nations.

Foreign acclaim

On the international front, however, interest in Greek film continues unabated.

Major retrospectives were held throughout the world, in New Zealand, South Africa, Germany and India. There was also a dual retrospective held in London in May–June, honouring both Angelopoulos and contemporary Greek production. Andreas Pantzis' **Slaughter of the Cock** won the Best Film award at the Naples and Barcelona film festivals. **Before the End of the World**, by Panayotis Maroulis, was an award-winner in Alexandria, Renos Haralambidis' **No Budget Story** in Istanbul, Andreas Thomopoulos' **Dharma Blues** in Kiev, and Vangelis' score for Iannis Smaragdis' **Cavafy** won the Best Music awards in Ghent and Valencia.

The first 10-screen multiplex in Athens (owned by Village Roadshow) provoked a real revolution in the habits of cinema audiences, with showings that begin at noon and continue during the summer months, when traditionally only outdoor theatres have been open. This multiplex alone accounted for more than 10 per cent of total admissions. Its operations were immediately extended to Thessaloniki, and rivals have

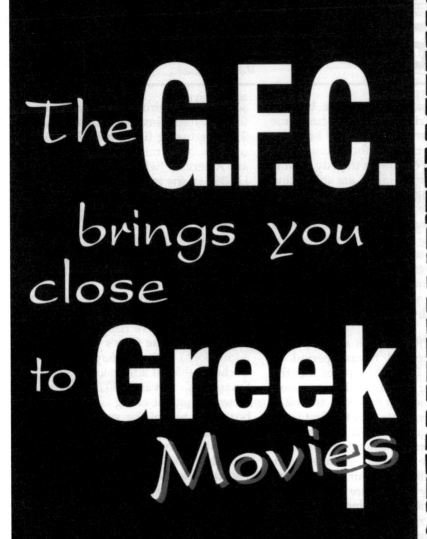

appeared on the scene. All indications suggest that the total number of theatres will double in the next couple of years. The increase in admissions, not officially confirmed, is now in the range of 15 per cent a year, thus raising the total to 12 million.

The lion's share belongs to American films, which once again exceeded the 80 per cent mark. *Titanic*'s success in Greece was amongst the most remarkable achieved by the film in any single territory, since in Athens alone it drew 850,000 admissions (almost four times that of the next most popular film) and perhaps as many as 1.8 million in all of Greece (equivalent to one in seven of every ticket sold!), an absolute all-time record for a single film, even for the pre-television period, when annual admissions reached a dizzying 140 million.

Still from IT'S A LONG ROAD

YANNIS BACOYANNOPOULOS is one of Greece's best-known film critics. Since 1960, he has worked for many newspapers and magazines, and for the past 20 years has been film critic of the Athens daily *Kathimerini* and Greek State Television ET-1.

Recent and Forthcoming Films

MIA EONIOTITA KE MIA MERA (Eternity and a Day)

Script and Dir: Theo Angelopoulos Players: Bruno Ganz, Fabrizio Bentivoglio, Isabelle Renauld, Alexandra Ladikou, Despina Bebedeli, Nikos Couros, Alekos Udinotis, Andreas Tsekouras. Prod: Angelopoulos/Greek Film Centre/Greek Television/Paradis Films/Intermedias/La Dept, with the participation of Canal+, Classic SRI, Istituto Luce and with WDR/ARTE.

A day from the past is relived by a terminally ill middle-aged writer, and a day in the present forces him to take stock of his life.

THE CHERRY ORCHARD

Script and Dir: Michael Cacoyannis, from the Chekhov play. Players: Alan Bates, Charlotte Rampling. Prod: Cacoyannis/Greek Film Centre.

I ANTIGONE TOU CABRAL (The Photographers)

Script: Nikos Konstandaras, Nikos Koundouros. Dir:

Koundouros. Players: Katerina Pavlaki, Manos Vakoussis, Michalis Comninos, Vangelis Mourikis, Dimitris Stratakis. Prod: Greek Film Centre/Lexikon/ETI Public TV Greece.

Based on Sophocles' ancient tragedy, Antigone, the film deals with the eternal questions of human conscience and the right to freedom of choice.

OLA INE DROMOS (It's a Long Road)

Script: Giorgos Skabardonis, Pantelis Voulgaris. Dir: Voulgaris. Players: Thanassis Vengos, Giorgos Armenis, Dimitris Katalifos. Prod: Thessaliniki/ Cultural Capital of Europe Organisation/ALCO-FILM/Greek Film Centre/ET-1.

Three people head towards a turning point in their lives.

O ADELPHOS MOU K'EGO (My Brother and I)

Script: Antonis Kokkinos, Nikos Panayotopoulos. Dir: Kokkinos. Players: Vangelis Germanos, Demosthenes Papadopoulos,

Pemy Zouni, Myrto Alikaki, Kyriakos Darivas, Stathis Livathinos, Stavros Mermingis, Yannis "Bach" Spyropoulos. Guest star: Eric Burdon. Prod: Greek Film Centre/Hyperion S.A./Greek State Television ET-1/P.P.V. S.A./Tonikon Ltd/ Spentzos Film/IOS Cultural Action.

A young man who idolises his older brother is disillusioned when he discovers things are not as they seemed.

PROSTATIS KIOYENIAS (Paterfamilias)

Script and Dir: Nikos Perakis. Players: Renos Haralambidis, Katerina Yiatzoglou, Alkis Panagiotidis, Cassandra Voyiatzi, Natalia Papaioannou, Evris Papanikolas. Prod: Greek Film Centre/Stefi S.A./ELKE/Nikos Perakis.

When an out-of-work schoolteacher and aspiring writer undertakes to "edit" the autobiography of a popular singer, Calypso, whose second husband is the business tycoon and owner of Hellas TV, Sotiris Mandrakas, he becomes the victim of a nightmarish conspiracy.

BLACK-OUT

Script and Dir: Menelaos Karamangiolis. Players: Hanna Schygulla, Myrto Alikaki, Cleon Grigoriadis, Marios Frangoulis. Prod: Greek Film Centre/Pausilypon Films Ltd/Stefi Films/MACT Production (France)/Animatografo Producao de Filmes (Portugal).

A woman's latest relationship is threatened by a former lover's interference.

HOMA KAI NERO
(Earth and Water)

Script and Dir: Panagiotis Karkanevatos. Prod: Greek Film Centre/Cinergon Productions.

The story of a village in the plains of Macedonia and the refugees who came from the Black Sea in 1922, built homes half-buried in the earth, and turned the surrounding marshes into fertile fields.

TO ISTORIKO SYNEDRIO TIS VOLVIS (The Historical Volvi Convention)

Script and Dir: Stavros Tsiolis. Players: Yannis Zouganelis, Argyris Bakirtzis, Sakis Boulas. Prod: Greek Film Centre/Sanyo-Alekos Papageorgiou/Elke Odeon/Stavros Tsiolis.

Three brothers-in-law who work in cottage industries in the Thessalonikistrial belt set off for the island of Thasssos in July to join their families on holiday, but a curious event en route in the Lake Volvis area interrupts their journey.

I ARITHMIMENTI
(The Numbered)

Script and Dir: Tassos Psarras. Prod: Tassos Psarras Productions/ET-1/Greek Television/Greek Film Centre.

Thriller about the political background to an assassination.

HELLADOS OR VENICE STREET

Script and Dir: Yiannis Ioannou. Players: Irene Papas, Sofiko Chiaourelli, Alexis Ionannou. Prod: Movie Makers/Kanina Film (Bulgaria)/Cinema Studio Camera (Russia)/Televisual Services J K (Cyprus)/Ioannou.

Drama about the friendship between a Greek boy and a Georgian boy during the Stalinist era.

TA RODINA AKROYALIA
(The Rosy Seashores)

Script and Dir: Efthimios Hatzis. Players: Stefanos Iatridis, Dimitris Poulikakos, Yannis Petinoudis, Dimitris Thermos, Tassos Palastzidis, Peggy Trikalioti, Maria Skoula, Despina Kourti, Evangelia Andreadaki, Vassilis Tsanglos. Prod: Greek Film Centre/Cinergon Productions/Hatzis.

A young man, Alexandros, is bewitched by a woman whom he dares not approach.

HONG KONG — Derek Elley

No one was really surprised by the body blow that hit the film industry in early 1998 – but many were shocked by its speed and force. Suddenly, hardly any films seemed to be shooting in Hong Kong. Foreign sales had plummeted, there were rumours of an imminent sell-off of the territory's one major studio, Golden Harvest, and production was expected to plummet by at least 40 per cent on the previous year – to around 50 titles.

The Asian currency crisis, which had begun in Thailand in July 1997, had finally worked its way up from Southeast Asia and hit the industry where it hurt – in exports. South Korea, which had served as a buffer against lost sales to traditional markets like Taiwan, almost disappeared off the map, and film-makers started to panic. Already suffering from an overvalued currency, a 25 per cent drop in tourism since the handover to China in July 1997, a shrinking economy and rising unemployment, Hong Kong suddenly looked like yesterday's success story.

In fact, the danger signs had been visible since the last film-making boom started to tail off in late 1993-early 1994, but the *carpe diem* philosophy which powered the run-up to the 1997 handover had disguised many of the industry's underlying weaknesses: too many poor-quality cinemas, rising ticket prices, the growth of other forms of home entertainment, and escalating stars' and directors' fees. However, when exports (by which Hong Kong's industry has always been driven) were hit, the truth finally hit home.

Such was the panic that a group of high-profile directors even started to discuss forming a cooperative (The Directors Co.), under which a revolving fund would finance a raft of lower-budget films in the $500,000 (HK$4m) range – an amount recoupable from foreign and ancillary sales if above-the-line costs are deferred. As of summer 1998, however, the idea had yet to come to fruition.

Tycoons' harvest

It now looks like production will top out at around 60 titles for 1998, against 82 released in 1997, 109 in 1996 and 140 in 1995 and 1994. If that means more money and care will be channelled into fewer titles, the shrinkage could be for the better. So far, Japan has held firm as Hong Kong's largest Asian market, and Golden Harvest – long alleged to be over-extended and looking for a buyer – is still around: in mid-June 1998, it was announced that a triumvirate of Malaysian tycoon Robert Kuok (who owns cinemas in Southeast Asia), Hong Kong's Li Ka-shing and Australian-born Rupert Murdoch were to buy a 16.5 per cent stake in the studio, worth $7.2m.

If Golden Harvest, as has been rumoured, manages to get a licence to distribute its movies in China, the tycoons' investment could be a canny one, especially for a Hollywood player like Murdoch. Certainly, now is the perfect time for China to loosen its regulations on importing Hong Kong films: previously, the bumptious territory looked like a threat to its own indigenous industry; now it looks more like the manageable partner China desperately needs. Hong Kong actors are already starting to appear in mainland Chinese productions as work and fees decrease back home.

Box-office receipts for Hong Kong movies fell again during 1997, to around $71m, down from $84m the previous year. For the first time since 1980, non-Hong Kong films outgrossed local product, taking $78.5m. Many of those were from the US, which launched an onslaught of big-budget productions in the second half of the year, although Hong Kong movies still occupied six spots in the year's top ten. The much-trumpeted "takeover" of the market by US movies is still a symptom of the local industry's problems rather than its cause, and far from the fait accompli in neighbouring Taiwan; in the 1960s and 1970s, western movies regularly made a heavy showing in Hong Kong's top ten.

The irony of all this is that none of the problems can be attributed to the territory's handover to China; so far, all the Red-scare stories have come to naught. What looks likely is that Hong Kong will evolve into a talent base for the region rather than being purely a production powerhouse: film-makers will come and go (as have several to Hollywood), rather than stay yoked to the one industry. There is still no sign of any other East Asian city replacing Hong Kong as an international, entrepreneurial base.

Chan matures, gangsters thrive

A further sign that the old days are over can be seen in the career realignment of Jackie Chan (whose latest, African-set extravaganza, **Who Am I?**, did well locally but looks a dodgy prospect outside Asia). The 44-year-old action superstar, long attached to Golden Harvest but now realising his own physical limitations, is actively managing his own movie legacy (having taken a stake in Media Asia, which owns GH's back catalogue), as well as adopting a less deferential attitude to the studio. Chan's personal ties were more with producer/exhibitor Leonard Ho, who died in February 1998, than with boss Raymond Chow.

Despite all the gloom and doom, striking work continues to come out of Hong Kong. One of the freshest new talents is Patrick

Leo Ku and Charlie Young in Patrick Leung's TASK FORCE

Yau, who with the off-beat gangster sagas *The Odd One Dies* and (especially) **The Longest Nite** showed that the genre is far from played out. With its stygian tone, mirrors-within-mirrors story, sweat-drenched Macau setting, and terrific performances by Lau Ching-wan and Tony Leung Chiu-wai as the hunter and hunted, *The Longest Nite* was one of the boldest stylistic exercises of the past year.

Former John Woo assistant Patrick Leung, another talent nurtured by relative newcomer Milkyway Image (co-run by director Johnnie To), continued to come up with impressive work in the crime genre with **Task Force**, an almost mystical blend of emotion and action. Also pursuing the trend towards more character-driven fare was Gordon Chan, whose **Beastcops**, co-directed with Dante Lam, proved a fine showcase for actor Anthony Wong, more often seen playing pure psychos in Category III movies.

Among established festival names, Ann Hui scored a solid success with **Eighteen**

Chingmy Yau and Sunny Chan in Stanley Kwan's HOLD ME TIGHT

Springs, a well-acted, unflashily directed 1930s Shanghai relationships saga (from a novel by Eileen Chang) with Anita Mui, Leon Lai and Wu Chien-lien. More ambitious, but ultimately capsized by the director's obsession with his (homo)sexuality, Stanley Kwan's **Hold Me Tight** proved a mixed blessing: a potentially fascinating examination of parallel lives (with a good performance by former sexbomb Chingmy Yau) that jumps the rails in the second half.

Style and substance

Fruit Chan's edgy, low-budget **Made in Hong Kong** – godfathered by local star Andy Lau and shot on bits of raw stock salvaged from other productions – fully deserved its festival accolades. A portrait of an amoral, confused Generation-Xer (played with veracity by newcomer Sam Lee), the film was a rare example of a truly independent production, along the lines of US indies, even though it goes overboard in its latter stages in a welter of blood and violence.

Equally bold stylistically, though in a commercial melodrama format, is Jacob Cheung's **Intimates**, charting the love story between two women (Carina Liu, Charlie Young) across 50 years of China's turbulent twentieth-century history. Unashamedly melodramatic in a Sirkian way, and constructed in complex flashbacks, the film even managed to get a limited release in its original 158-minute version, after being cut down to 116 minutes by Golden Harvest for its main run.

Following the less-than-happy experience of making the Jean-Claude Van Damme vehicle *Maximum Risk* for a US studio, Ringo Lam returned to Hong Kong in 1997 and came up with the dark and angry police thriller **Full Alert**, one of his finest action dramas and a terrific vehicle for actors Lau Ching-wan and Francis Ng. Showing similar revitalisation was Michael Mak, whose **Island of Greed**, an ambitious, *Godfather*-like portrait of political corruption in Taiwan, had an epic scope that's all too rare in Hong Kong cinema. The two-hour movie also reportedly exists in a so far unseen three-hour version.

The 17th Hong Kong Film Awards

Best Film: *Made in Hong Kong.*
Best Director: Fruit Chan (*Made in Hong Kong*).
Best Actor: Tony Leung Chiu-wai (*Happy Together*).
Best Actress: Maggie Cheung (*The Soong Sisters*).
Best Supporting Actor: Jiang Wen (*The Soong Sisters*).
Best Supporting Actress: Anita Mui (*Eighteen Springs*).
Best Script: To Kwok-wai (*The Mad Phoenix*).
Best Photography: Arthur Wong (*The Soong Sisters*).
Best Art Direction: Eddie Ma (*The Soong Sisters*).
Best Costume Design: Emi Wada (*The Soong Sisters*).

Best Action Design: Tung Wai (*Downtown Torpedoes*).
Best Editing: Wong Wing-ming (*Lifeline*).
Best Acting Newcomer: Sam Lee (*Made in Hong Kong*).
Best Original Music: Randy Miller (*The Soong Sisters*).
Best Original Song: "Happy Tonight" (from *Cause We Are So Young*).
Best Sound Effects: *Lifeline.*
Lifetime Achievement Award: director Chor Yuen.

Recent and Forthcoming Films

AND NOW YOU ARE DEAD...

Dir: Cory Yuen. Players: Shannon Lee, Jordan Chan, Anita Yuen. For Golden Harvest.

THE SUSPECT

Dir: Ringo Lam. Players: Koo Tin-lok, Julian Cheung, Ray Lui. For Sil-Metropole.

AWAY WITH WORDS

Dir: Christopher Doyle.

CITY OF GLASS

Dir: Mabel Cheung. Players: Leon Lai, Shu Qi. For UFO.

SO MUCH TO SAY

Dir: Ann Hui. Players: Loretta Lee, Tse Kwan-ho, Anthony Wong, Li Kang-sheng.

YOUNG AND DANGEROUS: THE PREQUEL

Dir: Andrew Lau. Players: Francis Ng, Shu Qi. For: Bob & Partners Co.

THE LOVE GENERATION

Dir: Wong Jing. Players: Leon Lai, Carina Liu, Shu Qi, Lee Ann. For Bob & Partners Co.

ILLUSION SQUAD

Dir: Jingle Ma. Players: Ekin Cheng, Jordan Chan. Kelly Chen.

EXPECT THE UNEXPECTED

Dir: Patrick Yau. Players: Lau Ching-wan, Simon Yam. For New Film City.

Producers

Bob & Partners Co.
22/F, 83 Austin Rd.
Tsimshatsui
Tel: (852) 2314 7198
Fax: (852) 2314 7120

Chang-Hong Channel Film & Video Co. (HK)
5/F, Blk A, Full View Bldg.
3-7 Liberty Ave.
Kowloon
Tel: (852) 2762 2689
Fax: (852) 2762 2692

China Star Entertainment Group
Unit 503C, Miramar Tower
1-23 Kimberley Rd.
Tsimshatsui
Tel: (852) 2313 1888
Fax: (852) 2191 9888

Eastern Production
Kimberly Mansion, GA
15 Austin Ave.
Tsimshatsui
Tel: (852) 2367 3328
Fax: (852) 2367 5797

Golden Harvest/Golden Communications
8 King Tung St.
Hammer Hill Rd.
Kowloon
Tel: (852) 2352 8222
Fax: (852) 2351 1683

Impact Films Production
6/F, Blk 2, Tien Chu Centre
1E Mok Cheong St.
Tokwawan, Kowloon
Tel: (852) 2715 6545
Fax: (852) 2713 3390

Ko Chi Sum Films Co.
Room 617, Hewlett Centre
52-54 Hoi Yuen Rd.
Kwun Tong
Tel: (852) 2793 1123
Fax: (852) 2793 1134

Long Shong Pictures (H.K.)
G/F, Blk D, 272 Prince Edward Rd.
West Kowloon
Tel: (852) 2338 2211
Fax: (852) 2336 9911

Mandarin Films (Singapore)
1801-2 Westlands Centre
20 Westland Rd
Quarry Bay
Tel: (852) 2579 1718
Fax: (852) 2579 1707

Media Asia Films
Rm 412-416, 4/F, World Commercial
Centre
11 Canton Rd
Tsimshatsui
Tel: (852) 2314 4288
Fax: (852) 2314 4247

Mei Ah Films Production Co.
Unit 15-28, 17/F, Metro Centre,
Phase 1
32 Lam Hing St
Kowloon Bay
Tel: (852) 2754 2855
Fax: (852) 2799 3643

**Milkyway Entertainment
Group**
22/F, Remington Centre
23 Hung To Rd
Kwun Tong
Kowloon
Tel: (852) 2718 8128
Fax: (852) 2718 8122

Mobile Film Production
Flat C, 2/F, Dorfu Court
5-6 Hau Fook St
Tsimshatsui
Tel: (852) 2301 3008
Fax: (852) 2732 5315

Pineast Pictures
Flat B, 8/F, Beauty Mansion
69-71 Kimberley Rd
Kowloon
Tel: (852) 2722 0896
Fax: (852) 2311 4167

Salon Films (H.K.)
6 Devon Rd
Kowloon Tong
Tel: (852) 2338 0505
Fax: (852) 2338 2539

Seasonal Film Corp.
12/F, Flat H, Kim Tak Bldg
328 Nathan Rd
Kowloon
Tel: (852) 2385 6125
Fax: (852) 2770 0583

Southern Film Co.
Rm 1902, Dominion Centre
43-59 Queen's Rd East
Hong Kong
Tel: (852) 2528 4787
Fax: (852) 2865 1449

Tomson (H.K.) Films Co.
Suite 1406-09, 14/F,
China Resources Bldg
26 Harbour Rd
Hong Kong
Tel: (852) 2848 1668
Fax: (852) 2877 0590

United Filmmakers Organisation
Unit B, 11/F, Prosperous Centre
1 Knutsford Terrace
Tsimshatsui
Tel: (852) 2336 3298
Fax: (852) 2339 0972

Win's Entertainment
2A Kimberley Mansion
15 Austin Ave
Tsimshatsui
Tel: (852) 2739 2877
Fax: (852) 2369 0981

Wong Jing's Workshop
PO Box 99093
Tsimshatsui
Tel: (852) 2314 7198
Fax: (852) 2314 7120

Useful Addresses

Hong Kong Film Archive
Rm 176, 7/F, Camplex
123A Fa Yuen St
Mongkok
Tel: (852) 2739 2139
Fax: (852) 2311 5229

Hong Kong Film Directors Guild
2/F, 35 Ho Man Tin St
Kowloon
Tel: (852) 2760 0331
Fax: (852) 2713 2373

Hong Kong Film Academy
PO Box 71311
Kowloon
Tel: (852) 2786 9349
Fax: (852) 2742 7017

Hong Kong Film Institute
6/F, 295 Lai Chi Kok Rd
Kowloon
Tel: (852) 2728 2690
Fax: (852) 2728 5743

Hong Kong Theatres Assn.
21/F, Hongkong-Chinese Bank
42 Yee Woo St
Causeway Bay
Tel: (852) 2576 3833
Fax: (852) 2576 1833

Performing Artists Guild of H.K.
145 Waterloo Rd
Kowloon
Tel: (852) 2794 0388
Fax: (852) 2338 7742

Derek
Elley

Judging by the figures for 1997, cinemagoing in Hungary is still on a roll, fuelled by a range of high-tech multiplexes opened since autumn 1996 and the success of several local films. At the end of the year, there were 32 multiplex screens in Budapest (42 per cent of all screens in the capital), which took in 66 per cent of the city's box-office revenues, up from 46 per cent in 1996. Hungary as a whole currently has almost 600 screens. Admissions for the year rose by 21 per cent, to 16.8 million, and revenue by 56 per cent, to $22.8m (4.7 billion forints). Hungarian films grabbed an amazing 8.4 per cent of the market, with the 16 new local productions seen by more than 1.4 million people – the first time since 1992 that this figure has topped the million mark.

The majority of new local movies were distributed by Budapest Film, which had a major hit with Péter Timár's 1960s retro musical **Dollybirds** (see *IFG 1998*), seen by half a million people. Most other films, however, did not get even close to that figure: in fact, the bulk of the remaining admissions for the year were accounted for by András Kern and Róbert Koltay's comedy **Out of Order**, which racked up 351,000 admissions for distributor InterCom in its first three weeks (after opening in December 1997) and has since become the fourth highest grossing Hungarian film ever.

That sobering fact showed how, beneath the rosy statistics, the position for local production is still extremely perilous. The vast majority of Hungarian movies scrape by with a few thousand admissions. Even titles that travelled to festivals did poorly at home: János Szász's splendid **The Witman Boys** clocked up 15,000 admissions, Attila Janisch's challenging Shirley Jackson adaptation, **Long Twilight**,

only 4,000, and Sándor Simó's affecting **Every Sunday** some 5,500. There is definitely a continuing trend towards making quality commercial fare, but many directors remain wedded to the art-for-art's sake ethos inherited from communist days. As a result, foreign sales of Hungarian films are still scarce.

The state-funded Motion Picture Foundation of Hungary, set up in April 1991 to aid the transition of film-making to a purely commercial basis, doled out $2.5m in 1997. The good news is that Hungarian TV (Magyar Televízió), which stood on the sidelines during the early days, is now an active partner in funding local production. Under the so-called TeleFilm agreement of 1996, and the Co-operation Contract signed in 1997, Hungarian TV is now bound to match the Foundation's contributions. A similar agreement with the country's two new commercial channels is also likely.

The long-debated Film Law – designed to replace the one that was swept away in 1989 – again hit the reefs in summer 1998. The arrival of a right-wing coalition in May put the whole issue of industry regulation (a favourite of the socialists) on the back burner. Draft proposals that included tripling the distribution tax from two to six per cent (to channel more money into local productions) had also been opposed by distributors and the US companies which supply them with product. Hungary's industry looks to remain resolutely free-market for the time being – which further increases the pressure on film-makers to come up with marketable, rather than purely art, movies.

Outrageous behaviour

The crop of new films shown at the 29th Hungarian Film Week in February 1998 did

András Kern (left) and Róbert Koltai (right) in OUT OF ORDER   *photo: Ferenc Somogyi*

not show much progress in the trend towards quality commercial fare. Kern and Koltay's *Out of Order* (*A miniszter félrelép* – literally, "The Minister Misbehaves"), produced by Hungarian-born Hollywoodite Andy Vajna, is a pleasantly amusing farce, based on Ray Cooney's English stage play about a politician's sexual escapades, but depends a lot for its humour on recognising the local stars going through their schtick.

Both Kern and Koltai have separately directed local box-office hits (*Stracciatella*, 1996, and *We Never Die*, 1993), but *Out of Order* evinces none of those films' very different styles: technically the film is functional rather than inspired, with the sheer mechanics of the plot and the lively performances keeping things going. Vajna plans a Hollywood remake in English.

After the entertaining *Dollybirds*, Péter Timár returned with a madcap comedy, **Feri's Gang** (*Zimmer Feri* – a pun on "Zimmer frei", the German for "room to rent"), about an entrepreneur who leases a boarding house near Lake Balaton and rips off any tourists stupid enough to stay there. Though the cast is good, the humour is manic rather than genuinely funny, and Timár's technical ticks, like accelerated action, become annoying as the movie progresses.

No other new films qualified for the "commercial" tag, though the Film Week showcased several items of solid quality. Károly Makk's **The Gambler**, a UK-Dutch-

Hungarian co-production shot in English, is a return to form by the veteran director, here taking Dostoyevsky's novel as the basis for a cleverly-constructed drama in which the creation of the novel (and Dostoyevsky's relationship with his secretary) parallels the author's own personal history. Michael Gambon is superb as the grouchy, indebted writer, and the film has a typically Makk feel for faded exotica and doomed love; as the secretary Dostoyevsky finally married, Jodhi May is, however, the weakest link in the strong cast.

Not quite a wandering star

Bence Gyöngyössy, son of film-makers Katalin Petényi and the late Imre Gyöngyössy, made a solid, if unexciting, debut with **The Law of the Gypsies** (*Roman kris/Cigánytörvény*), a kind of Romany *King Lear* with a powerful central performance by Djoko Rossich as a wandering teller of tales estranged from his youngest daughter. Beautifully shot by Tamás Sas (a director in his own right), the film is hampered by an over-loose script and too much semi-documentary detail of gypsy life, which dissipates the drama.

In his first film as a director, Sas came up with one of the most original films of the year, **Espresso** (*Presszó*), a portrait of the habitués of a small coffee bar over the course of a year that is entirely shot (apart from the opening and closing shots) from a single vantage point. Strongly scripted, and brightly coloured, with lively

Still from ESPRESSO

performances by a small cast, the movie intriguingly hovers somewhere between a commercial and art film in flavour.

Straightforwardly shot, and occasionally interesting, was Dezsö Zsigmond's **The Blood of the Rose** (*A rózsa vére*), a drama-cum-love story set on the Ukrainian border and centred on real-life trafficking in diesel fuel. Unfortunately, the fine actress Eszter Nagy-Kálózy, as an assured bar owner who dabbles in smuggling, is largely wasted in a film that never realizes its potential, due to an unfocused script and uninvolving characters. One of the smallest films of the year, but as fresh as it is fragile, was **Hungarian Fragment** (*Pannon töredék*), about a young man arrested for his part in the failed 1956 uprising. The film is basically a collection of flashbacks to his love affair with a Bulgarian girl, shot and acted with real tenderness, an advance on director András Sólyom's glossy, softcore *School of Senses*. The film will be remembered for, if nothing else, its shock final scene, featuring imaginative, excruciating sexual torture.

Auteurs and anarchy

The Week showcased the usual collection of auteurist movies that stand almost zero chance for any commercial career. The Russian co-production **Natasha** (*Natasa*), an unlikely, exotic romance set in Moscow University, is a severe disappointment from Tamás Tóth after the striking *Children of the Cast Iron Gods*. Györgyi Szalai and István Dárday's 143-minute, video-shot **Reflections** (*Tükröződések*) takes their normal experimentalism to ridiculous limits, an end-of-millennium fresco of images and memories (shot through ripple glass) revealed while an astrologer lies dying in a Venice hospital.

Such works were shamed by **Gangster Film** (*Gengszter film*), the latest blackly comic meld of reality and genre elements from middle-generation Gyorgy Szomjas, who continues to prove that it is possible to be anarchic and entertaining at the same time. Based on a true story, and centred on a group of bungling criminals, the film is

Still from GANGSTER FILM

much darker than a lot of Szomjas' work, but mixes superb performances, film, video and black-and-white in vigorous, virtuoso style.

Though it is entirely uncommercial, and demands considerable patience at times, the film of the year was undoubtedly **Passion** (*Szenvedély*), Béla Tarr disciple György Fehér's two-and-a-half-hour black-and-white transposition of James M. Cain's *The Postman Always Rings Twice* to a Hungarian setting. Shot over three years, Fehér's second feature is very similar in feel to his moody crime drama *Twilight* (1990), with grainy images, long silences, understated lighting and seemingly perpetual rain. However, for those willing to immerse themselves in the film there is a real sense of claustrophobia and animal passion, excellently incarnated by the experienced cast of Djoko Rossich as the brutish husband, Ildikó Bánsági as the wife, and János Derzsi as the lover.

29th Hungarian Film Week Awards

Best Film: *Passion* (György Fehér).
Best Director: György Fehér (*Passion*).
Best Actress: Ildikó Bánsági (*Passion*).
Best Actor: Djoko Rossich (*The Law of the Gypsies*) and János Derzsi (*Passion*).
Best First Film: *Espresso* (Tamás Sas).
Best Cinematography: Miklós Gurbán (*Passion*).
Best Script: Gábor Német, Tamás Sas (*Espresso*).
Best Experimental Film: *Altamira* (Attila Mispál).
Best Short: *Actor Benda Disappears* (Kata Nagy).
Special Prize: *Reflections* (Györgyi Szalai, István Dárday).

Best Documentary: *Helpless* (Tamás Almási) and *Fractions II* (Pál Schiffer).
Gene Moskowitz Prize (foreign critics): *Passion*.
Hungarian Assn. of Film Distributors Prize (most popular films of 1997): *The Conquest* (Gábor Koltay) and *Dollybirds* (Péter Timár).
Lifetime Achievement Awards: László Devényi (actor-director), Tibor Rajky (sound), Mrs Ferenc Szecsényi (editor).

Forthcoming Films

WERCKMEISTER HARMÓNIÁK (The Werckmeister Harmonies)

Script: László Krasznahorkai, Béla Tarr; based on Krasznahorkai's novel, *The Melancholy of Resistance*. Dir: Tarr. Players: Lars Rudolph, János Derzsi, Ildikó Pécsi. Prod: Goess Film, Telefilm (Hungary)/ Joachim von Vietinghoff (Berlin)/ Paul Branco Prods. (Paris).

KISVILMA (Little Vilma)

Dir: Márta Mészáros. Prod: Uj Dialog (Budapest)/Images Nouvelles (Paris)/Euroarts Intl. (Germany).

A prequel to Meszaros' *Diary* trilogy.

HANSEL AND GRETEL

Dir: Péter Gothár. Hungarian-French-Austrian coproduction.

Based on the Grimm Brothers' fairytale.

A WINTER BEHIND GOD'S BACK

Dir: Can Togay. Players: Florence Pernal, Yevgeni Sigikhin, Károly Eperjes, Lajos Kovács, Juli Básti. Hungarian-French-Belgian co-production.

Drama set in an isolated mountain village.

Producers

Béla Balázs Studio
Bajcsy-Zsilinszky ut 36-38
1054 Budapest
Tel/Fax: (36 1) 111 2809

Budapest Film Studio
Róna utca 174
1045 Budapest
Tel: (36 1) 251 8568
Fax: (36 1) 251 0478

Focus Film
Pasaréti út 122
1026 Budapest
Tel: (36 1) 176 7484
Fax: (36 1) 176 7493

Forum Film
Róna utca 174
1145 Budapest
Tel/Fax: (36 1) 220 5413

Hunnia Studio
Róna utca 174
1145 Budapest
Tel: (36 1) 252 3170
Fax: (36 1) 251 6269

InterPannonia
(animation, also distribution)
Gyarmat utca 36
1145 Budapest
Tel: (36 1) 267 6514, 267 6515
Fax: (36 1) 267 6516

Magic Media
Róna utca 174

1145 Budapest
Tel: (36 1) 163 3479
Fax: (36 1) 263 3479

Movie Innovation Partnership (MIP)
Kinizsi utca 28
1092 Budapest
Tel: (36 1) 218 3600, 218 0983
Fax: (36 1) 216 3601

Novofilm
(also services)
Hajógyárisziget 131
1033 Budapest
Tel: (36 1) 188 9304
Fax: (36 1) 155 9177

Objektiv Film Studio
Róna utca 174
1145 Budapest
Tel: (36 1) 252 5359
Fax: (36 1) 251 7269

Pannonia Film
(animation)
Hüvösvölgyi út 64
1021 Budapest
Tel: (36 1) 176 3333
Fax: (36 1) 176 3409

Transatlantic Media Associates (TMA)
(also services)
Táltos utca 4
1123 Budapest
Tel: (36 1) 155 3200
Fax: (36 1) 175 2444

Satellit-Film/Europe 2000
(also services)
Finkenstrasse 48
8130 Stamberg
Germany
Tel: (36 1) 8151 3551
Fax: (36 1) 8151 28544
ALSO
Róna utca 174
1145 Budapest
Tel/Fax: (36 1) 183 5930

Varga Studio
(animation, F/X)
Raktár utca 25-31
1035 Budapest
Tel: (36 1) 168 8296
Fax: (36 1) 168 6418

Distributors

Budapest Film
Báthori utca 10
1054 Budapest
Tel: (36 1) 132 8198
Fax: (36 1) 111 2687

Flamex
Labanc utca 22B
1021 Budapest
Tel: (36 1) 176 1534
Fax: (36 1) 176 0596

Hungarofilm
(also production services)
Báthori utca 10
1054 Budapest
Tel: (36 1) 111 0020, 131 4746
Fax: (36 1) 153 1850

InterCom
Bácskai utca 28-36
1145 Budapest
Tel: (36 1) 467 1400
Fax: (36 1) 252 2736

UIP-Dunafilm
Hüvosvolgyi ut 54
1021 Budapest
Tel: (36 1) 274 2180
Fax: (36 1) 274 2177

Useful Addresses

Assoc. of Hungarian Film & TV Artists
Városligeti fasor 38
1068 Budapest
Tel/Fax: (36 1) 342 4760

Assoc. of Hungarian Film Distributors
Karolina út 65
1135 Budapest
Tel/Fax: (36 1) 295 5001

Filmunio Hungary
(festivals, foreign promo)
Városligeti fasor 38
1068 Budapest
Tel: (36 1) 351 7760, 351 7761
Fax: (36 1) 268 0070, 351 7766

Hungarian Film Institute
Budakeszi út 51B
1012 Budapest
Tel: (36 1) 176 1018, 176 1322
Fax: (36 1) 176 7106

Motion Picture Foundation of Hungary (MMA)
Városligeti fasor 38
1068 Budapest
Tel: (36 1) 351 7696
Fax: (36 1) 268 0070

Mafilm Corp.
(studio complex)
Róna utca 174
1145 Budapest
Tel: (36 1) 252 2870
Fax: (36 1) 251 1080

S-media 2000
Szemlöhegy 28-30
1022 Budapest
Tel/Fax: (36 1) 326 0698

ICELAND

Ásgrímur Sverrisson

Film-making in Iceland remains a fight against huge odds. It is barely kept alive by meagre government funding, which has remained at around one million dollars for years. This amount is usually divided between three or four productions, with the producers having to find the remainder of their budgets (usually around 75 per cent) abroad.

Scandinavian and European film funds have provided assistance, but are evidently irritated at the lack of support from within Iceland for Icelandic-language films. The result is a vicious circle in which the Icelandic "film industry" is kept permanently below the poverty line and film-makers find themselves unable to work on a regular basis. Only Friðrik Thór

Pâll Banine in BLOSSI—810551

Friðriksson (*Cold Fever, Devil's Island*) has managed to keep himself constantly busy, thanks to his growing international stature.

How long can it go on like this? Increasingly, Icelandic film-makers are trying their luck elsewhere, but the grass is not necessarily greener on the other side and good stories about common human themes are usually rooted in the creator's culture. It is our perceptions of the little worlds we all live in that make the general specific – and therefore interesting.

Sophomores show progress

This rather sorry state of affairs was reflected in last year's films. Of the four features premiered, two were sophomore efforts by directors whose debuts, five years ago, were well-received. While both films, *BLOSSI/810551*, by Júlíus Kemp, and *Pearls and Swine*, by Óskar Jónasson, showed progress from their earlier efforts,

Still from Óskar Jónasson's PEARLS AND SWINE

the results were somewhat less than the sum of their parts. In spite of heartfelt subject matter, Einar Heimisson's debut feature, *Maria*, was also a disappoinment, unengaging and over-earnest. Ari Kristinsson's second feature, the entertaining *Count Me Out*, was the only one to deliver the goods.

BLOSSI/810551 takes place in the Iceland of tomorrow, where Reykjavík looks just like another urban desert and the barren Icelandic landscape is supposed to reflect the emotional bankruptcy of a generation gone astray. The main characters, Stella and Róbert, are pretty teenagers who want nothing – except constant stimulation in the form of clothes, music or drugs.

Watching their aimless circling around the country is amusing for a while, but soon grows tiresome and boring. The story is told with flashy style but, like its protagonists' lost souls, it has a hollow, pretentious core. There might be a message here, but it is like hearing breathing on your answering machine: you know somebody called but you do not know who and have no idea what the caller wanted to say.

Searching for a fast buck

Fuelled by a strong urge to make a fast buck, the middle-aged couple in **Pearls and Swine** embark on a series of questionable schemes. They buy a small, antiquated bakery and run it by any means necessary, selling dildos and other sex toys on the side. Their son accidentally double-crosses a bunch of hard-nosed Russian sailors on a shady car deal. What ensues is a comedy of errors where bad taste blends with good intentions. It all begins quite well, with funny and believeable characters you can laugh with and at; but in the latter half it seems as if writer–director Jónasson does not trust his characters to carry the story and instead he resorts to rather cheap tricks.

The fun remains, but is somewhat diminished as you watch real people change into caricatures. Still, with 21,475 admissions, *Pearls and Swine* ranked nineteenth in the year's box-office chart (the only Icelandic film in the top 20) and it would be interesting to see Jónasson flesh out these "little people with big dreams" in a stronger story.

Dry history, anarchic comedy

The title character in **Maria** is a refugee from post-war Germany, who is offered work on a farm in Iceland, along with several other women in similar circumstances. She finds farm life extremely boring and runs off to Reykjavík when the sex-starved farmer harasses her. There she meets a fellow countryman and refugee, a Jew who is soon dead of tuberculosis. She also bumps into the nice Icelandic sailor with whom she had a quick fling en route from Germany to Iceland. Now married, he is still willing to fool around, but she is having none of it and returns to Germany – relieved to get out of this rather dreary place.

Writer–director Heimisson, a historian who studied documentary-making at the Munich Film School, seems much more interested in the dynamics of history and politics than those of cinema. The outcome is a potentially interesting story buried in a dry, humourless and unfocused history lesson.

In **Count Me Out**, the adult world is amusingly complicated and ambiguous, but for the main characters, young Hrefna and her best friend, Yrsa, the objective could not be clearer: to locate Hrefna's long-absent father and get his recognition. In order to achieve their righteous aim they are prepared to tap-dance on the border of right and wrong. This is a slightly anarchic comedy disguised as social realism, a little fairytale within an everyday framework.

Writer–director Kristinsson has a light touch and handles the young cast very well, though the adult characters are a bit too sketchily drawn, resulting in uneven performances. Kristinsson's success in producing a film which can be enjoyed by young and old owes much to his vast

experience. One of the few true veterans of Icelandic film-making, he has worked mostly as a director of photography, but also as a producer and scriptwriter.

ÁSGRÍMUR SVERRISSON is a film-maker and the editor of the bi-monthly film magazine *Land & synir*.

Ingvar Sigurdsson and Nanna K. Magnúsdóttir in NO TRACE

Recent and Forthcoming Films

SPORLAUST (No Trace)

Script: Sveinbjörn I. Baldvinsson.
Dir: Hilmar Oddsson Prod: Jóna
Finnsdóttir/Tónabíó.

A young sports star wakes from a wild night to find an unknown girl in his bed.

ÓSKABÖRN (Plan B)

Script and Dir: Jóhann
Sigmarsson. Prod: Sigmarsson/
Friðrik Thór Friðriksson/The
Icelandic Film Corporation.

Petty criminals and drug addicts seek a way out of the seedy underworld.

DANSINN (The Dance)

Script: Agúst Guðmundsson,
Kristín Atladóttir, based on a
short story by William Heinesen.
Dir: Guðmundsson. Prod:
Guðmundsson/Nordisk Film/
Oxford Film Company/Hamburger
Kinokompanie.

On a small island in 1913, a wedding is disrupted by a shipwreck, looting, the disappearance of the bride and a close encounter with the devil.

MYRKRAHÖFDINGINN (Witchcraft)

Script: Hrafn Gunnlaugsson,
Bo Jonsson, Thórarinn Eldjárn.
Dir: Gunnlaugsson. Prod:
Gunnlaugsson/Friðrik Thór Frið-
riksson/Jonsson/Egil Ödegaard.

An idealistic seventeenth century priest is determined to save his flock from the devil, only to find demons raging within himself.

66°N

Script and Dir: Einar Thór
Gunnlaugsson. Prod: David
Pupkewitz/Focus Films UK/
Alliance Motion Pictures
Distribution/The Icelandic Film
Corporation.

A young hoodlum, on the run from the law, falls in love with a blind girl.

ENGLAR ALHEIMSINS (Angels of the Universe)

Script: Friðrik Thór Friðriksson,
Einar Már Guðmundsson, from
his Nordic Council Award-
winning novel. Dir: Friðriksson.
Prod. Friðriksson/The Icelandic
Film Corporation.

The tragi-comic story of a mentally ill man, told with humour and vitality.

FÍASKÓ (Fiasco)

Script and Dir: Ragnar Bragason.
Prod: Thórir Snær Sigurjónsson/
The Icelandic Film Corporation.

A funny look at the trials of a hapless family in downtown Reykjavík.

101 REYKJAVÍK

Script and Dir: Baltasar Kormákur,

from the novel *101 Reykjavík,* by Hallgrímur Helgason. Prod: Ingvar Thórðarson/101 Productions.

A comedy about a man whose mother is the father of his child.

UNGFRÚIN GOÐA OG HUSID (Honour of the House)

Script and Dir: Guðný Halldórsdóttir. From a short story by Halldór Laxness. Prod: Halldór Fiorgeirsson/Umbi Films/Nordisk Film.

Two sisters torture each other at the turn of the century, both in love with the man who has fathered the younger sister's child.

Still from Ágúst Guðmundsson's THE DANCE

Producers

The Icelandic Film Corporation
Contact: Friðrik Thór Friðriksson, Ari Kristinsson
Hverfisgata 46
101 Reykjavík
Tel: (354) 551 2260
Fax: (354) 552 5154
e-mail: icecorp@vortex.is
Website: www.saga.is/ifc

Pegasus Pictures
Contact: Snorri Thórisson
Sóltún 24
105 Reykjavík
Tel: (354) 511 4590
Fax: (354) 511 4595
e-mail: pegasus@islandia.is
Website: pegasus-pictures.com

Ísfilm
Contact: Ágúst Guðmundsson
Ooinsgata 20
101 Reykjavík
Tel: (354) 561 3395
Fax: (354) 552 3395

Umbifilm
Contact: Halldór Thorgeirsson, Guðny Halldórsdóttir
Melkot
270 Mosfellsbær
Tel: (354) 566 6874
Fax: (354) 566 8002

Distributors

Association of Icelandic Film Distributors
Laugarásbíó, Laugarási
104 Reykjavík
Tel: (354) 553 8150
Fax: (354) 568 0910

Useful Addresses

Icelandic Film Fund
Túngata 14,
101 Reykjavík
Tel: (354) 562 3580
Fax: (354) 562 7171
E-mail: iff@iff.is
Website: www.iff.is/

Association of Icelandic Film Producers
Pósthússtraeti 13
PO Box 476
121 Reykjavík
Tel: (354) 562 8188
Fax: (354) 562 3424

Ministry of Culture and Education
Sölvhólsgötu 4
101 Reykjavík
Tel: (354) 560 9500
Fax: (354) 562 3068

The Icelandic Film Makers Association
PO Box 5162
121 Reykjavík
Tel: (354) 552 1202
Fax: (354) 562 0958
e-mail: fk@isholf.is

The Association of Icelandic Film Directors
Laugarnestangi 65
105 Reykjavík
Tel: (354) 588 1706
Fax: (354) 588 1706

The Icelandic Producers Association
PO Box 5357
125 Reykjavík

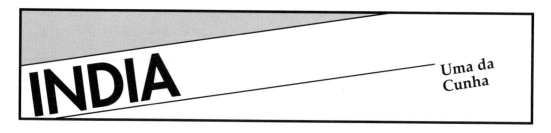

INDIA

Uma da
Cunha

In mid-1998, the Indian film industry hit the lowest ebb in its 67-year talkie history. Of the 58 new films released in the first five months of the year, only one, **Pyar Kiya to Darna Kya**, could be deemed a hit. This was worse even than 1988, when only 23 of the 140 Hindi films released recovered their costs. Film folk, in fear of their lives following 1997's gangster killings of movie magnates, now feared for their livelihood as well. Producers, exhibitors and stars floundered over a $23m loss.

The fall was hard on a cinema that has always prided itself on its infallible appeal. Even now it can boast an annual $1.25 billion turnover, employment for one million, the world's highest rate of film production, a national audience of 14 million per day and an ethnic one of 50 million outside India. Another 100 million in India watch movies on televison every day, as do a billion ex-patriots in 90 other countries. There is a great deal to lose.

For a year and more, Indian audiences have kept away from cinemas, ignoring the hyped-up new releases paraded before them by producers. Nothing seemed to work. Comedies, tragedies, musicals, fantasies, even big-budget, star-laden bonanzas - thumbs down greeted the lot. Young and old stars, paired and even tripled up for box-office safety, no longer drew the masses.

Why, asked the movie-makers, did 1997's *Virasat* (a warm, winsome film) succeed when 1998's **Saat Rang Ke Sapna** (a sugary sop) flop? Why did South India's top director Shankar's earlier *Hindusthani* (stirring songs) win and his current **Jeans** (an unconvincing mish-mash of characters and locations) fail? The answer is obvious.

A leading daily summed it up: "Cinema is a creative medium, not an assembly line which regurgitates pulp week after week." Besides, movie-going is pricey, with entertainment tax of more than 100 per cent added on to tickets. Cable television's movie-driven programming offers a cheaper alternative.

No pain, no gain?

The film industry's creativity goes into its financing. Bombay's film production maintains an outrageous flamboyance, despite its hair-raising risks on cash flow, with only one out of five films hitting the jackpot. By its speculative nature, film financing attracts money-lenders charging a 40 per cent annual interest rate. Perhaps 70 per cent of film finance comes from ready-cash traders in real estate, construction and jewellery, who are in awe of movie glamour. Only five per cent comes from the killer underworld.

Yet all this financial hurt may have a healing power. Films were being made at exorbitant production costs. Stars were spoilt brats getting sky-high fees. Now star prices are steady and falling. Distributors are refusing to accept films at huge pre-set prices. Theatres are rejecting the high, up-front costs of outright sales or minimum guarantee deals, preferring percentage agreements. This is a total reversal in India's film trade practice. Producers may finally learn to keep their costs down in order to survive.

The new BJP government's rulings may have their own remedial effect. At long last, the Ministry of Information and Broadcasting has recognised film-making as an industry, which will give it commercial status and benefits, for

Prashant and Aishwarya Rai in JEANS

instance enabling producers to approach reliable financing sources such as banks. In turn, the industry will have to learn management and marketing principles.

From a high of 938 films in 1994, India's film production rate has declined each year and was down to 681 in 1996. The 1997 total of 697 releases includes 523 new titles, with 174 dubbed from one Indian language into another. As usual, South India's lanuages dominate the output, with Telugu (151 films), Tamil (128), Malayalam (92) and Kannada (81) accounting for 65 per cent of the output. The remainder include Bengali (49 films), Oriya (20), Punjabi (14), Gujarati (10), Marathi (9), English (7) and Manipuri (5).

Foreign affairs and high-tech

Foreign film imports show an increase, with Hollywood hits coming to India at the same time as, or soon after their home release. In all, 191 foreign films were certified, of which 147 were from the US, 23 from Hong Kong, five each from Canada and Italy, two from South Africa and one each from the UK, Canada, Australia and Switzerland.

While Indian films are floundering, foreign films are thriving. Within eight weeks of its Indian release, *Titanic* took $4.25m, beating *Jurassic Park* even though it was released only in English, whereas Spielberg's dinosaurs won viewers in Indian language versions. Mira Nair's **Kamasutra**, dubbed in Hindi, rated among

the top three grossers. In 1997, 17 English language films were dubbed into Indian languages, and the sizeable market for such movies is beginning to worry the indigenous industry.

India's growing expertise in film technology is where the country scores. While digital high-definition studios are mushrooming within India, the country's special effects and computer technology is on demand internationally. Madras-based PentaFour, specialising in motion-capture computer technology, will handle the Hollywood film *Sinbad*, billed as the first 3-D animated motion capture feature.

At home, Hyderabad, the city that produced the most movies in India, now boasts the world's largest studio complex, the $110m Ramoji Film City, named after city magnate Ramoji Rao. In Bombay, the younger members of established film families are making waves in exhibition and distribution. Shravan Shroff, of Shringar Films, renovated a suburban theatre and renamed it Cinemax. With marvellous new seating and projection, it is now packed to capacity by the young. Shroff is also providing release opportunities to the young and gifted. Nagesh Kukunoor's first film, **Hyderabad Blues**, will be a landmark release at Cinemax. Roosi Modi, second-generation owner of another Bombay cinema, the old-world New Empire, followed Shroff's example. He refurbished the New Empire, preserving every nuance of its original art-deco style, while upgrading its technical facilities. Significantly, these renovated theatres screen mostly English-language movies.

Suffering for their art

The art-house Indian movie is also on the decline. Major film-makers, such as Shyam Benegal, are busy with television assignments linked to the fiftieth anniversary of Indian independence. The art film invariably subsists on low government funding and has no distribution outlet. They look to film festivals for recognition. Among those

Tabu and Kamal Haasan in CHACHI 420

braving the bleak scene with new ventures are Dev Benegal, with his English film, **Split Wide Open**, which should be released in the spring of 1999.

Rituparna Ghosh, whose *Dahan* got international notice, has started on his new film, **Asukh**. In Madras, Mani Ratnam has been completing his next, **Dil Se** (in Hindi). Jayaraaj, who established himself as a director with *Deadanam*, is ready with a new film, **Thalolam**. The year was dominated by Kamal Haasan. This multi-talented personality (actor, director, producer, dancer, writer) released an Indian take-off of *Mrs Doubtfire*, **Chachi 420**, which audiences lapped up, and is now working on a marathon project about Marudanaayagam, an eighteenth-century soldier-patriot.

India's film diaspora is increasingly active. Ismail Merchant produced **Side Streets**, a tale of immigrant life in the New

Kamal Haasan in MARUDANAAYAGAM

York suburbs, directed by newcomer Tony Gerber and starring Shashi Kapoor, Art Malik and Shabana Azmi. Merchant is now set to make an India-based feature, **Cotton Mary**. Shekhar Kapur has been making two more of the bio-pics that, starting with the raw *Bandit Queen*, have become his forte, directing *Elizabeth* in England and then moving on to *Mandela* in South Africa. Atlanta-based Nagesh Kukunoor's second feature, **Rockford – A Journey from Innocence**, is set in southern India.

Deepa Mehta's new film, **Earth**, will be released in the autumn. Her next is said to be an American film with Richard Gere in the lead. Mira Nair starts on her next film later this year, set in Bombay's glittery film community. UK-based Asians such as Fraz Hussein, with *Dirty British Boys*, and Ian Rasheed, with *Surviving Sabu*, are names to watch.

Film festivals are proliferating in India. The leader of the pack is the International Film Festival of India, run by Malti Sahai and held every January in Delhi, with awards for Asian films. November's

Art Malik (right) and Shashi Kapoor in SIDE STREETS

impressive Calcutta International Film Festival has gained FIAFP accreditation in just four years. Held in the sprawling Nandan Film Complex, it is managed by Ansu Sur. Each April, Kerala has been hosting its own creditable international event and now Bombay has entered the frame, with a November festival.

UMA DA CUNHA heads Medius (India) Services Private Ltd, a company that provides promotional and executive services for films shot in India, specialising in casting Indian actors. She is *Variety's* correspondent in India and a consultant on film programming and events for festivals in India and abroad.

Recent and Forthcoming Films

MARUDANAAYAGAM

Lang: Tamil. Dir: Kamal Haasan. Phot: Ravi K. Chandran. Story/Script: Sujatha Rangarajan. Players: Haasan, Om Puri. Prod: Haasan.

A three-part epic about Marudanaayagam, an obscure, eighteenth-century patriot-rebel. He paid with his life for sowing the seeds of India's independence and is regarded today as a folk-hero.

ENNU SWANTHAM JANAKIKUTTY
(Yours, Janakikutty)

Lang: Malayalam. Dir: T. Hariharan. Phot: Hari Nair. Story: M. T. Vasudevan Nair. Players: Sarath Das, Jomol, Valsala Menon, Chakyar Rajan. Prod: P. V. Gangadharan.

Neglected teenager Janakikutty discovers a fantasy world and is befriended by a Yakshi (a netherworld enchantress with a thirst for blood).

KALIYATTAM (The Play of God)

Lang: Malayalam. Dir: Jayaraaj. Phot: M. J. Radhakrishnan. Story: Balaram. Players: Suresh Gopi, Lal, Manju Warrier, Rajendran, Narendra Prasad, Bindu Panickar. Prod: M/S Jayalakshmi Films.

Shakespeare's *Othello* adapted to Kerala's Theyyam, a temple ritual dance form in which the costumed performer assumes a divine identity.

THAI SAHEB

Lang: Kannada. Dir: Girish Kasaravalli. Phot: H. M. Ramachandra. Story: Ram-Sha, Lokapur. Players: Jayamala, Suresh Hoblikar, Shivram, Vijaya Ekkundi. Prod: Jayamala.

India, from the 1930s to 1960s. Landowner Appa Sahib's wife, Thai Saheb, is the archetypal traditional woman. Their adopted son, unable to marry the daughter of Appa Sahib's mistress, goes to seed and Thai Saheb sets out to ensure his happiness.

CHHUTI KAR DOONGA
(Getting Even)

Lang: Hindi. Dir and Story: Roop Naik. Phot: Seetha Ram Sandhiri. Players: Mamta Kulkarni, Samir Soni, Anjan Srivastava, Vijayendra Ghatge. Prod: NFDC.

An upright bank official refuses to sanction a loan to a rich businessman. Both meet unexpectedly on holiday and problems begin when their off-spring fall in love.

EKTI NADIR NAAM
(The Name of the River)

Lang: Bengali. Dir: Anup Singh. Phot: K. K. Mahajan, Prasann Jain. Story: Anup Singh, Madan Gopal Singh. Prod: NFDC/BFI.

Documentary about the work of celebrated Bengali film-maker, Ritwick Ghatak, tracing his emotional and intellectual life as a refugee.

KUCH DIL NE KAHA
(A Whisper from the Heart)

Lang: Hindi. Dir: Purnima Prabhu. Story: Manjiri Prabhu. Phot: Debu Deodhar. Players: Divya Dutta, Rajiv Raj, Sulabha Deshpande, Anang Desai. Prod: NFDC.

Chandan, a soon-to-be-married psychiatrist, is troubled by memories of a mysterious woman and resorts to hypnosis as a cure. First film from a new woman director.

Suresh Gopi in KALIYATTAM

ASUKH (The Illness)

Lang: Bengali. Dir/Story/Script: Rituparna Ghosh. Phot: Aveek Mukherjee. Players: Soumitra Chatterjee, Debashree Roy, Gita Sen, Shilajeet. Prod: D. Rama Naidu.

The story of a film actress, and how the close relationship she shares with her father falters when her mother falls ill.

DIL SE (From the Heart)

Lang: Hindi. Dir: Mani Ratnam. Phot: Santosh Sivan. Players: Sharukh Khan, Manisha Koirala, Sabyasachi Chakroborty, Arundhati Nag. Prod: Quasar Productions.

This film deals with the current Assam terrorist movement and was made amid much secrecy. Ratnam's treatment of contemporary socio-political themes, enlivened with song, dance and cinematic panache, invariably invokes strong reactions.

DANCING HELL

Lang: Bengali. Dir: Nitish Mukherjee. Story: Manoj Mitra. Phot: Kanai De. Players: Debashree Roy, Sumanta Mukherjee, Anup Kumar, Chinmoy Roy. Prod: Sujeet Sen for Production SS.

A political satire in which mythological characters lord it over humdrum peasants in a symbolical presentation of heaven, hell and earth.

MY OWN COUNTRY

Lang: English. Dir: Mira Nair. Phot: Dion Beebe. Story: Abraham Verguese. Script: Sooni Taraporevala. Players: Naveen Andrews, Ellora Patnaik, Marisa Tomei, Hal Holbrook and Glenne Headly. Prod: Dufferin Gate for Show-Time Entertainment.

An India-born doctor raised in Ethopia finds himself in Tennessee's poor quarters, working with terminally ill Aids patients. The experience touches his soul but his wife is appalled and threatens to leave him.

Jayamala in THAI SAHEB

ANU

Lang: Bengali. Dir and Story: Shatumanya Sanyal. Phot: Kamal Nayak. Players: Indrani Haldar.

Anu is gang-raped to force her to divulge her insurgent boyfriend's hide-out. He is arrested and jailed. On his release they marry, but he finds he cannot cope with his wife's past ordeal.

TERRORIST

Lang: Tamil. Dir, Story and Phot: Santosh Sivan. Players: Ayesha Dharker, Vishnu Vardhan, Bhanu Prakash, K. Krishna. Prod: Modern Gallery Motion Pictures/Indian Image.

Young Malli, devastated when her brother, a revolutionary, is killed, joins a terrorist group and is chosen to kill a politician by serving as a 'human bomb'.

RAY

Lang: English. Script, Dir and Phot: Gautam Ghose. Prod: Satyajit Ray Archives/Ford Foundation.

A documentary about Ray's creative world – his music, movies, stories and illustrations. Ray's 'Khero Khata' (work books and personal diaries) form the spine of the film.

SIDE STREETS

Lang: English. Dir: Tony Gerber. Phot: Russell Lee Fine. Story: Lynn Nottage and Gerber. Players: Valeria Golino, Shashi Kapoor, Leon, Shabana Azmi, Art Malik. Prod: Ismail Merchant/Bruce Weiss, Cornerstone Films.

Five criss-crossing tales reflecting immigrant lifestyles in raucous New York surburbia. One concerns an ageing Indian ex-star (Kapoor) preparing for a doomed come-back.

SUCH A LONG JOURNEY

Lang: English. Dir: Sturla Gunnasson. Story: Rohinton Mistry. Script: Sooni Taraporewala. Phot: Jan Kiesser. Players: Naseeruddin Shah, Roshan Seth, Om Puri, Soni Razdan, Sam Dastoor. Prod: Filmworks/AmyInternational.

Gustad Noble, a member of Bombay's select Parsi family finds himself downgraded in life as a bank clerk and dreams of a bright future brought about by his son.

Marselli
Sumarno

The only Indonesian film that could be considered a box-office hit in 1997 was **Sugarcane Plantation Mystery** (*Misteri Kebun Tebu*). This was based on a true story of a 'sorcerer' in Medan, North Sumatra, who, with the assistance of his wives, deceived and murdered scores of women who were reportedly his patients. The film sparked great controversy because it was screened while the trial of the sorcerer was still going on. Some quarters branded the film as unethical. Its producer claimed to have paid the sorcerer for the rights to his story. As is usually the case, the controversy only served to boost the film's box-office success.

Gripped by economic crisis, Indonesia has all of a sudden become poor, film producers included. Even the country's growing television industry cannot escape the impact. In the last five years, the annual film production level has slipped to not more than 30 titles. Twenty were produced in 1997, but, in 1998, a question mark hangs over their quality because most have yet to return from the laboratory – producers simply cannot afford to pay the soaring costs of film processing and printing. The number of movie theatres has plummeted: 2,292 cinemas in 1994, half that number in 1997.

Demands for economic, political and legal reforms reverberated across the country and culminated in the resignation of President Suharto in May. The same cries could be heard within the film industry. The National Film Advisory Board, which is under the co-ordination of the Ministry of Information, has been criticised for being too bureaucratic, and film-maker Sophan Sophiaan believes the entire film infrastructure has totally collapsed. Scriptwriter Asrul Sani has said

there are too many speeches and slogans in the Indonesian film world. Chand Parwez, a producer and distributor, has recommended that the government scrap its import quotas and give distributors freedom to buy in as many movies as they want from America, Europe or Asia.

Matters of life and death

In the meantime, a number of films have been completed, as if unaffected by the gloomy economic atmosphere. They have been made by individuals who have obtained international funds and are oriented to the international market. It is becoming increasingly evident that the film industry urgently needs an injection of international funds to survive.

Young Garin Nugroho directed **Leaf on a Pillow** (*Daun Di Atas Bantal*), a film about the hard life experienced by three boys in Yogyakarta, Central Java. The three grow up on the streets, desperate for money. Luckily, they are taken care of by a batik-selling widow (excellently played by Christine Hakim, a celebrated actress who also produced the film). However, the hard life in a big city proves too much for the boys and, one after the other, they die.

Garin has earned a number of awards, although none of his films have been commercially successful. His second and third features, *Letter to an Angel* (*Surat Untuk Bidadari*) and *And the Moon Dances* (*Bulan Tertusuk Ilalang*), have not gained theatrical distribution, although they have been aired on the national TV channel.

Two years in the making, **Cul-de-sac** (*Kuldesak*) was finally scheduled for distribution in July 1998. The film, dwelling on the dead-end fate of a number of young people, is a collaboration

Still from Slamet Rahardjo's TELEGRAM

between four young film-makers – Nan Triveni, Mira Lesmana, Muhamad Rivai and Rizal Mantovani – who have each made a 30-minute segment of the two-hour project.

Return to sender

A more senior director, Slamet Rahardjo, showed his awareness of the need to find international finance with his latest work, **Telegram**, a co-production involving 70 per cent investment from his own company, Eka Praya, with producer Joel Farges of France's Artcam International contributing the remaining 30 per cent of a $500,000 budget.

Telegram is based on the novel by noted author Putu Wijaya. It tells the story of a journalist facing a lot of problems. One day, he receives a telegram from his mother in Bali asking him to return home immediately. However, his relations with a number of prostitutes, his adopted child and his busy work prevent him from returning home immediately. Telegrams keep arriving, telling him that his mother is seriously ill. When he finally journeys home he arrives to find his mother already dead.

Your correspondent made his directorial debut with **Sri**, focusing on a young woman who, after marrying an older man of noble blood, Hendro, becomes a famed Javanese classical dancer. When Hendro is seriously ill, Sri pleads with the god of death for leniency, namely to postpone his demise in order to enable him to carry out three important acts. The film is set in decadent Java, Surakarta City to be precise, where men gamble and womanise. Towards the end of the film, Hendro, beyond salvation, is as dead as the past. Sri is meant to symbolise every modern Javanese woman.

MARSELLI SUMARNO heads the Film Studies Department, Faculty of Film and Television, IKJ. He is also a film critic, scriptwriter and director.

Recent and Forthcoming Films

DAUN DI ATAS BANTAL
(Leaf on a Pillow)

Script: Armantono. Dir: Garin Nugroho. Phot: Nur Hidayat. Players: Christine Hakim, Sugeng, Heru, Kancil. Prod: Christine Hakim Film.

SRI

Script and Dir: Marselli Sumarno. Phot: Hadi Artomo. Players: Rina Ariyanti, Sardono W. Kusumo, R.M. Ronosuripto, Niniek L. Karim. Prod: Sinema Sejati & FFTV–IKJ.

MISTERI KEBUN TEBU
(Sugarcane Plantation Mystery)

Script: Joko Supriyono. Dir: Edd SS. Phot: Hadi Artomo. Players: Wawan Wanisar, Devi Ivone, Linda, Rina Martini, Chandra. Prod: Diwangkara Citra Film.

GAIRAH 100% (Total Passion)

Dir: Golden Koswara. Phot: Partogi. Players; Reynaldi, Meggie, Wilda Hidayat. Prod: Diwangkara Citra Film.

Producers

Sinema Sejati
Sentra Radio Dalam
Jalan Kramat Pela 39
Kebayoran Baru
Jakarta 12140
Tel: (62 21) 726 9937, 726 9938
Fax: (62 21) 720 3504

Star Vision
Jalan Cempaka Putih Raya 116 A–B
Jakarta Pusat 10510
Tel: (62 21) 425 3390
Fax: (62 21) 425 5477

Eka Praya Film
Jalan Pahlawan no. 4
Rempoa
Jakarta Selatan
Tel/Fax: (62 21) 743 0146

Cinevisi
Gedung PSKD
Jalan Kramat IV
Jakarta 10330
Tel: (62 21) 334 333/361 824
Fax: (62 21) 310 2133

Pancaran Indra Cine
Jalan KS Tubun 75B
Jakarta 10260
Tel: (62 21) 571 0998/571 1003
Fax: (62 21) 573 1636

Miles Production
Jalan Pelita 18
Cipete
Jakarta Selatan
Tel: (62 21) 720 7341
Fax: (62 21) 722 6569

Rapi Film
Jalan Cikini II/7
Jakarta Pusat
Tel: (62 21) 357 135/332 860

Parkit Film
Roxi Mas
Blok C–2, no. 31-34
Jakarta
Tel: (62 21) 386 7315/386 7316

Elang Perkasa Film
Jalan Kayu Putih 4/48
Jakarta Timur
Tel: (62 21) 470 0801
Fax: (62 21) 489 4574

Prasidi Teta Film
Jalan Dr. Sahardjo 149 J
Jakarta Selatan
Tel: (62 21) 828 2740/828 1324

Kanta Film
Jalan Kayu Putih VI B/28
Jakarta Tinur
Tel: (62 21) 489 6434

Bola Dunia Film
Jalan Pintu Air 51C
Jakarta Pusat
Tel: (62 21) 384 3983/384 8721

Sepakat Bahagia Film
Jalan Mangga Besar Raya 107
Blok D–7
Jakarta Pusat
Tel: (62 21) 649 6657/649 6657

Virgo Putra Film
Jalan KH Hasim Ashari Dalam 111
Jakarta Pusat
Tel: (62 21) 363 308

Studio 41
Jalan Kapten P. Tendean 41
Mampang
Tel: (62 21) 520 4356
Fax: (62 21) 520 1493

Distributors/ Importers

Satrya Perkasa Estetika
(European/American importer)
Subentra Building
Jalan Gatot Subroto Kav.21
7th Floor
Jakarta
Tel: (62 21) 522 0022

Suptan Film
(Mandarin importer)
Subentra Building
Jalan Gatot Subroto Kav.21
7th Floor
Jakarta
Tel: (62 21) 522 0022

Buanavista Indah Film
(Asia non-Mandarin importer)
Jalan Pintu Air 51C
Jakarta
Tel: (62 21) 384 3983/384 8721

Useful Addresses

Faculty of Film and Television – The Jakarta Institute of the Arts
Jalan Cikini Raya 73
Jakarta 10330
Tel: (62 21) 316 1258
Fax: (62 21) 323 603

Directorate for Film and Video Development
Ministry of Information
Jalan Merdeka Barat 9

Jakarta
Tel: (62 21) 377 408/385 4336
Fax: (62 21) 386 0830

National Film Advisory Board
Jalan MT Haryono
Kav. 47–48
Jakarta Selatan
Tel: (62 21) 790 2974/790 2975
Fax: (62 21) 790 2973

State Film Production Centre
Jalan Otto Iskandardinata 125–127
Jakarta Timur
Tel: (62 21) 819 2508
Fax: (62 21) 819 0339

Indonesian Film Producers Association
Pusat Perfilman H. Usmar Ismail
Jalan Rasuna Said
Jakarta 12940
Tel: (62 21) 526 8461
Fax: (62 21) 526 8460

Association of Film and TV Technicians
Pusat Perfilman H. Usmar Ismail
Jalan Rasuna Said
Jakarta 12940
Tel: (62 21)526 8459/526 8457
Fax: (62 21) 526 8457

Sinematek Indonesia
Pusat Perfilman H. Usmar Ismail
Jalan Rasun Said
Jakarta 12940
Tel: (62 21) 526 8455/527 8841
Fax: (62 21) 526 8454

Inter Pratama Studio & Lab
Jalan Raya Pasar Ragunan
Jakarta 12550
Tel: (62 21) 780 6030
Fax: (62 21) 780 6230

Televisi Republic Indonesia
(TVRI, state-owned TV network)
Jalan Gerbang Pemuda
Senayan
Jakarta
Tel: (62 21) 570 4720/570 4732
Fax: (62 21) 531 1195

PROMOTING
IRANIAN CINEMA

FARABI CINEMA FOUNDATION (FCF)

No. 55 Sie-Tir Ave.
Tehran 11358/I.R. IRAN
TEL: 98 21 671010, 678156
FAX: 98 21 678155
E-MAIL: FCFI@dpi.net.ir

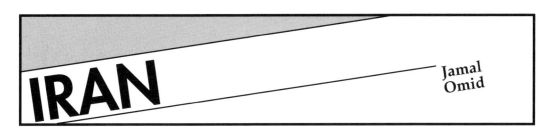

IRAN — Jamal Omid

The management of Iranian film affairs changed hands three times between 1994 and 1997 and, even if one were optimistically to assume that each successive Deputy Minister for cinematographic affairs had not made any mistakes, the negative effects of so much transition had undeniably created obstacles to the normal flow of film production.

The latest, extremely positive transition, however, came about in the wake of the election in May 1997 of Mohammad Khatami as Iran's president. Khatami, hitherto better known as a cultural personality than a political figure, gave cause for great hope by appointing Seifoliah Daad, a film-maker with 15 years' experience as a director (*Kani Manga, The Survivor*), scriptwriter, editor and producer, as cinema's new Deputy Minister.

Daad entrusted the sensitive task of managing the Supervision and Evaluation Department to Manuchehr Mohammadi, a highly successful executive producer in Daad's production corporation, Sina Cinema Organisation. The presence of two efficient industry figures in these key executive positions was an encouraging sign for film-makers: now they were dealing officials who had first-hand experience of the problems of film-making

Daad and Mohammadi both knew that the continued economic crisis – with salaries, film stock and equipment costs all soaring – could not be solved by issuing directives. They believed the solutions could only come from within the industry and, as a result, Daad disbanded the committees for screenplay approval, exhibition and production license, and turned over their functions to the House of Cinema, the association for various groups of Iranian film-makers.

The scheduling of the screening of films was transferred to an association of theatre managers and film producers. Thus Daad's office limited itself mainly to overseeing the implementation of the various duties, offering guidelines and creating suitable laws and regulations. It will take time, but these welcome measures may well create a new momentum in film production and exhibition.

Young talent bears fruit

With a few exceptions, the Iranian cinema in 1997 was characterised by commercial productions of low quality, and only a few pictures presented new vitality and surprisingly high artistic merit. One such was **The Apple**, scripted by Mohsen Makhmalbaf, and directed by his 17-year-old daughter, Samira. This was a bold account of the bitter real-life story of two girls and their mother, who were imprisoned in their home for several years by their beggar father. Samira's analytical method owes a great deal to her father's, but she brings her own sympathies and

Samira Makhmalbaf, director of THE APPLE, flanked by Zahra and Massume Naderi

Still from Farhad Mehranfar's THE TREE OF LIFE   *photo: Mohammad Zavvar Jalali*

sensitivities to the film, which was selected for Un Certain Regard at Cannes.

One of the most memorable Iranian films of recent years came from the exceptionally talented documentary-maker Farhad Mehranfar. **The Tree of Life** shows us the rites and values of the ancient Talesh tribe in northern Iran. Focusing mainly on one couple over the course of a year, Mehranfar fills the screen with scenes of exceptional pastoral beauty. Back in 1996, Ali Hatami, a peerless director when it came to depicting the culture and traditions of Iran's past, had died while filming **Takhiti, the World Champion**, about the life of the great Iranian wrestler. Last year, Behruz Ajkhami completed the project and the result was an exciting collage of imaginative scenes.

Iranian cinema witnessed exceptionally low box-office receipts in 1997, although **The Snowman**, directed by Davud Mirbaqeri, set a new Iranian box-office record of $500,000 (1.4 billion rials). The film, which was shot in 1994 and includes scenes of a man disguised as a woman, had been banned for four years, and was screened despite objections from certain groups. Aside from *The Snowman*, of the 48 domestic productions screened during the year, 30 failed to make back their production costs through admissions alone, and the other 18 fared even worse.

However, at a time when one would expect all production activities to have come to a halt, optimism about new measures from the Deputy Minister which may rekindle public interest in cinema (such as his decision to lift restrictions on the choice of themes suitable for feature films) has speeded up the production wheels.

By the time this report was prepared in April, more than 30 features were in production or post-production. Considering that twice that number will probably be shot during the summer and autumn, there could be a record total. The seventeenth Fajr International Film Festival, in February 1999, should offer greater variety in themes and styles.

JAMAL OMID has written 15 books on Iranian cinema in the past 30 years. He is best known for his 1,200-page *The History of the Iranian Cinema: 1900–1979*. The second, 1,500-page volume of this history has just been published. He also helped establish the Museum of Iranian Cinema, which opened in Tehran in May 1998.

Behruz Afkhami (left), directing Fariborz Arabnia in
TAKHTI – THE WORLD CHAMPION
photo: Ali Nikraftar

Recent and Forthcoming Films

SPECIAL CEREMONY

Script and Dir: Abbas Kiarostami. Phot: Mahmud Kalari. Players: Behzad Dowrani, ordinary people. Prod: Kiarostami.

SILENCE

Script and Dir: Mohsen Makhmalbaf. Phot: Ebrahim Ghaffuri. Players: Khorshid Nermatov, Nadere Abdolova.

THE WIND AND POPPY

Script and Dir: Ziaoddin Dorri. Phot: Ebrahim Ghaffuri. Players: Ezzatollah Entezami, Abolfuzi Poorarab, Landan Tabatabaie. Prod: Anti-Narcotics Information Department.

PAW IN THE DUST

Script: Mehdi Ab-bar, Sina Motallabi. Dir: Iraj Qaderi. Phot: Hussein Maleki. Players: Behzad Javanbakhsh, Akbar Abdi, Afsane Bayegan Prod: Shabanali Eslami.

A CHUNK OF THE MOON

Script: Ali Teimuri. Dir: Moharram Zeinaízade. Phot: Fazlollah Fáal Noori. Players: Changiz Vosuqi, Mahshid Afsharzade, Jamshid Shah-Mohammadi, Khosro Dastgir. Prod: Sacred Defense Foundation, Ormiye Cooperative 97.

TO BE OR NOT TO BE

Script and Dir: Kianush Ayari. Phot: Parviz Malekzade. Players: Asal Badiie, Farhad Sharifi, Hussein Ilbeigi. Prod: Farabi Cinema Foundation, K. Ayari.

THE RIOTERS

Script: Ah Asghar Amini. Dir: Mohammad Reza Aalami. Phot: Gholamreza Azadi. Players: Aryaz Alikhal, Behzad Khodaveisi, Jamshid Jahanzade, Krishma Ray. Prod: Amir Hussein Sharifi (Afagh Film).

THE WRONG MAN

Script: Farhad Towhidi. Dir: Mohammad Reza Honarmand. Phot: Mehrdad Fakhimi. Players: Parviz Parastui, Afsane Bayegan, Reza Zhiyan, Fateme Motamed-Aria. Prod: Soore Cinema Organization.

PASSION FOR LIFE

Script: Farzane Shabani. Dir: Farial Behzad. Phot: Gholamreza Azadi. Players: Dariush Arjomand, Mehrane Mahin Torabi. Prod: G. Azadi.

THE EAGLE'S EYES

Script and Dir: Shafi Aqamohmmadian. Phot: Faraj Heidari. Players: Framarz Qaribian, Jamshid Hashempoor,

Jalal, Akbar Abdi. Prod: Seyed Kamal Tabatabaie.

THE LEGEND OF THE GOLDEN POOPAK

Script: Mohsen Damadi. Dir: Khosro Shojaie. Phot: Farhad Saba. Players: Dariush Arjomand, Akbar Abdi, Jahanbakhsh Soltani. Prod: Majid Modarresi.

BITTER ALMONDS

Script and Dir: Kazem Masumi. Phot: Mojtaba Tahimi Players: Fariborz Arabnia, Hassan Joharchi, Amin Hayaie, Jamshid Mashayekhi. Prod: Seyed Mohsen Vaziri.

RED

Script and Dir: Freidun Jeirani. Phot: Mahmud Kalari. Players: Hedye Tehrani, Mohammad Reza Forutan, Shohre Soltani, Turan Mehrzad. Prod: Gholamreza Musavi, Habib Esmaili.

COMPANION OF THE ROAD

Script: Seyed Mehdi Madani, Hussein Irie. Dir: S. M. Madani. Phot: Naser Mahmud. Players: Mohammad Kasebi, Fathali Oveisi, Amir Badr Talei. Prod: Science and Culture Group, Channel One, I.R.I.B.

SURPRISE ATTACK

Script: Ataollah Salmanian. Dir: Abdolhussein Barzide. Phot: Masud Kramati. Players: Hussein Yari, Bahman Dan, Mohammad Jowzani.

DAWN OF VICTORY

Script: Alireza Akhlaqi. Dir: Hussein Bolande. Phot: Hussein Maleki. Players: Jafar Dehqan, Habib Allahyari.

THE LAST LONE RIDER OF THE TRIBE

Script: Mohammad Seifzade, Mohammad Taherian. Dir: M. Seifzade. Phot: Hassan Alimardani. Players: Behzad Frahani, Hadi Marzban, Mohammad Yegane. Prod: Khorramabad Cooperative 97.

THE FAMILIAR STRANGER

Script and Dir: Karim Atashi. Phot: Azim Javanruh. Players: Mahmud Dini, Atashi, Mehri Vedadian. Prod: Seventh Art Institute.

THE WHEEL

Script and Dir: Gholamreza Ramazani. Phot: Majid Farzane. Players: Ahmad Jan-Mohammadi, Abbas Taheri, Zahra Salehi.

THE SIN

Script and Dir: Mehran Taeedi. Phot: Mojtaba Rahimi. Players: Rambod Javan, Esmail Kamali, Negar Foruzande. Prod: M. Taeedi.

THE UGLY AND THE BEAUTIFUL

Script and Dir: Ahmad Reza Motamedi. Phot: Mohammad Aladpush. Players: Saeed Poorsamimi, Golchehre Sajjadiye, Asghar Hemmat. Prod: Farabi Cinema Foundation, Sima Film.

THE INNOCENT

Script: Jamshid Bahmani. Dir: Davud Towhidparast. Phot: Hassan Soltani. Players: Abolfazi Poorarab, Farhad Jam, Negar Foruzande, Mahbube Bayat. Prod: Ruhollah Khoshkam (Kowsar Film).

TWO WOMEN

Script and Dir: Tahmine Milani. Phot: Mehrdad Fakhimi. Players: Niki Karimi, Fariborz Arabnia, Athene Faqih Mofidi. Prod: Arta Film.

TOUGH TARGET

Script and Dir: Hushang Darvishpoor. Phot: Mahmud Akbari. Players: Bizhan Darvishpoor, Reza Samipoor, Turan Akbari. Prod: Ariyen Film.

SWEET AFFLICTIONS

Script and Dir: Alireza Davudnezhad. Phot: Asghar Rafiie Jam. Players: Mohammad Reza Davudnezhad, Fateme Davudnezhad, Zohre Miraqai, Hussein Miraqai, Hassan Joharchi. Prod: A. Davudnezhad.

FLIGHT OF THE SPIRIT

Script: Hussein Qasemi Jami, Javad Hashimi. Dir: Qasemi Jami. Phot: Abbas Baqerian. Players: J. Hashemi, Hassan Abbasi, Yusof Reza-Raisi. Prod: War Unit, Channel One, I.R.I.B.

LINES AND SHADOWS

Script and Dir: Behruz Faraji Qarkhuni. Phot: Ali Akbar Mazinani. Players: Framarz Qaribian, Fathali Oveisi, Jahangir Vosughi, Farimah Farjami.

THE STORY OF LOVE

Script and Dir: Ebrahim Vahidzade. Phot: Dariush Ayari. Players: Akbar Abdi, Soraya Qasemi, Amin Tarokh. Prod: Vahidzade.

THE TEST

Script and Dir: Majid Qarizade. Phot: Azim Javanruh. Players: Abolfazl Poorarab, Behruz Razavi, Hussein Kasbian, Marjan Shirmohammadi, Masume Taqipoor, Behzad Rahimkhani. Prod: Qarizade, Abbas Panahande.

THE WOUNDED

Script : Mohammad Taqi Zolqadr, Mohammad Saleh – Ala. Dir: Kamran Qadakchian. Phot: Reza Banki. Players: Jamshid Hashempoor, Afsane Bayegan, Mohammad Sadeqi.

Producers, Distributors and Co-operatives

Afaq Film
(Amir Hussein Sharifi)
No. 23 Shalid Amini
(Frahbod) St
Vali-e Asr Ave
Tehran
Tel: (98 21) 879 8588
Fax: (98 21) 8884 5141

Shekufa Film
(Dariush Babaiyan)
No.18 Amir Parviz, Abureyhan St
Enqelab Ave
Tehran
Tel: (98 21) 641 6939
Fax: (98 21) 640 2202

Hedayat Film
(Morteza Shayeste)
No.15 7th St
Khaled Eslamboli Ave
Tehran
Tel: (98 21) 872 7188/9
Fax: (98 21) 871 4220

Sobhan Film
(Saeed Hajimiri)
No. 45 Zay Alley, Vali-e Asr
Tehran
Tel: (98 21) 641 0816
Fax: (98 21) 641 5098

Iran Film Development
(Alireza Raisian)
No. 5 Arbabi Alley, Nesa St
Dastgerdi Ave
Tehran
Tel: (98 21) 222 1600
Fax: (98 21) 225 5621

Didar Film
(Shabanali Eslami)
No. 24 Behruzi Alley
North Kargar Ave
Tehran
Tel/Fax: (98 21) 928 034

Basir Film
(Habibollah Bahmani)
No. 12 J. St Moqaddas Ardabili
Vali-e Asr Ave
Tehran
Tel/Fax: (98 21) 204 0545.

Abgun Cultural Center
(Ali Akbar Saqafi)
No. 401 Avarez, Shariati Ave
Tehran
Tel: (98 21) 762 047

Cadre Film
(Majid Modarresi)
No. 39 Ashqian (Nilufar) St
Khorramshahr Ave
Tehran
Tel: (98 21) 876 6110
Fax: (98 21) 876 0488

Iran-Milad
(Bizhan Emkanian)
No. 1 Marivan St, South Sohreverdi
Tehran
Tel: (98 21) 831 549
Fax: (98 21) 752 4881

Children of Iran
(Mohammad Reza
Sarhangi)
No. 1 Sirus Alley, Shariati Ave,
Qolhak.
Tehran
Tel: (98 21) 267 708
Fax: (98 21) 269 496

Mahed Film
No. 27, Third Goldis, Danesh Blvd.
Gendarmerie Town.
Tehran
Tel: (98 21) 821 3042
Fax: (98 21) 22 8009

Hamrah Cooperative
(Hassein Zandbaf)

No. 40 Baharmastian Alley
7th of Tir Sq.
Tehran
Tel: (98 21) 883 4612
Fax: (98 21) 843 212

Nimruz
(Mehdi Sabbaghzade)
No. 1 Mohammadi Alley
North Bahar St
Tehran
Tel: (98 21) 753 6727
Fax: (98 21) 753 6727

**Soore Film Develepment
Organization**
(Mohammad Ah Hussein-Nezhad)
No. 213 Sornaye St
Nejatollahi Ave
Tehran
Tel: (98 21) 881 0270
Fax: (98 21) 889 3530

Sima Film
(Mohammad Mehdi Heidarian)
No. 53 Kuhyar Alley, Fereshte St
Tehran
Tel: (98 21) 221 8118
Fax: (98 21) 221 5889

Atlas Film
(Mohsen Shayanfar)
No. 26 Khorram Alley, Ansari St,
Jomhuri Ave
Tehran
Tel: (98 21) 646 6131

Dohol Film
(Mohammad Baqer Khosravi)
No. 246 (Opposite Mir Emad St)
Motahhari Ave
Tehran
Tel: (98 21) 882 5519

Ofoq Cinema Organisation
(Rasul Mollaqolipoor)
No. 23 Mansur Alley
(adjacent to Tehran Grand Hotel)
Motahhari Ave
Tehran
Tel: (98 21) 872 1871
Fax: (98 21) 872 1781

Arta Film
(Tahmine Milani, Abolhassan
Davudi)
No. 1/1 Etehad Alley
South Shiraz St, Molla Sadra Ave
Tehran
Tel/Fax: (98 21) 803 1193

Arman Film
(Ali Akbar Erfani)
No. 5 Ghaffari Alley, Fajr (Jam) St
Motahhari Ave
Tehran
Tel: (98 21) 882 2117
Fax: (98 21) 884 4025

Avishan Film
(Naser Shafaq)
No. 5 Fast Láal Alley
Parvin Etesami St
Dr. Fatemi Ave
Tehran
Tel: (98 21) 654 415
Fax: (98 21) 885 1720

Omid Film
(Sirus Taslimi)
No. 23 Tajbakhsh Alley, Nesa St
Mirdamad Ave
Tehran
Tel: (98 21) 227 6746
Fax: (98 21) 227 2310

Pakhshiran
(Harun Yashayaie)
No. 8 Somaye St, Bahar St
Tehran
Tel: (98 21) 882 4052
Fax: (98 21) 883 7684

Vara Honar
(Mehdi Karimi)
No.168 Avang Alley
Parvin Etesami St
Dr. Fatemi Ave
Tehran
Tel: (98 21) 800 0345
Fax: (98 21) 802 8853

Purika Film
(Seyed Mohammad Qazi
Samadollah Abedi)
No. 43 Ghaffari Alley, Fajr am St,
Motahhari Ave
Tehran
Tel: (98 21) 832 3540

Film Noor
(Fuad Noor)
No. 9 Azarshahr Alley, Iranshahr St
Tehran
Tel: (98 21) 834 889
Fax: (98 21) 272 310

Puya Film
(Hussein Farahbakhsh,
Abdollah Alikhani)
No. 10 Tavakko 1 Bldg., Jomhuri Ave
Tehran
Tel: (98 21) 673 574

Peyman Film
(Abolhassan Sanamari)
No. 11 Mehrzad Alley
South Iranshahr St
Tehran
Tel: (98 21) 883 9163
Fax: (98 21) 883 3789

Jozan Film
(Masud, Fathollah Jafari Jozani)
No. 20 Razmandegan Alley
Ghaffari, Fajr (Jam) St, Motahhari
Ave
Tehran
Tel: (98 21) 883 7271
Fax: (98 21) 882 6876

Iran Film Mansion
(Alireza Beheshti)
Tavakkol Bldg., Jomhuri Ave
Tehran
Tel: (98 21) 671 247
Fax: (98 21) 649 7106

Ama Medium
(Mohammad Mehdi Dadgu)
No. 138 Shahid Beheshti Ave
Tehran
Tel: (98 21) 874 4694
Fax: (98 21) 875 2976

Roshan Film
(Ali Mazinani)
No. 97 Arbab Jamshid, Kushk St
Ferdowsi Ave
Tehran
Tel: (98 21) 645 2975

Sepahan Film
(Mohammad and Asghar Banki)
No. 126 Razi Alley, Sheikh Hadi St
Jomhuri Ave
Tehran
Tel: (98 21) 673 047
Fax: (98 21) 676 268

Shahr Film
(Jalal Qazal-Ayaq)
No. 1/36 Kabkanian (Homa) St
Keshavarz Blvd.
Tehran
Tel: (98 21) 658 181
Fax: (98 21) 652 480

Shiraz Film
(Mohammad Hashem Sabuki)
No. 1/56 Neauphle-le-Chateau St
Tehran
Tel: (98 21) 677 952
Fax: (98 21) 672 985

Oruj Film
(Mohammad Shariati)
No. 335 Darband, Tajrish.
Tehran
Tel: (98 21) 801 8414
Fax: (98 21) 602 2193

Fanus Khiyal
(Gholamreza Azadi)
No. 75 Bakhtyar St, 7th of Tir Sq.
Tehran
Tel: (98 21) 883 4678
Fax: (98 21) 884 7795

Fajr Cinema Organization
(Abdolreza Sa'atchifard)
No. 52 Shahin Alley, Shoa Sq.
Qaem
Maqam Farahani St
Tehran
Tel: (98 21) 882 5650
Fax: (98 21) 883 7991

Andishe Film Workshop
(Seyed Mohsen Vaziri)
No. 728 Shariati Ave
Tehran
Tel: (98 21) 845 398

Kowsar Cinema Organization
(Ruhollah Khoshkam)
No. 363 Motahhari Ave
Tehran
Tel/Fax: (98 21) 872 5809

Gol Film
(Majid Ashtianipoor)
No. 2 Maraghe St, Villa St
Tehran
Tel: (98 21) 880 2151
Fax: (98 21) 881 0150

Lale Film
(Gholamhasan Bolurian)
No. 41 Amir Soleinani, Enqelab Ave
Tehran
Tel: (98 21) 649 4562
Fax: (98 21) 645 5518

Mehrab Film
(Jamal Shurle)
No. 86, 25th St, Jahan-Ara
Shahid Gomnam Express Way
Tehran
Tel/Fax: (98 21) 800 0076

**Institute of Film Affairs of
Mostazafan Foundation**
(Alireza Sarbakhsh)
Bldg. No. 343, Shahid Beheshti Ave

Tehran
Tel: (98 21) 871 6666
Fax: (98 21) 872 7330

Film Baharan
(Akbar Sadeqi)
No. 81/1 Baharmastan Alley
7th of Tir Sq.
Tehran
Tel: (98 21) 882 4432

Mahab Film
(Seyed Zia Hashemi)
No. 85 Bakhtyar Alley, 7th of Tir Sq.
Tehran
Tel: (98 21) 837 547
Fax: (98 21) 883 4332.

Misaq Film
(Hussein Yaryar)
No. 101 North Sohreverdi Ave
Tehran
Tel: (98 21) 875 7517

Milad Film
(Rasul Sadr-Ameli)
No.3 Fourth St, Asadabadi Ave
Tehran
Tel: (98 21) 872 7673
Fax: (98 21) 885 7119

Mina Film
(Mohammad Reza Alipayam)
No. 9, 11, Bldg. No. 1317, Vanak Sq.
Tehran
Tel: (98 21) 887 9314
Fax: (98 21) 879 9803

Nahid Film
(Hojjatollah Seifi)
No. 27 Sharif Alley, Sheikh Hadi St
Jami St
Tehran
Tel: (98 21) 676 473

Novin Film
(Hushang Nurollahi)
No. 15 48th Passage, Jomhuri Ave
Tehran
Tel/Fax: (98 21) 640 3697

Yaran Film
(Samuel Khachikian)
No. 78, 1st Haeri, Shahid Adibi St
Shariati Ave
Tehran
Tel: (98 21) 870 2552

IRELAND

Michael Dwyer

Film production continued apace in Ireland during 1997, with over 20 features completed. So many movies were set to shoot during the summer of 1998 that finding available Irish crew members became particularly difficult for domestic and international producers alike. There was also an encouraging burst of activity in Northern Ireland, with five features shooting there late in 1997.

The Minister for Arts secured first-year funding of $320,000 (200,000 Irish punts) for the first Screen Commission of Ireland, whose members include actors Pierce Brosnan and Sinead Cusack, with Mary Leonard, director of KPMG corporate finance, in the chair. The Irish Film Board, whose members include actor Gabriel Byrne, again funded a wide range of features, documentaries and shorts. It has been a notably good year for Irish short films, with the Northern Ireland production *Dance Lexie Dance*, directed by Tim Loane, achieving an Oscar nomination for Best Short Film (Drama), and Dublin director Martin Mahon's *Happy Birthday to Me* being selected for the shorts competition at Cannes.

However, with the admirable exception of Paddy Breathnach's **I Went Down**, 1997 was a very thin year indeed for Irish movies at Irish cinemas. Breathnach's comedy-thriller, which introduced two exciting new screen talents in writer Conor McPherson and actor Peter McDonald, took more than $800,000. Takings were substantially lower for *Gold in the Streets*, *The Disappearance of Finbar*, *Moll Flanders*, *Space Truckers* and *The Eliminator*. A number of other Irish movies are collecting dust as they await belated release.

There was no single commercial success

during 1997 to approach Neil Jordan's 1996 blockbuster, *Michael Collins*, which held the Irish record with takings in excess of $6.4m. Nevertheless, it was a very solid year for exhibitors, with the top four releases taking more than $14m between them. The biggest and most surprising hit of the year, the low-budget British comedy *The Full Monty*, comfortably topped the box-office chart, with takings in excess of $4.8m.

Top of the league

Cinema admissions in the Republic during 1997 equalled the previous year's figure of 11.5 million, almost double the number of admissions registered in 1988. Cinemas in Northern Ireland attracted 3.8 million

Daniel Day-Lewis in THE BOXER
photo: Frank Connor/Universal

admissions in the same period, up 100,000 on 1996. A European Union survey showed Ireland top of the cinema-going and video rentals league, with each member of the population attending the cinema on average 3.2 times a year, and every Irish household with a video renting an average of 37 films a year.

The boom in cinema-going in the Republic over the past decade can be gauged by the fact that seven years ago *The Commitments* made history as the first movie to break $3m, while in 1997 several films which made over $1.6m each (among them *Batman & Robin*, *Matilda* and *Space Jam*) could not even break into the year's top ten. Figures for the first four months of 1998 show admissions in the Republic at 4.7 million, up substantially on the corresponding figure of 3.9 million in 1997, a surge largely attributable to *Titanic*, which shattered *Michael Collins'* box-office record, taking more than $9m.

Fighting back

The first half of 1998 saw the release of new Irish movies from such heavy-hitters as Jim Sheridan, Neil Jordan and John Boorman. Sheridan's **The Boxer**, which was chosen to open the Berlin Film Festival in February, is a thoughtful and highly topical picture of life and conflict in Northern Ireland. Set in Belfast during a fragile cease-fire, it begins with the release from prison of 32-year-old Danny Flynn (an expressive, hypnotic Daniel Day-Lewis), a once promising Belfast boxer who is regarded with suspicion by the IRA, whom he has now rejected.

Determined to change his life, he sets out to make a comeback in the ring, channelling his energy and what is left of his youthful idealism into fighting by the rules. Reuniting with his old trainer (Ken Stott), who is now a homeless alcoholic, he sets out to re-build a dilapidated gym and re-open it as a non-sectarian venue. Danny is also reunited with his teenage sweetheart, Maggie (Emily Watson), the daughter of an IRA godfather (Brian Cox), and although she married another man while he was in prison, the two of them tentatively, and clandestinely, begin to rekindle their relationship.

Never shirking the complexities of the issues, Sheridan's film is firmly un-ambiguous in promoting the case for the paramilitaries to put down their guns and start talking peace. Calm in its reasoning and serious in its intent, the film builds to a powerful climax which ultimately delivers some glimmer of hope.

Meat is murder

Patrick McCabe's extraordinarily imaginative 1992 novel **The Butcher Boy** is fully complemented in Neil Jordan's surreal, startling and richly cinematic film version. With its internal structure and stream-of-consciousness narration, the novel seemed unfilmable, but Jordan and McCabe's screenplay triumphantly overcomes these problems. At the film's centre is the bravura performance Jordan elicits from the gifted 13-year-old newcomer Eamonn Owens, as Francie Brady, an outwardly cheerful youngster growing up in a small Irish town in the early 1960s, with his morose, alcoholic father (Stephen Rea) and his manic depressive, suicidal mother (Aisling O'Sullivan).

Losing each of his parents, and then the company of his cherished best friend, Francie is left perplexed, insecure and alone in a big, threatening adult world. When he snaps, he targets a neighbour, the snooty Mrs. Nugent (Fiona Shaw), whose lurid green outfits evoke the aliens of

Eamonn Owens (left) and Joe Purcell in THE BUTCHER BOY

Jon Voight and Brendan Gleeson in THE GENERAL

Francie's comic-books, and releases his confused rage in an explosion of violence. This remarkable picture precisely catches the repression and hypocrisy of an Irish town at a time when talk rarely sounded so small and the lace curtains were kept firmly drawn against anything that shattered the cosiness of the superficial contentment of daily life.

The wild black humour which permeates the movie and erupts uproariously at the most unlikely moments effectively counterpoints the intensity of the drama, as the smile is abruptly wiped off the viewer's face. Jordan well deserved the Best Director award he received at Berlin.

A life of crime

At Cannes, John Boorman received the Best Director award for **The General**, his factually based film about the notorious Dublin criminal Martin Cahill, who ran rings around the police before being gunned down by an IRA hit man in 1994. Boorman offers a thoughtful, compelling and ultimately responsible warts-and-all view of his subject, who is played, in his finest performance to date, by the formidable Brendan Gleeson.

Cahill, who was nicknamed the General, is depicted as a mischievous opportunist who sees himself as some kind of modern-day Robin Hood, dispensing stolen goods to those who claim to be needy. A man who eschews drink and drugs, he shares a most unorthodox ménage à trois with his wife and sister-in-law, fathering children by both. He is shown to be daring in his criminal activities, taking on elaborate heists at a jewellery firm and a major art collection.

Boorman's film does not flinch from dramatising Cahill's ruthlessness and propensity for violence: setting a bomb in the car of a forensic witness; knee-capping a gang member who has raped his own daughter, to keep the man out of court; crucifying another gangster, whom he wrongly believes has swindled him, on a pool table. The richly textured black-and-white cinematography by Seamus Deasy and a terrific, jazz-based score by Richie

Buckley enhance the film's evocation of the classic gangster movies which are its cinematic antecedents. *The General* is Boorman's most satisfying film since the autobiographical *Hope and Glory* 11 years ago.

MICHAEL DWYER is Film Correspondent of *The Irish Times*. He is president of the Federation of Irish Film Societies and the co-founder and former programme director of the Dublin Film Festival.

Recent and Forthcoming Films

ALL FOR LOVE

Script: Allan Cubbit. Dir: Harry Hook. Players: Jean-Marc Barr, Anna Friel, Michael Gough. Prod: Little Bird.

ANGELA'S ASHES

Script: Laura Jones and Frank McCourt. Dir: Alan Parker. Prod: PolyGram/Paramount.

DANCING AT LUGHNASA

Script: Frank McGuinness. Dir: Pat O'Connor. Players: Meryl Streep, Sophie Thompson, Brid Brennan, Catherine McCormack, Rhys Ifans, Michael Gambon. Prod: Ferndale Films.

THE GENERAL

Script and Dir: John Boorman. Phot: Seamus Deasy. Players: Brendan Gleeson, Jon Voight, Adrian Dunbar, Sean McGinley, Maria Doyle Kennedy, Angeline Ball. Prod: Merlin Films.

HOOLIGANS

Script: James Mathers. Dir: Paul Tickell. Phot: Reinier Van Brummelen. Players: Darren Healey, Jeff O'Toole, Viviana Verveen. Prod: Liquid Films.

HOW TO CHEAT IN THE LEAVING CERTIFICATE

Script: Graham Jones, Tadhg O'Higgins and Aislinn O'Loughlin. Dir: Jones. Phot: Robbie Ryan. Players: Garret Baker, Aileen O'Connor, John Wright. Prod: Graham Jones Productions.

THE LAST SEPTEMBER

Script: John Banville. Dir: Deborah Warner. Phot: Players: Fiona Shaw, Maggie Smith, Jonathan Rhys-Meyers. Prod:

LOVE AND RAGE

Script: Brian Lynch. Dir: Cathal Black. Phot: Slawek Idziak. Players: Greta Scacchi, Daniel Craig. Prod: Cathal Black Films.

MAD ABOUT MAMBO

Script and Dir: John Forte. Phot: Ashley Rowe. Players: Keri Russell, Willaim Ash, Brian Cox, Rosaleen Linehan. Prod: First City Features.

THE MAMMY

Script: John Goldsmith and Brendan O'Carroll. Dir: Anjelica Huston. Players: Huston, Gerard Depardieu. Prod: Hell's Kitchen.

METEOR

Script and Dir: Joe O'Byrne. Phot: Paul Sarossy. Players: Mike Myers, Brenda Fricker, Ian Costello. Prod: Paradox Pictures.

NIGHT TRAIN

Script: Aodhan Madden. Dir: John Lynch. Players: John Hurt, Brenda Blethyn. Prod: Subotica Films.

ORDINARY DECENT CRIMINAL

Script: Gerry Stembridge. Dir: Thaddeus O'Sullivan. Players: Kevin Spacey. Prod: Icon/Little Bird.

SUNSET HEIGHTS

Script and Dir: Colm Villa. Players: Toby Stephens, Jim Norton. Prod: Northland Films.

THE TALE OF SWEETY BARRETT

Script and Dir: Stephen Bradley. Phot: Thomas Mauch. Players: Brendan Gleeson, Lynda Steadman, Liam Cunningham. Prod: Temple Films.

Producers

Ferndale Films
4 Harcourt Terrace
Dublin 2
Tel: (353 1) 676 8890
Fax: (353 1) 676 8874

The Good Film Company
15 Vesey Place
Monkstown
Co Dublin
Tel: (353 1) 284 4881
Fax: (353 1) 284 4882

Hell's Kitchen Productions
92 Merrion Road
Ballsbridge
Dublin 4
Tel: (353 1) 667 5599
Fax: (353 1) 667 5592

Irish Screen
34 Lower Baggot Street
Dublin 2
Tel: (353 1) 662 3505
Fax: (353 1) 662 3507

Little Bird Productions
122 Lower Baggot Street
Dublin 2
Tel: (353 1) 661 4245
Fax: (353 1) 660 0351

Merlin Films Group
16 Upper Pembroke Street
Dublin 2
Tel: (353 1) 676 4373
Fax: (353 1) 676 4368

Parallel Film Productions
14-15 Sir John Rogersons Quay
Dublin 2
Tel: (353 1) 671 8555
Fax: (353 1) 671 8242

Samson Films
The Barracks
76 Irishtown Road
Dublin 4
Tel: (353 1) 667 0533
Fax: (353 1) 667 0537

Temple Films
4 Windmill Lane
Dublin 2
Tel: (353 1) 671 9313
Fax: (353 1) 671 9323

Treasure Films
Shamrock Chambers
Dame St
Dublin 2
Tel: (353 1) 670 9609
Fax: (353 1) 670 9612

Distributors

Abbey Films
35 Upper Abbey Street
Dublin 1
Tel: (353 1) 872 3422
Fax: (353 1) 872 3687

Buena Vista International
12 Parliament Street
Dublin 2
Tel: (353 1) 677 3484
Fax: (353 1) 671 0098

Clarence Pictures
13 Merrion Square
Dublin 2
Tel: (353 1) 661 4022
Fax: (353 1) 661 4186

Columbia TriStar Films
Seagrave House
20 Earlsfort Terrace
Dublin 2
Tel: (353 1) 616 3200
Fax: (353 1) 616 3210

Light House Cinema
12 Anglesea Street
Dublin 2
Tel: (353 1) 679 9585
Fax: (353 1) 679 9586

PolyGram Filmed Entertainment
Whitefriars
Aungier Street
Dublin 2
Tel: (353 1) 475 7700
Fax: (353 1) 475 7860

Warner Bros
9 Townyard Lane
Malahide
Co Dublin
Tel: (353 1) 845 1844
Fax: (353 1) 845 1858

United International Pictures
D'Olier Chambers
D'Olier Street
Dublin 2
Tel: (353 1) 679 2433
Fax: (353 1) 679 8801

Useful Addresses

Ardmore Studios
Herbert Road
Bray
Co Wicklow
Tel: (353 404) 286 2971
Fax: (353 404) 286 1894

The Arts Council
70 Merrion Square
Dublin 2
Tel: (353 1) 661 1840
Fax: (353 1) 676 0436

Espace Video Européen
(EVE)
6 Eustace Street
Dublin 2
Tel: (353 1) 679 5744
Fax: (353 1) 679 9657

Film Institute of Ireland
6 Eustace Street
Dublin 2
Tel: (353 1) 679 5744
Fax: (353 1) 679 9657

Film Makers Ireland
19 Duke Street
Dublin 2
Tel: (353 1) 671 3525
Fax: (353 1) 671 3505

Irish Film Board
Rockfort House
St Augustine Street
Galway
Co Galway
Tel: (353 91) 561398
Fax: (353 91) 561405

Irish Film Centre
6 Eustace Street
Dublin 2
Tel: (353 1) 679 5744
Fax: (353 1) 679 9657

Radio Telefis Eireann
(RTE)
Donnybrook
Dublin 4
Tel: (353 1) 208 3111
Fax: (353 1) 208 3080

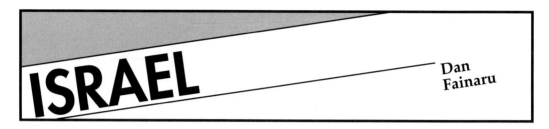

Dan
Fainaru

With the entire country watching its leaders juggle any number of hot potatoes for the past two years, Israeli culture has had no choice but to take a back seat to the political dramas. Everything one might look for – tragedy, melodrama and farce – is bountifully supplied on newspaper front pages, and nothing can match the popularity of the evening TV news. It seems as if the latest bulletins (plus the soccer World Cup) are all the entertainment Israelis wish to handle right now. Their interest in other branches of showbusiness, certainly in domestic films, is faint.

It is no secret that culture cannot survive in a small country like Israel without hefty government subsidies. But with the various factions within the ruling coalition tearing each other apart in search of a bigger slice of the state budget, any mention of the finer things in life falls on deaf ears. Cinema, traditionally the most neglected of Israel's cultural fields, has taken an unprecedented beating.

Its progress in the past may have been slow and painful, but at least the industry, such as it was, kept going. For the last couple of years, it has steadily regressed in every respect. More than half the production funds ($3m out of a promised $5m) have evaporated into thin air; facilities have become sadly depleted, and most of the country's discouraged movie players are looking for lucrative ventures elsewhere.

Most have headed for television, where they find deep pockets waiting to be picked – on one condition: that they provide the right kind of product. That means no feature films to speak of, but plenty of soaps, game shows, low-budget crime series and lots of documentaries. Making a feature is an almost impossible mission, but there is work aplenty for those film-makers willing to compromise; the choice is starkly simple.

A kind of magic

The two films which stood out in the first part of the year where **Afula Express** and **The 92 Minutes of Mr Baum**. The former marked the feature debut of talented documentarist Julie Schlez, and told the story of a would-be magician who tries to make it in the big city. Received more warmly by home audiences than foreign ones, it scored mainly through the popularity of TV personality Zwika Adar and the vivacious performance of Esti Zackheim as his girlfriend.

Mr Baum, which completes Assi Dayan's trilogy on the accidental meaning of life, sardonically follows a businessman through the last 92 minutes of his life, as he realises that all his existence was meaningless and nobody really cares if he lives or dies. Dayan, who drew fire from every quarter for his numerous rude and outspoken attacks on the political regime and its treatment of films, has justified once again his reputation as the *enfant terrible* of Israeli cinema.

The Jerusalem Film Festival, usually the mid-year barometer of the local industry, confirmed the bleak picture to which Dayan repeatedly referred: of the five feature films scheduled to be premiered at the July event, two withdrew at the last moment: actor-director Jonathan Sagall's *Urban Feel* was unfinished, while *Super Boy*, a children's film, may well have pulled out in fear of a critical drubbing.

Of the remaining three entries, **Nitza Gonen's Family Secrets**, based on a best-selling novel, failed to deliver either the painful family drama or the tragic undertones of Holocaust trauma it was supposed to contain, while the topic of battered women, an ever-present issue in the Israeli courts, was superficially and rather clumsily handled by Tzippi Trope's **Chronicle of Love**.

Far more challenging was **Day by Day**, Amos Gitai's portrait of present-day Israeli society. A slice-of-life picture which functions mainly as a metaphor, it lacks a dramatic structure and is quite content with light sketches of characters deserving better treatment. Still, thanks to remarkable performances by Moshe Ivgi (the most familiar face on Israeli screens) and two seasoned stage veterans, Hanah Maron and Yussuf Abu-Warda, as well as Renato Berta's precise camerawork, Gitai had no real competition for the festival's Best Feature Award.

Romi Aboulafia and Michael Hanegbi in FAMILY SECRETS   *photo: Yoni Hamenachem*

Truth seems stronger than fiction

Far more depressing than the films themselves was the feeling that better tidings for Israeli cinema cannot be expected. True, seven or eight more features should have been completed by October 1998 (when the Israeli Film Academy will distribute its awards), among them new work from Michal Bat-

Moshe Ivgi and Giuliano Mer in Amos Gitai's
DAY BY DAY

Adam and Shemi Zarhin, but all were made with budgets granted in previous years. With no cash in sight this year, there is little to look forward to for 1999. Except, that is, for documentaries.

A plentiful stream of non-fiction film and (mostly) video projects of every length and style has been emerging from the various television channels, with a special fund, The New Foundation for Cinema and Television, often supplying additional financial support. These documentaries tackle an immense range of political and social themes. The best of the year's crop, without doubt, was **Fragments of Jerusalem**, a six-hour portrait of the city.

Director Ron Havilio invested some seven years of his and his family's efforts and funds in this labour of love. First shown in full at the 1998 Berlin Forum, it is already doing the festival rounds and gaining international acclaim, while Havilio is trying to collect the resources necessary to add three more hours of footage to this already massive, personal and moving study of what may well be the world's most complex and troubled city.

Other documentaries likely to figure on the festival circuit include **Hide'n'Seek**, directed by Iris Rubin, about three married women who suddenly decide to join an amateur theatre group in Jaffa (a stunning decision in light of their families' old-fashioned values) and **Another Land**, produced by Amit Goren for ZDF (the second German state television channel), a chronicle of the recent past, in which personal conflicts and political events blend into a composite picture of the State of Israel struggling for its own identity at the end of its first half-century.

DAN FAINARU is an Israeli film critic and journalist, and Editor-in-Chief of *European Film Review*. A former director of the Israeli Film Institute, he is a familiar face at the world's major and minor festivals.

Recent and Forthcoming Films

AFULA EXPRESS

Script: Amit Lior. Dir: Julie Schlez. Phot: Itzik Portal. Players: Zwika Adar, Esti Zackheim, Arie Moscona, Orli Perl.

MESUKENETH (Dangerous Acts)

Script and Dir: Shemi Zarhin. Phot: David Gurfinkel. Players: Gila Almagor, Moshe Ivgi, Nathan Datner, Amos Lavi.

ZUR HADASSIM

Script: Eran Kolirin. Dir: Gideon Kolirin. Phot: Amnon Salomon. Players: Danny Shtag, Orly Ben-Garty, Albert Iluz, Daphna Rechter.

MR BAUM (The 92 Minutes of Mr Baum)

Script and Dir: Assi Dayan. Phot: Avi Koren. Players: Dayan, Rivka Neuman, Shira Geffen, Karin Ofir, Idan Alterman.

SODOTH MISHPAKHA (Family Secrets)

Script: Shemi Zarhin. Dir: Nitzz Gonen. Phot: Gideon Porath. Players: Romi Aboulafia, Michael Hanegbi, Eli Cohen, Galia Soudri, Adi Terrer, Alex Peleg, Aviva Joel.

HAKHAVERIM SHEL JANA (Jana's Friends)

Script: Arik Kaplun, Semion

Vinokur. Dir: Kaplun. Phot: ValentinBalonogov. Players: Evelyne Kaplun, Nir Levy, Mosco Alcalay, Dalia Friedland, Vladimir Friedman, Shmiel Ben-Ari.

KESHER IR (Urban Feel)

Script and Dir: Jonathan Sagall. Phot: Dror Dror Moreh. Players: Sagall, Daphna Rechter, Sharon Alexander, Ziv Baruch, Assi Levy.

CIRCUS PALESTINA

Script and Dir: Eyal Halfon. Phot: Valentin Balonogov. Players: Genia Dodina, Yoram Hatav, Vladimir Friedman, Bassam Zuamut, Amos Lavi.

AGADATH HA'ISH SHESHATAK (The Legend of the Silent Man)

Script and Dir: Doron Nesher. Phot: Beni Mali. Players: Israel Damidov, Shmiel Ben-Ari, Alona Dagan, Yoram Gal, Maya Bar-Shalom, Dorin Kaspi.

YOM YOM (Day by Day)

Script and Dir: Amos Gitai. Phot: Renato Berta. Players: Moshe Ivgi, Giuliano Mer, Hanah Maron, Dalith Kahan, Nathalie Atiah, Yussuf Abu-Warda.

AHAVA ME'MABAT SHENI (Love at Second Sight)

Script and Dir: Michal Bat-Adam. Phot: Yoav Kosh. Players: Michal Zuaretz, Yossi Yadin, Nathan Cogan, Alon Abutbul, Igal Sade.

CHRONIKA SHEL AHAVA (Chronicle of Love)

Script and Dir: Zippi Trope. Phot: Hanania Ber. Players: Semadar Kilshinski, Sharon Alexander, Ci Hyman, Tanya Sobolev, Nitzan Bar-Tana.

Producers

Marek Rosenbaum
22, Nahmani St Tel Aviv 65201
Tel: (972 3) 566 1484
Fax: (972 3) 566 1450

Screen Entertainment
Eitan Even and Effi Atad
Merkaz Baalei Melacha 40
Tel Aviv 63824
Tel: (972 3) 528 1191
Fax: (972 3) 528 1192

Paralite Productions
Uri Sabbag and Einat Bikel
57, Nahmani St
Tel Aviv
Tel: (972 3) 560 8217
Fax: (972 3) 560 7947

Cinema Factory
11, Hayei Adam St
Tel Aviv
Tel: (972 3) 691 4279
Fax: (972 3) 691 3982

Distributors

Globus Group (UIP, Warner)
10, Glickson St
Tel Aviv
Tel: (972 3) 526 6333
Fax: (972 3) 526 6373

A.D. Matalon & Co. (Columbia, TriStar, Fox)
13, Yona Hanavi St
Tel Aviv
Tel: (972 3) 5162020
Fax: (972 3) 5161888

Forum/Israeli Theatres (Buena Vista)
91, Medinath Hayehudim
PO Box 12598
Herzlyia Pituakh
Tel: (972 9) 952 6200
Fax: (972 9) 956 1581

Shapira Films
34, Allenby St
Tel Aviv
Tel: (972 3) 517 2923
Fax: (972 3) 510 1370

Shani Films
Lev Cinemas
Dizengoff Center
Tel Aviv
Tel: (972 3) 528 8282
Fax: (972 3) 620 4749

Useful Addresses

Israel Film Centre
Ministry of Industry and Trade
PO Box 299
Jerusalem
Tel: (972 2) 6220608
Fax: (972 2) 6236303

Israeli Film & TV Producers Association
PO Box 20486 Tel Aviv
Tel: (972 3) 5613919
Fax: (972 3) 5612529

Jerusalem Cinematheque & Israeli Film Archive
11, Hebron Rd
Jerusalem
Tel: (972 2) 672 4131
Fax: (972 2) 971 3044

Tel Aviv Cinematheque
2, Shprintzak St
PO Box 20370
Tel Aviv 61203
Tel: (972 3) 691 7181
Fax: (972 3) 696 2841

The Fund for the Promotion of Israeli Quality Films
12, Judith Blvd
Tel Aviv 67016
Tel: (972 3) 626 8180
Fax: (972 3) 562 5992

The New Fund for Cinema and Television
113, Hashmonaim St
Tel Aviv
Tel: (972 3) 561 5786
Fax: (972 3) 562 7991

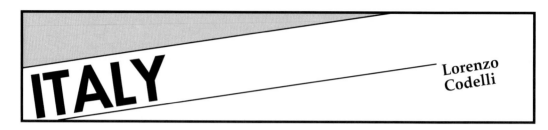

ITALY

Lorenzo
Codelli

After half a century of carelessness, and sometimes genuine obstruction, from the central power, Italian cinema's renaissance should have been almost guaranteed by the last two years of governmental measures, including increased public subsidy and unprecedented self-pride. Why is such an idea just wishful thinking? Paying customers still prefer American movies; distributors and exhibitors still bury many Italian movies, giving them a very limited release. These sleeping products, usually opening in the post-Easter months, amounted once again to half of the released titles, which numbered just over 70. Their stable, 27 per cent share of the gross – compared with 58 per cent for US imports – was again dominated by a few major comic hits.

Comedy remains the *only* commercial genre for Italian movies, preferably low-budget and starring TV names. The farce **Three Men and a Leg** (*Tre uomini e una gamba*), by Aldo, Giovanni & Giacomo, was a surprise blockbuster at Christmas. The male trio performs spontaneously and unpretentiously – as they did every Sunday afternoon in a popular sports broadcast. No ambitions, no plot, broad bar jokes between chums, that is their secret formula. Let us not forget that Roberto Benigni, Massimo Troisi and Carlo Verdone started the same way.

When a clown grows up, he wants to be Chaplin. That ancient adage fits Benigni's **Life is Beautiful** (*La vita è bella*), his own *Great Dictator* no less. This is a fable about Benigni's familiar Candide figure, this time a Jewish waiter, left unharmed by Fascist and Nazi evils, who tries to convince his young child that the concentration camp where they are both imprisoned is nothing but a big hilarious game. Benigni gets killed

off screen, but a tear-jerker ending blesses his boy with a dream-like liberation. Apart from some crazy monologues, the actor-director looks punchless and tediously didactic, letting his surrealist edge evaporate. *Life is Beautiful* won the Grand Prix at Cannes but one is still left hoping that Benigni will finally find a director stronger than himself. Protests against the film from orthodox Jews pushed Miramax to re-edit it for the US.

Leonardo Pieraccioni's Tuscan *oisiveté* shines in **Fireworks** (*Fuochi d'artificio*), his third consecutive hit. A thinner vehicle than *Il ciclone*, his massive 1997 hit, this is still built on similar sexual and romantic lines, designed to appeal to young post-yuppies like himself. Pieraccioni is so brilliant and good-looking that he could simply sit down or say anything and people would applaud. Maybe acting and directing is really too taxing a job for this nice guy, and, in any case, his powerful producer, Vittorio Cecchi Gori, would never let him change mask – his Chaplin days can wait.

News from the home fronts

Why, dear leftist intellectuals, is it no longer so easy, under the Olive centre-left government, to engage yourselves in social issues? This theme was shared by two of Cannes' most discussed selections, Nanni Moretti's **Aprile** and Mario Martone's **Theatre of War** (*Teatro di guerra*). Whereas the former engages in ironical self-flagellation for taking too much care of his newborn baby instead of worrying about Northern secessionists' menaces or poor Albanians sunk by the Italian navy, the latter audaciously compares Naples to Sarajevo, to understand why the war never ends in his home town. A film about film

Nanni Moretti in his APRILE

for Moretti, a film about theatre for Martone, both letting their audiences find the answers. Martone's keen episode from the portmanteau movie **The Vesuvians** (*I vesuviani*) analyses the troubles of a Neapolitan mayor symbolically climbing Vesuvius to attain some new civilisation.

Venice Festival award winner **Ovosodo**, by Paolo Virzì, revamps the highest traditions of 'commedia all'italiana' – thanks to Furio Scarpelli's expert screenwriting hand. It follows the mis-adventures at school and work of a shy Tuscan teenager. A splendid cast of fresh faces make this proletarian, bittersweet look at the 1990s generation wholly enjoyable .

The Last New Year's Eve (*L'ultimo capodanno*), Marco Risi's apocalyptic and quite expensive satire, inspired by Niccolò Ammanniti's gory best-seller, with special effects galore and a large ensemble of character actors, misfired to the point of being withdrawn by the director himself after the first weekend of release. Were the trailers and ads too repulsive? An angry attack against advertising concoctions is

Still from THEATRE OF WAR

Still from Paolo Virzì's OVOSODO

fought in Sandro Baldoni's **Commercial Break** (*Consigli per gli acquisti*), another picture unfortunately too dark for the audiences' taste.

Pupi Avati digs again into his family's very rich heritage in **The Best Man** (*Il testimone dello sposo*). This is a tale of repressed romance set during a wedding on the last day of 1899, peopled by a multitude of bizarre types. Above all, it is a metaphor for our century's fears about the future. Daniele Ciprì and Franco Maresco's **Toto who lived twice** (*Totò che visse due volte*) had at least one merit: it was briefly banned by retrograde censors, a move which finally convinced the legislators to reform the censorship laws, though alas not quite to kill them off. The paper storm did not convince many customers to pay to see this black-and-white bore, set, like the same team's *Lo zio d'America* (1996), in a Sicilian wasteland inhabited by male freaks. Every image attempts to be 'Pasolini-like' and/or 'Buñuel-like'.

Naked ambitions, old masters

Sexploitation – a trend once so dominant in the peninsula – seems to be coming back

into fashion. Giuseppe Ferlito, together with renowned playwright Giuseppe Patroni Griffi, allowed glittering Monica Guerritore some exciting naked exhibitions in **Female** (*Femmina*). Aurelio Grimaldi's **Il macellaio** did the same for TV plastic surgery icon Alba Parieti. In **Kid** (*Monella*), Tinto Brass exceeded even his spectacular voyeuristic instincts, turning rapacious teenager Anna Ammirati into an update of Clara Bow. Asia Argento does not really undress in **Viola Kisses Everybody** (*Viola bacia tutti*), a youthful comedy by Giovanni Veronesi, but her carnal appeal still punches us on the nose.

Popular actor Christian De Sica directed **Agreeable and Disagreeables** (*Simpatici e antipatici*), a funny portrait of Rome's privileged class. Davide Ferrario's **Hannibal's Children** (*I figli di Annibale*) mocked clichés about North and South tribes; similar ethnic differences were exploited in a more lowbrow vein by Carlo Vanzina's **Wandering Through Time – The Adventure Continues** (*A spasso nel tempo – L'avventura continua*).

Roberta Torre's acclaimed musical **Tano To Die For** (*Tano da morire*) poked fun at mafia bosses. Among major disappointments, let us include Mimmo Calopresti's **The Word Love Exists** (*La parola amore esiste*), a meaningless psychodrama, and Renzo Martinelli's **Porzûs**, a pamphlet about Resistance. Amateurish historic saga **Moons Above Earth and Sea** (*Giro di lune tra terra e mare*), by Giuseppe M. Gaudino, found its niche at some festivals.

In the book shops, some Italian masters could be seen in new lights. *Pietro Germi*, by Mario Sesti (Baldini & Castoldi), and *'Signore e Signori' di Pietro Germi*, edited by Lino Miccichè (Fondazione Philip Morris/Lindau Editore), analyse Germi's powerful vision. The Associazione Fellini (via Angherà 22, Rimini) crafted a trilogy of pearls: *Il mio amico Pasqualino* (1945?), a reprint of Fellini's lost first tome; *Fellini 1937-1947*; plus *Gli ultimi sogni di Fellini*.

Marco Ferreri, by Tullio Masoni (Gremese Editore), is an in-depth study of *Dillinger Is*

Dead's auteur. Just before flying happily to paradise, Carlo Ludovico Bragaglia, 103 years old, composed another brilliant memoir, *Bragaglia racconta Bragaglia* (Scheiwiller Editore). *Cinema Italiano Annuario 1997*, edited by Paolo D'Agostini and Stefano Della Casa (Il Castoro), offers a critical summary about features, shorts, television, restorations and more.

LORENZO CODELLI has written for many periodicals, including *Positif*. He is a member of the board of the Cineteca del Friuli, of the Pordenone Silent Film Festival, and of Udine Incontri Cinema.

Diego Abatantuono in THE BEST MAN

Recent and Forthcoming Films

APRILE (April)

Script and Dir: Nanni Moretti. Phot: Giuseppe Lanci. Players: Moretti, Silvia Nono Mortetti. Prod: Sacher Film (Rome)/Bac Films (Paris)/RAI1/Canal+.

**A SPASSO NEL TEMPO –
L'AVVENTURA CONTINUA
(Wandering Through Time –
The Adventure Continues)**

Script: Enrico Vanzina, Carlo Vanzina. Dir: Carlo Vanzina. Phot: Gianlorenzo Battaglia. Players: Massimo Boldi, Christian De Sica. Prod: Filmauro.

**AUGURI PROFESSORE
(Good Luck, Professor)**

Script: Sandro Petraglia, Stefano Rulli, Domenico Starnone, Riccardo Milani. Dir: Riccardo Milani. Phot: Alessandro Pesci. Players: Silvio Orlanddo, Claudia Pandolfi. Prod: Cecchi Gori Group Tiger Cinematografica.

BANZAI

Script: Enrico Vanzina, Carlo Vanzina. Dir: Carlo Vanzina. Phot: Sergio Salvati. Players: Paolo Villaggio, Francesca Romana Coluzzi. Prod: Video 80.

**CONSIGLI PER GLI ACQUISTI
(Commercial Break)**

Script: Sandro Baldoni, Johnny Dell'Orto. Dir: Baldoni. Phot: Renato Alfarano. Players: Ennio Fantastichini, Silvia Cohen. Prod: Strane Storie/Istituto Luce/RAI.

CUCCIOLO (Pup)

Script: Neri Parenti, Enrico Vanzina. Dir: Neri Parenti. Phot: Carlo Tafani. Players: Massimo Boldi, Claudia Koll. Prod: Filmauro.

DEL PERDUTO AMORE (About Lost Love)

Script: Michele Placido, Domenico Starnone. Dir: Placido. Phot: Blasco Giurato. Players: Michele Placido, Giovanna Mezzogiorno, Fabrizio Bentivoglio. Prod: Clemi Cinematografica.

FEMMINA (Female)

Script: Giuseppe Patroni Griffi. Dir: Giuseppe Ferlito. Phot: Mauro Marchetti. Players: Monica Guerritore, Roberto Farnesi. Prod: Cecchi Gori Group.

**FIGLI DI ANNIBALE
(Hannibal's Children)**

Script: Davide Ferrario, Diego Abatantuono, Sergio Rubini. Dir: Ferrario. Phot: Giovanni Cavallini. Players: Diego Abatantuono, Silvio Orlando. Prod: Colorado Film/Medusa Film/Mediaset.

**FUOCHI D'ARTIFICIO
(Fireworks)**

Script: Giovanni Veronesi, Leonardo Pieraccioni. Dir: Pieraccioni. Phot: Roberto Forza. Players: Pieraccioni, Massimo Ceccherini. Prod: Cecchi Gori Group Tiger Cinematografica.

**GIRO DI LUNE TRA TERRA E
MARE (Moons Above Earth
and Sea)**

Script: Giuseppe M. Gaudino, Isabella Sandri, Heidrun Schleff. Dir: Gaudino. Phot: Tarek Ben Abdallah. Players: Olimpia Carlisi, Aldo Bufi Landi. Prod: Gaundri Film (Rome)/ZDF (Mainz).

IL MACELLAIO (The Butcher)

Script: Aurelio Grimaldi from Alina Reyes' novel. Dir: Grimaldi. Phot: Romano Albani. Players: Alba Parietti, Miki Manojlovic. Prod: Freeway Production.

I MIEI PIU' CARI AMICI
(My Dearest Friends)

Script: Alessandro Benvenuti, Alberto Ongaro. Dir: Benvenuti. Phot: Maurizio Calvesi. Players: Benvenuti, Eva Robins, Athina Cenci. Prod: Cecchi Gori Group.

MONELLA (Kid)

Script: Tinto Brass, Barbara Alberti, Carla Cipriani. Dir: Brass. Phot: Massimo Di Venanzo. Players: Anna Ammirati, Serena Grandi, Patrick Mower. Prod: California Film/Cardinal Pictures/CRC/Production Group/PFC 2000.

OVOSODO

Script: Francesco Bruni, Paolo Virzì, Furio Scarpelli. Dir: Virzì. Phot: Italo Petriccione. Players: Edoardo Gabbriellini, Claudia Pandolfi. Prod: Cecchi Gori Group Tiger Cinematografica.

LA PAROLA AMORE ESISTE
(The Word Love Exists)

Script: Mimmo Calopresti, Francesco Bruni, Heidrun Schleef, Doriana Leondeff. Dir: Calopresti. Phot: Alessandro Pesci. Players: Valeria Bruni Tedeschi, Fabrizio Bentivoglio, Gérard Depardieu. Prod: Bianca Film (Rome)/Camera One, Area Films (Paris).

POLVERE DI NAPOLI
(Naples Dust)

Script: Antonio Capuano, Paolo Sorrentino. Dir: Capuano. Phot: Pasquale Rachini. Players: Silvio Orlando, Tonino Taiuti. Prod: Ama Film.

PORZUS

Script: Renzo Martinelli, Furio Scarpelli. Dir: Martinelli. Phot:

Giuliano Giustini. Players: Lorenzo Crespi, Gianni Cavina, Gastone Moschin, Gabriele Ferzetti. Prod: Videomaura/Progetto Immagine Martinelli Film Co./RAI.

SANTO STEFANO

Script: Angelo Pasquini, Roberto Nobile. Dir: Pasquini. Phot: Giuseppe Lanci. Players: Claudio Bigagli, Claudio Amendola. Prod: Alia Film.

LA SECONDA MOGLIE (The Second Wife)

Script: Ugo Chiti, Nicola Zavaglia. Dir: Chiti. Phot: Raffaele Mertes. Players: Maria Grazia Cucinotta, Lazar Ristovski. Prod: Cecchi Gori Group.

SIMPATICI & ANTIPATICI
(Agreeables & Disagreeables)

Script: Carlo Vanzina, Enrico Vanzina. Dir: Christian De Sica. Phot: Ennio Guarnieri. Players: De Sica, Alessandro Haber, Leo Gullotta. Prod: Taodue Film/Medusa Film.

LA STANZA DELLO SCIROCCO
(Scirocco's Room)

Script: Suso Cecchi D'Amico, Salvatore Marcarelli, Maurizio Sciarra, from Dino Campana's novel. Dir: Sciarra. Phot: Arnaldo Catinari. Players: Giancarlo Giannini, Tiziana Lodato. Prod: Fandango.

TANO DA MORIRE
(Tano To Die For)

Script: Roberta Torre, Gianluca Sodaro, Enzo Paglino. Dir: Torre. Phot: Daniele Ciprì. Players: Ciccio Guarino, Enzo Paglino. Prod: ASP/RAI3/Telepiù/Città di Palermo.

TEATRO DI GUERRA
(Theatre of War)

Script and Dir: Mario Martone. Phot: Pasquale Mari. Players:

Andrea Renzi, Anna Bonaiuto, Iaia Forte. Prod: Teatri Uniti/Lucky Red.

IL TESTIMONE DELLO SPOSO
(The Best Man)

Script and Dir: Pupi Avati. Phot: Pasquale Rachini. Players: Diego Abatantuono, Inès Sastre, Dario Cantarelli. Prod: Duea Film/Filmauro.

TI AMO MARIA (I Love You, Maria)

Script: Gianni Molino, Francesco Cardì, Chiara Tozzi from Giuseppe Manfridi's play. Dir: Carlo Delle Piane. Phot: Pasquale Rachini. Players: Delle Piane, Laura Lattuada. Prod: Duea Film.

TOTÓ CHE VISSE DUE VOLTE
(Toto Who Lived Twice)

Script: Daniele Ciprì, Franco Maresco, Lillo Iacolino. Dir: Ciprì and Maresco. Phot: Luca Bigazzi (b&w). Players: Salvatore Gattuso, Marcello Miranda. Prod: Tea Nova.

TRE UOMINI E UNA GAMBA
(Three Men and a Leg)

Script: Aldo Baglio, Giovanni Storti, Giacomo Poretti, Massimo Venier, Giorgio Gherarducci, Lucio Martignoni. Dir: Baglio, Storti & Poretti. Phot: Giovanni Fiore Coltellacci. Players: Baglio, Storti, Poretti, Marina Missironi. Prod: Rodeo Drive/AGIDI.

L'ULTIMO CAPODANNO
(The Last New Year's Eve)

Script: Niccolò Ammaniti, Marco Risi from Ammaniti's novel. Dir: Risi. Phot: Maurizio Calvesi. Players: Alessandro Haber, Monica Bellucci. Prod: Sorpasso Film/Istituto Luce/Cinecittà/RAI/Cinema Fiction.

I VESUVIANI (The Vesuvians)

Script: Antonio Capuano, Pappi Corsicato, Ivan Cotroneo, Antonietta De Lillo, Laura

Sabatino, Stefano Incerti, Mario Martone, Fabrizia Ramondino. Dir: Capuano, Corsicato, De Lillo, Incerti, Martone. Phot: Antonio Baldoni, Luca Bigzzi, Cesare Accetta, Pasquale Mari. Players: Tonino Taiuti, Anna Bonaiuto, Iaia Forte, Enzo Moscato, Toni Servillo. Prod: Megaris/Mikado Film/RAI/Telepiù.

IL VIAGGIO DELLA SPOSA
(The Bride's Voyage)

Script: Umberto Marino, Sergio Rubini, Filippo Ascione, Raffaele Nigro. Dir: Rubini. Phot: Italo Petriccione. Players: Rubini, Giovanna Mezzogiorno. Prod: Cecchi Gori Group.

VIOLA BACIA TUTTI
(Viola Kisses Everybody)

Script: Giovanni Veronesi, Rocco Papaleo. Dir: Giovanni Veronesi. Phot: Fabio Cianchetti. Players: Asia Argento, Massimo Ceccherini, Valerio Mastandrea. Prod: Cecchi Gori Group Tiger Cinematografica/Pacific Pictures.

LA VITA E' BELLA
(Life Is Beautiful)

Script: Vincenzo Cerami, Roberto Benigni. Dir: Benigni. Phot: Tonino Delli Colli. Players: Benigni, Nicoletta Braschi. Prod: Melampo Cinematografica.

Useful Addresses

Adriana Chiesa Enterprises
Via Barnaba Oriani, 24/A
00197 Roma
Tel: (39 6) 808 6052
Fax: (39 6) 858 7866

Agis
Via di villa Patrizi, 10
00161 Roma
Tel: (39 6) 884 731
Fax: (39 6) 4423 1838

Anica
Viale Regina Margherita, 286
00198 Roma
Tel: (39 6) 4423 1480
Fax: (39 6) 440 4128

Banca Nazionale del Lavoro
Piazza San Bernardo, 101
00187 Roma
Tel: (39 6) 47021
Fax: (39 6) 4702 5179

CAM
Via Cola di Rienzo, 152
00192 Roma
Tel: (39 6) 687 4220
Fax: (39 6) 687 4046

Carol Levi Company
00100 Roma
Via G. Carducci, 10
Tel: (39 6) 486 961
Fax: (39 6) 487 1150

Cinecittà
Via Tuscolana, 1055
00173 Roma
Tel: (39 6) 722 931
Fax: (39 6) 722 2155

Cecchi Gori Group
Via Valadier, 42
00193 Roma
Tel: (39 6) 324 721
Fax: (39 6) 3247 2302

Dipartimento dello spettacolo
Via della Ferratella in Laterano, 45/51
00184 Roma 4
Tel: (39 6) 77321

Ente Cinema
Via Tuscolana, 1055
00173 Roma
Tel: (39 6) 722 861
Fax: (39 6) 722 1883

Filmexport Group
Via Polonia, 7/9
00198 Roma
Tel: (39 6) 855 4266
Fax: (39 6) 855 0248

Fininvest/Mediaset/Rete Italia
Viale Europa, 48
20093 Cologno Monzese
Tel: (39 6) 25141
Fax: (39 6) 2514 9091
Via Aurelia Antica, 422/424
00165 Roma
Tel: (39 6) 663 901
Fax: (39 6) 6639 0510

Filmauro
Via XXIV Maggio, 14
00187 Roma
Tel: (39 6) 678 0097
Fax: (39 6) 678 0116

International Recording
Via Urbana, 172
00184 Roma
Tel: (39 6) 482 1066
Fax: (39 6) 474 5246

Istituto Luce
Via Tuscolana, 1055
00173 Roma
Tel: (39 6) 729 921
Fax: (39 6) 722 2493

Kinepolis SpA
Via Pontina, Km 23.270
00128 Roma
Tel: (39 6) 505 0545
Fax: (39 6) 505 0119

Loeb and Loeb
Piazza Digione, 1
00197 Roma
Tel: (39 6) 874 557

Rai – Radiotelevisione Italiana
Viale Mazzini, 14
00195 Roma
Tel: (39 6) 3686 4062
Fax: (39 6) 322 1023

Rai International
Largo Villy De Luca 5
00188 Roma
Tel: (39 6) 3354 2526
Fax: (39 6) 3317 0767

RCS Film & TV
Via Mecenate, 91
20138 Milano
Tel: (39 2) 50951
Fax: (39 2) 5095 5575

Sacher Film
Via Annia Faustina, 25
00153 Roma
Tel: (39 6) 574 5353
Fax: (39 6) 574 0483

Sacis
Via Teulada, 66
00195 Roma
Tel: (39 6) 374 981
Fax: (39 6) 372 3779

JAPAN

Frank
Segers

When things economic go sour, head for the cinemas. This time-honoured entertainment maxim was demonstrated in Japan, of all places, during 1997, when the frightening realities of a faltering marketplace, bumbling political leadership, high taxation and a tsunami of bank debt all hit home. By mid-1998, the true state of Japan's economy became alarmingly evident. Let's hope for another banner year at the cinemas.

Some 141 million people went to Japanese cinemas in 1997, sharply reversing a general two-decade decline in attendance that had prompted much handwringing by cineastes and industryites alike. In his keynote speech at the 42nd National Film Day ceremonies in early 1997, Shigeru Oakada, the powerful chairman of Toei Co., sounded like a man with – finally – something to crow about. Cinema attendance should jump by a full 25 per cent or more, said the man behind Tokyo's International Film Festival. Things did not turn out quite as rosily, but, after an abysmal 1996, when attendance hit an historic low, 1997 saw an 18 per cent jump in admissions, a 19 per cent increase in total box-office to $1.3 billion (182 billion yen) on a ticket price increase of only one per cent (reducing the traditionally steep per-ticket levy to a mere $8.95).

While the number of Japanese films released in 1997 remained constant, at 278 titles, the market share of national product increased more than five points to 41.5 per cent, the equivalent of $231m in rentals. Foreign films (read those from the US) still remained dominant, with 333 titles garnering $326m in rentals (58.5 per cent). Rentals for Japan's four key film importer-distributors jumped more than 10 per cent to nearly $135m. The total number of screens increased by 56 to 1,884.

Doe-eyed superstar

Powering the advances on the domestic side was **Princess Mononoke**, the animated feature from 57-year-old Hayao Miyazaki, whose work (*Whisper Of The Heart*, *Tombstone For Fireflies*, *Pon Pocco*) combines reverence for nature, nostalgia for traditional Japan and a loathing of violence. Miyazaki, whose family ran a prosperous aviation company during the Second World War, is an outspoken pacifist whose animation is as revered as Walt Disney's is in the US. Princess Mononoke is a doe-eyed young heroine, a familiar protagonist in Miyazaki's work. She lives with wolves in a forest being pillaged by various nasties who smelt steel and indiscriminately cut down trees. Inevitably, the God of the Mountain becomes outraged, and a raging battle ensues involving dozens of forest creatures.

Despite his pacifism, Miyazaki does not stint on the bloodshed: heads and arms are lopped off with abandon and wolves vomit blood. Some of this might have been excised by the time Miramax opens *Princess Mononoke* in the US. The film played extraordinarily well with families across Japan, grossing $76m and surpassing by more than $7m the 16-year-old record held by *E.T.* as Japan's most popular film ever. The film also established its producer, Studio Ghibli (a unit of Tokuma publishing, run by Yasuyoshi Tokuma, another power behind the Tokyo festival), as a player on the worldwide animation stage, and there has been talk of deals on future projects with Disney and DreamWorks.

Mourning the masters

Japan lost some of its most luminous film creators in 1997, and last December sadly validated the proposition that deaths often come in threes. Haruko Sugimura, best known in Japan for starring in more than 900 performances of the play *Life Of a Woman*, died of cancer in a Tokyo hospital. The 91-year-old actress was best known in film circles for her appearance in Yasujiro Ozu's classic *Tokyo Story*.

Later in the month came news that Toshiro Mifune, Japan's most internationally recognisable actor for a generation, had died at 77 after a lengthy illness. An extraordinary talent, Mifune powered such classics as *Rashomon*, *Seven Samurai*, *The Rickshaw Man* and a host of international productions, often of uneven quality. Whatever the film, Mifune's athletic majesty and surprising subtlety and sensitivity shone through. Not surprisingly, he was chosen as the embodiment of Japanese man in a cinema magazine poll in 1984. Recipient of countless international tributes, Mifune will probably be best remembered for his work in 15 Kurosawa films (and Kurosawa himself would pass away in September 1998).

The third December blow for the film world was the death of director Juzo Itami, Japan's most established international presence over the last decade. The circumstances of his death were as shocking as the event itself. It happened late on the night of Saturday, December 20, shortly before *Flash*, a weekly magazine, was to have reported an alleged affair involving the 64-year-old director and a 26-year-old woman. Itami, who was married at the time of his death to Nobuko Miyamoto, an actress who starred in his films, wrote a note to the effect that he would "prove his innocence" with his own death. He then went to the roof of his Tokyo office building and jumped.

Itami, born Yoshihiro Ikeuchi, left behind a legacy of topical satires exploring the many cultural curiosities of Japanese society. A former actor and the son of a film director, Itami moved behind the camera and first made his international mark with 1984's *The Funeral*. His renown as a master of trenchant, often cutting humour was enhanced with *Tampopo*, the story of a young woman who sets out to create the perfect noodle, and then *A Taxing Woman*, a send-up of the Japanese high art of tax evasion. His *Minbo no Onna*, about the blusterings of yakuza gangsters, drew a vicious response in 1992. Itami was set upon by a quintet of underworld thugs, slashed about the face and neck and hospitalised for weeks. He emerged from the grisly incident a national hero.

His 10th and last film, **Marutai No Onna**, continues Itami's fascination with the topical's effect on the egocentric. The film is a comedy about a self-centred actress who unwittingly witnesses the murder of a lawyer fighting a religious cult. She becomes a *marutai*, a person under police protection, who chafes at her condition's interferences with her acting career and her love life. The star of the film is Ms Miyamoto. In Itami's death, Japan lost one of its most serious – and commercially successful – directors.

A different Beat

Equally serious, but not as commercially successful as Itami, is Takeshi Kitano, the popular TV personality, actor and writer-director. At 50, "Beat" as he is familiarly known, is moving beyond the international cult status claimed by *Violent Cop*, his first directorial effort in 1989, *Sonatine*, *Getting Any?* and *Kids Return*. Kitano's **Hana-bi** – the title is hyphenated to symbolise the film's theme; *hana* meaning flower, *bi*

Director and star Takeshi Kitano in HANA-BI

meaning firearms – walked off with the Golden Lion at Venice in 1997. Much as his other films, *Hana-bi* is a formalist look at violence, involving a renegade detective whose wife is terminally ill and whose police partner is paralysed by a shooting incident that could have been avoided had not the detective abandoned a stakeout.

There are criminals, loansharks and much gunplay, some formally observed in the manner Kitano adopted in *Sonatine*. *Hana-bi* contains stretches of silence, and often its violent acts are played out onscreen but not heard. Kitano said he wanted to take a more abstract approach to his depictions of violence, a shift inspired partly by the near fatal motorcycle accident several years ago that left him with temporary partial facial paralysis.

The wealth of Japanese films with contemporary themes is sometimes overlooked on the foreign market. Masato Harada's **Leaving** is a case in point: a straightforward look at super-consumerist high-school girls who hang around Tokyo's trendy Shibuya area, engaging in prostitution and pornography. Director Masashi Yamamoto's **Junk Food** is a rivetingly realistic look at a group of gang members, druggies and other Tokyo crazies. On a more mainstream note, Koki Mitani's **Welcome Back, Mr McDonald**, produced by Fuji Television, takes a humorous approach to a grimly serious rehearsal of a radio drama thrown off kilter when cast members, one after another, demand script revisions shortly before airtime. And certainly worthy of mention

is **Kyoichi Sawada – The Life And Death Of A Pulitzer-Winning Photographer**, Sho Igarashi's documentary about the life of a Japanese photo-journalist remembered for his work during the Vietnam War.

The tenth Tokyo International Film Festival was dominated by the mass hysteria which greeted Leonardo DiCaprio's appearance for the *Titanic* premiere; young female fans regarding his visit as a virtual second coming. The 1997 jurors decided to share the top feature prize between *Perfect Circle*, from Bosnia, and Germany's *Beyond Silence*. Popular actor Koji Yakusho won Best Actor for his role in one of 1997's best films, Kiyoshi Kurosawa's **Cure**, the tale of a detective trying to solve a series of mysterious murders. Yakusho is on a roll after starring in 1996's smash hit, *Shall We Dance?*, and Imamura's *The Eel*.

Finally, a piece of historical revisionism. General Hideki Tojo led Japan's Second World War effort, and was executed as a war criminal by the victorious Allies. His granddaughter thinks he has been badly judged by history, and has turned to cinema to back up her case. The result is a mainstream film production – with no English title as yet from distributor Toei – pushing the view that Tojo was not such a bad sort after all. Popular actor Masahiko Tsugawa plays Tojo – funny spectacles and all.

FRANK SEGERS writes for *Variety* and specialises in Far Eastern entertainment issues.

Producers/ Distributors

Daiei Co. Ltd.
1-1-16 Higashi,
Shimbashi, Minato-ku,
Tokyo 105
Tel: (81 3) 3573 8716
Fax: (81 3) 3573 8720

Nikkatsu Corp.
3-28-12 Hongo,
Bunkyo-ku, Tokyo
Tel: (81 3) 5689 1002

Shochiku Co.
13-5 Tsukiji 1-chome
Chuo-ku, Tokyo
Tel: (81 3) 5550 1623
Fax: (81 3) 5550 1654

Shochiku-Fuji Co.
13-5 Tsukiji, 1-chome
Chuo-ku, Tokyo
Tel: (81 3) 5550 1623
Fax: (81 3) 5550 1654

Toei Co.
2-17, 3-chome,
Ginza, Chuo-ku,
Tokyo
Tel: (81 3) 3535 7621
Fax: (81 3) 3535 7622

Toho International Co.
Hibiya Park Building,
8-1 Yukucho, 1-chome,
Chiyoda-ku, Tokyo

SHIBATA ORGANISATION INC.

Distributes in Japan

Pedro Almodover – "LIVE FLESH"

Eric Rohmer – "CONTE D' AUTOMNE"

Théo Angelopoulos

"ETERNITY AND A DAY"

Emir Kusturica

"BLACK CAT, WHITE CAT"

Jean-Luc Godard

"LE(S) HISTOIRE(S) DU CINEMA"

●

2-10-8, Ginza, Chuo-ku, Tokyo
Tel: 813-3545-3411
Fax: 813-3545-3519

Tel: (81 3) 3213 6821
Fax: (81 3) 3213 6825

Distributors/ Sales Agents

Asmik Ace Entertainment, Inc.
5-24-5 Hongo
Bunkyo-ku, Tokyo 113
Tel: (81 3) 3817 6717
Fax: (81 3) 3817 6718

GAGA Communications Inc.
East Roppongi Building,
3-16-35 Roppongi,
Minato-ku, Tokyo 106
Tel: (81 3) 3589 7503
Fax: (81 3) 3589 7499

Nippon Herald Films Inc.
5-11-1 Ginza,
Chuo-ku, Tokyo 104
Tel: (81 3) 3248 1162
Fax: (81 3) 3248 1169

(*continued on page 234*)

KAZAKHSTAN — Eugene Zykov

In 1998, the state financing of the Kazakh film industry increased by 22 per cent. Nearly two dozen Kazakh features, with an average budget of $150,000 to $300,000, and documentaries ($40,000–$50,000) went into production. Twelve independent productions, plus a few documentaries, were produced by the Almaty-based National Centre Of Cinematography (NCC), which channels state financing to film productions of the Kazakh indies. Located at the sets of Kazakh Film Studios, NCC released **Abai**, an epic drama about the life of Abai, the great Kazakh poet. It was the first Kazakh-French feature to be made with Dolby sound.

This was a highly successful year for co-productions. Kazakh-French criminal drama **Killer**, directed and co-written by Darezhan Omirbayev, snatched the Grand Prix in Un Certain Regard at Cannes. It is the tale of a professional driver forced by gangsters to kill a political leader. Among other award-winners was the drama of shabby urban life, **Shankhai**, written and directed by Alexander Baranov, which won the Special Award at the International Young Film Festival in Artek (Ukraine).

In mid-1998, another four international co-productions were launched. A US-Kazakh historical drama, *Tomiris*, is currently in development to be shot in early 1999, with a record-breaking budget of $6m, raised by Almaty-based Orken Film Productions. Meanwhile Kazakh-Mongolian historical drama **Warrior** was produced for a record low budget of $80,000, and the forthcoming Kazakh-Kyrgyz period drama **The Last Love Of Genghis Khan**, directed by Bakhyt Karagulov, will probably cost about the same.

Toon trouble and a documentary boom

Kazakh animation is in deep crisis, with only one or two short films released every other year. However, a young Almaty-based indie, Rick Corporation, has launched *Funny Kaleidoscope*, a $180,000 series of ten, six-minute animations, based on local medieval comic stories in co-production with Khabar TV/Radio. The local TV boom has sparked scores of documentaries in Kazakhstan. Sergei Asimov, a former documentary film director, who now runs the state TV/Radio Centre, hires good film-makers and offers them good money. Within the last two years, he has produced 22 documentaries on subjects ranging from politics to archaeology and history, such as *Ancient Muslim Pantheon*.

An independent documentary producer and director, Igor Gonopolsky, has released a much-awarded 52-minute 35mm documentary, **It's Me Crossing The Street**, about Sergei Kalmykov, an insane but highly talented painter, whose art was banned in Kazakhstan. In late 1998 Gonopolsky also wrapped a 52-minute essay, **Unknown Eisenstein**, which explores the mass evacuation of Soviet film-makers to Almaty during the Second World War, and a seven × 52-minute documentary series, **The People From The Opposite Bank Of The River**, about the roots of Kazakhstan's Jews.

Kazakh buyers are gradually entering the global markets. Dariga Nazabaeva, director general of Khabar State TV/Radio regularly attends every MIP-TV and MIPCOM event to buy programmes. In June this year, Kazakh and Uzbek film and TV buyers, producers and distributors presented their potential jointly at the round-table discussion "East-Meets-West: Exploring Opportunities", held at the sixth DISCOP-98 feature market in Budapest. "The success of the [Kazakh delegation's] debut was way beyond our expectation," said Patric Jucaud, founder and president of DISCOP. "Western producers and distributors are truly interested in the region. They want to know more and do business there."

In October 1997, Kazakhstan launched the first International Film Festival in Almaty. The state-financed event was reinforced by lavish private donations to boost its exotic slate of films. The festival may attract state and private investments for the renovation of movie-houses in Almaty (in Kazakhstan, cinemas show mainly US titles, besides Kazakh, Russian and European films, while the top level attendance rarely exceeds 20 per cent). The highlight of the year for domestic exhibitors was the launch of *Titanic*. James Cameron's epic, nicknamed 'the exhibitor's delight', generated immense ticket lines in front of most cinemas and a record amount of press coverage.

On January 1, 1998, a new Criminal Code came into operation, but it is proving incapable of curbing rampant copyright violations and video piracy. The situation should improve when Kazakhstan joins the Berne Convention on anti-piracy measures, a move scheduled for the year 2000.

EUGENE ZYKOV is Moscow-based East European Bureau Chief for *Channel 21 International* (UK).

Recent and Forthcoming Films

DESANT (Paratroopers)

Script: Alexander Baranov, Rafad Samigullin. Dir: Leila Oranysheva. Phot: Valerii Mulgaut. Prod: Firma-Kino Studios

Action-adventure: three   teenagers

Still from EXECUTION AFTER DEATH

Useful Addresses

Caravan/BG Productions
017 11 Chaikovsky St
480004 Almaty
Tel: (7 3272) 620 413
Fax: (7 3272) 399 895
e-mail: root@caravan alma-ata.su

Gala-TV
23A Tole Bi
480100 Almaty
Tel: (7 3272) 617 613
Fax: (7 3272) 616 816
e-mail: galatv@galatv.almaty.kz

Rik Corp.
76 Zhibek Zholy St
Suite 603
Almaty
Tel: (7 3272) 47 91 54
e-mail: radiorik1@kazmail.asdc.kz

*The four companies below are
all based at:*
176 Al-Farabi Ave
480067 Almaty

Firm-Kino
Tel/Fax: (7 3262) 630 901

Kazakh Film Studios
Tel: (7 3272) 482 211
Fax: (7 3272) 480 909

**National Centre of
Cinematography**
Tel: (7 32 62) 48 23 23
Fax: (7 3272) 48 17 00

**Orken Film
Production/Distribution**
Tel/Fax: (7 3262) 48 07 55
e-mail: aigul@orkenfil.almaty.kz

recruited in the 'black beret' division become real men during border conflict.

PODLINNAYA ISTORIA ANGELOV (The Real Story Of Angels)

Script: Leila Akhinzhanova. Dir: Karpykov. Photo: Alexei Berkovich. Players: Farkhad Abdraimov, Kristina Arabkaite. Prod: Karpykov and National Centre Of Cinematography.

Mystery/criminal drama in which a charismatic invalid recovers thanks to willpower and friendship.

RAIYMBEK

Script: Odelshi Agishev. Dir: Boulat Kalymbetov. Phot: Alexei Berkovich. Prod: Kalymbetov/ National Centre Of Cinema-ography.

Historic drama about a strong warrior fighting to liberate his people from invaders.

KAZN' POSLE SMERTI (Execution After Death)

Script: Talgat Temenov, Nikita Dzhilkibaev. Dir: Temenov. Prod: National Centre Of Cinema-tography/Kazakh Film Studios.

Drama. A writer becomes the victim of a dangerous experiment: he is locked in a prison cell whose previous occupant – a serial killer who is a dead-ringer for the writer – has died shortly before execution.

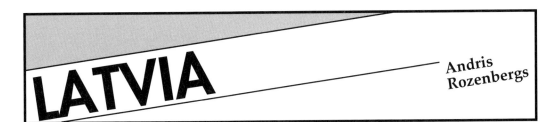

LATVIA

Andris Rozenbergs

The Consultative Film Council, a public advisory body at the National Film Centre, this year expressed its support for four fiction film projects. All of them were presented by young directors preparing to make their first or second full-length film. The ascent of this new generation is exciting to watch: suddenly it appears that a group of people with different backgrounds, different levels of education, experience and age, are sharing the same views and attitudes towards their social environment, history and cultural heritage.

Trying to define these film-makers' attitudes, one might say that they are more individualistic than the previous generation, not bothering very much about cinema's communicative role or social mission. The history in which the older generation were participants, victims or witnesses is for these youngsters nothing but a source of captivating stories. So Aivars Grauba, in **The Gruesome Summer** (*Big Vassal*), designs a fascinating love story, with elements of melodrama, against the background of political events during the summer of 1940, when Latvia, occupied by Soviet troops, lost its independence.

Anna Viduleja, a graduate of England's National Film and Television School, together with her producer Aris Dreimanis, in **The Colour of Lead** (*Svina Krāsa*) plan to explore some episodes from the youth of the Latvian painter Georgs Eliass, who is supposed to be the famous Peter the Painter, one of the participants in the Siege of Sidney Street, the 1910 incident in which Winston Churchill deployed 1,000 soldiers against two Latvian revolutionaries holed up in a London house.

Border crossings

Viduleja is not the only young Latvian film-maker to have studied or lived abroad

and thus developed a more open perspective on the world. So Una Celma, in **The Curse of Gravitation** (*Gravitācijas lāsts*), attempts to compare the Latvian and Swedish mentalities, and another of the projects approved this year, **Three Love Stories** (*Trīs Mīlas Stāsti*), an Estonian-Latvian-Lithuanian co-production, will play with cultural patterns. The film will consist of three immortal love stories – Carmen, Tristan and Isolde and King Solomon – recreated in contemporary settings in Baltic countries. Janis Putnins, in his **Hide-and-Seek** (*Paslēpes*), plays with the structures of detective fiction to tell a story of imaginary crime.

All producers, having obtained support from the Latvian government, are now seeking foreign production and marketing investment. They are fully aware of the necessity to incorporate national characteristics into a broader European context if funds are to be raised and, instead of perceiving this shift as a threat to their identities, they consider it as a natural development.

To facilitate and support those efforts, Latvia is preparing to join MEDIA II and Eurimages. The necessary contributions have been allocated, and a working party set up by the Minister of Culture has prepared amendments to the Radio and Television Law which will bring it into line with the EU's "Television without frontiers" directive, a precondition for joining EU audio-visual industry support mechanisms.

Now everything depends on hard political decisions. Latvia ardently wants to join the World Trade Organisation, and this has made it a hostage of the big dispute between the EU and US over audio-visual quotas. Finally, the Riga Film Studio was privatised last year, and most feature films will be made there.

Still from Laila Pakalnina's THE SHOE, with the considerate man dressed in KGB uniform
photo: Andrejs Grants

ANDRIS ROZENBERGS has directed seven fiction films and a dozen documentaries. He is Deputy Director of the National Film Centre, in charge of International Relations.

Recent and Forthcoming Films

BIG VASSAL
(The Gruesome Summer)

Script: Pauls Bankovskis, Guntars Gabranovs, Andrejs Ekis, Aigars Grauba. Dir: Grauba. Prod: PLATFORMA Filma.

GRAVITĀCIJAS LĀSTS
(The Curse of Gravitation)

Script: Lauris Gundars. Dir: Una Celma. Prod: KAUPO Filma (Latvia) and Bjerking Production AB (Sweden).

PASLĒPES (Hide and Seek)

Script: Lauris Gundars. Dir: Janis Putnins. Prod: KAUPO Filma.

TRISTAN AND ISOLDE

Script: Janis Einfelds Dir: Askolds Saulitis Prod: F.O.R.M.A.

Useful Addresses

National Film Centre
Smerla 3
Riga LV-1006
Tel: (371 2) 252 0411
Fax: (371 2) 754 19 56
e-mail: nfc@com.latnet.lv

Latvian Filmmaker's Union
Elizabetes 49
Riga LV-1050
Tel: (371 2) 728 8536
Fax: (371 2) 724 0542

Riga Film Studio
Smerla 3
Riga LV-1006
Tel: (371 2) 755 1706
Fax: (371 2) 782 8408

LITHUANIA — Gražina Arlickaite

Lithuanian cinema today is characterised by two tendencies. The first reflects the aesthetic aspirations of Lithuanian film-makers and demonstrates the continuum of the auteur tradition. Two of the three feature films made in Lithuania in 1997 are part of this tendency, which unites the middle and younger generation of Lithuanian directors.

The fourteenth film by productive middle generation director Algimantas Puipa, **A Wolf's Teeth Necklace** (*Vilko dantų karoliai*), considers a popular theme in European cinema: man against the totalitarian system. The film's hero, Tadas, an artist, grew up in a small village during the period of post-war Stalinist repression. His childhood memories bring back to life friends and family, the long wait for his father's return from Siberia, longing and grief. In the little boy's universe, the external manifestations of totalitarianism are not important. The camera seems to catch sight of the men in KGB uniforms, the deportation centres, Soviet posters and portraits of Stalin only by accident. The essential problem is the deformation of the human soul, and the film uncovers it in a rather unexpected form.

Puipa has created a sequence of images in which consistent story-telling has no

Still from A WOLF'S TEETH NECKLACE

importance; only psychological nuances reveal the incompatibility of humanism and the totalitarian system. The idea of the film is not to reveal the crimes of totalitarianism, but to highlight the psychological traumas of a child and later artist, which cannot be healed in an entire lifetime. Puipa's film has participated in a number of European festivals, as well as in Tehran, Cairo and Calcutta, winning numerous awards. However, it could not be called 'popular', because it failed to attract a wide public in Lithuania, or any other countries.

Home alone

Visual language and wordless expression are the dominant elements of another interesting film, **The House** (*Namai*), by young Lithuanian director Šarūnas Bartas. The film is free of story or character development, as the director creates his own magic world of visions, in which the question 'What's the story?' is replaced by 'How is the story told?'.

Like the other works of this original artist, the film is like a cinema fresco, reflecting one particular theme, in this case the home. The camera roams around a huge house which is sometimes empty and sometimes full of people. These people are always lonely, even if they are together. The film director wants to reveal the nature of 'home'. Bartas is a regular guest of Un Certain Regard at Cannes, and a film like *House* really needs not only a special exhibition outlet, but also a special kind of spectator. It is hard to believe that it could be understood by a public used to commercial fare.

The second tendency in Lithuanian cinema is much more prosaic, but no less important. The country's film production structure has begun to take on a much clearer shape. Following pleas from Lithuanian film-makers for greater state support of film production, the government has guaranteed annual finance for a minimum of three feature films, ten hours of shorts documentaries, one hour of animation and four hours of film chronicle.

Governmental institutions have been working to bring Lithuania's audio-visual sector into harmony with the directives of the European Union and European conventions; Lithuania wants to join the MEDIA II and Eurimages programmes. For that purpose, the Lithuanian Ministry of Culture and Audiovisual Eureka have jointly established Information Antenna. The task of this new body is to create a new film-financing structure by developing relations between Lithuanian audio-visual professionals and public authorities and European institutions.

DR GRAŽINA ARLICKAITE is Head of International Relations and Sales Service at the Lithuanian Film Studio, and Director of Information Antenna. She is also a lecturer in the Film and Theatre Department of the Lithuanian Music Academy and a film researcher.

Production Companies

Lithuanian Film Studio
Nemenčinės pl. 4
2016 Vilnius
Lithuania
Robertas Urbonas – Director
Tel: (370 2) 763 444
Fax: (370 2) 764 254

Kinema
Grybautojų g. 30
2000 Vilnius

Lithuania
Daiva Vaitiekūnaitė – Producer
Tel: (370 2) 770 148/769 594
Fax: (370 2) 619 507

Film and Video Studio 'Kopa'
P.O. Box 2581
2015 Vilnius
Lithuania
Alicija Žukauskienė – Producer
Tel: (370 2) 223 451

Film Studio Nominum
Nemenčinės pl. 4
2016 Vilnius

Lithuania
Arūnas Matelis – Producer
Tel/Fax: (370 2) 700 337

Studija 2000
Nemenčinės pl. 4
2016 Vilnius
Lithuania
Kęstutis Petrulis – Producer
Tel: (370 2) 768 909
Fax: (370 2) 483 690

Filmfocus
Birutės g. 18
2004 Vilnius

Lithuania
Audrius Kuprevičius – Producer
Tel: (370 2) 230 803
Fax: (370 2) 223 769

Litnek
Nemenčinės pl. 4
2016 Vilnius
Lithuania
Arūnas Stoškus – Producer
Tel: (370 2) 768 381
Fax: (370 2) 727 702

Distributors

Lietuvos Kinas
Ozo g. 4
2600 Vilnius
Lithuania
Stasys Karamza – General Director
Tel: (370 2) 772 696
Fax: (370 2) 770 994

BDG
B. Radvilaitės g. 1-309
2026 Vilnius
Lithuania
Romualda Daciūtė – Manager
Tel: (370 2) 610 935
Fax: (370 2) 611 141

Cinemark
Birutės g. 18
2004 Vilnius
Algis Šemeševičius – President
Tel: (370 2) 220 730
Fax: (370 2) 223 716

Bombos filmai
Žygimantų g. 6
2600 Vilnius
Lithuania
Gintaras Plytnikas – Manager
Tel: (370 2) 223 358/312 837
Fax: (370 2) 225 715

Amfiteatro filmai
Pylimo g. 17
2001 Vilnius
Lithuania
Tel: (370 2) 313 118
Fax: (370 2) 313 119

Useful Addresses

The Ministry of Culture of the Republic of Lithuania
Basanavičiaus g. 5
2683 Vilnius
Bonifacas Gintalas – Head of
Cinema Division
Tel: (370 2) 616 005
Fax: (370 2) 623 120

Lithuanian State Archive of Vision and Sound
O. Milašiaus g. 19
2016 Vilnius
Dainius Narvydas – Director
Tel: (370 2) 768 209 /762 587
Fax: (370 2) 764 489

Information Antenna
Nemenčinės pl. 4
2016 Vilnius
Tel/Fax: (370 2) 763 463
Gražina Arlickaitė – Director

Lithuanian Union of Cinematographers
Birutės g. 18
2004 Vilnius
Gytis Lukšas – President
Tel/Fax: (370 2) 220 759

The Association of Independent Producers
Nemenčinės pl. 4
2016 Vilnius
Tel: (370 2) 762 881
Fax: (370 2) 762 882

LUXEMBOURG
Jean-Pierre Thilges

The big film news in Luxembourg in 1997 was the leap in cinema admissions which followed the opening, in December 1996, of the 10-screen Utopolis multiplex. Attendance for the year shot up by more than 60 per cent, from 754,000 on 16 screens in 1996, to 1,186,000 on 27 in 1997. With major assistance from *Titanic*, which sold more than 130,000 tickets, attendance for 1998 may break the 1.4 million mark.

The number of films released went from 140 in 1996 to 231 in 1997, and is expected to rise yet again this year. Although art-house figures initially suffered a major blow from the opening of the multiplex, the trend was reversed toward the end of the year and figures are definitely looking like a viable 200,000 tickets at the five-screen Utopia miniplex in 1998. A Festival of Spanish Films and an extensive season of new British fare helped consolidate this trend. With Utopolis having reached saturation point much sooner than expected, the Utopia Group may build another five- to seven-screen complex in the south of Luxembourg, whose 410,000 inhabitants are among the most eager cinemagoers in Europe.

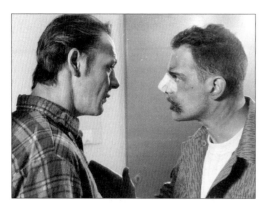

Still from Andy Bausch's BACK IN TROUBLE

While exhibition continued to soar in the Grand-Duchy, the ever-expanding production community (two production studios now operate all year round) felt a bit jittery towards the end of 1997, when the government failed to come through on its proposed 10-year extension (with minor changes) of the local tax-break scheme, which has been attracting brisk international business to the country. The old scheme has, however, been kept in place for another year, and the government recommitted to enact the updated legislation in 1999, which was generally welcomed as good news.

An endless boom?

Budgets spent in the country's fledgling film "industry " have constantly been going up. After having its sound-stages haunted by Russell Mulcahy's *Talos - The Mummy* and the more modestly budgeted *The First 9¹/₂ Weeks*, the Carousel Pictures Company opened its studio facilities to Chris Roberts' $27m sci-fi feature *Wing Commander - The Movie*, the most ambitious work shot in the country so far.

Delux Studios has been host to Peter Greenaway's forthcoming *Eight-and-a-half Women*, billed as an "erotic hommage to the universe of Federico Fellini", and expected to premiere at Cannes in 1999. Greenaway's last picture, *The Pillow Book*, was also shot at Delux. At press time, Iris Productions of Luxembourg, together with London-based Uli Meyer Production, had announced the $60m *Quack*, a feature

expected to blend live-action and animation, in the *Roger Rabbit* vein. According to the producers, several US majors were looking into the deal.

While studio shoots and international co-productions are on a constant increase (Samsa Film had a 10 per cent stake in Benoît Jacquot's Cannes competition entry, *L'Ecole de la Chair*) local film-makers seem to be taking a sabbatical year to either work (and gain experience) on the large international productions filming around the country, or venture into short subjects and documentaries.

Amongst local releases, Andy Bausch's **Back In Trouble** (Lynx Productions) had a so-so commercial career (15,000 tickets sold), while the heavily re-edited cut of Luis Galvão Teles' **Elles** (Samsa) did well with the art-house crowd in Luxembourg, Germany and Portugal. Samsa Film also supervised and co-financed *Pourquoi Se Marier le Jour de la Fin du Monde* and *Max et Bobo*, and produced one of the finest animated shorts ever made in this country, *Fragile* by Daniel Wiroth.

Although the internationalisation of the Luxembourg film scene is of major importance to the country, no new local talent in the directing or screenwriting fields has emerged lately, which is a shame, as all elements are now in place to give the country a viable industry. The fact that none of the existing producers, directors and/or writers are currently prepared to tackle typically 'Luxembourgish' subjects, is felt as the one major drawback to the current film-making boom in the Grand-Duchy. Although it is economically sensible to hedge one's bets and venture into international co-productions, local audiences are being left out in the cold.

JEAN-PIERRE THILGES is an ex-banker turned film critic, who helped bring the multiplex boom to Luxembourg. A compulsive collector of laser discs and now DVDs, he is still desperate for someone to release the work of Douglas Sirk on these formats.

MALAYSIA

Baharudin A. Latif

Regarded initially as a mere inconvenience that everyone had to put up with, the economic turmoil that swept Southeast Asia in mid-1997 had assumed the proportions of a life-threatening disaster by year end. By mid-1998, it became abundantly clear that Malaysians had to readjust their lifestyles as the price of goods and services soared by 50 per cent. The leisure and entertainment sector was the hardest hit. Television stations cancelled all new programmes, imposing a 15 to 25 per cent cut on existing deals. They also curtailed imports and showed extra repeats. More than 200 companies, which make features and TV programmes, have suspended all production.

Three of the biggest companies – Astro-Shaw (a joint venture between Hong Kong-based producer/exhibitor Shaw Brothers, and Astro, the 24-channel satellite company), Home Video Distributors, the biggest video producer/distributor, and new exhibition circuit Golden Screen Cinemas – all had ambitious plans to go into feature film production, but these have now been put on hold indefinitely. Even Grand Brilliance, which planned for 24 films a year, scaled down to half that figure. For the current 1998–99 season it has only four films, including the animated feature **Man Spider**, children's adventure **The Thing** and **The Last Malay Woman**. About a dozen movies shot last year remained unreleased.

Two is too few

Only two films released in the 1997–98 season, both youth-oriented, boy-meets-girl stories, made money: Aziz Osman's **Dream Princess** (a sequel is shooting) and Grand Brilliance's fourth production,

Yusof Haslam's **Maria Mariana II**. The directorial debut of Nurhalim Ismail, **Sizzling**, was critically acclaimed but, like all recent adult dramas, did not ignite the box office. Not surprisingly, *Titanic* became the top movie of all time, grossing $2.5m (RM10m) by April 30, 1998, after four months in release. Other top films were *Tomorrow Never Dies*, Jackie Chan's *Who Am I?*, *The Lost World: Jurassic Park* and *Men in Black*, which all grossed more than $1.5m.

The exhibition sector, surprisingly, is still growing like nobody's business. Two exhibitors, Golden Communications and Cathay Cinemas, were merged into Golden Screen Cinemas, becoming the country's biggest circuit, with 110 cinemas. It is 60 per cent owned by Golden Harvest, which is rumoured to be abandoning Hong Kong, and expecting to solidify its presence here. Its biggest multiplex will be the 18-screen site at the prestigious Mid-Valley project in Kuala Lumpur, scheduled for a 1999 opening.

Golden Harvest also has a 25 per cent stake in Tanjung Golden Village, the other big multiplex player. Its partners are Village Roadshow of Australia (25 per cent) and Tanjung PLC, a local company with the remaining 50 per cent. It is anybody's guess as to what lies around the corner, although the country has been assured by visiting money experts, including International Monetary Fund officials, that the Malaysian economy will recover by the last quarter of 1998.

BAHARUDIN A. LATIF is a professed film buff and historian and has written extensively on Malaysian cinema since the mid-1960s for more than 100 publications, including *Variety*, *Asiaweek*, *Movie/TV Marketing* and *Asia Magazine*.

Aleeza Kassim in HOT

Eman Manan in HITMAN

Recent and Forthcoming Films

PUTERI IMPIAN
(Dream Princess)

Script, Dir and Edit: Azis M. Osman. Phot: Badarudin Azmi. Music: Azman Abu Hassan. Players: Amy Mastura, Hairie Othman, Chiko, Harahap Rashid, NorAliah Lee. A Paradigm Production.

PANAS (Hot)

Script and Dir: Murhalim Ismail. Phot: Nuri Harmaini. Music: Ibraham Bachik. Edit: Elias Mydin. Players: Aleeza Kasim, Yusof Mohamed, Eizlan Yusuf, Shahrizan Ahmad, Omar Abdullah, Normala Omar. Nurhalim/Take One/Keris Motion Production.

LENJAN (Hitman)

Script and Dir: Ismail Yaacob. Phot: Badarudin Azmi. Edit: Elias Mydin. Players: Eman Manan, Rosyam Noor, Nina Juren, Pansha.

MARIA MARIANA II

Script and Dir: Yusof Haslam. Phot: Badarudin Azmi. Edit: Salehan Sallehudin. Players: Erra Fazira, Ziana Zain, Awie. A Skop Production.

Producers, Importers and Exhibitors

Grand Brilliance Sdn. Bhd.
99L, Jalan Tandak, off Jalan Bangsar
59100 Bangsar
Kuala Lumpur
Tel: (603) 284 6900
Fax: (603 284 6864

Golden Screen Cinemas Sdn. Bhd.
1 Jalan SS22/19, Damansara Jaya
47400 Petaling Jaya
Sellangor D.D.
Tel: (603) 719 5666
Fax: (603) 712 1655

Mega Pavilion Cinemas Sdn. Bhd.
Kompleks Bukit Jambul
3A-06-01 Jalan Rumbia
11900 Penang
Tel: (604) 646 7888
Fax: (604) 646 4113

Keris Motion Sdn. Bhd.
18B Jalan Tun Mohd. Fuad 1
Taman Dun Dr. Ismail
60000 Kuala Lumpur
Tel: (603) 716 6162
Fax: (603) 716 6167

Tanjung Golden Village Sdn. Bhd.
17th Floor, Menara Boustead
Jalan Raja Chulan
50200 Kuala Lumpur
Tel: (603) 244 3388
Fax: (603) 244 3301

Useful Address

FINAS
(The National Film Development Corporation Malaysia)
Studio Merdeka Complex
Lot 1661, Hulu Kelang
68000 Selangor D.E.
Tel: (603) 408 6722
Fax: (603) 407 5216

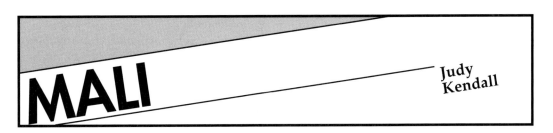

MALI — Judy Kendall

Although Malian film-makers have always relied heavily on support from France in terms of finance and production skills, they have succeeded in the past in leaving a definite Malian print on the international scene. This has been most obviously the case with the acclaimed Souleymane Cisse, but others have also made their mark.

In 1997, the films of two Malian directors were featured at Cannes: Adama Drabo's **Taafe Fanga**, and Abdoulatye Ascofare's **Faraw! (Une Mère des Sables)**. Both films then went on to have extensive runs on the international festival circuit, and both won awards at the Namur Film Festival. However, when it comes to the question of distribution, the success story pales significantly. Outside Mali, films tend only to be shown during festivals; internally, the privatisation of Mali's cinemas makes it difficult to gauge how many African films will now be shown to their local audience.

Hard times, African dreams

This comes at a time when local audiences are becoming more important. Generally, the film industry in Africa is falling on hard times, having to face further financial constraints as external funders initiate cutbacks. As a result, film-makers are tending to look more locally, both for an audience and for finance (through co-productions with neighbouring African countries).

An echo of these concerns can be heard in Souleymane Cisse's wish to provide a more "African" content to his films. In July last year he said that his current dream was "to make films in which the ancient depths of African culture will surge up again. To this end I spend my time visiting old men who tell me stories of the past, true or mythical. A cinema imitating that of America or Europe will be in vain. We must immerse ourselves in our own sources."

It is interesting therefore to see that in Chieck Oumar Sissoko's forthcoming **La Genese**, he has chosen to go to the Bible for inspiration – a new and surprising departure for African film. *La Genese* is Sissoko's fourth feature and deals with the story of Jacob and his sons as reported in Genesis. However, the story is very much set in a Mali context.

Salif Keita (the popular Malian singer) plays Esau, and Sissoko has drawn on similarities with Mali's own culture in terms of clothes, social relations and architecture – the film was shot in a reconstructed Malian stone village, which was abandoned 17 years ago. The biblical story tells of three communities in conflict: animal-raisers, hunters and peasants, and, as Sissoko says, the parallels with Malian society are easy to make: "It is rare [in Mali] to see a farming village without a village of animal-raisers nearby – with the related possibilities of conflict."

Useful Addresses

Centre de Services de Production Audiovisuelle (CESPA)
Route de Koulouba (derrière Le Musée National)
BP 1810 Bamako

Tel: (223) 220 450
Fax: (223) 228 070

Ministère de l'Industrie de l'Artisanat et du Tourisme
Quartier du Fleuve
BP 1759 Bamako

Tel: (223) 224 387/8058/9208
Fax: (223) 230 267

MCAC: Ambassade de France
BP 84 Bamako
Tel: (223) 226 429
Fax: (223) 228 339

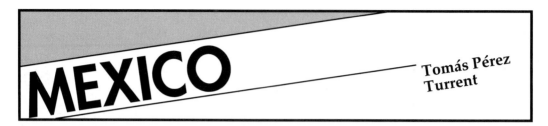

MEXICO

Tomás Pérez
Turrent

The trend for diminishing production levels, which began in 1994, has continued and there is no likelihood of a return to the boom period of the 1950s, or even 1982-87, when on average 80 films a year were produced, albeit not all of the best quality. In 1997, only 13 features were made, of which six were shown at the Guadalajara Film Festival. That four or five of the 13 should have been noteworthy for one reason or another is more than satisfactory.

This selection included Arturo Ripstein's **Divine** (*El evangelio de las maravillas*), which was invited to Cannes 1998, and Carlos Carrera's equally ambitious **The Enchantment** (*El embrujo*), set in a flea-bitten circus in the late 1920s. For the moment, an increase in production capacity cannot be contemplated: there is simply no money available and it is miraculous indeed that a dozen feature films and a couple of documentaries manage to get produced, as well as a handful of shorts showing the new trends in animation.

Rites of passage

The first feature as director by the exceptionally talented cinematographer

Still from WHO THE HELL IS JULIETTE?

Carlos Markovich, **Who the hell is Juliette?** (*¿Quien Diablos Es Juliette?*), was without doubt the best film of 1997 – and many other years. It takes a 16-year old Cuban girl and pairs her with a Mexican model who is at once her double and her opposite. Both hide behind the façade of young, pleasure-loving kids on a journey of initiation which moves between Cuba, Mexico and a snow-covered New York, confronting the realities and taboos of their respective societies. The film won a prize at the Sundance Festival.

The well-known veteran Gilberto Martinez Solares made his first film in Mexico in 1937, having first learnt the business in Hollywood. He went on to make 100 films in many different genres, his comedies being especially brilliant. He died a few months after the completion of **Crisis**, which he directed in conjunction with his son, Adolfo (his custom for the last decade of his life). It is a complicated tale of political and corporate corruption, adultery, mistaken diagnosis (an actor kills a senator who, supposedly, is terminally ill) and existential crises. Unfortunately, this is not one of the films for which Don Gilberto will be remembered.

There were many promising shorts made, but, like its big brother, the feature, the Mexican short film has no exhibition outlets. Multiple theatre chains such as Cinemex, Cinemark, General Cinemas all prefer to show *any* film from Hollywood. This year, for example, of the 20 Mexican films exhibited, all were produced before 1997. Supposedly the public is to blame for making their choices according to the laws of the free market. But is the market really that free? Of the 30 films with most admissions, only Luc Besson's *The Fifth*

Still from Arturo Ripstein's DIVINE

Element (number 19) is not Hollywood-produced, although it has all the characteristics of a Hollywood film. Hollywood's crushing supremacy makes the market for Mexican films as difficult as it is for any other foreign movie.

TOMÁS PÉREZ TURRENT has been awarded a scholarship from Mexico's Sistema Nacional de Creadores. During 1997 he gave courses on scriptwriting in various Mexican cities. His latest film script, *Birds Die of Fatigue*, will be filmed in 1998.

Recent and Forthcoming Films

EL AGUJERO (The Hole)

Script: Beto Gomez, Rabdull Fez. Dir: Gomez. Phot: Hector Ozuna. Edit: Nacho Ruiz Capillas. Players: Roberto Cobo, Pedro Altamirano, Lorenzo Felipe, Jose Pimentel Ramos. Prod: Raul Fernandez, Juan Gordon, with the collaboration of Elias Querejeta.

Pachuco returns to Mexico, disillusioned and disappointed, having spent 30 years in the US working without a permit. He goes back to his native Patzcuaro during the famous Hallowe'en festivities and ends up in jail.

ANGELUZ

Script and Dir: Leopoldo Laborde.

Phot: Francisco Bojorquez. Mus: Quinta Raza. Players: Roberto Trujillo, Jose Luis Badillo, Hugo Stieglitz, Arianne Pellicer, Tina French. Prod: H&S y Asociados, Filmo Imagen, Videovisa.

After two efforts in video, 28-year-old Laborde has attempted a feature film in that particularly difficult genre: fantasy/horror. The result shows plenty of ingenuity but little film-making skill — not everybody can be a Wes Craven.

CRISIS

Script: Gilberto Martinez Solares, Adolfo Martinez Solares, Diana Legarreta. Dir: Gilberto and Adolfo Martinez Solares. Phot:

Arturo de la Rosa. Players: Jose Alonso, Hector Bonilla, Manuel Ojeda, Lisa Owen, Tina Romero, Rafael Rojas. Prod: Filmo Imagen, S.A. de C.V.

DE NOCHE VIENES ESMERALDA (Esmeralda Comes by Night)

Script: Jaime Humberto Hermosillo, based on the story by Elena Poniatowska. Dir and Edit: Hermosillo. Phot: Xavier Perez Grobet. Players: Maria Rojo, Claudio Obregon, Pedro Armendariz, Marta Navarro, Ignacio Retes, Ernesto Laguardia, Alberto Estrella. Prod: Producciones Monarca, IMCINE,

Fondo de Fomento a la Calidad Cinematografica, Resonancia Production, Producciones Esmeralda

Esmeralda is a nurse, simultaneously married to five men whom she loves and makes happy. All five accept the arrangement until her youngest husband denounces her in a fit of jealousy and she has to confront an intolerant justice system.

FIBRA OPTICA (Optic Fiber)

Script and Dir: Francisco Athie. Phot: Rodrigo Prieto. Players: Roberto Sosa, Lumi Cavazos, Alberto Estrella, Angelica Aragon, Christian Gout. Prod: Erwing Neumaier, Mathias Erenberg para Hubert Balls Fund, IMCINE .

The murder of a union leader appears to be a crime of passion, but is really just a link in a major conspiracy. Marco, an unemployed journalist, is hired by an anonymous voice to investigate. The same voice hires a mediocre lawyer to defend the dead man's mistress, accused of being the murderess. A complex, visually rich film – one of the best of the year.

¿QUIEN DIABLOS ES JULIETTE? (Who the hell is Juliette?)

Script, Dir, Phot and Edit: Carlos Markovich. Mus: Alejandro Markovich. Players: Yuliet Ortega, Fabiola Quiroz, Oneida Ramirez, Francisco Clemente, Benny, Salma Hayek. Prod: Yolanda Andrade for El Error de Diciembre, Genesis, Etudios Churubusco Azteca, Beta Imagen Digital, Hubert Balls Fund, Alameda Films, IMCINE.

LA PRIMERA NOCHE (The First Night)

Script: Benjamin Cann. Dir: Alejandro Gamboa. Phot: Alfredo Kasem. Players: Oswaldo Benavides, Mariana Avila, Xavier Massini, Julio Casado, Audrey Vera, Margarita Magaña, Paul Choza, Amara Villafuerte, Martha Aura. Prod: Roberto Gomez Bolaños para Televicine.

A group of middle-class teenagers in Mexico City experience their first taste of sex. Typical rites of passage movie, made outstanding by its freshness and by the credibility which the very young actors give to the characters. Awarded the foreign critics' prize at the Festival of Guadalajara.

VIOLETA

Script: Alberto Cortes, based on the play by Nicolas Dorr. Dir: Cortes. Phot: Jorge Medina. Players: Blanca Guerra, David Ramy, Katia Elnecave, Enrique Lizalde, Reynaldo Leon Corro. Prod: Juan Jose Muñoz for ICAIC-IMCINE.

A Cuban rumba dancer tells her life story to a young journalist.

Producers

Alameda Films
Av. Division del Norte 2462-501
03300, Mexico D.F.
Tel: (52 5) 688 0330/5085/7318
Fax: (52 5) 605 8911

Amaranta Films
Eje 10 Sur,
Henriquez Urena 395
Col. Santo Domingo
Coyoacan
04369, Mexico D.F.
Tel: (52 5) 610 1037/1772/1171
Fax: (52 5) 610 1725

Direccion de Cortometraje
(formerly Didecine)
Av. Division del Norte 2462, 3 piso
03300, Mexico D.F.
Tel: (52 5) 688 7614/7079
Fax: (52 5) 688 7611

Producciones Rosas Priego
Av. Division del Norte 2462, 4 piso
03300, Mexico D.F.
Tel: (52 5) 688 7022/7223
Fax: (52 5) 688 7044

Rio Mixcoac, S.C.L.
Morelos 33-4
Col. Torriello Guerra
Tlalpan
14060, Mexico D.F.
Tel: (52 5) 665 6417/8998
Fax: (52 5) 665/9123

Tabasco Films
Cuernavaca 17
Col. Condesa
06140, Mexico D.F.
Tel: (52 5) 286 1860/1890
Fax: (52 5) 286 2063

Televicine
Benito Juarez 7
Col. del Carmen
Coyoacan
04100, Mexico D.F.
Tel: (52 5) 659 2961/7168
Fax: (52 5) 554 3698

Distributors

Cine Alternativo
Pereferico Sur 4121
Col. Fuentes de Pedregal
14141, Mexico D.F.
Tel: (52 5) 420 1309, 645 4080
Fax: (52 5) 645 5704

Columbia TriStar/Buena Vista
Edif. Plaza Reforma
Prol. Paseo de la Reforma 600, PH-331
Col. Santa Fe Pena Blanca
01210, Mexico D.F.
Tel: (52 5) 258 2700/2702
Fax: (52 5) 570 1012/0957

Gussi (Artecinema/Videomax)
Gob. Ignacio Esteva 70
Col. San Miguel Chapultepec
Mexico D.F.
Tel: (52 5) 277 8999, 271 0955
Fax: (52 5) 516 5729

Latina, S.A.
Estudios Churubusco
Atletas 2
Col. Country Club
04220, Mexico D.F.
Tel: (52 5) 544 7805
Fax: (52 5) 549 1820

Twentieth Century Fox
Queretaro 65B, 2 piso
Col. Roma
06700, Mexico D.F.
Tel: (52 5) 574 2869/7068
Fax: (52 5) 574 6150; 564 8111

United International Pictures
Ejercito Nacional 343, 2 piso
Col. Granada
11520, Mexico D.F.

Tel: (52 5) 255 2102/2203/5476
Fax: (52 5) 255 5657; 203 2881

VideoCine (incl. Warner)
America 173
Col. Parque San Andres
04040, Mexico D.F.
Tel: (52 5) 544 4405/549 3100
Fax: (52 5) 549 2911

VideoVisa
Av. Acoxpa 444
Col. Vergel del Sur
14340, Mexico D.F.
Tel: (52 5) 229 3100/3110
Fax: (52 5) 230 3332

**Camara Nacional de Cine
(CANACINE)**
Gen. Anaya 198
Col. San Diego Churubusco
04120, Mexico D.F.
Tel: (52 5) 688 0442/3258
Fax: (52 5) 688 8810

Cinemex
Montes Urales no 723
Col. Lomas de Chapultepec
México D.F. C.P. 11000
Tel: 540 6954/520 5184

Compañia Operadora de Teatros
Insurgentes Sur 453
C.P. 06170
Tel: (52 5) 264 0678/264 1358/
264 1340/264 5104
Fax: (52 5) 264 7701/164 5104

**Direccion General de
Actividades Cinematograficas,
UNAM**
San Ildefonso 43
Col. Centro
06020, Mexico D.F.
Tel: (52 5) 704 3700/702 4454
Fax: (52 5) 702 4503

Useful Addresses

**Asociacion de Productores y
Distribuidores de Peliculas
Mexicanas**
Av. Division del Norte 2462, 8 piso
03300, Mexico D.F.
Tel: (52 5) 688 7251/8705
Fax: (52 5) 688 7378

MOROCCO — Roy Armes

These are optimistic days for Moroccan cinema. The handful of locally produced films still has to confront 350 imported features each year, but the government is taking serious steps to raise output from two or three films a year to a planned eight (which would make Morocco the most prolific of all North African countries). Taxes on film exhibition have fallen sharply and although the number of cinemas has continued to fall there are firm plans to refurbish those still operating.

Local films, beginning with Abdelkadar Lagtaa's *A Love Affair in Casablanca* and Mohamed Tazi's *In Search of My Wife's Husband* in the early 1990s, have shown that they can rival the receipts from foreign films, and the system for state aid to production is being expanded. Above all, a new generation of feature directors is beginning to emerge from the ranks of those who have received funding for shorts over the past decade.

One of those to succeed has been 58-year-old Mohamed Lotfi, whose sole feature film, made in 1997, was **Rhesus, or Another Person's Blood** (*Rhésus, ou le sang de l'autre*), in which a young film-maker neglects his fiancée for an affair with a Canadian director, until an accident involving his mother brings him to his senses.

The search continues

Among the established directors who have profited from the new climate is Mohamed Abderrahman Tazi, whose latest film, **Lalla**

Hobby, is a sequel to *In Search...*, telling the further comic adventures of Haj Ben Moussa in Belgium, still looking for the husband of his (third) wife. After a gap of 16 years, Mohamed Abazzi has followed his first feature, *From the Other Side of the River*, with **The Treasures of the Atlas Mountains** (*Les trésors de l'Atlas*), a historical drama in which a spoilt elder son, who has been disinherited, unsuccessfully seeks to use the treasures of the Atlas to regain his lost power. But the treasures are not made up of gold, but of the laws which have traditionally ruled the people's activities.

Saâd Chraïbi, whose first feature, *Chronicle of a Normal Life*, appeared in 1991,

has followed this with **Women ... and Women** (*Femmes ... et femmes*), in which Zakia, a television presenter dismissed for her feminist views, and her three female friends have to rely on one another in a hostile world of male prejudice and violence. Amongst the younger Moroccan directors who, having made at least three shorts, are now obtaining funding for full-length projects, Nabil Ayouch (born in 1969), who studied in Paris, is the first to have completed a feature. In **Mektoub**, a young woman attending a conference in Tangier with her husband is kidnapped and raped, but rebuilds her relationship with her husband on a trip to the south of the country.

Recent Films

LES TRÉSORS DE L'ATLAS (TREASURES OF THE ATLAS MOUNTAINS)

Script and Dir: Mohamed Abazzi. Phot: Majid Rechiche. Players: Mohamed Bastaoui, Mohamed Khiyi, Mohamed Rzine, Abdelatif Khammouli, Benaissa Jirari, Hamid Basket, Fatima Herrindi, Saadia Ladib, Souad Nejjar. Prod: Thagmat Films.

MEKTOUB

Script and Dir: Nabil Ayouch. Phot: Vincent Mathias. Players: Rachid El Ouali, Faouzi Bensaïd, Amal Chabli, Mohamed Miftah, Malika Oufkir, Abdelkader Lotfi, Mohamed Zouhir. Prod: Shems Publicité – Playtime.

FEMMES ... ET FEMMES (Women ... and Women)

Script: Saâd Chraïbi & Jamal Belmejdoub. Dir: Chraïbi. Phot: Kamal Derkaoui. Players: Mouna Fettou, Fatema Khair, Touria Alaoui, Salima Benmoumen, Hamid Zoughi, Hamid Baskit, Abdellah Amrani, Ahmed Naji, Moulay Abdelaziz Tahiri, Moulay Tahar Al Asbahani. Prod: Cinautre.

RHÉSUS OU LE SANG DE L'AUTRE (Rhesus or Another Person's Blood)

Script: Mohamed Lotfi & Driss Chouika. Dir: Lotfi. Phot: Alain Levent. Players: Mohamed Mehdi, Cyrille Gaudin, Nadia El Jaouhari, Amal Chabli, Larbi Batma. Prod: Horizon Films.

LALLA HOBBY

Script: Noureddine Sail (from an idea by Tazi). Dir: Mohamed Abderrahman Tazi. Phot: Alain Marcoen. Players: Amidou, Amina Rachid, Naïma Lemercherqui, Ahmed Taib El Aly, Samia Akariou. Prod: ATA (Arts et Techniques Audiovisuels)/ Télévision Marocaine/Canal Plus Horizons/Cinétéléfilms (Ahmed Attia).

Useful Addresses

Centre Cinématographique Marocain
Quartier industriel, avenue Al-Majd, BP 421, Rabat
Tel: (212 7) 798 110
Fax: (212 7) 798 108

Chambre Marocaine des Distributeurs de Films
36 boulevard d'Anfa
Casablanca
Tel: (212 5) 272 081

Radio-Télévision Marocaine (RTM)
1 rue El Brihi
Rabat

NETHERLANDS — Pieter van Lierop

What could be a better boost for the national cinema of a small country than winning the Oscar for Best Foreign Language Film? This is exactly what director Mike van Diem pulled off with his debut film, **Character**, two years after Marleen Gorris won with *Antonia's Line*, and 12 years after Fons Rademakers' success with *The Assault*. The Oscar triumph for van Diem's powerful exploration of a tempestuous father-son relationship was euphorically greeted in the Dutch media, yet the 170,000 tickets sold for *Character* (including a post-Oscar re-issue) pale somewhat when compared to the million-plus sold for *Bean*.

For Laurens Geels, producer of *Character*, this disappointing box-office performance signalled his final frustration with the restrictions and complexity of the Netherlands' film situation. He announced that **The Red Swan**, the children's film which was nearing completion when this article went to press, would be his last movie within the Dutch system. This does not bode well, especially as Geels was closely involved in consultations with the Ministries of Economic Affairs, Finance and Culture, which had produced initiatives designed to make Dutch films more attractive to potential investors.

Alongside these incentives, the establishment of an intermediary body (FINE BV), which commenced operations in the summer of 1997 with government start-up capital of $7.5m (15m guilders), was of particular significance. This seed funding was designed as a magnet to attract sufficient private finance to enable an additional 50 films to be made within five years

The prospect of so much extra cash, in addition to the $8.7m to be provided by the Dutch Film Fund each year until 2000, brought an enthusiastic response within the industry. Only a few voices recommended a structured increase to the Fund budget as an alternative to a firm of intermediaries subject to the laws of the marketplace. However, if the enthusiasm of private investors is to be maintained, they will have to see a Dutch film occasionally make a profit; a phenomenon all too seldom encountered in the past.

Failing the screens test

The Netherlands has a population of approximately 17 million, and cinema admissions totalled 19 million in 1997, up 13 per cent on 1996. During the first months of 1998, 'the *Titanic* effect' also

Director Mike van Diem with his Oscar for CHARACTER
photo: Rob Keeris

resulted in a 25 per cent increase in box-office takings. Cinema owners are delighted, but it is salutary to note that 1997's list of the 20 most popular films (which bring in 60 per cent of total box-office) contained not a single Dutch production.

Growth is stagnating because, according to all distributors, there are too few screens. Plans have been in the pipeline for years for multiplexes in cities such as Amsterdam and Utrecht, but these inevitably become entangled in the red tape of local government. Furthermore, the most significant characteristic of programming in existing multiplexes is the provision of still more screens for the most popular films. As a result, the subsidised art-house cinemas, the *filmhuizen*, increasingly screen films from commercial distributors. The screening options for Dutch art films and 'difficult' movies from subsidised distributors are steadily dwindling.

In short, the pride of Dutch film-making has to be cherished primarily at festivals. Fortunately, such exposure is widespread. In Berlin, the Golden Bear for the best short film was won by Gerrit van Dijk with his autobiographical animated film, **I Move, So I Am**. The directorial debut of actor Jeroen Krabbe, **Left Luggage**, screened in competition at Berlin. The film deals with Jewish trauma and the exceptional bond between a nanny and a troubled five-year-old from a Hassidic family. Laura Fraser, Isabella Rossellini, Maximilian Schell and Krabbe himself take the lead roles in this English-language production, which was awarded two prizes and an honourable mention from the jury for Rossellini.

Down on the farms

The Rotterdam Festival witnessed a minor miracle when, from more than 600 titles, the Dutch production **The Polish Bride** (*De Poolse Bruid*) emerged as the most appreciated film in a questionnaire conducted among the 275,000 visitors. The film is a sober but profound drama about a Polish prostitute who, fleeing her Dutch pimps, finds sanctuary with a lonely farmer. Almost without words, a tender relationship develops between them. Algerian-born Algerijn Karim Traïda, a resident of the Netherlands, directed this as part of a quartet of low-budget productions funded by the Dutch VPRO broadcasting company and the Film Fund. Following its success in Rotterdam, *The Polish Bride* was invited to participate in the Critics Week at Cannes.

Even more praiseworthy was the recognition for **Little Tony** (*Kleine Teun*) in Un Certain Regard. This fourth feature film by Alex van Warmerdam is a bizarre

Still from THE POLISH BRIDE

Alex van Warmerdam in his own LITTLE TONY

drama set on the Dutch polders, in which a love triangle is fought out on a grotesquely designed farm during an idyllic spring. Once again, van Warmerdam proves that he is an inspired designer with a fascination for extreme contrasts. While the test of wills between the women (Annet Malherbe and Ariane Schluter) takes on mythic proportions, van Warmerdam (who plays the male lead) intersperses the action with absurd details and exceedingly dry dialogue, brimming with jet-black humour.

At the Mannheim Festival, Ben van Lieshout took first prize for **The Stowaway** (*De Verstekeling*), the touching story of an Uzbeki man who no longer sees a future in his birthplace beside the dried-up Aral Sea. He attempts to reach America as a stowaway, but gets no further than Rotterdam, where he finds solace with a sailor's wife whose marriage has become as barren as the Aral.

Public television organisations' increasing involvement in feature production offers a ray of hope. The 'Telefilmplan', developed to arrange special co-operation between the Film Fund and the television organisations in the creation of a 'movies of the week' system, is vital. There were more than 200 proposals submitted for the first series of six films. It is hoped that it will soon be possible to produce 12 'telefilms' per year, offering employment to the Netherlands' youngest film-makers, a few of whom have already demonstrated startling energy and originality.

These include debutante Miriam Kruishoop, who revealed her peculiar talent with **Vive Elle** during the Rotterdam Festival, and is already working on her next project. Ron Termaat, Ineke Houtman and Ger Poppelaars all have completed films awaiting premieres. There are high

Still from Ben van Lieshout's THE STOWAWAY

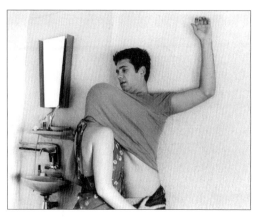

Still from SIBERIA

hopes for Robert Jan Westdijk, with **Siberia**, Eddy Terstal, with **Babylon**, and Lodewijk Crijns, with **Jesus was a Palestinian** – all three films set in the Amsterdam youth scene.

Quest for distribution

So many films are currently in production that they cannot all hope to achieve anything like a reasonable distribution. **Mrs Dalloway**, Marleen Gorris' first post-Oscar project, was only released in the Netherlands a year after its international premiere. Too few screens! George Sluizer has already made two films that will never be screened in the Netherlands. The same

applies to Rudolph van den Berg's **For My Baby**, a psycho-thriller filmed in Budapest, which was awarded the director's prize at the 1997 Netherlands Film Festival. The Golden Calf for best feature film went to *Character*. Jaap van Donselaar was named best actor for his part in the pseudo-documentary **Castro's Tears** (*De Tranen van Castro*). The best actress prize was awarded to the collective who appeared in **Brittle** (*Broos*), a drama about five sisters reflecting on their parents' impending golden wedding.

Disappointingly, Orlow Seunke's **Tropic of Emerald** (*Gordel van Smaragd*) won nothing. The film simultaneously offers a passionate love story and a historical chronicle of the Dutch Indies from 1939 to 1945. **Lagrimas Negras**, by Sonja Herman Dolz, which deals with elderly musicians in Cuba, and Heddy Honigmann's **The Underground Orchestra** (about street musicians in exile in Paris) were far and away the best documentaries of the past year, and were screened for 25 weeks on the normal cinema circuit.

PIETER VAN LIEROP has written about film since 1974 and is film editor of the Netherlands Press Association GPD (18 syndicated daily papers). He has been a correspondent for *IFG* since 1981.

Recent and Forthcoming Films

KLEINE TEUN (Little Tony)

Script, Music and Dir: Alex van Warmerdam. Phot: Marc Felperlaan. Players: van Warmerdam, Annet Malherbe, Arianne Schluter. Prod: Ton Schippers and Marc van Warmerdam for Graniet Film.

DE POOLSE BRUID
(The Polish Bride)

Script: Kees van der Hulst and Karim Traïdia. Dir: Traïdia. Phot: Jacques Laureys. Players: Monic Hendrickx, Jaap Spijkers, Rudi Falkenhagen, Roef Ragas. Prod: Jeroen Beker and Frans van

Gestel for Motel Films; Marc Bary and Ilana Netiv for IJswater Films.

BABYLON

Script and Dir: Eddy Terstall. Phot: Willem Nagtglas and Stefan Bijnen. Players: Rifka Lodeizen, Willem Ekkel, Daan Ekkel, Nick Leslie, Johanneke van Kooten, Arthur de Boer, Marc van Uchelen. Prod: Wim Louwrier for DKP Amsterdam.

BROOS (Brittle)

Script: Myke de Jong and Jolein

Laarman. Dir: de Jong. Phot: Joost van Starrenburg. Players: Maartje Nevejan, Marnie Blok, Adelheid Roosen, Leonoor Pauw, Lieneken le Roux. Prod: René Scholten for Studio Nieuwe Gronden.

FELICE.....FELICE....

Script and Dir: Peter Delpeut. Phot: Walter vanden Ende. Players: Johan Leysen, Toshie Ogura, Rina Yashima, Noriko Sasaki, Yoski Oida, Noriko Proett, Kumi Nakamura. Prod: Pieter van Huystee for Huystee Film & TV and Ariel Films.

FOR MY BABY

Script: Rudolf van den Berg and Michael O'Laughlin. Dir: van den Berg. Phot: Gabor Szabo. Players: Alan Cumming, Juliet Aubrey, Frank Finlay, Elisabeth Spriggs, Timothy Bateson, Hedi Temessy. Prod: van den Berg, Karel van Ossenbrüggen, Berry van Zwieten and Laszlo Helle for Hungrey Eye Features.

DE MAN MET DE HOND
(One Man and His Dog)

Script: Bennie Roeters. Dir: Anette Apon. Players: Ramsey Nasr, Monic Hendrickx, Viviane de Muynck, Truus te Selle, Titus Muizelaar, Janni Goslinga, Paul Kooij, Fred van der Hilst. Prod: Stienette Bosklopper for Circe Films.

DE VERSTEKELING
(The Stowaway)

Script: Ben van Lieshout and Bert Bisperink. Dir: van Lieshout. Phot: Stef Tijdink. Players: Bekzod Mukhamedkarimov, Arianne Schluter, Dirk Roothooft . Prod: Hans de Wolf and Hans de Weers for Egmond Film.

SIBERIA

Script: Robert Jan Westdijk and Jos Driessen. Dir: Westdijk. Players: Roeland Fernhout, Hugo Metsers III, Vlatca Simac, Nicole Eggert, Johnny Lion. Prod: Clea de Koning

JEZUS IS EEN PALESTIJN
(Jesus was a Palestinian)

Script: Lodewijk Crijns and Martin Lagestee. Dir: Crijns. Players: Hans Teeuwen, Kim van Kooten, Dijn Blom, Peer Mascini , Najib Amhali. Prod: Martin Lagestee for Lagestee Film.

HET VEERTIENDE KIPPETJE
(The Fourteenth Chick)

Script: Arnon Grunberg, Paul Ruven and Hany Abu-Assad. Dir: Abu-Assad. Players: Antonie

Kamerling, Thekla Reuten, Dirk Zeelenberg, Peter Paul Muller, Kaspar van Kooten, Michael Pas, Peer Mascini, Victor Löw. Prod: Marc Bary and Ilana Netiv for IJsater Films.

Producers

Added Films International
Lange Muiderweg 616
1398 PB Muiden
Tel: (31 29) 426 3277
Fax: (31 29) 426 4868

Argus Film Productions
PO Box 58188
1040 HD Amsterdam
Tel: (31 20) 693 1379
Fax: (31 20) 597 4412

Ariel Film Produkties
Prinsengracht 770
1017 LE Amsterdam
Tel: (31 20) 638 8199
Fax: (31 20) 638 0149

Belbo Film Productions BV
Sarphatikade 11
1071 WV Amsterdam
Tel: (31 20) 638 7999
Fax: (31 20) 638 8209

Cilia van Dijk
Ged. Voldersgracht 20
2011 WD Haarlem
Tel: (31 23) 531 4273
Fax: (31 23) 542 1097

CinéTé Film Prods.
Elisabeth Wolffstraat 45
1053 TR Amsterdam
Tel: (31 20) 685 5339
Fax: (31 20) 689 1954

Cine Ventura
Hudsonstraat 52
1057 SN Amsterdam
Tel: (31 20) 683 7439
Fax: (31 20) 616 0500

DNU Film BV
Rolf Orthel/Evelyn Voortman
Zoutkeetsgracht 116-1
1013 LC Amsterdam
Tel: (31 20) 622 0255
Fax: (31 20) 626 1885

Ecco Films
Orlow Seunke
PO Box 53223
1007 RE Amsterdam
Tel: (31 20) 623 9457
Fax: (31 20) 623 7900

Egmond
Keizersgracht 382
1018 GA Amsterdam
Tel: (31 20) 638 7886
Fax: (31 20) 427 2020

First Floor Features
PO Box 30086
1303 AB Almere
Tel: (31 36) 532 7003
Fax: (31 36) 532 7940

Graniet Film
Marc van Warmerdam/
Ton Schippers
Anjeliersstraat 470
1015 NL Amsterdam
Tel: (31 20) 421 2820
Fax: (31 20) 625 1024

Grote Broer Filmwerken
Clea de Koning/
Robert Jan Westdijk
PO Box 58141
1040 HC Amsterdam
Tel: (31 20) 616 1879/622 4705
Fax: (31 20) 616 1879

IJsater Films
Kromme Mijdrechtstraat 110–4
1079 LD Amsterdam
Tel: (31 20) 442 1760
Fax: (31 20) 442 1727

Lagestee Film BV
Martin Lagestee
Maarlemmer Houttuinen 307
Tel: (31 20) 627 3374
Fax: (31 20) 626 1049

Linden Film BV
Chopinstraat 25
1077 GM Amsterdam
Tel: (31 20) 679 3128
Fax: (31 20) 664 1046

Lowland Productions
Duivendrechtsekade 82
1096 AJ Amsterdam
Tel: (31 20) 668 0492
Fax: (31 20) 694 1018

Lucid Eye Productions
Oude Schans 69 A
1011 KW Amsterdam
Tel: (31 20) 623 0354
Fax: (31 20) 638 2968

MGS Film Amsterdam BV
Golden Egg Film
Singel 64
1015 AC Amsterdam
Tel: (31 20) 623 1593/662 9960
Fax: (31 20) 624 3181

Molenwick Film Productions
Tuinstraat 64-66
1015 PG Amsterdam
Tel: (31 20) 624 8805
Fax: (31 20) 638 6384
ext. 0005/6252296

Moskito Film
Oostelijke Handelskade 12
1019 BM Amsterdam
Tel: (31 20) 638 1924
Fax: (31 20) 638 1855

Movies Film Productions BV
Postbus 432
1200 AK Hilversum
Tel: (31 35) 261 500
Fax: (31 35) 248 418

Nico Crama Films
Nico Crama
Stevinstraat 261
2587 EJ The Hague
Tel: (31 70) 354 4964

Odusseia Films
Eddy Wijngaarde
Stadhouderskade 6
1054 E5 Amsterdam
Tel: (31 20) 607 1199
Fax: (31 20) 607 1198

Praxino Pictures BV
Onstein 190
1082 KN Amsterdam
Tel: (31 20) 646 6121
Fax: (31 20) 661 3411

Rolf Orthel Film Prods.
Zoutkeetsgracht 1161
1013 LC Amsterdam
Tel: (31 20) 622 0255
Fax: (31 20) 626 1885

Red Dog Productions
Valeriusstraat 111
1075 ER Amsterdam
Tel: (31 20) 662 5747
Fax: (31 20) 675 6901

Roeland Kerbosch Film Prods. BV
Keizersgracht 678
1017 ET Amsterdam
Tel: (31 20) 623 0390
Fax: (31 20) 627 9879

Shooting Star Filmcompany BV
Prinsengracht 546
1017 KK Amsterdam
Tel: (31 20) 624 7272
Fax: (31 20) 626 8533

Sigma Film Productions BV
Bolensteinseweg 3
3603 CP Maarssen
Tel: (31 34) 657 0430/0431
Fax: (31 34) 656 9764

Van der Staak Film Prods.
Jacob Oliepad 2
1013 DP Amsterdam
Tel: (31 20) 626 0634

Jos Stelling Film Prods. BV
Springweg 50-52
3511 VS Utrecht
Tel: (31 30) 313 789
Fax: (31 30) 310 968

Studio Nieuwe Gronden
Van Hallstraat 52
1051 HH Amsterdam
Tel: (31 20) 686 7837
Fax: (31 20) 682 4367
Telex: 12682 sngfp

Distributors

Cinemien
Entrepotdok 66
1018 AD Amsterdam
Tel: (31 20) 627 9501/623 8152/625 8357
Fax: (31 20) 6209857

Columbia TriStar Films (Holland) BV
PO Box 533
1000 AM Amsterdam
Tel: (31 20) 573 7655
Fax: (31 20) 573 7656

Concorde Film
Lange Voorhout 35
2514 EC The Hague
Tel: (31 70) 360 5810/392 4571
Fax: (31 70) 360 4925
Telex: 34568 cofil nl

Contact Film Cinematheek
PO Box 3100
6802 DC Arnhem
Tel: (31 85) 434 949
Fax: (31 85) 511 316

Express Film
Heemraadschapslaan 13
1181 TZ Amstelveen
Tel: (31 20) 641 2331

Filmtrust BV
Molenkade 57A
1115 AC Duivendrecht
Tel: (31 20) 695 7719/695 5503
Fax: (31 20) 695 6625

Holland Film Releasing BV
De Lairessestraat 111-115
1075 HH Amsterdam
Tel: (31 20) 575 1751
Fax: (31 20) 662 2085

Hungrey Eye Pictures BV
Duivendrechtsekade 82
1096 AJ Amsterdam
Tel: (31 20) 668 6126
Fax: (31 20) 668 3452

International Art Film
Vondelpark 3
1071 AA Amsterdam
Tel: (31 20) 589 1418/589 1426
Fax: (31 20) 683 3401

Melior Films BV
Steynlaan 8
1217 JS Hilversum
Tel: (31 35) 245 542
Fax: (31 35) 235 906

Polygram Filmed Entertainment
Postbus 432
1200 AK Hilversum
Tel: (31 35) 261 500
Fax: (31 35) 248 418

RVC Entertainment BV
and Argus Film BV
PO Box 142
1200 AC Hilversum
Tel: (31 35) 625 1200
Fax: (31 35) 624 7483

Shooting Star Film Distributors
Prinsengracht 546
1017 KK Amsterdam
Tel: (31 20) 624 7272
Fax: (31 20) 626 8533

Useful Addresses

Ministry of Education, Culture and Science
Department of Film
PO Box 3009
2280 ML Rijswijk
Tel: (31 70) 340 6148
Fax: (31 70) 340 5742

COBO Fund
Jeanine Hagen
Postbus 26444 (NOS TV)
1202 JJ Hilversum
Tel: (31 35) 775 348

Dutch Film and Television Academy
(Nederlandse Film en Televisie Academie)
Ite Boeremastraat 1
1054 PP Amsterdam
Tel: (31 20) 683 0206
Fax: (31 20) 612 6266

Maurits Binger Film Instituut
Nieuwezijds
Voorburgwal 4-10
1012 RZ Amsterdam
Tel: (31) 20 421 2048
Fax: (31) 20 638 3002

Dutch Film Fund
(Stichting Nederlands Fonds voor de Film)
Jan Luykenstraat 2
1071 CM Amsterdam
Tel: (31 20) 664 3368
Fax: (31 20) 675 0398

Holland Film
Jan Luykenstraat 2
1071 CM Amsterdam
Tel: (31 20) 664 4649
Fax: (31 20) 664 9171

MEDIA Desk/AV Platvorm
PO Box 256
1200 AG Hilversum
Tel: (31 35) 238 641
Fax: (31 35) 218 541

Netherlands Institute for Animation Film
Bachlaan 640
5011 BN Tilburg
Tel: (31 13) 562 925
Fax: (31 13) 562 428

Sources
(Stimulating Outstanding Resources for Creative European Screenwriting)
Jan Luykenstraat 92
1071 CT Amsterdam
Tel: (31 20) 672 0801
Fax: (31 20) 672 0399

Association of Dutch Film Theatres.
(Associated with the Netherlands Cinematographic Assn.)
Prinsengracht 770
1017 LE Amsterdam
Tel: (31 20) 626 7602
Fax: (31 20) 627 5923

Europe Cinema Nederland
PO Box 75242
1070 AE Amsterdam

GNS
(The Film-makers Society of the Netherlands)
PO Box 581
1000 AN Amsterdam
Tel: (31 20) 676 5088
Fax: (31 20) 676 5837

KNF
(Circle of Dutch Film Critics)
Snelliuslaan 78
1222 TG Hilversum
Tel: (31 35) 856 115

The Netherlands Cinematographic Foundation
(Nederlandse Federatie van Cinematografie)
Jan Luykenstraat 2
1071 CM Amsterdam
Tel: (31 20) 679 9261
Fax: (31 20) 675 0398

NBF
(The Association of Film and TV Directors)
Jan Luykenstraat 2
1071 CM Amsterdam
Tel: (31 20) 664 6588
Fax: (31 20) 664 3707

NEW ZEALAND — Peter Calder

It may well be that the best 'New Zealand movie' of the last few years was made in South Yorkshire, England, without a New Zealander in the cast or crew and went on to make a fortune for Fox. That, at least, is the contention of playwrights Anthony McCarten and Stephen Sinclair who (with the support of many of their compatriots) believe that *The Full Monty* was a systematic adaptation of their play, *Ladies Night*, the biggest theatrical success in this country's history, which – suitably rewritten – packed houses in the north of England and the West End of London as well.

The suit filed by McCarten and Sinclair was dismissed by a Los Angeles court in

June, and the writers will have to pursue their case in Britain, where the potential defendants are based. But if they were to win (and screenwriter Simon Beaufoy vigorously denies plagiarism) the makers of *The Full Monty* would have been adjudged guilty of stealing from the poor to give to the rich. For the New Zealand cinema industry – rich in world-beating technical talent – has always been hampered by a shortage of good scripts.

The New Zealand Film Commission is chronically underfunded, with an annual budget of less than $6m (NZ$12m), and the steady decline of the New Zealand dollar against major currencies has been eroding its spending power even further. The commission has in recent years attempted to address this imbalance by allocating its scant funds to script development and obliging producers to raise the bulk of their finance from other sources. A big slump in production followed (high interest rates offered foreign and local investors plenty of less risky propositions than feature film production) and the commission has finally moved to address the situation by recommitting itself to production finance.

The past year has also seen the launch of a new low-budget feature scheme, a partnership between the commission, New Zealand On Air (NZOA), which distributes government funds to local radio and television production, state broadcaster Television New Zealand and a British sales agent. The scheme, cutely entitled ScreenVisioNZ, initially proposed a budget of barely $500,000 per film, but that was boosted to $700,000 after sustained criticism from film-makers, who argued with some justice that they were being short-changed by a mean regime which effectively required them to subsidise production.

Long on ignorance, short on passion

Many of these criticisms were made under their breaths by film-makers reluctant to bite the only hand likely to feed them. But

Tim Balme and Rima Te Wiata in VIA SATELLITE

some of the leading hands were not so coy. Peter Jackson, director of *Heavenly Creatures* and *The Frighteners*, joined respected actor and film-maker Ian Mune and John O'Shea, a pioneering director who is now the industry's unofficial godfather, in a stinging attack on the commission as it celebrated its twenty-first birthday in 1998.

O'Shea said the commission lacked "passion or purpose", and Jackson characterised it as an organisation staffed by timid "career diplomats" whose policy-making was characterised by "wilful ignorance [and] flailing uncertainty". The only way the commission is likely to blunt such criticism is by making films and there is no doubt that the last year has seen production emerge from the doldrums.

The partnership between NZOA and the commission has deepened since Ruth Harley, who used to run the former, was appointed as chief executive of the latter in March 1997. Under her stewardship, the commission has encouraged quirky productions with a distinctive local identity, and has emphasised the need to make feelgood movies that can counter New Zealand's reputation as a producer of dark and deviant stories. The commission has earmarked $50,000 for assessment and development of these light or comic scripts – at least 30 are in the pipeline – and the slate for 1998 shows almost a dozen films in production or advanced stages of pre-production.

The commission took three films to Cannes – with mixed results. None of them had been screened here at press time, but word of mouth gave **Via Satellite** (the first of the ScreenVisioNZ projects and the feature debut as writer-director for Anthony McCarten of *Ladies Night* fame) the best prospects. The comedy, which screened in the buyers market at Cannes, is based on a successful stage play about skeletons rattling in the family closet of a New Zealand Olympic swimmer (played by Danielle Cormack) on the night she is to be joined – via live satellite feed – by her family on the other side of the world.

The response was reportedly less encouraging for the other two Cannes pictures. **Memory and Desire** is the debut for Niki Caro (whose short films have suggested an ostentatious and slightly derivative stylist) and was selected for Critics' Week – the first New Zealand film honoured in this way since *Desperate Remedies* in 1993 – but had rated no mention in dispatches by the end of proceedings. It is the story of two Japanese lovers who elope to New Zealand to escape the disapproval of the man's mother. The husband drowns during the honeymoon and tradition demands the wife return to Japan to live with her mother-in-law.

The third film at Cannes, **Saving Grace**, is the work of a poacher-turned-gamekeeper. Costa Botes, a former film critic for newspapers in Wellington, works with a script in which Duncan Sarkies has adapted his own highly-regarded play about the rocky relationship between a street kid and an unemployed carpenter who thinks he is Jesus.

Of the films well under way, perhaps the most notable is **When Love Comes**, the second feature from Garth Maxwell (*Jack Be Nimble*), since it provides the first starring role for Rena Owen since she played the battered wife in *Once Were Warriors*. And three other films which, at press time, did not have full finance or a confirmed start date are worthy of mention: Ian Mune (*Came A Hot Friday*; *The End of the Golden Weather*) hopes to start shooting *Bow Down, Shadrach* in the (southern) summer; the long-time producer/director team of

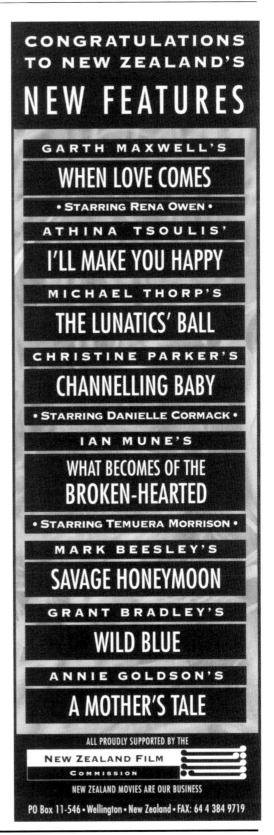

Simon Westerway and Rena Owen in Garth Maxwell's *WHEN LOVE COMES*

Still from Niki Caro's *MEMORY AND DESIRE*

Robyn Laing and Gaylene Preston were close to closing all the deals on *Ophelia*, adapted from Jean Betts' play. *What Becomes of the Broken-Hearted*, based on a novel which was the sequel to *Once Were Warriors*, has been delayed by wrangles over script rights, but will doubtless eventually go into production.

The big, the pregnant and the ugly

The biggest New Zealand-made movie released last year was not even a New Zealand film. Peter Jackson's ghostbusting spoof *The Frighteners* was a Universal picture and had Robert Zemeckis as executive producer. But its state of the art effects were another feather in the cap of Weta, the special effects and computer animation studio Jackson and partners operate out of an old factory in Wellington.

The films released locally in the last year met with mixed fortunes. **Topless Women Talk About Their Lives** was a spin-off from a late-night TV soap which screened in five-minute episodes. The work of the versatile Harry Sinclair, it was an infuriatingly aimless, yet infectiously energetic story of a group of twentysomethings dealing with the pregnancy of one of their number (Danielle Cormack). Distinguished mainly by the fact that Cormack was really pregnant during shooting, the film commanded a level of local support out of proportion to its merits. **The Ugly**, a dark and disturbing chamber piece about the fraught relationship between a serial killer and his psychiatrist was sold to more than 40

countries, although widespread theatrical success has proved elusive.

The local industry was saddened by two deaths. The last of the country's pioneer film-makers, Ted Coubray, who shot *Birth of New Zealand* in 1921, died, aged 97. And Murray Newey, the colourful producer of five features, from *Death Warmed Up* (1984) to *The Whole Of The Moon* (1995), took his own life in Auckland in April.

New Zealanders continued their enthusiastic cinemagoing. Admissions in 1997 topped 16.5 million on 285 screens – an increase of more than 10 per cent on the preceding year, and the latest stage in a steady renaissance since 1990 when six million tickets were sold for 140 screens. By general consensus, the boom has reached a plateau, but at 4.6 admissions per head per year, we lag behind only Singapore and Iceland among foreign markets.

PETER CALDER is a senior writer for the *New Zealand Herald*, for whom he has been a film critic since 1985.

Still from Michael Thorp's *THE LUNATICS' BALL*

Recent and Forthcoming Films

MEMORY AND DESIRE

Script and Dir: Niki Caro. Prod: Owen Hughes. Players: Yuri Kanagawa, Eugene Nomura.

VIA SATELLITE

Script: Anthony McCarten and Greg McGee. Dir: McCarten. Players: Danielle Cormack, Rima Te Wiata, Tim Balme, Jodie Dorday. Prod: Philippa Campbell.

SAVING GRACE

Script: Duncan Sarkies. Dir: Costa Botes. Players: Jim Moriarty, Kirsty Hamilton. Prod: Larry Parr.

WHEN LOVE COMES

Script: Garth Maxwell, Peter Wells, Rex Pilgrim. Dir: Maxwell. Players: Rena Owen, Dean O'Gorman, Simon Prast. Prod: Jonathan Dowling, Michele Fantl.

Love story about a faded singing star who flies back to New Zealand to revisit her roots.

I'LL MAKE YOU HAPPY

Script: Anne Tsoulis, Athina Tsoulis. Dir: Athina Tsoulis. Players: Jodie Rimmer, Jennifer Ward-Lealand, Michael Hurst, Lucy Lawless. Prod: Liz Stevens.

Comedy drama set among the prostitutes of urban Auckland.

THE LUNATICS' BALL

Script and Dir: Michael Thorp. Players: Russel Walder, Jane Irwin. Consultant Prod: Jamie Selkirk.

An obsessive psychologist fighting to help young patients, is confronted by a personal challenge.

CHANNELLING BABY

Script and Dir: Christine Parker.

Players: Danielle Cormack, Kevin Smith. Prod: Caterina De Nave.

Off-beat love story which follows a couple's relationship through three decades.

Producers

Communicado Ltd
PO Box 5779
Wellesley Street
Auckland
Tel: (64 9) 379 3734
Fax: (64 9) 377 7419

Essential Productions
Ltd PO Box 90 056
Auckland Mailing Centre
Auckland
Tel: (64 9) 378 9754
Fax: (64 9) 378 9734

Fiona Copland
PO Box 415
Albany
Auckland
Tel: (64 9) 413 8405
Fax: (64 9) 413 8403

Gibson Group
PO Box 6185
Te Aro
Wellington
Tel: (64 4) 384 7789
Fax: (64 4) 384 4727

Isambard Productions
PO Box 41066
St Lukes
Auckland
Tel: (64 9) 849 7772
Fax: (64 9) 849 7755

Larry Parr
Kahukura Productions
PO Box 31444
Lower Hutt
Wellington
Tel: (64 4) 619 0759
Fax: (64 4) 619 (64 9)44

Keir Film Productions Limited
PO Box 47-548
Ponsonby
Auckland
Tel: (64 9) 360 8233
Fax: (64 9) 360 8234

Kiwi Film Productions Limited
PO Box 9656
Auckland
Tel: (64 9) 630 9364
Fax: (64 9) 623 0336

Pacific Films
PO Box 6249
Wellington
Tel: (64 4) 382 9539
Fax: ((64 4)) 382 9916

Pinflicks Productions
PO Box 9438
Wellington
Tel: (64 4) 387 8741
Fax: (64 4) 387 8794

Plumb Productions
PO Box 2070
Wellington
Tel: (64 4) 385 1283
Fax: (64 4) 382 8787

Preston-Laing Productions
PO Box 9175
Wellington
Tel: (64 4) 384 6405
Fax: (64 4) 384 7406

South Pacific Pictures
PO Box 35656
Auckland
Tel: (64 9) 444 3000
Fax: (64 9) 443 5900

Top Shelf Productions
PO Box 9101
Wellington
Tel: (64 4) 382 8364
Fax: (64 4) 801 6920

James Wallace Productions Ltd
PO Box 5508
Wellesley Street
Auckland
Tel: (64 9) 302 5271
Fax: (64 9) 302 5272

Wingnut Films
PO Box 15208
Wellington
Tel: (64 4) 388 8388
Fax: (64 4) 388 9449

Distributors

Blue Angel Productions
PO Box 56 444
Dominion Road
Auckland
Tel: 360 6924
Fax: 360 6926

Buena Vista International (NZ)
[from 1/1/99]
PO Box 37524
Parnell
Auckland
Tel: (64 9) 302 7560
Fax: (64 9) 302 0201

Columbia Tristar Pictures
21 Falcon Street
Parnell
Auckland
Tel: (64 9) 366 9499
Fax: (64 9) 366 9488

Essential Films (Distribution)
PO Box 99 532
Newmarket
Auckland
Tel: (64 9) 523 1411
Fax: (64 9) 523 1811

Everard Films
PO Box 3664
Auckland
Tel:(64 9) 302 1193
Fax: (64 9) 302 1192

Footprint Films Ltd
PO Box 91(64 9)3
Auckland
Tel: (64 9) 360 0110
Fax: (64 9) 360 0320

Hoyts Entertainment (NZ)
PO Box 6923
Auckland
Tel: (64 9) 309 0955

REP Film Distributors (NZ) Ltd
PO Box 6789
Wellesley Street
Auckland
Tel: (64 9) 489 6896
Fax: (64 9) 360 2920

2 Brothers Films
PO Box 5653
Wellesley Street
Auckland
Tel: (64 9) 378 2123
Fax: (64 9) 378 1005

Useful Addresses

Screen Producers and Directors Association
PO Box 9567
Wellington
Tel: (64 4) 385 8055
Fax: (64 4) 385 8755

New Zealand Film Archive
PO Box 11449
Wellington
Tel: (64 4) 384 7647
Fax: (64 4) 382 9595

New Zealand Film Commission
PO Box 11546
Wellington
Tel: (64 4) 382 7680
Fax: (64 4) 384 9719

New Zealand On Air
PO Box 9744
Wellington
Tel: (64 4) 382 9524
Fax: (64 4) 382 9546

Film New Zealand
PO Box 24 142
Wellington
Tel: (64 4) 385 8055
Fax: (64 4) 385 8755

(*continued from page 207*)

Shibata Organisation Inc.
(France Eigasha)
2-10-8 Ginza
Chuo-ku
Tokyo
Tel: (81 3) 3545 3411
Fax: (81 3) 3545 3519

Tohokushinsha Film Co. Ltd.
4-17-7 Akasaka
Minato-ku
Tokyo 107
Tel: (81 3) 3582 0211
Fax: (81 3) 3589 4504

Toho-Towa Co. Ltd.
Playguide Building 3F
2-6-4 Ginza
Chuo-ku, Tokyo
Tel: (81 3) 3562 0109
Fax: (81 3) 3535 3656

Useful Address

Association for the Diffusion of Japanese Films Abroad
Nakamura Building 3F
Ginza 5-9-13, Tokyo
Tel: (81 3) 3572 5106
Fax: (81 3) 3572 8876

NORWAY

Trond Olav
Svendsen

In previous editions of *IFG* I have praised the arrival of new talent, as well as the more sensible system of government participation evident in the Norwegian film business in the 1990s. But is there an audience for the homegrown product? In 1997, the Norwegian share of the home market dropped to five per cent, and the top ten films were all English language, so the answer seemed to be 'Maybe not'.

The figures indicate that in this small country, with a population of 4.4 million, good films like *Junk Mail, Insomnia* (both reviewed in *IFG 1997*) and *Eggs* are likely only to do business in a handful of cities. An entire wave of Norwegian film-making may come and go with much of the country hardly noticing.

The low figures cannot be blamed on the cinemas. Thanks to the system of municipal management, Norwegian art films are as widely distributed as those with a broader appeal, and cinemas in the densely populated areas are optimistic. The Oslo region keeps expanding and now has more screens than ever. In December 1997, Oslo Municipal Cinema opened a new four-screen multiplex, and in Sandvika, a town just outside Oslo, a privately-owned multiplex with eight, mostly small screens replaced the municipal cinema. Good box-office returns in Sandvika will probably lead to the construction of more private cinemas – though all close to Oslo.

Cinema statistics do not go unnoticed by politicians – particularly those who believe that a film is only good when it appeals to everyone. There is, therefore, a danger that populist politicians may work against much of what is good in today's Norwegian cinema. This kind of cultural climate is tough on Norwegian producers and directors who know where the talent is, but at the same time feel obliged to search for a formula that will draw crowds in larger as well as smaller communities.

Crime wave

But what sort of formula will create good box office results in Norway in the last years of the century? Could the answer be a crime story told with a loose camera, and replete with jump-cuts, ellipses and high-powered performances by young, unfamiliar actors? No, but thanks for trying. It felt almost as though all of the Norwegian films of 1997-98 were crime dramas made in a fast, youth-oriented style, sometimes with references to the likes of Hitchcock and Kubrick. Most of them were also reminders of how easy it is in a small nation to make films which appeal neither to film buffs nor the general public.

The visually talented Trygve Allister Diesen made his debut with the Hitchcock-

Sofie Gråbøl in ISLE OF DARKNESS

inspired **Isle of Darkness** (*Mørkets Øy*), with bright Danish star Sofie Gråbøl in the female lead. A whodunit set on an island dominated by fundamentalist religion, it has some good scenes, but the plot is seriously underpopulated, making it fairly easy to spot the bad guy early on.

Scared to Death (*Livredd*), written and directed by Are Kalmars, tells the story of two brothers, one a talented writer, the other a drug smuggler: the former is pulled by the latter into the sordid Oslo underworld with tragic results. Kalmars' violent and efficient film could probably have reached a wide audience if it had not been made on such a miniscule budget.

That cannot be said of Erik Gustavson's **Weekend**, which had an aggressive gun-toting young woman speaking lines as literary as those of Tarantino's gangsters. Hopes were high, but the twists and U-turns of this narrative, going for exaggeration at every turn, would have been more exciting if they made sense.

Hopes were high also for TV veteran Carl Jørgen Kiønig with his theatrical debut, **Blessed Are Those Who Thirst** (*Salige er de som tørster*). It told a conventional police story adorned with a predictably unpredictable twist: the chief investigator is a lesbian. Based on a popular novel by Anne Holt, a mystery writer who once served as Minister of Culture, it failed to bring its boring police officers, whether homo- or heterosexual, to life, and the grainy images, jump-cuts and constantly moving camera did not help.

Intrigue, courage and cool jazz

Knut Erik Jensen, a veteran who makes films about northern Norway, gave us something in many ways more interesting in **Burned by Frost** (*Brent av frost*). His film is based on the true story of a Norwegian communist partisan from the Soviet campaign against the Germans in 1944. He keeps his Soviet contacts after the war, reporting on the U2 flights, and ends up with a long prison sentence for espionage. The film, although storywise a fragmented

Jørgen Langhelle in BLESSED ARE THOSE WHO THIRST   *photo: Helge Hansen*

puzzle that the patient observer has to put together, has some over-the-top images that linger in the mind afterwards, and did better than expected at the box office.

So did Sigve Endresen's documentary **Living Amongst Lions** (*Leve blant løver*), which dealt movingly with young people fighting cancer. Sometimes depressing, sometimes uplifting, it reconfirmed the talents of a stubborn, hard-working documentarist who always reaches a bigger audience than anyone expects.

Unni Straume's **Thrane's Method** (*Thranes metode*) was arguably the highlight of the season. Based on a story by renowned novelist Øystein Lønn, it takes place in Mr Thrane's flat, and deals with his futile attempt not to get involved with the beautiful woman next door. The film plays like cool jazz (the characters keep referring to Charlie Mingus, whose music adorns the soundtrack) and the dialogue, voice-over and camerawork give the film a well-judged theatricality. Straume creates a quiet atmosphere with telling long shots, but the beautiful Petronella Barker (as the neighbour) is often seen in sensual close-ups, her sudden, bright grin as broad as Gene Kelly's.

Sailor's blues

Finally, Bent Hamer followed the success of *Eggs* by making another personal, interesting and quite strange film. In **Water Easy Reach** (*En dag til i solen*), a young Norwegian sailor is stuck in a town in northern Spain. His watch is being

Ingrid Rubio and Erik Magnuson in WATER EASY REACH

repaired, but the local watchmaker is in no hurry to finish the job, and while he waits he meets an Australian seaman (Nicholas Hope) who has contacts in the underworld, and a lovely young woman (Ingrid Rubio).

Hamer has a curious habit of making anything but the 'important' events of the story carry weight; whenever the story is moved along this seems to happen in the background. One leaves the film a little bit undernourished: there is satisfaction on many levels, but nothing is emphasised, and at times it seems like Hamer is unsure

of what attracted him to the story in the first place. In a desperate mood, the Australian seaman douses the inside of a warehouse with gasoline, determined to create one hell of a bang, then cannot find his matches. That scene could stand for the whole Norwegian film season.

TROND OLAV SVENDSEN has a history degree from the University of Oslo. He works as a critic and film historian, and has published a *Theatre and Film Encyclopaedia*, as well as other books on film.

Recent and Forthcoming Films

LIVREDD (Scared to Death)

Script and Dir: Are Kalmar. Phot: Hallvar Bræin. Players: Åsmund Brede Eike, Bjarte Hjelmeland, Stig Henrik Hoff. Prod: Kappa Film A/S, Norwegian Broadcasting Corporation.

HALVVEIS TIL HAUGESUND (Halfway to Haugesund)

Script: Erling Dokk Holm, Harald Østgaard Lund. Dir: Østgaard Lund. Phot: Runar Hodne. Players: Geir Brink Nilsen, Yasmin Syed, Peter Garden. Prod: dBut Production A/S (Christian Fredrik Martin).

WEEKEND

Script: Arne Berggren, Erik Gustavson. Dir: Gustavson. Phot: Philip Øgaard. Players: Camilla Strøm Henriksen, Kim Kolstad, Thea Westby. Prod: A/S Film 21 (Olav Øen).

LEVE BLANT LØVER
(Living Amongst Lions)

Dir: Sigve Endresen. Phot: Hallgrim Ødegård. Prod: Motlys A/S (Sigve Endresen). Documentary.

THRANES METODE
(Thrane's Method)

Script and Dir: Unni Straume. Phot: Harald Paalgard. Players: Bjørn Sundquist, Petronella Barker. Prod: Speranza Film (Thomas Robsahm), Unni Straume Filmproduksjon A/S.

MED DØDEN TIL FØLGE
(Followed by Death)

Script: Leidulv Risan. Dir: Eva Isaksen. Phot: Erling Thurmann-Andersen. Players: Andrine Sæther, Sverre Anker Ousdal, Kelly Tainton. Prod: Yellow Cottage A/S (Aage Aaberge).

DESPERATE BEKJENTSKAPER
(Desperate Acquaintances)

Script: Svend Wam, Dag Anders Rougseth. Dir: Wam. Phot: Harald Paalgard. Players: Bjarte Hjelmeland, Anders Dale, Bjørnar Teigen. Prod: Mefistofilm A/S (Svend Wam).

STEREO

Script: Hans Petter Blad, Erik Poppe. Dir: Poppe. Phot: John Christian Rosenlund. Prod: BulBul Film A/S (Finn Gjerdrum).

MARERITTET HAR ET POSTNUMMER – HVA ER DITT?
(Every Nightmare Has a Zip Code – What's Yours?)

Script: Kjetil Indregaard. Dir: Karin Julsrud. Phot: Philip Øgaard. Players: Reidar Sørensen, Gaute Skjegstad, Trond Høvik, Stig Henrik Hoff. Prod: Norsk Film A/S (Tom Remlov).

ABSOLUTT BLÅMANDAG
(Absolute Lost Weekend)

Script: Axel Hellstenius. Dir: Petter Næss. Phot: Svein Krøvel.

Players: Ingar Helge Gimle, Brit Elisabeth Haagensli, Anette Hoff. Prod: Monolith Production AS (Christian Wildhagen).

1997: TØRST (1997: Thirst)

Script: Vigdis Hjort, Håvard Rem, Hans Petter Blad. Dir: Nathilde Overrein Rapp, Karoline Frogner, Maria Fuglevaag Wasinski. Phot: Svein Krøvel. Prod: Norsk Film A/S (Tom Remlov).

SOFIES VERDEN
(Sophie's World)

Script: Petter Skavlan. Dir: Erik Gustavson. Phot: Kjell Vassdal. Prod: Norwegian Broadcasting Corporation, Filmkameratene A/S.

BALLEN I ØYET
(The Ball in the Eye)

Script: Beate Grimsrud. Dir: Catrine Telle. Players: Laila Goody. Prod: Norsk Film A/S (Tom Remlov).

Producers

AS Film 21
Sollies gt. 2
N-0254 Oslo
Tel: (47) 2256 1650
Tel: (47) 2256 1210
Contact: Olav Øen

Barentsfilm A/S
PO Box 4383 Torshov
N-0402 Oslo
Tel: (47) 2202 3518
Tel: (47) 2202 3510
Contact: Jan Gammleng

BulBul Film A/S
Collets gt. 12 A
N-0169 Oslo
Tel: (47) 2246 9794
Tel: (47) 2246 9794
Contact: Bent Hamer

Caprino Filmcenter A/S
Mario Caprinos vei 3
N-1335 Snarøya
Tel: (47) 6753 3195
Fax: (47) 6758 1470
Contact: Ivo Caprino

Filmhuset A/S
President Harbitz gt. 22 A
N-0259 Oslo
Tel: (47) 2256 2100
Tel: (47) 2255 1540
Contact: Egil Ødegård

Filmkameratene A/S
PO Box 6868 St. Olavs plass
N-0130 Oslo
Tel: (47) 2200 7800
Tel: (47) 2233 2797
Contact: John M. Jacobsen

Kappa Film A/S
Hafrsfjordsgt. 37A
N-0268 Oslo
Tel: (47) 2255 8212
Tel: (47) 2255 8212
Contact: Are Kalmar

Magdalena Film A/S
President Harbitz gt. 21
N-0259 Oslo
Tel: (47) 2256 2278
Tel: (47) 2256 2279
Contact: Bente Erichsen

Mefistofilm A/S
Gyldenløves gt. 41
N-0260 Oslo
Tel: (47) 2243 8260
Tel: (47) 2255 7777
Contact: Svend Wam

Merkurfilm A/S
Munkedamsvn. 61
N-0270 Oslo
Tel: (47) 2283 2270
Tel: (47) 2283 2271
Contact: Petter Vennerød

Motlys A/S
Islandsgt. 6
N-0658 Oslo
Tel: (47) 2268 6063
Tel: (47) 2268 2191
Contact: Sigve Endresen

MovieMakers A/S
PO Box 6858 St. Olavs plass
N-0130 Oslo
Tel: (47) 2236 0990
Tel: (47) 2236 4128
Contact: Dag Nordahl

Nordic Screen Productions AS
Wedel Jarlsbergs vei 36
N-1342 Jar
Tel: (47) 6752 5460
Fax: (47) 6712 3773
Contact: Petter J. Borgli

Norsk Film A/S
PO Box 4
N-1342 Jar
Tel: (47) 6752 5300
Fax: (47) 6712 5108
Contact: Tom Remlov

Northern Lights A/S
PO Box 104
N-1342 Jar
Tel: (47) 6752 5330
Fax: (47) 6752 5340
Contact: Axel Helgeland

National Broadcasting Corporation
Drama
N-0340 Oslo
Tel: (47) 2304 8921
Fax: (47) 2304 5350
Contact: Oddvar Bull Tuhus

Parabel Film A/S
Parkveien 71
N-0254 Oslo
Tel: (47) 2243 6300
Tel: (47) 2256 3650
Contact: Emil Stang Lund

Regional Film A/S
Langesgt. 11
N-0165 Oslo
Tel: (47) 2220 6068
Tel: (47) 2236 0552
Contact: Trond G. Lockertsen

Speranza Film A/S
PO Box 619 Sentrum
N-0106 Oslo
Tel: (47) 2282 2470
Tel: (47) 2282 2471
Contact: Thomas Robsahm

Studio Regin A/S
Lofotgt. 2
N-0458 Oslo
Tel: (47) 2238 2223
Tel: (47) 2235 4699
Contact: Sverre Pedersen

Unni Straume Filmproduksjon A/S
Corso Anita Garibaldi 45
I-040 19 Terracina
Italy
Tel: (39) 773 7001 83
Contact: Unni Straume

ViPro A/S
PO Box 238
N-6101 Volda
Tel: (47) 7007 8194
Fax: (47) 7007 8819
Contact: Jørn Brente

Wildhagen Produksjon A/S
Kragsvei 9B
N-0391 Oslo
Tel: (47) 2214 8366
Tel: (47) 2214 8344
Contact: Christian Wildhagen

Yellow Cottage AS
Wedel Jarlsbergs vei 36
N-1342 Jar
Tel: (47) 6752 5345
Fax: (47) 6752 5349
Contact: Aage Aaberge

Distributors

Arthaus
Dronningens gt. 16
N-0152 Oslo
Tel: (47) 2247 4685
Tel: (47) 2247 4692
Contact: Svend B. Jensen

BV Film A/S
PO Box 17
N-4262 Avaldsnes
Tel: (47) 5284 2210
Fax: (47) 5284 3575
Contact: Bjørg Veland

Egmont Columbia Tristar Filmdistributors A/S
Kristian Augusts gt. 14
N-0164 Oslo
Tel: (47) 2298 9980
Tel: (47) 2298 9981
Contact: Bjørn Hoenvoll

Europafilm A/S
Stortingsgt. 30
N-0161 Oslo
Tel: (47) 2283 4290
Tel: (47) 2283 4151
Contact: Åge Hoffart,
Erik Sælen

AS Fidalgo
PO Box 2054 Posebyen
N-4602 Kristiansand
Tel: (47) 3802 4004
Fax: (47) 3802 2354
Contact: Arild Frøyseth

Kommunenes Filmcentral AS
PO Box 411 Sentrum
N-0103 Oslo
Tel: (47) 2236 9530
Tel: (47) 2242 1469
Contact: Knut Bohwim

Norsk FilmDistribusjon A/S
PO Box 1178 Sentrum
N-0107 Oslo
Tel: (47) 2282 7800
Tel: (47) 2282 7810
Contact: Frida Ohrvik

Scandinavian Entertainment Group
President Harbitz' gt. 22A
N-0259 Oslo
Tel: (47) 2256 2100
Tel: (47) 2255 1540
Contact: Egil Ødegård

SF Norge A/S
Box 6868 St. Olavs pl.
N-0130 Oslo
Tel: (47) 2200 7800
Tel: (47) 2200 7801
Contact: Rasmus Ramstad

Tour de Force AS
Georgernes V. 3
N-5011 Bergen
Tel: (47) 5532 2590
Fax: (47) 5532 3740
Contact: Tor Fosse

United International Pictures
PO Box 7134 Majorstua
N-0307 Oslo
Tel: (47) 2256 6115
Tel: (47) 2256 7181
Contact: Liv Jacobsen

Useful Addresses

The Audiovisual Production Fund
Dronningens gt. 16
N-0152 Oslo
Tel: (47) 2247 4650
Tel: (47) 2247 4691
Contact: Elin Erichsen

The National Association of Municipal Cinemas
Dronningens gt. 16
N-0152 Oslo
Tel: (47) 2247 4610
Tel: (47) 2247 4699
Contact: Lene Løken

National Centre for Screen Studies
PO Box 904 Sentrum
N-0104 Oslo
Tel: (47) 2282 2400
Tel: (47) 2282 2422
Contact: Toril Wien

The Norwegian Federation of Film Societies
Dronningens gt. 16
N-0152 Oslo
Tel: (47) 2247 4680
Tel: (47) 2247 4692
Contact: Jon Iversen

Norwegian Film and TV Producers' Association
Dronningens gt. 16
N-0152 Oslo
Tel: (47) 2247 4644
Tel: (47) 2247 4688
Contact: Tom G. Eilertsen

Norwegian Film Critics' Association
PO Box 352 Sentrum
N-0101 Oslo
Tel: (47) 2241 9409
Tel: (47) 2242 0356
Contact: Osman Kibar

Norwegian Film Distributors' Association
Øvre slottsgt. 12
N-0157 Oslo
Tel: (47) 2242 4844
Tel: (47) 2242 3093
Contact: Kristin Hoenvoll

Norwegian International Film Festival
PO Box 145
N-5501 Haugesund
Tel: (47) 5273 4430
Fax: (47) 5273 4420

The Norwegian Film Institute
PO Box 482 Sentrum
N-0105 Oslo
Tel: (47) 2247 4571
Tel: (47) 2247 4597
Contact: Jan Erik Holst

Norwegian Film Workers' Association
Dronningens gt. 16
N-0152 Oslo
Tel: (47) 2247 4640
Tel: (47) 2247 4689
Contact: Rolv Håan

PAKISTAN
Aijaz Gul

The first quarter of 1998 saw the sad demise of two film pioneers. Actress Asha Posley was never rated as a great artiste, but she was the leading lady in the very first Pakistani feature, *Memories* (*Teri Yaad*), in 1948. Retired from acting for a long time, she could still be seen in recent years driving her junky car through the crowded streets of downtown Lahore. Sadly, she died destitute.

The film industry also lost Agha Talish, one of the finest actors Pakistan has ever produced. Born in 1924, Talish began his film career in India in the mid-1940s. He came to fame a decade later playing a bum in *Money* (*Sat Lakh*) and his delivery and mannerisms were always perfect in a total of 270 Urdu and Punjabi films. Talish was particularly known for his roles in memorable films like *Martyr* (*Shaheed*), *Alien* (*Farangi*) and *Patriot* (*Zerqa*). He won numerous awards, including Pride of Performance, which is in the gift of the nation's president.

Producers Rashid Khawaja and Nadeem Mandviwalla joined forces on the most talked-about film of 1998, **Good and Bad** (*Very Good Duniya, Very Bad Log*). Shot in Mauritius, and starring Resham, Shan, Neeli and newcomer Fakhare Alam, it featured an extremely rich production design and lavish musical numbers – the melodies of Nisar Bazmi (the best film music composer of 1997–98) and Late Masroor Anwar's lyrics brimmed with style. However, director Suleman made a big mess with an extremely thin script, based loosely on John Landis' *Trading Places*, and the attractive box-office dividend in the initial three weeks following the film's January release owed much to a massive promotional campaign.

Produced by Sohail Butt and directed by

Syed Noor, **Bodyguard** (*Mohafiz*) was a smooth blend of two Kevin Costner films, *The Bodyguard* and *A Perfect World*. Made in Hong Kong, this was a powerful drama involving a tense tussle between a hired killer and a pious bodyguard, slightly marred by Noor's "all in the family" approach – he involved his wife and daughter in the film and gave himself a Hitchcock-like appearance.

Anything Hollywood can do...

Following the success of *Toy* (*Khilona*) and now **Motive** (*Ehsaas*), actress-director Sangeeta has become an important force in Pakistani film-making. She has been accused of being constantly fixated on Hollywood's brutal sex dramas (*Fatal Attraction*, *Basic Instinct* etc.), and her heroines have regularly been caught up in nightmarish scenarios that lead to their deaths.

However, at least Sangeeta has the courage to make films on female themes, unlike her counterpart Shamim Ara, who finds refuge in the escapist songs and dances of appalling movies like **Agree/Disagree** (*Kabhi Han Khabi Na*). *Motive* and Syed Noor's **Precious** (*Zever*) were two good films showing the greed and lust of women leading to vengeance. Unfortunately, these well-crafted titles were thrown into the theatres without publicity and sank without trace. In the National Film Development Corporation's awards, bestowed in April 1998, the most honoured titles of 1997 were **Love Crazy** (*Deewaney Terey Pyar Key*) and **Union** (*Sangam*), both directed by Syed Noor, which between them picked up 12 of the 19 major awards.

Love Crazy, filmed in Mauritius with newcomers Jia and Moammar, was the top-grossing film of the year. It certainly had plenty going for it: good music, impressive technical effects, a fresh leading pair, handsome production effects and the time-honoured poor boy-rich girl romance which must overcome many obstacles before finally prospering. Noor – the year's most prolific director, with 12 features –

Yasmin Ismail and Sohail in LOVE CRAZY

also claimed the number three spot on the year's box-office chart with *Union*, in which a gravely ill hero in a glass room becomes involved in a love affair with a TV singer. The film ends, unsurprisingly, with the hero's death. An impressive score and good acting from Shan and Resham were its saving graces.

Aiming low

Filled with sexy musical numbers, revealing outfits and tasteless settings, **Lost and Found** (*Khuda Janey*), **Pious** (*Sharafat*) and **Mafia** were all calculating, lowbrow efforts which enjoyed short-term box-office glory but no critical acclaim. *Pious* even featured the heroine Saima's well-endowed body inter-cut with shots of ripe mangoes. Director Altaf Hussain's cinematic vision is, to say the least, limited.

Usman Pirzada fared poorly at the box-office with **Debt** (*Qarz*), his low-budget, poor man's *Indecent Proposal*, though it was nominated for eight National Film Awards. The heroine agrees to become mistress to Javaid Sheikh in order to pay for medical treatment for her boyfriend (Babar). The film bombed partly due to a lack of promotion. Director Hassan Askari's well-made **Heartless** (*Dil Kisi Ka Dost Nahi*) did modest business but won award nominations in acting and music. This overlong film (180 minutes!) deals with the doomed relationship between a rich, debauched man and a dancer. Again, a shortage of pre-release advertising did not help the film's prospects.

Babar (*Debt*), Saud (*Heartless*), and Moammar (*Love Crazy*) were the bankable heroes of 1998. Resham and Reema were the leading ladies now obliged to strip off to entice audiences. As well as Noor, Masood Butt and Javaid Sheikh also had prolific years as directors. In all, 66 features bowed in 1997 (36 in Urdu, 20 Pushto, nine Punjabi and one Sindhi).

Successful Hollywood imports included *Daylight*, *Twister*, *Con Air* and *Face/Off*. Shazia Manzoor won a competitive race to be the year's most popular playback singer. Ailing 'Melody Queen' Noorjehan, who began her acting-singing career in the 1930s, received a special President Award, as did Dilip Kumar, the superstar for the last 50 years in India.

AIJAZ GUL earned his MA in Cinema from the University of Southern California, Los Angeles. He has written three books and numerous articles on film. He is presently working for Egypt's National Film Development Corporation and resides in Islamabad.

Recent and Forthcoming Films

DEEWANEY TEREY PYAR KEY (Love Crazy)

Dir: Syed Noor. Players: Jia Ali, Moammar Rana, Nadeem.

Poor boy–rich girl romance filmed in Mauritius with high-class production values.

MOHAFIZ (Bodyguard)

Dir: Syed Noor. Players: Nadee, Shahid, Saima.

The dramatic tussle between a hired hiller and a pious custodian over a rich girl. Filmed in Hong Kong.

DUPATTA JAL RAHA HAI (Burning Scarf)

Dir: Syed Noor. Players: Nadeem, Resham.

The tragic account of a bride who suffers because she brings a small dowry.

EHSAAS (Motive)

Dir: Sangeeta. Players: Mira, Shan, Javaid Sheikh, Laila.

The heroine seduces the man who betrayed her and then kills herself.

NIKAH (Wedding)

Dir: Sangeeta. Players: Reema, Shan.

Producers/ Distributors

Evernew Pictures (Producer-Distributor-Studio)
2-Abbot Road
Lahore
Tel: (92 42) 631 6959/631 7063

Eveready Pictures (Producer-Distributor)
Eveready Chambers
PO Box No. 139
I.I. Chundrigar Road
Karachi
Tel: (92 21) 263 4817–8
Fax: (92 21) 262 7843

Mandviwalla Entertainment (Producer-Distributor-Importer)
Nishat Cinema Building
M.A. Jinnah Road
Karachi
Tel: (92 21) 721 9505

Shera Films (Producer-Distributor)
Abbot Road
Lahore
Tel: (92 42) 636 2486

Useful Addresses

Ministry of Culture, Sports, Tourism & Youth Affairs
Block-D, Pak Secretariat
Islamabad
Tel: (92 51) 921 3121
Fax: (92 51) 922 1863

National Film Development Corporation Limited
NAFDEC Complex
56-F Jinnah Avenue
PO Box No. 1204
Islamabad
Tel: (92 51) 920 3853
Fax: (92 51) 922 1863

Pakistan Film Producers Association
Regal Cinema Building
Shahrah-e-Quaid-e-Azam
Lahore
Tel: (92 42) 732 2904
Fax: (92 42) 724 1264

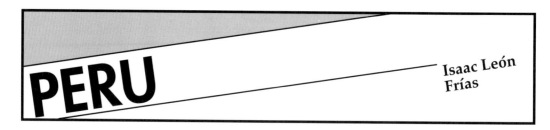

Isaac León Frías

In 1997, for the first time since 1979, there were no Peruvian feature film releases. None of the three feature projects awarded finance by the Consejo Nacional de Cinematografia (CONACINE) in 1996 could be made in 1997. However, the prospects turned out to be much better for the three scripts awarded prizes in CONACINE's 1997 contest. The successful scripts, awarded between $140,000 and $250,000 each, were Augusto Tamayo's **The Elusive Good** (*El bien esquivo*), Marianne Eyde's **The Bait** (*La carnada*) and Marite Ugaz and Mariana Rondón's **At Half Past Midnight** (*A la medianoche y media*). Happily, Alberto Durant's **Courage** (*Coraje*), which was one of the films awarded finance in 1996, *The Bait* and *At Half Past Midnight* were completed in the first months of 1998 and were expected to be in cinemas by the end of the year.

Francisco J. Lombardi directed an adaptation of Jaime Baily's novel **Don't Tell Anyone** (*No se lo digas a nadie*). This Spanish-Peruvian co-production was filmed mainly in Lima, with some scenes shot in Miami. Finally, Federico García announced the termination of the television miniserial **El Amauta**, about the Peruvian ideologist José Carlos Mariátegui. A feature film will be made using some parts of the serial. All these developments give some encouragement for the continuation of local feature film production, despite myriad financial problems, both with Peru's internal market and external distribution.

Short cuts

In 1997, two short film contests took place in Lima, in accordance with one of the laws governing Peruvian film production. In the first contest, 12 short films were awarded prizes, the largest number permitted by law, and eight were successful in the second . As in the first contest in 1996, most of the competing shorts had been filmed before 1992, when law Number 19327, which guaranteed cinema exhibition for short films, was revoked.

Among the short films awarded prizes of approximately $14,000 each in 1997 were four directed by Peruvian students attending film schools in the US: Alvaro Velarde directed *98 Thompson* and *C.Lloyd – A Tale of Crime and Punishment* (*Un cuento de crimen y castigo*), Javier Fuentes made *Rooms*, and Lisset Barcellos *The Tramp* (*La trampa*). Amongst the impressive debut shorts made in Peru were Fabrizio Aguilar's *The Loose Rope* (*La cuerda floja*) and Ricardo Tenaud's *Teeth Music* (*Música para los dientes*).

In general terms, however, these awards are not reactivating short film production because a number of short film producers have debts to pay and because the prize money on offer is not attractive enough in itself when the prospects of exhibition are so slim. There are very few film-makers willing to produce short films if the exhibition channels are not assured in movie theatres and on television.

This is one of the issues that has not been resolved, although (CONACINE) wants to establish that one of the principles contained in exhibition law would ensure that every feature shown in theatres would be preceded by a short. That proposal would not guarantee that the short would be Peruvian – but it gives Peruvian film-makers hope.

ISAAC LEÓN FRÍAS is a film critic and Professor of Language and Film History at the University of Lima. From 1965 to 1985 he was director of *Hablemos de Cine* magazine and is now a member of the editorial council of *La gran ilusión* magazine and director of Filmoteca de Lima.

Recent and Forthcoming Films

A LA MEDIANOCHE Y MEDIA (At Half-Past Midnight)

Script and Dir: Marité Ugaz and Mariana Rondón. Phot: Micaela Cajahuaringa. Players: Salvador del Solar, María Fernanda Ferro, Constanza Morales. Prod: Imagen Latina (Peru)/Sudaca Films (Venezuela).

EL AMAUTA (The Amauta)

Script and Dir: Federico García. Phot: José Riera. Players: Carlos García, Elena Passapera. Juan Carlos García, Kolela Derteano, César Urueta. Prod: Cinematográfica Kuntur.

LA CARNADA (The Bait)

Script and Dir: Marianne Eyde. Phot: César Perez. Players: Mónica Sánchez, Orlando Felices, Miguel Medina, Ana Cecilia Natteri. Prod: Kusi Films.

CORAJE (Courage)

Script: Alberto Durant and Ana Caridad Sánchez. Dir: Durant. Phot: Mario García Joya. Players: Olenka Cepeda, María Teresa Zúñiga, Ana Ponce, Jorge Chiarella, Aristóteles Picho, Salvador del Solar. Prod: Agua Dulce Films, Pontificia Universidad Católica, Fernando Colomo P.C. (Spain).

NO SE LO DIGAS A NADIE (Don't Tell Anyone)

Script: Giovanna Pollarolo and Enrique Moncloa. Dir: Francisco J. Lombardi. Phot: Carlos Gusi. Players: Santiago Magill, Christian Meier, Hernán Romero, Carmen Elías, Lucía Jimenez, Giovanni Ciccia. Prod: Inca Films (Peru)/Lola Films (Spain).

Useful Addresses

Conacine
Museo de la Nación
Av. Javier Prado 2465, 8º Piso
Lima
Tel: (51 14) 377 607 / 769 892

Sociedad Peruana de Directores y Productores Cinematográficos (SOCINE)
Tel/Fax: (51 14) 791 722

Asociacion de Cineastas
Tel: (51 14) 470 041

Filmoteca de Lima
Paseo Colón 125
Lima
Tel: (51 14) 234 732/235 149
Fax: (51 14) 236 332

Producciones Inca Films
La Florida 180
San Isidro
Lima
Tel: (51 14) 221 427
Fax: (51 14) 406 390

PHILIPPINES
Agustin Sotto

The election in May of movie actor Joseph Estrada as the Philippines' thirteenth president confirms the stranglehold of cinema on national politics. Rebuffed by the bourgeoisie, Estrada campaigned on a populist platform and based his winning strategy on his charismatic appeal to the vast underclass which has, justifiably, felt neglected by past administrations. Estrada gained political leverage when, in the early 1960s, he played unflagging people's champions on screen, largely illiterate characters who fought oppressive and corrupt social institutions. He was elected first as mayor of a Manila suburb, then as senator, and later vice-president.

The election of other movie stars to government positions, from town councillor to senator, once again demonstrated the depth of this controversial cinematic hegemony. It is now standard practice for movie stars to enter politics, especially when their showbiz careers start to wane. Other political leaders have joined in by encouraging their children to enter the movies, or by having biopics made about their lives.

Movies may have a high profile in the political arena, but box-office returns for local films have dipped to disastrous levels. The major studios have cut back on production and drastically reduced the budgets for those projects still being made. Many reasons have been proffered for this poor performance, including tough competition from a revitalised television industry, the growth of cable, relatively high ticket prices, onerous taxation, capricious and arbitrary censorship policies and the Southeast Asian financial crisis.

Independents' days

Ironically, local movies have never been so widely screened – thanks largely to the pirates. In remote areas, thousands of *betahan*, or videohouses, have sprung up, showing one or two movies a day without payment of royalties. Even buses show movies to entertain passengers caught in mammoth traffic jams.

Despite the prospect of the studios collapsing, the Philippines still produced a whopping 204 features in 1997. Most of the new films came from the independents who have been refused playdates in the more prosperous years. The present situation thus echoes the 1960s and 1970s, when more than 1,000 independent producers filled the vacuum created by the collapse of the studios. The economic crunch did not seem to affect Hollywood, with two movies breaking the $2.5m (100m pesos) mark: *Tomorrow Never Dies*, and, of course, the Philippines all-time box-office champ, *Titanic*.

Marilou Diaz-Abaya's poignant **Milagros** predictably swept the URIAN (film critics awards), and she is showing winning form again in **Jose Rizal**, the most expensive Filipino film ever made. Conceived to celebrate the centenary of Philippine independence, the film illustrates scenes from the life of the national hero whose example inspired Gandhi. Rizal's two novels, written in the 1880s, politicised the populace and prompted the uprising against the colonial power – the first such revolution in Asia. Abaya's film features a hugely ambitious production design and outstanding performances, especially from Cesar Montano in the title role.

Another standout is Carlito Siguion-Reyna's **The Man in Celia's Life** (*Ang Lalaki sa Buhay ni Selya*), which proved to be a box-office sleeper. The film focuses on Selyad, who is grossly disappointed with her boyfriend's macho posturings. She shacks up with a homosexual who needs a heterosexual cover as protection from society's prejudice. This genial comedy deftly avoids stereotyping and conventional resolutions.

AGUSTIN SOTTO is an archivist, film-maker and film critic. He is presently editing *Philippine Cinema in the 1990s*.

Recent and Forthcoming Films

TATULOK (Triangle)

Script: Jose F. Lacaba. Dir: Tiloy Aquiluz. Players: Albert Martinez, Amanda Page, Elizabeth Oropesa.

SA PUSOD NG DAGAT (In the Navel of the Sea)

Script: Jun Lana. Dir: Marilou Diaz Abaya. Players: Jomari Yllana, Elizabeth Oropesa.

JOSE RIZAL

Script: Peter Ong Lim, Jun Lana, Ricardo Lee. Dir: Marilou Diaz Abaya. Players: Cesar Montano, Joel Torre, Jaime Fabregas, Gloria Diaz.

CURACHA (Cockroach)

Script: Ricardo Lee. Dir: Chito Roño. Players: Rosanna Roces, Mike Magai, Richard Bonnin.

Useful Addresses

Film Development Foundation of the Philippines
Production Design Bldg.
CCP Complex

Roxas Blvd
Manila

Film Division
Cultural Center of the Philippines
Roxas Blvd
Manila

Film Committee
National Commission for Culture and the Arts
Intramuros
Manila

Society of Film Archivists
C63A Gueventville II
Libertad
Mandaluyong

Mowelfund Film Institute
66 Rosario Drive
Quezon City

Film Academy of the Philippines
Sampaguita Compound
Gilmore
Quezon City

POLAND — Wanda Wertenstein

The box-office statistics for 1997 brought the Polish film industry the best news imaginable. For the first time ever, a Polish movie was the biggest hit of the year. Juliusz Machulski's **Killer** attracted 1.6 million admissions, almost 200,000 more than the top American import, *Space Jam*, and more than double the number for *Dogs*, previously the biggest Polish hit of the past decade.

Made for $450,000, *Killer* was a comedy thriller whose title character was a hitman played by Cesary Pazura, best described as Poland's answer to Bruce Willis, and now the country's biggest movie star. The film is likely to be remade for the US by Disney, with *Men in Black*'s Barry Sonnenfeld as director. Hollywood producers Dale Pollock and Polish-born Kai Schoenhals of Open Door Entertainment have optioned the next script from *Killer*'s scriptwriter, Piotr Weresniak, and also acquired re-make rights to Jerzy Stuhr's 1997 feature, *Love Stories*.

Total admissions at Poland's 620 cinemas in 1997 were 23.7 million, up five per cent on 1996. Ticket prices climbed to between $5 and $6 in the first half of 1998. Meanwhile the Ministry of Culture has been advocating the introduction of a film

bill that would levy a 10 per cent gross revenue tax on theatre owners and oblige distributors to obtain government permission to release foreign films in Poland.

In 1996, there were no Polish films at all in the box-office top ten, but last year *Killer* was joined by two more local productions. At number seven was **Sara**, directed by Maciej Slesicki, whose mother worked as production manager on a number of Andrzej Wajda's films. His ordinary but enjoyable film charted the troubled romance between the daughter of a gangster and her decent teenage boyfriend. One place behind in the chart came **Night Graffiti**, directed by Maciej Dutkiewicz. This was a thriller based on the real-life search for a policeman who murdered a boy in Krakow when Poland was under martial law. The case was never solved.

Happily, the country's economic problems have not unduly slowed down the rate of film production, and by the end of 1998 we should have seen about 35 new titles, with the usual range of style and content. Of the projects currently in production, the two most eagerly awaited are both adaptations of Polish literary masterpieces, directed by veterans of the national cinema. Andrzej Wajda announced plans to make a multi-million dollar version of the epic poem **Master Taddeus or Last Raid in Lithuania**, written by national icon Adam Mickiewicz in 1834.

Jerzy Hoffman filmed the last part of novelist Henryk Sienkiewicz's late nineteenth-century trilogy, *Mister Wolodyjowski*, in 1968, and filmed the second part, *The Deluge*, in 1974. Now he is preparing to direct the first instalment,

With Fire and Sword, which was first published in 1887. It will star Izabella Scorupco, who played Pierce Brosnan's love interest in *GoldenEye*.

WANDA WERTENSTEIN is a veteran film critic who also worked with Jerzy Bossak in Warsaw Documentary Films' Studio; made some documentaries herself; and has translated film books from English and Italian. She has published a book on Wajda and a study of his famous Film Unit "X".

Recent and Forthcoming Films

AMOK (Amuck)

Script: Natalia Koryncka, Robert Brutter. Dir: Koryncka. Phot: Zdzisław Najda. Players: Mirosław Baka, Rafał Maćkowiak, Ewa Gorzelak. Prod: Fokus Film, F.S. Perspektywa, APF, TVP S.A.

AVE, MARUSIA

Script: Tadeusz Chielewski. Dir: Jacek Bromski. Phot: Ryszard Lenczewski. Players: Ira Łaczina, Jan Wieczorkowski, Krzysztof Dzierba, Artur Krajewskio, Iowa Szczęsna, Ryszard Doliński, Ilja Zmiejew. Prod: SF OKO, TVP S.A. APF.

SIEDRONECZKO, BIEDRONECZKO (Ladybird, Ladybird)

Script: Andrzej Gołda. Dir: Bolesław Pawica. Phot: Jarosław Szoda. Players: Michał Litwiniec, Katarzyna Groniec. Prod: Filmcontract, APF.

BILLBOARD

Script: Janusz Głowacki. Dir: Łukasz Zadrzyński. Phot: Łukasz Kośmicki. Players: Rafal/ Maćkowiak, Jekatierina Gusiewa, Bogusław Linda, Piotr Steczkowski, Andrzej Seweryn, Justyna Steczkowska. Prod: Vilm Production, Polish Television S.A.

CHŁOPCY Z MIELCZARSKIEGO (Boys from Mielczarski's)

Script: Marek Miller. Dir: Waldemar Dziki. Phot: Jarosław Żamojda. Prod: Pleograf, TV Polsat, Vision, WFDIF, APF.

CIEMNA STRONA WENUS (Dark Side of Venus)

Script: Radosław Piwowarski. Dir: Władysław Pasikowski. Phot: Grzegorz Kuczeriszka. Players: Agnieszka Wagner, Jan Englert, Paweł Deląg, Anna Przybylska, Marcin Jędrzejewski, Małgorzata Siatka, Eugeniusz Priwieziencew, Michał Lesień. Prod: SF Perspektywa, APF.

CUDZE SZCZĘSCIE (Somebody Else's Luck)

Script: Mirosław Bork and Hans Werner Honert. Dir: Bork. Phot: Grzegorz Kędzierski. Players: Danuta Stenka, Maciej Robakiewicz, Paweł Krucz, Jan Machulski, Piotr Fronczewski. Prod: Heritage Films, Saxonia Media.

CZAS ZDRADY (Time of Treason)

Script: Wojciech Marczewski, Witold Zalewski, Maciej Strzembosz. Dir: Marczewski. Phot: Krzysztof Ptak. Players: Janusz Gajos, Jerzy Radziwiłowicz, Kryzysztof Wakuliński, Agnieszka

Krukówna, Mariusz Benoit. Prod: Maciej Strzembosz, Jan Dworak – Studio A, TVP S.A.

DARMOZJAD POLSKI (Polish Sponger)

Script and Dir: Łukasz Wylężałek. Phot: Bartek Prokopowicz. Players: Adam Hutyra, Anna Samusionek, Ewa Kula, Janusz Michałowski, Andrzej Iwiński. Prod: Polish Television S.A., OTV Poznań.

DEMONY WOJNY WEDŁUG GOI (Demons of War After Goya)

Script and Dir: Władysław Pasikowski. Phot: Paweł Edelman. Players: Bogusław Linda, Tadeusz Huk, Olaf Linde-Lubaszenko, Zbigniew Zamachowski, Artur Żmijewski, Mirosław Baka. Prod: Vision Film Production, TV Polsat S.A., Kom. Kin. APF.

FARBA (Paint)

Script and Dir: Michał Rosa. Phot: Mieczysław Anweiler. Players: Agnieszka Krukówna, Ewa Gorzelak, marcin Władyniak, Karolina Łukaszewicz. Prod: TVP S.A., Foundation for Film Art.

FOTOMATOR (Photoamateur)

Script: Arnold Mostowicz, Andrzej Bodek, Dariusz Jabłoński. Dir:

Jabłoński. Phot: Tomasz Michałowski. Prod: Apple Film Prod. Broadcast A.V., TVP S.A., Canal+, MDR, Arte, Eurimages, Open Society Institute, Polish-German Collaboration Foundation.

I LOVE YOU

Script and Dir: Marek Kotarski. Phot: Bogdan Stachurski. Players: Katarzyna Figura, Cezary Pazura. Prod: Pleograf, Vision, Canal+, APF.

JAK NARKOTYK (Like a Drug)

Script and Dir: Barbara Sass. Phot: Wiesław Zdort. Players: Magda Cielecka, Krzysztof Pieczyński, Bartek Opania. Prod: TVP S.A., APF, Akson Studio.

KRONIKI DOMOWE (Home Chronicles)

Script and Dir: Leszek Wosiewicz: Phot: Marek Edelman. Players: Aleksander Ignatowicz, Grażyna Szapolowska, Krzysztof Kolberger, Stanisława Celińska, Halina Łabonarska, Artur Barciś, Ewa Szykulsak. Prod: Akson Studio for TVP S.A., APF.

KOCHAJ I ROB CO CHCESZ (Love and Do What You Want)

Script: Michał Arabudzki. Dir: Robert Gliński. Phot: Marian Prokop. Players: Rafał Olbrychski, Monika Kwiatkowska, Jerzy Trela, Paweł Dylag, Henryk Dylag, Agata Buzek. Prod: Filmcontract Ltd., TVP S.A., APF.

MATKIN ŻONY, KOCHANKI (Mothers, Wives, Mistresses)

Script: Juliusz Machulski, Ryszard Zatorski. Dir: Machulski. Phot: Witold Adamek, Zdzisław Najda. Players: Anna Romantowska, Gabriela Kownacka, Elzbieta Zającówna, Małgorzata Potocka, Jan Englert, Leon Niemczyk. Prod: Film Studio ZEBRA for TVP S.A.

Still from YOUNG WOLVES ½

photo: Justyna Grzybek

MATURA (Final Exams)

Script: Waldemar Szarek, Jacek Janczarski: Dir: Szarek. Phot: Wlodzimierz Głodek. Players: Karolina Gruszka, Dorota Kamińska, Krzysztof Kowalewski. Prod: Maxfilm, TVP S.A.

MEIR EZOFOWICZ

Script and Dir: Zbigniew Kuźmiński. Phot: Tomasz Tarazin. Prod: Fenix Film, APF, TVP S.A.

MLODE WILKI (Young Wolves)

Script and Dir: Jarosław Żamojda. Phot: Andrzej Jaroszewicz. Players: Krzysztof Antkowiak, Anna Mucha, Zbigniew Suszyński, Paweł Dylag, Jarek Jakimowicz-Kriegi, Alex Murphy, Jan Nowicki. Prod: TVP S.A., APF, Canal, ZCF, ITI Cinema.

MUSISZ ZYC (You Must Live)

Script: Maria Moneta-Majewska, Bozena Toeplitz, Konrad Szołajski. Dir: Szołajski. Phot: Krzysztof Pakulski. Players: Piotr Fronczewski, Marzena Trybala, Jacek Klata, Dominika Ostałowska, Sława Kwaśniewska, Krzysztof Kowalewski, Adam Ferency. Prod: TVP S.A.

NA KONIEC SWIATA (To the End of the World)

Script: Joanna Zołkowska and Magdalena Łazarkiewicz. Dir: Lazarkiewicz. Phot: Tomasz Kobrowolski. Players: Janusz Józefowicz, Justyna Steczkowska. Prod: Akson Studio, TVP S.A., APF.

NIC (Nothing)

Script and Dir: Dorota Kędzierzawska. Phot: Artur Reinhart. Players: Anita Kuskowska-Borkowska, Janusz Panasewicz, Jola Zawadzka, Adam Popielewski. Prod: KidFilm, TVP S.A., Łódź Film Center, Kom.Kin. APF.

FEUER REITER/OGNISTY JEZDZIEC (Fiery Rider)

Script: Susanne Schnieder. Dir: Lina Grosse. Phot: Egon Wergin. Players: Rafał Olbrychski, Monika Kwiatkowska, Agata Buzek, Jerzy Trela, Jan Frycz. Prod: SF TOR/Warsaw/, PROVOBIS/Germany

OGNIEM I MIECZEM (By Fire and Sword)

Script: based on Henryk Siekiewicz's novel. Dir: Hoffman. Phot: Grzegorz Kedzierski.

Players: Michał Żebrowski, Krzysztof Kowalewski, Izabella Scorupco, Zbigniew Zamachowski, Wojciech Malajkat, Bogusław Linda, Andrzej Seweryn. Prod: "ZODIAK"/Jerzy Hoffman i Jerzy Michaluk/, TVP S.A. APF, ZP OKOCIM, Kredyt Bank S.A. Euroford-Krakow.

FPAN TADEUSZ CZYLI OSTANTNI ZAJAZD NA LITWIE (Mister Thaddeus or The Last Raid in Lithuania)

Script: Andrzej Wajda from Adam Mickiewicz's epic poem. Dir: Wajda. Phot: Pawel Edelman. Dialogues: Piotr Wereśniak. Players: Bogusław Linda, Marek Kondrat, Michal Zborowski, Grażyna Szapołowska, Daniel Olbrychski, Andrzej Sweryn. Prod: Heritage Films, Canal+ Entertainment, APF, Kom.Kin.

PROSTYTUTKS (Prostitutes)

Script and Dir: Eugeniusz Priwieziencew. Phot: Ryszard Lenczewski. Players: Zuzanna Paluch, Mariusz Saniternik, Katarzyna Figura, Agnieszka Fitkau-Perepeczko, Władysław Komar. Prod: SF TOR, Polsat TV S.A. WFDIF, APF.

PRZYSTAN (Harbour)

Script: Jakub Duszyński. Dir: Jan Hryniak. Phot: Arkadiusz Tomiak. Players: Maja Ostaszewska, Rafał Krolikowski. Prod: Karol Irzykowski Film Studio.

SPONA

Script: Wojciech Tomczyk. Dir: Waldemar Szarek. Phot: Włodek Głodek. Players: Anna Ciepielewska-Więckowska, Łukasz Lewandowski, Radosław Elis, Władysław Kowalski, Krzysztof Kowalewski. Prod: MTL, Maxfilm, APF, TVP S.A.

U PANA BOGA ZA PIECEM (As a Bug in a Rug)

Script: Jacek Bromski, Zofia

Miler. Dir: Bromski. Phot: Ryszard Lenczowski. Players: Jan Wieczorkowski, Ira Łacina. Prod: SF Oko, TVP S.A.

WIESER DAWIDEK (Weiser Davy)

Script: Wojciech Marczewski and Toni Grisoni, based on Paweł Huelle's book. Dir: Marczewski. Phot: Krzysztof Ptak. Prod: FS TOR/Warsaw, Magic Hour Films, Kopenhagen, Pro Vobis/Berlin, Vega/Zurich.

WROTA EUROPY (Europe's Gates)

Script: adapted by Andrzej Kularczyk from Melchior Wańkowicz's novel "Hospital in Cichinicze". Phot: Witold Sobociński. Players: Agnieszka Sitek, Agata Bazela, Kasia Żochowska, Magda Teresa Wójcik, Maja Ostaszenko, Magdalena Cielecka, Piotr Szwedes, Marcin Ostaszenko, Henryk Boukołowski and others. Prod: Filmcontract, TVP S.A., APF and German coproducer.

WIELKA WODA (Flood)

Dir: Piotr Łazarkiewicz. Phot: Adam Sikora. Prod: Program II TVP S.A.

ZABIC SEKALA (Kill Sekal)

Script: Jiri Krizan: Dir: Vladimir Michalek: Phot: Martin Strba. Players: Bogusław Linda, Olaf Lubaçzenko, Jiří Bartoska, Agnieszka Sitek, Vlasta Hramostova, Jiri Holy. Prod: BucFilm, Apple Film Production, APF, TVP S.A. Canal+ Poland, Proast Prod./Slovakia, CDP/France.

ZLOTO DEZERTEROW (Deserters' Gold)

Script and Dir: Janusz Majewski. Phot: Witold Adamek. Players: Marek Kondrat, Wiktor Zborowski, Robert Koltai, Anna Gornostaj, Krzysztof Kowalewski, Wojciech Pokora. Prod: Heritage

Films, Canal+, TVP S.A., FS "Perspektywa".

ZOZKO WIERSZALINA (Wierszalin's Bed)

Script and Dir: Andrzej Domalik. Phot: Jack Bławut. Players: Piotr Fronczewski, Hanna Mikuć, Ewa Telega, Agnieszka Kruk, Władysław Kowalski, Mariusz Bonaszewski. Prod: TVP S.A., Filmcontract Sp.ooo.

ZLOTE RUNO (The Golden Fleece)

Script: Andrzej Kondratiuk. Dir: Janusz Kondratiuk. Phot: Tomasz Michałowski. Players: Zbigniew Buczkowski, Zbigniew Mazurek, Stanisława Celinska, Eugeniusz Priwieziencew. Prod. TVP S.A., IGA Film Productions.

Producers

Film Studio Dom
Puławska 61
02595 Warsaw
Tel: (48 22) 455 065

Film Studio Kadr
Puławska 61
02595 Warsaw
Tel: (48 22) 454 923

Film Studio Oko
Puławska 61
02595 Warsaw
Tel: (48 22) 454 041, ext. 222

Film Studio Perspektywa
Puławski 61
02595 Warsaw
Tel: (48 22) 455 494

Film Studio Tor
Puławska 61
02595 Warsaw
Tel/Fax: (48 22) 455 303

Film Studio Zebra
Puławska 61
02595 Warsaw
Tel/Fax: (48 22) 455 484

Film Studio Zodiak
Puławska 61

02595 Warsaw
Tel: (48 22) 452 047

Karol Irzykowski Film Studio
Mazowiecka 11
02595 Warsaw
Tel: (48 22) 276 653, 276 656

Film Studio Kronika
Chełska 21
00724 Warsaw
Tel/Fax: (48 22) 416 221

S.F. Semafor
Pabianicka 34
93513 Łódź
Iel/Fax: (48 42) 814120

Studio Indeks
Targowa 61/63
90323 Łódź
Tel: (48 42) 205 126

Łódź Film Centre
Łąkowa 29
90554 Łódź
Tel: (48 42) 367 500
Fax: (48 42) 360 487

WFDiF (Wytwórnia Filmów Dokumentalnych i Fabularnych)
Chełmska 21
00724 Warsaw
Tel: (48 22) 411 211
Fax: (48 22) 415 891

Independent Producers

Apple Film Production Ltd
Pl. Konstytucji 3/10
00647 Warsaw
Tel/Fax: (48 22) 290 754

Ekran Bis
Łąkowa 29
90554 Łódź
Tel: (48 42) 372 577
Fax: (48 42) 362 046

Feniks Film
Chełmska 21
00724 Warsaw
Tel/Fax: (48 22) 413 821

Figaro
Chełmska 21
00724 Warsaw
Tel/Fax: (48 22) 635 6130

Focus Producers Ltd
Ryżowa 42
02495 Warsaw
Tel: (48 22) 662 7586
Fax: (48 22) 662 7083

Fokus Film Ltd
Okrąg 4/45
Łódź
Tel: (48 42) 297 003

Gambit Productions
Przemysłowa 7
02496 Warsaw
Tel/Fax: (48 2) 667 4596

Heritage Films
Marsałkowska 2/6
00581 Warsaw
Tel: (48 22) 625 2601
Fax: (48 22) 625 2693

Marek Nowowiejski Film Productions
Chełmska 21
00740 Warsaw
Tel/Fax: (48 22) 644 3400

MS Film
Chełmska 21
00724 Warsaw
Tel: (48 22) 405 056
Fax: (48 22) 405 935

N (Independent Studio "Niezalezni")
Lajkonika 5
04110 Łódź
Tel: (48 42) 861 394

Pleograf Ltd
pl. Mirowski 18
00138 Warsaw
Tel/Fax: (48 22) 208 342

MM Potocka Productions
Puzonistów 4
02876 Warsaw
Tel: (48 22) 643 9556
Fax: (48 22) 643 9553

Skorpion Film
Chełmska 21
00724 Warsaw
Tel/Fax: (48 22) 416 171

Distributors

Film Agency Silesia-Film
Kościuszki 88

40519 Katowice
Tel/Fax: (48 832) 512 284
and
al. Ujazdowskie 20/10
00478 Warsaw
Tel/Fax: (48 22) 628 4518

Gentrum Filmowe Graffiti Ltd
Sw. Gertrudy 5
31046 Krakow
Tel: (48 12) 211 628
Fax: (48 12) 211 402

Fundacja Sztuki Filmowej
Andersa 1
00174 Warsaw
Tel: (48 22) 311 636
Fax: (48 22) 635 2001

MAF – Mlodziezowa Akademia Filmowa
Marsałkowska 28
00639 Warsaw
Tel/Fax: (48 22) 628 9698

Black Cat
Magnoliowa 2
20208 Lublin
Tel/Fax: (48 81) 774 654

Iti Cinema
Marsałkowska 138
00004 Warsaw
Tel: (48 22) 826 9862
Fax: (48 22) 826 8552

Solopan Film Centrum
Krakówskie Przedmiescie 21/23
00071 Warsaw
Tel/Fax: (48 22) 635 0044

Syrena Entertainment Group
Marsałkowska 115
00102 Warsaw
Tel: (48 22) 273 503
Fax: (48 22) 275 648

Vision
Rydygiera 7
01793 Warsaw
Tel: (48 22) 390 753
Fax: (48 22) 391 367

Imp Poland
Hoża 66/68
00950 Warsaw
Tel/Fax: (48 22) 628 7691

Imperial Entertainment
Kolska 12

01045 Warsaw
Tel: (48 22) 472 052
Fax: (48 22) 430 585

Artvision
Jerolimskie 125/127
01017 Warsaw
Tel: (48 22) 628 9315
Fax: (48 22) 467 239

Useful Addresses

Committee for Cinema
Krakowskie Przedmiescie 21/23
00071 Warsaw
Tel: (48 22) 826 7489
Fax: (48 22) 276 233

Film Polski
Mazowiecka 6/8
00048 Warsaw
Tel: (48 22) 826 8455
Fax: (48 22) 826 2370

PORTUGAL
Martin
Dale

In Manoel de Oliveira's latest film, **Anxiety** (*Inquietude*, Official Selection, Cannes 1998), the call of a croupier rings out loud and clear: "Ladies and gentlemen, please place your bets." Oliveira brilliantly captures the demi-monde of Oporto in the early twentieth century, in a film which interweaves three tales exploring unrequited desire, supernatural gifts and the contradictory emotions of growing old. The roulette wheel formed by a circle of hand-carved horses also perhaps hints at the current climate of risk-taking in Portuguese cinema. Since the election of a new Socialist Government in 1995, the government has upped its commitment to the sector and has reaped considerable commercial and critical success.

In the 1997–98 season, five out of the annual slate of ten films appeared in Official Selection at Venice, Berlin or Cannes: *Bones, Dribbling Fate, Anxiety, The Mutants* and *Gold River*. During the same period, the country has enjoyed its biggest ever local box-office hit, *Temptation*, with 375,000 admissions, and moderate hits such as *Black Shoes*, with over 60,000 admissions. On the basis of these achievements, the government is pumping an extra 50 per cent of state funds into the sector, and has adopted a transversal strategy embodied in the Institute of Cinema, Audiovisual and Multimedia (ICAM).

Portuguese films have a reputation for being somewhat slow and soul-searching, but it is precisely these qualities which have brought a high level of critical praise in recent years. Films such as *Anxiety*, or Paulo Rocha's **Gold River** (*O Rio do Ouro*), have a mesmerising effect as they explore private universes revolving around subtle, often frustrated emotions, and mythic spaces endangered by the tide of modernity. *Gold River* is set in 1960, and pays homage to the "golden river", the Douro. The images of golden landscapes, accompanied by the haunting songs of the local womenfolk, build to a magic realist finale orchestrated by veteran actress Isabel Ruth.

Pedro Costa's **Bones** (*Ossos*) is another sumptuous visual journey, which explores Lisbon's underbelly without falling into the traps of social realism. Most of the cast in *Bones*, as in Teresa Vilaverde's **The Mutants** (*Os Mutantes*), are non-professional actors and both films succeed in capturing primeval worlds hidden within modern Europe. **Le Bassin de JW**, written and directed by and starring João Cesar Monteiro, offers an even more personal and idiosyncratic universe, and includes a memorable scene, perhaps a commentary on the recent debate in Portugal about the need for film-makers to court the public, in which the mercurial

Joaquim de Almeida in TEMPTATION

Monteiro ascends a stage and urinates on his audience.

Forbidden fruits

Very different portraits of Portugal are found in films such as **Temptation** (*Tentação*) and **Black Shoes** (*Sapatos Pretos*). *Temptation*, written and directed by Joaquim Leitão and based on a true story, is about a Catholic priest in a sleepy town in the north of Portugal who falls in love with a heroin addict and succumbs to the twin temptations of flesh and needle. The film features a strong and subtle performance by local star Joaquim de Almeida, and is given particular force by newcomer Cristina Camara. The story addresses important social issues such as drug-taking and attacks on gypsy communities, but its real power lies in the romance between the lead characters, and their struggle with inner demons. João Canijo's *Black Shoes* is another factually-based tale of forbidden love, but has a far darker and more violent tone.

Both films were handled by Portugal's leading producers, *Temptation* by Tino Navarro and *Black Shoes* by Paulo Branco. Navarro also produced the local hit *Adão e Eva* in 1996, which marked a new populist trend in Portuguese films, and he is now moving into English-language territory with Bruno d'Almeida's debut feature, *On the Run*, a light comedy, in the style of Martin Scorsese's *After Hours* (and penned

M|C
Ministério da Cultura

I C A M |PORTUGAL

INSTITUTE OF CINEMA
AUDIOVISUAL
AND MULTIMEDIA

RUA DE S. PEDRO
DE ALCÂNTARA, 45, 1º
1250 LISBOA
PORTUGAL

Promoting and supporting Portuguese Cinema, Audiovisual and Multimedia

by the same screenwriter, Joseph Minion). Branco continues to be one of Europe's main promoters of classic auteur films, but with works such as *Black Shoes* is also branching out into slightly more mainstream territory. One of the most surprising signs of this progression was the announcement in Cannes in 1998 that the next film by Manoel de Oliveira, *La Princesse de Clèves*, will feature local rock star Pedro Abrunhosa and will be co-financed by schlockmeisters Menahem Golan and Yoram Globus.

Other notable Portuguese films included **Elles** by Luis Galvão Teles, a major European co-production which was selected as Luxembourg's entry to the Oscars in 1998. Fernando Vendrell's

Dribbling Fate (*Fintar o Destino*) is a promising debut feature which follows a retired football player in Cape Verde as he travels to Lisbon to recapture his childhood dreams. **Inês de Portugal**, by José Carlos de Oliveira, is based on the incredible true story of the Portuguese King Pedro I, who after the unjust assassination of his wife, Inês de Castro, ordered that she be exhumed and her skeleton placed by his side on her throne.

MARTIN DALE has lived in Lisbon since 1994 and is currently working for the Institute of Cinema, Audiovisual and Multimedia (ICAM). He has written several books on the film industry, including *The Movie Game* (Cassell, 1997).

Recent and Forthcoming Films

INQUIETUDE (Anxiety)

Script and Dir: Manoel de Oliveira. Phot: Renato Berta. Players: Luís Miguel Cintra, Leonor Silveira, Diogo Dória. Prod: Madragoa Filmes (Portugal)/Gemini Films (France).

RIO DE OURO (Gold River)

Script: Paulo Rocha, Cláudia Tomaz. Dir: Rocha. Phot: Elso Roque. Players: Isabel Ruth, Lima Duarte, Joana Bárcia. Prod: Suma Filmes.

OSSOS (Bones)

Script and Dir: Pedro Costa. Phot: Emmanuel Machuel. Players: Vanda Duarte, Nuno Vaz, Maria Lipkina, Inês de Medeiros. Prod: Madragoa Filmes.

OS MUTANTES (The Mutants)

Script and Dir: Teresa Villaverde. Phot: Accio de Almeida. Players: Alexandre Pinto, Nelson Varela, Ana Moreira. Prod: Mutante Filmes.

LE BASSIN DE JW

Script and Dir: João Cesar

Monteiro. Phot: Mário Barroso. Players: Monteiro, Hugues Quester, Pierre Clementi. Prod: Fábrica de Imagens.

TENTAÇÃO (Temptation)

Script and Dir: Joaquim Leitão. Phot: Carlos Assis. Players: Joaquim de Almeida, Cristina Câmara, Diogo Infante. Prod: MGN Filmes.

SAPATOS PRETOS (Black Shoes)

Script and Dir: João Canijo. Phot: Mário Castanheira. Players: Ana Bustorff, Vitor Norte, João Reis. Prod: Madragoa Filmes.

EM FUGA (On The Run)

Script: Joseph Minion. Dir: Bruno de Almeida. Phot: Igor Sunara. Players: Michael Imperioli, John Ventimiglia. Prod: MGN Filmes.

ELLES

Script and Dir: Luis Galvão Teles. Phot: Alfredo Maya. Players: Carmen Maura, Miou-Miou, Joaquim de Almeida. Prod: Samsa Film

FINTAR O DESTINO (Dribbling Fate)

Script: Fernando Vendrell, Carla Baptista. Dir: Vendrell. Phot: Luís Correia. Players: Carlos Germano, Betina Lopes. Prod: David & Golias.

TRAFICO (Traffic)

Script and Dir: João Botelho. Phot: Olivier Gueneau. Players: Rita Blanco, Adriana Luz. Prod: Madragoa Filmes.

LONGE DA VISTA

Script: João Mario Grilo, Paulo Filipe Monteiro. Phot: Laurent Machuel. Dir: Grilo. Players: Canto e Castro, Henrique Viana. Prod: Madragoa Filmes.

GLORIA

Script: Manuela Viegas, Joaquim Sapinho. Dir: Sapinho. Phot: João Gil, Artur Costa. Players: Jean-Christophe Bouvet, Francisco Relvas. Prod: Rosa Filmes.

Producers

Akademya Lusoh-Galaktika
Largo Santo Antoninho, 1
1200 Lisbon
Tel: (351 1) 346 1290
Fax: (351 1) 342 2494

Animanostra
Av. Cinco Outubro, 10, 7º, sala 2
1000 Lisbon
Tel: (351 1) 315 7692
Fax: (351 1) 353 4194

Animatógrafo
Rua de Rosa, 252, 2º
1200 Lisbon
Tel: (351 1) 347 5372
Fax: (351 1) 347 3252

David & Golias
Rua da Madalena 91, 3ºD
1100 Lisboa
Tel: (351 1) 888 2028
Fax: (351 1) 888 2046

Fábrica de Imagens
Largo do Contador Mor, 3
1100 Lisbon
Tel: (351 1) 888 1102
Fax: (351 1) 886 0 23

Filmógrafo
Rua Duque de Loulé, 141 R/C
4000 Oporto
Tel: (351 2) 208 6780
Fax: (351 2) 208 6861

Madragoa Filmes
Av. D. Manuel 1, nº 3
2890 Alcochete
Lisbon
Tel: (351 1) 234 2185/2225/2233
Fax: (351 1) 234 2202

MGN Filmes
Rua de S. Bento, 644, 4º Esq.
1200 Lisbon
Tel: (351 1) 388 7497
Fax: (351 1) 388 7281

Mutante Filmes
Rua Imprensa Nacional, 48, 3'E
1250 Lisbon
Tel: (351 1) 395 2975
Fax: (351 1) 395 2975

Produções Off/Rosi Burguete
Rua da Barroca, 72-3'
1200 Lisbon

Tel: (351 1) 347 0378
Fax: (351 1) 347 0370

Rosa Filmes
Campo de Cebolas, 17, 2º, Esqº
1100 Lisbon
Tel: (351 1) 882 0160
Fax: (351 1) 882 0169

S.P. Filmes
Rúa Das Pracas, 60, 1º DTº
Lisbon
Tel: (351 1) 396 4222
Fax: (351 1) 397 1352

Distributors

Filmes Castelo Lopes
Rua de Sto Amaro à Estrêla, 17A
1200 Lisbon
Tel: (351 1) 392 9750
Fax: (351 1) 395 5924

Filmes Lusomundo
Av. Liberdade, 266
1250 Lisbon
Tel: (351 1) 318 7300
Fax: (351 1) 352 3568

Atalanta Filmes
Rua Tomás Ribeiro 8, 2º
1050 Lisbon
Tel: (351 1) 353 1585/9
Fax: (351 1) 353 1636

Useful Addresses

Cinemateca Portuguesa
Rua Barata Salgueiro, 39
1250 Lisbon
Tel: (351 1) 354 6279
Fax: (351 1) 352 3180

IPACA/ICAM – Instituto da Cinema, Audiovisual e Multimedia
Rua São Pedro de Alcântara, 45-1'
1250 Lisbon
Tel: (351 1) 323 0800
Fax: (351 1) 343 1952

Media Desk, Portugal
Rua S. Pedro de Alcântara, 45, 1º
1200 Lisbon
Tel: (351 1) 347 8644
Fax: (351 1) 347 8643

Radiotelevisao Comercial (RTC)
Av. Fontes Pereira de Melo, 17-19,
2º-3º
1050 Lisbon
Tel: (351 1) 352 8835
Fax: (351 1) 355 7076

Radiotelevisao Portuguesa (RTP)
Av. 5 de Outubro, 197
1094 Lisbon Codex
Tel: (351 1) 757 5070/793 1774
Fax: (351 1) 796 6227

Sociedade Independente de Comunicaçao (SIC)
Estrada da Outurela, 119
Linda-A-Velha
2795 Carnaxide
Tel: (351 1) 417 3138/71
Fax: (351 1) 417 3119/20

Televisão Independente (TVI)
Rua Mário Castelhano, 40
Queluz de Baixo
2745 Queluz
Tel: (351 1) 435 5181
Fax: (351 1) 435 8747

Tobis Portuguesa
Praça Bernardino Machado
1700 Lisbon
Tel: (351 1) 759 5425
Fax: (351 1) 758 9622

PUERTO RICO
José Artemio Torres

The fiscal year June 1997 to July 1998 has been a busy one for Puerto Rican film production, especially considering that no features emerged during the two previous years. Those years involved important preparation, however, because new means of financing became available. This has been the trend followed in Puerto Rico since the 1980s: two or three years without a new film and then two or three come along at once. The past year has been exceptional because it saw the premieres of seven movies, five filmed in English, two in Spanish and nearly all low-budget. Only one, **The Disappearance of García Lorca**, had a potentially strong international appeal, but, unfortunately, all flopped at the local box-office.

The Disappearance of García Lorca, a co-production with Spain, directed by Puerto Rican Marcos Zurinaga and distributed by Triump Films, a division of Columbia Pictures, was the first of the seven to be released. It explored the mysterious murder of the Spanish poet during the Civil War, and featured Hollywood Latino actors Andy García, Edward James Olmos, Esaí Morales and Italian legend Giancarlo Giannini.

Local themes were handled by Luis Molina Casanova's **Short Stories to Remember** (*Cuentos para recordar*), which dealt with the life and work of Puerto Rican writer Abelardo Díaz Alfaro, and **Heroes from Another Land** (*Héroes de otra patria*), by Iván Dariel Ortiz, which focused on Puerto Rican soldiers who fought in Vietnam. The third wholly Puerto Rican-financed feature, **The Face at the Window**, was produced, photographed and directed, in English, by Radamés Sánchez. A horror story set in old San Juan, it was shot on 35mm but went straight to video.

Low budgets, no stars

Video stores will almost certainly be the main destination for the year's three other features, which were made with a mixture of US and local finance. **Undercurrent**, **Paradise Lost** and **The Survivor** are all low-budget American efforts featuring second- and third-division names like Lorenzo Lamas. They all secured financing from the Puerto Rico Investor's Tax Credit Enhanced Film Fund and Banco Popular, Puerto Rico's largest bank, via a scheme that has been one of the biggest developments in the industry in recent years. It is paving the way for the steady production of films that, for the moment, fall within two categories: local fare in Spanish and US low-budget pictures in English. As yet, none of the films produced has had international distribution or made a profit.

Over the last couple of years, the industry has also benefited from location shooting for major Hollywood films like *Assassins* and, more recently, *Contact* and *Amistad*. As a result, the American Screen

Jorge Castillo in HEROES FROM ANOTHER LAND
photo: César Silva

Actors Guild and the International Alliance of Theatrical Stage Employees have established local offices.

The government, more interested in promotion and infrastructure than production investment, is helping to establish a studio complex next to the El Comandante racetrack. A joint venture between Dean Hamilton Productions and the owners of the racetrack, the studio should open for business as home to *D.R.E.A.M. Team*, a cross between *Charlie's Angels*, *Miami Vice* and *Mission: Impossible*. We now have financing, infrastructure, government support and union presence –

it seems that soon we will have a film industry that is active every year.

Exhibition, meanwhile, is booming. In 1997, total box-office receipts hit $40m and multiplexes have taken hold of the shopping malls. Inevitably, Hollywood fare dominates, but plenty of foreign films can be seen thanks to the two local film festivals and the efforts of a small group of committed independent distributors.

JOSÉ ARTEMIO TORRES is a film-maker and writer. He heads La Linterna Mágica, a film and video production and distribution company.

Producers

Cine del Caribe
Muñoz Rivera 894
San Juan
Puerto Rico 00927
Tel: (1 787) 764 1589
Fax: (1 787) 764 1204
e-mail:cineca@hotmail.com

Nova Films
PO Box 22808
San Juan, Puerto Rico 00931
Tel/Fax: (1 787) 727 6039

Guede Films
PO Box 194140
San Juan, Puerto Rico 00919-4140
Tel: (1 787) 783 5656
Fax: (1 787) 782 8600
e-mail: guedpost@icepr.com

Paradiso Films
PO Box 11894
San Juan, Puerto Rico 00922-1894
Tel (1 787) 782 0020
Fax: (1 787) 783 8394
e-mail: lux1@caribenet.com

Distributors

Premiere Films
PO Box 8598
San Juan, Puerto Rico 00910-8598
Tel (1 787) 724 0762
Fax: (1 787) 723 4562
e-mail: premiere@caribe.net

La Linterna Magica, Inc.
667 Ponce de Leon Ave.

Box 132
San Juan, Puerto Rico 00907
Tel: (1 787) 723 2362
Fax: (1 787) 723 6412
e-mail: llmagica@.tld.net

Tropical Visions Entertainment Group
954 Ponce de Leon Ave.
Suite 208
San Juan, Puerto Rico 00907
Tel: (1 787) 725 3565
Fax: (1 787) 724 4333
e-mail: tvegsjpr@prtc.net

Useful addresses

Corporación para el Desarrollo del Cine en Puerto Rico
(Government organisation. Director: Manuel A. Biascoechea)
Apartado Postal 2350
San Juan
Puerto Rico 00936-2350
Tel: (1 787) 754 7110
Fax: (1 787) 756 5806

Asociación de Productores
(President: Ana María García)
PO Box 190399
San Juan
Puerto Rico 00919-0399
Tel: (1 787) 764 1589
Fax: (1 787) 764 1204

Puerto Rico Investor's Tax Credit Enhanced Film Fund
(Administrator: Laura Vélez)
Banco Popular Center
Suite 1414

San Juan
Puerto Rico 00917
Tel: (1 787) 759 8080
Fax: (1 787) 753 7510

Banco Popular de Puerto Rico
Motion Pictures and Allied Services
(Manager: Ingrid Acevedo)
PO Box 362708
San Juan, Puerto Rico 00936-2708
Tel: (1 787) 765 9800 ext. 5556
Fax: (1 787) 756 3909
e-mail: ikaacevedo@pppr.com

Archivo de Imágenes en Movimiento (Film archive)
(Director: Nelly V. Cruz Rodríguez)
Archivo General de Puerto Rico
PO Box 4184
San Juan
Puerto Rico 00901
Tel: (1 787) 722 2113/0331
Fax: (1 787) 722 9097

San Juan Cinemafest
PO Box 9020079
San Juan
Puerto Rico 00902
Tel: (1 787) 721 6125
Fax. (1 787) 724 4187
Director: Gabriel Suau
October 1999

Puerto Rico International Film Festival
Calle Mayagüez 17
Suite B-1
San Juan, Puerto Rico 00918
Tel: (1 787) 763 4997
Fax: (1 787) 753 5367
Director: Juan Gerard González
November 1999

ROMANIA

Cristina
Corciovescu

Last year, while Romanian cinema historians celebrated the centenary of the first films shot in Bucharest, Romanian film-makers celebrated a new beginning. A government act dated October 24, 1997, created The National Film Office (Oficiul National al Cinematografiei), with the aim of reforming the film industry on free market principles. Above all, the NFO's goal is to find solutions to the financial and creative crisis sparked by the revolution of 1989.

The NFO Board's main tasks are: to provide, on a competitive basis, development grants for screenplays and project grants for production and distribution; to support cinema modernisation; to ensure that Romanian productions account for at least five per cent of all cinema screenings; to secure Romania's inclusion in European Community film programs.

The government appointed Radu Gabrea, one of the country's most important directors, as NFO Chairman. Gabrea was awarded the Jury Prize at the 1970 Locarno Film Festival for *Too Little for Such a Big War*, and his talent was confirmed later, during his exile in Germany, with *A Man Like Eva* (*Ein Man wie Ewa*, 1984). He has considerable standing within the industry and proven management skills.

Political murders and untimely death

While his films have frequently been set in a non-specific time period, Dan Pita's latest, **Man of the Day** (*Omul zilei*), saw him on unmistakably contemporary ground. Based on a screenplay by Radu F. Alexandru, the film explores the world of late 1990s politicians, revealing the shady deals and the secrets of deeply immoral lifestyles protected by the "respectability" of money.

A prominent politician is accused of murdering his mistress' lover, and the "crime" becomes caught up in political games. The hero must choose between letting himself be destroyed or sanctioning his mistress' murder to clear his name. Served by an exceptional cast, led by Pita's favourite actor, Stefan Iordache (the lead in five of his previous films), the director's straightforward narrative formula highlighted the new *and* inherited diseases of Romania's transitional society.

The Woman in Red (*Femeia in rosu*) was the sixteenth and, unfortunately, the last film from Mircea Veroiu, the director whose premature death was mourned by Romanian film-makers in December. Moritz de Hadeln referred to Veroiu as a "friend of the Berlin Film Festival" and dedicated its 48th edition to Veroiu, among all the other recently deceased film-makers.

Based on the novel by Mircea Nedelciu, *The Woman in Red* is the story of Ana, the Romanian who emigrated to the US between the wars and became a brothel owner. She became the mistress of gangster John Dillinger and turned him in to the police when threatened with blackmail. Sadly, the tiredness and disappointment of a film director who expected more from life than it gave him are perceptible through his last film even more than through his previous one, *At the Orient's Gates*. Early in 1998, the Union of Romanian Film-makers paid its last respects to Veroiu, awarding him a posthumous prize.

CRISTINA CORCIOVESCU is chief editor of *ProCinema* magazine and the author of several books on cinema.

Producers

Atlantis Film
Str. Gral Berthelot nr 52
Bucharest
Tel: (401) 312 4850
Fax: (401) 312 4025

Castel Film
Str. Lucaci nr 44
Bucharest
Tel: (401) 621 5065
Fax: (401) 322 3879

Cinerom
Bd Mihail Kogalniceanu nr 11
Bucharest
Tel: (401) 311 2710
Fax: (401) 311 3080

Domino film
Str. Dr. Felix nr.59, et 1
Bucharest
Tel: (401) 210 3713 / 223 4669
Fax: (401) 312 9609

Filmex
Str. Pictor Verona nr. 2
Bucharest
Tel: (401) 315 8913/315 9038
Fax: (401) 312 1388

Distributors

Guild Film Romania
Bd Republicii nr 51 et 1
Bucharest
Tel: (401) 314 8846
Fax: (401) 312 5095

Media Pictures International
Str. Armeneasca nr. 8
Bucharest
Tel: (401) 314 0156
Fax: (401) 312 4140

QCB
Str Piscului nr. 16
Bucharest
Tel/Fax: (401) 675 4401

Romania Film
Str Thomas Massaryk nr. 25
70231 Bucharest
Tel: (401) 210 7398/210 7835
Fax: (401) 611 7660

Transglobal Media
Calea Floreasca nr.167 bis
72321 Bucharest
Tel: (401) 230 7020
Fax: (401) 212 1779

Independenta film
Bd. Nicolae Balcescu nr 24
Bucharest
Tel/Fax: (401) 613 9522

Useful Addresses

**Oficiul National al
Cinematografiei**
Str. Dem I. Dobrescu, nr 4-6
Bucharest
Tel: (401) 310 4301
Fax: (401) 310 4300

Uniunea Cineastilor
Str. Mendeleev nr 28-30
70169 Bucharest
Tel: (401) 650 4265
Fax: (401) 311 1246

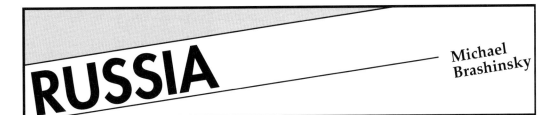

RUSSIA

Michael Brashinsky

After years of jobless bitterness, Russia's film-makers are beginning to regain their faith. The sense of revival in the film industry is palpable when you walk the lively corridors of Mosfilm and Lenfilm, the country's two biggest studios. In 1996, just one feature was shot at Lenfilm, based in St Petersburg, but in 1997 there were five, and 1998 will have marked a record of seven films. That is excellent for a Russian studio these days – but still only half as many as were originally scheduled for the year.

As the budgetary, political and, finally, coal-miners' crises shook the Russian parliament, the film-makers inevitably had to do without any state support. Yet 26 features were completed in the country during the first six months of 1998, and the expectations for the year are high: 60 to 70 films, compared to 53 in 1996.

But while production remains the strongest stage in the process connecting film-makers with their audience, distribution and exhibition are lagging a long way behind. On average, only three out of every 100 cinema seats are filled, while American product dominates the market, with about 80 per cent of the gross. Yet the success of Dolby-equipped cinemas (three in Moscow, one in St Petersburg) proves that, as Russia's middle-class grows, so does its movie audience. The average ticket price here stays at about 25 cents (though some people were paying an astonishing $30 to see *Titanic*), a rate which certainly cannot satisfy the industry, and makes the video market more important than cinema income.

While the rental field is undeveloped, retail prices are so cheap (videotapes sell for less than $5 at kiosks on almost every street corner in both capitals) that it is illegal to put a tape out for rent until the buying quotas, set by the producer, have been reached. Approximately one third of the population owns a VCR, but with about 25 feature films shown on the main television channels daily, video profits are low.

A tale of two cities

The Russian branch of Soviet cinema traditionally emerged from two schools of film-making, the "Moscow" and the "Leningrad", whose styles were as different as the cities themselves – the extrovert, "horizontal" Moscow is to the introvert, "vertical" St Petersburg what Los Angeles is to New York. St Petersburg, best known for the work of two contemporary directors, Alexei Gherman and Alexander Sokurov, produced sophisticated, highly stylised, often black-and-white art pictures, while Moscow made less personal, more popular, bigger films.

In the latest free-for-all production mini-boom, those differences have disappeared. No wonder: one works where one can and

Still from Maxim Pezhemsky's MOMMA, DON'T BE SAD

does what the producer tells one to do. Now it is common for a St Petersburg director to shoot a Moscow-financed picture at home. Young film-makers' movies such as Dmitry Meskhiev's **An American Bet** (*Amerikanka*) and Maxim Pezhemsky's **Momma, Don't Be Sad** (*Mama, ne goryui*) were made this way. This cannot help reflecting on the post-modern erasure of stylistic differences: the emerging style of film-making here is hip and clean to the point of sterility. It is comparable with that of many American independents, who are themselves nothing more than Hollywood wannabes.

One of the few young film-makers to retain an idiosyncratic "Leningrad" style (still shooting in black-and-white) is the self-appointed "necro-realist" and former avant-garde auteur Yevgeny Yufit, who showed **Silver Heads** (*Serebryannye golovy*) this season. It was, as usual from Yufit, about the "undead" – this time trying to interbreed men and trees in a secret experiment. Sardonically nonsensical in its "message", but no-nonsense in its starkly primitivist technique, this almost-silent movie played like George Méliès remade by George Romero.

Tales in two genres

Though the shoestring budget solution was thought to have been exhausted this year by many (average budgets are around $1m), the most interesting pictures emerged as a low-budget package from the Maxim Gorky Studio, led by Sergei Livnev. All imperfect in more ways than one, most were made by directors under 35 and offered fresh insights – if not into life, then into cinema.

Except for Natalya Pyankova's **Strange Time** (*Strannoye vremya*), a series of vignettes dealing with love, all of the Gorky features fell into two genre categories, both of which are cheap, quick and dirty. Alexander Khvan's **Good Asshole, Bad Asshole** (*Dryan' khoroshaya, dryan' plokhaya*), Valery Todorovsky's **Country of the Deaf** (*Strana glukhih*) and

Oleg Fomin's **Tax Collector** (*Mytar*) were all urban thrillers, drifting towards post-punk romanticism à la Leos Carax.

Pastiche pulp fictions, close to Hal Hartley or the Coen brothers, came courtesy of *Momma, Don't Be Sad,* **The Body Will Be Given to the Ground, And the Sailor Will Sing** (*Telo budet predano zemle, a starshyi michman budet pet'*), by Ilya Makarov, and **The Snake Spring** (*Zmeinyi istochnik*), by Nikolai Lebedev.

All of these cost around $200,000 – and it showed. Most did not make it across the national borders, which is a pity, because it is time for young Russian film-makers to measure themselves by an international yardstick. The only one to gain international exposure was Todorovsky Jnr.'s *Country of the Deaf,* a convoluted though stylish story of a deaf girl and a girl who 'learns' to be deaf to earn money. Despite a terrific performance by newcomer Dina Korzun, it went unnoticed in competition at Berlin.

Race for the Nikes

The general consensus this year was that four features would be in the running for the main Nikes – Russia's response to the Oscars, now in their eleventh year. The brilliant Kira Muratova's **Three Stories** (*Tri istorii*, reviewed in *IFG 1998*) fell out of the race early when the Academy failed to nominate it for anything. Then Alexei Balabanov's **The Brother** (*Brat*) – a thriller about a village boy who comes to the city to visit his big brother and becomes a mafia hitman – was surprisingly nominated only in the Best Picture and not in the Best Director category.

All eyes focused on the remaining two contenders: Vadim Abdrashitov's **Time of the Dancer** (*Vremya tantsora*) and Pavel Chukhrai's **The Thief** (*Vor*). After a decade of confusion, Abdrashitov, the country's leading social moralist, has emerged with a vibrant epic, reminiscent of John Woo's *Bullet in the Head.* It follows three friends, veterans of the Chechen war, who settle in

the occupied territories with unexpected and ultimately tragic results. No less confused and asymmetrical than his previous post-Soviet efforts, this one had a powerful, sensual energy – testimony to the artist's honesty and vitality.

It did not win, however. *The Thief* did. Russia's astonishing third successive Best Foreign Language Film Oscar nomination (following Nikita Mikhalkov's victory in 1995 with *Burnt by the Sun* and Sergei Bodrov's citation for *Prisoner of the Mountains*) it played well in the West and at home. Understandably so: it supplied melodrama where tragedy was in order. This post-war story of a beautiful single mother who falls victim to a charming burglar who masquerades as an army officer was bound to please those who like their history reduced to the level of a simple tear-jerker.

Long haul for the auteurs

Neither Nikita Mikhalkov, nor Gleb Panfilov – leading members of the Russian auteur generation that has suddenly become "old" – completed their epic canvases in time for Cannes. Mikhalkov shuttled between Paris and Florence, finishing post-production on **The Barber of Siberia** (*Sibirskiy tsyryulnik*), which features an international cast led by Julia Ormond and Oleg Menshikov. With a budget of more than $40m, it has already become the most expensive exclusively European production ever.

Panfilov continued labouring over **Romanovs: The Crowned Family** (*Romanovy: ventsenosnaya semya*), co-written by him with his son, Ivan, and wife, Inna Churikova, the undisputed First Lady of Russian stage and screen. As both Muscovites failed to meet the Cannes deadline, disappointed festival director Gilles Jacob turned to St Petersburg. There, Alexei Gherman was struggling to complete his long-awaited **Khrustalev, Get the Car!** (*Khrustalev, mashinu!*). As rotund and gifted as Orson Welles, with whom he is sometimes compared, Gherman, who in 25 years has made only three features,

RUSSIA INTERNATIONAL FILM GUIDE

worked on this one for more than six years.

He is famous for his prickliness and perfectionism, but his awesomely-crafted films – the most famous of which is *My Friend Ivan Lapshin* – are truly hand-made. A historical drama, set in the days of Stalin's death in 1953, *Khrustalev* is inspired by Joseph Brodsky's English-language essay "In a Room And a Half". As always with Gherman, its main focus is not the events of the story, but the textures of period life, richly and precisely reconstructed. On the Riviera, this brilliant and difficult picture was ignored by the jury and its theatrical life looks ominous.

The Cannes sidebar selectors passed on Karen Shakhnazarov's **Day of the Full Moon** (*Den' polnoluniya*), an Ophulsian *la ronde* of unconnected vignettes from the Russian present and past that tries too hard

for its own good to be "European" (Shakhnazarov, incidentally, has become chief executive of Mosfilm). Alexei Balabanov's controversial black-and-white period piece **On Freaks and People** (*Pro urodov i lyudei*) was chosen for Un Certain Regard. Its subject is porno-photography in the late nineteenth century, close to the birth of cinema. It should do well when released in Russia: ordinary people and freaks are equally welcome on the country's screens.

MICHAEL BRASHINSKY divides his time between New York and St Petersburg. He is a contributing editor to *Séance* film magazine and a film columnist at *Russian Telegraph*, a leading Moscow newspaper. He is co-author of *The Zero Hour: Glasnost and Soviet Cinema in Transition* and co-editor of *Russian Critics on the Cinema of Glasnost* (both with Andrew Horton).

Recent and Forthcoming Films

AMERIKANKA (An American Bet)

Script: Yuri Korotkov. Dir: Dmitry Meskhiev. Phot: Sergei Machilsky. Players: Natalya Danilova, Sergei Vasilyev, Oleg Fyodorov, Konstantin Vasilevsky, Alisa Grebenshchikova. Prod: Lenfilm Studio.

BOMBA (The Bomb)

Script: Sergei Radlov. Dir: Dmitry Meskhiev. Phot: Sergei Machilsky. Players: Alexander Polovtsev, Olga Tolstetskaya, Vasilina Strelnikova, Olga Tarasenko, Yuri Kuznetsov, Victor Bytchkov. Prod: Nikola-film.

BRAT (The Brother)

Script and Dir: Alexei Balabanov. Phot: Sergei Astakhov. Players: Sergei Bodrov, Jr., Viktor Sukhorukov, Svetlana Pismichenko, Yuri Kuznetsov, Vyacheslav Butusov. Prod: STV, Roskomkino.

DEN' POLNOLUNIYA (Day of the Full Moon)

Script: Alexander Borodyansky, Karen Shakhnazarov. Dir: Shakhnazarov. Phot: Gennady Karyuk. Players: Yelena Koreneva, Vladimir Ilyin, Valery Priemykhov, Valery Storozhik, Filipp Yankovsky. Prod: Mosfilm, Courier Studio.

DRYAN' KHOROSHAYA, DRYAN' PLOKHAYA (Good Asshole, Bad Asshole)

Script: Armen Petrosian. Dir: Alexander Khvan. Phot: Anatoly Susekov. Players: Armen Petrosian, Oksana Fandera, Alexander Tyunin.

GORKO! (Newlyweds' Toast)

Script: Arkady Tigai, Yuri Mamin, Vladimir Vardunas. Dir: Tigai and Mamin. Phot: Vladimir Brylyakov. Players: Kirill Lavrov, Svatlana Nemolyayeva, Andrei Zibrov, Svetlana Solovyeva. Prod: Nikola-film, Tvin.

IZ ADA V AD (From Hell to Hell)

Script: Oleg Danilov. Dir: Dmitry Astrakhan. Phot: Yuri Vorontsov. Players: Gennady Svir, Anna Kling, Gennady Nazarov, Alla Klyuka. Prod: Filmkunst, Belarusfilm.

KHRUSTALEV, MACHINU! (Khrustalev, Get the Car!)

Script: Alexei Gherman, Svatlana Karmalita. Dir: Gherman. Phot: Vladimir Ilyin. Players: Yuri Tsurilo, Nina Ruslanova, Misha Dementyev, Genrietta Yanovskaya.

KRIZIS SREDNEGO VOZRASTA (Mid-Life Crisis)

Script: Ivan Okhlobystin with Garik Sukachev, Yuri Razumovsky. Dir: Sukachev. Phot: Vladislav Opelyants. Players: Dmitry Kharatyan, Fyodor Bondarchuk, Ivan Okhlobystin, Garik Sukachev, Yevgeniya Dobrovolskaya, Mikhail Yefremov. Prod: Anatoly Voropayev Prod. Company.

MAMA, NE GORYUI (Momma, Don't Be Sad)

Script: Konstantin Murzenko. Dir: Maxim Pezhemsky. Players: Yevgeny Sidikhin, Valery Priemykhov Ivan Okhlobystin, Nina Ruslanova. Prod: STV, Maxim Gorky Studio.

MYTAR' (Tax Collector)

Script: Ivan Okhlobystin. Dir: Oleg Fomin. Phot: Igor Klebanov. Players: Oleg Fomin, Anna Molchanova, Mikhail Gluzsky, Alexander Porokhovshchikov, Yuozas Budraitis, Alexei Zharkov. Prod: Maxim Gorky Studio.

Still from CLASSWORK FOR THE VICTORY DAY

PRIYATEL POKOINIKA (Friend of the Deceased)

Script: Andrei Kurkov. Dir: Vyacheslav Krishtofovich. Phot: Vilen Kalyuta. Players: Alexander Lazarev, Jr., Anjelika Nevolina, Yelena Korikova. Prod: Dovzhenko Studio, Compagnie des films, Compagnie Est-Ous.

PRO URODOV I LYUDEI (On Freaks and People)

Script and Dir: Alexei Balabanov. Phot: Sergei Astakhov. Players: Sergei Makovetsky, Viktor Sukhorukov, Anjelika Nevolina, Dinara Drukarova. Prod: STV.

RETRO VTROYEM (Three-Way Retro)

Script: Piotr Todorovsky, Timur Suleimenov, Mira Todorovsky. Dir: Piotr Todorovsky. Phot: Nikolai Nemolyayev. Players: Yelena Yakovleva, Sergei Makovetsky, Yevgeny Sidikhin. Prod: Mirabel, Goskino, Krug Studio, Gosfilmofond.

SEREBRYANNYE GOLOVY (Silver Heads)

Script and Dir: Yevgeny Yufit, Vladimir Maslov. Phot: Alexei Burov. Players: Nikolai Marton, Vladimir Maslov, T. Verkhovskaya, V. Deryagin, N. Rudik. Prod: STV.

SERGEI EISENSTEIN: MEXIKANSKAYA FANTASIYA (Sergei Eisenstein: Mexican Fantasy)

Script, Dir and Edit: Oleg Kovalov (based on *El Viva Mexico* by Sergei Eisenstein). Phot: Eduard Tisse. Phot. coordination: Yevgeny Shermergor. Prod: STV.

SHIZOFRENIYA (Schizophrenia)

Script: Alexander Abdulov, Yevgeny Kozlovsky, Viktor Nevsky. Dir: Viktor Sergeyev. Phot: Yuri Shaigardanov. Players: Alexander Abdulov, Alexander Zbruyev, Kirill Lavrov, Armen Dzhigarkhanian, Nikolai Trofimov, Leonid Bronevoi. Prod: Lenfilm Studio.

SOCHINENIYE KO DNYU POBEDY (Classwork for the Victory Day)

Script: Gennady Ostrovsky. Dir: Sergei Ursulyak. Players: Mikhail Ulyanov, Oleg Yefremov, Vyacheslav Tikhonov, Vladimir Menshov. Prod: Maxim Gorky Studio.

STRANA GLUKHIKH (Country of the Deaf)

Script: Yuri Korotkov, Valery Todorovsky, based on a Renata Litvinova story. Dir: Todorovsky. Phot: Yuri Shaigardanov. Players: Dina Korzun, Chulpan Khamatova, Maxim Sukhanov, P. Poimalov. Prod: Maxim Gorky Studio.

STRANNOYE VREMYA (Strange Time)

Script: Natalya Pyankova with Ilya Narodovoi. Dir: Pyankova. Phot: Radik Askarov. Players: Oleg Fomin, Yelena Mayorova, Gleb Soshnikov, Sergei Vinogradov, Natalya Pyankova. Prod: Maxim Gorky Studio.

TELO BUDET PREDANO ZEMLE, A STARSHYI MICHMAN BUDET PET' (The Body Will Be Given to the Earth and the Sailor Will Sing)

Script: Konstantin Murzenko. Dir: Ilya Makarov. Players: Alexander Lazarev, Yevgeniya Igumnova, Alexander Stroyev, A. Barilo. Prod: Hard Time Studio, Maxim Gorky Studio.

TSAREVITCH ALEXEI (Prince Alexei)

Script and Dir: Vitaly Melnikov. Phot: Ivan Bagayev. Players: Alexei Zuyev, Viktor Stepanov, Stanislav Lyubshin, Vladimir Menshov. Prod: Golos Film Studio, Lenfilm, Goskino.

TSIRK SGOREL I KLOUNY RAZBEZHALIS' (The Circus Had Burnt and the Clowns Have Run Away)

Script and Dir: Vladimir Bortko. Phot: Sergei Lando, Yevgeny Shermergor. Players: Nikolai Karachentsov, Tatyana Vasilyeva, Zinaida Sharko, Pyotr Zaitchenko.

UPYR' (The Bloodsucker)

Script: Sergei Dobrotvorsky. Dir: Sergei Vinokurov. Players: Alexei Serebryakov, Nikolai Lavrov. Prod: Zhestkoye vremya (Hard Times) studio, Lenfilm.

V TOI STRANE (In That Country)

Script and Dir: Lidiya Bobrova. Phot: Sergei Astakhov with Valery Revich. Players: Dmitry Klopov, Vladimir Borchaninov, Alexander Stakheev. Zoya Buryak. Prod: Lenfilm, Narodny Film Studio.

VOR (The Thief)

Script and Dir: Pavel Chukhrai. Phot: Vladimir Klimov. Players: Vladimir Mashkov, Misha Filipchuk, Yekaterina Rednikova. Prod: NTV-Profit, Roissy Films, Productions le Pont.

VREMYA TANTSORA (Time of the Dancer).

Script: Alexander Mindadze. Dir: Vadim Abrashitov. Phot: Yuri Nevsky. Players: Andrei Yegorov, Yuri Stepanov, Sergei Garmash, Zurab Kipshidze, Chulpan Khamatova, Svetlana Kopylova, Vera Voronkova. Prod: Arc-film.

ZHELEZNAYA PYATA OLIGARKHII (The Iron Foot of Oligarchy)

Script and Dir: Alexander Bashirov. Players: Bashirov. Prod: Deboshir Films.

ZMEINYI ISTOCHNIK (The Snake Spring)

Script and Dir: Nikolai Lebedev. Players: Yevgeny Mironov, Olga Ostroumova. Prod: Maxim Gorky Studio.

Useful Addresses

Double D Agency
(sociological research, publishing)
7 Maly Gnezdnikovsky per
Suite 604
103877 Moscow
Tel: (7 95) 229 7921
Fax: (7 95) 369 1815

Intercinema Agency
(distribution, production)
Contact: Raissa Fomina at Kinocentre (see below)

Iskusstvo Kino Magazine
9 Usievich St., 125319 Moscow.
Tel: (7 95) 151 1833.
Fax: (7 95) 151 0272
e-mail: postmaster@filmartisk.ru

Kinocentre (programmes, publishing, museum, information)
15 Druzhinnikovskaya St.,
123242 Moscow
Tel: (7 95) 255 9489 or 255 9087.
Fax: (7 95) 973 2029
Telex: 411070 CENTRE

Kinotavr (Sochi International Film Festival)
15 Druzhinnikovskaya St.,
Kinocentre, Suite 301,
123242 Moscow
Tel: (7 95) 255 9661
Fax: (7 95) 255 9275

Lenfilm Concern
10 Kamennoostrovsky Ave.,
197101 St. Petersburg
Tel: (812) 232 8374
Fax: (812) 232 8881 or 233 2174.
Telex: 121534 FILM SU

Maxim Gorky Film Studios
8 Eisenstein St.,
129226 Moscow
Fax: (7 95) 188 9871
Telex: 411941

Mosfilm Concern
1 Mosfilmovskaya St.,
119858 Moscow
Tel: (7 95) 147 7042
Fax: (7 95) 938 2083
Telex: 411293 MSFILM SU

Premiere Film
Contact: Alexander Antipov
Fax: (7 95) 755 5982

Seance Film Project
(Production, publishing, film school)
10 Kamennoostrovsky Ave.,
197101 St. Petersburg
Tel: (812) 237 0842
Fax: (812) 232 4925
e-mail: seans@comset.net

Tri Te Studios
11 Maly Kozikhinsky Lane
103009 Moscow

SENEGAL

Judy Kendall

Senegal has had a longer history of film-making than many African countries, starting with Ousmane Sembene's *Borom Sarret* (1964), which is regarded as marking the birth of indigenous film art in French-speaking Africa. Djibril Diop Mambety continued this pioneering trend when his film, *Touki Bouki*, was screened at the Cannes Directors' Fortnight in 1973. Senegalese films have been marked by an insistence on social and (often hidden) political comment, despite pressures to the contrary. Sembene, some of whose films have been censored in Senegal, has stressed the importance of working to "remain close to our past and act as witnesses to our own times".

A second and not unrelated issue again touched upon by Sembene is that of language: "In order to reach a larger African audience, I must use French [rather than Wolof], but it is a double-edged sword: people in Senegal will not come to see [such] a film." This theme was continued in his address to colleagues at the 1997 PanAfrican Film-makers Federation: "Unfortunately, the films we make are not seen by [their] first audience, which is tragic for us. The distribution ... of our films is a goal we can reach. It is therefore essential that we ... take steps to recover our cinematographic and televisual areas."

Two weddings and a funny role

The above difficulties have been partially resolved by one film director, Moussa Sene Absa, who now resides in Paris so as better to further his career. It is interesting to see that he chose to make his most recent film, **Tableau Ferraille** (*Scrap Heap*), in both French and Wolof. Launched in 1997, *Scrap Heap* is a comedy dealing with the rise and fall of an idealistic politician, Daam, who becomes Minister for Development. Vigorous, youthful and popular, he marries the village beauty, Gagnesiri, but loses face when she fails to conceive.

He marries a second time, promising Gagnesiri that she will always be first in his heart, but faces further trouble when an influential sweatshop owner exploits this tricky marital situation. The film is a co-production between Senegal and France, and stars the popular Senegalese musician Ismael Lo as Daam, with Ndeye Fatou Ndaw and Ndeye Bineta Diop playing the two wives.

The PanAfrican *African Dreaming* compilation, an initiative of South Africa's M-Net channel and South African producer Jeremy Nathan, includes the Senegalese film **So Be It** (*Ainsi Soit Il*), which won the Silver Lion at the 54th Venice International Film Festival 1997. This is a 26-minute short, directed by Joseph Gaye Ramaga and featuring Félicité Wouassi and Alex Descas.

A woman tries to get her lover to leave the medical centre where they work after he befriends an albino boy, whom she fears is possessed by evil spirits. This sinister film has an assuredly slow pace, and, despite its brevity, is recommended for its ability to evoke the epic, as in one shot which shows the albino boy and a little girl talking in a courtyard as more than 100 cattle stream past in the background.

Useful Address

Consultants et Réalisateurs Associés
Parcelle No 2017
Usine Bene Tally
Dakar
Senegal
Tel: (221) 824 0408
Fax: (221) 825 1861

SERBIA & MONTENEGRO

Goran
Gocić

The Serbian film market experienced similar box-office growth compared to other Eastern European countries, with total admissions increasing from around 4.5 million in 1996 to 5.3 million in 1997. There were 187 films distributed in Serbia and Montenegro in 1997, compared to 140 in the previous year. The box-office split between the US majors (77 titles) and the domestic, international and independent distributors (110 titles) was almost exactly 50-50.

In the past season there were a few surprises concerning content as well. Serbian moviegoers had an opportunity to recognize their look-alikes in several foreign features, such as Michael Winterbottom's *Welcome to Sarajevo*. At times, Hollywood's condescending interest in ex-Yugoslavia's civil war was turned into a curious pleasure for the locals: at screenings of Mimi Leder's *The Peacemaker* (eleventh place at the domestic box-office in 1997) the Belgrade audience cheered and booed according to their own affections, regardless of the fact that George Clooney was playing the good guy and Marcel Iures was playing the Serbian terrorist who tries to nuke New York.

However, **Savior**, produced by Oliver Stone and shot in Montenegro with a Serbian director, Predrag Antonijević, was definitely the most gruesome of the lot, depicting a season in hell. Containing every single atrocity the screenwriters (Antonijević and US journalist Robert Orr) had ever heard of, *Savior* looked like premium footage from a Pulitzer-hungry CNN reporter.

On the other hand, European features about Serbian emigrants, such as *Yugofilm*, by Goran Rebić (made in Austria) or

Dennis Quaid in SAVIOR

Denmark's *Tired Passengers* (*Müde Weggefahrten*), by Branislav Solomun, were greeted almost as domestic projects. *Yugofilm*, a simple, understated story about the post-war angst of a Serbian youth in Austria, won an award at a local film festival.

Arms and the women

The stars of *Yugofilm* were Eva Mattes, who acted for Fassbinder, and Ljubisa Samardzic, a veteran actor from ex-Yugoslavia and also proud owner of Sinema Dizajn, a company which has so far

Mirjana Joković and Sergej Trifunović in HORNET

produced or co-produced seven features. The magnificent seventh was **Hornet** (*Strsljen*), directed by Gorcin Stojanović. This is a love story – sprinkled with action sequences – about a Serbian schoolgirl and an Albanian hitman from Kosovo. The result is notable, but flawed. Stojanović directs the actors well (especially Sergej Trifunović, the most talked-about Serbian actor of the moment), but the screenplay lets him down. Recent turmoil in Serbia's Kosovo province gave the film a topical edge.

The most curious feature of the season was that Serbian audiences saw several film debuts from female directors. Gordana Boskov's **Flashback**, a melodrama about a boxer traumatised by the war, was a straightforward failure which received minimal distribution, while **Superreality** and **Play**, both made by a prominent ex-Yugoslav actress, Sonja Savić, were MTV-style collections of performance pieces and computer animation, shot on video. However, **Three Summer Days** (*Tri letnja dana*), directed by Mirjana Vukomanović, had its moments. It is a pessimistic account of post-war Serbia, peopled by impoverished refugees and unscrupulous profiteers.

Three Palms for Two Punks and a Babe (*Tri palme za dve bitange i ribicu*), directed by Radivoje Andric, and *Three Summer Days* have several things in common. First, they both deal with marginal characters and their love affairs; second, they are both set in post-war Belgrade; third, they both feature a plot involving suspect, pyramid-bank financing. Finally, they have similar casting: Mirjana Karanović playing shady businesswomen, and Srdjan Todorović playing streetwise losers in both films. However, while *Three Summer Days* is thoroughly depressing, *Three Palms...* is a comedy, the latest example of the escapist "pink wave" of Serbian film-making, which began with Srdjan Dragojević's comedy *We Are No Angels*. *Three Palms...* was part-funded by Warner Bros, the first time a US major has had a hand in a Serbian feature.

No sense in dancing

Something completely different was offered by **The Tango Is a Sad Thought One Dances To** (*Tango je tuzna misao koja se pleše*). This bitter comedy is an unusual excursion even for eccentric Serbian veteran Puriša Djordjević. The loose, atmospheric story about Russian hookers stranded in Serbia had an air of nostalgia, but did not make much sense – a bit like real life in Serbia. **Birds Which Do Not Fly** (*Ptice koje ne polete*) was another film made by a band apart. The first feature film directed by Petar Lalović, a wildlife documentarist, it is an unusual yet universal story about a terminally ill young city girl and the healing power of nature. It has been warmly received at a handful of overseas festivals.

With films from established directors such as Emir Kusturica, Goran Paskaljević, Živojin Pavlović and Srdjan Dragojević still in production, Serbian cinema in the first half of 1998 was dominated by the outsiders and debutantes (Rebić, Vukomanović, Andvić, Boškov). It seems that it was up to the makers of videos, documentaries and shorts to defend the colours of the local feature film industry. For example, Milos Radojević received a dozen awards abroad for his effective short feature **My Country** (*Moja domovina*), and, two years after it was made, Zelimir Gvardiol's magnificent documentary about ageing, **I Don't Know Where, When Or How** (*Ne znam ni gde, ni kada, ni kako*), is still cruising the world and collecting prizes everywhere.

GORAN GOCIĆ is a film and art critic. He is currently employed as a culture page editor on the Belgrade daily *Dnevni Telegraf*. He has co-written four books on cinema and visual arts: *A Light in Dark*; *Pop Vision*; *Film and Video* and *When I'm Dead and White*, and authored a monograph, *Andy Warhol and Strategies of Pop*.

Recent and Forthcoming Films

BUDJENJE MRTVOG ČOVEKA (Wake Up, Dead Man)

Script and Dir: Darko Mitrevski, Aleksandar Popovski. Phot: Vladimir Samoilovski. Players: Lazar Ristovski, Nikola Ristanovski. Prod: Mirco & Slavco – First Partisans Production (Macedonia)/VANS.

BURE BARUTA (The Powder Keg)

Script: Dejan Dukovski, Filip David, Goran Paskaljević. Dir: Paskaljević. Phot: Milan Spasić. Players: Sergej Trifunović, Mirjana Karanović. Prod: VANS/ Mact Productions, Ticket Productions (France)/Gradska Kina (Macedonia)/Stefi (Greece)/Min (Turkey).

DRŽAVA MRTVIH (Land of the Dead)

Script: Siniša Kovacević. Dir: Živojin Pavlović. Phot: Aleksandar Petković. Players: Radko Polič, Katina Ivanova. Prod: Delfin film.

FLASHBACK

Script: Veroslav Rančić, Gordana Boškov. Dir: Boškov. Phot: Branko Perak. Players: Nebojša Dugalić, Tatjana Bošković. Prod: Impuls film.

KUPI MI ELIOTA (Buy me Eliot)

Script: Gordan Mihić. Dir: Dejan Zečević. Phot: Predrag Todorović. Players: Ivana Mihić, Nikola Kojo. Prod: Horizont 2000/Cobra Film Department.

LAJANJE NA ZVEZDE (Barking at the Stars)

Script: Milovan Vitezović. Dir: Zdravko Šotra. Phot: Veselko Krčmar. Players: Dragan Mićanović, Nataša Šolak. Prod: Komuna/RTV Serbia.

POVRATAK LOPOVA (Thief's Comeback)

Script: Biljana Maksić-Pajkić. Dir: Miroslav Lekić. Phot: Veselko Krčmar. Players: Maja Sabljić, Vojislav Brajović. Prod: RTV Serbia/E.O.L. film.

PRVA LJUBAV ANE MORAVE (The First Love of Ana Morava)

Script: Gordana Brajović. Dir: Mihailo Vukobratović. Phot: Milan Tvrdišić. Players: Milena Dravić, Svetozar Cvetković. Prod: Film danas/Večernje Novosti/RTV Serbia.

PTICE KOJE NE POLETE (Birds Which Do Not Fly)

Script, Dir and Phot: Petar Lalović.

Players: Ivana Šurdić, Velimir-Bata Živojinović. Prod: Media film/Avala film/Srbijašume.

RANE (The Wounds)

Script and Dir: Srđan Dragojević. Phot: Dušan Joksimović. Players: Predrag-Miki Manojlović, Dragan Bjelogrlić. Prod: Cobra Film Department/Le Studio Canal + (France).

STRŠLJEN (Hornet)

Script: Srđan Koljević, Zoran Popović. Dir: Gorčin Stojanović. Players: Sergej Trifunović, Mirjana Joković. Prod: Sinema Dizajn.

SAVIOR

Script: Robert Orr, Predrag Antonijević. Dir: Antonijević. Players: Dennis Quaid, Nataša Ninković. Phot: Ian Willson; Prod: IEG (USA)/Komuna.

TRI PALME ZA DVE BITANGE I RIBICU (Three Palms for Two Punks and a Babe)

Script: Milan V. Puzić. Dir: Radivoje Andrić. Phot: Miloš Spasojević. Players: Srdjan Todorović, Dubravka Mijatović. Prod: Dakar film.

Useful Addresses

Avala Film International DD
(Production company & studio facilities)
Kneza Višeslava 88
11030 Beograd
Tel: (381 11) 557 331
Fax: (381 11) 559 474

Beograd film
(Chain of theatres)
Terazije 40
11000 Beograd
Tel: (381 11) 688 940
Fax: (381 11) 687 952

Cobra Film
(Independent producer)
Kneza Miloša 7
11000 Beograd
Tel: (381 11) 323 1943
Fax: (381 11) 324 6413

First Production
(Independent distributor)
Kumodraška 176/6
11040 Beograd
Tel: (381 11) 471 403
Fax: (381 11) 473 207

Inex film
(Independent producer & distributor)
Francuska 12
11000 Beograd
Tel: (381 11) 323 9821
Fax: (381 11) 323 9821

Institut za film
(Yugoslav Film Institute)
Čika Ljubina 15
11000 Beograd
Tel: (381 11) 625 131
Fax: (381 11) 634 253

Komuna
(Producer and distributor)
Cakorska 2
11000 Beograd
Tel: (381 11) 367 2424
Fax: (381 11) 367 2525

Metrofilm International
(Independent distributor)
Trg Nikole Pašića 8
11000 Beograd
Tel: (381 11) 334 0318
Fax: (381 11) 323 5221

Monte Royal Pictures
(Independent producer)
Skerlićeva 30
11000 Beograd
Tel: (381 11) 431 726
Fax: (381 11) 444 1951

Sinema Dizajn
(Producer)
Ustanicka 125/1
11000 Beograd
Tel: (381 11) 488 2377
Fax: (381 11) 488 8011

Tuck
(Independent distributor)
Velikomoravska 11-15
11000 Beograd
Tel: (381 11) 424 666
Fax: (381 11) 413 177

Vans
(Independent producer and distributor)
Njegoševa 84
11000 Beograd
Tel: (381 11) 432 492
Fax: (381 11) 434 226

SINGAPORE

Yvonne Ng

After decades of inactivity in the country's film industry, the theatrical release last year of three local feature productions Eric Khoo's *12 Storeys*, about three unhappy households in a tower block, Hugo Ng's serial killer drama, *God or Dog*, and Lim Suat Yen's *The Road Less Travelled*, about starstruck graduates, generated considerable excitement among local film enthusiasts.

In the first five months of 1998, two locally produced films were released, with several more in the pipeline. The sense of artistic ferment in Singapore remains palpable and has been further stoked by the government's repeated announcements to transform the island into a "global city of the arts". The most recent development was the establishment of a Film Commission with a modest budget of $1.4m (S$2.5m) to assist local film-makers.

Having served as the country's de facto film institute for about 40 years, the Singapore Film Society (SFS) has been actively involved in the first local production to be released this year. With a loudly 'Singlish' title, **Money No Enough** is a comedy directed by T.L. Tay and produced by JSP Entertainment, a leading Singapore production house and multimedia organisation, which spent $485,000 on the film.

Three of a kind

Tay's film focuses on three characters with different lifestyles but the same problem: never having enough money. Scriptwriter and actor Jack Neo plays a long-serving manager in a small company, Mark Lee is a rough but good-hearted building contractor and Henry Thia is a coffee-shop assistant who yearns for a beautiful girlfriend.

Good friends in real life, all three actors also star in the Chinese-language *Comedy Night* series on TCS (Television Corporation of Singapore). Whereas Eric Khoo's *12 Storeys* is aimed at a more sophisticated audience, Neo declares: "Our market is more the lower- to middle-income group." According to Kenneth Tan, Chairman of the SFS, the Film Society had to request special permission from the Board of Film Censors to allow *Money No Enough*'s release, as almost all of its dialogue is in Chinese dialects (mainly Hokkien). Since the 1980s, when the government launched its Speak Mandarin campaigns, dialect films have usually been banned from exhibition, or dubbed into Mandarin. The film went on to reach number one in Singapore's box-office chart in May 1998.

Still from MONEY NO ENOUGH

Another 1998 release is Glen Goei's **Forever Fever**, inspired by the director's memories of the 1970s in Singapore, when John Travolta's *Saturday Night Fever* was all the rage. Until now, Goei has been better known for his theatre work, in particular, for his critically-acclaimed performance as Song Liling in a West End stage production of *M Butterfly* opposite Anthony Hopkins in 1989. He has also set up Mu-lan Arts, a Chinese theatre company based in London. Goei, who trained at New York University's film school and used his life savings, a mortgage and a bank loan to finance the film, could be set for international success after Miramax bought the rights to distribute *Forever Fever* in the US, Canada and Britain and signed him up to a three-film deal. Both *Forever Fever* and *Money No Enough* are entertaining, but are weakened by over-acting.

Growing pains and Indian rhythms

Meanwhile, **The Teenage Textbook**, which was supposed to have been made last year, has been rescheduled for filming this year. Based on the best-selling book by local writer Adrian Tan, the film will depict the adolescent pains of growing up in Singapore. The producer, Jonathan Foo, and director, Phillip Lim, are also producers at MTV Asia.

The Singaporean Indian classical dancer Shanta Rati Misra has sprung a pleasant surprise with her first film venture, the documentary **And Miles To Flow**, about the Indian Kathakali dance form. She has had a brief stint in New York as a TV anchor and a producer of short documentaries, which may explain why her film, made on 35mm, seems better suited for television. Nevertheless it is well-made, has a good sense of aesthetics and a pulsating rhythm.

Never afraid to scale the heights of technology, Singapore now boasts the interactive CineMania theatre. Built on the recently-opened Fantasy Island Theme Park, on Sentosa Island, CineMania fuses rides and movies to create the sensation of being completely immersed in the action. The films' audio-visual effects are created by shooting at 60 frames per second on 70mm film, with a full spectrum magnetic soundtrack. The audience watches from computer-synchronised motion seats. The idea originated from Douglas Trumbull, a special effects producer on movies such as *Jurassic Park, E.T.* and *Star Wars*.

YVONNE NG was born in Singapore, and graduated in film studies from the University of Waterloo, Ontario, Canada. She has written on the contemporary mainland Chinese cinema and is currently on the editorial board of *KINEMA* (published at the University of Waterloo).

Recent and Forthcoming Films

MONEY NO ENOUGH

Script: Jack Neo. Director: T. L. Tay. Players: Neo, Mark Lee, Henry Thia. Prod: JSP Entertainment.

FOREVER FEVER

Script and Dir: Glen Goei.

Players: Adrian Pang, Medaline Tan, Steven Lim, Pierre Png. Prod: Tiger Tiger Productions Pte Ltd.

TEENAGE TEXTBOOK

Script: Haresh Sharma. Director: Phillip Lim. Prod: Monster Film

Company and Springroll Creative Entertainment Agency.

AND MILES TO FLOW

Documentary. Script, Dir and Prod: Shanta Rati Misra.

Useful Addresses

Cathay Organisation
017 #05-00 Cathay Bldg
11 Dhoby Ghaut
Singapore 229233
Tel: (65) 337 8181
Fax: (65) 334 3373

Eng Wah Film Pte Ltd
#16-06 Orchard Towers
400 Orchard Road
Singapore 0923
Tel: (65) 734 0028
Fax: (65) 235 4897

**Golden Village Entertainment
Pte Ltd**
2 Handy Road
#15-04 Cathay Building
Singapore 229233
Tel: (65) 334 3766
Fax: (65) 334 8397
www.golden-village.com.sg/homep
age.html

National Arts Council
460 Alexandra Road
#35-00, PSA Building
Singapore 119963
Tel: (65) 270 0722
Fax: (65) 273 6880

Oak 3 Films
73A Pagoda St.
Singapore 059232
Tel: (65) 226 2338
Fax: (65) 226 2339
e-mail: oak3films@pacific.net.sg

Shanta Rati Misra
241-A Tanjong Katong Road
Singapore 437029
Tel: (65) 346 4776
Fax: (65) 346 7292

Shaw Organisation
Shaw Centre
1 Scotts Road
Singapore 229233
Tel: (65) 235 2077
Fax: (65) 235 2860
sunflower.singnet.com.sg/~javao/

Singapore Film Society
Golden Village Marina
5-A Raffles Avenue
#03-01 Marina Leisureplex
Singapore 039801
Fax: (65) 737 1543
www.sfs.org.sg

SLOVAKIA — Hana Cielová

The biggest studio in Slovakia, ex-state Štúdio Koliba, was privatised some time ago by a group of people centred around its ex-communist director, Vladimír Ondruš – a situation typical of nearly the whole Slovak film industry. Koliba's "old-new" management is naturally close to the government, which signed the privatisation deal, so its forthcoming projects are in line with the state cultural policy: monumental historical epics about heroic figures from Slovak history, such as Pribina, a mythical Slavic king, or Jánošík, a Slovak Robin Hood.

Another forthcoming film is **A Flock of Wild Geese** (*Kŕdeľ divých husí*), based on the book by Milan Ferko, the official "expert" on Slovak history. It describes Slovaks as a poor, suffering people, always oppressed by other nations. This is to be directed by Martin Ťapák, a prolific veteran from the "good old times". The governmental Pro Slovakia organisation, which distributes state film subsidy, is always willing to provide money for such nationalistic projects.

Life is much harder for films which take a critical look at Slovak history or, even worse, at the contemporary situation. The most talked-about example is the new film from Vladimír Balco, **Rivers of Babylon**, based on the two provocative best-sellers by Peter Pišťánek, *Rivers of Babylon I* and *II*, which are probably the most interesting novels published in Slovakia since the end of communism.

Pišťánek demolishes the myth of the "always suffering and always good" Slovaks. The idealised image of Slovakia is demolished. Pistanek peoples the main hotel in Bratislava, the capital, with cowardly staff, criminals and greedy women. The hotel (called the Ambassador, but modelled on Bratislava's real-life Kjev Hotel) serves as a metaphor for the whole country and Pišťánek paints a brutal picture of an insignificant country in Eastern Europe in the communist and post-communist eras.

Meet the new boss

Like the books, *Rivers of Babylon* the film combines realism with stylised, bizarre scenes, reminiscent of the magical realism of Gabriel García Márquez. Unfortunately, the reality in Slovakia is much more grey and bitter than in Márquez's fantastic town of Macondo. The film tells the story of Ràc, a primitive young man who comes to the capital from a small village to become a furnace stoker at The Ambassador. At the beginning, everything seems beyond his reach: he is only allowed to use the staff entrance at the rear of the hotel; to look at the stripper in the exclusive bar he must use a peep-hole.

But when winter comes, everybody in the hotel is dependent on Ràc and he quickly finds out the immense power he has. Desperate to stay warm, everybody starts to bribe or flatter him – with the exception of the hotel director, who reluctantly stays in his freezing room as Ràc becomes the real boss. Soon he is in control not only of the hotel, but of the whole city. The once-admired stripper is no longer good enough for him, so he finds a beautiful, highly-educated virgin from a good family. The girl's now ex-boyfriend, a petty criminal who had served Ràc as willingly as everyone else, mounts a short-lived rebellion.

Transferring to the screen the black humour of the books, their bitter irony and original style, balanced on the verge between reality and absurdity, would have been a very difficult task for anybody. Balco tried his best, and his film, though sadly much weaker than the books, is still an honest attempt to say something about Slovakia today.

The unhappy hookers

In contrast to Pistanek's contemporary vision, **The Camp of Fallen Women** (*Tábor padlých žien*), tries to remind audiences of an almost-forgotten chapter in Slovak history. At the very beginning of the communist era, the new regime created the so-called re-educational camps for prostitutes. The aim was to turn hookers

Still from THE CAMP OF FALLEN WOMEN

into proud socialist women. This, of course, offers great material for bitter comedy as well as strong drama, and there is no denying that the film deals with a subject never previously addressed by Slovak cinema – probably the reason why it was chosen for Berlin.

Unfortunately, the film itself is not as interesting on screen as the subject is on paper. We are shown an isolated camp run by an old, tired commander who had done a similar job for the Nazis. There is a cynical Jewish doctor, a young, naive teacher and a fanatical army lieutenant, who sees American spies everywhere and symbolises the coming era. To them are sent all the "fallen women" working the harbour in Bratislava: old, experienced Mandy, young and sensitive Ernička, exotic dancer Carmen and her admirer, mysterious Ria Amala, as well as Berta, the funny German. Even when the actors were trying really hard, the result was not very convincing and felt like a slightly old-fashioned TV production.

One of the most talented and internationally known directors of the younger generation, Martin Šulík, was hired to direct one episode from **Prague Stories** (*Praha ocima*), produced by Prague-based Frenchman Artemio Benki. Another project, **Fountain for Susannah III** (*Fontana pre Zuzanu III*), the third in a series of romantic, sentimental and blatantly commercial teen dramas, will be directed by Dušan Rapoš.

Slovak cinemas are, like those of almost

every country in the world, full of commercial, mostly American films. Only a few independent distributors, notably The Association of Slovak Film Clubs, are trying to bring something different to the cinemas, though it is good to see the audience for these alternative titles growing each year, especially amongst the young. That, perhaps, is a good sign for the future.

HANA CIELOVA is a freelance writer. She has a monthly show about film on Czech Television and also works as a programmer for the Karlovy Vary International Film Festival.

Producers

ALEF
Uršulínka 9
811 01 Bratislava
Tel: (421 7) 533 4812
Fax: (421 7) 531 9406

Ars Media
Odeská 13
821 06 Bratislava
Tel/Fax: (421 7) 552 4617

Atan Film
Rovniakova 1
824 95 Bratislava
Tel/Fax: (421 7) 838 486

Attack
Karpatská 2
811 05 Bratislava
Tel: (421 7) 392 520

Barok Film
Konventná 8
811 03 Bratislava
Tel: (421 7) 531 9480
Fax: (421 7) 531 9372

Charlie's
Špitálska 4
811 08 Bratislava
Tel: (421 7) 363 430, 363 396
Fax: (421 7) 323 678

Davay
Trnavská cesta 68
821 01 Bratislava
Tel: (421 7) 572 1498
Fax: (421 7) 572 1497

HQ Agency
Nevädzová 2
821 08 Bratislava
Tel/Fax: (421 7) 236 606

JMB Film and TV Production
Korničova 12
811 03 Bratislava
Tel: (421 7) 531 1041
Fax: (421 7) 531 5778

Partnerfilm
Brečtanová 1
833 14 Bratislava
Tel: (421 7) 371 966
Fax: (421 7) 371 126

Štúdio Koliba
Brečtanová 1
833 14 Bratislava
Tel: (421 7) 371 368, 378 8213
Fax: (421 7) 372 224

Distributors

Asociácia Slovenských Filmových Klubov
Grosslingova 32
811 09 Bratislava
Tel/Fax: (421 7) 325 533

Continental Film
Vajanského nábr. 17
P.O. Box 124
810 00 Bratislava
Tel: (421 7) 363 354, 325 427
Fax: (421 7) 536 1363

Intersonic Taunus Productions
Staré Grunty 36
842 25 Bratislava
Tel/Fax: (421 7) 722 070

Tatra Film
Priemyselná 1
821 09 Bratislava
Tel: (421 7) 526 7681
Fax: (421 7) 521 5685

Bioscop
Hviezdoslavovo nám. 17
811 02 Bratislava
Tel: (421 7) 533 5815

Saturn
Podháj 19
841 03 Bratislava
Tel: (421 7) 731 151
Fax: (421 7) 731 150

Solarfilm
Priemyselná 1
821 09 Bratislava
Tel: (421 7) 211 301
Fax: (421 7) 521 5685

Useful Addresses

Slovak Film Archive/National Cinematographic Center
Grosslingova 32
811 09 Bratislava
Tel: (421 7) 326 452
Fax: (421 7) 363 462

Slovak Television Archive
Mlynská Dolina
845 35 Bratislava
Tel (421 7) 723 086
Fax: (421 7) 729 440

SOUTH AFRICA — Martin Botha

In general, 1997 was not a good year for the South African film industry. Johan Blignaut, one of our best film-makers, took his life in the early morning of December 17, 1997. He worked in theatre, television and cinema for more than 20 years and scripted, produced and directed two of the milestones in South African cinema, *Mamza* (1985) and *Toyan* (1986). In 1989, he created Showdata, an on-line database on the local film industry which was a major source for the research into the restructuring of the industry.

A few months after Blignaut's suicide, producer Edgar Bold died of cancer at the age of 57. His impressive filmography includes features such as *Jock of the Bushveld*, *Lambarene*, *Taxi to Soweto* and *The Angel, the Bicycle and the Chinaman's Finger*. Just a few months later, director David Lister, who made *The John Ross Story*, and Koos Roets, one of our most outstanding cinematographers, announced their plans to emigrate to Australia because of the severe shortage of work within the local film industry, as well as the shocking crime situation.

Strained resources

Despite the fact that a government-appointed Task Group finished work on the White Paper for Film in early 1996, we are nowhere near a Film and Video Foundation (such as the French CNC or Australian Film Finance Corporation) to support the post-apartheid film industry.

The late Johan Blignaut, one of South Africa's outstanding film-makers

A scene from JOCK OF THE BUSHVELD, produced by the late Edgar Bold

The Department of Arts, Culture, Science and Technology, which is responsible for the facilitation of this Film Foundation, only provides $2m (R10m) annually to fund documentaries (almost 30 in 1997), short films and script development, scriptwriting seminars, and the Southern African International Film and Television Market.

However, each year that total has to be divided between almost 100 different projects: from documentaries like *Cecil Williams*, *Saartjie Baartman* and *Steve Biko*, to development funding for features such as Tertius Meintjies' *The Outcast*, Danie Pieterse's *Dying Breed* and Simon Bruinders' *Dream Weekend*. This Interim Film Fund is also used to support institutions like the Newtown Film School and the distributor of African cinema, the Film Resource Unit.

Thirty-three grants were given to develop feature films (with amounts ranging from $1,000 to $15,000); nine grants were given to the development of short films; two for $20,000 each were given to the production of shorts. No wonder the local film industry produced less than 10 features in 1997.

The only noteworthy local feature to reach our screens was director Katinka Heyns' third film, **Paljas**. Shot in Afrikaans, with English subtitles, this was a collaborative venture between Anant Singh, our most prominent producer, and Heyns' Sonneblom Films. *Paljas* deals with the relationship between a clown and a young boy from a dysfunctional Afrikaner family. It was accepted as the country's official entry for the Academy Award for Best Foreign Film – the first time a South African movie has been presented to the Academy's screening committee. Though it did not appear in the final list of nominees, it won major critical acclaim at home.

Just part of the scenery

Apart from *Paljas*, nothing else made any impression. South Africa has again become a mere backdrop for international films. Warner Brothers' *Tarzan and the Lost City* used the local soil to portray the white hero's fight against evil in the jungles of the mysterious Dark Continent. *Dark Two Zero* used our landscapes to depict a top-secret mission by British SAS troops to infiltrate Iraqi territory during the Gulf War. The sequel to *From Dusk till Dawn* was also made here. Are we back in the situation which prevailed in the mid-1980s, when several hundred international films were made in South Africa without ever reflecting an indigenous character?

Without a fully operational Film and Video Foundation it will never be possible to support the local industry adequately, and without clear film policy we will never be able to protect our local cinema. Until it has the wholehearted support of the ANC-led government our industry will never fulfil the promise of the small independent renaissance of the late 1980s.

DR MARTIN BOTHA has published four books on South African Cinema and was co-writer of the White Paper for the country's future film policy. He teaches film at the Cape Town Film and Television School and has completed a major study on gays in African, Asian and Latin American cinema.

Producers

Free Film Makers
Thabo Nel
41 Frost Avenue
Auckland Park
Johannesburg 2006
Tel: (27 11) 482 2131
Fax: (27 11) 482 4024

Independent Film Centre
Carl Fischer
Toron Studios
2 Johannesburg Road
Highlands North
Johannesburg 2192
Tel: (27 11) 786 2360
Fax: (27 11) 887 2975

M-Net
New Directions
Michael Cheze
137 Hendrik Verwoerd Drive
Randburg 2125
Tel: (27 11) 329 5162
Fax: (27 11) 329 5167

Anant Singh
134 Essenwood Road
Berea
Durban 4001
Tel: (27 31) 224 000
Fax: (27 31) 222 444

Scy Productions
Helena Spring
3rd Floor
Blairgowrie Plaza
70 Conrad Drive
Blairgowrie 2194
Tel: (27 11) 789 1353
Fax: (27 11) 789 1376

Sonneblom Films
Katinka Heyns
PO Box 3940
Honeydew 2040
Tel: (27 11) 794 2100
Fax: (27 11) 794 2061

Nu World Services
Danny Lerner
PO Box 3903
Booysens
Johannesburg 2000
Tel: (27 11) 494 4311
Fax: (27 11) 494 1236

Underdog Productions
Marc Schwinges
PO Box 78965
Sandton 2146
Tel: (27 11) 325 5252
Fax: (27 11) 325 6252
e-mail: Underdog@Global.co.za
www.safilm.org.za/underdog

Distributors

Nu Metro
PO Box 392026
Bramley
Johannesburg 2018
Tel: (27 11) 880 7040
Fax: (27 11) 442 7030

Ster Kinekor
Mike Ross
PO Box 76461
Wendywood 2144
Tel: (27 11) 455 7700
Fax: (27 11) 444 0659

UIP Warner
7 Junction Avenue
Castrol House
Parktown

Johannesburg 2000
Tel: (27 11) 484 4215
Fax: (27 11) 484 3339

Useful Addresses

Black Filmmakers Association
George Menoe
141 Commissioner Street
Kine Entertainment Center
Johannesburg 2000
Tel: (27 11) 331 1813
Fax: (27 11) 331 1805

The Camera Guild
Antoinette Steinhobel
11 Frenschhoek Bergbron
Northcliff x.19
1709
Tel: (27 11) 673 3889
Fax: (27 11) 673 3889

The Cape Film and Video Foundation
PO Box 16140
Gardens 8001
Tel: (27 21) 480 3158
Fax: (27 21) 480 3205

The Cape Film and TV School
John Hill
18 Rhodes Avenue
Mowbray 7700
Tel: (27 21) 685 4358
Fax: (27 21) 686 9410

Department of Arts, Culture, Science and Technology
Neville Sing
Private Bag x894
Pretoria 0001
Tel: (27 12) 314 6132
Fax: (27 12) 323 2720
(For information on the Film Development Strategy)

The Film Lab
Guido Rasura
Coode House
Portswood Business Park
Portswood Close
V & A Waterfront
Cape Town 8002
Tel: (27 21) 418 4030
Fax: (27 21) 418 4037

Film Resource Unit
Mike Dearham

Training, Distribution and Resource Centre
Gate 2
Newtown Cultural Precinct
1 President Street
Johannesburg 2001
Tel: (27 11) 838 4280/1/2
Fax: (27 11) 838 4451
e-mail: fru@wn.apc.org

The French Institute of South Africa
Alexandre de Clermont-Tonnerre
PO Box 542
Newtown 2113
Tel: (27 11) 836 0561/3
Fax: (27 11) 836 0564

National Television and Video Association of Southern Africa
Tel: (27 21) 480 3100
Fax: (27 21) 480 3101

Performing Arts Workers' Equity (PAWE)
Lennox Ntsimango
Room 409, Fourth Floor
Atlantic Hse.
16 Corporation Street
Cape Town 8000
Tel: (27 21) 461 6920
Fax: (27 21) 836 4425

Podium Digital Realiti
David Johnson
3rd Floor
Foretrust Building
Martin Hammeschlag Way
Foreshore
Cape Town 8001
Tel: (27 21) 410 8158
Fax: (27 21) 211 383
e-mail: dav@oppcom.co.za

Screen Africa
Angela van Schalkwyck
29 Linden Road
Strathavon
Sandton 2031
Tel: (27 11) 884 3162
Fax: (27 11) 883 9281

Showdata
Alan Hammond: Showdata
Webmaster
PO Box 15756
Vlaeberg
Cape Town 8018
Tel: (27 21) 683 7280

e-mail: admin@showdata.org.za
www.showdata.org.za

Six Street Studios
Graham Beaumont
Longkloof Studios
Darters Road
Gardens
Cape Town 8001
Tel (27 21) 480 3100
Fax (27 21) 480 3101

South African Guild of Editors
PO Box 66105
Broadway
Kensington
Johannesburg 2020
Tel/Fax: (27 11) 614 7596

**Southern African
International Film &
Television Market**
Dezi Rorich
PO Box 3832
Johannesburg 2000
Tel: (27 11) 714 3229
Fax: (27 11) 714 3275
e-mail: saftvm@sabc.co.za
www.showdata.org.za/market

**South African Scriptwriters'
Association**
Dermod Judge
Tel: (27 21) 483 1653
Fax: (27 21) 438 3268
e-mail: dermod@aztec.co.za

The Whole Lot Directory
Barry Lucas
50 Montrose Avenue
Oranjezicht
Cape Town
South Africa
Tel: (27 21) 462 4523
Fax: (27 21) 461 4282
e-mail: tetra@aztec.co.za
www.wholelot.co.za
(Excellent informations base on the
South African film industry)

Women in Film
Merrilee Kick
PO Box 130982
Bryanston 2021
Tel: (27 11) 706 5784

SOUTH KOREA
Frank Segers

Korea's cinema landscape offers a bleak prospect. Domestic production is down, acquisition of foreign films is but a memory, red ink is flowing on the books of the smaller independent producers as well as the much-vaunted *chaebols*, the big conglomerates. It is hard to believe that the economic plight of this nation of 46.4 million citizens could get much worse. The International Monetary Fund bail-out, designed in part to stem the haemorrhaging local currency, the won, is exacting its toll. The entertainment industry is said to be in a state of near paralysis.

Koreans in recent years grew accustomed to an economy generating annual growth rates of seven or eight per cent. Imagine the chagrin when the 1997 figure came in at 4.9 per cent, followed by negative growth of 3.4 per cent in the first half of 1998. Conglomerates like Samsung, Daewoo, Hyundai and SKC, which have in recent times become formidable producers, accounting for more and more of the nation's domestic film funding, are by no means exempt from the economic sting.

Samsung's audio-visual subsidiary registered a 13 per cent fall in revenue in 1998's first quarter; the comparable unit at Daewoo dropped eight per cent. To compound that bad news, some of the more traditional sources of production finance, so-called chungmu-re capital from smaller independents, disappeared as more indies went out of business.

The current period is considered the most turbulent in South Korea's 75-year film history (foreign films were introduced on the peninsula in the early 1900s, but the first domestic film from a Korean producer did not emerge until 1923). A total of 59 films – new issues and some re-releases from domestic producers – were distributed in 1997, down from 64 in each of the two preceding years. The number of new productions dipped to 53, down from 70 in 1996, but the number of foreign imports, largely American, remains formidable – 271 in 1997, or roughly five titles a week. Attendance at the year's most popular imported feature, Steven Spielberg's *The Lost World: Jurassic Park*, was nearly twice as high as the figure for

The Contact, 1997's top Korean title, which in turn outperformed the second most popular local feature, *Downfall,* by 40 per cent.

In addition, the strong exposure in recent years of Korean cinema internationally seemed to have diminished in 1997. To pick up the slack, film festivals of various sizes and persuasions were mounted. The second Pusan International Film Festival kicked off in October, featuring 170 films from 30 countries. The first Puchon International Fantastic Film Festival, staged in August and early September, drew large audiences. The 42nd Asia-Pacific Film Festival was hosted in October in Cheju Island. The first Seoul Feminist Film Festival and the second Seoul Documentary Film Festival – documentary features still find a commercial niche in South Korea – were held in April, followed by the International Children's Festival in the capital city in July.

Innocence and experience

Despite the troubled landscape, Korean cinema managed to produce worthwhile features that, miraculously, proved popular with critics and public. **The Contact**, directed by 31-year-old Jang Yoon-Hyun, won the grand prize at Korea's Grand Bell Awards. This tells the sweetly melodramatic tale of a forlorn young couple who extricate themselves from tangled relationships via computer communication (talk about a *deus ex machina*). **Downfall** came from the dean of domestic directors, 62-year-old Im, Kwon-Taek, whose body of work (15 films since 1962) warrants considerable inter-national attention. *Downfall's* protagonist is a hardened prostitute who finds that the kindly man who appears occasionally in her life is her key to emotional freedom. Im's subject seemed to appeal to general audiences but not to all of the critics, some of whom rated *Downfall* as one of his lesser works.

With his feature debut, **Green Fish**, 34-year-old Lee Chang-Dong delivered the biggest critical hit of 1997. The film, which played at the 1998 Hong Kong

Shin Zun-Kyung in DOWNFALL

International Film Festival, concerns the tribulations of a young, somewhat innocent man who befriends a ruthless club-owner's moll given to riding trains at night. The film contains a sense of romantic longing set against explicit violence, paralleling the tension in Korean life between a longing for family tradition and get-rich-at-all-costs materialism.

Another of 1997's most acclaimed outings, **Push! Push!**, came from 50-year-old director Park Cheol-Soo, and appealed to the continuing Korean fascination with things genital (another popular 1997 feature was *Mr Condom*). A low-budget social satire set in an obstetrics clinic, *Push! Push!* presents the differing styles and philosophies of two women physicians. Amid routine deliveries and abortions, there is a dramatically crucial birth of test-tube twins. What's next as a feature subject – open heart surgery?

Chung, Ji-Young walked off with the Grand Bell for Best Director. His **Black Jack** is an engaging if convoluted tale of a self-involved embezzler's precarious involvement with a none-too-bright but very pretty woman who turns out to be smarter than she appears. Critics loved it, the public was less keen.

Heartbreak motel

Among the most internationally marketable of 1997's new domestic films were three from first-time directors. **Motel Cactus**, from 37-year-old Park Ki-Yong, appears to have the greatest commercial appeal of the trio. Set in a "love hotel", the film picks out moments in the lives of four couples as they start or end an affair, yearn for a new liaison or resume an old one. What is not said or shown is as important as what is.

A bit more down-to-earth is **Bath House: 3pm Paradise** from Kwak, Kyung-Taek, a pleasantly watery exercise about afternoons in a small, neighbourhood bath house in the coastal city of Pusan, the director's home patch (although he studied at New York University's film school). *Bath House* is a light-hearted, episodic effort, a solid showcase for locals known for hot tempers and warm hearts. The plot, such as it is, turns on the comic encounters of strangers confronting one another nude in a public place – a very Korean ritual.

As mentioned earlier, documentary features still sometimes have commercial life in South Korea. One of 1997's best, Byun Young-Joo's **Habitual Sadness**, concerns another national fascination – the plight of the "comfort women" commandeered by the Japanese Imperial Army to service the troops in the colonial period of 1930-40. Byun wrenchingly surveys the horrible past of these ageing grandmothers, who became increasingly comfortable with the director's cameras as the shoot progressed. Byun, a graduate of Ehwa Women University's law department, is perhaps Korea's most perceptive documentarist. Her mission in letting these women tell their stories is much the same as those Western documentarists addressing the Holocaust: "Lest we forget."

Han Seok-Kyu and Chun Do-Yun in THE CONTACT

The year's greatest fiasco was **Insh Allah**, which, with a budget of almost $1.15m, was hugely expensive for a Korean production. Backed by the giant Jeiljedang corporation, it was lavishly mounted and shot in a number of foreign locations, including the Sahara. But when it opened in Seoul cinemas, customers, as the old adage goes, could have shot deer in the balcony. Total admissions hit 42,000, a fraction of the audience pulled by *The Contact*. What went wrong is still being debated by critics. One has concluded that *Insh Allah* destroyed the "illusion" that the film business is capable of producing a "golden egg" project. Many such illusions are being similarly tested in the tough 1997–98 period.

Grand Bell Awards

Best Film: *The Contact*, directed by Jang, Yoon-Hyun, produced by Myung Film Co.
Best Director: Chung, Ji-Young for *Black Jack*.
Best Actor: Han, Suk-Kyu for *The Contact*.
Best Actress: Shim, Hye-Jin for *Green Fish*.
Best New Director: Jang, Yoon-Hyun for *The Contact*.

SPAIN

Peter
Besas

The surge of new film-making that swept total feature production in Spain close to the hundred mark in 1996 slackened off slightly last year, with 73 pictures completed, and a similar figure is expected for 1998. The commercial success of a dozen of these films proves that many local film-makers and writers are well attuned to their audiences' tastes.

This high volume of production is made possible thanks to a solid industrial infrastructure. With such major financing groups as Sogetel, Telefónica, Spanish Television (RTVE), Antena 3 TV, as well as regional television networks and provincial governments involved, the economic basis for production finance is firm. Major producers such as Lolafilms, Aurum, Elias Querejeta, Cartel, Fernando Colomo, Gerardo Herrero and Mate Production assure a steady flow of highly professional, high-quality product.

Even if it fails to make a big splash abroad, Spanish cinema is doing well at home. In the first four months of 1998, domestic films succeeded in cornering a 13.2 per cent audience share, the highest for 13 years. Moreover, 35 films went into production during the same period. The local scene is buzzing. It is also significant that the most successful Spanish films last year were not just tasteless boulevard pap. The hits included work from established directors – Pedro Almodóvar's **Live Flesh** (*Carne Trémula*) and Juanma Bajo Ulloa's eclectic **Airbag** – and sensitive, intimate films like Ricardo Franco's **The Good Star** (*La Buena Estrella*) and Montzo Armendariz's **Secrets of the Heart** (*Secretos del Corazón*).

The scope of filmgoers' interests within Spain is wide. One of the most successful efforts of the year was a madcap comedy-spoof geared to the youth market: actor-turned-director Santiago Segura's **Torrente – The Dumb Arm of the Law** (*Torrente – El*

The drunken, sexist cop "hero" of TORRENTE

Brazo Tonto De La Ley). The film's "hero" is a patriotic, fascist, sexist, racist drunken policeman. At the other end of the scale was Carlos Saura's lyrical **Tango**, featuring exquisite dance sequences (cinematographer Vittorio Storaro received the Technical Prize at Cannes 1998), although the plot was rather wobbly.

Local heroes

The "new generation" of hard-hitting Spanish film-makers is now well established. One can expect a film a year from such directors as Bajo Ulloa, Alex de la Iglesia (*Perdita Durango*) and Rafael Moleón, who made **Question of Luck** (*Cuestión de Suerte*) and **Liquid Glance** (*Mirada Liquida*). Perhaps the "hottest" director at the moment is Alejandro Almenabar, who followed up his amazingly successful debut *Thesis* (*Tesis*), about a snuff murder, with an equally popular thriller, **Open Your Eyes** (*Abre Los Ojos*).

Established directors now in their fifties and sixties help keep the local scene lively.

In 1997–98, this group was represented by Mario Camus, who scored with **The Colour of the Clouds** (*El Color de Las Nubes*), Vicente Aranda, with **The Other Man's Look** (*La Mirada de Otro*), Fernando Colomo, with **That** (*Eso*) and Bigas Luna. The last named's **The Chambermaid of the Titanic** (*La Camarera del Titanic*) was a "difficult" and convoluted film, which had little to do with the famous ship. Bigas is now preparing the Latin-titled **Volaverunt**, based upon a historical whodunit. The murder victim in this case was the Duchess of Alba, better known as the model for Goya's *Maja Unclothed*, and one of the suspects is the painter himself.

Deaths and disappointments

Unfortunately, two of the country's top veteran directors passed away in the course of the year: Pilar Miró, whose **The Dog in the Manager** (1997) had been a great success, and Ricardo Franco, who died during the final week's shooting on **Black Tears** (*Lágrimas Negras*). The film was completed by his assistant.

The diversity in Spanish production is astounding; but, whatever the subject, most films continue to languish at the box-office. Many never get released, or wind up on pay-TV, or run a week in an art-house cinema before being forgotten forever. Nevertheless, enough local films strike box-office gold to keep production on an upbeat scale.

Meanwhile, more and more screens are opening around the country, as multi-national companies set up multiplexes in shopping centres and satellite cities, as well as in major provincial capitals. Co-productions with other countries (Argentina, France, the US) provide not only welcome financing, but also introduce new talent, such as Argentinian director Adolfo Aristarain, or actors Federico Luppi, also from Argentina, and Luis Alberto García, from Cuba.

While quantity does not necessarily assure quality, the large number of projects certainly provides an outlet for new talent in all phases of film-making. Thus a fine, relatively unknown middle-aged actor, Ramón Barea, has been directing his first feature, **Pecata Minuta**, the unknown Pilar Tavora is making a new version of Lorca's **Yerma**, and well-known Peruvian director

Dancers in Carlos Saura's TANGO

Francisco Lombardi is making **Don't Tell Anyone** (*No Se Lo Digas a Nadie*). All this makes for an effervescent film scene, which at present is one of the most dynamic in Europe.

PETER BESAS has lived in Madrid since the mid-1960s and is chief of *Variety's* Latin American bureau. He has written various books, including a history of Spanish cinema.

Goya Awards

Best Film: *Lucky Star*.
Best Director: Ricardo Franco (*Lucky Star*).
Best Actor: Antonio Resines (*Lucky Star*).
Best Actress: Cecilia Roth for Martin (*H*).
Best Supporting Actor: Jose Sancho (*Live Flesh*).
Best Supporting Actress: Charo Lopez (*Secrets of the Heart*).
Most Promising Young Actor: Andoni Erburu (*Secrets of the Heart*).
Most Promising Young Actress: Isabel Ordaz (*Chevrolet*).

Best Original Screenplay: Ricardo Franco and Angeles Gonzalez Sinde (*Lucky Star*).
Best Adapted Screenplay: Bigas Luna and Cuca Canals (*The Chambermaid of the Titanic*).
Best Cinematography: Jaume Peracaula (*The Colour of Clouds*).
Best Original Music: Eva Gancedo (*Lucky Star*).
Best Animation Film: *Megasonics*.
Best Short: *Hunters* (Dir. Achero Manas).
Best European Film: *The Full Monty* (Dir. Peter Cattaneo; UK).
Best Spanish-Language Foreign Film: *Ashes of Paradise* (Dir. Marcelo Piñeyro; Argentina).
Honorary Academy Award: Rafael Azcona.

Recent and Forthcoming Films

VOLAVERUNT

Script: Bigas Luna and Cuca Canals, based on the novel by Antonion Larretta. Dir: Luna. Phot: José Luis Alcaine. Players: Aitana Sánchez-Gijón, Penelope Cruz, Jorge Perrugoria. Prod: Mate Production.

LA SOLEDAD ERA ESTO (That Was Solitude)

Script: Imanol Uribe and Juan José Millás, based on the novel by Millás. Dir: Uribe. Phot: Javier Aguirresarobe. Players: Charo López, Héctor Alterio, Ingrid Rubio, Giancarlo Giannini. Prod: Enrique Cerezo P.C.

EXTRAÑOS (Strangers)

Script: Imanol Uribe and Lourdes Iglesias. Dir: Uribe. Phot: Gonzaolo Fernández Berridi. Players: María Casal, Carmelo Gómez. Prod: Enrique Cerezo P.C.

EL REGRESO DE FUMANCHU (The Fiendish Trap of Fu Manchu)

Script: Alex de la Iglesia and Jorge Guerricaechevarria. Dir: de la Iglesia. Prod: Lolafilms.

EL EMBRUJO DE SHANGHAI (The Shanghai Gesture)

Script and Dir: Víctor Erice, based on the novel by Juan Marsé. Players: Fernando Fernán Gómez. Prod: Rocabruno

LAS HUELLAS BORRADAS (The Faded Footprints)

Script: Enrique Gabriel and Lucía Lipschutz. Dir: Gabriel. Photo: Raúl Pérez Cubero. Players: Federico Luppi. Prod: Trastorno Films.

LA NIÑA DE TUS OJOS (The Girl of Your Dreams)

Script: Rafael Azcona and David Trueba. Dir: Fernando Trueba. Phot: Jaime Aguirresarobe. Players: Penelope Cruz, Enrico Lo Verso, Antonio Resines, Jorge Sanz. Prod: Lolafilms.

LISBOA (Lisbon)

Script: Antonio Hernández and Enrique Braso. Dir: Hernández. Phot: Juan Carlois Gómez. Players: Carmen Maura, Federico Luppli, Vittorio Gassman. Prod: Blue Legend Productions.

LA NOVENA PUERTA (The Ninth Door)

Script: Enrique Urbizu, Roman Polanski, John Brown, based on the novel *The Club Dumas*, by Arturo Pérez Reverte. Dir: Polanski. Phot: Darius Khondji. Players: Johnny Depp, Lena Olin, Frank Langella. Prod: Origen P.C./Kinovision, S.L./Orly Films/ Roman Polanski Productions/ Live Entertainment.

Producers

Aurum Films
Isla Fuerteventura 21
28700 San Sebastián
de los Reyes, Madrid
Tel: (34 91) 663 9000
Fax: (34 91) 663 9320

Avanti Films
Rda. Sant Pere, 46, 5è
08010 Barcelona
Tel: (34 93) 268 1233
Fax: (34 93) 268 1617

Bailando en la Luna
Plaza de España 18, piso B, 11
28008 Madrid
Tel: (34 91) 548 3090
Fax: (34 91) 547 9821

Boca a Boca Producciones
Marqués de Valdeiglesias 5, 2 Izqa
28004 Madrid
Tel: (34 91) 532 0900
Fax: (34 91) 532 8381

Cartel
Lanzarote 4
Polígono Ind. "Los Alamillos"
San Sebastián de los Reyes
28700 Madrid
Tel: (34 91) 654 2857
Fax: (34 91) 654 3455

El Deseo SA
Ruiz Perelló, 15, bajo centro
28028 Madrid
Tel: (34 91) 725 0106/7
Fax: (34 91) 355 7467

Elías Querejeta PC
Maestro Lasalle 21
28016 Madrid
Tel: (34 91) 345 7139
Fax: (34 91) 345 2811

Els Films de la Rambla
Casp, 59, 3er, 2°
08010 Barcelona
Tel: (34 93) 265 3026
Fax: (34 93) 232 2870

Enrique Cerezo PC
Ferrán González 28
28009 Madrid
Tel: (34 91) 431 4790
Fax: (34 91) 431 7555

Esicma
Maestro Lasalle 15
28016 Madrid
Tel: (34 91) 345 8708
Fax: (34 91) 359 6683

Fernando Colomo PC
Génova 7, 2°, escalera interior
28004 Madrid
Tel: (34 91) 310 3834
Fax: (34 91) 310 4613

Fernando Trueba PC
Antonio Cavero, 37
28043 Madrid
Tel: (34 91) 759 6264
Fax: (34 91) 300 0104

Igeldo Komunikazioa
Aldamar 9, 5° izda.
20003 San Sebastián
Tel: (34 43) 431 252/3
Fax: (34 43) 427 794

Lola Films
Velázquez 12, 7°
28001 Madrid
Tel: (34 91) 431 246
Fax: (34 91) 435 5994

Mate Producciones
Hortaleza 59, 1A
28004 Madrid
Tel: (34 91) 532 0225
Fax: (34 91) 532 9450

Sogetel
Gran Via 32, 4°
28013 Madrid
Tel: (34 91) 524 7200
Fax: (34 91) 522 2297

Samarkanda
Capitán Haya, 51, 3°, 2 (Portal)
28020 Madrid
Tel: (34 91) 571 5334
Fax: (34 91) 571 5620

Starline
Principe de Vergara, 39
Madrid
Tel: (34 91) 431 5908
Fax: (34 91) 575 1181

Tornasol
Plaza Emilio Jiménez Millás, 2, 1°B
28008 Madrid
Tel: (34 91) 542 9564
Fax: (34 91) 542 8710

Distributors

Alta Films
Martin de los Heros 12
28008 Madrid
Tel: (34 91) 542 2702
Fax: (34 91) 542 8777

Araba Films
Avenice del Doctor Arce, 13
28002 Madrid
Tel: (34 91) 564 9498
Fax: (34 91) 564 5738

Buena Vista International (BVI)
José Bardasano Baos,
(Edif. Gorbea 3)
28016 Madrid
Tel: (34 91) 384 9460
Fax: (34 91) 766 9241

Columbia TriStar Films de España
Hernández de Tejada, 3
28027 Madrid
Tel: (34 91) 377 7100
Fax: (34 91) 377 7129

Cine Company
Zurbano 74, 2 dcha
28010 Madrid
Tel: (34 91) 442 2944
Fax: (34 91) 441 0098

Cine Mussy
Princesa 17, 2°
28008 Madrid
Tel: (34 91) 541 6869
Fax: (34 91) 541 5482

Filmayer
Edificio Bronce
Avda. de Burgos, 8A, 10°-1
28036 Madrid
Tel: (34 91) 383 1572
Fax: (34 91) 383 0845

Golem Distribucción
Avda. de Bayona 52
38008 Pamplona
Tel: (34 48) 174 141
Fax: (34 48) 171 058

Hispano Fox Films
Avda. de Burgos, 8A, Pl.11
28036 Madrid
Tel: (34 91) 343 4640
Fax: (34 91) 343 4655

Lauren Films
Balmes 87, principal
08008 Barcelona
Tel: (34 93) 451 4243
Fax: (34 93) 323 6155

Lider Films
Calle Isla Fuerteventura, 21, 1°
28700 San Sebastián de los Reyes
Madrid
Tel: (34 91) 657 9600
Fax: (34 91) 663 9320

Musidora Films
Princesa 17, 2
28008 Madrid
Tel: (34 91) 541 6869
Fax: (34 91) 541 5482

Prime Films
Aurelio Nuñez 5, 7°C
28002 Madrid
Tel: (34 91) 519 0181
Fax: (34 91) 413 0772

Sogepaq
Gran Via 32, 1°
28013 Madrid
Tel: (34 91) 524 7220
Fax: (34 91) 521 0875

Tripictures
Doce de Octubre, 28
28009 Madrid
Tel: (34 91) 574 9007/8
Fax: (34 91) 574 9005

U Films
Maestro Huerroero, 4
28015 Madrid
Tel: (34 91) 547 6585
Fax: (34 91) 542 7887

United International Pictures (UIP)
Plaza Callao 4, 6°
28013 Madrid
Tel: (34 91) 522 7261
Fax: (34 91) 532 2384

Vertigo
Silva 2, 4°, officina 4
28013 Madrid
Tel: (34 91) 542 2225
Fax: (34 91) 541 6985

Still from THE OTHER MAN'S LOOK

Wanda Films
Avda. Europa 9, Portal 3 bajo
Pozuelo 28224
Tel: (34 91) 352 8376
Fax: (34 91) 352 8371

Warner Sogefilms
Manuel Montilla 1
28016 Madrid
Tel: (34 91) 350 6200
Fax: (34 91) 345 1948

Sales Agents

Lauren Films International
Balmes 87, principal
08008 Barcelona
Tel: (34 91) 451 4243
Fax: (34 91) 323 6155

Lola Films International
Velázquez 12, 7°
28001 Madrid
Tel: (34 91) 431 4246
Fax: (34 91) 435 5994

Multimedia
Antonio Ruíz, 4
Pozuelo de Alarcón
28224 Madrid
Tel: (34 91) 351 3747
Fax: (34 91) 351 3748

RTVE
Dirección de Operaciones
Comerciales

Edificio Prado del Rey, 3°
Centro RTVE
28223 Madrid
Tel: (34 91) 581 7963
Fax: (34 91) 581 7757

Sogepaq International
Gran Via 32, 1°
28013 Madrid
Tel: (34 91) 524 7220
Fax: (34 91) 521 0875

Useful Addresses

Catalan Films & TV
Portal Santa Madrona, 68
08001 Barcelona
Tel: (34 93) 412 5640
Fax: (34 93) 412 1958

Federación de Asociaciones de Productores Audiovisuales Espanoles (FAPAE)
Capitán Haya, 50, 6° D
28020 Madrid
Tel: (34 91) 571 1682
Fax: (34 91) 571 1841

Instituto de la Cinematografia y de las Artes Audiovisuales (ICAA)
Plaza del Rey, 1
28071 Madrid
Tel: (34 91) 532 5089
Fax: (34 91) 522 9377

SRI LANKA — Amarnath Jayatilaka

In the early part of 1998, public outcry against the unavailability of major American movies in Sri Lanka came sharply into focus. In a letter to the *Sunday Observer* in April, the distinguished resident and science-fiction writer Arthur C.Clarke asked: "When will we have the chance to see the latest *Titanic* movie here, or for that matter any good foreign movies!"

The Film Exhibitors Association (FEA), which represents practically every cinema on the island, has laid the blame for Clarke's lament, shared by thousands of moviegoers, at the doors of the National Film Corporation (NFC). The FEA has been persistently lobbying for a relaxation in the NFC's rigorously imposed import restrictions. According to FEA Joint Secretary Sunil Siriwardena, the NFC's "intransigence, which heeds neither the interests of the industry nor the public, is pushing a once vibrant industry down the slope."

According to Imtiaz Carder, Executive Director of Liberty Cinemas Ltd, the terms and conditions imposed by the NFC are such that it is no longer feasible to import films. Although the Motion Picture Association of America is willing to send the latest Hollywood releases to Sri Lanka, their global policy prevents them from dealing with the NFC, who are not willing to review their policies. In 1994, when *Jurassic Park* was being screened, the average occupancy of cinemas was 64 per cent, but by 1997 it had dropped to merely 27 per cent. Managing director of Ceylon Theaters Ltd, Anthony Page, who has been involved in the industry for more than 25 years, said that over the last ten years admissions have dropped by just under a million – a fall of 46 per cent.

Tied by red tape

The drastic drop in cinema attendance, which is forcing the closure of many theatres, is being attributed by their owners to the poor quality films imported by the NFC. Academy Award winners of yesteryear can be screened, but do not draw the same crowds as the latest releases. Every exhibitor has to go through a large amount of 'red tape' in order to obtain a film. After the copy has been approved by the preview committee and the Public Performance Board (Censor Board) it can be screened. The cost of importing and the operational costs incurred while screening cannot be covered by revenue, especially since 23 per cent of income has to be handed to the NFC. Exhibitors, said Carder, are therefore running at a loss and are reduced to screening old movies, virtually to empty houses.

Exhibitors are also calling for the NFC to invest in cinema refurbishment to help bring back lost audiences, and resent the fact that the 23 per cent levy is not ploughed back into such work. Carder and Page argue that the film industry in Sri Lanka is probably the only private sector industry still subject to state control. With the public turning to the videos, video compact discs and DVDs which are storming the market, they believe the moviegoing habit is dying fast. Television also provides a variety of domestic and foreign programmes.

Under the prevailing conditions in the exhibition sector, not a single English-language movie enjoyed box-office success. Most of the Sinhala films released in 1997 were failures, except for **Giniawi**

Sha-Ginikeli, a crime thriller, and one soft porn film that clicked. The Tamil films imported from south India continue to thrive in Sri Lankan cinemas.

AMARNATH JAYATILAKA is a filmologist and one of the leading personalities in Sri Lankan cinema. He has been the country's *IFG* liaison for the last 25 years.

Useful Addresses

Ceylon Entertainment Ltd.
Liberty Cinemas Ltd.
35 Sri Anagarika Dharmapala
Mawata
Colombo 7
Tel: (94 1) 325 764
(Importer/exhibitors)

Ceylon Theares Ltd.
8 Sir C. Gardner Mawata
Colombo 2
Tel: (94 1) 431 243/431 109
(Producer/importer/exhibitor)

EAP Films & Theatres Ltd.
122 Ward Place
Colombo 7
Tel: (94 1) 694 517/694 608
Fax: (94 1) 694 845
(Producer/importer/exhibitor)

Film Location Services Ltd
Taprobane Pictures Ltd
790 Kotte Road, Etul Kotte
Tel: (94 1) 864 928/875 120
Fax: (94 1) 875 119
(Producer/importer/services)

National Film Corporation
224 Bauddhaloka Mawata
Colombo-07
Tel: (94 1) 580 247
Fax: (94 1) 585 526

SWEDEN

Bengt Forslund

It has been said that to get quality in film, you also need a certain quantity of films. I doubt it very much. Very good films can be made in countries with a very small production output and lack of money is not necessarily the main problem. It is more a question of a nation's film-making climate, of optimism, self-confidence and ensuring that the right people are in the right positions.

Sweden in 1997 is a good example. More films have been released than ever (meaning since 1963, when the Swedish Film Institute was founded): 30 films compared to an average of 20 or 25. But only half a dozen reached an audience of 100,000, and about the same proportion received half-way decent reviews. Almost none had any international success. The only film prized at big festivals was Liv Ullmann's *Private Conversations*, from the television drama by Ingmar Bergman, which was shown in Un Certain Regard in Cannes.

The shadow of Bergman looms yet again. He directed arguably the best film of the year: **In the Presence of a Clown** (*Larmar och gör sig till*), a television drama which was a fascinating homage to theatre, film and television. The best film of the year, according to the critics, was **Tic Tac**, directed by Daniel Alfredson, based on a script by Hans Renfäll, which picked up

Skinheads and soon-to-be victim in Daniel Alfredson's TIC TAC

three Golden Bugs. Like Daniel Bergman's **Expectations,** it is a Swedish *Short Cuts* about daily life in the 1990s, but both films had problems: the former being too smartly arranged for its own good, and the latter too ambitious, including stories about all kinds of Swedes from north to south.

Bringing up baby

Richard Hobert's **Run for Your Life**, with five Bug nominations, was an intelligent thriller about a family taking care of a baby born to a pair of illegal immigrants who are being chased by the Swedish police. Bergman-prized Hobert may finally make his breakthrough with his new film, *The Eye*. Advance word on it was favourable. The only film grabbing the attention of critics and public was the comedy hit **Adam & Eva**, by Måns Herngren and Hannes Holm. It may have a future as an American re-make, since the script has been bought by Hollywood. Another good comedy was **Unmarried Couples**, but like **Svensson, Svensson**, a trivial movie based on a popular Swedish soap opera, it is probably too Swedish in its concept to be appreciated abroad.

Best youth films of the year were Christina Olofsson's **Truth or Dare**, about teenage friendship and rivalry, and Christer Engberg's **Wild Angel**, about a group of problem kids putting on a musical. Best long documentary was Jan Troell's **A Frozen Dream** and best Nordic co-production was Nils Malmros' Danish epic, **Barbara**. This year kicked off with Anders Grönros' expensive and much delayed children's film **The Glassblower's Children**. Honoured by many critics, and well made, it had one major flaw: like the book on which it is based, it is a fairytale with more to offer grown-ups than children, which means a rather limited audience.

Action men

Two thrillers will be more lucky: **Hamilton**, the fourth movie in the series featuring Hamilton, Sweden's answer to James Bond, and Kjell Sundvall's **The Last Contract**, a film speculation about the murder of Swedish prime minister Olof

Lena Endre and Göran Stangertz in RUN FOR YOUR LIFE *photo: Nille Leander*

Palme in 1986. Both films are highly professional, proving that Scandinavians can also make Hollywood-style action movies – but so what? *Hamilton* is too cruel, with a detestable motorsaw-massacre replacing Bond's playful humour; *The Last Contract* is both too close and too far away from the reality of Palme's murder.

The negotiations regarding a new agreement for the Swedish Film Institute collapsed late last autumn and, in March this year, Lars Engquist, head of the Institute since 1994, was picked up by the government to become Secretary of Integration! His interim replacement, pending the announcement of that elusive new agreement (now due in 1999) is the Institute's administrative managing director, Hans Ottosson. Moreover, Svensk Filmindustri, the only heavy production centre in Sweden, with a glorious past from the silent era to Bergman, has once again reorganised. The new head is Jan Edholm, 34, but, like last year, we still await new declarations and visions.

Due to the film industry's economic problems in 1997, a general political instability and the circumstances mentioned above, very few films are now in production – with empty studios and unemployment the inevitable consequence. It is not easy to be optimistic, but it is a necessity – and if an artistic catastrophe like *Titanic* can be the success of the century, then nothing is impossible.

BENGT FORSLUND was a well-known film producer for 30 years at Svensk Filmindustri, the Swedish Film Institute and Nordic Film and TV Fund. He is also a film historian and author of several books on cinema, including the definitive study of Victor Sjöström, and a volume on Sven Nykvist.

The Golden Bugs 1998

Best Film: *Tic Tac*.
Best Direction: Daniel Alfredson (*Tic Tac*).
Best Actress: Johanna Sällström (*Under the Surface*).
Best Actor: Göran Stangertz (*Run for Your Life*).
Best Script: Annika Thor (*Truth or Dare*).
Best Camera: Jens Fischer (*Under the Surface*).
Best Supporting Actress: Tintin Anderzon (*Adam & Eva*).
Best Supporting Actor: Emil Forselius (*Tic Tac*).
Best Foreign Film: *The Ice Storm*.

Recent and Forthcoming Films

COMEDIA INFANTIL

Script: Tommy Karlmark, Solveig Nordlund. Dir: Nordlund. Phot: Lisa Hagstrand. Players: Sérgio Titos, Joao Manja. Prod: Torromfilm/Swedish Film Institute/ Prole Filme(Portugal)/ Avenida Producoes (Mocambique).

**DET SJUNDE SKOTTET
(The Seventh Shot)**

Script: Thore Soneson. Dir: Ulf Aldevinge. Phot: Hans-Åke Lerin. Players: Lena Nilsson, Örjan Rahmberg, Harriet Andersson. Prod: Pandora Film/Canal +/ Triangel Film/Viking Vision/ Swedish Film Institute.

**GLASBLÄSARENS BARN
(The Glassblower's Children)**

Script and Dir: Anders Grönros. Phot: Philip Øgaard. Players: Pernilla August, Stellan Skarsgärd, Jasmine Heikura, Oliver Pedius. Prod: Birkeland Film/Nordic Screen Prod/ Zentropa/Spice/TV 1000/Mutter Media/Danish, Norwegian and Swedish Film Institutes/Nordic Film & TV Fund/Eurimages.

HAMILTON

Script: Jonas Cornell, William Aldridge. Dir: Harald Zwart. Players: Peter Stormare, Lena

Olin, Mark Hamill. Prod: Moviola Film & Tele-vision/TV4/Yellow Cottage (Norge)/Nordic Film & TV Fund.

LUCKY PEOPLE CENTER INTERNATIONAL

[Documentary] Script and Dir: Erik Pauser, Johan Söderberg. Phot: Jan Röed. Prod: Memfis Film/ SVT Dok/Stockholm Records/Swedish Film Institute/ Nordic Film & TV Fund/Zentropa – TV2 – Statens Filmcentral (Denmark)/NRK (Norway)/Eurimages.

OGIFTA PAR (Unmarried Couples)

Script and Dir: Peter Dalle. Phot: Esa Vuorinen. Players: Lena Endre, Susanne Reuter, Peter Dalle John Ulveson. Prod: Cinema Art/Svensk Filmindustri/ SVT Drama/Zip Zap Prod/TV 1000/Swedish Film Institute.

**SANNA ÖGONBLICK
(True Moments)**

Script: Anders Wahlgren, Lena Koppel, Niklas Rädström, Peter Kandimaa. Dir: Koppel, Wahlgren. Phot: Jens Fischer. Players: Lena Endre, Krister Henrikson, Anita Björk. Prod: Omega Film & Television/ Sandrew Film/Rip Off/Tonservice/

Suecia Film/SVT/Jˆrn Donner Prod (Finland)/ (Metronome (Denmark)/Swedish Film Institute/ Nordic Film & TV Fund/ Eurimages.

**SANNING OCH KONSEKVENS
(Truth or Dare)**

Script: Annika Thor. Dir: Christina Olofsson. Phot: Robert Nordström. Players: Tove Edfeldt, Alexandra Dahlström, Anna Gabrielsson. Prod: CO Film/Sandrew Film/duR Film/Swedish Film Institute.

SISTA KONTRAKTET (The Last Contract)

Script: Mats Arehn, Johan Bogaus, Börje Hansson. Dir: Kjell Sundvall. Phot: Kjell Lagerros. Players: Mikael Persbrandt, Michael Kitchen, Pernilla August, Reine Brynolfsson. Prod: Filmlance Int/TV 4/Svensk Filmindustri/Yellow Cottage – Norsk Film (Norway)/Kinoprod Oy (Finland)/Norway and Swedish Film Institute/Finnish Film Foundation/Nordic Film & TV Fund/Eurimages.

SJÖN (The Lake)

Script: Hans Iveberg. Dir: Hans Åke Gabrielsson. Phot: Björn Blixt. Players: Regina Lund, Fredrik Hammar, Gösta Bredefeldt. Prod:

Omega Film & Television/Spice Prod/Nordisk Film & TV (Denmark)/Swedish Film Institute.

SPRING FÖR LIVET
(Run for Your Life)

Script and Dir: Richard Hobert. Phot: Lars Crépin. Players: Camilla Lundén, Göran Stangertz, Lena Endre. Prod: Cimbria Film/SVT Malmö/Swedish Film Institute.

SVENSKA HJÄLTAR
(Expectations)

Script: Reidar Jönsson. Dir: Daniel Bergman. Phot: Esa Vuorinen. Prod: Svensk Filmindustri/TV 4/Swedish Film Institute/Per Holst Film (Denmark)/Nordic Film & TV Fund.

SVENSSON, SVENSSON

Script: Michael Hjort, Johan Kindblom, Tomas Tivemark. Dir: Björn Gunnarsson. Phot: Mats Olofsson. Players: Susanne Reuter, Allan Svensson. Prod: SVT Drama/Svensk Filmindustri.

TIC TAC

Script: Hans Renfäll. Dir: Daniel Alfredson. Phot: Peter Mokronsinski. Players: Tintin Anderzon, Thomas Hanzon, Jacob Nordenson. Prod: Sandrew Film/Swedish Film Institute.

Stellan Skarsgård in THE GLASSBLOWER'S CHILDREN
photo: Anders Birkeland

UNDER YTAN
(Under the Surface)

Script and Dir: Daniel Fridell. Phot: Jens Fischer. Players: Johanna Sällström, Mikael Persbrandt, Tove Appelqvist. Prod: Reaction Pictures/Swedish Film Institute/Nordisk Film (Denmark)/Nordic Film & TV Fund.

VERANDA FÖR EN TENOR
(Veranda for a Tenor)

Script: Klas Östergren, Lisa Ohlin. Dir: Ohlin. Phot: Anders Bohman. Players: Johan Hson Kjellgren, Krister Henrikson, Lena B Eriksson. Prod: Svensk Filmindustri/Migma Film/Swedish Film Institute.

Producers

Cimbrua Film
Östra Parkskolan
S-272 31 Simrishamn
Tel: (46) 4141 6660
Fax: (46) 4141 6661

Cinema Art Productions
Box 20105
S-161 02 Bromma
Tel: (46) 8799 6900
Fax: (46) 898 1005

FilmLance International
Box 27156
S-102 52 Stockholm
Tel: (46) 8665 1100
Fax: (46) 8662 0444

Götafilm
Haraldsgatan 6
S-413 14 Göteborg
Tel: (46) 3182 5570
Fax: (46) 3182 0860

Memfis Film & Television
Upplandsgatan 35
S-113 28 Stockholm
Tel: (46) 833 5576
Fax: (46) 830 9934

MovieMakers Sweden
Råsundavägen 150
S-171 30 Solna
Tel: (46) 8730 2850
Fax: (46) 8730 2853

Moviola Film
Box 20102
S-161 02 Bromma
Tel: (46) 8799 6900
Fax: (46) 829 1386

Omega Film & Television
Box 27888
S-115 93 Stockholm
Tel: (46) 820 0555
Fax: (46) 820 0595

Pictures in Motion
Box 16371
S-103 26 Stockholm
Tel: (46) 8762 7700
Fax: (46) 8762 7760

Reaction Pictures
Drakens gränd 6
S-111 30 Stockholm
Tel: (46) 820 3450
Fax: (46) 820 3423

Sandrew Film
Box 5612
S-114 86 Stockholm
Tel: (46) 823 4700
Fax: (46) 810 3850

Spice Produktion
Box 20105
S-161 02 Bromma
Tel: (46) 8799 6900
Fax: (46) 898 6863

Svensk Filmindustri
S-127 83 Stockholm
Tel: (46) 8680 3500
Fax: (46) 8710 4460

Sveriges Television/Drama
S-105 10 Stockholm
Tel: (46) 8784 0000
Fax: (46) 8664 5418

Sweetwater
Grev Turegatan 21
S-114 38 Stockholm
Tel: (46) 8662 1470
Fax: (46) 8662 1471

Viking Film
Sturegatan 8
S-114 35 Stockholm
Tel: (46) 8679 9115
Fax: (46) 8679 9120

Distributors

Atlantic Film
Box 21112
S-100 31 Stockholm
Tel: (46) 830 5230
Fax: (46) 830 5280

Buena Vista International
Box 5631
S-113 86 Stockholm
Tel: (46) 8440 5200
Fax: (46) 8678 0728

Columbia TriStar Films
Box 9501
S-102 74 Stockholm
Tel: (46) 8658 1140
Fax: (46) 884 1204

Egmont Film
Box 507
S-183 25 Taby
Tel: (46) 8510 10050
Fax: (46) 8510 12046

Folkets Bio
Box 2068
S-103 12 Stockholm
Tel: (46) 8402 0820
Fax: (46) 8402 0827

Fox Film
S-127 83 Stockholm
Tel: (46) 8680 3500
Fax: (46) 8710 4460

Novemberfilm
Nidarosgatan 4, 2tr.
S-164 34 Kista
Tel: (46) 8751 5144
Fax: (46) 8632 0185

Polfilm
Östra Rönneholmsvägen 4
S-211 47 Malmö
Tel: (46) 812 4044
Fax: (46) 812 4044

Sandrew Film
Box 5612
S-114 86 Stockholm
Tel: (46) 823 4700
Fax: (46) 810 3850

Scanbox Sweden
Box 111 28
S-161 11 Bromma
Tel: (46) 828 5111
Fax: (46) 828 4111

Sonet Film
Box 20105
S-161 02 Bromma
Tel: (46) 8799 6900
Fax: (46) 828 5834

Svensk Filmindustri
S-127 83 Stockholm
Tel: (46) 8680 3500
Fax: (46) 8710 4460

Triangel film
Box 285
S-201 22 Malmö
Tel: (46) 4012 5547
Fax: (46) 4012 9099

United International Pictures
Box 9502
S-102 74 Stockholm
Tel: (46) 8616 7400
Fax: (46) 884 3870

Warner Bros
Box 9503
S-102 74 Stockholm
Tel: (46) 8658 1050
Fax: (46) 8658 6482

Willmar Andersson Film
Box 5612
S-114 86 Stockholm
Tel: (46) 823 4700
Fax: (46) 810 3850

Useful Addresses

The National Archive of Recorded Sound and Moving Image
Box 27890
S-115 93 Stockholm
Tel: (46) 8783 3700
Fax: (46) 8663 1811

The Swedish Film Distributors' Association
Box 49084
S-100 28 Stockholm
Tel: (46) 8785 0400
Fax: (46) 8653 2425

Swedish Film Institute
Box 27126
S-102 52 Stockholm
Tel: (46) 8665 1100
Fax: (46) 8661 1820

Swedish Film Producers' Association
Box 1008
S-171 21 Solna
Tel: (46) 8730 5780
Fax: (46) 827 3745

The Swedish Institute
Cultural Film Events
Box 7434
S-103 91 Stockholm
Tel: (46) 8789 2000
Fax: (46) 820 72 48

SWITZERLAND — Pierre Lachat

Fredi Murer's **Full Moon** was the cinema event of the year. It was one of the most costly Swiss productions of recent years, with a budget of $4.5m (7m Swiss francs; more than three times the average for a domestic feature), and with about half that amount coming from state funds, it was the most convincing argument yet in favour of concentrating state film finance on large, single projects.

However, it fared relatively poorly at the box-office – a particular disappointment in light of the new system under which subsidised film are awarded premiums based on their commercial success, the money being channelled into the producer and director's next feature. This new set-up is possibly the last chance for the 30-year old film support system to justify its continued existence, after the meagre results evinced since the mid-1980s. If these new attempts fail at least to effect a return to the results of the 1970s and early 1980s, then the days of the current system may be numbered.

At 58, strong-minded documentarist and story-teller Murer (a 1960s pioneer of experimental film), only partially managed to follow up on the success of *Alpine Fire* (1985), the present-day 'Greek tragedy' of

Mariebelle Kuhn and Felix Rellstab in FULL MOON
photo: Luca Zanetti

children doing away with their parents, which was the last internationally noted milestone in Swiss cinema. *Full Moon* is a fantastical story of a police inspector's search for mysteriously disappearing children who turn out to have entered a parallel world. The truth of the matter is that the film denies any rational explanation and owes its uniqueness to the unexplainable. Many cinemagoers simply did not know what to make of it.

At first glance, the theme is children, but they appear in isolation, because the actual

theme is the generations which have lost touch with each other. Murer's initial plan was a double film which should have reflected both sides of abandonment: how parents become childless and children parentless. This comprehensive project was significantly too expensive for Switzerland and had to be separated into two features; a split that was of little benefit.

The concentration of means on this single project paid off artistically, but not commercially. No other feature to date displays a scale or ambition to match this one: neither the love story **L'amour fou**, from Michel Rodde, nor the emigrant drama **Waalo Fendo** from Mohammed Soudani, nor Jean-Luc Wey's elegiac comedy **L'année du Capricorne**. We must wait to see how forthcoming projects will fare, namely those from Alain Tanner (*Requiem*), Claude Champion (*Fin de siècle*), Francis Reusser (*Guerre dans le Haut-Pays*) or Rolando Colla (*Le monde à l'envers*).

Captain courageous

Like Murer in fiction, Richard Dindo continues on his own tenacious path in documentary. His **Grüninger's Fall** is artistically and politically one of the most urgently needed films in a long time. A foolish TV premiere, to which the film-maker unwisely agreed, unfortunately defused its potential public impact. Television, which in Switzerland as in so many other countries has become enslaved to sensationalism, insisted on airing a massively shortened version. The broadcast of the 60-minute version received little response, in spite of a large audience, and achieved but one thing: no one could be motivated to see the full, 100-minute version, which is not a moment too long, in the cinemas.

And yet the story of Captain Grüninger, who, contrary to all orders, allowed Jewish refugees to enter Switzerland during the Second World War, for which he was later ostracised, is an exemplary Swiss topic: solidarity versus political stiffness, discipline versus human sympathy – a classic conflict between duty and

A skater from Peter Entell's documentary, ROLLING

inclination. The director guides the survivors of those years as if they were actors, and carefully dramatises without straining the documentary aspect. With his 30 years of experience, Dindo is one of the few European film-makers who also knows from a practical aspect no absolute 'either/or' between fiction and documentary. His films are never pure reporting, but are always, additionally, a commentary on form and methods.

Swiss documentary film-making remains as rich as ever. Fine examples from the past year included: Christian Davi's **Die Regierung**, about an orchestra of the disabled, Peter Entell's **Rolling**, on the art of in-line skating, Erich Langjahr's **The Farmers' War**, about agricultural endurance, Bruno Moll's **Brain Concert**, exploring consciousness research, and Karl Saurer's **Steinauer, Nebraksa**, focusing on descendants of Swiss emigrants in America. These documentaries have won for themselves a small but passionate cinema audience. In this way they contribute fundamentally to keeping the documentary tradition alive.

PIERRE LACHAT has published extensively on film in magazines and newspapers, as well as broadcasting on radio and television in Switzerland. He is a lecturer on film history at the University of Fribourg.

Recent and Forthcoming Films

L'AMOUR FOU (Requiem Glove)

Script and Dir: Michel Rodde. Phot: Denis Jutzeler. Players: Eléonore Hirt, Wojtek Pszoniak. Prod: Stalker Films/Balzli & Fahrer GmbH.

L'ANNÉE DU CAPRICORNE
(The Year of Capricorn)

Script: Jean-Luc Wey, Philippe Morand, Claude-Inga Barbey. Dir: Wey. Phot: Edwin Horak. Players: Claude-Inga Barbey, Maria Blanco, Károly Eperjes, Patrick Lapp, Maurice Aufair, Leyla Aubert. Prod: Bernard Lang AG/Wega Film.

BAUERNKRIEG
(The Farmers' War)

Script, Dir and Phot: Erich Langjahr. Prod: Langjahr Film-produktions GmbH. Documentary.

BRAIN CONCERT

Dir: Bruno Moll. Phot: Hansueli Schenkel. Prod: T & C Film. Documentary.

CROWDED JUNGLE – TUMULT IM URWALD

Script and Dir: Lisa Faessler. Phot: Pio Corradi, Jürg Hassler. Prod: Andromeda Film. Documentary.

FIN DE SIÈCLE

Script and Dir: Claude Champion. Phot: Yves Pouliquen. Players: Mireille Perrier, Robert Bouvier, Laurent Sandoz, Julien Basler, Pascale Vachoux. Prod: Intermezzo Films.

VOLLMOND (Full Moon)

Script and Dir: Fredi M. Murer. Phot: Pio Corradi. Players: Hans-Peter Müller, Lilo Baur, Benedict Freitag, Yolande Moreau. Prod: T & C Film/Pandora/Arena Films.

MADE IN HONG KONG

Script: Luc Schaedler, Reto Tischhauser. Dir and Phot: Schaedler. Prod: Schaedler/Universität Zürich. Documentary.

MESCHUGGE

Script: Dani Levy, Maria Schrader. Dir: Levy. Phot: Carl F. Koschnick. Players: Levy, Schrader, David Strathairn, Nicole Heesters, Jeffrey Wright. Prod: X-Filme creative pool/Condor Films/Jugend Film.

LE MONDE À L'ENVERS

Script: Rolando Colla, Hansjörg Schertenleib, Jean Jourdheuil, Gianluigi Toccafondo, Elena Pedrazzoli. Dir: Colla. Phot: Peter Indergand. Players: Laurence Côte, Denis Lavant, Sara Capretti, Roshdy Zem, Yann Collette, Jean-Claude Grenier, Paolo M. Scalondro. Prod: Peacock/Gaïa Films/Fandango.

DIE REGIERUNG

Script and Dir: Christian Davi. Phot: Hans Schurmann. Prod: Magic Lantern Productions. Documentary.

REQUIEM

Script: Alain Tanner, Bernard Comment, Antonio Tabucchi, based on a novel by Tabucchi. Dir: Tanner. Phot: Hugues Ryffel. Players: Francis Frappat, André Marcon. Prod: CAB Productions/Gemini Films/Madragoa Filmes/Filmograph.

ROLLING

Script and Dir: Peter Entell. Phot: Camille Cottagnoud. Prod: Catpics Coproductions/Show and Tell Films. Documentary.

GELD ODER LEBEN
(working title)

Script and Dir: Marco Hausammann-Gilardi, Stephan Laur, Phot: Brian Dean Goff, Nicola Belucci. Prod: Mahagi Film/Tara Film.

L'AMOUR EN GUERRE
(working title)

Script: Francis Reusser, Jean-Claude Carrière, based on a novel by Charles Ferdinand Ramuz. Dir: Reusser. Phot: Christophe Beaucarne. Players: Yann Tregouet, Antoine Basler, François Marthouret, Marion Cotillard, Patrick Le Mauff, Eric Cousteaud, François Perrot, François Morel, Robert Bouvier. Prod: CAB Productions/Arena Films/Saga Films.

IRRLICHTER

Script: Carlo Meier, Christoph Kühn. Dir: Kühn. Phot: Peter Indergand. Players: Barbara Auer, Tobias Langhoff, Adolph Spalinger, Walo Lüönd, Christian Redl. Prod: Ventura Film/Cinecas Filmproduktion/Dor Film.

JOURNAL DE RIVESALTES 1941-42

Script and Dir: Jacqueline Veuve. Phot: Edwin Horak, Thomas Wütrich. Prod: Ciné Manufacture. Documentary. (Winner of the Swiss Film Prize 1998, Best Documentary).

DIE KINDER VON FURNA/JAHRE SPÄTER (Furna's Children)

Script, Dir, Phot and Prod:

Christian Schocher. Documentary.

LÉOPOLD R.

Script and Dir: Jean-Blaise Junod. Phot: Denis Jutzeler. Prod: Junod.

SPUREN VERSCHWINDEN

Script and Dir: Walo Deuber. Phot: Guido Noth. Prod: Rose-Marie Schneider Doc Productions/ Deuber. Documentary.

STEINAUER NEBRASKA

Script and Dir: Karl Saurer. Phot: Rolf Rosenberg, Hansueli Schenkel, John Spence. Prod: Saurer. Documentary.

STEPS OF MINDFULNESS – A JOURNEY WITH THICH NHAT HANH

Script, Dir and Phot: Thomas Lüchinger. Prod: roses for you/Beat Curti. Documentary.

TANZ DER HÄNDE
(Dance of Hands)

Script and Dir: Phil Dänzer, Peter Hemmi. Phot: Enrico de Marco. Prod: Etoile Productions. Documentary.

THREE BELOW ZERO

Script and Dir: Simon Aebi, Phot: Jamie Silverstein. Prod: Aebi/Kuhn.

WAALO FENDO (Là où la terre gèle)

Script: Mohammed Soudani, Saidou Moussa Ba. Dir: Soudani. Phot: Soudani, Alessio Viola. Players: Saidou Moussa Ba, Souleymane Ndiaye, Baara NíGom. Prod: Amka Films Productions. (Joint winner of the Swiss Film Prize 1998, Best Picture).

WER HAT ANGST VOR DEM UMBRISCHEN WOLF (Who's Afraid Of The Big Bad Wolf?)

Script, Dir and Phot: Clemens Klopfenstein. Players: Anne-Christine von Gablenz, Erika-Juliane Fischer, Johannes Hartmann, Muzzu Muzzulini, George Meyer-Goll. Prod: Ombra Films.

ZAKIR AND HIS FRIENDS

Script and Dir: Lutz Leonhardt. Phot: Felix von Muralt. Prod: Horizonte Film/interartes. Documentary.

Producers

Alhena Films SA
(production and distribution)
8, rue des Moraines
CH-1227 Carouge
Tel: (41 22) 823 0303
Fax: (41 22) 823 0304

Ascot/Elite
(production and distribution)
see address under Distributors

Balzli & Cie Filmproduktion
Altenbergstrasse 16
CH-3013 Bern
Tel/Fax: (41 31) 332 9438

Boa Filmproduktion AG
Neugasse 6
CH-8005 Zürich

Tel: (41 1) 271 0464
Fax: (41 1) 271 0518

CAB Productions SA
17, rue du Port-Franc
CH-1003 Lausanne
Tel: (41 21) 321 15 00
Fax: (41 21) 321 15 09

Carac Film AG
Zinggstrasse 16
CH-3007 Berne
Tel: (41 31) 372 00 40
Fax: (41 31) 372 04 81

Catpics Coproductions AG
Steinstrasse 21
CH-8003 Zürich
Tel: (41 1) 451 23 58
Fax: (41 1) 462 01 12

Ciné Manufacture SA
21, rue du Bugnon
CH-1003 Lausanne
Tel/Fax: (41 21) 311 58 58

Arthur Cohn
Gellertstrasse 18
CH-4052 Basel
Tel: (41 61) 312 12 42
Fax: (41 61) 312 07 17

Condor Films AG
Restelbergstrasse 107
CH-8044 Zürich
Tel: (41 1) 361 96 12
Fax: (41 1) 361 95 75

Dschoint Ventschr
Filmproduktion AG
Zentralstrasse 156
CH-8003 Zürich
Tel: (41 1) 456 3020
Fax: (41 1) 456 3025

Fama Film AG
(production and distribution)
Balthasarstrasse 11
CH-3014 Bern
Tel: (41 31) 992 9280
Fax: (41 31) 992 6404

J.M.H. Productions SA
PO Box 58
CH-2005 Neuchâtel 5
Tel: (41 32) 729 0020
Fax: (41 32) 729 0029

Bernard Lang AG
(production and distribution)
Dorfstrasse 14d
CH-8427 Rorbas-Freienstein
Tel: (41 1) 865 6627
Fax: (41 1) 865 6629

Les Productions
Crittin & Thiébaud SA
3, rue des Sources
CH-1205 Geneva
Tel: (41 22) 329 5983
Fax (41 22) 321 2512

T & C Film AG
Seestrasse 41a
CH-8002 Zürich
Tel: (41 1) 202 3622
Fax: (41 1) 202 3005

Thelma Film AG
Josefstrasse 106
CH-8031 Zürich
Tel: (41 1) 271 8124
Fax: (41 1) 271 3350

Triluna Film AG
Neugasse 6
CH-8005 Zürich
Tel: (41 1) 273 0053
Fax: (41 1) 273 0106

Vega Film AG
Kraftstrasse 33
CH-8044 Zürich
Tel: (41 1) 252 6000
Fax: (41 1) 252 6635

Distributors

Alexander Film
Lägernstrasse 6, PO Box 590
CH-8037 Zürich
Tel: (41 1) 362 8443
Fax: (41 1) 361 1603

Alhena Films SA
(production and distribution)
see Producers

Alpha Films SA
PO Box 176
CH-1211 Geneva 12
Tel: (41 22) 789 4545
Fax: (41 22) 789 3555

Buena Vista Int. Ltd
Am Schanzengraben 27
CH-8002 Zürich
Tel: (41 1) 289 2200
Fax: (41 1) 289 2222

Columbus Film AG
Steinstrasse 21
CH-8036 Zürich
Tel: (41 1) 462 7366
Fax: (41 1) 462 0112

Elite Film AG
Molkenstrasse 21
CH-8026 Zürich
Tel: (41 1) 298 8181
Fax: (41 1) 298 8189

Fama Film AG
(production and distribution)
see Producers

Filmcooperative
Heinrichstrasse 114, PO Box 1366
CH-8031 Zürich
Tel: (41 1) 448 4422
Fax: (41 1) 448 4428

Focus Film AG
Mittelstrasse 14, PO Box
CH-8034 Zürich
Tel: (41 1) 382 3388
Fax: (41 1) 382 3389

Frenetic Film AG
Bachstrasse 9, PO Box
CH-8038 Zürich
Tel: (41 1) 483 0660
Fax: (41 1) 483 0661

Bernard Lang AG
(production and distribution)
see under Producers

Look Now!
Staffelstrasse 10
CH-8045 Zürich
Tel: (41 1) 201 2440
Fax: (41 1) 201 2442

Monopole Pathé Films SA
Neugasse 6, PO Box 1827
CH-8031 Zürich
Tel: (41 1) 271 1003
Fax: (41 1) 271 5643

Praesens Film AG
Münchhaldenstr. 10, PO Box 322
CH-8034 Zürich
Tel: (41 1) 422 3832
Fax: (41 1) 422 3793

Rialto Film AG
Neugasse 6
CH-8005 Zürich
Tel: (41 1) 444 2277
Fax: (41 1) 444 2280

Sadfi SA
8, rue de Hesse, PO Box
CH-1211 Geneva 11
Tel: (41 22) 311 7767
Fax: (41 22) 781 3119

Stamm Film AG
Löwenstrasse 20, PO Box
CH-8023 Zürich
Tel: (41 1) 211 6615
Fax: (41 1) 212 0369

Trigon-Film, Filmverleih Dritte Welt
Bahnhofstrasse 11
CH-4118 Rodersdorf
Tel: (41 61) 731 1515
Fax: (41 61) 731 3288

Twentieth Century-Fox
PO Box 1049
CH-1211 Geneva 26
Tel: (41 22) 827 1717
Fax: (41 22) 343 9255

UIP (Schweiz) GmbH
Signaustrasse 6, PO Box 295
CH-8032 Zürich
Tel: (41 1) 383 8550
Fax: (41 1) 383 6112

Warner Bros. Inc.
Studerweg 3, PO Box
CH-8802 Kilchberg
Tel: (41 1) 715 5911
Fax: (41 1) 715 3451

Useful Addresses

Swiss Film Center
Neugasse 6, PO Box
CH-8031 Zürich
Tel: (41 1) 272 5330
Fax: (41 1) 272 5350

Swiss Short Film Agency
2, rue du Maupas
CH-1004 Lausanne
Tel: (41 21) 311 0906
Fax: (41 21) 311 0325

Federal Office of Culture
Film Department
Hallwylstrasse 15
CH-3003 Berne
Tel: (41 31) 322 9271
Fax: (41 31) 322 9273

Pro Helvetia
Arts Council of Switzerland
Film Department
Hirschengraben 22, PO Box
CH-8024 Zürich
Tel: (41 1) 267 7171
Fax: (41 1) 267 7108

**Swiss Film Producers'
Association SFP**
Zinggstrasse 16
CH-3007 Berne
Tel: (41 31) 372 4001
Fax: (41 31) 372 4053

Swiss Film and Video Producers
Weinbergstrasse 31
CH-8006 Zürich
Tel: (41 1) 266 6446
Fax: (41 1) 262 2996

Procinéma
Swiss Association of Exhibitors and
Motion Pictures Distributors
PO Box 8175
CH-3001 Berne
Tel: (41 31) 387 3700
Fax: (41 31) 387 3707

SYRIA
Rafik Atassi

A continuous recession in Syrian film production: this is the headline that might gave a true image of Syrian cinema last year. Not one new film was produced in spite of all the promises from the National Film Organisation (NFO) director about new plans and new films under preparation. Even the project announced in the previous year, Samir Zekra's **The Dust of Strangers**, about the Syrian historical figure Ak-Kawakbi, is still unfinished, due to a shortage of finance.

Al-Kawakbi spent the last period of his life in Cairo, where he was poisoned and buried. Most of his works and books were written there and his rich, modern thoughts spread firstly in Egypt at the beginning of this century when Syria was under the Turkish Ottoman occupation. Thus it was natural enough for the film-makers to plan to shoot some scenes on location in Cairo, but this has yet to happen and some observers say the film will stay unfinished for a long while yet.

The other film screened last year, **On the Move**, directed by Raymon Butrus, represented Syrian cinema in the 10th Damascus Film Festival last November, and won the silver medal. But it was a disastrous failure in the country's cinemas. Very few people were interested in this tale of 1920s life in the city of Hama, 200 kilometres north of Damascus, although critics have praised it. The film was Syria's entry in the Festival of Arab Films organised by the Institute of the Arab World in Paris in July 1998.

More money worries

As reported in last year's *IFG*, the country's economic hardships forced the NFO, part of the government's general section, to find its own resources to fund production, while independent producers turned to TV, which offers them better distribution prospects, thanks to the many Arab satellite stations operating within the Arab world and beyond.

Another NFO-produced film which started shooting this past year, **The Breeze of Soul**, written and directed by Abdullatif Abdulhamid (*Nights of the Jackal, Verbal Messages* and *Ascent of Rain*), is still waiting to raise the money needed for completion. In the meantime, Osama Muhammad, whose first film, *Stars of Midday*, was banned in Syria and only screened at various film festivals overseas, announced his new project, called **The Box of Dunia**. The other Syrian films mentioned in *IFG 1998*, namely Nabil Maleh's **Hassiba**, Ghassan Shmeit's **Zahr al-Rumman** and Waha Raheb's **Dreams**, are no nearer to completion.

The most surprising announcement of the last year came from independent producer Bashir Ghaiah, hitherto known only in the field of TV, who has taken on the risk of producing a film about the late Egyptian President Nasser, directed by the Anglo-Syrian film-maker Anwar Kawadri (*Nutcracker, Out of Time*). It will feature Egyptian and Syrian actors and is based on the book by Anthony Nattings, who was a minister in the British Cabinet during the Suez Crisis of 1956.

RAFIK ATASSI has been a film critic for more than 25 years and has written many articles and books on Arabic cinema. A member of the high organising committee of the Damascus Film Festival, he has served as a jury member at many regional and international film festivals. He is currently director of programmes for the Syrian Satellite Channel.

Producers

National Film Organisation
Rawda
Damascus
Tel: (963 11) 333 4200

Haya for Artistic Production
Bashir Ghaiah
Salheia
Damascus
Tel: (963 11) 221 8144
Tel: (963 11) 224 0373

Nader Atassi
Fardous St
Damascus
Tel: (963 11) 221 6009

Tahseen Kawadri
Tigheez St
Damascus
Tel: (963 11) 223 0767

Ghanem Films
Malki
Damascus
Tel: (963 11) 333 6279

Igraa Films
Khateeb St
Damascus
Tel: (963 11) 444 1446

Cham Al-Dawkia
Mezz
Damascus
Tel: (963 11) 613 3382

Aleppo Al-Dawlia
Sabeel
Aleppo
Tel: (963 11) 312 752

Syrian TV
Omayad Square
Damascus
Tel: (963 11) 221 2000
Fax: (963 11) 222 5374

Momen Mulla
Rokn El-deen
Damascus
Tel: (963 11) 512 284

Ara for Artistic Prod
Fine Arts Square
Damascus
Tel: (963 11) 442 008

Distributors

Tiba and Abboud
Fardous St
Damascus
Tel: (963 11) 222 1096

Mamoun Serri
Fardous St
Damascus
Tel: (963 11) 221 1188

Shamra
Mezza
Damascus
Tel: (963 11) 442 7008

Venus
Mezza
Damascus
Tel: (963 11) 611 5433

Useful Addresses

Cham Cinemas
Maysaloun St
Damascus
Tel: (963 11) 223 2300

Boruq
Mazraa
Damascus
Tel: (963 11) 444 9306

Saad
Baghdad St
Damascus
Tel: (963 11) 442 7153

Daoud Sheikhani
Rawda
Damascus
Tel: (963 11) 333 3491

Haysam Hutahet
Salheia
Damascus
Tel: (963 11) 222 2212

Abdul Masih Atia
Tijara
Danascus
Tel: (963 11) 232 0021

Khaled Saad deem
Bahsa
Damascus
Tel: (963 11) 221 8065

Syndicate of Artists
Baghdad St
Damascus
Tel: (963 11) 444 5809

TAIWAN — Derek Elley

Nothing much has changed during the past year to pull Taiwan out of its film-making doldrums. Locally, the box-office is totally dominated by US movies whose supremacy was underlined by the news earlier this year that Taiwan had agreed to abolish any quotas on American films, as part of its application to join the World Trade Organisation. Hong Kong films make little impact nowadays: even Michael Mak's ambitious, big-budget triad drama *Island of Greed*, set in Taiwan and shot in Mandarin, flopped disastrously. Internationally, a small number of names make regular appearances on the festival circuit with art movies that die at home and pick up few sales abroad.

After an interval of two years, Hou Hsiao-hsien returned to Cannes in May 1998 with the third (and last) of his films under a deal with Japan's Shochiku. **Flowers of Shanghai** (*Haishang hua*) is a gorgeously photographed but extremely leisurely paced movie, set in and around the city's upper-class brothels in the late nineteenth century. Following the tepid reception to his previous *Good Men, Good Women* (1995) and especially *Goodbye South, Goodbye* (1996), Hou seems to have taken stock of his career, though perhaps not quite as thoroughly as he needs to. Gone are many of the annoying stylistic ticks he has accumulated over the years –

confusing off-screen action, large ellipses in the narrative, mind-bendingly static set-ups – replaced here by wonderfully fluid camerawork and a dialogue-rich script which is essentially a series of conversation pieces, totally set in the brothels' interiors. His pacing is, however, still needlessly slow: shorn of half an hour, the 120-minute movie could have been among his best works.

The characters are not the down-market hookers and clients that usually populate such movies; Hou is at pains to show that the brothels were more like Japanese geisha houses, places where men dined, relaxed and chatted, away from their families, sharing companionship with educated young women. The film perfectly captures the obsessive, closed lives of the characters, gossiping about others' affairs as if in a soap opera. Performances by the star-rich cast (with Hong Kong-based actors like Carina Liu, Tony Leung Chiu-wai and Michele Reis alongside Taiwanese regulars like Jack Kao) are also finely pointed, and the film breaks ground by being almost entirely in Shanghainese dialect. Immaculately researched on an art direction and costume design level (despite being entirely shot in a Taiwan studio), the whole film is bathed in warm, amber lighting that recalls cinema-

Carina Liu (left) in Hou Hsiao-hsien's FLOWERS OF SHANGHAI

tographer Lee Ping-bin's previous Hou outing, *The Puppetmaster*.

Shallow hole, solid passion

FIPRESCI favourite Tsai Ming-liang, was also in Cannes with another chamber film, **The Hole** (*Dong*), featuring two of his regular actors, Lee Kang-sheng and Yang Kuei-mei, in a parable about loneliness and lack of communication. Part of French company Haut & Court's series of films set on the eve of the millennium, *The Hole* looks too much like an over-extended short that should have run 30 rather than 90 minutes. As rain pours down endlessly outside, a young man and a woman gradually connect after the former hacks a hole in the floor of his apartment. Tsai pads out the running time with fantasy musical numbers in which the two perform songs by 1950s pop diva Grace Chang; though these have a camp appeal, and liven up the almost dialogue-free film considerably, the idea is more a conceit than a valid contribution to the action.

Far more substantial is Lin Cheng-sheng's third feature, **Sweet Degeneration** (*Fanglang*), a slow-burning mood piece spun around a past incestuous relationship between a brother and sister. In plotting and character, the script is richly constructed but, unlike in Lin's superbly realised *Murmur of Youth* (1997), much of its potential remains unmined. As the brother who returns from military service and avoids his sister (Chen Hsiang-chi), Lee Kang-sheng is less brooding than in his films with Tsai, but never builds a character worthy of the audience's attention. Lin remains one of 1990s Taiwanese cinema's more interesting talents, but seems here to be surrendering to the negative, dysphoric elements that have helped to all but kill off quality film-making on the the island.

Present-day parables

Wang Shau-di made a better showing with the contemporary comedy **Yours and Mine**

Lee Kang-sheng in SWEET DEGENERATION

yue), the first movie in six years by Ko Yi-cheng, one of Taiwan's original New Wavers from the early 1980s. Made to be shown with the projectionist playing the five reels in any order, the film is a refreshing change from the joyless, anally retentive movies that have dominated Taiwanese production in the 1990s: a portrait of a basically likeable group of young people who gather at a bar-restaurant called Blue Moon, it has an ensemble warmth that often recalls the films of French veteran Claude Sautet. Each reel is fairly self-contained, so the stunt of them being shown in random order casts interesting shadows as new information is divulged on the characters.

(*Wode shenjingbing*) than with her chaotic *Accidental Legend* (1996), but mismatched direction robs the film of almost all its inherent energy and fun. Four tales that ingeniously criss-cross into an ironic commentary on 1990s Taiwan consumer-ism, the film is a two-hour hawl of static camerawork, long takes and a rather condescending attitude by the director towards her manic characters. The film flopped locally, but did better on video.

The black comedy **Wolves Cry under the Moon** (*Guodao fengbi*), the second feature of young Ho Ping, is also meant to be read as a parable of modern Taiwan, in this case tackling the frustrations of a people with too much wealth and energy and too little social sophistication to handle the island's transition to democracy and personal freedom. The film, however, ends up going in as many circles as its characters: a motley collection of hitman, hooker, chauffeur and traditional puppeteers, all thrown together when the island's main highway is closed to traffic for 12 hours one night.

Potentially far more pretentious, but in fact highly enjoyable, is **Blue Moon** (*Lan*

Golden Horse Awards 1997

Best Film: *Comrades, Almost a Love Story.**
Best Director: Fruit Chan (*Made in Hong Kong*).*
Best Actor: Che Kwan-ho (*The Mad Phoenix*).*
Best Actress: Maggie Cheung (*Comrades, Almost a Love Story*).*
Best Supporting Actor: Chen Chin-hsing (*Love Is Here*).
Best Supporting Actress: Liao Hui-chen (*Love Is Here*).
Best Original Script: Fruit Chan (*Made in Hong Kong*).*
Best Adapted Script: To Kwok-wai (*The Mad Phoenix*)*
Best Photography: Christopher Doyle (*Happy Together*).*
Best Visual Effects: no award.
Best Art Direction: Eddie Ma (*The Soong Sisters*).*
Best Costume Design: Eddie Mok (*Eighteen Springs*).*
Best Action Direction: Jackie Chan's Stunt Team, Cho Wing (*Mr. Nice Guy*).*
Best Original Music: Kitaro (*The Soong Sisters*).*
Best Original Song: *Eighteen Springs.**
Best Editing: Clifton Ko (*The Mad Phoenix*).*
Best Sound Effects: *The Soong Sisters.**
Best Short: *Wild Sparrows.*
Best Documentary: *Visiting the Homeland.*
Best Animated Film: *A Chinese Ghost Story – The Tsui Hark Animation.**
Lifetime Achievement Awards (posthumous): King Hu, Li Han-hsiang, Lo Wei.
Special Jury Prize: Ho Ping (*Wolves Cry under the Moon*).
* Hong Kong production

Forthcoming Films

SHANDINGSHANGDE ZHONGSHENG (Sound of a Bell on a Hilltop)

Dir: Yeh Hung-wei. Players: Shu Qi, Annie Wu. Shot in Yunan province, China.

HONG ZHU SHAONIAN

Dir: Sylvia Chang. Players: Maggie Cheung, Stephen Fung.

IN GOD WE TRUST

Dirs: Edward Yang, Stanley Kwan, Shunji Iwai. Prod: Pony Canyon (Japan) and others.

Projected triptych of features about US influence on Asian culture.

Useful Addresses

Central Motion Picture Corp. (CMPC)
8/F 116 Hanchung St
Taipei
Tel: (886 2) 371 5191
Fax: (886 2) 331 0681

Chang-Hong Channel Film & Video Co.
3/F, No. 9, Alley 6, Lane 166
Section 3, Hsinyi Rd
Taipei
Tel: (886 2) 705 2603
Fax: (886 2) 709 0334

Long Shong Pictures
2/F, 113 Hankou St
Section 2
Taipei

Tel: (886 2) 311 0249
Fax: (886 2) 314 5157

Scholar Films Co.
10/F, 88 Omei St
Taipei
Tel: (886 2) 361 5850
Fax: (886 2) 311 9692

3-H Films
3/F, No. 19, Lane 2
Wanli St
Taipei
Tel: (886 2) 230 0136

Taiwan Film Centre
4/F, No. 19, Lane 2
Wanli St
Taipei
Tel: (886 2) 239 6026
Fax: (886 2) 239 6501

THAILAND
Anchalee Chaiworaporn

Once again the news is doom-laden: Thai movies are getting into a deadlock. Because of local economic turmoil, audiences are becoming more selective, and US blockbusters are the clear winners. Of the 335 movies released in Thailand in 1997, only 30 were local productions (down from 40 in 1996), while 219 came from Hollywood and 87 from Hong Kong. Unfortunately, these Thai films took only about 11 per cent of the total ticket sales of $75m (Bt3,000m), compared to a 20 per cent share in 1996. Since the devaluation of the Baht was announced on July 2, the prospects for Thai films – already likely to be at the bottom of a local moviegoer's list – diminished considerably. All post-July 2 Thai releases lost money.

Despite these low box-office receipts, 1997 was still a year to remember because of the emergence of some talented newcomers. More feature opportunities have been given to directors who had started out in TV commercials, in the same way as happened with music video directors a few years ago. One of Thailand's legends came to life in **Daeng Bailey and Young Gangsters**, thanks to a team of newcomers led by commercials director Nonsee Nimitbut. Based on the exploits of real-life criminal Daeng Bailey in the 1950s, this action-packed film broke the all-time record for a Thai movie, taking almost $2m, and also collected numerous awards.

Much of *Daeng Bailey*'s success was due to incidental factors. The film opened in March, when no Hollywood blockbusters were launched, and before the Asian economic crisis began. Most importantly, the film's treatment of real-life events generated a great deal of front-page coverage when various figures from the 1950s came forward claiming the film-makers had distorted the truth. That kind of publicity can only boost ticket sales. The film also succeeded not only in attracting the teenagers who are always the main target audience, but also adults aged 50 and over who remembered the real Daeng Bailey.

Out of tune

Another director who cut his teeth in advertising, Penen Ratanaruang, directed **Fun Bar Karaoke**, but did not enjoy the same success as Nimitbut. Though it became the talk of the town after being invited to many leading festivals, the film was still too sophisticated and drawn out for a mass audience. Also, it was released two months after the devaluation, when most people were being very cautious with their daily expenses, and was up against major Hollywood movies.

Several graduates of foreign film schools tried their hands as first-time directors in the last year. These included New York University PhD candidate Theeranit Tamrongvinitchai, with a story set in the Thai fashion world, **Dream Society**, and UCLA graduate Supachai Surongsain, whose **Miracle in April** focused on the reasons why girls from northern Thailand go into the sex trade.

Despite these fresh visions, the majority of Thai movies are ignored by the public for one major reason – their weak, idiotic scripts. Over the past decade, they have relied on the same old boys-meet-girls or boys-kick-boys plots. Classroom drama, teen action and teen comedy have been repeated again and again and their appeal is waning. Yet, with *Daeng Bailey*'s success, we are seeing one genre variation replaced by another – action drama.

Teens, tears and guns

Thailand's oldest studio, Five Star Productions, and two record companies that have now branched out into film production, RS Film and Grammy Films, still base their storylines around tears and guns as well as teen idols and pop soundtracks. Since the industry is

Still from DAENG BAILEY AND YOUNG GANGSTERS

controlled by a few companies, who have production capital and movie theatres, film-makers have little choice but to accept these behind-the-scenes rules. They know that if they protest they will never have *any* opportunities.

But there is hope. Away from the teen flicks and action movies, some have decided to go out on their own with independent financing. Hong Kong director Oxide Pang Chun, who has been working in Thailand for years, made his directorial debut, **Who's Running**, with funding from well-known production lab Kantana Production. This story about a man fighting against destiny was well received by local audiences and critics.

Established director Prince Chatree C. Yukol started work on **Klong**, a comedy about the relationship between a short man and a beautiful woman. With a famous comedian, Udom Taephanich, and a former Miss Thailand, Metinee Kingphayom, in the starring roles, commercial success seems likely.

We are also seeing the emergence of alternative film-makers who are self-sufficient and usually show their works in private art-houses or cultural centres. One of these is Pimpaka Tohveera, whose experimental film **Mae Nak**, about a famous Thai ghost, was funded by the Goethe Institute and received a prize from Japan's Image Forum. Also, after the inaugural short films competition held in Bangkok in 1997, many people made low-budget shorts knowing they would be able to find an outlet for their work at the 1998 event.

ANCHALEE CHAIWORAPORN is a freelance film and drama writer for Thai and international periodicals, including *Variety*, and a volunteer with the Thai Film Foundation.

Producers

Five Star Productions Co. Ltd.
157/9 Soi Areesamphan 2
Bangkok 10310
Fax: (66 2) 246 2105/245 7931

Grammy Film
209/1 CMIC Tower B
Sukhumvit 21
Bangkok 10110
Fax: (66 2) 664 0246

Kantana Production
333 Soi Ratchadanivej 19
Pracha-u-tit Rd
Huay Kwang
Bangkok 10310
Fax: (66 2) 275 4530

N.K. Entertainment
261/107 Charansanitwong Rd
Bangkok 10700
Fax: (66 2) 412 8102

New Breed Pictures
301/61 Soi Panich-a-nun
Sukhumvit 71
Bangkok 10110
Fax: (66 2) 392 3447

RS Film
419/1 Ladphrao 15
Jatujark
Bangkok 10900
Fax: (66 2) 511 2324

Saha Mongkol Film Co., Ltd
1081/5 Phaholyothin Rd
Phyathai
Bangkok 10400
Fax: (66 2) 271 0620

Star Pictures International
61/1 Soi Thaweemitr 2
Rama 9 Rd
Huaykwang
Phyathai
Bangkok 10400
Fax: (66 2) 278 1486

Tai Entertainment
79/23 Srinakarin Rd
Nongbon
Pravej
Bangkok 10260
Fax: (66 2) 366 0377

Still from DREAM SOCIETY

Useful Address

Thai Film Foundation
21/1 Sukhumvit 61
Klong Toey
Bangkok 10110
Fax: (66 2) 437 9818

TUNISIA

Roy
Armes

Tunisian cinema, buoyed up by local enthusiasm for indigenous films, but hampered by a domestic distribution circuit of just 50 cinemas (down from 75 in the mid-1950s), continues to produce no more than two or three films a year. The seven-year gap separating Ali Abidi's debut, **Nocturnal Lighting** (*Barg Ellil*), released in 1990, from last year's second feature, **Redeyef '54**, is far from abnormal. Abidi's first film, adapted from a novel by the well-known Tunisian writer Bechir Khraief, was set in the sixteenth century; *Redeyef '54*, from an original script, is set in the recent past, specifically the events in Abidi's home town of Redeyef during the struggle against the French in 1954.

Born in 1959, Mohamed Zran is – at almost 40! – the first representative of a new generation of directors in Tunisia, where virtually all currently active film-makers are at least 50. Zran has finally released **Essaïda** (mentioned in *IFG 1997*). Unlike much recent Tunisian cinema, this is a look at the nation's contemporary face, bringing out the social tensions between the westernised artistic centre of Tunis and the outlying working-class district of Essaïda.

Another welcome feature debut is that of Kaltoum Bornaz (born 1945), one of the few North African women directors, who is already well-known for her short films. Her first feature is **Keswa – The Lost Thread** (*Keswa – Le fil perdu*). The film's action unfolds during 24 hours in today's Tunis: 27-year-old Nozha returns home feeling confused after a long absence which followed a row with her family, prompted by her decision to divorce against their wishes.

Together alone

The major reappearance of the year was that of Nouri Bouzid, who made an enormous impact with his first three features, made in quick succession between 1988 and 1992, but who has since been confined to scriptwriting (excellent work on Ferid Boughedir's *Halfaouine* and Moufida Tlatli's *Silences of the Palace*). His new film, **Girls from Good Families** (*Bent familia*), is a major event and a fascinating depiction of life in contemporary Tunis.

It tells the stories of three women friends: Amina, who is trying to leave her brutal, adulterous husband, Aïda, a divorcee bringing up her son single-handed, and Fatiha, an Algerian refugee struggling to come to terms with the memory of her murdered sister. The film paints a vivid picture of women's problems in a male-dominated society. The women share moments of togetherness, but at the end their lives are driven apart: Amina returns to her husband, Aïda starts up her life again after being deserted by her lover and Fatiha sets out for new opportunities in Europe.

Other directors with features in production include the newcomer Mohamed Ben Smail, who has worked extensively as an actor in France and in Tunisia, where he appeared in *Wandering Heart* (Fitouri Belhiba, 1990) and *The Sultan of the Medina* (Moncef Dhouib, 1993). He recently finished shooting **Tomorrow I Burn**.

Naceur Khemir, a man of many talents – sculptor, writer, film animator and oral storyteller – is already well-known for his first two features, which have received wide festival showings. His new project is **The Prince Who Contemplated his Soul**. Another director planning his return is Mahmoud Ben Mahmoud, best known for his debut feature, *Crossings*, who has signed a Belgian-Tunisian co-production deal for a new film, **Grenadan Siestas**.

Recent Films

BENT FAMILIA (Girls from Good Families)

Script and Dir: Nouri Bouzid. Phot: Armand Marco. Players: Amel Hedhili, Nadia Kaci, Leila Nassim, Raouf Ben Amor, Kamel Touati, Alia Laaouad, Abderrazek

Useful Addresses

Carthage Image (Formerly SATPEC: Film Laboratory)
017 20 avenue Taeib Mehri
Gammarth 2003
Tel: (216 1) 740 944.

Canal Horizons Tunisie
(Television Company),

Hammami. Prod: Cinétélefilms/ Lucie Films/SFP Cinema.

ESSAÏDA

Script and Dir: Mohamed Zran. Phot: Jean-Claude Coty. Players: Hichem Rostom, Chadly Bouzayen, Myriam Amarou-chene, Faouzia Badre, Abdallah Maymoun. Prod: Sangho Films.

rue de la Monnaie
Tunis 1000, Tel: (216 1) 333 100.
Fax: (216 1) 333 104

Journées Cinématographiques de Carthage (Biennial Film Festival)
5 rue Ali Belhouane
2070 La Marsa
Tel: (216 1) 745 355.
Fax: (216 1) 745 564

KESWA – LE FIL PERDU
(Keswa – The Lost Thread)

Script and Dir: Keltoum Bornaz. Players: Rim Turki, Mouna Noureddine. Prod: Les Films de la Mouette.

REDEYEF '54

Script and Dir: Ali Abidi (from a novel by Mohamed Jabra Zabrini.

SeptièmArt
(Film journal), B.P. 992 –
1045 Tunis
Tel: (216 1) 256 904

Festival International du Film Amateur de Kelibia (FIFAK)
(Film Festival), B.P. 116,
1015 Tunis.
Tel: (216 1) 280 298

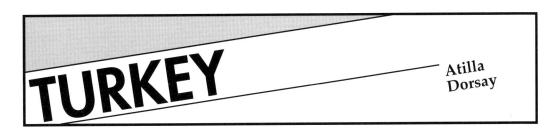

TURKEY

Atilla Dorsay

This was another good year for Turkish film, and for cinema in this country in general. The box-office wonder of recent years, **The Bandit** (*Eşkíya*), continued its astonishing career, nearing three million admissions. Mustafa Altioklar, whose hugely successful account of Ottoman history, *Istanbul Beneath My Wings*, was a breakthrough in Turkish cinema two years ago, delivered another blockbuster. **Cholera Street** (*Ağır Roman*) successfully transported to the screen the "unfilmable" novel of the same name, depicting the way of life of Istanbul gypsies in ghetto-like quarters and picturesque, but miserable streets. The critics were sceptical, but the film notched up more than 850,000 admissions.

The only director who survives from the 1950s "cinéastes generation", the ever-active Atıf Yılmaz, made a pleasant fantasy,

Miracle, ma Non Troppo (*Nihavent Mucize*), about a man whose sex life is threatened by night-time visions of his beautiful dead mother, who proceeds to return to earth to help her dear son solve his problems! *Miracle* gave the unique star Türkan Şoray the chance to make a much-appreciated comeback.

The so-called middle generation who, in the 1970s and 1980s, contributed so much to the international image of Turkish cinema, returned, but with disappointing results. Ali Özgentürk, for instance, whose *Hazal* and *The Horse* are considered milestones, made **The Letter** (*Mektup*), about a man searching for traces of his father, who was executed by the police for being a communist. Unfortunately, this was not a patch on Özgentürk's best work. Erden Kıral, whose *A Season in Hakkari* and *Dilan* are fondly remembered, came back with **The Hunter** (*Avci*), an unnecessary remake of *Rashomon*.

Old city, new life

Newcomers were far more successful. Ferzan Özpetek, Turkish-born but resident in Italy for many years, made a very remarkable debut with **The Turkish Bath** (*Hamam*), the story of a typically bourgeois Italian couple, finding, at least as far as the man is concerned, new values and worthwhile relationships in old Istanbul. The international success of this film (it was sold to practically every European country) was maybe due to its offering a return to the nearly-lost values of the past.

In his second film, **Innocence** (*Masumiyet*), Zeki Demirkubuz continued to prove his sensitivity as a director. He skilfully presented us with a trio of marginalised people, and demonstrated a remarkable talent for depicting suffering souls. Nuri Ceylan Bilge, whose documentary, *Koza*, was selected for the short films competition at Cannes in 1996, presented his first feature, **The Town** (*Kasaba*). This was a sharp observation of a small family (Bilge's own), in their daily life in the country, surrounded by nature. Throughout the year, Derviş Zaim, another first-time director, continued to witness the incredible success of his **Somersault in a Coffin**, which was screened and awarded prizes in many a festival, from Thessaloniki to San Francisco.

Another debutant, Umur Turagay, with his **Mixed Pizza** (*Karışık Pizza*), has proved to be one of a number of young film-makers heavily influenced by Tarantino. His film pleased the audiences, but not the critics. Ersin Pertain, in his third film, **Love Under Siege** (*Kuşatma Altında Aşk*), wasted a unique opportunity, as this was the first Turkish film ever to consider the conquest (or fall) of Constantinople from the Byzantine point of view. But his ambitious film was ill-conceived and over-theatrical. With the exception of **The Collapse** (*Çökertme*), by the veteran Tunca Yönder, all the films produced by the state television company, TRT, looked too much like TV movies.

Still from MIXED PIZZA

More than 160 foreign films were shown, with better box-office results than in previous years. That prompted the importers to increase the variety of foreign pictures on offer. Cinemas, mainly in the form of multiplexes, become more numerous and comfortable in the big towns, but remain few and far between in rural areas. Eurimages was the main source of international finance, and there was an increase in private investment. State subsidies, which had been suspended for a while, have resumed, but we must wait to see the on-screen fruits of this investment.

At the 17th Istanbul Film Festival, Istvan Szabo and Francesco Rosi collected lifetime achievement awards and an honorary award was made to Bertrand Blier. A jury presided over by Krzysztof Zanussi gave the Golden Tulip award to the Iranian film *The Mirror*, directed by Jafar Panahi. The FIPRESCI awards went to the Greek *No Budget Story*, by Renos Haralambidis, and Bilge's *The Town*. *Innocence* and *Hamam* were winners in the national festivals in Istanbul, Ankara and Antalya.

ATILLA DORSAY was born in 1939 in Izmir and has been a film critic since 1966. He is the author of 15 books on the cinema, is president of SIYAD, the Turkish film critics' association, and a member of the organising committee of the Istanbul Film Festival.

Recent and Forthcoming Films

HAMAM

Script: Ferzan Özpetek, Stefano Tummolini. Dir: Özpetek. Players: Alessandro Gassman, Francesca d'Aloja, Halil Ergün, Şerif Sezer. Prod: Sorpasso Film.

KARISIK PIZZA (Mixed Pizza)

Script: Tamer Baran, Uygar Şirin. Dir: Umur Turagay. Players: Meltem Cumbul, Cen Özer, Olgun Şimşek. Prod: United Film Production.

NİHAVENT MUCİZE (Miracle, ma Non Troppo)

Script: İpek Çalişlar, Atıf Yılmaz. Dir: Atıf Yilmaz. Players: Türkan Şoray, Haluk Bilginer, Lale Mansur. Prod: Delta Film.

AVCI (The Hunter)

Script: Oman Şahin. Dir: Erden Kıral. Players: Jale Arıkan, Fikret Kuşkan. Ahmet Uğurlu. Prod: Erden Kıral Film prodüksion.

KASABA (The Town)

Script: and Dir: Nuri Bilge Ceylan. Players: Mehmet Emin Toprak, Havva Sağlam. Prod: NBC films.

MASUMIYET (Innocence)

Script and Dir: Zeki Demirkubuz. Players: Hauk Bilginer, Derya Alabora, Güven Kıraç. Prod: Mavi Filmcilik.

Useful Addresses

CASOD
(The Association of Actors)
Istiklal Caddesi
Atlas Sinemasi Pasaji–C Blok 53/3
Beyoğlu
Istanbul
Tel: (90 212) 251 9775
Fax: (90 212) 251 9779

FILM-YÖN
(The Association of Directors)
Ayhan Işik Sokak, 28/1
Beyoğlu
Istanbul
Tel: (90 212) 244 0138
Fax: (90 212) 245 7194

Istanbul Kültür ve Sanat Vakfi
(The Istanbul Culture and Arts Foundation)
Istiklal Caddesi, Louvre Apt. 146
800070 Beyoğlu
Istanbul
Tel: (90 212) 293 3133
Fax: (90 212) 249 7771

SIYAD–Sinema Yazarları Derneği
(The Association of Film Critics)
Mr Atilla Dorsay–Akçam Sokak 17/6
4. Levent
Istanbul
Tel: (90 212) 264 0683
Fax: (90 212) 269 8284

Still from THE HUNTER

TÜRSAK
(The Turkish Cinema and Audiovisual Culture Foundation)
Gazeteci Erol Dernek Sokak
11/2 Hanif Han
Beyoğlu
Istanbul
Tel: (90 212) 244 5251
Fax (90 212) 251 6770

Umut Sanat
Halaskargazi Caddesi

Gezi Ethem Paşa Sitesi, 214/7
80220 Şişli
Istanbul
Tel: (90 212) 230 4041
Fax: (90 212) 232 3583

Özen Film
Sakızağaci Caddesi, 21
Beyoğlu
Istanbul
Tel: (90 212) 7070/71
Fax: (90 212) 244 5851

UKRAINE

Konrad
Will

Since becoming independent in 1991, Ukraine has earned increasing international recognition as a country whose cinema has a distinctive and distinguished past. Sadly, however, continuing economic instability, a corrupt and xenophobic government, and lack of support for new ideas and talent now threaten the present and future of the Ukrainian film industry.

Like their neighbours in the CIS and the Baltic states, Ukrainian film-makers are struggling to cope with the disappearance of the largest government-sponsored production system in the world. In the late 1980s, thanks to a steady flow of government contracts, studios turned out 20 to 30 feature films a year. Production dropped precipitously after the break-up of the Soviet Union, finally levelling off in 1995 at an average annual output of five or six features.

It is taking time for private finance to replace state investment. All five of the Ukrainian films released in 1997 were made with government funding, but three were co-financed to varying degrees by independent investors. These "independent" features tend to be more interesting and successful than the average state-funded project, reflecting the level of sophistication and initiative a director needs to attract private – usually foreign – money.

Victory for the pirates

Making films in and for Ukraine is not a profitable business, and output is unlikely to increase until Ukrainians start going to the movies again. In the last ten years, annual per capita attendance has plummeted from 13 to 0.17 – equivalent to one in every five Ukrainians visiting a cinema just once a year. The number of cinemas in the country has fallen by 50 per cent since 1989, with more closures looming.

The infamously dilapidated state of the movie theatres is one of many factors behind this decline. Another is the skill with which video pirates on both sides of the Atlantic make many films available soon after, or even before they open in the US. Rising crime rates and the shortage of disposable income also help keep people at home. Understandably, few people will pay to sit in an uncomfortable and potentially dangerous theatre, with poor projection and sound, to see a film that came out on video six months earlier.

The demise of communism meant the demise of government censorship, and many Ukrainian intellectuals assumed a cultural renaissance would accompany such political and ideological independence. Five years later, however, many film-makers feel as if the rug has been pulled out from under their feet. Regardless of their political affiliations, directors are still trying to find their bearings after the belief system that underpinned their art evaporated. Few established professionals have the energy, initiative or desire to invent capitalist techniques of film financing and production.

A killer in Kiev

Vyacheslav Kryshtofovych's **Friend of the Deceased** (*Pryatel Nebizchyka*) serves as an introduction to the present mentality of Ukrainian film-makers. Set in modern Kiev, the film uses a standard plot (man hires an assassin to kill him, then decides he wants to live) to illustrate the clash of two cultures. Shuffling through the town's medieval architecture, Anatoly contemplates the disappearance of his breed: the superfluous intellectual dreamer who can no longer survive in a capitalist jungle which values money over friendship.

The new Kiev is populated by wealthy but wary businessmen, their trophy wives and expensive escorts, who move through a world of glitzy nightclubs, casinos and shopping arcades. But Anatoly is given a new lease of life by a chance encounter with a vivacious, idiosyncratic prostitute, and, after suffering a symbolic death when he kills his would-be assassin, he rises again in the image of his victim. A showing in the 1997 Directors Fortnight at Cannes led to *Friend of the Deceased* being purchased by Sony Classics and given a limited release in the US in May 1998.

Recent films by veterans Mykhaylo Illenko, Mykhaylo Belikov and Vilen Novak have all abandoned the mythic past of their previous work in favour of stories set in the present, but they are still choosing escapist plots which side-step the most pressing issues of the day. Only Kira Muratova appears to have the courage to look the present straight in the face and say what she thinks (her *Three Stories* was reviewed in the Russia section of *IFG 1998*).

Elena Korikova and Alexandre Lazarev in A FRIEND OF THE DECEASED

However, recent announcements that the big three of Ukrainian film – Muratova, Yuri Illienko and Roman Balayanó – are to make new films, have given cause for optimism. There is also hope that the young generation of film-makers will find their voice again. One of them, Alyona Demyanenko, who shocked us with her award-winning debut **Cruel Fantasy**, is completing her second film. She will be the second director under 35 to finish a full-length feature since 1995.

KONRAD WILL has lived for most of the 1990s in Russia and Ukraine, working in the field of film, most recently as Managing Director of the Kiev International Film Festival. He currently resides in New York, working as a freelance translator and film journalist.

Recent and Forthcoming Films

TRI ISTORII (Three Stories)

Script: Igor Boshko, Renata Litvinova, Vera Storosheva. Dir: Kira Muratova. Phot: Gennady Karyuk. Players: Sergei Makovestsky, Leonid Kushnir; Renata Litvinova, Natalia Buzhko; Oleg Tabakov. Prod: NTV-Profit/Odesa Film Studio/Ministry of Culture and Art of Ukraine.

PRYATEL NEBIZHCHYKA (Friend of the Deceased)

Script: Andriy Kurkov. Dir:

Vyacheslav Kryshtofovych. Phot: Vilen Kalyuta. Players: Aleksandr Lasarev, Yevgen Pashin, Tetyana Kryvytska, Olena Korikova, Kostyantyn Kostyshyn, Serhiy Romanyuk. Prod: Ministry of Culture and Art of Ukraine/ Compagnie des Films (France)/ Dovzhenko National Film Studio.

SYOMY MARSHRUT (The Seventh Route)

Script: Seven film students from Mykhaylo Illenko's class at the Institute of Theater Art in Kiev.

Dir: Illenko. Phot: Yuriy Garmash. Players: Viktoria Malektorovych, Yuriy Yevsukov, Bohdan Benyuk, Viktor Polischuk. Prod: Ministry of Culture and Art of Ukraine/ Dovzhenko National Film Studio.

PRYNTSESA NA BOBAKH (The Princess and the Pea)

Script: Maryna Mareeva. Dir: Vilen Novak. Phot: Viktor Krutin. Players: Yelena Safonova, Serhiy Zhygunov. Prod: Ministry of Culture and Art of Ukraine/Odesa Film Studio/Studio Shans.

SVVYATE SIMEYSTVO (The Holy Family)

Scrip and Dir: Mykhaylo Belikov. Phot: Vasyl Trushkovsky Players: Daryna Loboda, Olena Balashova, Yuriy Odynoky, Aleksandr Pashutin, Nina Sharalapova. Prod: Ministry of Culture and Art of Ukraine/Dovzhenko National Film Studio.

DVA MICYATSI, TRI SONTSYA (Two Moons and Three Suns)

Script: Marina Mareeva. Dir: Roman Balayan. Players: Vladimir Mashkov, Olena Schevchenko, Ada Rogatseva, Kostyantyn Stepankov. Prod: Studio 1+1/NTV-Profit (Russia)/Ministry of Culture and Art of Ukraine/Goskino (Russia)/Illusion Films.

DVE IYULII (Two Julies)

Script and Dir: Alyona Demyanenko. Phot: Volodymyr Bass. Players: Serhiy Ivanov, Viktoria Malektorovich, Kostyantyn Shaforenko, Oksana Kolakova. Prod: Ministry of Culture and Art of Ukraine/Sepro/Dovzhenko National Film Studio.

TUPIK (Dead End)

Script: Andriy Kokotyukha, Evhen Onoprienko Dir: Hrihory Kokhan. Phot: Vitaly Zimovetz. Players: Irena Melnik, Taras Postnikov, Yuriy Evtzukhov, Oleksandr Bystrushkin. Prod: Ministry of Culture and Art of Ukraine/Meyster Video/Dovzhenko National Film Studio.

CHORNA RADA (The People's Parliament)

Script: Hrihory Stoyn, based on the book by Panteleymon Kulysh. Dir: Mykola Zaseev-Rudenko. Photo: Oleksandr Chorny. Players: Bohdan Stupka, Vasyl Lanovy, Bohdan Benyuk, Serhiy Romanyuk, Ada Rogatseva, Ruslana Pysanko, Kostyantyn Shaforenko, Mykola Dzhygurda. Prod: Ministry of Culture and Art of Ukraine/National Teleradio Company of Ukraine/Dovzhenko National Film Studio

GENERAL ARMII BESSMERTIA (General of the Immortal Army)

Script: Vasyl Portyak. Dir: Les Yanchuk. Prod: Ministry of

Culture and Art of Ukraine/ Ukrainian Congressional Committee/Dovzhenko National Film Studio.

NA POLI KROVY (On a Field of Blood)

Dir: Yarsoslav Lupy. Phot: Viktor Krutin. Prod: Ministry of Culture and Art of Ukraine/Odesa Film Studio.

YAK KOVAL SCHASTE SHUKAL (How the Ironsmith Sought Happiness)

Script: Anatoly Vasylevsky. Dir: Radomyr Vasylevsky. Phot: Leonid Burlaka. Players: Andriy Plakhotnyuk, Lev Persilov, Vasyl Pendas. Prod: Ministry of Culture and Art of Ukraine/Odesa Film Studio.

PRIMKHY DOLI (The Fickleness of Fate)

Script: Renata Litvinova. Dir: Kira Muratova Prod: Odesa Film Studio/independent producer.

Useful Addresses

Dovzhenko National Film Studio
pros. Permogy 44
252057 Kyiv
Tel: (380 44) 446 9231
Fax: (380 44) 446 4044

Odesa Film Studio
Frantsuzky b-r. 33
27044 Odesa
Tel: (380 44) 286 508
Fax: (380 44) 600 355

National Cinematheque of Ukraine
vul. Kioto 27
252156 Kyiv
Tel: (380 44) 513 0766
Fax: (380 44) 513 1244

Ukranimafilm
(government animated film studio)
PO Box 462
253094 Kyiv

Tel: (380 44) 513 8292/513 9355
Fax: (380 44) 227 3130

Studio 1+1 (independent TV and film production company)
vul. Menchnikova 14/1, Fifth Floor
252023 Kyiv
Tel: (380 44) 224 5291, 224 3157
Fax: (380 44) 225 0280

Ministry of Culture and Art of Ukraine
vul. Franka
252300 Kyiv
Tel: (380 44) 226 2645
Fax: (380 44) 225 3257

Union of Cinematographers of Ukraine
House of Cinematographers
252033 Kyiv
Tel: (380 44) 227 7557
Fax: (380 44) 227 3130

Kyiv International Film Festival Molodist
vul. Saksagansky 6, Suite 115
252033 Kyiv
Tel: (380 44) 227 4557
Fax: (380 44) 227 4557
e-mail: molodist@gu.kiev.ua

Department of Film
Kyiv State Institute of Theater Art
vul. Sichnevogo Postanya 35
Kyiv
Tel: (380 44) 212 0200
Fax: (380 44) 212 1003

KinoKolo (film journal)
Volodymyr Voytenko, editor
vul. Klovsky uzviz 6, kv. 41
252021 Kyiv
Tel: (380 44) 293 1977
Fax: (380 44) 227 4557

UNITED KINGDOM
Philip Kemp

After the party, the hangover. Last year's post-election euphoria, when the incoming Labour administration seemed to usher in a glorious new dawn for British film-making, could hardly last. The tax breaks for film-makers; the three new Lottery-funded production franchises; the appointment of a cine-literate Arts Minister; the rejoining of Eurimages; as yet none of these, nor other promising initiatives has delivered as hoped. Meantime the one problem that needs above all to be tackled, the inflexible, Hollywood-skewed distribution system, retains its stranglehold on the industry. If anything, its grip has tightened.

Still, it is far too soon to write off the much-hailed 'British film renaissance'. Production continues to flourish, only marginally down from last year's record levels. Despite the strong pound, British studios are still showing healthy bookings for months ahead, and Britain is now reckoned second only to Hollywood as an international production centre. The same goes for the network of post-production houses in London's Soho district, where every kind of cutting-edge technological expertise is on offer. British films (so long as one interprets the term 'British' fairly loosely) score worldwide hits at the box-office.

Most crucial of all to a healthy film culture, movies in Britain are still putting bottoms on seats. Cinema attendances continued their steady rise, and in the first quarter of 1998 were reported to have reached their highest level since 1972. While the National Cinema Day on Sunday, June 7 pulled in only 850,000 admissions, as against last year's 1.4 million, that was probably because this year the concession was less generous: half-price seats instead of all seats for $1.60 (one pound). But given that the average daily figure is 250,000, it was still a respectable showing.

The increase in screens continues to keep pace with the surge in admissions, with gleaming new multiplexes sprouting everywhere. Twenty-five new ones are scheduled to open in 1998 – that is 'plexes, not just screens – bringing the proportion of UK screens housed in these leviathans to over 30 per cent. Britain's first Warner Bros megaplex, nearing completion in Birmingham, will have 30 screens.

More cinemas, less choice

But while the number of available screens grows, the range of films they show is narrowing. Hollywood product swamps the new outlets; despite promises, few multiplexes set aside even a single screen for minority-appeal films, or at best do so only briefly and intermittently. The art-house exhibition sector steadily shrinks: the loss of the Curzon Phoenix and the closure (supposedly temporary but indefinite) of London's oldest rep cinema, the Hampstead Everyman, diminished the capital's dwindling stock of art-house outlets yet further.

The trend may be reversed if current moves to build 'artplexes' come to fruition. Two overseas exhibitors, Australia's Hoyts and South African Ster-Kinekor, have announced plans for UK chains of five- to eight-screen multiplexes dedicated to art-house fare. Ster-Kinekor has picked a possible site for a six-screen artplex in Covent Garden, central London. Warner Bros, meanwhile, intends its megaplexes to include two or three screens set aside for art-house product, separately branded as Cinema Europa, with their own entrances and cafés.

Such plans, if they materialise, could help unblock the backlog of British films awaiting release. Otherwise, it is estimated that six out of ten of the British films completed in 1998 will have to wait more than a year for a cinematic release, and many will never get one at all. Not for years has it been so easy to produce films in Britain – nor so hard to get them shown. Far too many people, it is suggested, are making films just because they can; shoot first, think about distribution later.

In many ways, the current situation looks like a replay of the 1960s. Then, as now, the British film industry was fizzing with fresh creative talent. Then, as now, the Hollywood majors were taking notice and eagerly buying into the lucrative scene: in 1967, the US provided 90 per cent of the funding behind British films; in 1997, it was 60 per cent and rising. Now pessimists with long memories warn that the whole balloon could suddenly burst, as it did in 1969, when Hollywood decided the Swinging London vogue had passed, took its dollars and went home.

For the moment, though, the American presence grows stronger by the week. Virtually every Hollywood player of significance has set up a London subsidiary or acquired an interest in a British company. Or in some cases both: Miramax, already one of the strongest US presences on the London scene, lost no time in bankrolling HAL Films, the new outfit set up by David Aukin and Colin Leventhal, former leading lights of Channel Four Films, plus Leventhal's wife Trea Hoving, ex-Miramax executive.

The influx of US finance seems likely to become a flood in the wake of the phenomenal world-wide box-office success of **The Full Monty**. This utterly unforeseen sleeper about six unemployed Sheffield workers who stage a striptease show is said to have made more money for its backers, Fox, than James Cameron's lumbering *Titanic* – and infinitely more in relation to its cost. *The Full Monty* (like last year's left-field hit, *The English Patient*) was hailed as a triumph of British cinema despite having received no UK funding –

Gwyneth Paltrow and John Lynch in SLIDING DOORS
photo: Alex Bailey

or returning a penny of profit to Britain. To rub salt in the wound, before it fetched up at Fox the project was turned down by both Film Four and Granada.

The *Four Weddings* wannabes

Other moneyspinners spurned by cautious British financiers included the Rowan Atkinson vehicle **Bean** (funded by Polygram) and the alternative-reality comedy **Sliding Doors** (picked up by Miramax). The conceit behind the latter, that one tiny incident like catching or not catching a train can send us off on a whole other life, had already been done – and, many would say, better – by Kieslowski in his 1981 film *Blind Chance*. Still, Peter Howitt's film skilfully interweaves its bifurcated narrative strands, constantly cross-cutting but never leaving us in doubt which version of events we are watching at any given moment.

The film's weakness is that it is so delighted by its own ingenuity that it forgets to give its characters any depth or a credible existence outside the demands of the plot. As the doubled heroine, Gwyneth Paltrow relies on her vulnerable appeal – and a strikingly convincing English accent – to engage our sympathies; but neither she nor John Hannah, playing her lover in what looks suspiciously like a role Hugh Grant turned down, amount to much more than a deftly applied set of cultural reference points. Even so, as a soft-hearted romantic comedy tricked out with the lightest of metaphysical superstructures, *Sliding Doors* exerts an undemanding charm.

Films like this, old-fashioned comedies with a light veneer of modish Brit sophistication, can trace their lineage back to the movie that kick-started the whole current British revival, *Four Weddings and a Funeral*. Other recent specimens include the vacuous **Martha – Meet Frank, Daniel and Laurence**; Stefan Schwartz's heist-comedy **Shooting Fish**; Simon Moore's bitter-sweet quasi-musical, **Up on the Roof**; and perhaps even, in costume-drama guise, the engaging historical two-hander, **Mrs Brown**.

Making a sophisticated comedy, of course, is no guarantee of box-office success; the hitherto triumphant *Trainspotting* team of Danny Boyle, Andrew MacDonald and John Hodge took the first tumble of their career with **A Life Less Ordinary**. Their mistake may have been in trying to tackle a Stateside setting, never an easy trick for British film-makers to pull off – though it can be done, as Richard Kwietniowski proved with his fastidious, *Lolita*-lite comedy of manners, **Love and Death on Long Island**.

Neglected gems

In general, it seems UK film-makers currently stand a better chance of

Samantha Morton and Matthew Delamere in UNDER THE SKIN   *photo: BFI*

acceptance, and even acclaim, if they keep it light and likeable. Few serious British films of recent months have received the publicity support they deserved, or been allowed the time to build their audience by word-of-mouth. Among those that vanished after barely a week or two on release were Michael Winterbottom's searing account of the Bosnian tragedy, **Welcome to Sarajevo**; **My Son the Fanatic**, a shrewd study of racial and generational conflict scripted by Hanif Kureishi and directed by Udayan Prasad; **Face**, Antonia Bird's high-energy gangster movie; Alan Rickman's directorial debut **The Winter Guest**; and another exceptional debut, Carine Adler's **Under the Skin**, a stark and uncompromising look at female sexuality.

But perhaps the most ineptly distributed, and unjustly neglected, British film of the year was **Regeneration**, Gillies MacKinnon's masterly adaptation of Pat Barker's WWI trilogy. Set mainly in Craiglockhart Hospital, near Edinburgh, where shell-shocked officers were sent to be patched up and returned to the carnage of the trenches, the film (like the novel) mixes real figures – the poets Wilfred Owen and Siegfried Sassoon – with fictional characters to explore questions of class, guilt, medical ethics and a whole snakes' nest of metaphoric connections between war and insanity. The film is shot in subdued, brooding tones: dark blues and greys within the hospital, and outside it a bleak, wintry countryside whose stripped trees and stark contours evoke the ravaged landscape of Flanders. The trenches themselves intermittently figure,

Danny Boyle, director of A LIFE LESS ORDINARY photo: Darren Michaels/PolyGram

Still from Gillies MacKinnon's REGENERATION
photo: Artificial Eye

but as hallucinatory excursions sparked by the mental conflicts being played out at Craiglockhart. In a uniformly superb cast Jonathan Pryce stands out as the humane, tormented Dr Rivers who, through wrestling with the demons in his patients' minds, comes to suffer shell-shock by contagion. Refusing to indulge in facile anti-war polemic, *Regeneration* leaves us with no easy answers.

MacKinnon's film was a prime victim of Britain's cruelly distorted distribution system, which allots all but a fraction of the cake to mainstream Hollywood product and leaves a few small independents to squabble over the crumbs. Five distributors, all tied to Hollywood – Fox, Buena Vista, UIP, Columbia, Warner – control over 80 per cent of UK distribution, guaranteeing massive blanket releases to the latest blockbusters and pushing smaller, independent, non-US-funded films to the margins. By February 1998, 74 per cent of solely UK-funded films made the previous year had failed to be picked up for distribution.

Since then, the situation has worsened. The London-based PolyGram, the only independent distributor capable of mounting a challenge to the Hollywood majors, has been sold by its Dutch parent company Philips to the Canadian liquor giant Seagram. Since Seagram already controls Universal, absorption seems likely – or else a further sell-on, perhaps to another Hollywood-linked outfit. Carlton, who last year bought Rank Distribution amid pious promises to maintain the UK's independent distribution sector, six

months later announced the closure of the operation – having secured the 700-plus titles film library that went with it. One of the smaller independents, Electric, was bought by a Canadian corporation; and another, First Independent, folded.

Punch-drunk and pitiless

In such a skewed set-up, even having a Hollywood major as your distributor is no guarantee of fair treatment. If a magisterial figure like Martin Scorsese cannot secure proper handling for *Kundun*, what hope is there for a fiercely localised, small-scale, relentlessly downbeat study of dead-end lives on a squalid South London estate? Gary Oldman's first film as director, **Nil by Mouth**, was as shocking and immediate as a punch in the face (plenty of which featured in the action). It had Luc Besson as co-producer, Fox as distributor, awards from Cannes and universally ecstatic reviews. Yet, despite creditable box-office takings, it disappeared from cinemas in short order, elbowed aside by flashier, more crowd-pleasing product.

Working to his own script and shooting mainly in pitiless close-up, Oldman creates a stifling sense of personal and cultural claustrophobia. He draws intense, rawly honest performances from his star-free cast (especially Ray Winstone and Kathy Burke as abusive husband and battered wife), sparing us nothing of the rage and futility of his characters' lives. Not for a moment are they patronised or sentimentalised; this is Oldman's own background, and he knows it intimately from the inside. The dialogue is mumbled, oblique, overlapping; we are plunged straight into this world, with no helpful expository speeches, and forced to live with these people and work out for ourselves who they are. *Nil by Mouth* is a bruising yet strangely exhilarating experience. Its subject-matter may be anything but uplifting, but there's a joy in watching film-making of such a high order.

Change must come

If films like Oldman's and MacKinnon's –

Ray Winstone and Kathy Burke in NIL BY MOUTH   *photo: Fox*

and indeed lesser but still worthwhile British movies – are to get a fair crack at an audience, bold initiatives to reform the industry are long overdue. On the production side, activity all over the UK remains at its highest for 50 years. Plans for the first Scottish studio are afoot – indeed two rival projects are now mooted, one fronted by the uncrowned king of Scotland, Sean Connery, the other by young pretender Ewan McGregor. A unified Welsh film body, Sgrin, is being set up. With the prospect of peace in Northern Ireland, film shoots in the province were on the up. A new cottage-style studio on the Ealing pattern is proposed for the West Country. And The Film Consortium, undeterred by the abdication of Carlton, is about to release the first fruit of the Lottery-funded franchises: Gillies MacKinnon's *Hideous Kinky*.

But in the absence of radical change on the distribution and exhibition fronts, all this energy and creativity could soon be stifled. The Government, having promised action and deliberated for a year, muttering of great things, has brought forth a mouse: the Till Report, from the Film Policy Review Group (FPRG) chaired by Stewart Till, head (at least for the time being) of PolyGram Films. The report suggests: a voluntary, industry-wide levy, designed to raise some $24 (£15m), to subsidise training and independent distribution; lifting the $24m budget ceiling on films qualifying for tax write-off; easing the restrictions on what counts as a 'British film' to access subsidies. Experimental, minority-appeal films are largely disregarded; the FPRG's ideal British film would seem to be *The Full Monty*.

Industry response has varied from guardedly optimistic to openly dismayed. But the general reaction is that 'voluntary' equals 'unworkable', and that far bolder measures will be needed if the brave new British movie industry is not to become a fully-funded outpost of Hollywood, restricted to producing anodyne comedies and tasteful costume dramas. While the debate continues, two rival film versions of Oscar Wilde's *An Ideal Husband* are in the pipeline, along with no less than three films about Mary Queen of Scots. Let us hope this is not a portent.

PHILIP KEMP is a freelance writer on film, a regular contributor to *Sight and Sound, Film Comment* and *Variety*. He is currently working on a biography of Michael Balcon.

Recent and Forthcoming Films

ALL THE LITTLE ANIMALS
Script: Eski Thomas. Dir: Jeremy Thomas. Phot: Mike Molloy. Players: John Hurt, Daniel Benzali, Christian Bale. Prod: Recorded Picture Co.

ARLINGTON ROAD
Script: Ehren Kruger. Dir: Mark Pellington. Phot: Bobby Bukowaki. Players: Jeff Bridges, Tim Robbins, Joan Cusack, Hope Davies. Prod: Samuelson/Lakeshore/Polygram.

BEDROOMS AND HALLWAYS
Script: Robert Farrar. Dir: Rose Troche. Phot: Daf Hobson. Players: Simon Callow, Jennifer Ehle, Christopher Fulford, Julie Graham. Prod: Berwin & Dempsey.

DAD SAVAGE
Script: Steven Williams. Dir: Betsan Morris Evans. Phot: Gavin Finney. Players: Patrick Stewart, Kevin McKidd, Helen McCrory, Joe McFadden. Prod: PolyGram.

DIVORCING JACK
Script: Colin Bateman. Dir: David Caffrey. Phot: James Welland. Players: David Thewlis, Rachel Griffiths, Richard Grant, Laura Fraser. Prod: BBC Films/Winchester/Scala.

DREAMING OF JOSEPH LEES
Script: Catherine Linstrum. Dir: Eric Styles. Phot: Jimmy Dibling. Players: Samantha Morton, Lee Ross, Rupert Graves, Miriam Margolyes. Prod: Midsummer/Fox Searchlight.

EYES WIDE SHUT
Script: Stanley Kubrick, Frederic Raphael. Dir: Kubrick. Players: Tom Cruise, Nicole Kidman, Marie Richardson, Vanessa Shaw, Sydney Pollack. Prod: Warner Bros.

THE GOVERNESS
Script and Dir: Sandra Goldbacher. Phot: Ashley Rowe. Players: Minnie Driver, Tom Wilkinson, Jonathan Rhys-Myers, Harriet Walter. Prod: Parallax.

GREY OWL
Script: William Nicholson. Dir: Richard Attenborough. Phot: Roger Pratt. Players: Pierce Brosnan, Annie Galipeau, Nathaniel Arcand, Renee Asherson. Prod: Beaver/Ajwaan.

GURU IN SEVEN
Script and Dir: Shani Grewal. Phot: James Bishop. Players: Saeed Jaffrey, Jacqueline Pearce, Nitin Chandra Ganatra, Lea Rochelle. Prod: Ratpack/Balhar.

HIDEOUS KINKY
Scr: Bill McKinnon. Dir: Gillies McKinnon. Phot: John de Borman. Players: Kate Winslet, Saïd Taghmaoui. Prod: L Films/Greenpoint/The Film Co.

I WANT YOU
Script: Eoin McNamee. Dir: Michael Winterbottom. Phot: Slawomir Idziak. Players: Rachel Weisz, Alessandro Nivola, Labina Mitevska. Prod: Revolution/Polygram.

A KIND OF HUSH
Script and Dir: Brian Stirner. Phot: Jacek Petrycki. Players: Darren Smith, Marcella Plunkett, Ben Roberts, Paul Williams. Prod: First Film Co.

THE LAND GIRLS
Script: David Leland, Keith Dewhurst. Dir: Leland. Phot: Henry Braham. Players: Catherine McCormack, Rachel Weisz, Anna Friel, Steven Mackintosh. Prod: Greenpoint/West Eleven.

LOVE AND DEATH ON LONG ISLAND
Script and Dir: Richard Kwietniowski. Phot: Oliver Curtis. Players: John Hurt, Jason Priestley, Fiona Loewi, Sheila Hancock. Prod: Skyline.

THE LIFE OF STUFF
Script and Dir: Simon Donald. Phot: Brian Tufano. Players: Ewen Bremner, Liam Cunningham, Jason Flemyng, Ciaran Hinds. Prod: Prairie Pictures/BBC Films.

THE LOST SON
Script: Margaret Leclere, Eric Leclere, Mark Mills. Dir: Chris Menges. Phot: Eduardo Serra. Players: Daniel Auteuil, Natassja Kinski, Katrin Cartlidge, Ciaran Hinds. Prod: Scala/Ima/Canal Plus.

METROLAND
Script: Adrian Hodges. Dir: Philip Saville. Phot: Jean-François Robin. Players: Christian Bale, Emily Watson, Lee Ross, Elsa Zylberstein. Prod: Blue Horizon/Mact/Filmania/BBC Films/Canal Plus.

John Hurt in LOVE AND DEATH ON LONG ISLAND

MICKEY BLUE EYES

Script: Mark Lawrence, Adam Scheinman, Andrew Scheinman, Robert Kuhn. Dir: Kelly Makin. Phot: Donald Thorin. Players: Hugh Grant, Jeanne Tripplehorn, James Caan. Prod: Simian/Castle Rock.

MOJO

Script: Jez Butterworth, Tom Butterworth. Dir: Jez Butterworth. Phot: Bruno de Keyzer. Players: Ian Hart, Ewen Bremner, Ricky Tomlinson, Harold Pinter. Prod: Mojo/Portobello.

MONK DAWSON

Script: James Magrane. Dir: Tom Waller. Phot: Teoh Gay Hian. Players: John Michie, Ben Taylor, Paula Hamilton, Martin Kemp. Prod: De Warenne.

MY LIFE SO FAR (aka THE WORLD OF MOSS)

Script: Simon Donald. Dir: Hugh Hudson. Players: Colin Firth, Irène Jacob, Mary Elizabeth Mastrantonio, Rosemary Harris, Malcolm MacDowell. Prod: Hudson/Enigma.

MY NAME IS JOE

Script: Paul Laverty. Dir: Ken Loach. Phot: Barry Ackroyd. Players: Peter Mullan, Louise Goodall, David McKay, Annemarie Kennedy. Prod: Parallax/Road Movies.

MY SON THE FANATIC

Script: Hanif Kureishi. Dir: Udayan Prasad. Phot: Alan Almond. Players: Om Puri, Rachel Griffiths, Stellan Skarsgård, Akbar Kurtha. Prod: Zephyr/BBC Films.

"THE NOTTING HILL FILM"

Script: Richard Curtis. Dir: Roger Michell. Phot: Michael Coulter. Players: Hugh Grant, Julia Roberts, Tim McInnerny, Gina McKee. Prod: Notting Hill Films/Working Title.

PLUNKETT AND MACLEANE

Script: Selwyn Roberts. Dir: Jake Scott. Phot: John Mathieson. Players: Robert Carlyle, Liv Tyler, Jonny Lee Miller, Michael Gambon. Prod: Working Title/Polygram.

THE RISE AND FALL OF LITTLE VOICE

Script: Jim Cartwright. Dir: Mark Herman. Phot: Andy Collins. Players: Jane Horrocks, Michael Caine, Brenda Blethyn, Ewan McGregor. Prod: Scala/Miramax.

THE SECRET LAUGHTER OF WOMEN

Script: O.O.Sagay. Dir: Peter Schwabach. Phot: Martin Fuhrer, Jacques Renoir. Players: Colin Firth, Mia Long, Fissy Roberts, Joke Jacobs. Prod: Paragon/HandMade/Elba.

STIFF UPPER LIPS

Script: Paul Simpkin, Gary Sinyor. Dir: Sinyor. Phot: Simon Archer. Players: Peter Ustinov, Prunella Scales, Georgina Cates, Samuel West. Prod: Cavalier/Impact.

STILL CRAZY

Script: Dick Clement, Ian La Frenais. Dir: Brian Gibson. Phot: Ashley Rowe. Players: Stephen Rea, Billy Connolly, Jimmy Nail, Timothy Spall. Prod: Marmot Tandy.

THE TICHBORNE CLAIMANT

Script: Joe Fisher. Dir: David Yates. Phot: Peter Thwaites. Players: John Kani, Robert Pugh, Robert Hardy, Barry Humphries. Prod: Bigger Picture Co.

TO WALK WITH LIONS

Script: Keith Leckie. Dir: Carl Schultz. Players: Richard Harris, John Michie, Julie Delpy, Ian Bannen. Prod: Studio Eight/Kingsborough Greenlight.

TWO LIVES

Script: John Hay, Rik Carmichael. Dir: Hay. Players: John Hannah, Brian Cox, Ian Bannen. Prod: Movie Screen Entertainment/McGuffin.

THE WAR ZONE
Script: Alexander Stuart, Tim Roth. Dir: Roth. Players: Ray Winstone, Tilda Swinton, Lara Belmont, Freddie Cunliss. Prod: Portobello/Channel Four/Fandango/Mikado/JVC.

WHAT RATS WON'T DO
Script: Steve Coombes, Dave Robinson, Will Osborne. Dir: Alastair Reid. Phot: Brian Tufano. Players: James Frain, Natascha McElhone, Charles Dance, Parker Posey. Prod: Working Title/Polygram.

Producers

Berwin & Dempsey
37 Artesian Road,
London W2 5DA
Tel: (44 171) 792 5152
Fax: (44 171) 792 5153

British Film Institute Productions
29 Rathbone Street,
London W1P 1AG
Tel: (44 171) 636 5587
Fax: (44 171) 580 9456

Company Pictures
National House,
60-66 Wardour Street,
London W1V 4ND
Tel: (44 171) 734 8114
Fax: (44 171) 734 8124

Dakota Films
12A Newburgh Street,
London W1V 1LG
Tel: (44 171) 287 4329
Fax: (44 171) 287 2303

Enigma Productions
13 Queens Gate Place
Mews, London SW7 5BG
Tel: (44 171) 581 0238
Fax: (44 171) 584 1799

Figment Films
2-4 Noel Street,
London W1V 3RB
Tel: (44 171) 287 3209
Fax: (44 171) 287 3503

Fragile Films
97-99 Dean Street,
London W1V 5RA
Tel: (44 171) 287 6200
Fax: (44 171) 287 0069

Granada Film
The London Television Centre,
Upper Ground,
London SE1 9LT
Tel: (44 171) 737 8681
Fax: (44 171) 737 8682

Greenpoint Films
5A Noel Street,
London W1V 3RB
Tel: (44 171) 437 6492
Fax: (44 171) 437 0644

Gruber Brothers
5th Fl., 41-42 Foley Street,
London W1P 7LD
Tel: (44 171) 436 3413
Fax: (44 171) 436 3402

HAL Films
45A Brewer Street,
London W1R 3FD
Tel: (44 171) 434 4408
Fax: (44 171) 434 4409

Imagine Films
53 Greek Street,
London W1V 5LR
Tel: (44 171) 287 4667
Fax: (44 171) 287 4668

Little Bird Co.
7 Lower James Street,
London W1R 3PL
Tel: (44 171) 434 1131
Fax: (44 171) 434 1803

Oxford Film Co.
Leeder House,
6 Erskine Road,
London NW3 3AJ
Tel: (44 171) 483 3637
Fax: (44 171) 483 3567

Pagoda Film & TV Corp.
20th Century House,
31-32 Soho Square,
London W1V 6AP
Tel: (44 171) 534 3500
Fax: (44 171) 534 3501

Parallax Pictures
7 Denmark Street,
London WC2H 8LS

Tel: (44 171) 836 1478
Fax: (44 171) 497 8062

Pathé Distribution
4th Fl., Kent House,
14-17 Market Place,
Great Titchfield Street,
London W1N 8AR
Tel: (44 171) 323 5151
Fax: (44 171) 631 3568

Portobello Pictures Ltd.
14-15 D'Arbley Street,
London W1V 3FP
Tel: (44 171) 379 5566
Fax: (44 171) 379 5599

Prominent Studios
68A Delancey Street,
London NW1 7RY
Tel: (44 171) 284 0242
Fax: (44 171) 284 1004

Rafford Films
26-27 Oxendon Street,
London SW1Y 4LT
Tel: (44 171) 839 1800
Fax: (44 171) 839 3600

Recorded Picture Company
24 Hanway Street,
London W1P 9DD
Tel: (44 171) 636 2251
Fax: (44 171) 636 2261

Renaissance Films
34-35 Berwick Street,
London W1V 3RF
Tel: (44 171) 287 5190
Fax: (44 171) 287 5191

Revolution Films
10 Little Turnstile,
London WC1V 7DX
Tel: (44 171) 242 0372
Fax: (44 171) 242 0407

Rocket Pictures
7 King Street Cloisters,
Clifton Walk,
London W6 0GY
Tel: (44 181) 741 9090
Fax: (44 181) 741 9097

Samuelson Productions
23 West Smithfield,
London EC1A 9HY
Tel: (44 171) 236 5532
Fax: (44 171) 236 5504

Scala Productions
39-43 Brewer Street,
London W1R 3FD
Tel: (44 171) 734 7060
Fax: (44 171) 437 3248

Skreba-Creon Films
The Old Malthouse,
Westwood,
Bradford-on-Avon,
Wiltshire BA15 2AG
Tel: (44 1225) 864 905
Fax: (44 1225) 866 831

The Jones Company
6 Kings Avenue,
London N10 1PB
Tel: (44 181) 444 7211
Fax: (44 181) 444 1979

Toledo Films
30 Oval Road
London NW1 7DE
Tel: (44 171) 428 4000
Fax: (44 171) 284 2218

Working Title Films
Oxford House, 76 Oxford Street,
London W1N 9FD
Tel: (44 171) 307 3000, 580 2626
Fax: (44 171) 307 3001

Zenith Productions
43-45 Dorset Street,
London W1H 4AB
Tel: (44 171) 224 2440
Fax: (44 171) 224 3194

Distributors

Alliance Releasing
2nd Fl.,184-192 Drummond Street,
London NW1 3HP
Tel: (44 171) 391 6900
Fax: (44 171) 383 0404

Artificial Eye Film Ltd.
13 Soho Square,
London W1V 5FB
Tel: (44 171) 437 2552
Fax: (44 171) 437 2992

Blue Dolphin Film & Video Ltd.
40 Langham Street,
London W1N 5RG
Tel: (44 171) 255 2494
Fax: (44 171) 580 7670

British Film Institute
21 Stephen Street,
London W1P 1PL
Tel: (44 171) 255 1444
Fax: (44 171) 436 7950

Buena Vista International
Beaumont House,
Kensington Village,
Avonmore Road,
London W14 8TS
Tel: (44 181) 222 2890
Fax: (44 181) 222 2795

Columbia TriStar Film Distributors
Sony Pictures Europe House
25 Golden Square
London W1R 6LU
Tel: (44 171) 533 1111
Fax: (44 171) 533 1015

Entertainment Film Distributors
27 Soho Square,
London W1V 6HU
Tel: (44 171) 439 1606
Fax: (44 171) 734 2483

Feature Film Co.
68-70 Wardour Street,
London W1V 3HP
Tel: (44 171) 734 2266
Fax: (44 171) 494 0309

Film Four Distributors
Castle House,
75-76 Wells Street,
London W1P 3ER
Tel: (44 171) 436 9944
Fax: (44 171) 436 9955

Gala Film Distributors
26 Danbury Street,
London N1 8JU
Tel: (44 171) 226 5085
Fax: (44 171) 226 5897

ICA Projects
12 Carlton House Terrace,
London SW1Y 5AH
Tel: (44 171) 930 0493
Fax: (44 171) 873 0051

Mainline Pictures
37 Museum Street,
London WC1A 1LP
Tel: (44 171) 242 5523
Fax: (44 171) 430 0170

Metrodome Films
3rd Fl., 25 Maddox St.
London W1R 9LE
Tel: (44 171) 408 2121
Fax: (44 171) 409 1935

Metro Tartan
79 Wardour Street,
London W1V 3TH
Tel: (44 171) 734 8508
Fax: (44 171) 287 2112

Twentieth Century Fox
20th Century House,
31 Soho Square,
London W1V 6AP
Tel: (44 171) 437 7766
Fax: (44 171) 434 2170

U.I.P.
37-41 Mortimer Street,
London W1A 2JL
Tel: (44 171) 636 1655
Fax: (44 171) 636 4118

Warner Bros.
135 Wardour Street,
London W1V 4AP
Tel: (44 171) 734 8400
Fax: (44 171) 437 5521

Sales Companies

Jane Balfour Films
Burghley House,
35 Fortess Road,
London NW5 1AQ
Tel: (44 171) 267 5392
Fax: (44 171) 267 4241

Capitol Films
23 Queensdale Place,
London W11 4SQ
Tel: (44 171) 471 6000
Fax: (44 171) 471 6012

Film Four International
24 Horseferry Road,
London SW1P 2TX
Tel: (44 171) 306 8602
Fax: (44 171) 306 8361

Goldcrest Film International
65-66 Dean Street,
London W1V 6PL
Tel: (44 171) 437 8696
Fax: (44 171) 437 4448

Goldwyn Films
10 Stephen Mews, Office 718
London W1P 1PP
Tel: (44 171) 333 8877
Fax: (44 171) 333 8878

Handmade Films
19 Beak Street,
London W1R 3LB
Tel: (44 171) 434 3132
Fax: (44 171) 434 3143

IAC Films
19-21 Tavistock Street
London WC2E 7PA
Tel: (44 171) 836 6545
Fax: (44 171) 836 6564

Icon Films
56 Kingsdown Parade,
Bristol BS6 5UQ
Tel: (44 117) 924 8535
Fax: (44 117) 942 0386

Intermedia
81 Picadilly
London W1V 9HF
Tel: (44 171) 495 3322
Fax: (44 171) 495 3993

J&M Entertainment
2 Dorset Square,
London NW1 6PU
Tel: (44 171) 723 6544
Fax: (44 171) 724 7541

PolyGram Film International
4th Floor, Oxford House,
76 Oxford Street,
London W1N 0HQ
Tel: (44 171) 307 1300
Fax: (44 171) 307 1301

Portman Entertainment Group Ltd.
167 Wardour Street
London W1V 3TA
Tel: (44 171) 468 3434
Fax: (44 171) 468 3469

Smart Egg Pictures
11-12 Barnard Mews,
Barnard Road
London SW11 1QU
Tel: (44 171) 924 6284
Fax: (44 171) 924 5650

The Sales Company
62 Shaftesbury Avenue,
London W1V 7DE

Tel: (44 171) 434 9061
Fax: (44 171) 494 3293

Summit Entertainment N.V.
118-120 Wardour Street,
London W1V 3LA
Tel: (44 171) 494 1724
Fax: (44 171) 494 1725

Victor Film Co.
2B Chandos Street,
London W1M 9DG
Tel: (44 171) 636 6620
Fax: (44 171) 636 6511

Vine International Pictures
Astoria House,
62 Shaftesbury Avenue,
London W1N 7DE
Tel: (44 171) 437 1181
Fax: (44 171) 494 0634

Winchester Film & TV Sales
29-30 Kingly Street,
London W1R 9LB
Tel: (44 171) 434 4374
Fax: (44 171) 287 4334

Useful Addresses

British Academy of Film and Television Arts (BAFTA)
195 Piccadilly,
London W1V 0LN
Tel: (44 171) 734 0022
Fax: (44 171) 734 1792

British Board of Film Classification (BBFC)
3 Soho Square,
London W1V 6HD
Tel: (44 171) 439 7961
Fax: (44 171) 287 0141

British Actors Equity Association
Guild House,
Upper St. Martins Lane,
London WC2H 9EG
Tel: (44 171) 379 6000
Fax: (44 171) 379 7001

The British Council
Films, Television, & Video Dept.
11 Portland Place,
London W1N 4EJ
Tel: (44 171) 389 3065
Fax: (44 171) 389 3041

British Film Commission
70 Baker Street,
London W1M 1DJ
Tel: (44 171) 224 5000
Fax: (44 171) 224 1013

British Screen Finance
14-17 Wells Mews,
London W1P 3FL
Tel: (44 171) 323 9080
Fax: (44 171) 323 0092

Cinema Exhibitors' Association (CEA)
22 Golden Square,
London W1R 3PA
Tel: (44 171) 734 9551
Fax: (44 171) 734 6147

Directors' Guild of Great Britain
15-19 Great Titchfield Street,
London W1P 7FB
Tel: (44 171) 436 8626
Fax: (44 171) 438 8646

Independent Television Association
ITV Network Centre,
200 Grays Inn Road,
London WC1X 8HF
Tel: (44 171) 843 8000
Fax: (44 171) 843 8158

Independent Television Commission
33 Foley Street,
London W1P 7LB
Tel: (44 171) 255 3000
Fax: (44 171) 306 7800

London Film Commission
20 Euston Centre
Regent's Place
London NW1 3JH
Tel: (44 171) 387 8787
Fax: (44 171) 387 8788

PACT
45 Mortimer Street,
London W1N 7TD
Tel: (44 171) 331 6000
Fax: (44 171) 331 6700

Scottish Screen
74 Victoria Crescent Road,
Glasgow G12 9JN
Tel: (44 141) 302 1700
Fax: (44 141) 302 1711

UNITED STATES — Harlan Jacobson

nevitably, the past 12 months must be slugged as the year a US film cost $200 million and made more than a billion, instead of sinking like the Titanic and living out the drama of media hand-wringing over auteurist insanity. In this particular instance, the copy desk staff of virtually every newspaper in America must have gone home dejected the night the critical reviews of James Cameron's adolescent remake of *Lady and the Tramp* on a boat all came in raves. Out went all the banked headlines – "*Titanic* Tanks Again", etc. – and in came a thousand versions of "The Ship Sails On".

Only the more curmudgeonly op-ed writers got their licks in, and then only after the film had globally wracked up Bill Gates' weekly pay-cheque, carted off a record-tying 14 Oscars, and Cameron had the ill grace to give two billion or so people a glimpse inside the rather ungracious mindset of what passes for auteurship, *fin de millénnium*, with a "Top of the world" nod not to Ma but to himself.

While true US auteurs have mostly become an endangered species, the prevailing celebrity culture that has supplanted film-making and everything else shifted over the question of heroics. Given the euphoria over the gazelle-like US stock market, the demand for triumphant cinematic heroes slacked off. They function better in bear markets, when the national spirit needs a bit of reassurance. No bucking up needed now: pension fund managers for the Baby Boom continued to buy. No end in sight. How high is up? The sky is falling, the sky is falling – but up, that's how high.

Who this past year would refute the new American economic model of global commerce in which the US exports labour

John Travolta (centre) in PRIMARY COLORS
photo: François Duhamel/Universal

and sells information, capital formation and protection, entertainment and services – only the obsessive Michael Moore (*The Big One*, with a $736,000 US gross)? If there is a Euro-union of countervailing power on the horizon, it has not made a dent in the national dreamwork. No evil German central bankers or wily French economic espionage characters have showed up onscreen. Topics were mostly local.

Presidents galore

The most interesting development was the return of the political genre, from agit prop to satire to generic alarums. Mike Nichols struck out with **Primary Colors** ($39m gross) which anecdotally addressed the power of the spin that has come to substitute for truth. The conventional wisdom was that Monicagate made *Primary Colors* obsolete, but the hard fact is that while Nichols framed the donut shop refuge of the president-to-be like some beautiful Hopper painting, he failed to get a complex performance from John Travolta as Jack Stanton. The Arkansas, good times po-boy was there, but the Yale-Oxford-Georgetown intelligence was missing, as was the charisma. Bill Clinton simply is a hotter media presence than Travolta is a movie star.

And so much for leadership, which in film-making is sometimes called auteurism, or final cut, or, lastly, artistic integrity: *Primary Colors* sacrificed whatever internal punch remained from the not-so-Anonymous (Joe Klein) novel after Nichols cut an inter-racial love scene between the First Lady and Henry Burton, the black presidential aide and story narrator. Focus groups got distracted, he told the media at Cannes, whose organisers compounded the film's press agony by misguidedly inviting it to open the festival.

Far more successful was Barry Levinson's **Wag the Dog** ($30m), which eerily evoked the breaking Monicagate scandal. The film directly assaulted the subject of spin, in partnership with Dustin Hoffman, on a month's hiatus with Levinson from the dreadful **Sphere**, and Robert De Niro. The original Larry Beinhart novel was written to lampoon the Bush presidency, and Hillary Henkin's script sat in a drawer until it was given a polish by David Mamet and rushed into production for a 28-day shoot when *Sphere* was delayed for financial reasons.

Call it slumming, or a Hollywood independent film, *Wag the Dog* was ultimately less insightful about Washington than it was about Hollywood's resentment over its anti-social scapegoating. This is an odd film – funnier on second viewing than first, after the Clinton *à clef* aspect recedes into the background and the film reveals itself more as an open Hollywood letter to lawmakers that, in the guise of satire, addresses the issue of violence in film; as if to say: "At the end of the day, our dead guys leave the set and go home, well paid, to dinner. Yours don't get off the tarmac."

Wolfgang Petersen's **Air Force One** ($172m) and Clint Eastwood's **Absolute Power** ($60m) assumed opposite sides of the same tarnished presidential coin to no effect, as both skimmed along the surface as thrillers. Warren Beatty tried fusing agit prop about race with satire about anti-spin in **Bulworth**. Michael Winterbottom's UK-financed *Welcome to Sarajevo* ($300,000) failed to cut through the media clutter (the film's meta-subject) to register much impact.

Dustin Hoffman, nominated for an Academy Award in WAG THE DOG, Barry Levinson's low-budget political satire
photo: Entertainment Film Distributors

Politics and thrills

Alan J. Pakula reiterated American melting pot mythology and aversion to foreign involvement in **The Devil's Own** ($42 million). Steven Spielberg's **Amistad** ($39m) and Martin Scorsese's **Kundun** ($4m), both wonderfully intentioned, failed to connect, though the latter, beautifully framed and shot, with Morocco standing in for Tibet, was as strange and wonderful in its *mise-en-scène* as a sci-fi visit to a distant planet.

Even the lowly **Con Air** ($101m), more produced by Jerry Bruckheimer than it was directed by Simon West, managed to take a political stab at things – mounting a simplified argument against the death penalty that eluded critics, probably because it was deeply buried in cheap thrills that screeched to a halt in an idiotic *Silver Streak* ending.

Then, too, there were the generic anti-Fascist jeremiads, with John Sayles capably setting **Men with Guns** in a generic Latin American country, and Wallace Shawn crafting an alarum in his disastrous **The Designated Mourner**, which used direct address to make its case. Unwittingly, in *Mourner,* Mike Nichols, cast as a disaffected intellectual of the *real politik* inclination, sheds light on *Primary Colors* by playing Miranda Richardson's husband, who is judged as wanting for his amoral cynicism, and incapable of coming between Richardson and her steadfast loyalty to her intellectual-giant of a father. Sounds like a perfectly plausible reading of the Clinton-Rodham marriage to me – certainly better than Nichols filigreed in *Colors.*

On the independent front, the slambang release of the year was *The Full Monty* ($38m), which took a small fact – frontal male nudity – and filmed it simply, to the point of amateurishly. Audiences accepted it as fun, mostly because it shied away from any large scale ambitions about objectification and went for the belly laugh. When matters got more serious, as in Todd Solondz' **Happiness**, a nasty piece of work about men, molesters and suburban living,

Anthony Hopkins (left) and Djimon Hounsou in AMISTAD   *photo: A. Cooper/DreamWorks*

the dragon of studio propriety reared its ugly head. October bought the film out of the Quinzaine at Cannes, and reportedly dropped it at the insistence of Universal, uncomfortable more about its sardonic approach to child molestation than its graphic jokes about precious bodily fluids. At press time, *Happiness* was still unreleased in the US.

October gave it a brave go, however, by purchasing Robert Duvall's **The Apostle** ($9m), at the 1997 Toronto Film Festival. Manifestly, it was the bravest male performance of the year (Duvall as producer-director-writer-actor), and was simply gypped on Oscar night.

New values, tragic heroes

Matt Damon was new kid on the block for his onscreen acting and script work with Ben Affleck for **Good Will Hunting** ($135m), a mishmash of independent and major elements: directed by Gus van Sant; written by relative unknowns who also starred opposite Robin Williams; produced by Miramax with an eye to the future; and serving up some feelgood, self-help treacle in Cambridge, Mass., America's brain capital. Well, at least the youngsters are for something, which – after watching so many of the ironic, navel gazing, talky heroes who have ruled independent films since the late 1980s – is a positive sign.

Such heroes, as promulgated by slacker and Gen X directors, and subsequently Hollywoodised in Tarantino, were repudiated, or at least met with indifference (**Jackie Brown**, $38m). The cutting edge seemed to move toward larger politics. Good times have created a perhaps brief but dramatic reappearance of the tragic hero this year. Said hero, too good for this or any other world, had to die to register with the American public, however, which continues to like its received opinions framed in British class schematics (Leonardo DiCaprio in *Titanic* and Diana, Princess of Wales, in life).

At press time, Tom Hanks in Spielberg's **Saving Private Ryan** may be the apotheosis of this trend, as Spielberg finally Americanised the tragic hero's context and so is likely to be canonised next Spring with Oscars. Honorable failures, or tragic heroes without the guts to go all the way, playing out the attendant trappings of sadder-but-wiser endings (Curtis Hanson's **L.A.Confidential**, $41m, Iain Softley's **The Wings of the Dove**, $9m), did all right for themselves with the Academy of Motion Picture Arts and Sciences this past year by regurgitating corrupt social systems where the truth outing itself becomes the noble redemption of dark characters trying to make it through a *faux noir* world.

Perhaps that was why, in mid-summer 1998, the big news (as defined by Hollywood landing on the front page of *The New York Times* for something other than convenient scapegoating when another of America's errant children went on a killing spree) was not about one picture doing well. In fact, a number of summer films had done only middling business. It was that Miramax chief Harvey Weinstein had rescued that paragon of Oxbridge class, Tina Brown, from *The New Yorker*, which had passed critical mass in taking on Titanic levels of water.

Tina's New Mission for Miramax: nothing less than vertical aesthetic reintegration, which sounds like the back to-the-future synergy talk of the Reagan 1980s. Tina and Ron Galotti will soon preside over a magazine-to-film cycle designed to exploit a "reality generates

Guy Pearce in L.A. CONFIDENTIAL
photo: Merrick Morton/Regency

media coverage, generates movie deals for Miramax" formula. With Clinton-related events in the real world continuing to outstrip anything the more imaginative writers could possibly dream up – Andrew Niccol's script for Peter Weir's **The Truman Show** ($120m), for instance – the bet is that Tina will likely revert to themes from her *Vanity Fair* days of Good Women Done Wrong by Bad Men. How she will adjust to an editorial budget somewhat below the astonishing $30m at her disposal at *The New Yorker* is a concern – though selling tickets to the editorial meetings is an untapped source of revenue.

No avoiding the iceberg

Jeffrey Spaulding, assessing the 1997 box-office year in the April 1998 issue of *Film Comment*, was misguided in dismissing **Titanic** as a "bizarre footnote" to 1997 and more a 1998 story. *Titanic* was always a 1997 story, starting with its missed release dates, its postponement from July to December (in part to placate Harrison Ford, who publicly warned about a conflicting summer release with *Air Force One*), and the subsequent carrying charges borne by both Paramount and Twentieth Century Fox, partners in the film.

The studios' deal was more fun than the film, starting as a 50-50 cost split with Paramount capping out at a $65m contribution in exchange for North America, which had generated about $594m in takings by August 1998. Fox paid the rest, somewhere above $135m, which resulted in something close to a 30-70 cost share between the two companies. Fox retained foreign sales, which had turned up $1.18 billion through July 26. What those numbers yielded in true rentals, and the nature of the ultimate revenue split, is anyone's guess, since it involves a Byzantine recoupment formula and profit participation schedule beyond all but a Hollywood accountant's genius.

The film defied gravity where the boat did not. At about $1.8 billion worldwide, it doubled *Jurassic Park*'s 1993 worldwide take of $917 million. It did this at some three-and-a-quarter hours in length – with interminable nautical miles going by as a pair of muling kids discovered their bodies, and before anyone worth a damn fell into the drink. It did this despite critics failing to notice that Cameron was far more at home in the boiler room scene than in the cauldron of the heart, or that his best shot, at the end, of corpses bobbing around ice cube gargantua was lifted from Ingmar Bergman's *Shame.*

"Try explaining why the bumble bee flies," remarked Len Klady, *Variety*'s box-office reporter, charting *Titanic*'s progress. "It defies physics." Was it DiCaprio's non-threatening peach fuzz masculinity that roped in every young girl on the planet - five times over? Leo's charms certainly failed artistially, if not commercially, in Randall Wallace's remake of **The Man in the Iron Mask**. Was it one more example of the renewed public appetite for the good dying young? For the sad ending that

makes adults glad to be alive in Pottstown and teens all the more anxious to clear out and begin to live? Who knows?

Curly-haired studio merlins are staying up nights trying to understand why *Titanic* held in theatres for months, suspended in air, pouring out money, and how it can be done again – only cheaper. The studios *say* that *Titanic* is a one-time shot and will not spawn a round of mega-budgets and cost over-runs. They *say* the sweat caused by *Waterworld* is not forgotten. They said it after *Heaven's Gate*, too, and *Cleopatra* and...

Weaker by the week

Spaulding was right on the money, however, by noting that *Titanic*'s staying power flew in the face of the most notable crystalisation of trends in the past year – the precipitous demise in Week Two grosses. For most films it was a case of here this week, gone or greatly reduced – by as much as 50-60 per cent – the next. Which means more production and promotion dollars flying out the door for most of the 507 films released in 1997, up 7.7 per cent over the 471 released in 1996, according to the MPAA (whose release figures have seemed consistently high since member companies were concerned about anti-competitive charges of a managed "product shortage" 20 years ago). *Variety*, by contrast, charted 386 releases down to the $44,000 budget level, up from 379 a year earlier.

At any rate, 1997 was undeniably a good year, including the first two weeks or so of *Titanic*, with the MPAA computing total box-office revenue at $6.4 billion, up 8.4 per cent over 1996's $5.9 billion. Admissions climbed to 1.4 billion, up 7.7 per cent, while ticket inflation was nil.

Finally, one truly quirky American success story. Critics usually rate Federico Fellini's *8½*, *La Dolce Vita* and *La Strada* as his masterpieces, with **Nights of Cabiria** somewhere down the list. Bruce Goldstein, of the Film Forum in New York, decided it was time for a reappraisal of *Cabiria* – it presaged the post-war Italian search for meaning that Fellini gave Marcello Mastroianni in *La Dolce Vita* three years later.

Working with European sources and funding, Goldstein helped to mount a restoration and succeeded in retrieving a crucial seven-minute sequence in which Giulietta Masina makes night-time rounds with an anonymous Samaritan, dispensing alms to the forgotten, living in caves and craters. The sequence was only shown at Cannes in 1957 and then excised by Dino De Laurentiis, the film's producer, after the Catholic church leaders correctly understood the implied comparison and demanded Dino cut it. Now the irony: at press time, European exhibitors were waiting to see how *Cabiria* did in the US before booking it back home. It was a rare chance to strike a blow for US cultural imperialism and go see a Fellini.

Additional reporting by Susan Jacobson.

HARLAN JACOBSON covered the entertainment industries from New York for seven years for *Variety*, edited *Film Comment* for eight, and for nearly 25 years has written worldwide on film and pop culture. In 1992, with his wife, Susan Jacobson, he formed Talk Cinema, a preview screenings-and-discussion series, with sites in seven US cities.

Producers

Alliance Communications Corporation
301 N. Cannon Drive #321
Beverly Hills, CA 90210
Tel: (1 310) 275 5501
Fax: (1 310) 275 5502

American Zoetrope
916 Kearny Street
San Francisco, CA 94133
Tel: (1 415) 788 7500
Fax: (1 415) 989 7910

Beacon Communications Inc.
1041 N. Formosa Ave.
Santa Monica Bldg., #207
Los Angeles, CA 90046
Tel: (1 213) 850 2651
Fax: (1 213) 850 2613

Brillstein-Grey Entertainment
9150 Wilshire Blvd., #350
Beverly Hills, CA 90212
Tel: (1 310) 275 6135
Fax: (1 310) 275 6180

Cappa Production
(Martin Scorsese)
445 Park Ave., 7th Floor
New York, NY 10022
Tel: (1 212) 906 8800
Fax: (1 212) 906 8891

Caravan Pictures
3000 West Olympic Blvd., Bldg. 5,
Santa Monica, CA 90404
Tel: (1 310) 264 4400
Fax: (1 310) 264 4404

Castle Rock Entertainment
335 N. Maple Drive, #135
Beverly Hills, CA 90210
Tel: (1 310) 285 2300
Fax: (1 310) 285 2345

Cinergi Pictures Entertainment
2308 Broadway
Santa Monica, CA 90404
Tel: (1 310) 315 6000
Fax: (1 310) 828 0443

Columbia Pictures Television
(TV production)
3400 Riverside Drive
Burbank, CA 91505
Tel: (1 818) 954 6000

Donner Productions Warner Bros., Richard
4000 Warner Blvd.,
Burbank, CA 91522
Tel: (1 818) 954 4437
Fax: (1 818) 954 4908

DreamWorks SKG
100 Universal City Plaza,
Bungalow 477,
Universal City, CA 91608
Tel: (1 818) 777 4600
Fax: (1 818) 733 6153

The Robert Evans Company
The Lubitsch Bldg., #117
5555 Melrose Ave.
Hollywood, CA 90038
Tel: (1 213) 956 8800
Fax: (1 213) 862 0070

Finerman Productions, Wendy
10202 West Washington Blvd.,
Tristar 224
Culver City, CA 90232
Tel: (1 310) 244 4650
Fax: (1 310) 244 1495

40 Acres & a Mule Filmworks
(Spike Lee)
124 Dekalb Ave.
Brooklyn, NY 11217
Tel: (1 718) 624 3703

Fox Filmed Entertainment
10201 W. Pico Blvd.,
Los Angeles, CA 90035
Tel: (1 310) 369 3583
Fax: (1 310) 369 3155

Hanna Barbera Productions
3400 Cahuenga Blvd. West
Hollywood, CA 90068
Tel: (1 213) 851 5000
Fax: (1 213) 919 1201

Hollywood Pictures
(Distributed through Buena Vista)
500 South Buena Vista St.
Burbank, CA 91521
Tel: (1 818) 560 1000/6990
Fax: (1 818) 560 1930

Imagine Entertainment
1925 Century Park East, 23rd Floor
Los Angeles, CA 90067
Tel: (1 310) 277 1665
Fax: (1 310) 785 0107

James Cameron directs Leonardo DiCaprio and Kate Winslet on the set of TITANIC

photo: Fox/Paramount/Lightstorm

King World Productions
12400 Wilshire Blvd. #1200
Los Angeles, CA 90025
Tel: (1 310) 826 1108
Fax: (1 310) 207 2179

Kopelson Entertainment
2121 Avenue of the Stars, Ste. 1400
Los Angeles, CA 90067
Tel: (1 310) 369 7500
Fax: (1 310) 369 7501

Kushner-Locke Intl.
11601 Wilshire Blvd., 21st Floor
Los Angeles, CA 90025
Tel: (1 310) 445 1111
Fax: (1 310) 445 1191

The Ladd Company
Chevalier 117
5555 Melrose Ave.
Hollywood, CA 90038
Tel: (1 213) 956 8055
Fax: (1 213) 862 1115

Metro-Goldwyn-Mayer Inc.
2500 Broadway St., Ste. E-2029
Santa Monica, CA 90404
Tel: (1 310) 449 3000
Fax: (1 310) 449 3069

Miramax Films
7920 Sunset Blvd., #230
Los Angeles, CA 90046-3353
Tel: (1 213) 951 4280
Fax: (1 213) 845 4214

Morgan Creek Productions
4000 Warner Blvd., Bldg. 76
Burbank, CA 91522
Tel: (1 818) 954 4800
Fax: (1 818) 954 4811

New Line Cinema Corp.
(Distributor/Producer)
116 North Robertson Blvd. #200
Los Angeles, CA 90048
Tel: (1 310) 854 5811
Fax: (1 310) 854 1824

New Regency Productions Inc.
4000 Warner Blvd., Bldg. 66,
Room 5
Burbank, CA 91522
Tel: (1 818) 954 3044
Fax: (1 818) 954 3295

Northern Lights Ent.
100 Universal City Plaza, Bldg. 489

Universal City, CA 91608
Tel: (1 818) 777 8080
Fax: (1 818) 866 0689

Peters Entertainment, John
4000 Warner Blvd.
Burbank, CA 91522
Tel: (1 818) 954 4960
Fax: (1 818) 954 4983

PolyGram Filmed Ent.
9333 Wilshire Blvd.
Beverly Hills, CA 90210
Tel: (1 310) 777 7700
Fax: (1 310) 777 7709

Red Wagon Productions
10202 W. Washington Blvd., Ste. 112
Culver City, CA 90232
Tel: (1 310) 244 4466
Fax: (1 310) 244 1480

Ruddy-Morgan Organization
9300 Wilshire Blvd., Ste. 508
Beverly Hills, CA 90212.
Tel: (1 310) 271 7698
Fax: (1 310) 278 9978

Rysher Entertainment
2401 Colorado Avenue,
Ste. 200,
Santa Monica, CA 90404
Tel: (1 310) 309 5200
Fax: (1 310) 309 5210

Saban Entertainment
4000 West Alameda Avenue, Ste.
500
Burbank, CA 91505
Tel: (1 818) 972 4800
Fax: (1 818) 972 4895

Silver Pictures
4000 Warner Blvd., Bldg. 90
Burbank, CA 91522
Tel: (1 818) 954 4490
Fax: (1 818) 954 3237

Spelling Entertainment Group Inc.
5700 Wilshire Blvd., #375
Los Angeles, CA 90036
Tel: (1 213) 965 5700
Fax: (1 213) 965 5895

Tisch Company, Steve
3815 Hughes Ave., Culver City
CA 90232
Tel: (1 310) 838 2500
Fax: (1 310) 204 2713

Trimark Pictures
(Distributor/Producer)
2644 30th St., 2nd Floor,
Santa Monica
CA 90405
Tel: (1 310) 399 8877
Fax: (1 310) 392 0252

Universal Television Group
100 Universal City Plaza
Universal City, CA 91608
Tel: (1 818) 777 1000
Fax: (1 818) 866 1429

Wildwood Enterprises Inc.
(Robert Redford)
1101 Montana Ave., #E
Santa Monica, CA 90403
Tel: (1 310) 395 5155
Fax: (1 310) 395 3975

Wind Production Group
500 South Buena Vista St.
Burbank, CA 91521
Tel: (1 818) 560 1151
Fax: (1 818) 953 7401

Winkler Films Inc.
211 S. Beverly Drive, #200
Beverly Hills, CA 90212
Tel: (1 310) 858 5780
Fax: (1 310) 858 5799

Distributors

Alliance Releasing Corp.
121 Bloor Street, 14th Floor
Toronto
Ontario M4W 3M5, Canada
Tel: (1 416) 967 1141
Fax: (1 416) 967 4358

Buena Vista Pictures (Disney)
500 South Buena Vista St.
Burbank, CA 91521
Tel: (1 818) 560 4020
Fax: (1 818) 841 6847

King World Entertainment
12400 Wilshire Blvd., Ste. 1200,
Los Angeles, CA 90025
Tel: (1 310) 826 1108
Fax: (1 310) 207 2179

Miramax Films
375 Greenwich Street
New York, NY 10013
Tel: (1 212) 941 3800
Fax: (1 212) 941 3949

October Films
65 Bleeker Street
New York, NY 10012
Tel: (1 212) 259 4030
Fax: (1 212) 358 7662

Paramount Pictures
5555 Melrose Ave.
Hollywood, CA 90038
Tel: (1 213) 956 5000
Fax: (1 213) 862 1703

Sony Pictures Entertainment Inc.
10202 West Washington Blvd.
Culver City, CA 90232
Tel: (1 310) 244 4000
Fax: (1 310) 244 2626

TriStar
10202 West Washington Blvd.
Culver City, CA 90232
Tel: (1 310) 244 7700
Fax: (1 310) 244 1468

Twentieth Century Fox
10201 West Pico Blvd.
Los Angeles, CA 90035
Tel: (1 310) 369 1000
Fax: (1 310) 369 2735

Universal Pictures Inc.
100 Universal Plaza
Universal City, CA 91608
Tel: (1 818) 777 1000

Warner Bros. Pictures
(Distributor)
4000 Warner Blvd.
Burbank, CA 91522
Tel: (1 818) 954 6000
Fax: (1 818) 954 2222

Useful Addresses

Academy of Motion Picture Arts and Sciences
8949 Wilshire Blvd.
Beverly Hills, CA 90211
Tel: (1 310) 247 3000
Fax: (1 310) 859 9619

American Film Institute
John F. Kennedy Center for the
Performing Arts
Washington D.C. 20566
Tel: (1 202) 828 4090
Fax: (1 202) 659 1970

The Directors Guild of America
7920 Sunset Blvd., #230
Los Angeles, CA 90046
Tel: (1 310) 289 2000
Fax: (1 310) 289 2029

Independent Feature Project
104 W. 29th Street, 12th Floor
New York, NY 10001
Tel: (1 212) 465 8200
Fax: (1 212) 465 8525

Motion Picture Association of America (MPPA)
15503 Ventura Blvd.
Encino, CA 91436
Tel: (1 818) 995 6600
Fax: (1 818) 382 1784

NATO/ShoWest
116 North Robertson Blvd., Ste. F
Los Angeles, CA 90048
Tel: (1 310) 657 7724
Fax: (1 310) 657 4758

VENEZUELA

Irene
Herrera

Although the level of film production in Venezuela is low, it ranks fourth behind Argentina, Brazil and Mexico amongst Latin American countries. In the wake of the creation in 1993 of the government-financed Autonomous National Centre for Cinematography (CNAC), the nation's film landscape has experienced its most significant and optimistic revival since the mid-1970s. Not only have budgets and production volume increased, but co-productions have become a viable option.

Venezuela has signed co-production agreements with Canada, France and Spain. Last year, for example, three films (*Tokyo Paraguaipoa, The Valley* and *At Half Past Midnight*) received funding from the French Fond-Sud, while *Out in the Open*, directed by Luis Armando Roche, had funding from Venezuela, France and Canada and was the year's only movie with a budget above $1m (average feature budgets are around $500,000).

In 1997, Caracas hosted a meeting of the Conference of Iberian-American Film Authorities at which a multilateral fund was created to strengthen each nation's film industry. The Venezuelan Film Commission, meanwhile, is functioning well. Established in 1995, it helped bring more than $2.5m into the country in 1997, from international productions shooting at Venezuelan locations.

Most Venezuelan films' budgets depend mainly on CNAC grants and very few

Salsa band Salserin, the stars of Luis Alberto Lamata's THE FIRST TIME

incentives for private sector investment have succeeded. Since 1993, 28 films have been finished and eight more are expected for 1998. The country's 228 screens continue to be filled with Hollywood pictures, and attempts to pass a law in favour of the exhibition of Venezuelan films have failed. Of the 120 releases in 1997, about 100 were American, nine were Venezuelan, and 10 came from other countries, mainly Spain and France.

The only feature made entirely with private funding was **The First Time** (*La Primera Vez*) and it made the top ten for several weeks to finish with a gross of $472,590. Luis Alberto Lamata's film was based partially on the story of local salsa band Salserín, and boosted their popularity considerably. The other domestic releases were less commercially successful.

News from the underground

Roman Chalbaud, the most prolific film-maker in Venezuela, directed his sixteenth feature, **Pandemonium**. This impressive, apocalyptic comedy-drama follows Adonai, a poet who lives in the basement of an unfinished building and transmits news, music and poetry over a loudspeaker. He lives with his mother and Demetria, his lover, who forms a love triangle with two street boys. The drama climaxes when the inhabitants of the barrio rise up and take to the streets. This movie was recognised internationally, picking up awards in Havana and Biarritz – recognition for Chalbaud's unique vision.

Alberto Arvelo's dream-filled debut **One Life and Two Trails** (*Una Vida y Dos Mandados*), was selected for the official competition at the World Film Festival of Montreal, while Luis Armando Roche's historical drama **Out in the Open** (*Aire Libre*) deserved the Public Award at the International Film Festival in San Diego. In all, Venezuelan pictures travelled to festivals in 60 cities in 1997.

For 1998, hopes were high for three debut features from young film-makers: Gustavo Balza with **The Valley** (*El Valle*), Fernando Venturini with **Tres Noches**

Still from Alejandro Saderman's 100 YEARS OF FORGIVENESS

(*Three Nights*) and co-directors Mariana Rondón (a Venezuelan) and Marité Ugás (from Peru) with **At Half-Past Midnight** (*A la medianoche y media*), in which three lonely people – Sebastián, Ana and an apocalyptic girl – turn their city into a game board, where love, loneliness and the end of the world are at stake.

From the older generation, Alejandro Saderman's **100 Years of Forgiveness** (*100 Años de Perdon*), about four childhood friends planning a Christmas bank heist, and Carlos Azpurua's controversial **A Rude Awakening** (*Amaneció de Golpe*), about a coup in a Latin American country, sounded promising. Venezuela lacks film schools, but aspiring film-makers learn their trade by working with the veterans or studying overseas. Short films continue to be the best option for youngsters keen to experiment. Since 1995, 53 short films have been made in Venezuela, winning 19 international awards.

IRENE CAROLINE HERRERA has worked as art director on several 35mm short films and TV series. As a journalist, she has written for important Venezuelan publications such as *Verbigracia* (*El Universal*) and *Estilo* and is Venezuelan correspondent for *Producción & Distribución* and editor of their film magazine. She has written her first short film, scheduled to be filmed this year.

Recent and Forthcoming Films

PIEL (Skin)

Script: Armando Coll, Blanca Strepponi, Oscar Lucien. Dir: Lucien. Players: Indhira Serrano, Gabriel Blanco, Eileen Abad, Luke Grande, Sarah Sander. Prod: Antonio Llerandi.

Story of young lovers: an African-American girl and Juan Carlos, a white Venezuelan boy, who suffer racist prejudice because of their affair.

EL RIZO (The Loop)

Script and Dir: Julio Sosa Pietri. Players: Jean Carlo Simancas, Arcelia Ramírez (Mexico), Luly Bossa (Colombia), Claudio Obregón, Julio Medina, Daysi Granados (Cuba). Prod: Mauricio Walerstein.

The life of the outstanding playwright Alejandro del Rey. His anxieties, principles and lovers are portrayed in this tale of carnal passions and aesthetic obsession. Made in the best tradition of the great European cinema of the 1960s.

AMANECIÓ DE GOLPE
(A Rude Awakening)

Dir: Carlos Azpúrua. Script: José Ignacio Cabrujas. Players: Ruddy Rodríguez, Daniel Lugo, Héctor Myerston, Gabriel Retes (Mexico), Beatriz Santana (Spain), Vicente Tepedino. Prod: Alfredo D'Ambrosio (Venezuela), Enrique Vera (Canada), Carlos Orengo (Spain).

During a military coup in a Latin American country, a group of characters suffer the most terrifying experience of their lives.

ANTES DE MORIR
(Before Dying)

Script and Dir: Pablo de la Barra. Players: Rolando Padilla, Eileen Abad, Manuel Escolano, Juan Carlos Gardié, Bettina Grand. Prod: Philippe Toledano, Diana Sánchez, MBP (France).

Andrés is tormented by the memory of witnessing the murder of his family as a child. When the murderer returns to Venezuela, Andrés begins a quest for vengeance.

EL VALLE (The Valley)

Script: Armando Coll, Gustavo Balza. Dir: Balza. Players: Luis Fernández, Iván Tamayo, Pedro Durán, Luke Grande, Eliana López. Prod: Antonio Llerandi, Liz Mago.

Aixa, a pregnant teenager surrounded by friends and family offering conflicting advice, must decide whether or not to keep her baby.

DESPEDIDA DE SOLTERA
(Bridal Shower)

Script and Dir: Antonio Llerandi. Players: Dora Mazzone, Martha Tarazone, Claudia Reyes, Tatiana Padrón, Elaiza Gil, Laura Altieri. Prod: Liz Mago and Luis Zambrano.

Marisabel, her maid, and 11 girlfriends get together to have a bridal shower. The party starts off with all kinds of jokes and games, then a terrible storm endangers them all.

TRES NOCHES (Three Nights)

Script and Dir: Fernando Venturini. Players: Victor Mayo, Juan Carlos Vellido (Spain), Adriana Velásquez. Prod: Carmen Helena Nouel, Alexandra Medialdea.

A mysterious trip through a modern city is taken by a maverick detective and Picasso, a yuppie bar owner, in search of a top drug dealer's killer.

CORAZONES NEGROS
(Black Hearts)

Dir: Gabriel Rangel. Players: Francisco Alfaro, Rafael Briceño,

William Mujica, Francisco Salazar, Mercedes Mayo. Prod: Górgola Films CA and Tango Bravo Producciones.

Black comedy about four men who work with death: a mortician, a watchman, a hearse driver, and a salesman of religious articles. Problems begin when Julian, the mortician, steals the corpse of a beautiful young woman and takes it home.

TOKYO PARAGUIAPOA

Script: Juan Astorga and Leonardo Henríquez. Dir: Henríquez. Players: Adolfo Cubas, Kenji Satos, Eileen Abad, Asdrúbal Meléndez, Violeta Alemán. Prod: Antonio Llerandi.

Ryuzo, a young Japanese boy who has committed a crime of passion in Tokyo is sent by his industrial tycoon father to Paraguaipoa, a small western Venezuelan town, where he finds love and adventure.

AIRE LIBRE (Out in the Open)

Dir: Luis Armando Roche. Players: Christian Vadim (France), Roy Dupuis (Canada), Carlos Cruz, Dora Mazzone. Prod: Marie-Francoise Roche, Lidia Córdoba (Venezuela), Morelba Pacheco (France), Suzane Girardi (Canada).

This imaginary fable tells of the friendship between two famous explorers, Alexander von Humboldt and Aimeé Bonpland, and a young native half-breed during their visit to Venezuela in the early nineteenth century.

SANTERA

Script and Dir: Solveig Hoogesteijn. Players: Laura del Sol (Spain), Hirma Salcedo, Gledys Ibarra. Victor Cuica. Daniel López. Prod: Delfina Catalá, Cristian Playersillo.

Paula, an Amnesty International worker, visits Venezuela to inspect local prisons. In one of the women's jails she meets Soledad, who has been arrested for practicing witchcraft, and a strange relationship begins.

UNA VIDA Y DOS MANDADOS
(One Life and Two Trails)

Script: Freddy Sosa, Jorge Chacín, Alberto Arvelo. Dir: Arvelo. Players: Jordany Montilola, Germán Mendieta, Ramona Pérez, Bernardino Angel. Prod: Alexia Montilla, Gerardo Montilla.

Romer receives an old photograph as a fiftieth birthday gift. This makes him homesick and he has a strange dream and a premonition of his mother's death, prompting him to climb the mountain where he grew up.

ROSA DE FRANCIA
(Rose of France)

Script and Dir: César Bolívar. Players: Ninibeth Leal, Victor Cámara, Julie Restifo, Alberto Alifa, Lourdes Valera. Prod: Arnaldo Limansky, Valentina Ferrer.

Rose, a beautiful Indian girl, turns to prostitution to survive when she is threatened by a man of immense power.

LA VOZ DEL CORAZÓN
(Voice of the Heart)

Script: Salvador Garmendia, Carlos Oteyza. Dir: Oteyza. Players: Henry Soto. Lupe Barrado (Spain), Beatríz Valdes (Cuba), Asdrúbal Meléndez, Toco Gómez. Prod: Yekuana Films.

Tomás, an agent for the Green Americaenvironmentalist organisation, is investigating deforestation in South American jungles when he falls for Bilbao, a community leader. Together they struggle against the multinational sawmill company that is destroying the region.

PANDEMONIUM

Script: David Suárez, Román Chalbaud, Orlando Urdaneta. Dir: RChalbaud. Players: Urdaneta, Amalia Pérez Díaz, Miguelángel Landa, Elaiza Gil, Frank Spano. Prod: Arnaldo Limansky.

100 AÑOS DE PERDON
(100 Years of Forgiveness)

Dir and Script: Alejandro Saderman. Players: Orlando Urdaneta, Daniel Lugo, Mariano Alvarez, Aroldo Betancourt. Prod: Antonio Llerandi and Liz Mago.

Producers

Alter Producciones
Ave. Diego de Losada
Qta. Alter
San Bernardino
Caracas
Tel: (58 2) 527 197/511 923
Fax: (58 2) 552 7297

Bolivar Films
Av. Luis Guillermo Villegas Blanco
Edif. Bolívar Films. Sta
Eduvigis
Caracas
Tel: (58 2) 283 8455

Fax: (58 2) 284 1011
web page: www.bolivarfilms.com

Caral Cine
2da transversal.
Qta. El Laurel.
Sta. Eduvigis
Caracas
Tel: (58 2) 283 9944
Fax: (58 2) 285 9056

Centro de cinematografía de La Universidad de los Andes
Altos Comedor
Universitario
Entrada Vía Chorros de Milla
Mérida

Tel: (58 74) 401 725/401 720/441 514

Cine Marte
Calle Santa Ana con Calle Lecuna
Boleíta Sur
Caracas
Tel: (58 2) 239 5376
Fax: (58 2) 239 2073

Cine Sur C. A.
Av. Principal de San Marino
Qta. Siboney
Chacao
Caracas
Tel: (58 2) 261 8685/266 7667
Fax: (58 2) 266 7667

Pablo de la Barra Producciones
3era transversal con 4ta avenida.
Edificio Elite
Apto. 105, Los Palos Grandes
Caracas
Tel: (58 2) 283 4990/284 3484
Fax: (58 2) 149 355 057
e-mail: amaru@truevision.net

Premiere Producciones
Primera Av. De los Palos Grandes
Edif. Roxul
piso 3. Ofc. 31
Caracas
Tel: (58 2) 286 1291/6967
Fax: (58 2) 284 338
e-mail: alopezsojo@cantv.net

Producciones 800
Edifcio Torre Financiera
Oficina Mezanina M-O
Ave. Beethonven (al lado de Maxy's)
Urbanización Bello Monte
Caracas 1060
Tel: (58 2) 751 7076/752
1821/166243862

Producciones Doble Ele
Avenida Principal de Prados
del Este
Residencias
los Copigües
piso 7, apto. 7-4
Lomas de Prados del Este
Caracas
Tel: (58 2) 976 8273/261 8685
Fax: (58 2) 266 7667
Cel. (58 2) 16.6302854

Producciones Tango Bravo
4ta Avenida entre 9na
Y 10ma. Transversal
Qta. Turandot
Los Palos Grandes
Caracas
Tel: (58 2) 283 4829/285 9237
Fax: (58 2) 285.9213
e-mail: tango.bravo@cantv.net

T&M Films
Ave. Luis Guillermo Villegas Blanco
Edif. Rivera, Piso 1,
oficina 11, Santa Eduvigis
Caracas
Tel: (58 2) 283.4653/285 4747
Fax: (58 2) 283 4653
e-mail: tymfilms@facilnet.com

Luke Grande in Gustavo Balza's THE VALLEY

TVA
Av. El Retiro
Qta. 34, El Rosal
Caracas 1060
Tel: (58 2) 952 5727
Fax: (58 2) 953 0778

Distributors

Blancica
3era Av. Las Delicias
Sabana Grande
Edif. Las Delicias PB
Caracas
Tel: (58 2) 762 9781
Fax: (58 2) 762 4264

Cineven 2.000
Alberto Benaim
4ta Avenida entre 9na
Y 10ma.
Transversal
Qta. Turandot
Los Palos Grandes
Caracas
Tel: (58 2) 283 4829/283 7156
Fax: (58 2) 285 9237

Di Fox
Av. Las Palmas
Edif. Las Palmas
Piso 3
Caracas
Tel: (58 2) 781 7511
Fax: (58 2) 782 5087

Korda Films
Ed. Teatro Altamira PH
Altamira Sur
Caracas
Tel: (58 2) 762 6030

Movie Movie Asesoramientos
Av. Libertador, cruce con
Av. Las Palmas
Edif. Teatro Las Palmas
Sótano 1. Of. 7
Caracas
Tel: (58 2) 793 7158

Roraimex
Av. Las Palmas
Ed. Las Palmas
Mezzanina
Caracas
Tel: (58 2) 793 7377

Tepuy Films
Av. Libertador
Torre EXA, PH 1
El Rosal
Caracas 1060
Tel: (58 2) 953 3363/953 0942
Fax: (58 2) 953.6880
e-mail: tepuy@hdq.true.net

Venefilms
Av. Rómulo Gallegos
Esq. El Carmen
Ed. Torre Samán, piso 1
of. 11, Los Dos Caminos
Caracas
Tel: (58 2) 762 9781/239 6417

Useful Addresses

Asociación Nacional de Autores Cinematográficos (ANAC)
Urb. Avila, Av
San Gabriel
Qta. Primavera
Alta Florida
Tel: (58 2) 740 366/741 954

Asociación Nacional de Exhibidores
Av. Rómulo Gallegos
Esq. El Carmen
Ed. Torre Samán
psio, 1, of. 11
Los Dos Caminos
Caracas
Tel: (58 2) 237 0397/237 1262
Fax: (58 2) 239 6417

Cámara de la Industria del Cine y del Video
Tel: (58 2) 283 4829/283 7156
Fax: (58 2) 285 9237

Cámara Venezolana de Productores de Largometrajes (CAVEPROL)
4ta Avenida entre 9na
Y 10ma
Transversal
Qta. Turandot
Los Palos Grandes
Caracas.
Tel: (58 2) 283 4829/283 7156
Fax: (58 2) 285 9237

Centro Nacional Autónomo de Cinematografía (CNAC)
Av. Ppal de Los Ruices
Edificio Centro Monaca
Ala Sur, Piso 2
Los Ruices
Caracas
Tel: (58 2) 238 6494/238 1050
Fax: (58 2) 237 4942
e-mail: presidencnac@true.net

Film Comission
Av. Ppal de Los Ruices, Edificio
Centro Monaca
Ala Sur
Piso 2. Los Ruices
Caracas
Tel: (58 2) 238 6494/238 1050
Fax: (58 2) 237 4942
e-mail: venefilmcomis@true.net

Sindicato Profesional de Trabajadores de Radio, Cine, TV y Afines del
Distrito Federal y Estado Miranda
Av. Nivaldo
Qta. San Joseph
no. 175, La Florida
Caracas
Tel: (58 2) 744 444
Fax: (58 2) 731 0976

ZIMBABWE — Judy Kendall

When the Burkinabe/Zimbabwean/French/British co-production about enduring friendship, *Kini and Adams*, reached the official selection at Cannes 1997, it heralded a first for Southern Africa. In the same year, the Zimbabwean *Flame* was a number one hit at the domestic box-office. In 1998, new films have been thin on the ground, perhaps because of the country's weak financial situation. But Manu Kurewa's

Mangwana, exploring the relationship between an ageing Scottish farmer and a Zimbabwean elder, graced the new Cinefoundation category for young film-makers at Cannes 1998.

Given that finance has always been a major hurdle for Zimbabwean directors, it is not surprising that most recent films have been co-productions. In 1997, as well as *Kini and Adams*, there was the Cameroon director Jean-Pierre Bekolo's **Aristotle's Plot** (*Le Complot d'Aristote*, France/ Zimbabwe). Its story – local fans of American action movies harass a film-maker trying to screen more African pictures – was a poignant reminder of current pressing concerns for African cinema.

Dreaming of love

The new South African M-Net project, **Africa Dreaming**, is a co-production of six 26-minute love stories from Zimbabwe, Mozambique, Namibia, Senegal, South Africa and Tunisia. Zimbabwean Farai Sevenso's entry, **The Last Picture** (produced by Framework International), focuses on a young photographer who falls in love with an old man's third young wife when taking her photograph.

A second series, *Mama Africa* (films by African women directors), is now planned, including another Zimbabwean contribution, 30 per cent funded by M-Net. Forthcoming projects include the first ever East African co-production. Somalian director Adulkadir Ahmed Said's **The Errant Knights**, which deals with the environment and history of East Africa, will have finance from Djibouti, Kenya, Yemen, Ethiopia and Zimbabwe.

Shot in late 1996, Olly Maruma's **The Big Time** (Moonlight Productions), in which a woman leaves her lover for a big-time advertising executive-cum-gangster, is the first all-black, all-Zimbabwean production and should soon be ready for release. Another film at the post-production stage when this report went to press was Norbert Fero's romantic love triangle, **Matters of the Spirit**, produced by Chameleon Films.

Rory Kilalea's **Journey from the Jacarandas**, produced by Joel Phiri and Mary-Anne Amato of Chiaroscuro, deals with a relationship between two women in 1960s Rhodesia and features Anna Chancellor (*Four Weddings and a Funeral*), Sophie Ward, Mekhi Phifer, Nthati Mosesh (*Kini and Adams*) and Martin le Maître.

The Captain, the second feature from *Flame* director Ingrid Sinclair, will explore issues around the genocide in Rwanda (this looks likely to be yet another co-production, with investment from Zimbabwe, Canada, Rwanda and South Africa). Finally, there is **Itai Tione**, directed by Albert Chimedza, which promises to be the first ever Shona language feature. During the summer, Zimbabwean movie enthusiasts were looking forward to the biannual Southern African Film Festival, scheduled to be held in Harare in September 1998.

Producers

Black and White Film Company
51a Selous Avenue
Harare
Tel: (263 4) 727 495/708 426
Fax: (263 4) 708 426

Framework International Pty Ltd
Box A4
Avondale
Harare
Tel: (263 4) 720 026
Fax: (263 4) 737 491
email: framewk@icon.co.zw

Itai Tione Film Project
Box HG 496
Highlands
Harare
Tel/Fax: (263 4) 498 309

Useful Addresses

Artvark, CFL
7 Kenilworth Road
Newlands
Box CH 914
Harare
Tel: (263 4) 746 387/746 389/ 746 607
Fax: (263 4) 746 376
email: mikhail@artvark.icon.co.zw

Central Film Laboratory
Box HG 496
Highlands
Harare
Tel: (263 4) 746 257/8/9
Fax: (263 4) 746 252

Ministry of Information, Post and Telecommunications
PO Box 8
232 Causeway
Harare
Tel: (263 4) 703 891
Fax: (263 4) 707 213

Media for Development Trust
Box 6755
Harare
Tel: (263 4) 733 364/5
Fax: (263 4) 729 066

Z Promotions
PO Box 6109
Harare
Tel: (263 4) 726 795
Fax: (263 4) 726 796

Top: Don Ameche, a guest of the Flanders festival for the 1985 opening night screening of COCOON
Above: The 1997 Flanders jury: (left to right) Thom Hoffman, Giancarlo Esposito, Jean-Pierre De Decker, Gina Lollobrigida and Irvin Kershner.

FESTIVALS

The Flanders International Film Festival's First 25 Years

by Jacques Dubrulle

The Flanders International Film Festival – Ghent is Belgium's most prominent annual film event. It is attended by over 70,000 visitors and receives wide attention in the Benelux media. Regarded as one of the best organised festivals of its kind, it enjoys a good reputation on the international film circuit. Over the past 25 years, the festival has introduced hundreds of film-makers to Belgian audiences and welcomed a pantheon of internationally renowned guests. It combines glamour with the cosy atmosphere of art cinema

The festival is competitive, with a thematic competition focusing on "The Impact of Music on Film", which is also the festival's overall theme. This includes presentations of silent classics with live music, concerts of film music and other activities designed to showcase the contribution made by composers to a film's overall impact on its audience.

The festival also has a general programme designed to emphasise a wide variety of styles and genres, showcasing the best of contemporary international cinema by screening films from all over the world: works by new film-makers as well as internationally-renowned names. The titles chosen are "commercial" and "art" films, old and new, long and short.

Jacques Dubrulle greets Jeremy Irons before the opening night screening of CHINESE BOX in 1997

A brief history

Founded in January 1974 by the owner of Ghent's art-house cinema, Studio Skoop, and the Ghent University film club as a modest venture, presenting just 18 films, the Flanders festival quickly evolved into a large-scale event attracting thousands of film buffs, all seeking a unique opportunity to see movies which would never otherwise reach their local cinemas. By 1978, more than 50 films were shown, but the festival clearly needed a more solid structure. Various problems – mainly financial – threatened its very existence.

This resulted, in 1979, in the founding of a Non-Profit Organisation which gave the festival a financial backbone, through recognition by national and regional authorities, particularly the City of Ghent, the Province of East Flanders and the national (later Flemish) government. This recognition enabled the festival to become a "mature" event. Its organisers no longer had complete freedom to do what they wanted, but the pioneering spirit of the early days has never faded. At the end of

Festival juror Paul Bartel with producer Fred Roos in 1991

Michael Nyman conducted a concert of his film music in Ghent in 1991

1981, Decascoop, a revolutionary cinema multiplex, was opened in Ghent, allowing the festival to grow, and by 1982 some 100 films were shown each year, using four of Decascoop's 12 screens.

In 1985, the festival evolved into a new stage. I set out to create the conditions which would allow for constant growth and a long-term policy. The festival became a member of the International Federation of Film Producers Associations (IFFPA). This was the time of the hailed synergy between culture and economy. World cinema was going through a crisis and film producers and sellers had become concerned about their interests. The festival therefore was to pay more attention to the interests of the market and at the same time safeguard the artistic interests of film-makers.

Belgian cinema became a fixed item in the festival's programme. Since 1984, the festival has organised The Night of Film, at which the national film prizes, the Joseph Plateau Awards, are distributed. Plateau,

incidentally, was the professor at Ghent University who defined the principle of the persistence of vision – the basis of the concept of "moving images".

And the winner is...

The festival moved into its competitive phase in 1985. Its theme was "The Impact of Music on Film", making Flanders the only festival in the world to pay attention to the contribution of composers and musicians to the art of cinema. It enabled the festival to go beyond the boundaries of traditional film presentation. Since then, the festival has organised concerts of film music, with renowned composers such as Ennio Morricone, Michael Nyman, David Newman, Nicola Piovani, Stanley Myers, Peer Raben, Carl Davis, Georges Delerue and Jean-Claude Petit conducting their music in Ghent.

The competition emphasises the creative role of music in the general concept and effect of a film. The international jury, whose members have included Paul Bartel,

Mike Figgis, Sam Fuller, Jerry Leiber, Krzysztof Zanussi and many others, are invited to take the films into consideration as a whole, paying attention to the way music is applied to reinforce the dramatic and visual impact. It is, therefore, not merely a competition for film music. Whether a film uses original compositions or existing music has no bearing on its eligibility for the competition.

The international jury confers 3 prizes: The Grand Prix of the Flemish Community for Best Film (Gilded Spur), the Prize of the Flemish Community for Best Director (Silver Spur) and the Prize of the Flemish Community for Best Composer (original music, Georges Delerue Prize). All prizes include money, with about $26,000 (one million Belgian francs) going to the winner of the Gilded Spur.

Ennio Morricone signing autographs at Flanders in 1987

During the 1990s, the number of foreign guests has kept on increasing and the budget has kept pace with this growth, assisted by the festival's corporate sponsors, including Kinepolis, Canal+, ASLK, National Lottery, VRT, Sofitel, American Airlines and Tuborg. In 1993, the festival was appointed Cultural Ambassador of Flanders and, since then, has been represented in Paris, London and the US. This recognition from the Flemish government enabled the festival to offer the substantial cash prizes to competing films, as well as better accommodation for its guests. In 1997, the festival was appointed as City Ambassador of Ghent, an honour acknowledging the festival's role in promoting the city's overseas profile.

A six-part showcase

The Flanders festival is basically a showcase offering filmgoers an oppor-tunity to see films before they reach the regular cinema circuit – or films which will never reach mainstream theatres at all. Some 15 films compete for the three prizes and the festival also serves as a promotion platform for Belgian distributors and producers who want to launch their new acquisitions or productions to public, press and industry. The programme is divided

into six main sections, supplemented by special events and sidebars, as follows:

Official Selection – Premiere screenings of films in and out of the competition: "The Impact of Music on Film".

Previews – A showcase of films from Belgian distributors, scheduled for autumn release in Belgian theatres.

Filmspectrum: A Panorama of World Cinema – An anthology of films from all over the world in search of distribution in the Benelux. Originality, contents and innovative use of the film medium are primary criteria. Included are films by new film-makers ("New Horizons"), a survey of remarkable films shown at various festivals ("World Cinema Today"), special items, short films and documentaries.

The Memory Of Film – A retrospective section focusing on classics from the history of cinema. This section is either conceived as an anthology or as a thematic section, focusing on some specific theme.

Tributes – Prominent living personalities from the world of international cinema are celebrated with a retrospective of their work.

Belgian Cinema Today – Drawing attention to film-making in Belgium, with feature films, shorts of Belgian origin and a competition for Belgian shorts, encouraging young talent with cash prizes. The festival's international jury confers two prizes: Prize of the Flemish Community for the best Flemish short film and the Prize of the Flemish Community for the best Belgian short film.

Special Events – including concerts of film music, presentations of classic silent films with live music, presentations of films in an unusual venue.

Sidebar Activities – including seminars such as "Flanders Meets the European Cultural Alliance", for film-makers from the smaller European territories, as well as the traditional presentation of the annual national film awards, the Joseph Plateau Awards at the Night of Film, and other events.

The 1991 festival's swimming pool screening is still being talked about

Musicians and orchestras who have performed at various screenings, such as the opening and closing sessions of the festival include Claude Bolling Band, the Big Jazz Orchestra of the Ghent Music Conservatory, Lazy River Big Band, the Flanders Youth Orchestra, François Glorieux, Pim Jacobs and his orchestra, Jean 'Toots' Thielemans, Michel Legrand, Cantabile, The Beau Hunks, Joost Vanhove, Archie Shepp and Michel Herr, Johan Verminnen and La Piovra.

You must remember this

The most successful of the festival's many screenings in unusual venues was the screening of a compilation of film excerpts in a swimming pool in 1991. The spectators were *in* the water, watching a floating screen. Other screenings included *Much Ado About Nothing* in the Ghent theatre, *Underground* in the Ghent Opera House, *Escape from Alcatraz* in Ghent's prison and *The Hunchback of Notre Dame* in St Peter's Church. These screenings usually attract massive attention. The swimming pool event is still talked about.

Some festival screenings became memorable because they produced a moment of "magic". The screening of Lawrence Kasdan's *Silverado* gave us one of these, when cowboys on horseback rode into the screening room, and the horses,

frightened by the noise on screen and the cheering of the crowds, started staggering. Hal Ashby, unable to attend, came through live and clear on the loudspeakers via a direct phone call from Los Angeles in 1986, to welcome the crowd to the screening of his last film, *8 Million Ways to Die*. Other memorable moments: the magic of veteran art director Alexandre Trauner at the screening of Bertrand Tavernier's *Round Midnight*, or veteran film-maker Leonid Trauberg witnessing the rebirth of his 1927 film, *New Babylon*, in 1983.

Some of the many distinguished visitors will surely remember their visit to Ghent for a long time. There was Michel Piccoli, who was stopped by customs when crossing the border. Or, in 1986, Anthony Perkins, who left for a walk in town and was found hours later, when half the festival crew had gone in search of him (this was, of course, long before the days of mobile phones).

Some of these guests came to Ghent long before they were famous. Andy Garcia had just done his first film. Aki Kaurismäki came to Ghent in 1988, only to be extensively interviewed by Belgian journalists half a year later in Berlin, where the word was that everyone had to see *I Hired a Contract Killer*. Mel Brooks conducted the festival orchestra back in 1987, probably the first (and last) time he acted as a conductor.

The guest list

Some of the festival's guests have come to Ghent on more than one occasion and become real friends of the event, such as Georges Delerue, Robert Wise, Norma Heyman and Krzysztof Zanussi. The complete list of guests who have honoured the festival is far too long for inclusion here, but among the most notable are Robert Altman, Jean-Jacques Annaud, Patricia Arquette, Anne Bancroft, Elmer Bernstein, Luc Besson, Jane Birkin, Kenneth Branagh, Mel Brooks, Youssef Chahine, Toni Collette, Willem Dafoe and Terence Davies.

Flanders has also welcomed Atom Egoyan, Julius Epstein, Mike Figgis, Stephen Frears, Andy Garcia, Terry Gilliam, Danny Glover, Elliott Gould, Peter Greenaway, Melanie Griffith, Christopher Hampton, Michael Haneke, George Roy Hill, John Hurt, Jeremy Irons, James Earl Jones, Aki Kaurismäki, Irvin Kershner, Emir Kusturica, Patrice Leconte, Ken Loach, Gina Lollobrigida, Karl Malden, Nino Manfredi, Paul Mazursky, Ennio Morricone, Armin Muller-Stahl, Ornella Muti, Michael Nyman and Arthur Penn.

Not forgetting Anthony Perkins, Michel Piccoli, Brad Pitt, Sydney Pollack, David Puttnam, Charlotte Rampling, Fernando Rey, Jonas Rosenfield, Leonard Rosenman, John Schlesinger, Paul Schrader, Mrinal Sen, Jerzy Skolimovski, Max Von Sydow,

Mel Brooks conducting the Flanders festival orchestra in 1987

Alain Tanner, Bertrand Tavernier, Joseph Vilsmaier, Bo Widerberg, Michael Winterbottom and Frederick Wiseman.

The festival paid tribute to Georges Delerue, Elliott Gould, Gina Lollobrigida, Sydney Pollack, Robert Wise, Anthony Perkins, Frederick Wiseman, George Roy Hill, Henri Colpi, Paul Cox, Raoul Servais, Peer Raben, Sam Fuller, Julius Epstein, Aki Kaurismäki, Fons Rademakers, American Zoetrope, Alejandro Agresti, David Raksin and others. As the Flanders International Film Festival – Ghent prepares for its second quarter-century, we look forward to wecloming and honouring many more great names.

JACQUES DUBRULLE has been Secretary General of the Flanders International Film Festival – Ghent since 1979.

Anthony Perkins went walkabout in Ghent during the 1986 festival

Flanders tribute recipient Leslie Caron with Tom Hulce in 1996

Flanders tribute recipient James Earl Jones in 1995

Robert Altman visited Ghent for a festival screening of SHORT CUTS in 1993

Opening Films: 1974 to 1997

1974 – *Der Händler der 4 Jahreszeiten* (Rainer Werner Fassbinder)

1975 – *Film d'Amore e d'Anarchia* (Lina Wertmüller)

1976 – *The Apprenticeship of Duddy Kravitz* (Ted Kotcheff)

1977 – *Die Verrohung des Franz Blum* (Reinhard Hauff)

1978 – *Why Shoot The Teacher?* (Silvio Narizzano)

1979 – *A Woman of Paris* (Charles Chaplin)

1980 – *Zerkalo* [*The Mirror*] (Andrei Tarkovsky)

1981 – *Le Coup de Torchon* (Bertrand Tavernier)

1982 – *A Midsummer Night's Sex Comedy* (Woody Allen)

1983 – *Local Hero* (Bill Forsyth)

1984 – *Nineteen Eighty-Four* (Michael Radford)

1985 – *Cocoon* (Ron Howard)

1986 – *Round Midnight* (Bertrand Tavernier)

1987 – *The Untouchables* (Brian De Palma)

1988 – *To Kill A Priest* (Agnieszka Holland)

1989 – *Casualties of War* (Brian De Palma)

1990 – *Ju Dou* (Zhang Yimou)

1991 – *The Fisher King* (Terry Gilliam)

1992 – *Daens* (Stijn Coninx)

1993 – *The Age of Innocence* (Martin Scorsese)

1994 – *Taxandria* (Raoul Servais)

1995 – *Brylcream Boulevard: Blueberry Hill 2* (Robbe De Hert)

1996 – *Shine* (Scott Hicks)

1997 – *Chinese Box* (Wayne Wang)

Winners of the Gilded Spur for Best Film

1985 – *Stop Making Sense* (Jonathan Demme)

1986 – *My First Wife* (Paul Cox)

1987 – *Un Zoo la Nuit* (Jean Claude Lauzon)

1988 – *The Ice Palace* (Per Blom)

1989 – *Kuroi Ame* [*Black Rain*] (Shohei Imamura)

1990 – *Zamri, Oumi, Voskresni* [*Stand Still, Die and Rise Again*] (Vitali Kanevski)

1991 – *Europa* (Lars von Trier)

1992 – *A Woman's Tale* (Paul Cox)

1993 – *Passion Fish* (John Sayles)

1994 – *La Partie d'Echecs* (Yves Hanchar)

1995 – *Cyclo* (Tran Anh Hung)

1996 – *Village of Dreams* (Yoichi Higashi)

1997 – *The Witman Boys* (János Szász)

Silent Classics with Live Music

1983 – *New Babylon* (L.Trauberg & G.Kozintsev, 1928) – Music: Dmitri Shostakovich

1984 – *Borinage* (Joris Ivens & Henri Storck, 1932) – Music: André Asriel
L'Hirondelle et la Mésange (Andre Antoine & Henri Colpi 1924) – Music: Raymond Alessandrini; *Nosferatu* (F.W. Murnau, 1922) – Musical concept: Lothar Prox
La Passion de Jeanne d'Arc (C.Th. Dreyer, 1927) – Music: Jo Van den Booren

1986 – *Berlin: Symphony of a Great City* (Walther Rutmann 1927) – Music: Edmund Meisel

The 'Opus' Trilogy (Walther Rutmann 1921-24) – Music: Tilo Medek
L'Inhumaine (Marcel L'Herbier 1924) – Music: Christophe Desnoux

1987 – *Casanova* (Alexandre Volkoff, 1925) – Music: Georges Delerue

1988 – *Cabiria* (Giovanni Pastrone, 1915) – Music: Ildebrando Pizzetti
Visages d'Enfants (Jacques Feyder 1924) – Music : Dirk Brossé

1990 – *Battleship Potemkin* (Sergei Eisenstein, 1925) – Music: La Marmite Infernale

1993 – *Γaust* (1924) and *Nosferatu* (1922, both F.W. Murnau) – Music : Art Zoyd.

1994 – *A Page of Madness* (Teinosuke Kinugasa, 1926) – Music: the Blindman Quartet

1995 – *Rapsodia Satanica* (Nino Oxilia, 1915) – Music: Pietro Mascagni
Die Frau im Mond (Fritz Lang 1928) – Music: Denis Levaillant

Jane Birkin opens the Flanders Film Ball in 1985 with former Belgian Prime Minister Wilfred Martens

1996 – *Witchcraft through the Ages* (Benjamin Christensen, 1922) – Music: Art Zoyd

1998 – *La Chute de la Maison Usher* (Jean Epstein, 1928) – Music: the Blindman Quartet

Concerts of Film Music

1985 – Tribute to Nino Rota

1987 – A Night to Remember: Ennio Morricone

1988 – A Night of Great Movie Music with Frédéric Devreeze, Georges Delerue, Bruce Broughton, David Newman and Jean-Claude Petit

1989 – Film music in Europe with Frédéric Devreeze, Dirk Brosse, Nicola Piovani, Peer Raben, Stanley Myers and Lukas Karitinos

1991 – Michael Nyman in Concert

1992 – Simon Fisher Turner – Music from films by Derek Jarman

1993 – Double Bill Concert: Bernard Herrmann & Classical Music In Film

1994 – Double Bill Concert: Georges Delerue & Classical Music In Film

1997 – The Birth of a Score with Dirk Brossé on the history of film music, and guest performances by Leonard Rosenman, Jean-Claude Petit and Frédéric Devreese.

The Festival Staff

Jacques Dubrulle, *Secretary General & Delegate of the Board*

Gwen Vande Pitte, *Administration Executive & Sponsor Relations*

Walter Provo, *Programme Director*

Marian Ponnet, *Guest Officer & Public Relations*

Peter Bouckaert, *Press Relations & Assistant Manager*

Vera Lambersy, *Secretary*

Antoon Wyffels, *Member of the Board*

Wim De Witte, *Print Traffic Supervisor*

Daniëlla De Decker, *Accountant*

Composers (left to right) Frédéric Devreese, Jean 'Toots' Thielemans, Jean Claude Petit, Georges Delerue, David Newman and Bruce Broughton

Festival Addresses

Flanders International Film Festival (Ghent)
1104, Kortrijksesteenweg
B 9051 Ghent
Belgium
Tel: (32 9) 242 8060
Fax: (32 9) 221 9074
e-mail: info@filmfestival.be
Website: www.filmfestival.be

Denise Breton
(Festival contact in France)
Rue Fbg St.Honoré 25
F-75008 Paris
Tel: (33 1) 4266 2002
Fax: (33 1) 4742 1885

Charlotte Tudor
(Festival contact in UK)
Corbett & Keene
122 Wardour Street
London W1V 3LA
Tel: (44 171) 494 3478
Fax: (44 171) 734 2024

Chasen & Co. – Ronni Chasen
(Festival contact in US)
8599 Beverly Bvd # 407
Los Angeles
CA 90048
Tel: (1 310) 274 44 00
Fax: (1 310) 274 44 67

Lucius Barre
(Festival contact in US)
45, West 67th Street
Apt 7J
10023 NY New York
Tel: (1 212) 595 1773
Fax: (1 212) 769 9601

Above: Secretary General Jacques Dubrulle and the Flanders team
Top left: Peter Greenaway (right) at the festival in 1983 for a screening of THE DRAUGHTSMAN'S CONTRACT
Top right: Danny Glover was a festival guest for THE SAINT OF FORT WASHINGTON in 1993

Moritz de Hadeln, Festival Director, with Gwyneth Paltrow and Robert De Niro at the 1998 Berlinale

Guide to Leading Festivals

Adriaticocinema

June 1999

The first festival on the Adriatic coast which simultaneously involves three seaside resorts, Bellaria Igea Marina, Cattolica and Rimini, known for their formerly individual film festivals (Mystfest, Riminicinema and Anteprima). This new event combines research, experimental and independent cinema with entertainment. It includes films, conferences, awards, meetings and debates with film-makers and actors in the native region of Federico Fellini. There are special competitions for Italian independents and international film schools, as well as international preview and music and cinema sections. Director: Marco Bellocchio. Organising director: Gianfranco Miro Gori. *Inquiries to:* Adriaticocinema, Via Gambalunga 27, 47900 Rimini, Italy. Tel: (39 5) 412 6399/2627. Fax: (39 5) 412 4227. e-mail: adriaticocinema@comune.rimini.it

Amiens

November 5–14, 1999

A competitive festival in northern France for both shorts and features. There are also retrospectives ("Leo McCarey and the Renaissance of Brazilian Cinema" in 1998), as well as a "Cinémas du Monde" series, which includes works from Africa, Latin America and Asia. *Inquiries to:* Amiens International Film Festival, MCA, Place Leon Gontier, 80000 Amiens, France. Tel:

Kris Kristofferson attends the Sam Peckinpah tribute at Amiens

(33 3) 2271 3570. Fax: (33 3) 2292 5304. e-mail: amiensfilmfestival@burotec.fr

Austin Film Festival

October 1999

The original film festival dedicated to recognising the screenwriter's contribution to the motion picture and television industry. As such, Austin holds the Heart of Film Screenplay Competition, the four-day Heart of Film Screenwriter's Conference, which features more than 40 panels on the art, craft and business of screen writing conducted by over 80 industry professionals. The festival lasts one week and includes a competition for Best Narrative Film. *Inquiries to:* Austin Film Festival, 1600 Nueces, Austin, TX USA. Tel: (1 512) 478 4795. Fax: (1 512) 478 6208.

Annecy/MIFA

May 1999

Long-established international and competitive animated film festival in the spectacular Savoy region of south-eastern France, with a useful market (MIFA) to further the sale and distribution of animated films. Also offers retrospectives and exhibitions in a relaxed atmosphere much appreciated by the many animators who flock to Annecy. *Inquiries to:* Centre International du Cinéma d'Animation, B.P. 399, 74013 Annecy Cedex, France. Tel: (33 4) 5057 4172. Fax: (33 4) 5067 8195. Website: www.annecy-animation-festival.tm.fr.

Berlin

February 11–22, 1999

Approaching its Golden Jubilee, Berlin is generally accepted to be the most efficiently-organised of the world's festivals, although arrangements should be made as far in advance as possible. In addition to the competitive programme (with its Golden Bears and Silver Bears

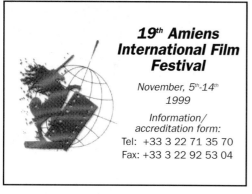

19th Amiens International Film Festival

November, 5th-14th 1999

Information/ accreditation form:
Tel: +33 3 22 71 35 70
Fax: +33 3 22 92 53 04

dispensed by an international jury) and information section, there is a retrospective as well as screenings of all new German films, and the Forum of Young Cinema, directed by Ulrich Gregor, where many of the most imaginative films are screened. Festival Director: Moritz de Hadeln. *Inquiries to:* Berlin International Film Festival, Budapesterstrasse 50, D-10787 Berlin, Germany. Tel: (49 30) 254 890. Fax: (49 30) 254 89249. Telex: 185255. e-mail: info@berlinale.de. Website: www. berlinale.de

AWARDS 1997

Golden Bear: **The People vs. Larry Flynt** (USA), Forman.
Special Jury Prize: **The River** (Taiwan/China), Ming-Liang.
Best Director: Eric Heumann for **Port Djema** (France/Italy/Greece).
Best Actor: Leonardo Di Caprio for **William Shakespeare's Romeo + Juliet** (US).
Best Actress: Juliette Binoche for **The English Patient** (US).
Best Short: **Heroines of Love** (Germany).

Brisbane

July 29–August 8, 1999

Now in its eighth year, Brisbane screens shorts, fiction features and documentaries on film and video. There is also the Chauvel Award for a distinguished contribution to Australian feature film-making, retrospectives, and an Asia Pacific Focus. *Inquiries to:* Brisbane International Film Festival, G.P.O. Box 909, Brisbane 4001, Australia. Tel: (61 7) 3224 4114. Fax: (61 7) 3224 6717. e-mail: pftc@pftc.com.au

Cannes

May 12–23, 1999

Cannes remains the world's top festival, attracting key American independents and personalities, as well as entries from more obscure countries. Cannes includes two major sections: the Competition and Un Certain Regard. There are also the Directors' Fortnight screenings, as well as the much-improved Marché (MIF), the Critics' Week, and innumerable other useful screenings (e.g. the Australian, New Zealand, and Scandinavian films). The great advantage of Cannes is that everyone of importance attends the event. *Inquiries to:* Festival International du Film, 99 boulevard Malesherbes, 75008 Paris, France. Tel: (33 1) 4561 6600. Fax: (33 1) 4561 9760. Website: www.festival-cannes.fr

AWARDS 1998

Palme d'Or: **Eternity and a Day** (Greece, Italy, France), Angelopoulos.
Grand Prix: **Life is Beautiful** (Italy/France), Benigni.
Best Actor: Peter Mullan for **My Name is Joe** (UK/Germany).

The 8th Brisbane International Film Festival
29 July - 8 August, 1999

colour your world

Shorts, fiction features and documentaries on film, experimental film and video

World Cinema
Asia Pacific Focus
Queensland Images
Chauvel Award for Distinguished Contribution to Australian Feature Filmmaking
BIFF Fast Film Short Film Competition
Retrospectives

Entries close 13 May 1999

Brisbane International Film Festival
Pacific Film and Television Commission
GPO Box 1436, Brisbane Qld 4001
Level 15, 111 George Street, Brisbane, Qld, 4001
Ph: + 61 7 3224 4114 Fax: + 61 7 3224 6717
Website: www.pftc.com.au Email: pftc@pftc.com.au

Presented by Pacific Film and Television Commission

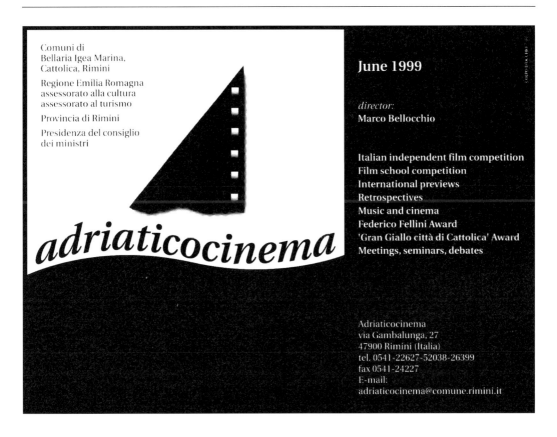

Comuni di
Bellaria Igea Marina,
Cattolica, Rimini

Regione Emilia Romagna
assessorato alla cultura
assessorato al turismo

Provincia di Rimini

Presidenza del consiglio
dei ministri

adriaticocinema

June 1999

director:
Marco Bellocchio

Italian independent film competition
Film school competition
International previews
Retrospectives
Music and cinema
Federico Fellini Award
'Gran Giallo città di Cattolica' Award
Meetings, seminars, debates

Adriaticocinema
via Gambalunga, 27
47900 Rimini (Italia)
tel. 0541-22627-52038-26399
fax 0541-24227
E-mail:
adriaticocinema@comune.rimini.it

Roberto Benigni receives the Federico Fellini Award at Adriaticocinema

Best Actress: Elodie Bouchez, Natacha Régnier for **La vie rêvée des anges** (France).
Best Direction: John Boorman for **The General** (Ireland/UK).
Best Screenplay: Hal Hartley for **Henry Fool** (US).
Jury Prize (shared): **The Class Trip** (France), Miller; **The Celebration** (Denmark), Vinterberg.
Technical Prize: Vittorio Storaro for **Tango** (Argentina/Spain).
Caméra d'Or: **Slam** (US), Levin.

Chicago

October 7–21, 1999

Now in its fourth decade, the Chicago International Film Festival is the oldest competitive event in North America. It spotlights the latest work by established international directors and seeks out works by new directors. The festival bestows its highest honour, the Gold Hugo, on the best feature film in its International Competition, with separate prizes for documentaries, student films and shorts. Chicago is the only US site to award the FIPRESCI prize for first and second time directors, judged by a jury of top international film critics. *Inquiries to:* Chicago International Film Festival, 32 W. Randolph St., Suite 600, Chicago, IL 60601, USA. Tel: (1 312) 425 9400, Fax: (1 312) 425 0944. e-mail: filmfest@wwa.com. Website: www.chicago.ddbn.com/filmfest/

AWARDS 1997

Gold Hugo: **The Winter Guest** (UK), Rickman.
Special Jury Prize: **The River** (Taiwan), Ming-Liang.
FIPRESCI prize: **La Vie de Jesus** (France), Dumont.
Best Director: Michael Haneke for **Funny Games** (Austria).
Best Documentary: **The Long Way Home** (US), Harris.
Best Short Narratives: **Crocodile Snap** (UK), Wright and **The Time of the Wolf** (Switzerland), Pluss and Mifsud.
Best Animated Short: **How Wings Are Attached to the Backs of Angels** (Canada), Welch.

Cinéma Tout Ecran

September 20–26, 1999

The first and, until recently, the only festival to devote its programme to films of artistic quality produced by television. The main criteria for selection are the film-maker's distinct view of the world and his story-telling style. Highlights of the festival include the International Competition

(three major prizes), New TV Series, Retrospective, Thematic Night, an international selection of shorts, and professional seminars. *Inquiries to:* Cinéma Tout Ecran, Maison des Arts de Grütli, 16 rue de Général-Dufour, CP 5305, CH-1211 Geneva 11, Switzerland. Tel: (41 22) 328 8554. Fax: (41 22) 329 6802. e-mail: info@cinema-tout-ecran.ch Website: www. cinema-tout-ecran.ch.

Clermont-Ferrand

January 29 – February 6, 1999

The ideal destination for anyone who wants to explore over 200 of the best short films of the year, the volcanoes of the Auvergne and the exquisite cuisine of the region. Now in its 21st year, this major event for short films (entries from 73 countries, 116,000 spectators and 1,500 professionals in 1998) offers both national and international competitions alongside retrospectives, children's and African programmes, debates and an accessible marketplace for shorts. *Inquiries to:* Clermont-Ferrand Short Film Festival, 26

CLERMONT-FERRAND SHORT FILM FESTIVAL

January 29 - February 6, 1999

11th International Competition
21st French Competition
14th Short Film Market

ADDITIONAL PROGRAMMES :
Italian Panorama
Short Film Noir
Elvis for Ever
African Perspectives
Children's Programme

FOR INFORMATION :
26, rue des Jacobins
63000 Clermont-Ferrand - France

Tél. (33) 473.91.65.73 - Fax : (33) 473.92.11.93
E-mail: festival@gdebussac.fr
Web : http://shortfilm.gdebussac.fr

rue des Jacobins, 63000 Clermont-Ferrand, France. Tel: (33 4) 7391 6573. Fax: (33 4) 7392 1193. e-mail: festival@gdebussac.fr. Website: www.shortfilm.gdebussac.fr.

MAIN AWARDS 1998
International Festival:
Les Mots Magiques (Canada), Vallée.
El Origen del Problema (Spain), Ponte.
La Carte Postale (Belgium), Goffette.
La Matta dei Fiori (Italy), Stefanelli.
National Festival:
Ma Place sur le Trottoir, Pollet-Villard.
Le Petit Frère d'Huguette, Mitsch.
La Vieille Barrière, Boukhitine.

Denver
October 14–21, 1999

The 22nd Denver International Film Festival is an invitational exposition of film that presents approximately 150 films over eight days and hosts more than 60 film artists, some of whom will be honoured with tributes. New international features, cutting-edge, independently-produced fiction films and documentaries, shorts, and children's programmes are among the genres screened. Awards

include a Lifetime Achievement Award, the John Cassavetes Award, the Krzysztof Kieślowski Award for Best European Film, and the Encore People's Choice Award for both feature-length film and documentary. The Denver Film Society also produces the Aurora Asian Film Festival in May, the Denver Jewish Film Festival in August, and KidsFilmFest in early Fall. Inquiries to: DIFF, Denver Film Society, 1430 Larimer Square, Ste. 201, Denver, Colorado 80202 USA. Tel: (1 303) 595 3456. Fax: (1 303) 595 0956. e-mail: dfs@denverfilm.org. Website: www.denverfilm.org

Edinburgh
August 1999

The oldest continually-running film festival in the world, Edinburgh is also one of the most accessible. Emphasis on new films, innovation and excellence in film-making world-wide, UK films and young directors, with retrospectives and seminars particularly well-chosen by Lizzie Francke. There's an offbeat sparkle to the Edinburgh mix of local audiences. The event also features the New British Expo, a unique

22nd Denver International Film Festival
OCTOBER 14 - 21, 1999

Inquiries to:
Denver International Film Festival   Phone   303.595.3456
1430 Larimer Square, Suite 201   Fax   303.595.0956
Denver, Colorado 80202 U.S.A.   e-mail   dfs@denverfilm.org
www.denverfilm.org

DENVER FILM SOCIETY

Bryan Brown and Danny Glover help celebrate the Denver International Film Festival's 20th anniversary
photo: Larry Laszlo

showcase of British film production. *Inquiries:* Edinburgh International Film Festival, 88 Lothian Road, Eduinburgh EH3 9BZ, Scotland. Tel: (44 131) 228 4051. Fax: (44 131) 229 5501. e-mail: info@edfilmfest.aug.uk. Website: www. edfilmfest.aug.uk

Espoo Ciné

August 17–22, 1999

One of the top annual showcases of contemporary European primarily full-length feature cinema in Finland, Espoo Ciné celebrates its tenth anniversary this year. The festival combines traditional selections appealing to both mainstream and art-house audiences with a growing number of fantasy films. Also included are US independents, as well as new highlights from other continents, the best of contemporary Finnish cinema, outdoor screenings, retrospectives, sneak previews, seminars and film-maker guests of honour. *Inquiries to:* Espoo Ciné. PO Box 95, FIN-

02101 Espoo, Finland. Tel: (358 9) 466 599. Fax: (358 9) 466 458. Website: www. espoo.fi / cine

Fajr International Film Festival

February 1–11, 1999

The Festival has flourished as a competitive event and aims to provide a bridge between Eastern and Western cinemas. Fajr focuses mainly on Iranian films but, since 1998, has incorporated an international competition section. *Inquiries to:* Fajr International Film Festival, Farhang Cinema, Dr. Shariati Ave., Gholhak, Tehran 19139, Iran. Tel: (98 21) 200 2088-90. Fax: (98 21) 267 082.

AWARDS 1998
Best Film: **La Promesse** (Belgium), Jean-Pierre and Luc Dardenne.
Best Director: Petr Vaclav for **Marian** (Czech Republic).
Best Actor: Chu Yuk for **King of Masks** (Hong Kong).
Best Actress: Golshifte Farahni for **The Pear Tree** (Iran).
Best Screenplay: Wan Jen and Ching-Sung for **Supercitizen Ko** (Taiwan).
Special Jury Prize: **Lady of the Month of May** (Iran), Rakhshan Banietemad.

Fantasporto

February 26–March 6, 1999

Specialises in fantasy and science-fiction films in its official competitive section. Also includes the 9th New Directors Week, with an official competition and a retrospective section dedicated to German cinema, with retrospectives on Werner Herzog and Alfred Hitchcock, the Early Years. Festival director Mario Dormingsky is preparing, with the help of the Portuguese Film Institute, a programme of Portuguese films for the benefit of foreign guests in Fantasporto. The Festival, now in its 19th year, runs in 12 theatres (3000 seats) and screens close to 300 feature films each year. Press coverage of the Festival by major newspapers, radio stations and television networks allows for press dossiers of about 1,500 clippings every year. *Inquiries to:* Fantasporto/Oporto International Film Festival, Multimédia

Center Vinema Novo, Rua da Constituição, 311, P-4200 Porto, Portugal. Tel: (351 2) 507 3880/1/2. Fax: (351 2) 550 8210. e-mail: fantas@caleida.pt.Website: www.caleida.pt/fantasporto

AWARDS 1998

Best Film: **Retroactive** (US), Louis Morneau.
Best Director: Hector Carré for **Dame Algo** (Spain).
Best Actor: Nancho Novo for **Dame Algo** (Spain).
Best Actress: Rebecca Hobbs for **The Ugly** (New Zealand).
Best Screenplay: Frank Stapleton and Nina Fitzpatrick for **The Fifth Province** (Ireland).
Best Special Effects: **Photographing Fairies** (UK).
Best Short: **Flying Saucer Rock'n' Roll** (Northern Ireland, UK), Edna Hughes.

Festival Des 3 Continents

November 1999

The only annual competitive festival in the world for films originating solely from Africa, Asia and Latin and Black America. The aim of the 21-year-old festival is to present the cultural values of these groups in a non-paternalistic and objective way. One of the few festivals where genuine

discoveries may still be made. *Inquiries to:* Alain and Philippe Jalladeau, Directors, Festival des 3 Continents, B.P. 43302, 44033 Nantes Cedex 1, France. Tel: (33 2) 4069 7414. Fax: (33 2) 4073 5522.

Figueira da Foz

September 1999

One of Portugal's most established film events. Held in early September in an exquisite seaside resort, the 28 year-old

Fruit Chan receives an award at the Festival des 3 Continents in Nantes

festival focuses on "quality" cinema with a wide range of competitive sections for features, shorts, medium-length features, children's films, and videos, plus tributes and panorama of lesser-known national cinemas. Round-table discussions, special publications and a good international turn-out of stars and directors add flavour to this event. *Inquiries to:* José Vieira Marques, Director, Figueira da Foz International Film Festival, Post Box 50 407, 1709 Lisbon Codex, Portugal. Tel: (351 1) 812 6231. Fax: (351 1) 812 6228.

Filmski Festival Ljubljana

November 1999

A Slovenian event that concentrates on retrospectives (Kiarostami in 1998, for example), offering world premieres of Slovenian films, and presenting independent productions by highly creative and promising directors. The winner in this latter section receives the Kingfisher Award (10,000 DEM), and there are also documentaries and a round-up of the cream of other festivals. *Inquiries to:* Cankarjev Dom, Prešernova 10, 1000 Ljubljana, Slovenia. Tel: (386 61) 176 7150. Fax: (386 61) 22 42 79. E-mail: jelka.stergel@cd-cc.si

Flanders International Film Festival (Ghent)

October 5–16, 1999

Belgium's most prominent yearly film event, which celebrates its Silver Jubilee in 1998 and attracts an annual attendance of over 70,000, with the prime focus on "The Impact of Music on Film". The competitive Ghent Festival awards grants up to $130,000 and screens around 150 features and 80 shorts, most without a Belgium distributor. Outside the competitive section, screenings include Country Focus, a Film Spectrum of international titles receiving their world, European or Benelux premieres as well as a tribute to an important film-maker. Deadline for entry forms: August 15. *Inquiries to:* Flanders International Film Festival-Ghent, 1104 Kortrijksesteenweg, B-9051 Ghent, Belgium. Tel: (32 9) 221 8946, 242 8060. Fax: (32 9) 221 9074. e-mail: info@filmfestival.be Website: www.filmfestival.be

28 FESTIVAL INTERNACIONAL DE CINEMA · FIGUEIRA DA FOZ

SEPTEMBER 1999 - PORTUGAL

"The Figueira da Foz Festival provides a kind of laboratory of the moving image"
Helma Sanders-Brahms. Director. Germany

Apartado dos Correios 50407
1709 Lisboa Codex
Tel. (+ 351.1) 812 62 31
Fax (+ 351.1) 812 62 28

In September have good films, good food and good wine in one of the best seaside resorts in Portugal: Figueira da Foz

The 14th Annual
**Fort Lauderdale
International Film Festival**
A vacation from ordinary film
October 24 - November 14, 1999

Presented by Blockbuster

(954) 760-9898
fax: (954) 760-9099

AWARDS 1997

Best film: **The Witman Boys** (Hungary), János Szász.
Best director: **Junk Mail** (Norway), Pål Sletaune.
Best composer of music: **Cavafy** (Greece), by Iannis Smaragdis and music by Vangelis.

Fort Lauderdale

October 24 – November 14, 1999

Presents more than 100 films from around the world, including features, documentaries, shorts, and student films. The festival will present Lifetime Achievement Awards to outstanding industry leaders in the fields of acting, directing, producing, writing and composing. The popular event (61,000 admissions in 1997) also offers film competition with cash prizes and a host of gala events on the beaches and waterways of South Florida. *Inquiries to:* The Fort Lauderdale International Film Festival, 1402 East Las Olas Blvd., Fort Lauderdale, FL 33301, USA. Tel: (1 954) 760 9898. Fax: (1 954) 760 9099. e-mail: Brofilm@aol.com. Website: www.ftlaudfilmfest.com.

AWARDS 1997

Best Film: **Ma Vie en Rose** (Belgium) and **The Sweet Hereafter** (Canada).

Best Foreign Film: **Ma Vie en Rose** (Belgium).
Best Director: Paul Chart for **American Perfekt** (US).
Best Actor: Nick Nolte for **Afterglow** (US).
Best Actress: Michele Laroque for **Ma Vie en Rose** (Belgium).

Geneva Film Festival

October 21–26, 1999

Annual event aims to introduce "Stars of Tomorrow" — actors known in their own country but not yet on a global scale. There is a lively competitive section and numerous guest appearances, tributes and seminars. In the past decade, at least four films starring winners of the main Geneva prize have gone on to triumph at the Academy Awards. *Inquiries to:* Festival du film de Genève, 35 rue des Bains, C.P. 5615, CH-1211 Genève, Switzerland. Tel: (41 22) 809 9450. Fax: (41 22) 809 9444. e-mail: info@festival-ffg.ch Website: www.festival-ffg.ch.

Gijón International Film Festival

November 20–27, 1998

With a calling card of "the best young cinema worldwide", the 36-year-old Gijón Festival has become a springboard for edgy, independent and first-time directors. Set in lovely northern Spain, Gijón features an official competition section and is perhaps one of Spain's top five festivals. Festival Director: José Luis Cienfuegos. *Inquiries to:* Gijón International Film Festival, Paseo de Begona, 24-entlo., P.O. Box 76, 33205 Gijón, Spain. Tel: (34 98) 534 3739. Fax: (34 98) 535 4152.

Göteborg

January 29–February 7, 1999

Now in its 22nd year, Göteborg has established itself as among the best film festivals in Norden and as one of the key events in Europe, with an attendance of almost 105,000 enthusiastic spectators always ready to give spontaneous applause. Hotels and cinemas are conveniently close to one another. Swedish TV broadcasts live from the festival and selects a couple of films to screen each year. *Inquiries to:* Göteborg Film Festival, PO Box 7079, S-402 32 Göteborg, Sweden. Tel: (46 31) 410 546. Fax: (46 31) 410 063. e-mail: goteborg@filmfestival.org. Website: www.goteborg.filmfestival.org.

Heartland Film Festival

November 1999

Established in 1991 in Indianapolis, Indiana, to honour and reward film-makers whose work explores the human journey, artistically expressing hope and respect for positive values of life. $100,000 in cash prizes and Crystal Heart awards are awarded to the winners each year. *Inquiries to:* Heartland Film Festival, 613 N. East Street, Indianapolis, Indiana 46202, USA. Tel: (1 317) 635 9405. Fax: (1 317) 635 4201. e-mail: hff@pop.iquest.net. Website: www.heartlandfilmfest.org.

Helsinki Film Festival – Love & Anarchy

September 19–28, 1999

An important film festival in Finland, now in its 11th year. Helsinki promotes international and daring quality film-making to Finnish audiences and distributors. True to its subtitle, "Love and Anarchy", the event uncompromisingly challenges limits of cinematic expression and experience alike. Non-competitive. *Inquiries to:* Helsinki Film Festival, Unioninkatu 10, FIN-00130 Helsinki, FInland. Tel: (358 9) 629 528. Fax: (358 9) 631 450. e-mail: la@cultnet.fi. Website: love-and-anarchy.cultnet.fi.

Helsinki Film Festival, Unioninkatu 10, FIN-00130 Helsinki, Finland.
Tel +358-9-629 528 Fax +358-9-631 450, E-mail: la@cultnet.fi Http://love-and-anarchy.cultnet.fi

Hong Kong

March 31 – April 15, 1999

Regularly includes a selection of Asian product and a Hong Kong Cinema Retrospective among 200 films and videos shown at various venues. The festival has been recognised as a valuable showcase of Asian works that allows the West to discover the riches of Chinese cinema. *Inquiries to:* Senior Manager, Festivals Office, Urban Services Department, Level 7, Administration Building, Hong Kong Cultural Centre, 10 Salisbury Road, Tsimshatsui, Kowloon, Hong Kong. Tel: (852) 2734 2903. Fax: (852) 2366 5206.

Huelva

November 21–28, 1998

The Festival de Cine Iberoamericano in Huelva, Spain, has become one of the world's key rendezvous for anyone connected with Latin American movies. It enables European buyers and film buffs to catch the latest developments from across the Atlantic. *Inquiries to:* Festival de Cine Iberamericano, Casa Colon, Plaza del Punto, s/n, 21003 Huelva, Spain. Tel: (34 959) 210 170. Fax: (34 959) 210 173.

Independent Feature Film Market

September 1999

The Independent Feature Film Market (IFFM) is the only market devoted to new, emerging American independent film talent. Since 1979, the IFFM has presented the industry with its first look at such landmark films as: *American Dream, Badlands, Blood Simple, The Big Slacker, The Brothers McMullen, Clerks, Daughters of the Dust, El Norte, Let's Get Lost, Metropolitan, My Dinner with Andre, One False Move, Poison, Stranger Than Paradise, Swoon, Welcome to the Dollhouse, Roger & Me* and many others. The IFFM screens over 300 film projects, including Works-in-Progress, and presents over 100 newly copyrighted scripts. Deadline: mid-May. *Inquiries to:* Independent Feature Project, 104 West 29th Street, 12th Floor, New York, NY, 10001-5310, USA. Tel: (1 212) 465 8200. Fax: (1 212) 465 8525. Website: www.ifp.org

India

January 10–20, 1999

Annual, non-competitive event recognised by IFFPA. There is a substantial inform-ation section, a new competition for features made by Asian women, a comprehensive "Cinema of the World" section, foreign and Indian retrospectives, and a film market, as well as a valuable panorama of the best Indian films of the year, subtitled in English. *Inquiries to:* International Film Festival of India, 4th Floor, Lok Nayak Bhavan, Khan Market, New Delhi 110 003, India. Tel: (91 11) 461 5953, 469 7167. Fax: (91 11) 462 3430.

International Film Camera Festival "Manaki Brothers"

September 22–26, 1999

Held in the last week of September each year in Bitola, Republic of Macedonia, in remembrance of the brothers Yanaki and Milton Manaki, the first cameramen in the Balkans. In the main programme, producers and directors of photography of 15 international feature films compete for the Gold, Silver and Bronze Camera 300 prizes, awarded by an international three-member jury assembled by various film industry professionals (directors, actors, critics, cinematographers). The festival also includes various sidebars, workshops and spotlights on both domestic and international cinema. This year's event includes a special 20th anniversary celebration. Festival Director: Delcho Mihajlov. *Inquiries to:* International Film Camera Festival "Manaki Brothers", 8-mi Mart #4, 91100 Skopje, Republic of Macedonia. Tel/fax: (389 91) 211 811.

INTERNATIONAL FILM CAMERA FESTIVAL "MANAKI BROTHERS"

Bitola. Republic of Macedonia

Encounters in İstanbul

Contact: Hülya Uçansu, Director
Address: İstiklal Caddesi, 146
Beyoğlu 80070 İstanbul-Turkey
Phone: (90-212) 293 31 33 (pbx)
Fax: (90-212) 249 77 71
Internet Address: http://www.istfest.org
e-mail: film.fest@istfest-tr.org

İSTANBUL FOUNDATION FOR CULTURE AND ARTS

18ᵗʰ INTERNATIONAL İSTANBUL FILM FESTIVAL

FILM

17 April - 2 May 1999

Corporate Sponsors

KOÇBANK   IBM   MARMARA İSTANBUL   RENAULT   DHL

Francesco Rosi visiting Istanbul in 1998, with festival director Hülya Uçansu

AWARDS 1997
Best Fiction Film: **The Stowaway** (Netherlands), Ben Van Lieshout.
Best Documentary: **Ghetto** (Switzerland), Imbach.
Best Short: **Sea Space** (US), Farley.
Rainer Werner Fassbinder Prize: **Burnt by Frost** (Norway), Jensen.

International Film Festival Mannheim-Heidelberg

October 8–16, 1999

A festival for young independent film-makers from all over the world. The event which gave early recognition to Truffaut, Fassbinder, Kieslowski, Jarmusch and, more recently, Bryan Singer presents features, shorts and documentaries in competition, with 30,000 DM going to the best fiction feature, 10,000 DM to the best documentary and for the Rainer Werner Fassbinder Prize, and 5,000 DM to the best short film. Films in competition are shown in the Independent Market Service, reserved for international buyers and distributors. There is also a parallel "Project Mark" for those seeking co-producers in Western Europe. Deadline: June 30. *Inquiries to:* Dr. Michael Koetz, International Filmfestival Mannheim-Heidelberg, Collini-Center, Galerie, D-68161 Mannheim, Germany. Tel: (49 621) 102 943. Fax: (49 621) 291 564. e-mail: ifmh@mannheim-filmfestival.com. Website: www.mannheim-filmfestival.com

Internationale Hofer Filmtage

October 27–31, 1999

Dubbed the "Home of Films" by Wim Wenders, Hof is famous for its thoughtful selection of some 50 features. Founded by the directors of the New German Cinema, Hof enjoys a high reputation among German film-makers and American cult figures like Roger Corman, Monte Hellman, John Sayles and Henry Jaglom, all of whom have attended retrospectives in their honour. Directed by one of the most respected German film enthusiasts, Heinz Badewitz, Hof has enjoyed a rising reputation these past 33 years. A screening in Hof can often result in a distribution deal. *Inquiries to:* Postfach 1146, D-95010 Hof, Germany: or Heinz Badewitz, Lothstr. 30, D-80335 Munich, Germany. Tel: (49 89) 129 7422. Fax: (49 89) 123 6868.

Istanbul

April 17 – May 2, 1999

The only film festival which takes place in a city where two continents meet, the Istanbul International Film Festival, recognised as a specialised competitive event by IFFPA, acts as a valuable showcase for distributors

internationally. Attendance reaches 100,000 every year. Now in its 18th edition, this dynamic event focuses on features dealing with the arts (literature, music, cinema, dance, etc.) with other thematic sections such as tributes, selections from World Festivals, "A Country – A Cinema", and a panorama of Turkish cinema. *Inquiries to:* Ms. Hülya Uçansu, Istanbul Kültür ve Sanat Vakfi, Istiklal Cad. Luvr Apt. No. 146, Beyoglu 80070, Istanbul, Turkey. Tel: (90 212) 293 3133/34/35. Fax: (90 212) 249 7771. e-mail: film.fest@istfest-tr.org. Website: www.istfest.org

Jerusalem

July 8–17, 1999

One of Israel's most prestigious cinematic events, which brings to Jerusalem over 150 films in a wide spectrum of themes and categories: Best of International Cinema, Documentaries, Israeli Cinema, Mediterranean Cinema, Animation, Short Films, American Independents, Avant Garde, New Directors, Jewish Themes, Classics and Restorations and Special Tributes. Prize categories include the Wolgin Awards for Israeli Cinema, Lipper Award for Best Israeli Screenplay, international awards, like the Wim van Leer "In Spirit of Freedom" for films focusing on human rights, the Mediterranean Cinema Award and the Films on Jewish Themes Award. *Inquiries to:* Jerusalem Film Festival, P.O. Box 8561, Jerusalem 91083. Tel: (972 2) 672 4131. Fax: (972 2) 673 3076. e-mail: jer.cine@inter.net.il. Website: www.cine.jer.org.il

Enthusiasts gather at the Hof Film days
photo: Bernd Schramm

34th Karlovy Vary International Film Festival

The most prestigeous cinema event in the Czech Republic

2nd – 10th July 1999

- **Two official competitions**
  Feature Films and Documentaries
- **Hors Concours Sections**
  Horizons – The Best of Last Seasons
  Another View
  Forum of Independents
  East of the West
- **Czech Cinema**
- **Retrospectives**
- **Special Events**

Contact address: Karlovy Vary Film-Festival Foundation, Panská 1, 110 00 Praha 1, Czech Republic
Tel: +420 2 24 23 54 12, Fax: +420 2 24 23 34 08, E-mail: foundation@iffkv.cz, Internet: http:www.iffkv.cz

Juraj Jakubisko, Agnès Varda and Deana Horvatova (Mrs. Jakubisko) at the 1998 Festival de La Rochelle
photo: Régis d'Audeville

Karlovy Vary

July 3–11, 1999

One of the oldest film festivals in the world. The annual programme includes international competition of features and documentaries with international juries awarding prizes for the Best Film, Director, Actor/Actress and a Special Jury Award as well. There is a major focus on the latest Czech features, as well as those from other formerly communist countries. The 1998 festival featured US independents, an overview of new Spanish cinematography, tributes to Joris Ivens and Sergei Eisenstein, and to the late Lithuanian director Vitautas Zhalakiaviscus, a retrospective of the Czech animation films, and profiles of Paul Morrissey and Takeshi Kitano. *Inquiries to:* Karlovy Vary International Film Festival, Panská 1, CZ 11000 Prague 1, Czech Republic. Tel: (420 2) 2423 5412. Fax: (420 2) 2423 3408/7735. e-mail: iffkv@tl.cz. Website: www.tlp.cz/internet/iffKarlovyVary

AWARDS 1997

Grand Prix: **Ma Vie en Rose** (Belgium/France) Alain Berliner.
Award of the Jury: **La Buena Vida** (Spain) David Trueba.
Best Director: Martine Dugowson for **Portraits Chinois** (France).
Best Actress: Lena Endre for **Christmas Oratorio** (Sweden).
Best Actor: Boleslav Polivka for **Forgotten Light** (Czech Republic).

AWARDS 1998

Grand Prix: **Le cœur au poing (Streetheart)** (Canada), Binamé.
Special Prize: **Full Moon** (Russia), Shakhnazarov.
Best Director: Charles Binamé for **Le cœur au poing (Streetheart).**
Best Actress: Julia Stiles for **Wicked** (US).
Best Actor: Olaf Lubaszenko for **Sekal Has To Die** (Czech Republic/Poland/France/Slovakia).

La Rochelle

June 25 – July 5, 1999

Fighting against the inroads of television, that cinematic polymath Jean-Loup Passek builds a bridge between past and future cinema with his popular and distinguished festival held in this French resort. The event includes a profusion of new features and thematic programmes, sometimes with magnificent discoveries (the Francesca Bertini retrospective in 1993 for example). La Rochelle attracted 66,000 spectators in 1998, despite the World Cup! *Inquiries to:* Festival International du Film de La Rochelle, 16 rue Saint Sabin, Paris 75011, France. Tel: (33 1) 4806 1666. Fax: (33 1) 4806 1540.

Locarno

August 4–14, 1999

Under director Marco Müller, Locarno has become a place where world and European premieres are regular occasions, and where serious buyers go to discover creative film-makers. More than 1,000 accredited journalists from over 30 countries are surrounded by an international attendance of 170,000. Every night 7,000 people sit in front of the giant screen in Piazza Grande to discover the lively and varied programmes. Müller can justifiably claim that Locarno is now one of the world's top half-dozen festivals. *Inquiries to:* Festival Internazionale del Film, Via della Posta 6, CH-6600 Locarno, Switzerland. Tel: (41 91) 751 0232. Fax: (41 91) 751 7465. e-mail: pardo@tinet.ch. Website: www.pardo.ch

AWARDS 1997

Golden Leopard: **The Mirror** (Iran), Panahi.
Silver Leopard (New Cinema): **Fools** (France/South Africa/Mozambique/Zimbabwe), Bidou.
Bronze Leopard (Actress): Rona Hartner for **Gadjo Dilo** (France).
Bronze Leopard (Actor): Valerio Mastandrea for **Tutti giù per terra** (Italy).
FIPRESCI Prize: **Tutti giù per terra** (Italy), Ferrario.

London

November 1999

Presented at the National Film Theatre and at cinemas throughout the capital. The programme comprises around 180 features and documentaries, as well as a showcase

Agnès Varda visiting the 1998 Festival de La Rochelle

XXVIIe FESTIVAL INTERNATIONAL DU FILM DE LA ROCHELLE

directed by jean-loup passek   **25 JUNE - 5 JULY, 1999**

100 LONG FEATURE FILMS   300 SCREENINGS   NON COMPETITIVE

3 MAIN SECTIONS

• Retrospectives devoted to the work of past filmmakers

• Tributes to contemporary directors, in their presence

• Le Monde Tel Qu'il Est (The World As It Is), a selection of unreleased films from all over the world.

Festival International du Film de la Rochelle
16, rue Saint Sabin, 75011 Paris
Phone: (1) 48 06 16 66 Fax: (1) 48 06 15 40

for shorts. Aside from the British section there is a very strong international selection including the *Evening Standard* Film on the Square, Asia, Africa, and Latin America as well as Europe's largest and most influential selection of US independents. The festival attracts over 400 UK and international press and provides a buyers/sellers liaison office. *Inquiries to:* London Film Festival, South Bank, London SE1 8XT, UK. Tel: (44 171) 815 1322. Fax (44 171) 633 0786. e-mail: sarah.lutton@bfi.org.uk

Los Angeles International Film Festival

October 21–29, 1999

Continuing the tradition started by Filmex, this event is the largest of its kind in the US. Collaborating with over 30 film and arts organisations, the Festival is dedicated to different aspects of film-making each year. *Inquiries to:* Carla Sanders, AFI Festivals, 2021 N. Western Avenue, Los Angelos, CA 90027, USA. Tel: (1 213) 856 7707. Fax: (1 213) 462 4049. e-mail: afifest@afionline.org. Website: www. afionline.org

Málaga Spanish Film Festival

May – June 1999

This event aims to establish itself as one of the most important festivals for Spanish productions (prizes here amount to more than $150,000), offering each year a comprehensive round-up of Spanish-language cinema past and present. Set in the sunny southern resort, the festival includes official sections for features and shorts, as well as tributes and retrospectives. The documentary section, organised in 1998 by Chilean Patricio Guzmán, also had terrific press. *Inquiries to:* Salomon Castiel, Director, Málaga Spanish Film Festival, Ramos Marin 2-2c, 29012 Málaga, Spain. Tel: (34 95) 222 8242. Fax: (34 95) 222 7760.

AWARDS 1998
Best Film: **La primera noche de mi vida**, Abadalejo.
Second Prize: **Subjudice**, Forn.
Best New Director: Manuel Toledano for **Shampoo Horns**.
Best Short: **En medio de ninguna parte**, Rebollo.

Rendezvous in Mill Valley: from right to left – Barry Levinson, Saul Zaentz, James Toback and IFG Editor Peter Cowie
photo: Margot Duane

MIFED (Milan)

November 1999

Long-established film market held in the expansive Milan Fair, particularly well-attended by buyers and sellers from all over the world. Third on the annual calendar after the American Film Market and the Cannes Film Festival, Mifed's atmosphere is more sober and business-like. Even in gloomy November, Milan is still attractive. *Inquiries to:* Mrs Elena Lloyd, E.A. Fiera Internationale di Milano, Largo Domodossola 1, 20145 Milano, Italy. Tel: (39 2) 4801 2912/4801 2920. Fax: (39 2) 4997 7020. e-mail: mifed@fmd.it. Website: www.fmd.it/mifed

Mill Valley

October 7–17, 1999

The Mill Valley Film Festival presents a wide variety of international programming that is shaped by a commitment to cultural and artistic excellence. This intimate and welcoming event of unusually high calibre and dedication is set in a beautiful small town just north of San Francisco. The 11-day, non-competitive festival includes the prestigious Videofest, as well as tributes, seminars and special events. *Inquiries to:* Mill Valley Film Festival, 38 Miller Avenue. Suite 6, Mill Valley, CA 94941, USA. Tel: (1 415) 383 5256. Fax: (1 415) 383 8606. e-mail: finc@well.com. Website: www.finc.org

Montpellier

October 22–31, 1999

A major meeting-place of Mediterranean cinema, the 21st annual Montpellier Festival has a rich programme covering present and past productions and three events that receive close attention from professionals: a competition with full-length feature and short film sections, development grants for full-length fiction projects, and a "test bench" section testing the marketing potential of films in order to stimulate their release in Europe. Total value of the awards is about $50,000. Deadline for the submission of film projects: August 15. *Inquiries to:*

WORLD FILM FESTIVAL
MONTRÉAL 1999
August 26 – September 6

Official Competition • Hors Concours section (official selection, non-competitive) •
Cinema of Today: Reflections of Our Time • Cinema of Tomorrow: New Trends
• Latin American Cinema • Focus on One Country's Cinema: Ireland • Panorama Canada
• TV films • Tributes • and

AIR CANADA

The International Film, TV and video Market

Information:
INTERNATIONAL FILM FESTIVAL OF MONTREAL
1432 Bleury St., Montréal (Québec) Canada H3A 2J1 / Tel.: (514) 848-3883 / fax: (514) 848-3886
E-mail: ffm@Interlink.net / Internet: http://www.ffm-montreal.org

Montpellier International Festival of Mediterranean Film, 6 rue Vieille-Aiguillerie, 34000 Montpellier, France. Tel: (33 4) 6766 3636. Fax: (33 4) 6766 3637. e-mail: cinemed@mnet.fr. Website: www.cinemed.tm.fr/

MAIN AWARDS 1997
Features:
Gipsy Magic (Republic of Macedonia), Popov.
Bent Familia (Tunisia), Bouzid.
Tabutta Rovasata (Turkey), de Dervis Zaim.
Ovosodo (Italy), Virzi.
Shorts:
Moja Domovina (Yugoslavia), Radović.
Libre Indirecto (Spain), Gimenez.
Tourbillon (Italy), Pellegrini.
Development grant:
Le Vent de l'oubli (Algeria), Hadjadj.

Montréal World Film Festival

August 26 – September 6, 1999

Established as a major competitive festival in Montreal in late summer, it is the only such event recognised by the IFFPA in North America. There are several categories (Official Competition, Hors Concours Section, Cinema of Today: Reflections of Our Time, Cinema of Tomorrow: New Trends, Latin American Cinema, Focus on One Country's Cinema, Panorama Canada, TV films, tributes). Public attendance is extremely high, and the number of foreign personalities swells each year. With its bilingual facilities and its proximity to several major North American outlets, Montreal is the ideal location for such an event. *Inquiries to:* World Film Festival (International Film Festival of Montreal), 1432 de Bleury St., Montreal, Quebec, Canada H3A 2J1. Tel: (1 514) 848-3883. Fax: (1 514) 848 3886. e-mail: ffm@interlink.net. Website: www.ffm.montreal.org

AWARDS 1997
Grand Prix of the Americas (best film): **The Children of Heaven** (Iran), Majidi.
Special Grand Prix of the Jury: **Homer–Portrait of an Artist as an Old Man** (Italy/France), Capri.
Best Director: **Pajarico** (Spain), Saura and **Tokyo Lullaby** (Japan), Ichikawa.
Best Actress: Frances O'Connor for **Kiss or Kill** (Australia).
Best Actor: Sam Rockwell for **Lawn Dogs** (UK).
Best Screenplay: **Homer–Portrait of an Artist as an Old Man** (Italy/France), Capri.

Netherlands Film Festival

September 22 – October 1, 1999

Since 1981, Holland's only event presenting an overview of the entire output of Dutch film-making for the year. A selection of Dutch features, shorts, documentaries, and television dramas are screened and judged. The Grand Prix of the Dutch Cinema are the Golden Calf Awards which are further broken down into 12 categories. Retrospectives on the history of Dutch cinema and special programmes address various aspects of Dutch film. The Holland Film Meeting, the international sidebar of the festival, informs film buffs, festival directors, distributors and critics from around the world about are recent Dutch productions and developments. *Inquiries to:* Nederlands Film Festival. P.O. Box 1581, 3500 BN Utrecht, The Netherlands. Tel: (31 30) 232 2684. Fax: (31 30) 231 3200. e-mail: ned.filmfest@inter.NL.net. Website: www.netherlandfilm.nl

AWARDS 1997

Golden Calf for Best Full-Length Feature: **Character**, Lauren Geels and Mike van Diem.
Golden Calf for Best Director: **For My Baby**, Rudolf van den Berg.
Golden Calf for Best Actor: Jaap van Donselaar for **De Tranen van Castro.**
Golden Calf for Best Actress: Blok, Nevejan, Pauw, Roosen, and le Roux for **Brittle.**
Golden Calf for Best Short Film: **Sientje**, Christa Moesker.

New York

September 24 – October 10, 1999

Now in its 37th year, the New York Film Festival has resisted the temptation to grow into a major market offering hundreds of films, instead limiting the programme to 25-30 international features and shorter works selected from nearly 1,000 entries annually. Cineastes of every type have hailed the Festival as a leading American forum for groundbreaking films, introducing first-rate artists whose works are often recognised as contemporary classics. Attendance has been well over 95 per cent for the past decade, and each selection receives extensive coverage in local, national and even international media. *Inquiries to:* Film Society of Lincoln Center, 70 Lincoln Center Plaza, New York, NY 10023-6595, USA. Tel: (1 212) 875 5638. Fax: (1 212) 875 5636. Website: www.film. linc.com

Nordische Filmtage

November 4–7, 1999

Annual event held in the charming medieval town of Lübeck (north of Hamburg). The Festival throws a spotlight on Scandinavian and Baltic cinema,

41. NORDIC FILM DAYS LÜBECK
4 – 7 November 1999

LARGEST SCREENING OF NORDIC FILMS IN GERMANY

THE BEST FILMS OF THE YEAR BIG SHOTS AND NEWCOMERS

Information:
NORDISCHE FILMTAGE LÜBECK
D-23539 Lübeck
Fax +49 451 12-24106

enabling members of the trade, critics and other filmgoers to see the best of the new productions. It also features a large documentary section. Deservedly celebrated its 40th anniversary in 1998. *Inquiries to:* Nordische Filmtage Lübeck, D-23539 Lübeck, Germany. Tel: (49 451) 122 4105. Fax: (49 451) 122 4106. e-mail: filmtage@luebeck.de. Website: www. luebeck.de/filmtage

Norwegian International Film Festival

August 21–29, 1999

Held in the west coast region of Haugesund every summer, the Norwegian International Film Festival has become one of the country's major film events, attended by many international visitors and over 1,000 representatives from the Norwegian and Scandinavian film world. Award-winning films receive Amanda Statuettes, and the New Nordic Film market runs parallel to the Festival. Festival Director: Gunnar Johan Løvvik. Programme Director: Kristin Berg. Honorary President: Liv Ullmann. *Inquiries to:* P.O. Box 145, N-5501 Haugesund, Norway. Tel: (47 52) 734 430. Fax: (47 52) 734 420.

Nyon

April 19–25, 1999

Specialises in creative documentaries. This recently rejuvenated event, entitled "Visions du Réel," includes two competitions, market screenings, film-makers, spectators, buyers, forums, and is a stimulating source of ideas for new projects. *Inquiries to:* Visions du Réel, case postale 593, CH-1260 Nyon, Switzerland. Tel: (41 22) 361 6060. Fax: (41 22) 361 7071. e-mail: docnyon@iprolink.ch

Oberhausen

April 23–28, 1999

Now in its 45th year, the International Short Film Festival, Oberhausen remains one of the world's premiere short film festivals. It includes a wide selection of

We look forward to greeting you again!
HAUGESUND
The NORWEGIAN INTERNATIONAL FILM FESTIVAL
AUG 21 - AUG 29, 1999

It is the aspiration of the Festival to maintain and enhance its particular blend of artistic ambition, business focus and conviviality. Also including 'New Nordic Films' a separate market and a unique opportunity for distributors and others to see the best of new Nordic cinema.

Gunnar Løvvik
Festival Director
Christin Berg
Programme Director

PO Box 145 N-5501
Haugesund, Norway
Tel: +47 52 73 44 30
Fax: +47 52 73 44 20
E-mail: haugfest@online.no
Honorary President: Liv Ullmann

international and German issues in the media field. *Inquiries to:* Oberhausen International Short Film Festival, Grillostrasse 34, D-46045 Oberhausen, Germany. Tel: (49 208) 825 2652/2318. Fax: (49 208) 825 5413. e-mail: kurzfilmtage_oberhausen@uni-duisburg.de. Website: www.uni-duisburg.de/HRZ/IKF/home.html

Odense
August 1999

Denmark's only international short film festival invites unusual films that displays an original and delightful sense of imagination – along the lines of the fairytales of Hans Christian Andersen. All 16mm and 35mm films can participate. Maximum length is 45 minutes. *Inquiries to:* Odense Film Festival, Vindegrade 18, DK-5000 Odense C, Denmark. Tel: (45) 6613 1372, ext. 4044. Fax: (45) 6591 4318. e-mail: filmfestival@post.odkomm.dk. Website: www.filmfestival.dk

AWARDS 1997
Grand Prix: **Signing Off** (New Zealand), Sarkies.
Most Imaginative Film: **Say My Name** (Sweden), Seth.
Most Surprising Film: **Surprise** (Germany), Helmer.

Ökomedia
November 1999

Held in the picturesque town of Freiburg, gateway to the Black Forest in Germany. There are screenings of international film and television productions which offer an up-to-date review of ecological and environmental issues. Regular categories of the awareness-raising programme include Children's Films, Films from Third World Countries and Nature Films. *Inquiries to:* Ökomedia International Ecological Film Festival, Ökomedia Institute, Habsburgerstr. 9a, D-79104 Freiburg, Germany. Tel: (49 761) 52 024. Fax: (49 761) 555 724. e-mail: oekomedia@T-online.O.K.de

Oulu International Children's Film Festival
November 12–28, 1999

The only annual festival of full-length feature films for children in Scandinavia. The event is competitive and screens both recent films and retrospective seasons. Oulu is set in northern Finland and contains some excellent modern acrhitecture. *Inquiries to:* Oulu International Children's Film Festival, Torikatu 8, SF-90100 Oulu, Finland. Tel: (358 8) 881 1293. Fax: (358 8) 881 1290. e-mail: raimo.kinisjarvi@oufilmcenter.inet.fi. Website: www.ouka.fi./oek

Palm Springs
January 7–18, 1999

Celebrating its 10th anniversary this year, the Nortel Palm Springs International Film Festival is a glittering event, screening over 150 films from 25 countries, including US and international premieres. Founded by former Congressman Sonny Bono, the festival offers seminars, panels, and workshops on various aspects of film-making and hosts a black-tie Awards Gala. The event has grown rapidly from a three-day event in 1990, to its current length of 12 days. *Inquiries to:* Nortel Palm Springs

International Film Festival, 1700 E. Tahquitz Canyon Way #3, Palm Springs, CA 92262, USA. Tel: (1 760) 322 2930. Fax: (1 760) 322 4087. Website: www.psfilmfest. org

Pesaro
June 1999

Focuses on the work of new directors and emergent, innovative cinemas, including non-fiction, animation, shorts and videos. For the past 34 years, this Mediterranean resort has been the centre for lively screenings and debates. In recent seasons, the Festival programme has been devoted in part to a specific country or culture. The main festival is coupled each year with a special retrospective of Italian cinema. In addition, each October the Festival organises a five-day themed retrospective. *Inquiries to:* Mostra Internazionale del Nuovo Cinema (Pesaro Film Festival), Via Villafranca 20, 00185 Rome, Italy. Tel: (39 6) 445 6643 491 156. Fax: (39 6) 491 163. e-mail: pesarofilmfes@mclink.it. Website: www. abanet.it/pesaro/cinema.html

Conductor John Lanchberry and director Mario Monicelli at Pordenone, 1997

Pordenone

October 9–16, 1999

Pordenone, wrote Hemingway in *A Farewell to Arms*, is "not much of a place" but that was before this unique festival existed. Now, for one week each autumn, this little Italian town is overrun by a devoted band of scholars, collectors, archivists and enthusiasts who travel from around the world for the "Giornate del Cinema Muto", established in 1982 and dedicated to silent films. David Robinson became director in 1997, the year that saw the start of the Griffith Project, a long-term commitment to show every extant film by D.W. Griffith. They show alongside a wealth of other rarities and rediscoveries all presented with live musical accompaniment. There is also a Film Fair devoted to scripts and books on the cinema. *Inquiries to:* Le Giornate del Cinema Muto c/o La Cineteca del Friuli, Palazzo Gurisatti, Via Bini 33013 Gemona (UD), Italy. Tel: (39 0432) 980 458. Fax: (39 0432) 970 542. e-mail: gcm@proxima. conecta.It. Website: www.cinetacadelfriuli. org/gcm/

Portland

February 11–28, 1999

The 22nd Portland International Film Festival is an invitational event presenting over 100 films from two dozen countries. New international features, documentaries and shorts enjoy an audience of over 35,000 people from throughout the Northwest. Special programmes include classic silents with live orchestra performances, visiting artists, children's programming, an annual Pacific Rim Showcase and "Cine-Lit," a special selection of new Hispanic-language films and symposiums on literature. Inquiries to: Portland International Film Festival, Northwest Film Center, 1219 S.W. Park Avenue, Portland, OR 97205, USA. Tel: (1 503) 221 1156. Fax: (1 503) 294 0874. e-mail: info@nwfilm.org. Website: www. nwfilm.org

Raindance Film Showcase

October 1999

A screening forum for the dynamic independent film sector, Raindance takes place annually during the London pre-MIFED screenings each October. Over five years, nearly 600 films have been screened, of which 75% are by first-time directors. Various related events occur alongside and within Raindance. *Inquiries to:* Elliott Grove, Director, Raindance Film Showcase, 81 Berwick Street, London W1V 3PF. Tel: (44 171) 287 3833. Fax: (44 171) 439 2243.

Rotterdam

Janurary 27 – February 7, 1999

The largest film festival in Benelux, the 27th Rotterdam International Film Festival has a reputation for programming innovative, independent new work alongside more commercial productions. New film talents from all over the world compete for three Tiger Awards ($10,000, plus guaranteed theatrical and television release in the Netherlands). More than 200 features – including 60 international or European premieres – offer an overview of contemporary world cinema. The festival also hosts Cinemart, the leading co-production market for independent film-makers, producers, sales agents, distributors and financiers. Rotterdam's Hubert Bals Fund supports film-makers from developing countries. *Inquiries to:* Rotterdam Film Festival, P.O. Box 21696, 3001 AR Rotterdam, Netherlands. Tel: (31 10) 411 8080. Fax: (31 10) 413 5132. e-mail: iffr@luna.nl. Website: www.iffrotterdam.nl

Outside the Verdi Theatre on the opening night at Pordenone in 1997

Saint Louis Film Festival

October 28 – November 7, 1999

Premieres over 70 US and international independent and studio "art" films prior to their commercial releases. Festival films range from avant-garde to traditional works and classics, plus documentaries. Last years' sidebars included: "A Separate Cinema", a celebration of 50 years of black culture and cinema, the annual New Film-

makers Forum, which showcases first-time directors, a Documentary Sidebar, and a Shorts Programme. Awards include both cash prizes and industry goods and services. The event will also feature guest film-makers, panel discussions, a Star Tribute and Opening Weekend Film Retrospective. *Inquiries to:* Saint Louis Film Festival, 55 Maryland Plaza, Suite A, St. Louis, MO 63108-1501, USA. Tel: (1 314) 454 0042. Fax: (1 314) 454 0540. e-mail: info@sliff.org. Website: www.sliff.org.

San Francisco

April – May 1999

The oldest film festival in the Americas, in its 42nd year, the San Francisco International Film Festival continues to rise in importance and popularity. Last year's event broke box-office records for the sixteenth year in a row, with over 78,000 filmgoers. The festival presents over 100 features and 70 shorts from around the world. Special awards include the recently-established Sky Prize, a $10,000 cash award designed to launch an emerging film-maker into the US marketplace. Attendees at last year's event included festival honoree Nicolas Cage, Robin Williams, Sharon Stone, Jeremy Irons, and directors Wayne Wang and Im Kwon-Taek. Inquiries to: San Francisco International Film Festival, 1521 Eddy Street, San Francisco, CA 94115-4102, USA. Tel: (1 415) 929 5000. Fax: (1 415) 921 5032. e-mail: sfiff@sfiff.org

San Juan Cinemafest

October 1999

One of the leading film festivals in Latin America and important in the Caribbean. The Caribbean Competition accepts both film and video, and an international jury awards the Pitirre Prize in the categories of fiction, documentary and animation. The World Cinema Section shows the best of the latest crop of international cinema. *Inquiries to:* San Juan Cinemafest, Box 9020079, San Juan, Puerto Rico 00902. Tel: (1 787) 721 6125. Fax: (1 787) 724 4187.

INTERNATIONAL FILM FESTIVAL ROTTERDAM
p.o.box 21696 3001 AR Rotterdam
t +31 10 4118080 f +31 10 4135132
e iffr@luna.nl w www.iffrotterdam.nl

DONOSTIA-SAN SEBASTIAN
INERNATIONAL FILM FESTIVAL

THE SEPTEMBER FESTIVAL

Apartado de correos, 397
Tel: (34) 943 48 12 12
Fax: (34) 943 48 12 18
Internet: http://www.sansebastianfestival.com
E-mail: ssiff@mail.ddnet.es
20080 DONOSTIA - SAN SEBASTIAN (Spain)

Official Sponsor

SPAIN

San Sebastian

September 1999

Held in an elegant Basque seaside city, San Sebastian remains one of the most important film festivals in Spain in terms of glamour, facilities, attendance, competition, partying and number of films. Events include the Official Competitive section, Zabaltegi, and a variety of meticulous retrospectives. The city is known for its superb gastronomy, beautiful beaches and quaint streets. The festival usually attracts a large number of international celebrities, national and international press, talent and film buffs. A special jury awards the New Director's Prize to a first or second-time producer and director, worth 25 million pesetas (approx. $160,000). Director: Diego Galan. *Inquiries to:* San Sebastian International Film Festival, Apartado de Correos 397, 20080 Donostia, San Sebastian 20080, Spain. Tel: (34 943) 481 212. Fax: (34 943) 481 218. e-mail: ssiff@mail.ddnet.es. Website: www.ddnet.es/sansebastianfestival.com

Michael Douglas receiving the Donostia Prize at San Sebastian   *photo: Alvaro Etxeberrid*

AWARDS 1997

Jury Prize: **I Went Down** (Ireland), Breathnach.
Best Photography: Nick Morris for **Firelight** (UK).
Best Actor: Federico Luppi for **Martin (Hache),** (Spain/Argentina).
Best Actress: Julie Christie for **Afterglow** (US).
Best Director: Claude Chabrol for **Rien ne va plus** (France).
Special Jury Prize: **Firelight** (UK), Nicholson.
Golden Shell for Best Film: **Rien ne va plus** (France), Chabrol.
New Director's Prize: Paddy Breathnach for **I Went Down** (Ireland).

Santa Barbara International Film Festival

March 4–14, 1999

An eleven-day event held each March in the glamorous seaside resort of Santa Barbara, California, just 90 minutes north of Los Angeles. Under the artistic direction of seasoned producer Renée Missel, the SBIFF has received worldwide recognition for its diverse programming and has grown to be a major cultural event since its inception in 1986. A jury of industry professionals select winners in several

categories, including Best US Feature Film, Best Foreign Feature Film, Best Director, Best Documentary Feature, Best Short, and Best of the Fest Audience Award. This year's theme will be American Comedy. *Inquiries to:* SBIFF 1216 State Street, Ste 710, Santa Barbara, CA 93101-2623, USA. Tel: (1 805) 963 0023. Fax: (1 805) 962 2524. e-mail: sbiff@west.net. Web: www.sbfilmfestival

Shots in the Dark

June 3–13, 1999

Britain's unique festival celebrating the crime, mystery and thriller genres, featuring an impressive line-up of previews of thrillers and special guests. The festival also includes major themed retrospectives, a "Mystery" film and short film programme, as well as a summer school and "In the Frame" young people's video making competition. *Inquiries to:* Shots in the Dark, Broadway, 14-18 Broad Street, Nottingham, NG1 3 AL. UK Tel: (44 115) 952 6600. Fax: (44 115) 952 6622.

Sitges '99: Festival Internacional de Cinema de Catalunya

October 7–16, 1999

The 32nd edition of Sitges: Festival Internacional de Cinema de Catalunya presents films from all over the world in its usual sections: Fantàstic, the Festival's core competitive section devoted to fantasy, Gran Angular, for non-fantasy films, a selection of the most recent international productions, Seven Chances, seven films with little chance of being commercially

distributed, chosen by seven critics, Anima't, a selection of the latest animation trends, Retrospectiva, a selection of classics from the history of cinema, and Brigadoon, an alternative space with projections in new formats. *Inquiries to:* Sitges '99: Festival Internacional de Cinema de Catalunya, c/o Roselló, 257, 3E, 08008, Barcelona, Spain. Tel: (34 93) 415 3938. Fax: (34 93) 237 6521. e-mail: cinsit@sitgestur.com

Solothurn Film Festival

January 26–31, 1999

Held every year since 1966, the Festival is a source of up-to-date information and gives a representative survey of all forms of creative film and video in Switzerland of the preceding year. It presents a selection of films and videos by Swiss directors and foreign directors resident in Switzerland, as well as co-productions between Switzerland and foreign countries. The event allows the Swiss and foreign mass media to be informed about the latest Swiss films. This year there will be a special programme with international short fiction films. *Inquiries to:* Solothurn Film Festival, Postfach 140, CH 4504, Solothurn, Switzerland. Tel: (41 32) 625 8080. Fax: (41 32) 623 6410, e-mail: filmtage@cuenet.ch. Website: www. filmtage-solothurn.ch

Stockholm

November 12–21, 1999

Celebrating its 10th anniversary this year, the Festival has established itself as the leading competitive festival in Scandinavia and one of the major festival events in northern Europe. It is the only Scandinavian festival recognised by IFFPA and also hosts a FIPRESCI jury. Quentin Tarantino, Steve Buscemi, Joel and Ethan Coen, Lars von Trier, Dennis Hopper and Elia Kazan are among the many personalities who have enjoyed the only festival in the world that operates 24 hours per day. When leaving Stockholm, Hopper stated, "I just wish my whole life was like this festival." *Inquiries to:* The Stockholm International Film Festival, PO Box 3136 S-103 62 Stockholm, Sweden. Tel: (46 8) 677 5000. Fax: (46 8) 20 0590. e-mail: info@cinema.se. Website: www.filmfestivalen.se.

AWARDS 1997

Best Film: **Unmade Beds** (US), Barker.
Best Director: Marc Evans for **House of America** (UK).
Best Actress: Pamela Rabe for **The Well** (Australia).
Best Actor: Sylvester Stallone for **Cop Land** (US).
Best Screenplay: Jones and Joshua Pate for **Liar** (US).
Life Time Achievement Award: Elia Kazan.
FIPRESCI Awards:
Best Film: **House of America** (UK).
Best Nordic Film: **Junk Mail**.
Metro Audience Award: **Lawn Dogs** (UK), Duigan.

Sundance Film Festival

January 21–31, 1999

Sponsored by Robert Redford's Sundance Institute, this winter festival ranks among America's most respected exhibition events of American independent cinema. The several hundred dramatic and documentary films presented in the Independent Feature Film Competition each year are indicators of the current trend prevalent in American independent cinema. *Inquiries to:* Sundance Film Festival, PO Box 16450, Salt Lake City, UT 84116, USA. Tel: (1 801) 328 3456. Fax: (1 801) 575 5175.

AWARDS 1998

Grand Jury Prize (Dramatic): **Slam**, Levin.
Grand Jury Prize (Documentary): **Frat House**, Phillips & Gurland and **The Farm**, Stack & Garbus.

10th anniversary

P.O. Box 3136
S-103 62 Stockholm
Sweden
Phone: +46 8 677 50 00
Fax: +46 8 20 05 90
e-mail: program@cinema.se
www.filmfestivalen.se

Film-Makers Trophy (Dramatic): **Smoke Signals**, Eyre.
Film-Makers Trophy (Documentary): **Divine Trash**, Yeager.

Taipei

December 1999

Held annually, the Taipei Golden Horse Film Festival aims to appreciate the art of film, to promote both domestic and international film, and to encourage understanding among different cultures through film art. Founded in 1964, the Festival is sponsored by the Government of the Republic of China (ROC) and the Motion Picture Development Foundation of ROC. The two main divisions of the film festival include Golden Horse Awards, a competition of Chinese-language films, including features, shorts, documentaries and animation, and the International Film Exhibition, a non-competitive showcase of wide range of outstanding film from all over the world. Entry form deadline: August 31. *Inquiries to:* Ya-Mei Li (programmer), Taipei Golden Horse Film Festival, 7F, No. 45 Chilin Road, Taipei, Taiwan. Tel: (886 2) 2567 5861. Fax: (886 2) 2531 8966. e-mail: tghff@ms14.hinet.net. Website: www.goldenhorse.org.tw

Tampere

March 10–14, 1999

The 29th year of one of the leading short film festivals in the world. This event attracts entries from 60 countries and traditionally offers an interesting collection from eastern Europe. The International competition has sections for short documentary, animation and fiction films

Tampere Film Festival
Box 305, 33101 Tampere, Finland
tel +358-3-213 0034, fax +358-3-223 0121
Film.Festival@tt.tampere.fi, www.tampere.fi/festival/film

Elia Kazan at the Stockholm Festival in 1997
photo: Urban Brådhe

as well as open seminars and debates. The market includes a special section on shorts and documentaries from northern and eastern European countries. *Inquiries to:* Tampere Film Festival, PO Box 305, 33101 Tampere, Finland. Tel: (358 3) 213 0034. Fax: (358 3) 223 0121. e-mail: film.festival@tt.tampere.fi. Website: www.tampere.fi/festival/film

AWARDS 1998
Grand Prix International: **Un Jour** (France), Paccou.
Special Prize of the Jury: **Le Signaleur** (Belgium), Mariage.
Public's International Prize: **Killer Boots** (Sweden), Olsson.

Telluride

September 3–6, 1999

A friendly gathering in the historic mining town of Telluride, a spectacular location in the mountains of Colorado. The Festival continues to be one of the world's most influential, as famous directors, players and critics descend on the Sheriden Opera House and other theatres. The dedication of both organisers and participants to the art of cinema gives Telluride a sincere, authentic feel – not forgetting the "surprise" element, with the programme only announced on the first day! *Inquiries to:* The National Film Preserve Ltd., PO Box B1156, Hanover, New Hampshire 03755, USA. Tel: (1 603) 643 1255. Fax: (1 603) 643 5938. e-mail: Tellufilm@aol.com. Website: www.telluridenm.com/filmfesthtml

Thessaloniki International Film Festival

November 1999

In its 40th year, the oldest and one of the most important film events in Greece. Thessaloniki targets a new generation of film-makers as well as high-quality independent films made by established directors. The International competition (for first or second features) awards the Golden Alexander (approx. $38,000) and the Silver Alexander (approx. $23,000). Other sections include the Greek film panorama, retrospectives, Balkan survey, New Horizons and a number of special galas and exhibitions. *Inquiries to:* International Thessaloniki Film Festival, 36 Sina Street, 106 72 Athens, Greece. Tel: (30 1) 644 8194. Fax: (30 1) 644 8143. e-mail: info@filmfestival.gr. Website: www. filmfestival.gr

AWARDS 1997

Special Jury Prize: **Somersault in a Coffin** (Turkey), Zaim.
Best Director: Patty Breathnach for **I Went Down** (Ireland).
Best Actor: Ahmet Ugurly for **Somersault in a Coffin** (Turkey).
Best Actress: Lena Kitsopoulou for **No Sympathy for the Devil** (Greece).
Artistic Achievement Award: **The Collector** (Finland), Auli Mantila.

Torino Film Festival

November 12–20, 1999

Well-organised event (formerly known as the Festivale Internazionale Cinema Giovani) which takes place each autumn and focuses exclusively on films made by new directors. There is a competitive section for shorts, features, and Italian independents, as well as a section for retrospectives and spotlights. The Festival has been recognised as a top showcase for hot new international talent and dubbed second only to Venice on the crowded Italian festival circuit. *Inquiries to:* Torino Film Festival, Via Monte di Pietà 1, 10121 Torino, Italy. Tel: (39 11) 562 3309. Fax: (39 11) 562 9796. e-mail: info@torinofilmfest.org. Website: www.torinofilmfest.org

ALL FESTIVALS LOOK THE SAME. TRY SOMETHING DIFFERENT.

17ᵗʰ TORINO FILM FESTIVAL

NOVEMBER 12-20, 1999

"THE BEST ITALIAN FILM FESTIVAL"
Nanni Moretti

Director:
Alberto Barbera

Torino Film Festival
Via Monte di Pietà 1
10121 Torino (Italia)
Ph. +39 011 5623309
Fax +39 011 5629796
http://www.torinofilmfest.org
info@torinofilmfest.org

Toronto International Film Festival

September 1999

A rich diversity of world cinema featured yearly with over 250 films in 10 days. The event offers hundreds of films and film-makers, in a wide range of international programmes: Galas, Special Presentations, Contemporary World Cinema, Planet Africa, Dialogues, Talking with Pictures, Material Spotlight, Reel to Reel, Directors Spotlight, Midnight Madness, Perspective Canada Discovery, and Masters events. There is also a Sales Office and an industry Symposium. *Inquiries to:* Toronto International Film Festival, 2 Carlton St., 16th Floor, Toronto, Ontario, Canada M5B 1J3. Tel: (1 416) 967 7371. Fax: (1 416) 967 9477. Public Box Office: (416) 968-FILM. e-mail: tiffg@torfilmfest.ca. Website: www. bell.ca / filmfest

Tromsø International Film Festival

January 1999

Possibly the world's northernmost film event, far beyond the Arctic Circle, this "Winter Wonderland" festival focuses on contemporary art films and documentaries, 35mm feature-length films from all continents. *Inquiries to:* The Arctic Film Festival, Tromsø, Postbox 285, N - 9001 Tromsø, Norway. Tel: (47) 7762 0607. Fax: (47) 7762 0616. e-mail: tromso filmfestival@lofotnett.no. Website: www. tromsokino.no / filmfestival

Udine Far East Film

April 1999

In April 1998 the town of Udine organised the largest showcase ever of Hong Kong cinema in Europe. The event brought together a dozen major film-makers and stars, such as Ringo Lam, Johnnie To, Peter Chan, Anita Yuen, Yim Ho and Lau Chin. Future festivals will be devoted to the cross-fertilisation among East Asian countries, focusing on popular genres, and will include retrospective and tributes.

Inquiries to: Centro Espressioni Cinematografiche, Via Gregorutti 25, 33100 Udine, Italy. Tel: (39 432) 522 717. Fax: (39 432) 601 421. e-mail: cecudine@tin.it

Umeå

September 17–25, 1999

Now in its 14th year. An annual, non-competitive event screening around 100 features and 50 shorts, including a number of Swedish premieres from around the world. The Festival has gained considerable standing as a gateway for film distribution in Sweden and the Nordic countries and is the largest film festival in Northern Scandinavia. Director Thom Palmen's lively programme includes an international panorama, innovative, funny shorts, Swedish and Nordic documentaries and special guests. The popular "Camera Obscura" section features obscure films and restored or neglected classics. The Festival also organises seminars and workshops. *Inquiries to:* Umeå International Film Festival, Box 43, S-901 02 Umeå,

Anita Yuen, top Hong Kong star, at the Udine Festival in 1998

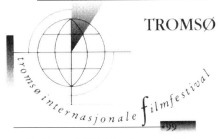

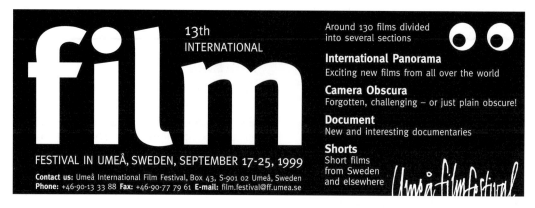

Sweden. Tel: (46 90) 133 388/356. Fax: (46 90) 777 961. e-mail: film.festival@ff.umea.se. Website: www.ff.umea.se

Valladolid

October 22–30, 1999

Now in its 44th year, an annual, well-organised, popular Spanish festival offering competition for features, shorts and documentaries. It also features a non-competitive section for retrospectives, film schools, and Spanish cinema and exhibits. The 1998 sidebars featured Liv Ullmann, Takeshi Kitano, Bert Haanstra, José Luis Dibildos, the Academia de Teatru Si Film, Bucharest and films based on the works of Mario Benedetti. *Inquiries to:* Semana Internacional de Cine de Valladolid, Spain. Tel: (34 983) 305 700,77,88. Fax: (34 983) 309 835. e-mail: festvalladolid@seminci.com. Website: www.seminci.com.

AWARDS 1997
Golden Spike: **The Sweet Hereafter** (Canada), Egoyan. *Silver Spike (shared):* **Cosas que dejé en la Habana** (Spain), Aragón; **Career Girls** (UK), Leigh.

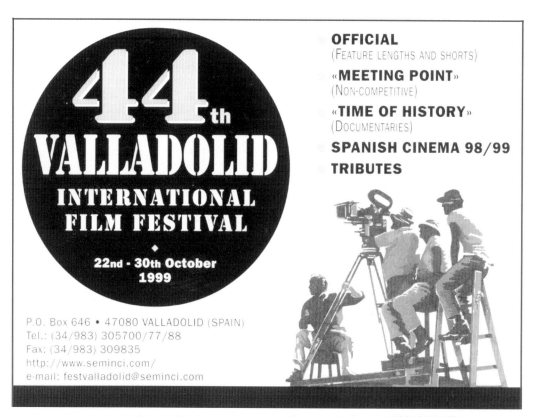

Best New Director: Wolfgang Becker for **Das Leben ist eine Baustelle** (Germany).
Best Actor: Nick Nolte for **Affliction** (US).
Best Actress: Pernilla August for **Private Conversations** (Sweden).
Best Cinematography: Paul Sarossy for **Affliction** (US) and **The Sweet Hereafter** (Canada).

Vancouver
September 24–October 10, 1999

Now in its 18th year, this festival has grown into an event of considerable stature. About 130,000 people attend more than 250 films from all parts of the world, and the Canadian city's natural beauty adds to the hospitality offered to guests. Areas of special focus are East Asia, Canada, Documentaries and the Annual Trade Forum. *Inquiries to:* Alan Franey, 410-1008 Homer Street, Vancouver, B.C., Canada V6B 2X1. Tel: (1 604) 685 0260. Fax: (1 604) 688 8221. e-mail: viff@viff.org. Website: www.viff.org

Venice
August–September 1999

Founded in 1932, this remains the world's oldest film festival. Recent editions have boasted a substantial US presence from both studio and independent sectors. Held in the Lido de Venezia every autumn, the Festival rekindles the once-cosmopolitan spirit of this old-fashioned beach town, and has been rejuvenated by the programming zeal of Felice Laudadio. The event includes special tributes and cultural meetings, plus art exhibitions all over town. *Inquiries to:* La Biennale di Venezia, San Marco, Cà Giustinian, 30124 Venice, Italy. Tel: (39 41) 521 8711. Fax: (39 41) 520 0569. e-mail: dip.spettacolo@labiennale.it. Website: www.labiennale.it

AWARDS 1997
Golden Lion: **Hana-bi** (Japan), Kitano.
Special Jury Award: **Ovosodo** (Italy), Virzi.
Best Actor: Wesley Snipes for **One Night Stand** (US).

The 1996 Modem Film Festival closed and became an archive

See page 399

Best Actress: Robin Tunney for **Niagara, Niagara** (US).
Best Original Screenplay: Gilles Taurand, Anne Fontaine for **Nettoyage à sec** (France).

Viennale
October 1999

Presents a line-up of new international films, independent and new cinema, creative documentaries, shorts, tributes programmes dedicated to directors, actors or producers (to Catherine Deneuve, Albert Brooks and Paulo Branco in 1997) and a large thematic/historical retrospective (Robert Rossellini in 1997). *Inquiries to:* Viennale, Stiftgasse 6, A - 1070 Vienna, Austria. Tel: (43 1) 526 59 7. Fax: (43 1) 523 4172. e-mail: office@viennale.or.at. Website: www.viennale.or.at

Vue sur les Docs
September 1999

Specialising in documentaries, the event includes both the Vue sur les Docs International Documentary Festival and the International Documentary Market "Sunny Side of the Dock", both held in Marseille. The Festival is a rich showcase for talent, an opportunity for a wide variety of cinematic styles to be presented to an audience of around 20,000. The Market deals with the prospects and economic aspects of the sector. *Inquiries to:* Vue sur les Docs, 3 Square Stalingrad, 13001 Marseilles, France. Tel: (33 4) 9504 4490. Fax: (33 4) 9184 3834.

AWARDS 1997
Grand prix: **Free Fall** (Hungary), Forgács.
Prix Planète Câble: **Jeckes, German Jews in Israel** (Germany), Meurer, Hueck.

Warsaw
October 8–18, 1999

Audience-oriented, 12-day event which has been screening current, invitation-only productions since 1985. It attracts around 40,000 spectators yearly. Sections include New Polish Films, Europa Europa, Panorama of World Cinema and Films from the North. *Inquiries to:* Warsaw Film Festival, PO Box 816, 00-950 Warsaw 1, Poland. Tel: (48 22) 847 1826. Fax: (48 22) 644 1184. e-mail: festiv@wff.org.pl. Website: www.wff.org.pl.

Roberto Benigni at Adriaticocinema 1988

Wellington

July 1999

Twenty-nine-year-old festival screening an invited programme of around 100 features and 50 shorts. Along with its Auckland sibling, the event provides a non-competitive New Zealand premiere showcase for a striking diversity of film and video styles. An archival component, co-ordinated by Jonathan Dennis, also enjoys considerable prominence. Now in their second decade under the direction of the apparently tireless Bill Gosden, the latest editions played to audiences totalling 65,000 in Wellington and 86,000 in Auckland. *Inquiries to:* Wellington Film Festival, Box 9544, Te Aro, Wellington, New Zealand . Tel: (64 4) 385 0162. Fax: (64 4) 801 7304. e-mail: enzedff@actrix.gen.nz. Website: www.enzedff.co.nz

Wine Country Film Festival

July–August, 1999

Set in the heart of Northern California's premium wine country, the event accepts feature film, shorts, documentaries, animation, student films and videos. The five categories are: independent features, international films, films that have a social comment, films about the arts and films about the environment. Generally non-competitive, but with short film, documentary and new directors' prizes. Many of the films are shown outdoors in spectacular wine country settings. *Inquiries to:* PO Box 303, Glen Ellen, CA 95442, USA. Tel: (1 707) 996 2536. Fax: (1 707) 996 6964.

JULY 1999

Presenting

THE WELLINGTON FILM FESTIVAL

THE AUCKLAND INTERNATIONAL FILM FESTIVAL

PO Box 9544 Te Aro
Wellington 6035
New Zealand

Telephone **+64–4 385–0162**
Fax **+64–4 801–7304**
E-mail **enzedff@actrix.gen.nz**
Website **http://www.enzedff.co.nz**

WorldFest-Flagstaff

November 1999

Previously held in Charleston, South Carolina, this annual Independent film festival, now held in Flagstaff, Arizona, offers premieres of independent and international features, shorts, documentaries and video. The 10-day event also offers in-depth film and video production seminars, from screenwriting to directing and producing independent feature films. Screenings are held in a three-screen theatre, and a select programme of 40-50 new features and 60 shorts are premiered with directors in attendance. Worldfest screens only independent films, and no major studio films are accepted. It is the sister festival to the spring WorldFest-Houston. *Inquiries to:* WorldFest-Flagstaff, PO Box 56566, Houston, TX 77356, USA. Fax: (1 713) 965 9960. e-mail: worldfest@aol.com. Website: www.vannevar.com/worldfest

WorldFest-Houston

April 1999

Celebrating its 32nd year, the Festival offers competition for independent features, shorts, student films, TV Productions and commercials, music videos and screenplays. WorldFest is the largest film and video competition in the world in terms of the number of entries received. It is the only truly independent film festival in North America as it no longer accepts major studio films. Festival Founding Director J. Hunter Todd operates a new Discovery Festival programme which automatically notifies the major 200

international film festivals of the WorldFest winners. The programme co-ordinators also submit all student, short and screenplay winners to the top US agents and agencies. *Inquiries to:* WorldFest-Houston, PO Box 56566, Houston, TX 77256, USA. Fax: (1 713) 965 9960. e-mail: worldfest@aol.com. Website: www.vannevar.com/worldfest

World Festival of Animated Films

June, 2000 (Biennial event, not held in 1999)

The organisers of Zagreb Festival aim to make the festival a gathering place for creators and fans of animated films from all over the world, where recent world production is judged and the past is recalled with relevant national, personal or thematic retrospectives. There are also meetings, exhibitions and lectures to promote and advance the art of film animation and animated film production in general. The event features a competitive section but still reserves a segment, entitled "Below the Line", for those works that just missed selection for the prize category. *Inquiries to:* Koncertna direkcija Zagreb Animafest, Kneza Mislava 18, 10000 Zagreb, Croatia. Tel: (385 1) 410 134, 410 128. Fax: (385 1) 443 022, 410 134. e-mail: kdz@zg.tel.hr. Website: www.animafest.hr.

Mike Bongiorno (left) with Nicola Piovani, who received the prestigious Nino Rota Award from CAM

photo: Antonio Brancaleone

Other Festivals and Markets of Note

Alcalá de Henares Film Festival, Plaza del Empecinado 1, 28801 Alcalá de Henares, Madrid, Spain. Tel: (34 91) 881 3934. Fax: (34 91) 881 3906. *(Competition for Spanish shorts and new directors, plus a panorama of international shorts and cartoons Nov. 13–20.)*

Alexandria International Film Festival, 9 Orabi Str. 111, Cairo, Egypt. Tel: (20 2) 574 1112. Fax: (20 2) 768 727. *(Competitive, mainly for Mediterranean countries and for first films internationally – Sept.)*

American Film Market, 10850 Wilshire Blvd., 9th floor, Los Angeles, CA, 90024. USA. Tel: (1 310) 446 1000. Fax: (1 310) 446 1600. *(Efficiently-run market primarily for English-language theatrical films. Buyers must be accredited Feb. 25 – March 5.)*

Ann Arbor Film Festival, PO Box 8232, Ann Arbor, MI 48107, USA. Tel: (1 734) 995 5356. Fax: (1 734) 995 5396. Website: aafilmfest.org *(Presenting experimental films from all over the world – March 16–21.)*

Asian American International Film Festival, Asian Cinevision, 37 East Broadway, New York, NY. 10002, USA. Tel: (1 212) 925 8685. Fax: (1 212) 925 8157. *(Showcases works by established and emerging Asian and Asian American film-makers – July.)*

Aspen Shortfest & Filmfest, 110 E. Hallam, Ste. 102, Aspen, CO. 81611, USA. Tel: (1 970) 925 6882. Fax: (1 970) 925 1967. e-mail: aspenfilm.org. Website: www.aspenfilm. org. *(Features documentaries – Sept. 23–27. Short subject competition – April 7–11.)*

Atlantic Film Festival, PO Box 36139, Halifax, NS B3J 3S9 Canada. Tel: (1 902) 422 3456. Fax: (1 902) 422 4006. e-mail: festival@atlanticfilm. com. Website: www. atlanticfilm.com. *(Features documentaries, shorts and workshops. Incorporates Screen-scene children's festival – Sept. 18–26.)*

Auckland International Film Festival, PO Box 9544, Wellington 6035, New Zealand. Tel: (64 4) 385 0162. Fax: (64 4) 801 7304. e-mail: enzedff@actrix.gen.nz. *(A leading showcase of over 100 features and 50 shorts. Twinned annually with the Wellington Film Festival – July 10–25.)*

Augsburg Children's Film Festival, Filmbüro Augsburg, Schroeckstrasse 8, 86152 Augsburg, Germany. Tel: (49 821) 349 1060. Fax: (49 821) 349 5218. *(New international feature films for children – Nov.)*

Banff Festival of Mountain Films, The Banff Centre for Mountain Culture, Box 1020, Stn. 38, Banff, AB, Canada TOL OCO. Tel: (1 403) 762 6125. Fax: (1 403) 762 6277. e-mail: cmc@banffcentre.ab.ca. Website: www.banffcentre.ab.ca/cmc/ *(International competition for all films and videos related to mountains and the spirit of adventure – Nov.)*

Birmingham International Film & Television Festival, 9 Margaret St., Birmingham B3 3BS, UK. Tel: (44 121) 212 0777. Fax: (44 121) 212 0666 *(Growing provincial festival which features both film and television – Nov.)*

Bite the Mango Film Festival, National Museum of Photography, Film & TV, Pictureville, Bradford, BD1 NQ West Yorkshire, UK. Tel: (44 1274) 773 399. Fax: (44 1274) 770 217. *(Annual film festival for South Asian and Black Film and TV – Sept.)*

Bogota Film Festival, Calle 26 No. 4-92, Santa Fe de Bogota, Colombia. Tel: (57 1) 282 5196, 243 1901. Fax: (57 1) 342 2872. e-mail: cidc@coll.telecom.com.co. *(International competition for new directors. France is the Guest of Honour this year Sept.)*

Boston Film Festival, PO Box 516, Hull, MA. 02045, USA. Tel: (1 781) 925 1373. Fax: (1 781) 925 3132. *(Approximately 50 films including studio releases, American independents, documentaries and short subjects – Sept.)*

Bradford Film Festival, National Museum of Photography Film & TV, Pictureville, Bradford, BD1 1NQ West Yorkshire, UK. Tel: (44 1274) 773 399. Fax: (44 1274) 770 217. *(Features a competitive section for new European film-makers, previews of new releases, sections of unreleased film, retrospectives and Widescreen Weekend – Jan. 12.)*

Breckenridge Festival of Film, PO Box 718, Riverwalk Centre/150 W. Adams, Breckenridge, CO 80424, USA. Tel: (1 970) 453 6200. Fax: (1 970) 453 2692. *(Independent US and international fare with tributes, receptions and educational activities – Sept.)*

British Short Film Festival, Room A214 – BBC TV Centre, Wood Lane, London W12, UK. Tel: (44 181) 743 8000. Fax: (44 181) 740 8540. *(Only competitive short film festival in UK – Sept. 16–23.)*

Brussels Festival of Cartoons and Animated Films, Folioscope, rue de la Rhetorique 19, B-1060 Brussels, Belgium. Tel: (32 2) 534 4125. Fax: (32 2) 534 2279. e-mail: Folioscope@skynet.be *(Showcase for the newest, most interesting works in animation – Feb. 8–29.)*

Brussels International Festival of Fantasy, Thriller and Science Fiction Films, 144 Avenue de la Reine, 1030 Brussels, Belgium. Tel: (32 2) 201 1713. Fax: 210 1469. *(Competitive international selection. Special side-events include the Unusual Fashion Show and Painting and Sculpture competitions – March 12–27.)*

Brussels International Film Festival, 30 chaussée de Louvain, 1210 Brussels, Belgium. Tel: (32 2) 227 3980. Fax: (32 2) 218 1860. *(Competitive festival featuring films from all countries – Jan. 19–30.)*

Cairo International Film Festival, 17 Kasr El Nil St., Cairo, Egypt. Tel: (20 2) 392 3562. Fax: (20 2) 393 8979. *(Competitive, aimed at showing major international films, usually not available – Nov./Dec.)*

Cairo International Children's Film Festival, 17 Kasr El Nil Str., Cairo, Egypt. Tel: (20 2) 392 3562. Fax: (20 2) 393 8979. *(Organised by the General Union of Arab Artists. Competitive – March.)*

Camerimage, Foundation Tumalt, Rynek Nowomiejski 28, 87 100 Torun, Poland. Tel: (48 56) 652 2179. Fax: (48 56) 621 0019. Website: www.man.torun.pl/camerimage. html. *(International event celebrating the art of cinematography. Includes a competition, film workshops and equipment presentations – Nov/Dec.)*

Cape Town International Film Festival, University of Cape Town, Private Bag, Rondebosch 7700, South Africa. Tel: (27 21) 238 257.Fax: (27 21) 242 355 e-mail: filmfest@hiddingh.uct.ac.za *(Longest established event in South Africa. Non-competitive, progressive tone – Oct./Nov.)*

Cartegena, Baluarte de San Francisco, Calle San Juan de Dios, A.A. 1834, Cartagena, Colombia. Tel: (57 5) 660 0966. Fax: (57 5) 660 0970, 660 1037. *(Accent on Ibero-American features – March).*

Chicago International Children's Film Festival, Facets Multimedia, 1517 W. Fullerton, Chicago, IL 60614, USA. Tel: (1 773) 281 9075. Fax: (1 773) 929 5437. *(Largest competitive festival for children's films in North America, screening films and videos from 25 countries – Oct.)*

Chicago Latino Cinema, 600 S. Michigan Ave., Chicago, IL 60605, USA. Tel: (1 312) 431 1330. Fax: (1 312) 360 0629. Website: www.chicagolatinocinema.org *(Aims to promote awareness of Latino culture through film and video – April 9–19.)*

Cinefest: The Sudbury Film Festival, 21840 Elm Street, Sudbury, Ontario P3C 1S8, Canada. Tel: (1 705) 688 1234. Fax: (1 705) 688 1351. Website: www.cinefest.com *(Aims to programme the best of contemporary Canadian cinema – Sept.)*

Cinekid, 249, 1017 XJ Amsterdam, The Netherlands. Tel: (31 20) 624 7110. Fax: (31 20) 620 9965. e-mail: engelzx@xsyall.nl. *(International film and TV festival for children and young adults – Oct.)*

Cinemagic Festival for Young People, Fourth Floor, 38 Dublin Road, Belfast BT2 7HN, Ireland. Tel: (44 1232) 319 709. Fax: (44 1232) 239 918. *(Children's films in competition Dec.)*

Cinéma Italien Rencontres d'Annecy, Bonlieu Scene Nationale, 1 rue Jean Jaurès, BP 294, 74007 Annecy Cedex, France. Tel: (33 4) 5033 440. Fax: (33 4) 5051 8209. *(Feature films from Italy, with tributes and retrospectives. Competitive – Sept.)*

Cinequest San Jose Film Festival, PO Box 720040, San Jose, CA, USA. Tel: (1 408) 995 5033. Fax: (1 408) 995 5713. e-mail: sjfilmfest@aol.com. Website: www.cinequest.org. *(Competition of features, documentaries and shorts, with accompanying tributes, seminars, entertainment – Jan. 28–Feb. 3.)*

CineVision International Film Festival, Museumstrasse 31, A-6020 Innsbruck. Austria. Tel: (43 512) 580 723. Fax: (43 512) 581762. *(Films about Africa, America and Asia, Austrian premieres – June.)*

Cleveland International Film Festival, 1621 Euclid Ave. #428, Cleveland, OH 44115-2017, USA. Tel: (1 216) 623 0400. Fax: (1 216) 623 0103. *(International "World Tour" progamme with specials like family films, American independents and lesbian and gay films – March 18–28.)*

Cork Film Festival, Hatfield House, Tobin Street, Cork, Ireland. Tel: (353 21) 271 711. Fax: (353 21) 275 945. e-mail: ciff@indigo.ie

Website: www.corkfilmfest.org/ciff/ *(Features documentaries, animation, art films, fiction and sponsored shorts. Competitive for shorts – Oct.)*

Deauville Festival of American Film, 36 rue Pierret, 92200 Neuilly-sur-Seine, France. Tel: (33 1) 4640 5500. Fax: (33 1) 4640 5539. *(Showcase for US features and independent films – Sept.)*

Dublin Film Festival, 1 Suffolk Street, Dublin 2, Ireland. Tel: (353 1) 679 2937. Fax: (353 1) 679 2939. e-mail: dff@iol.ie. Website: www.iol.ie/dff/ *(Amicable Irish festival focusing on world cinema with special emphasis on Irish film – April 15–25.)*

Duisburg Film Week, Am König-Heinrich-Platz, D-47049 Duisburg, Germany. Tel: (49 203) 283 4171. Fax: (49 203) 283 4130. e-mail: filmwoche.vhs@duisburg.de *(Dedicated to German-language documentaries – Nov.)*

Emden International Film Festival, An der Berufsschule 3, 26721 Emden, Germany. Tel: (49 21) 915 535. Fax: (49 21) 915 591. *(Focusing on North-Western European films, particularly from Germany and the UK – end of May.)*

European First Film Festival (Premiers Plans), Festival d'Angers, 54 Rue Beaubourg, F-75003 Paris, France. Tel: (33 1) 4271 5370. Fax: (33 1) 4271 0111. *(Competitive festival for European first films, including features, shorts, and film schools – Jan. 22–31.)*

femme totale International Women's Film Festival Dortmund, c/o Kulturbüro Stadt Dortmund, Kleppingstr. 21-23, D-44122 Dortmund, Germany. Tel: (49 231) 502 5162. Fax: (49 231) 502 2497. e-mail: femmetotale@compuserve.com Website: www.inter-net-work.de *(Biennial festival with changing themes highlighting films made as a result of women's efforts. Non-competitive – March 10–14.)*

Festival of French Cinema, Tel Aviv Cinematheque, 2 Sprintzak Street, Tel Aviv, Israel. Tel: (972 3) 691 7181. *(Screens new French fare, many Israeli premieres, with tributes and retrospectives – April.)*

Festival International du Film Francophone de Namur, 175 rue des Brasseurs, 5000 Namur, Belgium. Tel: (33 81) 241 236. Fax: (33 81) 224 384. *(Feature films, shorts and documentaries from French-speaking countries,* with retrospectives and first-time directors. *Competitive – Sept. 24 – Oct. 3.)*

Festival International du Film Juif & Israelian de Montpellier, 500 Boulevard d'Antigone, 34000 Montpellier, France. Tel: (33 4) 6715 0876. Fax: (33 4) 6715 0872. *(Showcases Jewish and Israeli films. Competitive – Nov.)*

Festival Dei Popoli, Borgo Pinto 82r, 50121 Firenze, Italy. Tel: (39 55) 244 778. Fax: (39 55) 241 364. e-mail: fespopol@dada.it. Website: www.festivalpopoli.org. *(Includes documentaries on social issues and films on history. Partly competitive – Nov.)*

Festival du Cinema International en Abitibi-Temscamingue, 215 Avenue Mercier, Rouyn-Noranda, Quebec J9X 5WB, Canada. Tel: (1 819) 762 6212. Fax: (1 819) 762 6762. e-mail: fcuat@fciat.qc.ca. Website: www.fciat.qc.ca. *(Short and medium length features from animation to documentary – end of Oct.)*

Filmfest Hamburg, Friedensallee 1, 22765 Hamburg, Germany. Tel: (49 40) 398 26210. Fax: (49 40) 3982 6211. *(International productions, retrospectives, tributes, children's films shorts and presentation of Hamburg productions – Sept.)*

Filmfest München, Kaiserstrasse 39, D-80801, Munich, Germany. Tel: (49 89) 381 9040. Fax: (49 89) 381 90426. *(International screenings, TV movies and retrospectives – June.)*

Filmfestival Max Ophüls Prize, Mainzerstrasse 8 66111 Saarbrucken, Germany. Tel: (49 681) 39452. Fax: (49 681) 905 1943. *(Competitve event for young directors from German-speaking countries – Jan. 19–24.)*

Florida Film Festival, Enzian Theatre,1300 South Orlando Ave. , Maitland, Florida 32751, USA. Tel: (1 407) 629 1088. Fax: (1 407) 629 6870. Website: www.enzian.org. *(Specialises in independent American films with special sections for features, shorts, documentaries and non-competitive spotlight films – June.)*

Fribourg International Film Festival, Rue de Locarno 8, 1700 Fribourg, Switzerland. Tel: (41 26) 322 2232. Fax: (41 26) 322 7950. e-mail: info@fiff.ch. *(Features, shorts and documentariess from Asia, Africa, and Latin America. Competitive – March 7–14.)*

Fukuoka International Film Festival, c/o

Fukuoka City Hall, 1-8-1, Tenjin, Chuo-ku, Fukuoka 810, Japan. Tel: (81 92) 733 5170. Fax: (81 92) 733 5595. (*Dedicated to the promotion of Asian Film. Non-competitive – Sept.*)

Galway Film Fleadh, Cluain Mhuire, Monivea Road, Galway, Ireland. Tel: (353 91) 751 655. Fax: (353 91) 770 746. e-mail: gafleadh@iol. Ie Website: ireland.iol.ie/ ~galfilm/fleadh (*Screens Irish, European, and international features and premieres. Last year's theme was "The Urban Jungle". Accompanied by the Galway Film Fair, Ireland's only film market – July*)

Haifa International Film Festival, 142 Hanassi Avenue, Haifa 34 633, Israel. Tel: (972 4) 838 3424. Fax: (972 4) 838 4327. (*Includes a broad spectrum of new films from around the world, special tributes, retrospectives and other events – Sept./Oct.*)

Hawaii International Film Festival, 1001 Bishop Street, Honolulu, Hawaii 96813, USA. Tel: (1 808) 528 3456. Fax: (1 808) 528 1410. (*Seeks to promote cross-cultural understanding – Nov.*)

Holland Animation Film Festival, Hoogt 4, 3512 GW Utrect, Holland. Tel: (31 30) 233 1733. Fax: (31 30) 233 1079. (*Animation from all over the world, competition for applied animation – Nov.*)

Hometown Video Festival, The Alliance for Community Media, 666 11th Street, NW #806, Washington, DC 20001, USA. Tel: (1 202) 393 2650. Fax: (1 202) 393 2653. (*Independent community producers from the US and abroad – Dec.*)

Hungarian Film Week, Magyar Filmunio, Varosligeti, Fasor 38, 1068 Budapest, Hungary. Tel: (36 1) 351 7760. Fax: (36 1) 351 7766. (*Competitive national festival showcasing Hungarian production from the past year – Feb.*)

Independent Film Days, Filmbüro Augsburg, Schroeckstrasse 8, 86152 Augsburg, Germany. Tel: (49 821) 349 1060. Fax: (49 821) 349 5218. (*International event for documentary and independent features, with retrospectives, national focus and symposium of film students – March.*)

International Documentary Film Festival-Amascultura, Rua Angola, Olival Basto, 2675 Odivelas, Portugal. Tel: (351 1) 938 8407. Fax: (351 1) 938 9347. e-mail: amascultura@mail.telepac.pt. (*International documentaries – Nov.*)

International Documentary Filmfestival – Amsterdam (IDFA), Kleine-Gartmanplantsoen 10, 1017 RR Amsterdam, The Netherlands. Tel: (31 20) 627 3329. Fax: (31 20) 638 5388. e-mail: info@idfa.nl. Website: www.idfa.nl (*Creative documentary films of all lengths, including numerous awards and a special "Kids & Docs" section. Includes the Forum, a market for international co-financing of documentaries – Nov/Dec.*)

International Festival of Film and Video For Children and Young Adults, Farhang Cinema, Dr. Shariati Ave., Gholhak, Tehran 19139, Iran. Tel: (98 21) 200 2988. Fax: (98 21) 267 082. (*Promotes film and video production for children – Oct.*)

International Festival of New Latin American Cinema, Calle 23 No. 1155, Vedado, Havana, Cuba. Tel: (53 7) 34169. Fax: (53 7) 334 273. (*Competitive event and market for Latin American and International Films – December.*)

International Film Forum "Arsenals," Marstalu 14, PO Box 626, Riga, LV 1047, Latvia. Tel: (371 7) 221 620. Fax: (371 7) 820 445. e-mail: programm@arsenals.lv (*Latvia's biggest film event, dedicated to innovative filmmaking – Sept.*)

International Student Film Festival, Tel Aviv Cinémathèque, 2 Sprintzak Street. Tel Aviv, Israel. Tel: (972 3) 691 7181 (*Workshops, retrospectives, tributes, premieres – June.*)

International Tournée of Animation, 30101 Agoura Court, Suite 110, Agoura, CA 91301, USA. Tel: (1 818) 991 2884. Fax: (1 818) 991 3773. Website: www.animag. com. (*Feature-length touring showcase of international short animated films – in over 40 locations.*)

International Women's Film Festival, Maison des Arts, Palace Salvador Allende, 94000 Creteil, France. Tel: (33 1) 4980 3898. Fax: (33 1) 4399 0410. e-mail: filmsfemmes@ wanadoo.fr. Website: www.g.debussac.fr/ filmfem. (*Features, shorts and animated films all made by women March 10–14.*)

Israel Film Festival, Israfest Foundation, 6404 Wilshire Blvd., Suite 1240, Los Angeles, CA. 90048, USA. Tel: (1 213) 966 4166. Fax: (1 213) 658 6346. (*US showcase for Israeli features, shorts, documentaries and TV dramas with an American Film and TV* *symposium at the Tel-Aviv Cinematheque. 15th anniversary celebration in NY, LA and Miami – Jan.)*

Junior Dublin Film Festival, Irish Film Centre, 6 Eustace Street, Dublin 2, Ireland. Tel: (353 1) 671 4094. Fax: (353 1) 677 8755. *(Showcases the best in world cinema for young people and includes workshops and seminars – Nov.)*

Kidfilm Festival, USA. Film Festival, 2917 Swiss Ave., Dallas, Texas 75204, USA. Tel: (1 214) 821 6300. Fax: (1 214) 821 6364. *(Showcases new and classic children's films from around the world – Jan.)*

Klamata International Documentary Festival, Center of Greek Documentary, Kifissias Ave. 125-127, Athens, Greece 11524. Tel: (30 1) 649 0060. Fax: (30 1) 649 0905. *(New festival screening short and feature-length documentaries (16mm, 35mm, Beta) with accompanying programmes and sidebars – First edition in late May.)*

Kraków International Short Film Festival, c/o Apollo Film, ul. Pychowicka 7, 30-364 Kraków, Poland. Tel: (48 122) 676 340. Fax: (48 122) 671 552. *(Poland's oldest international film festival and respected short film showcase – May.)*

Kudzu Film Festival, PO Box 1461, Athens, GA 30603, USA. Tel: (1 706) 227 6090. Fax: (1 706) 227 6090. *(Celebrates emerging talent and cultural diversity through features, shorts and documentaries – Oct.)*

Kyiv International Film Festival "Molodist", 6 Saksagansky Street, 252033 Kyiv, Ukraine. Tel: (380 44) 246 6798. Fax: (380 44) 227 4557. e-mail: molodist@ gu.kiev.ua. *(Ukraine's largest international film event and annual competition – last week in Oct.)*

Latin American Film Festival, Metro Pictures, 79 Wardour Street, London W1V 3TH, UK. Tel: (44 171) 434 3357. Fax: (44 171)287 2112. *(Films from Latin American countries, including features, documentaries and shorts Sept. 3–16.)*

Leeds International Film Festival, Town Hall, Headrow, Leeds LS1 3AD, UK. Tel: (44 113) 247 8389. Fax: (44 113) 247 8397. *(Premieres, previews, retrospectives, director tributes, workshops and special events – Oct. 2–17.)*

Ljubljana International Film Festival, Cankarjev Dom, Presernova 10, 1000 Ljubljana, Slovenia. Tel: (386 61) 212 600.

Fax: (386 61) 224 279. *(Independents and previews of films coming to Slovenian cinemas. Also featuring Irish cinematography and an Abbas Kiarostami retrospective – Nov.)*

Local Heroes International Screen Festival, National Screen Institute, 3rd floor, 10022-103 St., Edmonton, Canada T5J 0X2. Tel: (1 403) 421 4084. Fax: (1 403) 425 8098. E-mail: . Website: . *(Independent, non-competitive, seminars etc. – March 7–13)*

London Lesbian & Gay Film Festival, National Film Theatre, South Bank, London SE1 8XT. UK. Tel: (44 171) 815 1323. Fax: (44 171) 633 0786. *(Films made by or about gays and lesbians –April 8–18.)*

Lucas International Children's and Young People's Film Festival, Deutsches Filmmuseum, Schaumainkai 41, 60596 Frankurt/Main, Germany. Tel: (49 69) 620 167. Fax: (49 69) 630 2185. *(New films for children and young people – Sept.)*

Margaret Mead Film & Video Festival, American Museum of Natural History, 79th St. at Central Park West, New York, N.Y. 10024, USA. Tel: (1 212) 769 5305. Fax: (1 212) 769 5329. *(International documentary and ethnographic festival includes shorts and features –Nov.)*

Melbourne International Film Festival, PO Box 2206, Fitzroy 3065, Melbourne, Victoria, Australia. Tel: (61 3) 9417 2011. Fax: (61 3) 9417 3804. *(The oldest festival in the Southern hemisphere incorporating international features, animation, documentary and experimental works – Aug.)*

"Message to Man" Film Festival, Karavannaya 12, 191011, St. Petersburg, Russia. Tel: (7 812) 235 2660. Fax: (7 812) 235 3995. *(Programme includes international competition and special programmes, such as Russian documentaries, French films, a children's programme, Nordisk Panorama and retrospectives – July.)*

Miami Film Festival, Film Society of Miami, 444 Brickell Ave. no.229, Miami, Florida 33131. USA. Tel: (1 305) 377 3456. Fax: (1 305) 577 9768. e-mail: mff@gate.net. Website: www.miamifilmfestival.com.

(Festival emphasis is on Hispanic cinema, featuring an Audience Award – Jan/Feb.)
Midnight Sun Film Festival, Malminkatu 36 B 102, 00100 Helsinki, Finland. Tel: (358 9) 685 2242. Fax: (358 9) 694 5560. *(International and silent films, as well as award-winners from Cannes, Berlin, Locarno, and Stockholm film festivals June 16–20.)*
Minneapolis/St. Paul International Film Festival, University Film Society, Minnesota Film Center, 425 Ontario Street SE, Minneapolis, MN 55414. Tel: (1 612) 627 4431. *(Event built up over 16 years by the reliable Al Milgrom. Screens scores of foreign films, especially Scandinavian – April.)*
Montreal International Festival of New Cinema and New Media, 3668 Boulevard Saint-Laurent, Montreal, Quebec H2X 2V4, Canada. Tel: (1 514) 843 4725. Fax: (1 514) 843 4631. e-mail: montrealfest@fcmm.com. Website: www.fcmm.com *(Focuses on independent cinema and seeks to explore quality experimental films as an alternative to conventional commercial cinema – Oct. 14–24.)*
NAT-Annual Film Festival of Denmark, NatFilm Festivalen, Festivalsekretariat, Store Kannikestræde 6, 1169 Copenhagen, Denmark. Tel: (45) 3312 0005. Fax: (45) 3312 7505. e-mail: natfilm@centrum.dk. Website: www.filmfest.dk. *(Offers offbeat retros and tributes from various countries Feb. 26 – March 14.)*
New Directors/New Films, The Film Society of Lincoln Center, 70 Lincoln Center Plaza, New York, N.Y. 10023, USA. Tel: (1 212) 875 5610. Fax: (1 212) 875 5636. *(A forum for works by new directors co-sponsored by the Museum of Modern Art and The Film Society of Lincoln Center – March.)*
New England Film and Video Festival, Boston Film/Video Foundation, 1126 Boylston Street, #201, Boston, MA 02215, USA. Tel: (1 617) 536 1540. Fax: (1 617) 536 3576. e-mail: Devon@bfvf.org Website: www.bfvf.org *(Since 1976, competitive regional festival devoted to new works by professionals and students in New England. Residency required for eligibility – April 26 – May 1.)*
New Orleans Film and Video Festival, PO Box 50819, New Orleans, LA. 70150, USA. Tel: (1 504) 523 3818. Fax: (1 504) 529 2430. *(Eleventh annual festival includes international features, workshops and indie film competition – Oct. 8–14.)*

New York Exposition of Short Film and Video, New York Expo, 532 LaGuardia Place, Suite 330, New York, NY 10012, USA. Tel: (1 212) 505 7742. e-mail: nyexpo@aol.com Website: www.yrd.com/nyexpo *(Showcases both traditional, well-crafted work and challenging, experimental productions – Dec.)*
Northwest Film and Video Festival, Northwest Film Center, 1219 S.W. Park Ave., Portland, Oregon 97205, USA. Tel: (1 503) 221 1156. Fax: (1 503) 226 4842. Website: www.nwfilm.org *(Annual survey of new moving-image art produced in the US Northwest. Features, shorts and documentaries – Nov.)*
Oslo Animation Festival, Skippergt. 17, Box 867 Senturn 0104 Oslo, Norway. Tel: (47 23) 119 300. Fax: (47 23) 119 310. *(Nordic and international animation, with retros and student films. Competitive – April).*
Palm Beach International Film Festival, 1555 Palm Beach Lakes Blvd., Suite 403, West Palm Beach, Florida 33401 USA. Tel: (1 561) 233 1044. Fax: (1 561) 683 6655. *(Approximately 50 films, which include studio releases, American independents, documentaries and short subjects – April.)*
Palm Springs International Short Film Festival, 1700 E. Tahquitz Way, #3, Palm Springs, CA 92262, USA. Tel: (1 760) 322 2930. Fax: (1 760) 322 4087. *(Largest competitive short film festival in North America. Student, animation, documentary and international competition. Seminars and workshops – Aug.)*
Pia Film Festival, 5–19 Sanban-cho, Chiyoda-ku, Tokyo, Japan. Tel: (81 3) 3265 1425. Fax: (81 3) 3265 5659. *(Aims to nurture new, unique voices and emergent talent. Competitive for amateurs, with an invitational showcase – Dec.)*
Philadelphia Festival of World Cinema, International House, 3701 Chestnut Street, Philadelphia, PA 19104, USA. Tel: (1 215) 895 6593. Fax: (1 215) 895 6562. *(Festival screens a world-wide range of features, documentaries and shorts – May.)*
Rio de Janiero Film Festival, Rua Voluntarios da Patria 97, Rio de Janeiro, RJ 22270-000 Brazil. Tel: (55 21) 539 1505. Fax: (55 21) 539 1247. *(Screens about 150 films from all over the world and includes special programmes. Non-competitive – Sept.)*

Rouen, Festival du Cinéma Nordique, 22 rue de la Champmesle, 76000 Rouen, France. Tel: (33 2) 35 98 28 46. Fax: (33 2) 35 70 92 08. Telex: 771444. *(Competitive festival of Nordic cinema, including retrospective and information sections – March.)*

St. Petersburg Festival of Festivals, 190 Kamennostrovsky Ave., St. Petersburg 197101, Russia. Tel: (7 812) 237 0304, 237 0072. Fax: (7 812) 394 5870. *(Features international productions as well as local fare. Non-competitive – June 23–29.)*

San Francisco International Asian American Film Festival, c/o NAATA, 346 9th Street, San Francisco, CA., 94103, USA. Tel: (1 415) 863 0814. Fax: (1 415) 863 7428. e-mail: festival @naatanet. *(Film and video works by Asian-American and Asian artists – March 11–18.)*

San Francisco International Lesbian and Gay Film Festival, Frameline, 346 Ninth Street, San Francisco, CA. 94103, USA. Tel: (1 415) 703 8652. Fax: (1 415) 861 1404. *(Focus on gay and lesbian themes – June.)*

São Paulo International Film Festival, Alameda Lorena, 937 no. 303, 01424-001 Sao Paulo, Brazil. Tel: (55 11) 883 5137. Fax: (55 11) 853 7936. *(Competitive event with features and shorts from around 60 countries. Emphasis on independents – Oct.)*

Seattle International Film Festival, 801 East Pine Street, Seattle, Washington 98122, USA. Tel: (1 206) 324 9996. Fax: (1 206) 324 9998. e-mail: mail@seattlefilm.com Website: www.seattlefilm.com *(Unusual Northwest Pacific coast event that has done a great deal to establish Dutch cinema in the US – May/June.)*

Singapore International Film Festival, 29A Keong Salk Road, 089136 Singapore. Tel: (65) 738 7567. Fax: (65) 738 7578. *(Showcases the best of Asian and world cinema. Competitive Asian section – April.)*

Sydney Film Festival, PO Box 950, Glebe, NSW 2037, Australia. Tel: (61 2) 9660 3844. Fax: (61 2) 9692 8793. e-mail: sydfilm@ ozonline.com.au. *(Broad-based, non-competitive event screening new international films and Australian features and shorts June.)*

Taormina International Film Festival, Corso Umberto 19, 98039 Taormina, Italy. Tel: (39 94) 221 142. Fax: (39 94) 223 348. *(Competitive and non-competitive event in Sicily, stressing films by new directors – July.)*

Troia International Film Festival, Avenida Luisa Dodee 65, 2900 Setubal Codex, Portugal. Tel: (351 65) 525 908. Fax: (351 65) 525 681. *(Held in a summer recreational area on the tip of a peninsula. Features a wide variety of categories. Competitive – June 3–12.)*

Tokyo International Film Festival, 4th floor, Landic Ginza, Bldg. II 1-6-5 Ginza, Chuo-ku, Tokyo 104-0061, Japan. Tel: (81 3) 3563 6305. Fax: (81 3) 3563 6310. *(Major international event with competition and sidebars – Oct./Nov.)*

Uppsala Short Film Festival, PO Box 1746, S-751 47 Uppsala, Sweden. Tel: (46 18) 120 025. Fax: (46 18) 121 350. e-mail: uppsala@shortfilmfestival.com Website: www.shortfilmfestival.com. *(The only international short film festival in Sweden. Competitive – Oct.)*

USA Film Festival, 2917 Swiss Ave., Dallas, Texas 75204, USA. Tel: (1 214) 821 6300. Fax: (1 214) 821 6364. *(Eight-day festival featuring new US and foreign independents. Competition for US shorts with cash prizes – April.)*

Valencia Film Festival, Plaza Arzobispo, 2 acc. B, Valencia 46003, Spain. Tel: (34 96) 392 1506. Fax: (34 96) 391 5156. *(Competitive section for films made in and around the Mediterranean – Oct.)*

Vila do Conde Festival Internacional de Curtas Metragens, Auditório Municipal, Praça de República, 4480 Vila do Conde, Portugal. Tel: (351 52) 641 644. Fax: (351 52) 646 516. *(Competitive for both Portugese and international short films. Adjoining market for shorts – July.)*

Virginia Film Festival, Dept. of Drama, Culbreth Road, Charlottesville, VA 22903, USA. Tel: (1 804) 982 5277. Fax: (1 804) 924 1447. Website: www.virginia .edu / ~vafilm. *(Annual event dedicated to the study of American cinema in relation to international films, with classics, premieres and discussions – Oct.)*

Washington, DC International Film Festival (Filmfest DC), PO Box 21396, Washington, DC 20009, USA. Tel: (1 202) 724 5613. Fax: (1 202) 724 6578. *(Celebrates the best in world cinema – April 21 – May 2.)*

FILM SCHOOLS

AUSTRALIA

Australian Film, Television and Radio School, PO Box 126, North Ryde, NSW 2113.

AUSTRIA

Hochschule für Musik und darstellende Kunst, Abteilung für Film und Fernsehen, Metternichgasse 12, A-1030 Vienna. Director: Mr. Wolfgang Gluck, member of AMPAS, Director's Branch.

BELGIUM

Archimedia, European Training Network for the Promotion of Cinema Heritage, Cinémathèque Royale, 23 rue Ravenstein, 1000 Brussels. Tel: (32 2) 507 8403. Fax: (32 2) 513 1272

Hogeschool voor Audiovisuele Communicatie (R.I.T.S.), Naamsestraat 54, 1000 Brussels. (32 2) 507 1411

Institut des Arts de Diffusion (I.A.D.), Rue des Wallons No. 77, B 1348 Louvain-la Neuve.

Institut National des Arts du Spectacle et Techniques de diffusion (I.N.S.A.S), Rue Thérésienne, 8, 1000 Brussels.

Koninklijke Academie voor Schone Kunsten-Gent, Academiestraat 2, B-9000 Gent.

BRAZIL

Universidade de São Paulo, Escola de Comunicacões e Artes, Departamento de Cinema, Radio e Televisão, Av. Prof. Lúcio Martins Rodrigues 443, São Paulo 05508. Tel: (55 11) 813 3222. Fax: (55 11) 815 3083.

CANADA

Queen's University, 160 Stuart St., Kingston, Ontario K7L 3N6.

Website: www.film.queensu.ca. In its four-year B.A. (Honours) degree programme and three-year B.A. degree programme, the Department of Film Studies provides an integrated approach to film criticism, history and production.

Sheridan College, Faculty of Visual Arts, 1430 Trafalgar Road, Oakville, Ontario, L6H 2L1. Tel: (1 905) 845 9430 ext. 2700. Dean: Donald Graves. Intensive and award-winning diploma programmes in: Classical Animation, International Summer School of Animation, Computer Animation, Computer Graphics and Media Arts. Summer workshops available from May to August.

Simon Fraser University, School for the Contemporary Arts, Burnaby, B.C. V5A 1S6. Tel: (1 604) 291 3363. Fax: (1 604) 291 5907.

Vancouver Film School, 400-1168 Hamilton Street, Vancouver B.C. V6B 2S2. Tel: (1 604) 685 5808. Fax: (1 604) 685 5830. President: James Griffin. A unique training centre that offers five programmes in communication production: Film Production, Multimedia Production, Classical Animation, Computer Animation, and Acting for Film and Television. All programmes have been designed with industry consultation and are taught by industry proffesionals. Specialising in shorter (one year) and intensive formats, students create their own graduate productions.

University of Manitoba, 450 University College, Winnipeg, Man R3T 2M8. Basic film-making and screenwriting.

University of Windsor, Ontario N9B 3P4. Film, radio, TV.

York University, Faculty of Fine Arts, Film & Video Dept., 4700 Keele Street, Toronto, Ontario M3J 1P3. Offers studies in Film, Video, Screenwriting, and Theory over a four-year Honours B.A. or B.F.A. programme, also two-year M.F.A.

CZECH REPUBLIC

FAMU, Film and Television Faculty, Academy of Performing Arts, Smetanovo nábr. 2, CZ 116 65 Prague 1. Tel: (420 2) 2422 9176. Fax: (420 2) 2423 0285. Dean: Jan Bernard.

DENMARK

European Film College, DK-8400 Ebeltoft. Tel: (45) 8634 0055. Fax: (45) 8634 0535. Principal: Kjeld Veirup. Summer season: international, intensive training courses for professionals of the industry. Sept.-April: eight-month undergraduate courses for students from all over the world. No special qualifications required except English language.

The National Film School of Denmark, Theodor Christensen's Plads 1, 1437 Copenhagen K. Tel: (45) 3268 6400. Fax: (45) 3268 6407.

EGYPT

High Film Institute, Academy of Arts, Gamal El Din El Afaghani Str., Al Ahram Ave., Giza. Tel: (20 2) 585 4801. Fax: (20 2) 585 4701.

FINLAND

Taideteollinen korkeakoulu, elokuvataiteen osasto, University of Art and Design Helsinki UIAH, Department of Film and TV, Pursimiehenkatu, 29-31 B, SF-00150 Helsinki.

FRANCE

Institut de Formation et

d'Enseignement pour les Métiers de L'Image et du Son, 6 rue Francoeur, 75018 Paris. Chairman: René Bonnell. Director: Patrice Beghain.

Conservatoire Libre du Cinéma Français (C.I.C.F.), 9 quai de l'Oise, 75019 Paris. Tel: (33 1) 4036 1919. Fax: (33 1) 4036 0102.

ESEC, 21 rue de Citeaux, 75012 Paris. Tel: (33 1) 4342 4322. Fax: (33 1) 4341 9521. L'ESEC gives a national diploma.

GERMANY

Deutsche Film and Fernsehakademie Berlin GmbH, DFFB, Heerstrasse 18-20, 14052 Berlin.Tel: (49 30) 300 9040. Fax: (49 30) 300 90461. Director: Prof. Reinhard Hauff. Four-year course deals with theories of film-making, film-history, and all aspects of practical film and TV production, script-writing, direction, camerawork, editing and special effects.

Hochschule für Fernsehen und Film, Frankenthaler Strasse 23, D-81539 München. President: Prof. Dr. Albert Scharg. Approx. 300 students, 70 staff. Four-year course provides instruction in the theory and practice of film and TV. Facilities provide for work in 16 and 35mm as well as video equipment. Studies are free and begin each Fall. Ask for details about the two-step admission process in Jan. each year.

Hochschule für Film und Fernsehen "Konrad Wolf," Karl Marx Strasse 33/34, 14482 Potsdam-Babelsburg. Rector: Prof. Dr. Dieter Wiedemann.

HONG KONG

Hong Kong Academy for Performing Arts, School of Film and Television, 1 Gloucester Road, GPO Box 12288, Wanchai, Hong Kong. Dean: Mr. Richard Woolley. Tel: (852) 2584 8626/8679. Fax: (852) 2802 4372.

HUNGARY

Szinbáz-es Filmmiivészeti

Föiskola, Vas u. 2/c, 1088 Budapest. Rector: Péter Huszti. General Secretary: Lászlo Vadäsz.

INDIA

Film and Television Institute of India, Law College Road, Pune 411 004. Director: John Shankaramangalam. Chairman: Mahesh Bhatt.

IRELAND

European School of Animation, Senior College, Ballyfermot Road, Dublin 10. Tel: (353 1) 626 9421. Fax: (353 1) 626 6754.

ISRAEL

Department of Cinema and Television, Tel Aviv University, Ramat Aviv, Tel Aviv. Tel: (972 3) 640 8111. Fax: (972 3) 640 9935.

ITALY

Instituto di Storia del Cinema e dello Spettacolo, Universitá di Torino Facoltá di Magistero, Via San Ottavio 20, 10124 Torino.

Scuola Nazionale di Cinema, Via Tuscolana 1524, 00173 Rome. Tel: (39 6) 722 941. Fax: (39 6) 721 1619. President: Vittorio Caldiron. Director: Angelo Libertini.

JAPAN

Nihon University College of Art, Asahiganoka 2-42, Nerimaku, Tokyo, 176. Head of Film Department: Professor Toru Otake.

NETHERLANDS

Maurits Binger Film Institut, Nieuwezijds Voorburgwal 4-10, 1012 RZ Amsterdam NL. Tel: (31 20) 421 2048. Fax: (31 20) 638 3002. e-mail: binger@mbi.ahk.nl. Core programme of around 15 film-makers per half-year working together to develop numerous feature film projects. Also serves as a centre for the film community at large to exchange ideas, gain inspiration, and use the facilities.

Nederlandse Film en Televisie Academie, Ite Boeremastraat 1, 1054 PP Amsterdam. Managing Director: Richard Woolley. 260 students, 60 staff. Four-year programme.

POLAND

Panstwowa Wyzsza Szkola Filmowa, Telewizyina c Teatralna, im Leona Schillera, ul. Targowa 61/63, 90 323 Lódz.

ROMANIA

Academia de Teatru si Film, str. Matei Volevod nr. 75-77, 73226, Bucharest. Tel: (40 1) 642 2720.

RUSSIA

Vserossuyski Gosudarstvenni Institut Kinematografi (VGIK) (All-Union State Institute of Cinematography), ulitsa Vilgelma Pika 3, Moscow 129226. Fax: (7 095) 187 7174.

SERBIA & MONTENEGRO

Fakultet dramskih umetnosti (pozorista, filma, radija i televizije), Bulevar umetnosti 20, 11070 Belgrade. Tel: (381 11) 135 684. Fax: (381 11) 130 862.

SPAIN

University of Valladolid, Cátedra de Historia y Estética de la Cinematografica, 47002, Valladolid. Tel: (34 983) 423 611. Fax: (34 983) 423 007. Director: Sr. Dr. Francisco Javier de la Plaza.

ECCAM (Escuela de Cinematografia de la Comunidad de Madrid), Ciudad de la imagen, Crtra. Madrid-Boadilla del Monte M511-Km. 22 Pzuelo de Alarcón 28223 Madrid. Tel: (34 91) 411 0497.

SWEDEN

Department of Cinema Studies University of Stockholm, Borgvägen 1-5, Box 27062, S-102 51 Stockholm. Tel: (46 8) 647 7627. Fax: (46 8) 665 0723.

Dramatiska Institutet (College of Theatre, Film, Radio, and Television), Borgvägen, Box

The London
International
Film School

- Training film makers for 40 years •
- Graduates now working worldwide •
- Located in Convent Garden in the heart of London •
- 16mm documentary & 35mm studio filming •
- Two year Diploma course in film making •
- Commences three times a year: January, May, September •

London International Film School,
Department IG13. 24 Shelton Street, London WC2H 9HP
Tel: 0171 836 9642/0171 240 0168 Fax: 0171 497 3718
Email: lifs@dial.pipex.com Web Page: http://www.tecc.co.uk/lifs/index.html

27090, S-102 51 Stockholm. Head of School: Kjell Grede. Provides instruction in production techniques for theatre, film, radio and television. Equipped with film and TV studios and other up-to-date professional production and post-production equipment.

UNITED KINGDOM

University of Bristol, Department of Drama, Film and Television Studies, Cantocks Close, Woodland Road, Bristol BS8 1UP. Tel: (44 117) 928 7838. Fax: (44 117) 928 8251.

University of Derby, School of Arts and Design, Britannia Mail, Mackworth Road, Derby DE22 3BL. Tel: (44 13) 3262 2281. Fax: (44 13) 3262 2760. MA/FT/PT in Film with TV studies. B.A. (Honours) – subject to validation.

University of Westminster, Harrow School of Design and Media, Watford Road, Northwick Park, Harrow, HA1 3TP. Tel: (44 171) 911 5903.

London International Film School, 24 Shelton Street, London WC2H 9HP. Principal: Martin M. Amstell. Offers a practical, two-year Diploma course to professional levels, accredited by the British Film Technician's Union (B.E.C.TU.). About half of each term is devoted to film production and the other half to practical and theoretical tuition. All students work on one or more films each term and are encouraged to experience different skill areas. Facilities include two cinemas, shooting stages, rehearsal stages, and 15 cutting rooms. Equipment includes 16 and 35mm Panavision, Arriflex and rostrum cameras, Nagra recorders, Steenbeck editing machines and U-matic video. Faculty is permanent and visiting professionals. Entrance require-ments: a degree or art or technical diploma, with exceptions for special ability or experience. Applicants must submit samples of their work and be proficient in English. New courses commence each Jan., April and Sept.

Middlesex University, Faculty of Art and Design, Cat Hill, Barnet, Herts EN4 8HT. Tel: (44 181) 368 1299.

National Film and Television School, Station Road, Beaconsfield, Bucks, HP9 1LG. Tel: (44 1494) 671 234. Fax: (44 1494) 674 042. Director: Stephen Bayly. Head of Production: Sandy Lieberson. Training in all areas of film and television programme making.

Newport School of Art and Design, University of Wales College, Newport, College Crescent, Caerieon, Gwent NP6 1YG. B.A. (Hon.) Film and Video, Animation, and Media and Visual Culture.

University of Westminster, School of Communication, 18/22 Riding House Street, London W1P 7PD.

Royal College of Art, Department of Film and Television, Kensington Gore, London SW7 2EU. 35 Students.

The Surrey Institute of Art and Design, Farnham Campus, Falkner Road, Farnham, Surrey GU9 7DS. Tel: (44 1252) 722 441. Fax: (44 1252) 892 616.

University of East Anglia, School of English and American Studies, Norwich NR4 7TJ.

University of Stirling, Film and Media Studies, Stirling FK9 4LA. Head of Department: Dr. Mike Cormack.

UNITED STATES

Information on the thousands of US film schools and courses can be obtained in the *American Film Institute's Guide to College Courses in Film and Television*, which can be ordered at Publications, The American Film Institute, 2021 North Western Avenue, Los Angeles, CA 90027.

URUGUAY

Escuela de Cinematografia, Chucarro 1036, CP 11300 Montevideo. Tel: (598) 776 389. Fax: (598) 494 572.

FILM ARCHIVES

ARGENTINA

Cinemateca Argentina, Salta 1915, CP 1137 Buenos Aires. Tel: (54 1) 306 0548/0561. Fax: (54 1) 306 0592. Executive Director: Mrs. Paulina Fernandez Jurado. Established in 1949. Stock: 12,000 film titles, 6,250 books, collection of film periodicals, 352,000 film stills, 6,600 film posters. The collection of micro-filmed clippings holds files on individual films and on foreign and Argentine film personalities. The library is open to researchers and students. The Cinemateca operates one film theatre with daily screenings.

AUSTRALIA

Archives office of Tasmania, 77 Murray Street, Hobart, Tasmania, Australia 7000. Tel: (61 3) 6249 9013. Fax: (61 3) 6249 9015. State Archivist: Ian Pearce.

State Film Archives, Library and Information Service of Western Australia, Alexander Library Building, Perth Cultural Centre, Perth, WA 6,000. Tel: (61 9) 427 3310. Film Archivist: Robin Faulkner. Stock: 1,800 film titles.

AUSTRIA

Österreichisches Filmarchiv, Obere Augartenstr. 1, 1020 Vienna. Tel: (43 1) 216 1300.

Österreichisches Filmmuseum, A-1010 Vienna, Augustinerstr. 1. Tel: (43 1) 5337 0540. Fax: (43 1) 5337 05625. Directors: Peter Konlechner and Prof. Peter Kubelka. Stock: app. 14,000 film titles, and an extensive library and collection of stills and photographs.

BELGIUM

Royal Film Archive, 23 rue Ravenstein, 1000 Brussels. Tel: (32 2) 507 8370. Fax: (32 2) 513 1272.

BRAZIL

Cinemateca Brasileira, Caixa Postal 12900, 04092 São Paulo. Tel: (55) 577 4666. Fax: (55) 577 7433. Director: Thomaz Farkaz.

Cinemateca do Museu de Arte Moderna, Caixa Postal 44, CEP 20021, Rio de Janeiro, RJ. Tel: (55 21) 210 2188. Telex: 21 22084 FTVRBR. Director: João Luiz Vieira.

BULGARIA

Bulgarska Nacionalna Filmoteka, ul. Gourko 36,1000 Sofia. Tel: (359 2) 987 3740, 871 392. Fax: (359 2) 876 004.

CANADA

La Cinémathèque Québécoise, 335 boul de Maisonneuve est. Montréal, Québec H2X 1K1. Tel: (1 514) 842 9763. Curator: Robert Daudelin.

Conservatoire d'Art Cinématographique de Montréal, 1455 de Maisonneuve West, Montréal, Québec. Director: Serge Losique.

National Archives of Canada, Visual and Sound Archives, 344 Wellington Street, Room 1036, Ottawa, Ontario, K1A 0N3. Tel: (1 613) 995 7504. Fax: (1 613) 995 6575. Director: Betty Kidd.

CHINA

Cinémathèque Chinoise, 25B rue Xin Wai, Beijing. Tel: (86 10) 201

4316. Telex: 22195.

CZECH REPUBLIC

Národní filmovy archiv, Malesicka 12-14, 130 00 Praha 3. Tel: (420) 894 363. Fax: (420) 897 3057. Director/Curator: Vladimir Opéla.

DENMARK

Det Danske Filmmuseum, Gothersgade 55, DK-1123 Copenhagen K. Director: Dan Nissen. Stock: 26,000 film titles, 48,000 books, 350 periodicals subscribed to, 1,950,000 film stills, 18,000 posters, three cinemas (178, 140, and 142 seats) used for daily screenings and for researchers and students. The Museum also publishes a magazine, "Kosmorama."

EGYPT

National Archive of Egyptian Film, c/o National Film Centre, City of Arts, Al Ahram Road, Giza. Tel: (20 2) 585 4801/0897. Fax: (20 2) 585 4701. President: Prof. Dr. Madkour Thabet.

FINLAND

Suomen elokuva-arkisto, Pursimiehenkatu 29-31 A, P.O. Box 177, SF-00150 Helsinki. Tel: (358 9) 615 400. Fax: (358 9) 6154 0242. Director: Matti Lukkarila. Stock: 7,200 feature film titles, 26,000 shorts and advertising film (spots), 20,000 video cassettes, 20,000 books, 160 magazines (currently subscribed), 10,500 dialogue lists and scripts, 326,000

The Archive for the 1996 Modem Film Festival has developed a shop window

See page 409

different stills, 110,000 posters and 41,000 documentation files. The archive arranges regular screenings in Helsinki and eight other cities.

FRANCE

100 rue du Faubourg Saint-Antoine, 75012 Paris
Tel: (33 1) 5302 2230
Fax: (33 1) 5302 2259
Web: www.bifi.fr

Cinémathèque française, 4 rue de Longchamp, 75116 Paris. President: Sean Saint-Gedurs.

Cinémathèque de Toulouse, rue du Taur, BP 80024, 31080 Toulouse Cedex 6. Tel: (33 5) 6230 3010. Fax: (33 5) 6230 3012. Director: Pierre Cadars.

Cinémathèque Universitaire, 3 rue Michelet, 75006 Paris. Tel: (33 1) 4586 4853.

Institut Lumière, 25 rue du Premier-Film, 69008 Lyon. Tel: (33 4) 7878 1895. President: Bertrand Tavernier.

Musée du Cinéma de Lyon, 69 rue Jean Jaurès. 69100 Villeurbanne. Tel: (33 4) 7853 2769. Fax: (33 4) 47233 7925. President: Paul Génard. Stock: 1,600 film titles, 1,000 film stills, 50 posters.

Service des Archives du Film du Centre National de la Cinématographie, 7 bis rue Alexandre Turpault, 78392 Bois d'Arcy Cedex. Tel: (33 1) 3014 8000. Fax: (33 1) 3460 5225.

GERMANY

Arsenal/Kino der Freunde der Deutschen Kinemathek, Welserstrasse 25, 10777 Berlin. Tel: (49 30)

219 0010. Fax: (49 30) 218 4281. The nearest equivalent of Britain's NFT. Programming: Ulrich and Erika Gregor, Milena Gregor. The Freunde also runs a non-commercial distribution of about 800 films, most of them from the International Forum, the independent second main programme of the Berlin Film Festival, organised by the Freunde.

Bundesarchiv-Filmarchiv, Fehrbelliner Platz 3, 10707 Berlin. Tel: (49 30) 86811. Fax: (49 30) 868 1310.

Deutsches Filmmuseum Frankfurt am Main, Schaumainkai 41, D-60596 Frankfurt am Main. Tel: (49 69) 2123 8830. Fax: (49 69) 2123 7881. e-mail: filmmuseum@stadt-frankfurt.de Director: Prof Walter Schobert. Deputy Director: Herbert Gehr. Head of Archives: Hans-Peter Reichmann. Cinema: Kitty Vincke.

Deutsches Institut für Filmkunde, Schaumainkai 41, 60596 Frankfurt am Main. Tel: (49 69) 961 2200. Telefax: (49 69) 620 060. e-mail: mieles@em.uni-frankfurt.de Website: www.filminstitut.de Director: Claudia Dillmann. Administrative Director: Helmut Possmann. Stock: 10,000 film titles, 70,000 books, 260 periodicals, 140,000 programmes, 16,000 dialogue lists, 5,000 scripts. Also newspaper clippings, advertising material.

Münchner Stadtmuseum/Filmmuseum, St. Jakobsplatz 1, D-80331 München. Tel: (49 89) 2332 2348. Fax: (49 89) 2332 3931. e-mail: 101657.3365@compuserve.com. Director: Dr. Jan-Christopher Horak. Founded in 1963, this municipal film archive runs a daily cinema programme. Film archive holds approx. 5,000 titles, including many restored silent German film classics, New German cinema, and the Orson Welles Collection. Estate holdings from G. W. Pabst, Dr. Arnold Fanck etc. Library holds over 6,000 film books, 10,000 film periodicals.

Stiftung Deutsche Kinemathek, Heerstrasse 18-20, 14052 Berlin. Tel: (49 30) 300 9030. Fax: (49 30) 300 90313. Director: Hans Helmut Prinzler. Stock: 8,000 film titles, 1,500,000 film stills, 15,000 posters, 60,000 film programmes, 10,000 scripts etc. The Kinemathek's library of books and periodicals is amalgamated with that of the Deutsche Filmund-Fernsehakademie-Berlin, in the same building.

HUNGARY

Magyar Filmintézet, Budakeszi ut 51b, 1021 Budapest. Tel: (36 1) 200 8739. Director: Vera Gyürey. Stock: 7,022 feature titles, 8,713 short films, 3,756 newsreels, 13,224 books, 3,710 periodicals, 2,708 scripts, 5,381 manuscripts, 143,159 stills, 15,365 posters. In addition to housing the archive, the institute does research into the history of cinema, particularly Hungarian cinema, and encourages the development of film culture in Hungary.

Szinház-és Filmmüvészeti Foiskola, Vas utca 2/c, Budapest 1088. Tel/Fax: (36 1) 329 4790. Rector: Péter Huszti. General Secretary: Lajos Tiszeker.

ICELAND

Kvimyndasafn Islands (National Film Archive of Iceland), Vesturgtu 11213, Hafnarfjolgur 220. Tel: (354) 565 5993. Fax: (354) 565 5994. Nearly 400 titles in the collection, documentaries being the larger part of it. Numerous sources of information regarding Icelandic films and the national film history.

INDIA

National Film Archive of India, Ministry of Information and Broadcasting, Government of India, Law College Road, Pune 411 004, India. Tel: (91 212) 352 259. Fax: (91 212) 370 027. Director: Suresh Chabria. Stock: 13,596 films, 1,650 video cassettes, 22,838 books, 145 periodicals, 21,889 scripts, 7,768 pamphlets/folders, 136,273 press clippings, 102,681 stills, 4,295 slides, 7,525 wall posters, 7,558 song booklets, 2,471 disc records, 161 audio tapes, 1,957 micro films, 42 microfiches, 658 pre-recorded cassettes, 35 audio compact discs.

IRAN

National Iranian Film Archive, Baharestan Square, Tehran. Tel: (98 21) 324 1601. Director: Mohammad Hassan Khoshnevis.

ISRAEL

Israel Film Archive/Jerusalem Cinémathèque, P.O. Box 8561, Jerusalem 91083, Israel. Tel: (972 2) 672 4131. Fax: (972 2) 673 3076. Director: Lia van Leer. Stock: 18,000 prints: international, Israeli, Jewish film collections. Books, periodicals, stills, posters and scripts. Israeli and Jewish film documentation and educational programme for school children and adults. Permanent exhibition of early cinema apparatus and cinema memorabilia. Organisers of the Jerusalem Film Festival.

Tel Aviv Cinémathèque (The Doron Cinema Centre), 2 Sprintzak Street, Tel Aviv. Postal address: PO Box 20370, Tel Aviv 61203. Tel: (972 3) 6917 1818. Fax: (972 3) 696 2841. Director: Alon Garbuz. Stock: 20,000 video cassettes, 7,000 books, periodicals, stills, posters, scripts. 1,500 screenings yearly, various activities, lectures and seminars for the general public, and special morning educational programmes for schools. Publishes Israel's only film magazine, "Cinematheque."

ITALY

Cineteca del Friuli, Via Bini, Palazzo Gurisatti, 33013 Gemona del Friuli (Udine). Tel: (39 432) 980 458. Fax: (39 432) 970 542. e-mail: c d f @ p r o x i m a . c o n e c t a . i t Established in 1977, this excellent Italian archive conceived the idea for the Pordenone Silent Film Festival, and organises regular screenings. Stock: 2,000

film titles, 3,000 newsreels, 18,000 books.

Cineteca Nazionale, Via Tuscolana n. 1524, 00173 Rome. Tel: (39 06) 722 941. Fax: (39 6) 721 1619. Director: Angelo Libertini.

Fondazione Cineteca Italiana, Via Palestro 16, 20121 Milano. Tel: (39 2) 799 224. Fax: (39 2) 798 289. President: Gianni Comencini.

Museo Internazionale del Cinema e dello Spettacolo (M.I.C.S.), Casella Postale 6104-00195 Rome. Tel: (39 6) 370 0266. Fax: (39 6) 3973 3297. Director: Jose Pantieri.

JAPAN

Kawakita Memorial Film Institute, (Japan Film Library Council), 18 Ichibancho, Chiyodaku, Tokyo. President: Mrs. Masayo Okada.

National Film Center, 3-7-6 Kyobashi, Chuoku, Tokyo. Chief Curator: Masatoshi Ohba.

LATVIA

Riga Film Museum, Smerla str. 3. Postal address: PO Box 391, Riga LV 1047. Tel: (371 2) 520 655, 529 845. Tel/Fax: (371 2) 754 5099. e-mail: kinomuz @com.latnet.lv.

LUXEMBOURG

Cinémathèque Municipale de la Ville de Luxembourg, 10 rue Eugene Ruppert, L-2453 Luxembourg. Tel: (352) 4796 2644. Fax: (352) 407 519.

MEXICO

Cinemateca Luis Buñuel, Calle 5, Oriente 5, Apdo. Postal 255, Puebla, Pue. Curator: Fernando Osorio Alarcon.

Cinemateca Mexicana, Museo Nacional de Antropologia, Calzada M. Gandhi, México 6, D.F. Director: Galdino Gomez Gomez.

Cineteca Nacional, Av. Mexico-Coyoacán 389, Col. Xoco, C.P. 03330 Mexico, DF. Tel: (52 5) 688 8814. Fax: (52 5) 688 4211. e-mail: srm@spin.com.mx. Director: Alejandro Pelayo Rangel. Deputy

Director: Fernando Osorlo Alarcón. Mexico's main film archive, supported by the Federal government. Stock: 5,600 films, 100,500 stills, 4,500 posters, 5,000 books, 1,300 scripts and 6 film theatres.

Direccion General de Actividades Cinematograficas UNAM, San Ildefonso 43 Centro, 06020 Mexico, D.F. Tel: (52 57) 043 700. Fax: (52 57) 024 503. General Director: Biol. Ivan Trujillo Bolio.

NETHERLANDS

Netherlands Audiovisual Archive – The Hague, PO Box 1799, 2280 DT Rijswijk. Tel: (31 70) 356 4109, 390 7200. Fax: (31 70) 364 7756, 307 0428. Head: Mr. Paul Kusters, MA.

Nederlands Filmmuseum (Stichting), Vondelpark 3, 1071 AA Amsterdam. Postal Address: Postbus 747 82, 1070 BT Amsterdam. Tel: (31 20) 589 1400. Fax: (31 20) 683 3401. e-mail: nfmpubl@xs4all.nl. Director: Ms. Hoos Blotkamp-de Roos. Deputy Director: Mr. R.A.M. Visschedijk.

NEW ZEALAND

The New Zealand Film Archive, PO Box 11-449, cnr. Cable Street and Jervois Quay, Wellington. Tel: (64 4) 384 7647. Fax: (64 4) 382 9595. e-mail: n2fa@actrix.gen.n2. Website: www.n2fa.org.n2.

NORWAY

Henie-Onstad Art Centre, 1311 Hovikodden, Oslo. Director: Per Hovdenakk. Tel: (47 67) 543 050.

Norsk Film Institut, P.B. 482 Sentrum, 0105 Oslo. Tel: (47 22) 474 500. Fax: (47 22) 474 599. e-mail: nfi@nfi.no Director: Erling Dale. Curator: Vigdis Lian. Head of Cinémathèque: Kjell Billing. Stock: 13,000 film titles, 1,800 books, 2,000 periodicals and a large collection of stills and posters. Also over 500 pieces of early cinema apparatus and a theatre for screening films.

PANAMA

Cinemateca del GECU, Universidad de Panama, Apartado 6-1775, El Dorado, Panama. Tel: (507) 223 9324. Fax: (507) 264 2737. e-mail: gecu@ancon.up.ac.pa Stock includes films, books, periodicals, film stills and posters. It has a small theatre with three daily screenings. Director: Roberto Enrique King.

POLAND

Filmoteka Narodowa, ul. Pulawska 61, 00-975 Warszaw. Tel: (48 22) 455 074. Fax: (48 22) 455 074. Telex: 813 640.

Muzeum Kinematografn, Pl Zwyciestwa 1, 90312 Lódz. Tel: (48 42) 674 0957. Fax: (48 42) 674 9006.

PORTUGAL

Cinemateca Portuguesa, Rua Barata Salgueiro 39-1250 Lisboa. Tel: (351 1) 354 6279. Fax: (351 1) 352 3180. Director: João Bénard da Costa.

ROMANIA

Arhiva Nationala de Filma, Str. Thomas Massaryk nr.25, 70231 Bucharest. Tel/Fax: (40 1) 211 2260, 685 3720. Director: Anca Mitran.

RUSSIA

Gosfilmofond of Russia, Belye Stolby, Moskovskaia oblast. Tel: (7) 546 0516, 546 0513.Telex: 411700 LASTI 007913.

SERBIA & MONTENEGRO

Jugoslovenska Kinoteka, Knez Mihailova 19, 11000 Belgrade. Tel: (381 11) 622 555, 550 471 (Archive). Fax: (381 11) 622 587, 555 015 (Archive). Director: Radoslav Zelenović Head of Archive: Stevan Jovičić. Programme Director: Dinko Tucaković.

SOUTH AFRICA

South African National Film, Video and Sound Archives, Private Bag X236, Pretoria 0001.

SPAIN

Filmoteca Española, Carretera Dehesa de la Villa, s/n. 28040 Madrid. Tel: (34 91) 549 0011. Fax: (34 91) 549 7348. Director: José María Prado.

Filmoteca de la Generalitat de Catalunya, Portal de Santa Madrona, 6-8 Barcelona 08001. Tel: (34 93) 412 5640. Director: Antoni Kirchner.

SWEDEN

Asta Nielsen Filmmuseum, Vapenkroken 29, S-226 47. Lund. Established in 1946 by G.D. Postén, Head of the Film History section at the Dept. of History, University of Lund.

Cinemateket, Svenska Film Institutet. Filmhuset, Box 27126, S-102 52 Stockholm. Tel: (46 8) 665 1100. Fax: (46 8) 661 1820. Director: Jan-Erik Billinger. Curator: Rolf Lindfors. Head of Documentation: Margareta Nordström. Stock: 17,800 film titles, 41,000 books, 250 subscriptions to periodicals, 1,500,000 film stills, 31,000 posters, and unpublished script material on 7,600 foreign films and 1,900 Swedish films. The collection of microfilmed clippings holds 52,000 jackets on individual films, 16,500 jackets on film personalities and jackets on general subjects classified by the FIAF scheme. Cinemateket has four daily screenings at two theatres in Stockholm. A selection of the yearly programme is also shown in Göteborg and Malmö.

SWITZERLAND

Cinémathèque Suisse, 3 Allée Ernest Ansermet, 1003 Lausanne (Postal address: P.O. Box 2512, 1002 Lausanne). Tel: (41 21) 331 0101. Fax: (41 21) 320 4888. Curator: Hervé Dumont. Stock: 25,000 titles (300,000 reels), 260 apparati, 35,000 posters, 300,000 film references, 15,000 books, and 1,000,000 stills. Three projections each day.

TAIWAN

Chinese Taipei Film Archive, 4F, No. 7 Ching-Tao East Road, Taipei, Taiwan, R.O.C. Tel: (886 2) 392 4243, 2396 0760. Fax: (886 2) 2392 6359. Director: Edmond K. Y. Wong.

THAILAND

The National Film Archive of Thailand, 4 Chao Fa Road, Bangkok 10200. Tel: (66 2) 282 0170/1847. Director: Penpan Jarernport.

TURKEY

Turkish Film and Television Institute, 80700 Kislaönü-Besiktas, Istanbul. Tel: (90 212) 232 1200. Prof. Sami Sekerog_lu. The Institute is a science and art centre which is engaged in education, research and archiving on cinema and television. Stock: 6,000 film titles, 3,500 video titles. Library of books, periodicals, newspaper clippings and photos available to researchers. Price list available upon request.

UNITED KINGDOM

Imperial War Museum, Lambeth Road, London SE1 6HZ. Tel: (44 171) 416 5291/2. Fax: (44 171) 416 5299. Keeper of the Film and Video Archive: Roger Smither. Deputy: Paul Sargent. Stock: over 40 million feet of actuality film relating to conflict in the 20th Century, from Britain and other countries. Viewing facilities for students and researchers *by appointment only*; public film screenings.

National Film and Television Archive, 21 Stephen Street, London W1P 1LN. Tel: (44 171) 255 1444. Fax: (44 171) 580 7503. Curator: Anne Fleming. Deputy Curator: Henning Schou. Stock: 275,000 film and television titles, over 5,000,000 black-and-white stills, 700,000 colour transparencies, 18,000 posters, 2,500 set-designs. Viewing service for students and researchers.

The Scottish Film and Television Archive, 74 Victoria Crescent Road, Glasgow G12 9JN. Tel: (44

141) 302 1742. Fax: (44 141) 302 1713.

UNITED STATES
Academy of Motion Picture Arts and Sciences, Centre for Motion Picture Study, Academy Film Archive, 333 South La Cienega Blvd., Beverly Hills, California 90211. Director: Michael Friend. Curator: Daniel Woodruff.

American Cinematheque, 1800 N. Highland Ave., #717, Hollywood 90028. Executive Director: Barbara Zicka Smith. A viewer-supported arts organisation dedicated exclusively to the public exhibition of film and video. Permanent home at the Egyptian Theatre (6712 Hollywood Blvd.) will open in Dec. 1998.

American Film Institute/National Center for Film and Video Preservation, 2021 North Western, Los Angeles, CA 90027. Tel: (1 213) 856 7600.

George Eastman House/ International Museum of Photography and Film, 900 East Avenue, Rochester, N.Y. 14607. Tel: (1 716) 271 3361 Fax: (1 716) 271 3970. e-mail: film@geh.org Website: www.eastman.org Senior Curator of Film: Dr. Paolo Cherchi Usai.

Harvard Film Archive, Carpenter Center for the Visual Arts, Harvard Univ, 24 Quincy Street, Cambridge, MA 02138. Tel: (1 617) 4954700. Curator: Vlada Petrić. Films (16mm and 35mm); 4,000 titles, including the Film Study Center collection (Robert Gardner, Producer/Director).

The Library of Congress, Motion Picture, Broadcasting and Recorded Sound Division, Washington, DC 20540-4690. Tel: (1 202) 707 5840. Fax: (1 202) 707 2371. Telex: 64198. Chief: Devid Francis.

Museum of Modern Art, Department of Film and Video,11 West 53rd Street, New York, NY 10019. Tel: (1 212) 708 9602. Telex: 62370. Chief Curator: Mary Lea Bandy. Curators: Steve Higgins, Larry Kardish. Stock: 12,000 film titles, 2,500 books, 250 periodicals, 4,000,000 film stills. The excellent research and screening facilities of the department are available to serious students only by appointment with the supervisor, Charles Silver; 1,000 of its films are available for rental, sale, and lease. Stills Archive open by appointment with Mary Corliss.

National Museum of Natural History/Human Studies Film Archives, Rm E307, 123 Smithsonian Institution, Washington DC 20560. Tel: (1 202) 357 3349. Fax: (202) 357 2208. Director: John P. Homiak.

Pacific Film Archive, University Art Museum, 2625 Durant Avenue, Berkeley, California 94720.

UCLA Film and Television Archive, 302 East Melnitz Hall, University of California, 405 Hilgard Avenue, Los Angeles, CA 90024. Tel: (1 310) 206 8013. Fax: (1 310) 206 3129.

The Wisconsin Center for Film and Theater Research, 816 State Street, Madison, Wisconsin 53706. Tel: (1 608) 264 6466. Fax: (1 608) 264 6472. Head of Archive: Maxine Fleckner Ducey.

URUGUAY
Cinemateca Uruguaya, Lorenzo Carnelli 1311, Casilla de Correo 1170, Montevideo. Tel: (598 2) 408 2460, 409 5795. Fax: (598 2) 409 4572. Curator: M. Martinez Carril.

BOOK REVIEWS

The year was invigorated by a blast from the past, in the shape of a weighty tome entitled **Positif, Revue de Cinéma, Nos 1–15, Mai 1952-Novembre 1955** (Jean Michel Place, Paris). *Positif* has outlasted *Cahiers du Cinéma* as by far the most influential European film magazine. Founded by a doughty Lyonnais named Bernard Chardère, the monthly featured writers as diverse as Georges Sadoul, Jean Rouch and Jacques Doniol-Valcroze. To leaf through these early numbers is to get a whiff of an era bereft of cynicism, when cinema came closest to poetry in the critic's eye, and when Gilles Jacob could write in mischievous mood about the genius of Groucho Marx, and Jacques Prévert could extol the virtues of Jean Vigo.

If, for an older generation, the *Positif* facsimile constituted the "Book of the Year", another French publication ran it close. Jean-Loup Passek's splendid series of illustrated, scholarly, yet readable companions to national cinemas achieved something of a peak with **Le Cinéma Japonais,** by Tadao Sato (Centres Georges Pompidou, Paris), in two volumes. Stuffed with rare stills, and written with the consummate skill and assurance of probably Japan's finest critic, this is an altogether splendid work of scholarship (with state-of-the-art filmographies as a bonus).

Film theory attracted some of the year's brightest writing. David Bordwell's **On the**

History of Film Style (Harvard, Cambridge, Mass., and London) is a kind of "historiography" of the cinema, discussing the criticism of luminaries like Bazin and Burch, while offering close readings of a huge range of films, from *Ingeborg Holm* to *The Hunt for Red October*.

In **Surfing the Zeitgeist** (Faber, London), Gilbert Adair, the archetypal British intellectual, reprints some of his weekly newspaper columns on a range of modern icons and sacred cows, whether it be Mae West or Tintin, film noir, *The Triumph of the Will*, or his favourite theme, post-modernism. The writing is personal, even chatty, calling upon a considerable reservoir of references both arcane and witty.

If a theorist ever gets his or her hands on a camera, the result is usually avant-garde. **Lovers of Cinema: The First American Film Avant-Garde 1919-1945**, edited by Jan-Christopher Horak (University of Wisconsin Press, Madison) assembles a host of articles that somehow conjure up the long-forgotten magic of film-makers like Mary Ellen Bute, Theodore Huff, and Douglass Crockwell - the sort of talent that Amos Vogel unspooled at his memorable "Cinema 16" meetings in New York during the late 1940s and 1950s. A rare treasure of a book.

More mainstream in approach, **A Personal Journey with Martin Scorsese through American Movies**, by Martin Scorsese and Michael Henry Wilson (Faber, London; Miramax Books/Hyperion, New York), stems from a documentary series that Scorsese hosted on television. It is a candid, passionate voyage of rediscovery, as the director sifts through the B-movies and cinematic byways of his youth, resurrecting in the process a host of off-beat film-makers. The book is enhanced by some evocative illustrations, immaculately reproduced in duotone printing.

Biography

Books from the house of Harry N. Abrams (New York and London) are always luscious to behold, and the updated edition of **The Films of Merchant Ivory**, by Robert Emmet Long, is no exception. Now including coverage of such modern classics as *Howards End* and *The Remains of the Day*, this spectacular volume contains more than a hundred colour plates.

Another revival is even more comprehensive: Gerald Pratley's **The Films of Frankenheimer**

(Cygnus Arts, London; Leigh University Press, Bethlehem). Originally published in the late 1960s, Pratley's book set a standard for exhaustive interviews with directors. Since 1964, Pratley has visited Frankenheimer on location for almost every one of his films, and their conversations cover every aspect of the film-making process. With Frankenheimer about to make a real comeback with *Ronin*, this is a timely publication.

The best of the new biographies must be Rob van Scheers's **Paul Verhoeven** (Faber, London), translated - very well - from the Dutch by Aletta Stevens. By dwelling in detail on Verhoeven's early life and work, van Scheers illuminates and explains the obsessive themes of the director's recent Hollywood blockbusters. He also sets such underrated films as *Showgirls* and *Starship Troopers* in their context as a European's satirical vision of American society.

Although not yet available in English, Sven Nykvist's autobiography, **Vördnad för ljuset** (Albert Bonniers Förlag, Stockholm) traces one of the most successful careers in the history of cinematography. Nykvist talks frankly about his relationship behind the camera with Ingmar Bergman, Woody Allen, Louis Malle and Andrei Tarkovsky. Edited by Bengt Forslund, this Swedish-language memoir deserves publication in America, France and Britain.

Stanley Kubrick has always eschewed collaboration with a biographer. No year passes without some analysis of his intermittent career, but Vincent LoBrutto's **Kubrick** (Faber, London; Donald A. Fine Books, New York) can claim to be the first true biography. Indeed, its early chapters are almost too prolix in detail, studded with dates of births, marriages and movements by Kubrick's ancestors and relatives. But LoBrutto warms to his task midway through this lengthy volume, and his background information about the great films shows that he has talked to probably more sources than any preceding Kubrick scholar.

Two further entries have appeared in Fabers "directors on directors" series. **Lynch on Lynch**, edited by Chris Rodley, is the more allusive of the pair, throwing intriguing light on some of Lynch's more outlandish work and describing why he dwells on "the horror and sickness" of American society, along with "the very innocent, naive quality to life" in the United States. As a companion piece, read the screenplay by Lynch and Barry Gifford for **Lost Highway** (Faber, London).

Sayles on Sayles, edited by Gavin Smith, finds the maverick American film-maker in excellent voice. You finish the book in admiration for a man who has, like Ken Loach and Mike Leigh, fought throughout his life for the cause of the underprivileged – and the imaginative – among the population. Faber has also released, in one paperback, the Sayles screenplays for **Men with Guns** and **Lone Star**.

The Unknown James Dean, by Robert Tanitch (Batsford, London) provides an illustrated reference guide to the late star's work in theatre and television, when he acted alongside many of the best directors, and mediocre actors (Ronald Reagan among them!) of the day.

Like Albert Speer, Leni Riefenstahl remains caught in that sinister limbo between outright enthusiasm for the Nazi cause and unintentional complicity in the most disastrous regime of the century. **A Portrait of Leni Riefenstahl**, by Audrey Salkeld (Pimlico Books, London), confronts the controversy surrounding this seemingly ageless German director. She charts the rise to fame of an energetic, glamorous and hugely gifted film-maker from her earliest appearances on camera to her post-war studies of Nubian tribes.

Orion Books in London have launched a welcome new series of pocket-sized hardbacks. Each profiles a director of the "movie brat" generation. **Martin Scorsese**, by Andy Dougan, and **Oliver Stone**, by Chris Salewicz, are readable surveys, laced with plenty of quotes from their subjects, and bolstered by the full *Variety* reviews of each man's films. They are available through Thunder's Mouth Press in the United States.

Not quite at home in this category, but as revealing of John Huston the man and the director as any official biography, Lillian Ross' classic **Picture** (Faber, London; Modern Library/Random House, New York) still sets the benchmark as far as "the making of" books are concerned. Too bad that the film in question, *The Red Badge of Courage*, failed to please either critics or public. Published originally in 1952, *Picture* reads like a thriller.

Screenplays

Among the most sparkling titles of the past year published by Faber in London are Kevin Smith's **Clerks** and **Chasing Amy**, and Neil LaBute's **In the Company of Men**. All three screenplays resound with terse, streetwise

dialogue, and a savvy understanding of how scenes are paced and structured. Conversely, a script like Eric Bogosian's **subUrbia** depends more on visual impact rather than eloquent exchanges of dialogue, and so gives the reader but a murky shadow of the actual film.

None of these American screenwriters can match the unostentatious profundity of the Polish duo, Krzysztof Kieślowski and Krzysztof Piesiewicz in the monumental **Three Colours Trilogy: Blue, White, Red** (Faber, London). For once the printed word grasps some portion of the magic achieved by films such as these. It is due in part to the detailed description of each small incident, as well as the fluent translation by Danusia Stok.

Four more screenplays from Faber epitomise the British renaissance. Frank Cottrell Boyce wrote **Welcome to Sarajevo**, transformed by Michael Winterbottom into a respectable, sharp-eyed picture of choice and compromise in modern war. Mike Leigh's **Career Girls** marks a relaxed, amusing change of gear after the anguish of *Secrets and Lies*, while Sally Potter's **The Tango Lesson** strikes an altogether more emotional note than this director's earlier work, perhaps because she is personally involved in the story and is also its leading actress.

The General is prefaced, like all John Boorman's screenplays, with a lucid account of how this trenchant, unsentimental film came to be made. Based on the true exploits of a Dublin criminal during the 1980s, this is Boorman's finest achievement in decades, and the screenplay captures its intelligence and smirking guile.

During the 1960s, first *L'Avant-Scène* in Paris, and then Andrew Sinclair and his Lorrimer Books in London pioneered the publication of screenplays in extenso. Today, Faber rules the roost, and under the rubric "Classic Screenplay" has reissued one of those early and long out of print Lorrimer titles: **Bonnie and Clyde**. Three further screenplays, **Peeping Tom**, **The Apartment** and **Sweet Smell of Success**, make up the first quartet of paperbacks in this welcome series. How exasperating that neither camera movements nor music are included in such texts.

The playwright Christopher Hampton has become increasingly involved in the cinema, and in a single paperback Faber have published his screenplays for **The Secret Agent** (directed by Hampton himself) and **Nostromo**, the gigantic and still unfilmed Conrad adaptation that drifted into limbo after the death of David Lean. Hampton's introduction recalls his fascinating collaboration with Lean in his waning months.

Evoking the expectation of *Waiting for Godot*, **The Winter Guest** (Faber, London) never arrives in Alan Rickman's film of that name. But a Scottish seaside town and its often clenched inhabitants stir to life in a frozen climate, both on screen thanks to Emma Thompson and Phyllida Law, and on the page by virtue of the spare style of Sharman Macdonald and Rickman.

Substantial novels present a challenge to even an experienced screenwriter like Laura Jones, who adapted both *An Angel at My Table* and *The Portrait of a Lady* for Jane Campion. Her compressed, even distilled version of **Oscar and Lucinda** (Faber, London) lets slip the intricate subtlety and nuances of Peter Carey's long, award-winning novel.

Finally, high praise for Paul Thomas Anderson and his sizzling yet sensitive depiction of the porn movie business. **Boogie Nights** became one of the sleepers of 1997, and its salty dialogue makes even Tarantino pale by comparison. Faber, again, are the publishers.

Reference and History

Charles Drazin makes a game attempt to resurrect some unsung talent in **The Finest Years: British Cinema of the 1940s** (Andre Deutsch, London). For once, Michael Powell is not extolled as the saviour of the period. Lesser-known figures like the quaint, roguish Robert Hamer and the self-effacing, elegant Anthony Asquith contributed just as much to that curious and colourful tapestry that forms the British cinema from the Blitz to the end of rationing.

New Zealand Film, 1912–1996, by Helen Martin and Sam Edwards (Oxford University Press, Auckland) pays handsome tribute to one of the world's youngest cinemas. New Zealand

directors like Jane Campion and Roger Donaldson have found fame around the world, while Kiwi actors include Sam Neill, Kerry Fox and that legendary athletic presence of the silent cinema, Annette Kellerman. The book contains credits and commentary on every feature film produced in New Zealand.

Even more scholarly, and thus a trifle arid, is **Nordic National Cinemas** (Routledge, London and New York), by a team of academics (Tytti Soila, Astrid Söderbergh Widding and Gunnar Iversen). Individual films receive short shrift at the expense of cultural generalities and the intricacies of state economic policy. Five languages have posed a problem for the translators, and there are some glaring howlers (the Swedish national awards are Golden Bugs, not Rams!) All too little is available on the Scandinavian cinema, however, so this book belongs on all good library shelves.

Joel W. Finler devoted a lifetime to the acquisition and study of stills from the American cinema. His **Silent Cinema** (Batsford, London) offers a feast of vanished images, and covers the entire spectrum of film-making prior to the late 1920s with a narrative text that is not so much nostalgic as astute in its judgements.

The British Cinema Book, edited by Robert Murphy (BFI Publishing, London), provides a solid anthology of pieces on everything from quota quickies to censorship, although it seems not to embrace any films made beyond the late 1960s. More engaging is **The Chaplin Encyclopedia**, by Glenn Mitchell (Batsford, London), which includes full entries not only on every film made by Chaplin, but also on his collaborators, his stage work and themes such as "Race", "Radio" and, of course, "Politics".

The reliable lexicographer David Quinlan slices and dices his research every which way and just about every other year. Now he has published a revised paperback version of **Quinlan's Film Character Actors** (Batsford, London), with more than 1,100 impeccably-researched entries and a similar number of thumbnail portraits.

Slightly longer entries, on somewhat fewer stars, make up another Batsford book, **Hollywood, The New Generation**, by James Cameron-Wilson. Taking 1955 as an arbitrary date, Cameron-Wilson looks at the hottest young stars to have been born since then, and writes about them with quote-sprinkled enthusiasm.

Anyone entering the industry at studio or laboratory level should have a copy of Ira

Konigsberg's **The Complete Film Dictionary** (Bloomsbury, London) with its 4,000 entries on all aspects of the craft. Line illustrations and the occasional still leaven the mass of information and definitions between these sturdy covers.

For youngsters intrigued by the concept of film studies, the veteran "Teach Yourself" series has issued **Film Studies**, by Warren Buckland (Hodder & Stoughton, London). There are sections on film aesthetics, narrative, genres and documentary films, as well as a section on how to become a film reviewer! A pity, however, that such a primer does not even mention names like Bergman, Coppola or Antonioni.

The neophyte film critic would do better to dip into **Projections 8** (Faber, London), the annual anthology edited by John Boorman and Walter Donohue. A wide range of critics around the world respond to Bruce Willis' scornful comment that "Nobody up here pays attention to reviews" and some, like Alexander Walker, are surprisingly candid and personal about the ideals that first prompted them to write about the movies. The 1998 volume also contains some engrossing interviews with Francesco Rosi, Abbas Kiarostami and Hector Babenco, among others.

Despite the travails besetting the British Film Institute, its publishing wing continues to put out its admirable pocket-format series of "Film Classics" and "Modern Classics". The purist may wince at the thought of *Independence Day* being regarded as a "classic", let alone "modern", but this year there have been interesting entries on **La Nuit Américaine**, by Roger Crittenden, **The Birds**, by Camille Paglia, and **Pépé le Moko**, by Ginette Vincendeau. And where colour appears in these tiny books, it is used to startling effect, as in **Once Upon a Time in America**, by Adrian Martin.

Peter Cowie

FILM BOOKSHOPS POSTERS & RECORDS

AUSTRALIA

Electric Shadows Bookshop, City Walk, Akuna Street, Canberra, ACT 2601. Tel: (61 262) 488 352. Fax: (61 262) 471 230. Free quarterly catalogue available listing new books.

Movie Buffs, P.O. Box 508, Hawthorn, Victoria 3122. Free catalogue available listing movie books, magazines, posters and memorabilia.

CANADA

Theatrebooks, 11 St. Thomas Street, Toronto, M5S 2B7. Tel: (1 416) 922 7175. Fax: (1 416) 922 0739. e-mail: action@ theatrebooks.com. Website: www. theatrebooks.com. Founded first as a source of theatre, opera and dance books. Theatrebooks has also been developing a first-class film book collection since 1982. Worldwide mail-order is handled.

FRANCE

Atmosphère, Librairie du Cinéma, 10 rue Broca, 75005 Paris. Tel: (33 1) 4331 0271. Fax:

(33 1) 4331 0369. Atmosphère offers a wide range of film publications, with a large stock of stills, postcards, posters of new and old movies of all origins and sizes. Also stocks back issues of magazines. Open every day except Sunday from 11-7. Atmosphère sets up shop during the Cannes festival, too.

Cinédoc, 45-53 Passage Jouffroy, 75009, Paris. Tel: (33 1) 4824 7116. Fax: (33 1) 4483 0634. e-mail: cinedocuments@thema.net. Website: www.cinedoc.com. Posters, books, stills, pressbooks, magazines, etc.

Ciné-Folie, La Boutique du Cinéma, 14 rue des Frères Pradignac, 06400 Cannes. Tel: (33 4) 9339 2299. Stills, books, posters, postcards.

Cinémagence, 12 rue Saulnier, 75009 Paris. Tel: (33 1) 4246 2121. Fax: (33 1) 4246 2020. Stills, posters, magazines, books. Mail-order service. Free catalogue.

Contacts Champs-Elysées, 24 rue du Colisée, 75008 Paris. Tel: (33 1) 4359 1771. Fax: (33 1) 4289 2765. Cinema bookshop established 41 years ago in the Champs-Elysées area, close to the film production companies. Amply stocked with French and foreign-language books on technique, theory, history and director monographs. Also magazines. Reliable mail-order service. Free "new aquisitions" list. Open year round.

GERMANY

Bulchhandlung Walther Konig, Ehrenstr. 4, 56072 Koln. Tel: (49 221) 205 960. Fax: (49 221) 205 9640. Offers a comprehensive catalogue of international titles in the film department, also useful antiquarian department.

Buchhandlung Langenkamp, Beckergrube 19, D-2400 Lübeck. Tel: (49 451) 76479.

H. Lindemann's Bookshop, Nadlerstrasse 4+10, D-70173 Stuttgart 1. Tel: (49 711) 2489 9977. Fax: (49 711) 236 9672. Photography and film literature. Catalogue available.

Kiepert Taschenbuchladen, Hardenbergstr. 4-5, D-10623 Berlin. Tel: (49 30) 311 880. Good selection of film paperbacks.

Sautter· + Lackmann, Film-buchhandlung, Admiralitädstr. D-20459 Hamburg or Postfach 11 04 31, 20404 Hamburg. Tel: (49 40) 373 196. Fax: (49 40) 365 479. Books, videos, etc.

Marga Schoeller Bucherstube, Knesebeckstr. 33, D-10623 Berlin. Tel: (49 30) 881 1122. Fax: (49 30) 881 8479. One of the fabled literary haunts of western Europe, Marga Schoeller's shop is justly proud of its film book selection.

Verlag fur Filmschriften Christian Unucka, Am Kramerburg 7A, D-85241 Herbertshausen. Tel: (49 8131) 13922. Fax: (49 8131) 10075.

Books, posters, programmes, stills, postcards, videos, rare items, etc.

ITALY

Libreria dello Spettacolo, via terraggio 11, 20123 Milan. Tel: (39 2) 864 51730.

Il Leuto, via Monte Brianzo 86, 00186 Rome. Tel: (39 06) 868 687. Fax: (39 06) 869 269.

SPAIN

Alphaville, Martin de los Heros 14, 28008 Madrid. Tel: (34 91) 559 3836.

Filmoteca Espanola, Cine Doré, Santa Isabel 3, Madrid. Well-stocked bookstore dealing with movie topics.

SWEDEN

Movie Art of Sweden, Sodra Hamngatan 2, 411 06 Goteborg. Tel: (46 31) 151 412. Fax: (46 31) 115 1445. e-mail: info@essemposters. se. Website: www.movieart ofsweden.com. New and vintage film posters, stills, postcards, props, t-shirts. Postal service available.

SWITZERLAND

Filmbuchhandlung Hans Rohr, Oberdorfstr. 3 CH-8024 Zurich. Tel: (41 1) 251 3636. Fax: (41 1) 251 3344. In its long existence, Hans Rohr has offered an efficient and reliable service when it comes to dealing with mail-order inquiries for literally any film, book or magazine in print.

Librairie du Cinéma, 9 rue de la Terrassiere, CH-1207, Geneva. Tel: (41 22) 736 6616. Immaculate display of posters, books, stills, postcards, photos, soundtrack CDs and videos. A veritable treasure trove for the movie buff.

UNITED KINGDOM

The Cinema Bookshop, 13-14 Great Russell Street, London WC1B 3NH. Tel: (44 171) 637 0206. Fax: (44 171) 436 9979. Fred Zentner's film bookshop close to the British Museum has succeeded by virtue of prompt and friendly service and an eye for rare items.

The Cinema Store, Unit 4B/C, Orion House, Upper Saint Martin's Lane, London WC2H 9EJ. Tel: (44 171) 379 7838. Fax: (44 171) 240 7689. e-mail: cinemastor@aol.com. Website: www.atlasdigital.com/cinemasto re. Fine selection of magazines, toys and models, laser discs, posters etc. in Paul McEvoy and Neil Palmer's friendly and recently expanded store now stocking rare/new VHS, soundtracks and trading cards. Mail-order catalogue £1.

Anne FitzSimons, 62 Scotby Road, Scotby, Carlisle, Cumbria CA4 8BD. Tel: (44 1228) 513 815. Small stock of ephemera and second-hand and out-of-print books on the cinema, and other entertainment. Catalogue twice a year. Private premises. Postal only.

Flashbacks, 6 Silver Place, (Beak Street) London W1R 3LJ. Tel/Fax: (44 171) 437 8562. e-mail: flashbacks @compuserve.com. Most impressively stocked West End establishment which caters for those interested in movie ephemera – posters, stills, pressbooks – from many countries and every period of cinema history. Also extensive mail-order service. (No catalogues issued, but individual requests responded to. Monday to Saturday, 10:30-7).

Greenroom Books, 11 Bark Lane, Addingham, Ilkey, West Yorkshire LS29 ORA. Tel/Fax: (44 1943) 830 497. Mail-order service for books on the preforming arts.

David Henry, P.O. Box 9146, London W3 8WZ, England. Tel: (44 181) 932 5152. e-mail: filmbook@netcomuk.co.uk. Mail-order business catalogues upon request.

Hollywood Superstore, 16-18 St. Giles High Street, London WC2H 8LN. Tel: (44 171) 836 3736. Movie photos, posters, books, magazines, and vintage memorabilia. Open Mon-Fri. 10-6; Sat. 10-7)

Ed Mason, c/o Rare Discs, 18 Bloomsbury Street, London WC1B 32A. Tel: (44 171) 580 3516. Recently re-located, large and carefully assembled stock of memorabilia. Contact Ed Mason on (171) 736 8511 for further info.

Movie Boulevard, 3 Cherry Tree Walk, Leeds LS2 7EB. Tel: (44 113) 242 2888. Fax: (44 113) 243 8840. Welcome north of England addition to the ranks of shops specialising in soundtracks, videos, laserdiscs and memorabilia. Headed by the enthusiastic Robert Wood.

National Film Theatre Shop, South Bank, London SE1 8XT. Tel: (44 171) 928 3535. Visitors to the National Film Theatre now have a comprehensive bookshop in the foyer, to complement the stock of posters, postcards, toys and videos available at the MOMI shop.

The Reel Poster Company, 22 Great Marlborough Street, London W1V 1AF. Tel: (44 171) 734 4303. Fax: (44 171) 734 4260. London's first gallery dedicated

to original vintage film posters. An extensive yet selective stock includes posters of all genres, from Westerns to science-fiction, and Hollywood classics to cult titles, seen through the eyes of artists from various countries.

Zwemmer Media, 80 Charing Cross Road, London WC2. Tel: (44 171)240 4157. Fax: (44 171) 240 4186. Large selection of new and out-of-print film books, from early film-making to digital video. Mail-order inquires.

UNITED STATES

Applause, 211 West 71st Street, New York, NY 10021. Tel: (1 212) 496 7511. Fax: (1 212) 721 2856. Now one of the few – and certainly the only uptown – film and showbiz bookstores in Manhattan.

Cinema Books, 4753 Roosevelt Way NE, Seattle, WA 98105. Tel: (1 206) 547 7667. Fine selection of film books and magazines, with space also devoted to TV and theatre. Mail-orders welcome.

Cinema Paradiso, 162 Bleecker Street, New York, NY 10012. Tel: (1 212) 677-8215. Specialising in international movie posters, stills, vintage, originals. Open 365 days a year.

Cinemonde, 138 Second Ave North, Suite 104, Nashville, TN 37201. Tel: (1 615) 742 3048. Fax: (1 615) 742 1268. Installed in a capacious gallery in Old Nashville, Cinemonde is a poster store for movie buffs. Items are meticulously stored and displayed, and the colorful catalogue is a collector's item. In addition, Cinemonde has a search service in San Francisco for hard-to-find vintage posters, headed by the movie poster consultant for Sotheby's, New York (1932 Polk St., San Francisco, CA 94109. Tel: (1 415) 776 9988. Fax: (1 415) 776 1424).

Dwight Cleveland, P.O. Box 10922, Chicago, IL 60610-0922. Tel: (1 773) 525 9152. Fax: (1 773) 525 2969. Buys and sells movie posters.

Collectors Book Store, Dept. 10, 1708 North Vine Street, Hollywood, CA. 90028. Tel: (1 213) 467 3296. Fax: (1 213) 467 4536. Offers a superlative range of posters, stills, lobby cards, TV and film scripts.

Larry Edmund's Bookshop, 6644 Hollywood Blvd., Hollywood, CA 90028. Tel: (1 213) 463 3273. Fax: (1 213) 463 4245. The stills collection alone is a goldmine for any film buff. Back numbers of movie annuals, posters, lobby cards and largest collection of new and used books in the world.

Samuel French's Theatre & Film Bookshop, (2 Locations) 7623 Sunset Boulevard, Hollywood, CA 90046. Tel: (1 213) 876 0570. Fax: (1 213) 876 6822. Extended evening hours at 11963 Ventura Boulevard, Studio City, CA 91604. Tel: (1 818) 762 0535. e-mail: samuelfrench@earthlink.net. Website: www.samuelfrench. com. The world's oldest and largest play publisher (est.1830) operates a separate film and preforming arts bookshop. Complete range of new movie and preforming arts books available: directories, reference, writing, acting biography, screenplays, etc. World-wide mail-order service. The staff prepares meticulous catalogues that include more data than similar publications, and they strive to have any book in the English language from publishers throughout the world.

Gotham Book Mart, 41 West 47th Street, New York, NY 10036. Tel: (1 212) 719 4448. This famous literary bookshop in mid-Manhattan, est. 1920, is the only New York City bookstore offering new, used and out-of-print film and theatre books. Also, an extensive stock of "quality" film magazines dating from the 1950s to present.

Limelight Film and Theatre Bookstore, 1803 Market Street, San Francisco, CA 94103. Tel: (1 415) 864 2265. Derek G. Mutch runs this lively store for film and theatre books. Collection includes plays, screenplays, biographies, history and criticism of films and film and television technique.

Movie Madness, 1083 Thomas Jefferson Street, Washington, DC 20007. Current, classic and campy movie posters available at this unique store in Georgetown.

Jerry Ohlinger's Movie Material Store Inc., 242 West 14th Street, New York, NY 10011. Tel: (1 212) 989 0869. Jerry Ohlinger's emporium stocks a wealth of stills from the 1930s through the 1990s, specialising in colour material. Posters are also plentiful, and there are some magazines as well.

MAGAZINES

The following list amounts to a selection only of the world's hundreds of film publications. Editors wishing to receive a free listing must send sample copies (preferably opening a sample subscription for us). Address: IFG, Variety, 6 Bell Yard, London WC2A 1EJ, UK.

ALGERIA

MEDIASUD

Maison de la presse, Tahar Djaout, 1 rue Bachir Attar, Place du 1er Mai, Algiers. New Algerian film publication.

ARGENTINA

ENTERTAINMENT HERALD

Corrieres 2817 3-A 1015, Buenos Aires, Argentina.

AUSTRALIA

CINEMA PAPERS

116 Argyle Street, Fitzroy, Victoria, Australia. Excellent large-format Australian bi-monthly, packed with information and pictures, useful for anyone monitoring the industry in Oz.

FATAL VISIONS

PO Box 133, Northcote 3070, Victoria, Australia. Irregular but lively title dedicated to horror, sci-fi and sexploitation flicks with interviews, reviews and a Chinatown beat.

THE MAGUFFIN

177 Simpson Street, East Melbourne 3002, Australia. Scholarly newsletter focusing on the films of Alfred Hitchcock. Intelligent and jargon-free.

BELGIUM

CINE-FICHESDEGRANDANGLE

Rue d'Arschot 29, B-5660 Mariembourg, Belgium. Monthly review of new films and videos.

FILM EN TELEVISIE + VIDEO

Haachtesteenweg, 35, B-1210 Brussels, Belgium. Extensive reviews of major new film and video releases, profiles and interviews, festival news.

CINE & MEDIA

Rue du Saphir 15, 1040 Brussels, Belgium. Multilingual (French, English and Spanish) bi-monthly published by the International Catholic Organisation for Cinema and the Audiovisual, with reports from all continents.

MEDIAFILM

Haachtsesteenweg 35, B-1210 Brussels, Belgium. Serious Belgian quarterly, with extensive reviews, analysis and focus on directors. Quarterly.

SOUNDTRACK!

Astridlaan 171, 2800 Mechelen, Belgium. Excellent quarterly for film music collectors.

STARS

Rue d'Arschot 29, B-5660 Mariembourg, Belgium. Quarterly publication giving actors' biographies and filmographies.

BOLIVIA

IMAGEN

Casilla 1733, La Paz, Bolivia. Magazine of the Bolivian New Cinema Movement.

CANADA

CINÉ-BULLES

4545 avenue Pierre-de-Coubertin, CP 1000, Succursale M. Montréal, Canada H1V 3R2. Remarkable and informative Québécois quarterly that may just be the best in Canada.

KINEMA

Fine Arts (Film Studies), University of Waterloo, Waterloo, Ont. N2L 3G1, Canada. A journal of history, theory and aesthetics of world film and audiovisual media. Twice yearly.

THE NIGHTINGALE REPORT

45 Barclay Road, Toronto, Ontario M3H 3EZ, Canada. Fortnightly newsletter aimed at Canadian film and television industry. News and comprehensive listings.

24 IMAGES

3962, rue Laval, Montréal, QC H2W 2J2, Canada. Exceptionally attractive French/Canadian quarterly, witty and well-informed.

CHILE

ENFOQUE

Publicaciones y Audiovisuales, Linterna Mágica Ltda., Casilla 15, Correo 34, Santiago, Chile. Occasional quarterly taking an in-depth look at the Chilean/Latin American markets and new-releases.

CHINA

CITY ENTERTAINMENT

6/F, Flat A, Tung Nam Bldg, 475–481 Hennesssy Road, Causeway Bay, Hong Kong, R.O.C. Glossy, indispensable Hongkong monthly for anyone interested in Chinese cinema. In Chinese.

FILM APPRECIATION

The National Film Archive of the R.O.C., 4th Floor, 7 Ching-tao East Road, Taipei, Taiwan R.O.C. Taiwan's premier serious film journal, published as a bi-monthly. Focus on the cinematic output of Taiwan, Hong Kong and mainland China, as well as from Chinese communities overseas.

POPULAR CINEMA

(Dazhong dianying), 22 Beisanhuan donglu 22, Peking, China. Leading mainland Chinese monthly, also carrying pieces on Hongkong, Taiwan and foreign cinema.

WORLD SCREEN

China Film Press, 22 Beisanhuandonglu, Beijing 100013, China. Monthly, primarily devoted to new/classic features from around the world, with artist profiles and events.

COLOMBIA

KINETOSCOPIO

El Palo No. 53-24, Apdo. Aereo 8734, Medellin, Colombia. Bi-monthly covering international and Latin American cinema, Colombian directors and festival news.

CUBA

CINE CUBANO

Calle 23, no. 1115 Apdo. 55, Havana, Cuba. Vital information on all Latin American cinema, unfortunately only in Spanish.

CZECH REPUBLIC

FILM & DOBA

Halkova 1, 120 72 Prague 2, Czech Republic. The principal Czech film monthly.

DENMARK

KOSMORAMA

The Danish Film Museum, Vognmagergade 10, 1120-Copenhagen K, Denmark. A changed, chunkier, more academic format for *Kosmorama*, which appears twice yearly (in Danish).

FINLAND

FILMJOURNALEN

Finlandssvenskt filmcentrum, Nylandsgatan 1, 25700 Åbo, Finland. Passionate Swedish-language quarterly focusing on Nordic and Finnish cinema.

FILMIHULLU

Malminkatu 36, FI-00100 Helsinki, Finland. Finnish film and TV magazine with perverse if passionate critical approach, appearing eight times a year.

LA STRADA

PO Box 432, 33101 Tampere, Finland. Finland's largest film magazine, this quarterly is provocative and entertaining, with lots of news and reviews. In Finnish.

FRANCE

CAHIERS DU CINEMA

Editions de l'Etoile, 9 passage de la Boule Blanche, 75012 Paris, France. Celebrated French journal now enjoying a second lease of life after a long spell in the wilderness.

POSITIF

19 Villa Croix Nivert, 75015 Paris, France. In-depth interviews, articles, all immaculately researched and highly intelligent. By a clear margin, this is Europe's best film magazine. New large format.

PREMIERE

151 rue Anatole France, 92534 Levallois-Perret Cedex, France. France's familiar movie monthly, packed with information, reviews and filmographies.

STUDIO MAGAZINE

116 bis, avenue des Champs-Elysées, 75008 Paris, France. Glossy, beautifully designed monthly with reviews, articles and interviews.

GERMANY

ENTERTAINMENT MARKT

Stahlgruberring 11a, 81829 Munich, Germany. Bi-weekly business magazine that covers the German video, CD-ROM and computer games market.

KINO: GERMAN FILM + INTL. REPORTS

c/o Holloway, Helgoländer Ufer 6, 10557, Berlin, Germany. Excellent quarterly devoted to both German cinema and international festival reports. Features reviews, interviews and credits.

THE LIMITED EDITION

The Score Company, Linzer Str. 5, 53604 Bad Honnef, Germany. Quarterly devoted to soundtracks and the art of film scoring.

MEDIUM

Postfach 50 05 50, Frankfurt am Main, Germany. Highbrow German publication covering film, radio, TV, and the press. Bi-monthly.

WELTWUNDER DER KINEMATOGRAPHIE

Postfach 100 274, D-10562 Berlin, Germany. Fascinating, well-researched new title, with detailed articles on the past, present and future of cinematography and the technical art of film-making. Yearly.

HUNGARY

FILMKULTURA

Solymár u. 8, 1032 Budapest, Hungary. Essays and reviews on Hungarian and international cinema. Six times a year.

FILMVILAG

Pozsonyi út 20, H-1137 Budapest, Hungary. Monthly with reviews and interviews.

INDIA

CINEMAYA

B 90 Defence Colony, New Delhi 110 024, India. Informative, elegant magazine, published quarterly in English since 1988, on all aspects of the Asian film industry. Is the official journal of NETPAC (Network for promotion of Asian Cinema).

SPECIAL EFFECT

B/4, Balgachia Villa, Calcutta 700 037, India. Formerly *Magic Lantern*, this Indian film quarterly mixes interviews and reviews with insightful comment, and surveys different trends in Indian cinema.

IRAN

CINEMA

No. 123 Jami, Hafez Avenue, Tehran. Reports and reviews on local and international cinema.

CINEMA AND THEATRE

No. 1/1 Omrani Alley, North Bahar Street, Tehran. Articles on theoretical aspects of cinema and theatre.

CINEMA AND VIDEO

No. 1073, Rudaki Street, Jomhuri Square. Reports and features on cinema and video.

CULTURE AND CINEMA

P.O. Box 15175-338 Tehran, Iran. Monthly magazine featuring Iranian cinema.

FILM AND CINEMA

No. 18 Safa Alley, Kushk Street, Saadi Avenue, Tehran. Features focusing on theoretical aspects of cinema.

FILM AND VIDEO

No. 5 Laal Alley, Etesami Street, Fatemi Avenue, Tehran. Reports and features on cinema and video.

FILM INTERNATIONAL

No. 12 Sam Alley, Hafez Avenue, Tehran. English-language quarterly journal that offers a cross-cultural review of international cinema, focusing on the film art in Asia.

FILM MONTHLY

P.O. Box 11265-5872 Tehran. Reviews and features on the latest releases.

FILM REPORT

3rd Floor, 123 Jami St., Hafez Ave., Tehran, Tehran, Iran. Reviews and features on the latest releases.

THE IMAGE

No. 15 Golriz Street, Motahhari Avenue. Reports and features on cinema and photography.

WORLD OF IMAGE

No. 46 Khorshid Alley, Tus Street, Talequani Avenue Theoretical aspects of cinema and photography.

ISRAEL

CINEMATHEQUE

PO Box 20370, Tel Aviv 61203, Israel. Fine monthly Israeli magazine (with summary in English) dwelling on seasons at the Tel-Aviv Cinémathèque but also reporting on world festivals etc.

ITALY

BIANCO E NERO

1524 via Tuscolana, 00173 Rome, Italy. Italian yearly that boasts a reputation for scholarship second to none in its country.

CINECRITICA

Via Yser, n.8-00198 Rome, Italy. Dense Italian quarterly focussing on world cinema.

CINEMA & CINEMA

1 via Battibecco, 40123 Bologna, Italy. Respected quarterly.

CINEMA & VIDEO INTERNATIONAL

Via Tevere 46B, 00198 Rome, Italy. Monthly for audiovisual professionals in English and Italian.

CINEMA NUOVO

PO Box 362, 70100 Bari, Italy. Polemical, academic Italian quarterly with excellent articles

CINEMAZERO

Piazza Maestri del Lavoro 3, 33170 Pordenone, Italy. Serious Italian bi-monthly covering international cinema, with festival news and book reviews.

GRIFFITHIANA

Cineteca del Friuli, 26 via Osoppo, 33013 Gemona del Friuli (Udine), Italy. Italian quarterly devoted exclusively to the study of silent cinema and animation. Each issue is a miracle of scholarship and devotion. In English and Italian.

IMMAGINI & SUONI

FIAIS, Casella postale 6306, 00195 Rome, Italy. Published by the International Federa-tion of Film Archives. In French and Italian.

LA MAGNIFICA OSSESSIONE

Piazza Palermo, 10B, 16129 Genova, Italy. Published by the Cinema department of Genova University, this academic quarterly has numerous articles on cinema history.

NUOVO CINEMA EUROPEO

Via delle Cinque Giornate 15, 50129, Florence, Italy. Chunky bi-monthly report on Italian film industry, in English with Italian summary. Includes industry news, such as box-office, markets and foreign sales.

QUADERNI DI CINEMA

Via Benedetto Varchi 57, 50132 Florence, Italy. Wide-ranging Italian bi-monthly, striving to match cultural politics with an enthusiastic appreciation of film.

RIVISTA DEL CINEMATOGRAFO

Via Giuseppe Palombini, 6-165 Rome, Italy. Important Italian monthly.

SEGNOCINEMA

Via G Prati 34, Vicenza. Glossy Italian bi-monthly packed with profiles, reviews and photographs. September issue lists complete guide to all titles released the previous season.

KOREA

FILM

(Yeonghwa), Motion Picture Promotion Corporation of Korea, 34-5, 3-ga, Namsan-dong, Junggu, Seoul. South Korea's only serious film magazine, packed with information. Bi-monthly.

NETHERLANDS

HOLLAND ANIMATION NEWSBRIEF

Hoogt 4, 3512 GW Utrecht, The Netherlands. Quarterly newsletter from the Holland Animation Foundation.

SKRIEN

p/a Filmmuseum, Vondelpark 3, 1071 AA Amsterdam, The Netherlands. Excellent Dutch magazine that appears with regularity and enthusiasm. Bi-monthly.

NEW ZEALAND

ONFILM

PO Box 6374, Wellington, New Zealand. A film, television and video magazine for New Zealand, with location reports and a production survey.

NORWAY

Z FILMTIDSSKRIFT

Dronningensgate 16, 0152 Oslo, Norway. Enthusiastic quarterly with a focus on film theory and history, both Norwegian and international. Now with useful summaries in English.

PERU

EL REFUGIO

José Granda 460, Lima 27, Peru. South American monthly with reviews and features on world cinema.

LA GRAN ILUSIÓN

Universidad de Lima, Oficina de Distribución y Venta de Publicaciones, Av. Javier Prado Este s/n Monterrico, Apartado 852, Lima, Peru. Weighty journal with essays on international contemporary and classic cinema.

POLAND

FILM

Pulawska 61, 02595 Warsaw, Poland. Popular Polish monthly with international slant.

FILM NA SWIECIE

Polish Federation of Film Clubs, Plocka 16/34, 01138 Warsaw, Poland.

KINO

Chelmska 19/21, 00-724 Warsaw, Poland. Culturally inclined Polish monthly designed to promote European cinema, with interviews, reviews and essays.

PORTUGAL

CINEMA NOVO

Apartado, 78, 4002 Porto Codex, Portugal. Bi-monthly Portuguese magazine dealing with international and Portuguese topics.

ROMANIA

PRO CINEMA

Str. Luterana_ 11, et. II, sector 1, Budapest, Romania. Romanian monthly covering mainstream European and Hollywood fare. Plenty of colour pics, reviews, profiles and interviews.

RUSSIA

ISKUSSTVO KINO

9 ul. Usievicha, 125319 Moscow, Russia. Chunky, theoretical, most authoritative Russian film monthly.

SLOVENIA

EKRAN

1000 Ljubljana, Miklosiceva 38, Slovenia. Provides critical evaluation and topical consideration of Slovene and foreign films. Bi-monthly.

SPAIN

CINEMANIA

Gran Via 32, 2°, 28013 Madrid, Spain. Founded in 1995. Upmarket monthly with news, interviews, reports, feature articles and TV and video coverage.

DIRIGIDO POR

Conseil de Cent 304, 2°, 1°, Barcelona 08007, Spain. This handsomely-produced Spanish monthly throws the spotlight each issue on a particular genre, studio or director of international renown.

FANTASTIC

Gran Via de les Corts Catalanes 133, 2°, 08014 Barcelona, Spain. Breezy consumer monthly focusing on young stars. 46,000 readers.

FOTOGRAMAS

Gran Via de les Corts Catalanes 133, 3°, 08014 Barcelona, Spain. An institution, fifty years old in 1997. A glossy monthly with authoritative film reviews, news, on-location reports and features.

IMAGENES DE ACTUALIDAD

Consell de Cent, 304, 2.°, 1.ª, 08007 Barcelona, Spain. Glossy, well-presented international magazine with strong Hollywood bias. Monthly.

INTERFILMS

Valportillo Primera 16, Poligono Industrial Alcobendas, Alcobendas 28100, Madrid, Spain. Monthly film magazine for consumer.

NICKELODEON

Bárbara de Braganza 12, 28004 Madrid, Spain. Important new quarterly from Spain, very well illustrated and researched. First issue offers an in-depth look at Spanish cinema.

SRI LANKA

CINESITH

142 Abeyratne Mawatha, Boralesgamuwa, Sri Lanka. Sri Lanka's only serious film magazine focuses on national and international cinema with special reference to Asia.

SWEDEN

FILMHÄFTET

Box 101 56, 100 55 Stockholm, Sweden. Egghead periodical with features on international directors, retrospectives, and Scandinavian television.

FILMRUTAN

Box 82, 851 02 Sundsvall, Sweden. Organ of the Swedish Federation of Film Societies, this unpretentious monthly has, with the demise of *Chaplin*, become Sweden's most important film magazine. Features, film, book and record reviews.

SWITZERLAND

AVANT PREMIERE

Case Postale 5615, 1211 Geneva 11, Switzerland. Colourful monthly with lengthy reviews of new releases, as well as a pullout brochure on Swiss production and distribution.

CINE-BULLETIN

Swiss Film Centre, P.O. Box, Neugasse 6, CH-8031 Zürich, Switzerland. Serious Swiss monthly in French and German with box office and films in production.

FILM BULLETIN

Postfach 137, CH-8408 Winterthur, Switzerland. Informative, straightforward look at international cinema, with useful Swiss material also. Bi-monthly.

RECTANGLE

CAC Voltaire, Rue Général-Dufour 16, 1204 Geneva, Switzerland. Only film magazine in the Suisse romande, and admirably poised between the theoretical and researchist approach to the cinema, with a fresh and lively layout.

ZOOM

Bederstrasse 76, Postfach, 8027 Zürich, Switzerland. Swiss monthly highlighting new releases, with interviews and good festival coverage. In German.

TURKEY

VE CINEMA

Hil Yayinlari, Cagaloghi, Istanbul, Turkey. Quarterly published in Turkish.

UNITED KINGDOM

EMPIRE

1st Floor, Mappin House, 4 Winsley Street, London W1N 7AR, UK. Supercharged fanzine monthly with profiles, reviews and behind-the-scenes reports. Often far ahead of its rivals in breaking news and interviews.

FILM DOPE

74 Julian Road, Nottingham NG2 5AN. Not so much a magazine, more a part-work film dictionary, this (alas!) irregular British quarterly is to be welcomed for its exhaustive research.

FILM HISTORY

John Libbey and Co. Ltd., 13 Smiths Yard, Summerley Street, London SW18 4HR, UK. Articles on the historical development of the motion picture, in a social, technological and economic context. Quarterly.

MUSIC FROM THE MOVIES

1 Folly Square, Bridport, Dorset DT6 3PU, UK. Informative quarterly devoted to all aspects of film music and its composers, with articles, interviews and soundtrack reviews.

NEON

2nd Floor, Mappin House, 4 Winsley Street, London W1N 7AR, UK. Attractive new monthly; hipper, wittier and more intelligently written than *Empire.*

PICTURE HOUSE

5 Coopers Close, Burgess Hill, W. Sussex RH15 8AN. Admirable quarterly devoted to the cinema buildings of the past.

PRODUCER

162–170 Wardour Street, London, W1V 4LA, UK. Welcome voice for the independent British producer.

SIGHT AND SOUND

British Film Institute, 21 Stephen Street, London W1 1PL, UK. Apart from its reference guide to most films released in the UK, this once-celebrated magazine is still a pale shadow of its former authority. Slight improvement in the past year.

TALKING PICTURES

3b Glengarry Road, East Dulwich, London SE22, UK. Quarterly booklet with interviews, reviews and articles on film culture in the UK, now expanding in size and coverage.

TOTAL FILM

Future Publishing, Beauford Court, 30 Monmouth Street, Bath BA1 2BW, UK. Lively UK monthly focusing on mainstream Hollywood action fare.

VERTIGO

7–9 Earlham Street, London WC2H 9LL, UK. New quarterly for independent British film-makers and audiences. A forum for critical debate.

VIDEO MAKER

Oasis Publishing, Media House, Boxwell Road, Berkhamsted, Herts, England. Film and video monthly that concentrates on the craft of making your own films.

UNITED STATES

AMERICAN PREMIERE

8421 Wilshire Blvd., Penthouse; Beverly Hills, CA 90211, USA. Bi-monthly industry magazine, free to members of the Academy of Motion Picture Arts and Sciences.

ANIMATION JOURNAL

AJ Press, 2011 Kingsboro Circle, Tustin, California 92680-6733, USA. The only peer-reviewed scholarly journal devoted to animation history and theory. Quarterly.

ANIMATION MAGAZINE

Terry Thoren, Agoura Court, Suite 110, Agoura, California 91301, USA. International guide to the animation industry in a new eye-catching format. Bi-monthly.

AUDIENCE

PO Box 215, Simi Valley, CA93062-0215, USA. Billed as an "informal commentary on film", this witty, well-informed bi-monthly features articles and reviews, both recent and retrospective.

CINEASTE

Suite 1601 200 Park Avenue South, New York, NY 10003, USA. Perhaps the finest anti-establishment movie magazine, never afraid to tackle controversial issues and never prone to Hollywood worship. Interviews are especially good in *Cineaste.*

CINEFANTASTIQUE

PO Box 270, Oak Park, Ill. 60303, USA. An enthusiastic, well-written, beautifully produced monthly with a special emphasis on horror, fantasy and s-f films.

CINEMA JOURNAL

University of Texas Press, Journals Division, Box 7819, Austin, Texas 78713-7819, USA. Essays concerned with the study of the moving image from diverse methodological perspectives, with information on upcoming events and research opportunities.

CLASSIC IMAGES

PO Box 809, Muscataine, IA52761, USA. Formerly "Classic Film Collector," a good source for film buffs eager to enlarge their library of movies. Monthly.

FILMMAKER MAGAZINE

110 West 57th Street, New York, Ny 10019-3319, USA. Tel: 212-581-8080. Fax: 212-581-1857. Aimed at independent film-makers, this quarterly offers interviews, news and sound advice.

FILMS IN REVIEW

P.O. Box 589, New York, NY 10021, USA. Compact bi-monthly journal, reviewing notable new releases with interviews, retrospective articles and television/video reports.

FILM COMMENT

Film Society of Lincoln Center, 70 Lincoln Center Plaza, New York, NY 10023, USA. Informative, feisty, and usually uncompromising articles as well as interviews on wide-ranging international topics. Still the best US bi-monthly on the cinema.

FILM CRITICISM

Allegheny College, Box D, Meadville, PA 16335, USA. Scholarly essays on film history, theory and culture. Quarterly.

FILM JOURNAL INTERNATIONAL

The Sunshine Group, 244 West 49th Street, Suite 200, New York, NY 10019, USA. Monthly magazine covering international exhibition.

FILM LITERATURE INDEX

Film and Television Documentation Centre, State University of New York, 1400 Washington Avenue, Albany, NY 12222, USA. The most comprehensive international index to the journal literature of film and television.

FILM QUARTERLY

University of California Press, 2120 Berkeley Way, Berkeley, California 94720, USA. Publishes readable discussions of issues in contemporary film, TV and video, and analyses of independent, documentary, avant-garde and foreign films.

HONG KONG FILM MAGAZINE

601 Van Ness Avenue, Suite E3728, San Francisco, California 94102, USA. Quarterly focusing on the Hong Kong cinema scene, featuring news, reviews and interviews. In English.

INTERNATIONAL DOCUMENTARY

1551 South Robertson Boulevard, Suite 201, Los Angeles, CA 90035, USA. The only publication to focus exclusively on non-fiction film and video. Presents new work and ideas in the documentary field with informative articles, reviews and interviews. Published ten times a year.

JUMP CUT

PO Box 865, Berkeley, California 94701, USA. Published only once or twice a year, this tabloid contains an extraordinary amount of closely-woven text.

LITERATURE/FILM QUARTERLY

Salisbury State University, Salisbury, Maryland 21801, USA. Scholarly quarterly with film and book reviews, interviews and articles. Manuscripts invited for submission.

MOVIELINE

1141 South Beverly Drive, Los Angeles, CA 90035, USA. Intelligent, irreverent and refreshingly candid Hollywood monthly. Great interviews.

PREMIERE

1990 South Bundy Drive, Suite 250, Los Angeles, CA 90025, USA. Diluted in size and scope since its launch seven years ago, but still has its finger on the pulse of Hollywood and retains a huge circulation.

WIDE ANGLE

The Johns Hopkins University Press, Baltimore, Maryland 212180, USA. Scholarly, thematically arranged journal. Wide range.

URUGUAY

CINEMATECA REVISTA

Lorenzo Carnelli 1311, Casilla de Correo 1170, Montevideo, Uruguay. Bright magazine with international slant published by Cinemateca Uruguaya. Ten times a year.

Trade and Technical

BELGIUM

MONITEUR DU FILM

36 rue des Frambosiers, 1180 Brussels, Belgium. Monthly.

FRANCE

LE FILM FRANÇAIS

90 rue de Flandre, 75947 Paris Cedex 19, France. Lightweight weekly with news, reviews, box-office and production schedules.

GERMANY

BLICKPUNKT-FILM

Stahlgruberring 11a, 81829 Munich, Germany. Strong on box-office returns and marketing, this German weekly also covers the video and TV market.

FILM-ECHO/FILMWOCHE

Marktplatz 13, 65183 Wiesbaden, Germany. Doyen of the German trade. Weekly.

MÜNCHEN FILM NEWS

Kaiserstrasse 39, 80801 Munich, Germany. A monthly put out by Munich's Informationbüro Film containing festival reports, films in production, personalities and other news concerning the Munich film scene. Specials in English.

ITALY

ECOMONOPRESSACTINGNEWS

Via Belluno 1, 00161 Rome, Italy. Comprehensive weekly reports on Italian film starts. Four market issues have English translations.

CINEMA D'OGGI

Viale Regina Margherita 286, 00198 Rome, Italy. Fortnightly. Interviews with producers.

GIORNALE DELLO SPETTACOLO

Via di Villa Patrizi 10, 00161 Rome, Italy. Box-office data, legal requirements, technical information etc.

JAPAN

MOVIE/TV MARKETING

Box 30, Central Post Office, Tokyo, 100-91 Japan. Monthly from Japan – in English.

NORWAY

FILM OG KINO

Dronningensgate 16, 0152 Oslo, Norway. Wide-ranging and with a more expressive layout. Covering new releases in cinema as well as national and international trade matters and festival reports. Now the best film magazine in Scandinavia.

SPAIN

CINEINFORME & TELE

Grand Via 64, 28013, Madrid, Spain. 35-year-old monthly that covers Spanish and international film, video and TV development.

CINEVIDEO 20

Apartado 2016, 28080 Madrid. Features technologies of film, video, computer, studio facilities, satellite and cable for a Spanish readership.

EURO-MOVIES INTERNATIONAL

News-Movies, SCP, San Gaudencio 7, Sitges, 08870, Barcelona, Spain. Spanish and Latin American panorama, with reviews, festival news and television section.

UNITED KINGDOM

IMAGE TECHNOLOGY — JOURNAL OF THE BKSTS

67-71 Victoria House, Vernon Place, London WC1B 4DA, UK. Covers technologies of motion picture film, television and sound at professional level. Ten times yearly.

MOVING PICTURES INTERNATIONAL

6 Bell Yard, London WC2A 2JR, UK. European-orientated trade paper published in London, with daily editions at numerous festivals.

SCREEN INTERNATIONAL

33–39 Bowling Green Lane, London, EC1R 0DA, UK. Weekly, UK-oriented trade organ.

UNITED STATES

AMERICAN CINEMATOGRAPHER

ASC Holding Corp., 1782 N. Orange Dr., Hollywood, CA 90028, USA. Glossy monthly on film and electronic production techniques.

BOXOFFICE

6640 Sunset Blvd, Suite 100, Hollywood, California, 90028-7159, USA. Business monthly for the Hollywood and movie theatre industries.

FILM JOURNAL

Pubsun Corp., 244 West 49 Street, New York, NY 10019, USA. Monthly magazine aimed at US exhibitors.

THE HOLLYWOOD REPORTER

5055 Wilshire Boulevard, Los Angeles, CA 90036-4396, USA. Daily.

VARIETY

5700 Wilshire Boulevard, Suite 120, Los Angeles, CA 90036. The world's foremost newspaper (daily and weekly) of the entertainment business.

National Organs

AUSTRALIA

AFC NEWS

GPO Box 3984, Sydney NSW 2001, Australia. Monthly, with regular production and multimedia reports, industry statistics, funding approvals and Australian films at international markets and festivals and awards won.

BELGIUM

CINEMA, CINEMA

Ministère de la Culture Française, avenue de Cortenbur 158, 1040 Brussels, Belgium.

CANADA

FILM CANADA YEARBOOK

Cine-communications, Box 152, Station R, Toronto, Ontario M4G 3Z3, Canada. Comprehensive directory of the Canadian film industry for over a decade.

BURKINA FASO

FEPACI NEWS

01 BP. 2524 Ouagadougou 01, Burkina Faso. Monthly newsletter of the Pan-African Federation of film-makers.

GERMANY

KINO

Export-Union des Deutschen Films, Türkenstr. 93, D-80799 München. Information on new German features (in production and already released), and selected personalities of the German film industry. Published three times a year in English, French, Spanish and German, with a yearbook also available.

ISRAEL

ISRAEL FILM CENTRE INFORMATION BULLETIN

Ministry of Industry and Trade, 30 Agron Street, Jerusalem, Israel. Yearly review of Israeli film industry and catalogue of Israel films.

NEW ZEALAND

NZ FILM

PO Box 11-546, Wellington, New Zealand. News from the New Zealand Film Commission, a twice yearly round-up of the country's film industry.

SPAIN

ACADEMIA

Sagasta 20, 3° drcha., 28004 Madrid, Spain. Excellent quarterly with articles, news and opinions of members of Spain's Academy of the Arts and Cinematographic Sciences.

Index to Advertisers